The SAGE Handbook of
Risk Communication

The SAGE Handbook of
Risk Communication

Edited by

Hyunyi Cho
Purdue University

Torsten Reimer
Purdue University

Katherine A. McComas
Cornell University

Los Angeles | London | New Delhi
Singapore | Washington DC

SAGE

Los Angeles | London | New Delhi
Singapore | Washington DC

FOR INFORMATION:

SAGE Publications, Inc.
2455 Teller Road
Thousand Oaks, California 91320
E-mail: order@sagepub.com

SAGE Publications Ltd.
1 Oliver's Yard
55 City Road
London, EC1Y 1SP
United Kingdom

SAGE Publications India Pvt. Ltd.
B 1/I 1 Mohan Cooperative Industrial Area
Mathura Road, New Delhi 110 044
India

SAGE Publications Asia-Pacific Pte. Ltd.
3 Church Street
#10-04 Samsung Hub
Singapore 048763

Acquisitions Editor: Matthew Byrnie
Editorial Assistant: Janae Masnovi
Production Editor: Jane Haenel
Copy Editor: QuADS Prepress (P) Ltd.
Typesetter: Hurix Systems Pvt. Ltd.
Proofreader: Laura Webb
Indexer: Rick Hurd
Cover Designer: Candice Harman
Marketing Manager: Liz Thornton

Printed in the United States of America

Library of Congress Cataloging-in-Publication Data

The Sage handbook of risk communication / edited by Hyunyi Cho, Purdue University, Tursten Reimer, Purdue University, Katherine A. McComas, Cornell University.

pages cm
Includes bibliographical references and index.

ISBN 978-1-4522-5868-3 (hardcover : alk. paper)

1. Risk communication. I. Cho, Hyunyi. II. Reimer, Tursten. III. McComas, Katherine.

T10.68.S34 2015
658.15′5—dc23   2014019028

This book is printed on acid-free paper.

14 15 16 17 18 10 9 8 7 6 5 4 3 2 1

Contents

Acknowledgments

The editors wish to thank the following reviewers of the book's proposal and chapters.

Linda Aldoory, University of Maryland

Amanda D. Boyd, Washington State University

Noel Brewer, University of North Carolina

Wändi Bruine de Bruin, University of Leeds and Carnegie Mellon University

Nick Carcioppolo, University of Miami

Michael F. Dahlstrom, Iowa State University

James Dillard, Pennsylvania State University

Edna Einsiedel, University of Calgary

Danielle Endres, University of Utah

Amelia Greiner, Johns Hopkins University

Jakob D. Jensen, University of Utah

Se-Hoon Jeong, Korea University

William J. Kinsella, North Carolina State University

Erin K. Maloney, Memorial Sloan-Kettering Cancer Center

Xiaoli Nan, University of Maryland

Bryan H. Reber, University of Georgia

Sandi Smith, Michigan State University

Brian Southwell, RTI International and University of North Carolina, Chapel Hill

Teresa L. Thompson, University of Dayton

Daniëlle Timmermans, VU University Medical Center, Amsterdam

Introduction

Explicating Communication in Risk Communication

Hyunyi Cho, Torsten Reimer, and Katherine A. McComas

Premises and Goals

The essential role of communication in understanding and managing risk has been inherent in various intellectual perspectives. Claude Shannon, the developer of the earliest theory of communication (1948), thought the goal of communication was to reduce uncertainty (McGrayne, 2011). Symbolic interactionism (Blumer, 1969) may assign a role greater than uncertainty reduction to communication: By connecting two or more entities with shared meanings, communication can create, as well as change, perceptions of uncertainty or certainty, of insecurity or security, and of danger or safety. Danger is the transgression from culturally established classifications, asserted Douglas (1966); purity protects cultural orders. Innate in the social process of establishing and protecting such categorizations and orders is communication.

The utility of communication in managing and reducing risk may not have gone unnoticed. Enter the term risk communication in Google Books Ngram Viewer: It yields a steep slope of increase in the occurrence of the term since the 1980s. Industrialization may have brought "risk society" the inhabitants and hierarchies of which have to wrestle with the unforeseen concerns and consequences it engendered (Beck, 1986/1992).

And, individuals, groups, and institutions may have increasingly looked on communication as a desirable feature and important element determining the efficacy of risk decision-making processes (National Research Council, 1989).

Despite the growth, however, *communication* in risk communication remains rather amorphous. A salient conflation in the current literature is about risk perception and risk communication. Unlike perceptions, communication frequently involves materiality such as rhetoric, numbers, stories, images, the media, informed consent documents, protests on streets, and town hall meetings. Messages contained and permeated through these forms and venues influence perceptions about risk and energize and orient actions concerning risk issues.

This book aims to emphasize and articulate communication in risk communication, which is defined as interactions and exchanges among individuals, groups, and institutions in the processes of determining, analyzing, and managing risk (National Research Council, 1989). In seeking to lay a conceptual foundation for explicating the nature and role of communication in risk communication, this book integrates developments in theory and research in a range of disciplines, including decision science, psychology, and sociology, as well as communication. By bringing together perspectives that may have traditionally been distinct but which nonetheless serve to articulate the role of communication in risk communication, this book bridges historical disciplinary divides that impede rather than strengthen collective scientific progress.

Improved knowledge about communication in risk communication can in turn enhance the efforts to understand, manage, and reduce risk in diverse applied domains, including health, environment, science, technology, and crisis. If risk are the things, forces, or circumstances that pose danger to people or to that which they value (National Research Council, 1989), risk conceptually and practically pertains to multiple contexts ranging from public health to environmental and even financial well-being. The author and topic list of this book reflects a commitment to placing into conversation with one another studies that have ranged in focus from medical contexts to municipal boardrooms to social media websites.

With these premises and approaches, this book pushes the boundaries of communication research with the aim to advancing risk communication theory and practice. Furthermore, the multidisciplinary theories that this book pulls together under the rubric of risk lay a productive ground for developing new perspectives on communication theory and offers new directions for communication research. These goals are reflected in the organization of the book.

Structure and Contents

Providing a foundational understanding of risk perception necessary to engaging in effective risk communication is the aim of Part 1, Foundations of Risk Communication. The two keystones of this foundation are the psychology of risk perception and the sociology of risk construction. Based on this foundation, Part 2, Components of Risk Communication, aims to explicate effective risk communication, which requires an integrative knowledge about the models, audiences, messages, and the media of risk communication. Part 3,

Contexts of Risk Communication, describes the divergence in participants, goals, and processes of risk communication situated in interpersonal and organizational contexts and the public sphere.

Part I: Foundations of Risk Communication

Part I, Foundations of Risk Communication, consists of two sections: (1) Risk Perceptions of Individuals and (2) Risk as Social Construction. The Risk Perceptions of Individuals section focuses on psychological frameworks explaining risk-related cognitions, affect, and judgments. Chapter 1 by Bodemer and Gaissmaier offers an overview of concepts and conceptual frameworks fundamental to understanding risk perceptions. Bodemer and Gaissmaier start with the psychometric paradigm that was fundamental for many models of risk perception and describe major factors, moderators, and mediators that have been shown to systematically influence our perception of risks. In Chapter 2, Hertwig and Frey focus on the description–experience gap in risk perception, showing that risk decisions that are based on personal experience and risk decisions that are based on description often systematically differ from each other. The description–experience gap can help understand why expert and lay perceptions of risk are often at odds with each other and offers novel insight about the perception and communication of risk. In Chapter 3, Dickert and colleagues present research that looks at the feelings of risk and demonstrate how emotions influence the perception of risk. Dickert et al. argue and illustrate that risks are naturally intertwined with emotional reactions, and proffer communication strategies that take into account the important ways in which risk information triggers feelings and emotions.

Whereas the preceding section focuses on intraindividual processes, the Risk as Social Construction section is devoted to a discussion about how social exchanges shape and alter risk perceptions. Burgess opens this section with a rich analysis and synthesis of extant perspectives on the social and cultural processes in which the problems and solutions of risk issues are constructed (Chapter 4). Binder and colleagues offer a communication-focused account of the social amplification of the risk framework in Chapter 5. In particular, Binder et al. focus on explicating the role of news media in the amplification or attenuation of risk perception among the general public. In Chapter 6, Jensen describes the relationship between rhetoric and social construction of risk and extant convergence and divergence in theoretical perspectives on this matter and delineates considerations for engaging in discursive construction of risk.

Part II: Components of Risk Communication

Part II, Components of Risk Communication, includes four sections: (3) Models of Risk Communication, (4) Audiences of Risk Communication, (5) Risk Communication Messages, and (6) Risk Communication and the Media.

In the section on Models of Risk Communication, the contributors describe two theoretical frameworks explaining and predicting risk-germane communication processes. Dunwoody and Griffin (Chapter 7) discuss the risk information seeking and processing model. After describing the model's predictions about the information behaviors leading to risk decision making, they offer new evidence demonstrating the model's consistency across different risk issues over time. Cho and Kuang (Chapter 8) introduce the societal risk reduction motivation model. Integrating theories of media effects, social processes, and collective behaviors, this new risk communication model describes the predictors and processes of the path between societal risk perception and societal risk reduction action.

The Audiences of Risk Communication section explicates two primary audience factors to consider in developing and evaluating risk communication: edgework and numeracy. In Chapter 9,

Brust-Renck and colleagues focus on numeracy. Following a critical review of research and evidence on how people comprehend numerically presented risk information, the authors describe fuzzy-trace theory, a new framework that integrates analysis and intuition for explaining numeracy. Guided by fuzzy-trace theory, they offer recommendations for enhancing numeracy and for facilitating the comprehension of numeric risk information. Lyng and colleagues discuss edgework, a social psychological theory of voluntary risk taking, in Chapter 10. Deviating from prevalent risk communication premises, the theory of edgework posits that the dangers associated with activities only enhance their appeal for edgeworkers. Lyng et al. in this chapter examine the ramifications of these paradoxes for risk communication research and practice.

The section on Risk Communication Messages spans numeric, narrative, and visual messages. Reimer and colleagues, in Chapter 11, describe four major hurdles in the communication of numeric risk information and offer tools for the presentation of common quantitative information. The tools are evidence based and have been shown to effectively alleviate the described problems. In Chapter 12, Cho and Friley delineate the roles of narratives in risk communication. The authors distinguish accuracy and acceptance goals of risk communication and posit that narratives may be less able to achieve the accuracy goal than the acceptance goal. In Chapter 13, King describes and critiques conceptual and theoretical bases of understanding the role of visual messages in risk communication, with an eye on advancing theory of visual communication of risk. Furthermore, on the basis of an extensive review of available evidence, King offers cautious guidance for developing and evaluating visual messages in risk communication.

The Risk Communication and the Media section examines the content and effects of the media in influencing risk perceptions, behaviors, and policies. Priest describes the forces that shape risk-related media content. Risk news is the product of interplay of factors operating at organizational, institutional, and societal levels, all of which are vulnerable to cultural, economic, and political constraints and conventions, discusses Priest (Chapter 14). In Chapter 15, Nisbet presents the role of the media in risk communication from the standpoint of framing. Conceptualizing media framing as cognitive and social process, Nisbet discusses the central role that it plays in policy debates about risk issues. Rains and colleagues review available research on the uses and effects of social media for risk communication and explore its ramifications for developing a theory that inform future risk communication practice using social media (Chapter 16).

Part III: Contexts of Risk Communication

Part III, Contexts of Risk Communication, spans three sections, including (7) Interpersonal Contexts of Risk Communication, (8) Organizational Contexts of Risk Communication, and (9) Risk Communication in the Public Sphere. A prominent interpersonal context in which risk communication is engaged in may be medical encounters. In Chapter 17, Bylund and colleagues discuss health care provider–patient communication. After offering an overview of theoretical bases of research in this area and its extant findings showing how providers and patients mutually influence each other during their interactions, the authors point to gaps in the current knowledge and suggest directions to address the gaps. In Chapter 18, Yang focuses on informed consent and its indivisible relationship with risk communication. Yang elucidates the communication challenges for protecting participants in informed consent, on the basis of a review of research on variables influencing informed consent and a historical overview of research on informed consent.

Organizational contexts may foster unique communication and decision-making processes about risk, which is the focus of the Organizational Contexts of Risk Communication section. Russell and Reimer, in Chapter 19, offer an information-processing framework to conceptualize research on

risk communication in groups and teams. The review draws on classic studies and paradigms on risk perception in groups as well as studies in judgment and decision making that are highly relevant for our understanding of risk communication in groups. Sellnow in Chapter 20 offers a state of the art analysis of the literature on crisis communication—organizational response to disasters. After examining the interface between risk and crisis communication, Sellnow explicates three primary phases of crisis communication and their theoretical underpinnings and practical implications.

The Risk Communication in the Public Sphere section explores the communicative actions that are intended to influence societal perceptions and decisions about risk issues. In Chapter 21 on social movements, Boudet and Bell illuminate the precursors and dynamics of social mobilization for controversial risk issues. Based on the survey of extant approaches from sociology and communication disciplines, Boudet and Bell provide readers with a set of rich research questions that can strengthen the cross-disciplinary basis of the scholarship on social movements. Besley in Chapter 22 draws from broad areas of social sciences to offer a review of intellectual roots of public engagement and empirical findings about the effect of public engagement in risk decision processes gathered in diverse settings ranging from face-to-face to new media platforms. On the basis of this review, Besley calls risk communication scholars to engage with broad social sciences and social problems to harness the theory and practice of public engagement for risk decision making.

Across these parts, sections, and chapters, this book emphasizes theory and research to guide practice. Each chapter includes the Reflections for Theory and Research section to set agenda for risk communication scholarship. Each chapter offers the Recommendations for Practice section to illustrate the pathways from theory and research to practice and to provide specific pragmatic guidance for risk communicators. Suggested Additional Readings at the end of each chapter directs readers to resources for expanding knowledge about a subset of concepts covered in each chapter, and a Glossary at the end of the book provides an easy access to definitions of key concepts covered in this book.

References

Beck, U. (1992). *Risk society: Towards a new modernity*. London: Sage. (Original work published 1986)

Blumer, H. G. (1969). *Symbolic interactionism: Perspective and method*. Englewood Cliffs, NJ: Prentice Hall.

Douglas, M. (1966). *Purity and danger: An analysis of the concepts of pollution and taboo*. London: Routledge & Kegan Paul.

McGrayne, S. B. (2011). *The theory that would not die: How Bayes' rule cracked the enigma code, hunted down Russian submarines, and emerged triumphant from two centuries of controversy*. New Haven, CT: Yale University Press.

National Research Council. (1989). *Improving risk communication*. Washington, DC: National Academy Press.

Shannon, C. E. (1948). A mathematical theory of communication. *Bell System Technical Journal, 27,* 379–423, 623–656.

PART I

FOUNDATIONS OF RISK COMMUNICATION

SECTION 1

Risk Perceptions of Individuals

CHAPTER 1

Risk Perception

Nicolai Bodemer and Wolfgang Gaissmaier

Introduction

Natural hazards, health hazards, terrorist attacks, new technologies, transportation—all of them represent risks in our life. We face some of these risks daily, others rarely, if ever. Some risks constitute a threat to individuals, some to the entire society. We overestimate some risks, while underestimating others. Some risks trigger a strong emotional response, others are perceived more "cold" and rational.

In this chapter, we start with a definition of the concept of risk and how it differs from the concept of uncertainty. We then outline major theories, models, and mediators that influence our perception of risk. Although the models stem from different research programs, highlight different mechanisms, and are often discussed in isolation from each other, they serve as psychological explanations for how we perceive risks in our daily life.

Defining Risk and Risk Perception

Risk is a highly interdisciplinary concept and its measurement differs across and even within disciplines. For instance, in a health context, risk can refer to the number of fatalities, which can be measured through the probability of death, expected life-years lost, deaths per person exposed, or total deaths (Fischhoff, 2009, p. 943). More generally, most definitions of risk have in common that risk comprises two factors: (1) the probability of harm and (2) the magnitude of harm, where harm refers to threats to humans and things they value (Hohenemser, Kates, & Slovic, 1985). In this sense, risks are measureable and risky situations are conditions in which outcomes (i.e., the harm) and probabilities are known. For instance, one can access the risk of losing in the casino, the risk of an adverse event of a specific treatment, or the risk of a car accident for a given population. Risky situations have to be distinguished from uncertain situations that are conditions in which either both, the outcomes and probabilities, or at least the probabilities are unknown (see Meder, Le Lec, & Osman, 2013). This distinction goes back to Knight (1921) who defined uncertainty as immeasurable in contrast to measureable risks. However, more recent approaches broaden the definition of uncertainty as they consider probabilistic parameters such as standard deviations, expert confidence ratings, or ranges as (quantifiable) indicators of uncertainty (e.g., Politi, Han, & Col, 2007). Throughout this chapter, we mainly refer to risks, that is, situations in which outcomes and probabilities are measureable. Furthermore, when talking about uncertainty, we mean that probabilities are not measureable, and we use the term *ambiguity* to designate situations in which probabilistic parameters are used to quantify uncertainty of risk estimates.

Risk perception refers to the "subjective assessment of the probability of a specified type of accident happening and how concerned we are with the consequences" (Sjöberg, Moen, & Rundmo, 2004, p. 8z). Pidgeon, Hood, Jones, Turner, and Gibson (1992) defined risk perception as "people's beliefs, attitudes, judgments and feelings, as well as the wider social or cultural values and dispositions that people adopt, towards hazards and their benefits" (p. 89) and thereby stressed that risk perception is not simply an individual process but has to be understood against the societal and cultural background (see also Kasperson, Kasperson, Pidgeon, & Slovic, 2003).

Furthermore, evaluating a risk from different perspectives has different implications for the evaluation of such a risk, as well as consequences for behavior. Imagine a woman who knows that of 100,000 women like her, 15 will have cervical cancer. She might decide not to participate in prevention, such as screening with a pap smear (a test to identify early stages of cervical dysplasia), because her baseline risk is rather low. Now imagine a health policy maker: Pap smear screening reduces the annual incidence of cervical cancer in Germany by a total 10,400 women. In this case, a national program to implement pap smear screening might be appreciated (example from Neumeyer-Gromen, Bodemer, Müller, & Gigerenzer, 2011). Thus, depending on whether a policymaker or an individual layperson decides about the screening, the benefit will be evaluated differently.

Social and Cultural Components of Risk Perception

Although the focus of this chapter is on risk perceptions of individuals, it is important to remember that risk perception always takes place in a social and cultural context (see Part I, Section 2). The social amplification of risk framework is an integrative model of risk perception that is grounded on the assumption that "risk . . . is not only an experience of physical harm but the result of processes by which groups and individuals learn to acquire or create interpretations of risk" (Kasperson et al., 2003, p. 13). Hence, risk perception has to be understood as a communication process along a chain from the sender to the receiver, with different stations in between that may amplify or attenuate risks. Such stations can be social (e.g., news media), individual (e.g., attention filter), or institutional (e.g., political and social actions).

The way we perceive and react to risks is further shaped by our values. In their cultural theory of risk, Douglas and Wildavsky (1983) distinguished between different cultural worldviews. The major dimensions are individualism (e.g., defending individual freedom) versus communitarian (e.g., supporting collective action) and hierarchical (e.g., leaving important decisions to experts) versus egalitarian (e.g., striving for equality). For instance, people with hierarchical–individualist worldviews value markets and commerce and feel uneasy when these activities are restricted. On the other hand, people with egalitarian–communitarian worldviews are ambivalent about markets. The interaction of personal values and risk perception idea is also implemented in the cultural cognition of risk thesis.

The Psychometric Paradigm

One of the earliest and most influential models in risk perception is the psychometric paradigm (Slovic, 1987). Based on the assumption that risks are quantifiable and predictable, the psychometric paradigm uses psychophysical scaling and multivariate techniques to explain laypeople's reactions to hazards. In their seminal study, Fischhoff, Slovic, Lichtenstein, Read, and Combs (1978) asked participants to rate 30 activities and technologies (e.g., fire fighting, nuclear power, pesticides, motor vehicles, smoking, food coloring) on nine different dimensions they had previously identified in the literature: (1) voluntariness of risk, (2) immediacy of effect, (3) knowledge about risk by scientist, (4) knowledge about risk by exposed person, (5) control over risk, (6) newness, (7) catastrophic potential, (8) dreadfulness, and (9) severity of consequences. Each dimension was assessed on a 7-point scale. A factor analysis based on the correlation of the mean ratings revealed two orthogonal factors: dread risk and unknown risk (sometimes called novelty). High dread risk means that perceived lack of control, dread, and catastrophic potential and fatal consequences are high (e.g., nuclear reactor incidents); high unknown risk means that the hazard is unobservable, unknown, new, and delayed (e.g., chemical and DNA technologies; Slovic, 1987). Note that unknown risk is different from uncertainty and ambiguity as defined above, as unknown risk is a psychological construct and refers primarily to the fact that the risk is novel, yet it could, in theory, be objectively quantified. The two factors (dread and unknown risk) have been observed in various studies across countries to predict laypeople's reactions to hazards and have therefore been assumed as robust across different cultures and environments (Boholm, 1998; Slovic, 2000). The factor dread risk was found to better predict laypeople's risk perception and desire for risk regulations compared with the factor unknown risk (Slovic, 1987). It is important to keep in mind that the model was primarily intended to explain risk perception in laypeople, because they give relatively little weight to actual risk assessment (Covello, von Winterfeldt, & Slovic, 1987). Experts, in contrast, defined risks strictly in terms of annual fatalities, at least, according to findings from the psychometric paradigm on small expert samples (Slovic, Fischhoff, & Lichtenstein, 1979).

The psychometric paradigm is not without its critics (Sjöberg, 2002b, 2003). For instance, the model primarily predicts risk perception on an aggregated level—that is, using average ratings across participants and across hazards. In this case, up to 80% of the variance of perceived risk can be explained with the two factors, however, if one considers only one specific hazard each time the explained variance drops to about 20% (Gardner & Gould, 1989; Sjöberg, 1996, 2002b). Hence, the original aggregated analysis of perceived risk in the psychometric paradigm does not give information about individual variation as well as intraindividual perceptions across different hazards. Sjöberg (2002a) challenged the assumption that experts differ in their underlying processes and assess risks via annual fatalities only. In fact, he found that experts' and laypeople's risk perceptions were rather similar. However, one possible explanation is that laypeople and experts follow different definitions of risk, as experts primarily refer to an objective, numerical assessment, whereas laypeople are more affect driven (Slovic, 1999). In sum, the psychometric paradigm has been an influential model for describing risk perceptions and has yielded important insights and impulses. At the same time, its application to predict individual risk perception is limited and it does not provide a process model that explains the cognitive mechanisms underlying risk perception.

Dread Risk: The Role of the Social Circle

As proposed by the psychometric paradigm, dread is an important predictor in people's perception of and reaction to hazards. The dread hypothesis further proposes that people have a strong tendency to avoid risks that kill many people at once, compared with risks that cause the same number of fatalities over a longer period of time (Slovic, 1987). For instance, the terrorist attack of 9/11 represents a dread risk. As a consequence of the attack, many people avoided airplanes and switched to cars instead, which increased fatalities in car accidents (Gaissmaier & Gigerenzer, 2012; Gigerenzer, 2004, 2006). At the same time, the fact that between 44,000 and

98,000 patients die in the United States annually due to preventable medical errors is not perceived as a dread risk. At least four possible explanations can account for the fact that people tend to fear dread risks more than continuous risks, even if both cause the same number of fatalities (Galesic & Garcia-Retamero, 2012; Gigerenzer, 2006). First, dread risks are perceived as less controllable. The findings from the psychometric paradigm suggest that lack of control loads highly on the factor dread risk (Slovic, 1987). Whereas we may assume high control when driving, which yields in low risk perception, we may assume low control over earthquakes and terrorist attacks, which yields in high risk perception. Second, people are not aware of the actual underlying statistical information. In particular, knowledge about continuous, everyday risks may be underestimated as they are less salient compared with dread risks that, in turn, may be overestimated. Third, from an evolutionary perspective, an event killing many group members once imposed a substantial threat to the survival of the group when still living in hunter–gatherer societies. Hence, people might be prepared to fear particularly those risks that threaten survival of their group. Galesic and Garcia-Retamero (2012) examined this hypothesis and tested to what extent risks that affect a number of people corresponding to the typical size of our social circle (e.g., family, friends) are perceived as more relevant. They defined the social circle as a group of up to 200 people. Results of nine experiments consistently showed that people perceived a risk killing 100 people as more dreadful and frightening than a risk killing 10 people. However, a risk killing 1,000 people was rated equal to a risk killing 100 people, suggesting that the number of people corresponding to the social circle is crucial in defining the dread potential and related fear. Fourth, and related, is the finding that dread risks have a stronger impact on the population size over time than continuous risks causing the equivalent number of fatalities (Bodemer, Ruggeri, & Galesic, 2013). The reason is that a fatal event strikes twice: (1) it

kills a number of people immediately and (2) it reduces the number of future offspring by reducing the number of their potential parents. Hence, a risky event that kills young people—potential parents for future generations—strongly influences population size. Due to the fact that dread risks kill many people once and often affect younger generations also, it takes longer for the population to recover from dread risks than from equivalent continuous risks.

The Role of Affect: Risk-as-Feelings and the Affect Heuristic

Affective reactions provide important signals about how we perceive and "feel" about our environment (see also Chapter 3, this volume). Affect emerges automatically and quickly, often before a cognitive and conscious evaluation of the situation takes place. Affective reactions allow evaluation of the target, guide what information we search for and focus on, motivate behavior, and allow comparison of different events and situations on a common level (Peters, 2006). Risks can trigger emotions in two dimensions: (1) immediate emotion, when one is confronted with the risk as integral emotions that are caused by the risk itself or incidental emotions that are caused by other, unrelated factors yet influence risk perception, and (2) anticipated emotions, which are expected to be experienced in the future.

Two major approaches have been proposed to study the role of affect in risk perception. The risk-as-feelings hypothesis (Loewenstein, Weber, Hsee, & Welch, 2001) assumes a dual-process model according to which people assess risks cognitively and emotionally. In general, the emotional appraisal is considered as stronger than the cognitive appraisal. The affect heuristic describes how affective reactions influence risk perception. According to this heuristic, people consult their "affect pool" as a cue about the judgment of a risk (Finucane, Alhakami, Slovic, & Johnson, 2000; Pachur, Hertwig, & Steinmann, 2012). For instance, when comparing two risks, a person might infer that the risk that evokes a stronger emotional reaction (in terms of dread) is more prevalent.

Affective reactions also account for how people simultaneously perceive benefits and risks. Benefits and risks of technologies or medical treatments are usually positively correlated in our environment: A greater benefit goes along with a greater risk. Yet people's perceptions of benefits and risks are usually negatively correlated. Technologies with high benefits are perceived as less risky, and high-risk technologies are perceived as less beneficial. Alhakami and Slovic (1994) explained this pattern with participants' affective evaluation of technologies. Favorable affective evaluations result in high-benefit and low-risk perceptions, whereas unfavorable affective evaluations result in the opposite pattern (see also Slovic, Finucane, Peters, & MacGregor, 2002).

Availability Heuristic

Another strategy is to judge risks via the availability heuristic, that is, to judge "the frequency of a class or the probability of an event by the ease with which instances or occurrences can be brought to mind" (Tversky & Kahneman, 1974, p. 1127). Whether and when this heuristic leads to accurate risk perception depends on the structure of the environment. Assuming that more frequent events are easier to recall, risk perception should be quite accurate. However, factors such as memorability, imaginability, or disproportional media coverage of an event can bias risk perception. In their seminal work, Lichtenstein, Slovic, Fischhoff, Layman, and Combs (1978) used two different methods to elicit participants' frequency judgments. In one method, they presented participants pairs of causes of death and asked them first to state which causes a higher number of deaths and second to estimate the ratio of their frequencies. In another method, participants had to estimate the frequency of an event and prior to estimation

received either a high anchor (motor vehicle accidents cause 50,000 deaths per year) or a low anchor (electrocution causes 1,000 deaths per year). Participants' absolute risk judgments were influenced by the anchor. When the high anchor was provided, risk estimates were about two to five times higher than when the low anchor was provided. When it comes to relative judgments, participants performed better, and more frequent risks were generally identified as more likely when compared with a less frequent risk. However, two biases were obtained. First, participants overestimated low frequencies and underestimated high frequencies (primary bias). Second, participants assigned different ratios to different pairs of causes of death even when the ratio was the same (secondary bias). The availability heuristic was proposed to explain these biases: People base their estimates on recalled instances. If the recall of available instances in the mind is proportional to the actual frequency of the event, then people correctly assess the risk. However, when the recall of instances is not proportional to the actual frequency, then people may misjudge risks that could explain the primary bias.

Two major criticisms with respect to the availability heuristic have been raised (e.g., Hertwig, Pachur, & Kurzenhäuser, 2005). First, the heuristic has often been used as a post hoc explanation rather than to predict risk perception patterns. Second, the original definition does not distinguish between ease of recall and actual number of recalled instances. Hertwig and colleagues (2005) addressed the two criticisms and compared several models that specified these processes precisely. Their results were similar to those from Lichtenstein et al. (1978). Moreover, the authors compared two different versions of the availability heuristic: First, availability-by-recall operationalized by the number of instances one recalls from one's social circle (e.g., family members, friends, colleagues). Second, fluency operationalized by the anticipated ease of recall with which instances can be brought to mind. Fluency was modeled in two ways: (1) the speed with which instances come to mind and (2) the occurrence of events in the media. Availability-by-recall better predicted people's choice than fluency, and it suggests that, at least in this context, availability may be primarily defined by the number of recalled instances. However, it should be noted that there are situations in which availability-by-recall is not applicable, namely, when a risky event has not (yet) occurred in one's social circle. Yet the social environment seems to play an important role in the evaluation of risks. Furthermore, the authors also tested other possible mechanisms that could explain the data. For instance, regressed frequency assumes that people monitor the occurrence of risks but tend to overestimate small and underestimate low risks as a consequence of a regression-to-the-mean effect. In a later study, Pachur et al. (2012) also compared whether availability-by-recall or the affect heuristic better described people's risk judgments and found that availability-by-recall was a stronger predictor than affect for frequency estimates, although the affect heuristic described participants' value of a statistical life and perceived risk similarly well.

Optimism Bias

When asked about their risk in comparison to the average risk, people often show unrealistic optimism: They believe themselves to be better off and less likely to experience negative life events (or more likely to experience positive events) than others (Weinstein, 1987). Optimism bias, also termed the *above-average effect* and *comparative optimism*, serves as an explanation of why people often do not take precautions and instead simply discount their personal risk ("It won't happen to me"). For example, when Weinstein (1987) presented participants with 32 different life hazards, participants on average rated their chance of experiencing the hazard to be below average on 25 of them. However, it is important to note that optimism bias is primarily defined on a group level as it compares average

ratings with average population risks. This is due to the fact that one has usually no knowledge about the actual risk of an individual.

Different explanations for optimism bias have been proposed. Shepperd, Carroll, Grace, and Terry (2002) identified four broad categories: (1) the desired end state of comparative judgments (e.g., self-enhancement), (2) cognitive mechanisms (e.g., representativeness heuristic), (3) information about self versus target (e.g., person–positivity bias; discounting background information), and (4) underlying affect (e.g., mood congruency; for an overview, see also Chambers & Windschitl, 2004).

But is thinking to be better than average always a bias? Studies found that the majority of people believe that they drive more safely than the average (Johansson & Rumar, 1968; Svenson, 1981)—which is considered a bias as it is simply not possible that the majority are better than average. However, a closer look at the distribution of car accidents shows that most drivers have few accidents, and few drivers have many accidents. In such a nonsymmetric distribution, the median and the mean are not identical (Gigerenzer, Fiedler, & Olsson, 2012). Hence, the majority of drivers (i.e., more than 50%) have actually less accidents than the average. For instance, of 7,800 drivers in the United States, 80% had fewer accidents than average; and of 440 German drivers, 57% had fewer accidents than average. Hence, in this case, the better-than-average effect is no bias.

Representation of Risk: Fuzzy-Trace Theory

The way we perceive risks strongly depends on how we mentally represent them. Fuzzy-trace theory addresses this issue and distinguishes between two kinds of representations: verbatim and gist (Reyna, 2008; Reyna & Brainerd, 1995). Verbatim representations encode the stimulus objectively—that is, as it actually happened. For example, imagine that mammography screening reduces breast cancer mortality for women aged

50 and older by 1 in 1,000 (i.e., from 5 in 1,000 without screening to 4 in 1,000 with screening) (Gøtzsche & Nielsen, 2011). The verbatim representation would encode the exact wording and numerical information from the statement. In contrast, gist representations are more fuzzy and encode the information subjectively, that is, they interpret the information. For instance, a risk reduction of 1 in 1,000 could be translated into a "small" effect. Although individuals have different gist representations due to experience, knowledge, and emotional reactions, they do not differ in their verbatim representations. Moreover, in contrast to other dual-process approaches, fuzzy-trace theory states that the two representations are encoded, stored, and retrieved in parallel rather than sequentially.

Fuzzy-trace theory has been applied to a wide range of tasks in judgment and decision making and risk perception to explain framing effects, denominator neglect, and the role of emotions in the encoding of risk information (Reyna & Brainerd, 2011). Generally, findings suggest that people rely more heavily on gist than on verbatim representation. This tendency increases with age and expertise. The advantage of gist representations is that they are more stable and less prone to interference, whereas verbatim representations are more error prone and can be easily forgotten. Errors in gist representations can occur (because gist reflects understanding). So a woman might interpret reducing breast cancer with mammography as reducing cancer mortality. However, reliance on gist is generally associated with lower levels of unhealthy risk taking and more developmentally advanced decision making (e.g., Reyna et al., 2011).

Media and Risk Perception

The media are commonly perceived as an important mediator in the perception of risk (see also Part II, Section 4). If the media covered hazards proportional to their actual occurrence, the media would represent a good proxy for the actual frequency of such events. However, if media coverage is disproportional to the actual frequency of a hazard—for instance, if dramatic, low-probability events are covered more often—the media could contribute to people's tendency to misrepresent risks. In an early study, Combs and Slovic (1979) found that the frequency of newspaper reports about causes of death correlated more highly with laypeople's estimates than with the actual frequency. In contrast, Freudenburg, Coleman, Gonzales, and Helgeland (1996) systematically analyzed whether the media primarily exaggerated risks and found only little support: The objective severity of events (i.e., number of casualties) predicted media content. Hence, the frequency of reports in the media is not necessarily biased; just as the media's reaction to events is often quick and dramatic, so, too, is the rate at which such instances diminish in the media and get substituted by other news.

Does the frequency of reporting influence risk perception? In the above-mentioned study by Hertwig and colleagues (2005) on the availability heuristic, fluency—operationalized through the occurrence of instances in the media—did not predict participants' risk judgments of societal risks compared with, for instance, availability-by-recall. Although the media are one source providing information about risks and its occurrence in the environment, it is only one of many factors influencing risk perception, and effects of selective and short-term intensive media coverage may only be temporary (Sjöberg et al., 2000; Wahlberg & Sjöberg, 2000).

However, not only does the frequency of information in the media matter (i.e., *which* information is provided) but also the format of the information (i.e., *how* the information is provided). Media coverage is often biased as it presents incomplete and nontransparent information. For instance, newspaper and Internet reports about the human papillomavirus vaccine lacked fundamental statistical information about its benefits and harms (Bodemer, Müller, Okan, Garcia-Retamero, & Neumeyer-Gromen, 2012). Studies covering participants from nine European countries showed that a vast majority of people overestimates the benefits of cancer screening, or does not know (Gigerenzer, Mata, & Frank, 2009); those who acquired more information about it did not know better, but even tended to know less well. This suggests that many information channels, including the media, often fail to provide adequate information about health risks.

Moderators in Risk Perception

Besides the media, other factors moderate risk perception. We briefly summarize these below.

Age

Risk Perception in Adolescents

. The prevalence of risks and its perceptions is also not constant, but changes across the life span. Whereas some risks are more prevalent in young age (e.g., sexually transmitted diseases, crimes, alcohol), others are more prevalent in older age (e.g., cardiovascular diseases, cancer). A widely held but unsupported belief is that adolescents engage in risky behavior because they feel invulnerable. In fact, the opposite may be true. Quadrel, Fischhoff, and Davis (1993) found that adolescents are less inclined to optimism bias compared with adults. In addition, adolescents provide higher risk estimates than adults for various natural hazards and behavior-linked outcomes (Millstein & Halpern-Felsher, 2002) and overestimate their risk of dying in the near future (Fischhoff, Bruine de Bruin, Parker, Millstein, & Halpern-Felsher, 2010). A second common belief is that adolescents are less rational—however it may be defined—than adults. Yet studies applying fuzzy-trace theory on risk perception obtained the opposite finding: Gist-based representation increased from childhood through adolescence to adulthood (Reyna & Farley, 2006). In other words, adolescents base their decisions more often on verbatim

representations corresponding to the classic notion of "rational" and deliberate thinking.

Risk Perception in Older Adults

Only few studies systematically investigated how older adults perceive risks. Hermand, Mullet, and Rompteaux (1999) compared risk perception across different age groups and included older adults but found no support that older adults show higher risk perceptions than younger adults across 91 hazards (only a slightly higher perception of risks for surgery and radiation therapy). When it comes to the understanding of risks, older adults have difficulties in correctly interpreting health statistics compared with younger adults. Yet adequate communication formats such as graphical tools can overcome shortcomings (Galesic, Garica-Retamero, & Gigerenzer, 2009).

Expertise and Risk Perception

Laypeople's and experts' risk perceptions are often discussed in a dichotomous manner: Experts assess risk objectively, analytically, and wisely, whereas laypeople are more emotional and irrational in their risk perception (Slovic, 1999). However, this may be a very general assumption as it may only hold for some situations, but not all. Sjöberg (1998) proposed three areas in risk perception to illustrate a more fine-grained analysis of the commonalities and differences between laypeople and experts: (1) common, well-known risks (e.g., fatalities for common diseases), (2) technological risks (e.g., nuclear waste disposal), and (3) lifestyle and job environment risks (e.g., domestic radon, smoking, alcohol). In line with the psychometric paradigm, laypeople may show higher risk perception than experts for technology risks. However, the pattern might be reversed for lifestyle and job environment risks. Furthermore, the two groups may, on average, have very similar perceptions in the case of common and well-known risks, where both, laypeople and experts, assess the frequency relatively precisely.

Risk Perception and Values

How we perceive risks also depends on our personal and cultural values, as proposed by the cultural theory of risk (Douglas & Wildavsky, 1983). In one study, Kahan, Braman, Slovic, Gastil, and Cohen (2009) investigated laypeople's perception of the risk of nanotechnology. At the time of the study, the vast majority of participants had never heard of nanotechnology, and risk perception did not depend on cultural values initially. However, after they received balanced information about this technology, participants with different cultural values interpreted the information in different ways: Only a minority (23%) of those with an egalitarian–communitarian worldview (people who tend to take environmental risks seriously) now thought that the benefits of nanotechnology would outweigh the risks. In contrast, a large majority (86%) of those with a hierarchical–individualist worldview (people who tend to dismiss claims of environmental risk) now thought that the benefits of nanotechnology would outweigh the risks.

The White Male Effect

First observed by Flynn, Slovic, and Metz (1994), the white male effect states that white men fear and worry about risks less than women or minorities. Socioeconomic status and education were proposed as possible mechanisms underlying this effect; yet even when controlling for both, the white male effect occurs (Finucane, Slovic, Mertz, Flynn, & Satterfield, 2000). A possible explanation for the effect stems from its interaction with values, worldviews, and culture–identity protection (Kahan, Braman, Gastil, Slovic, & Metz, 2007). First, worldviews correlate with demographic variables. Second, culture/identity-protective cognition suggests that we act in a way to protect identity, that is, our worldviews, interests, and in-group. For instance, people who hold hierarchical and individualistic worldviews may consider guns as less dangerous

(i.e., their perception of risk is lower), as they value guns as part of their social roles and individual virtues. This pattern was most dominant among people with hierarchical and individualistic worldviews, which in turn was most prominent in a subgroup of white males. Hence, the distribution of worldviews in line with culture–identity protection can explain why specific subgroups fear some risks more than others.

The Role of Numeracy in Risk Perception

Individuals differ in their ability to deal with numerical and statistical information, which in turn influences the perception of risks. For instance, people low in numeracy give higher estimates of actual risks and treatment effectiveness than people high in numeracy (Dillard, McCaul, Kelso, & Klein, 2006; Schwartz, Woloshin, Black, & Welch, 1997). Less numerate people are also more sensitive to the way risks are framed, that is, whether a risk is presented in a gain or loss frame, or in percentage or frequency format (Garcia-Retamero & Galesic, 2010; Peters et al., 2006). What actually underlies this effect and whether it is primarily due to less numerate people having difficulties adequately interpreting and using scales measuring risk perception remain open questions (Reyna, Nelson, Han, & Dieckmann, 2009).

Reflections for Theory and Research

With the rise of new technologies in our world, and new developments in cognitive psychology, models and theories have been developed and applied to the perception of risk. The social amplification of risk framework considers risk perception as a communication process within social and institutional contexts. Thereby, it suggests possible factors that influence how we perceive risks and how risk perception develops across different stations; yet it does not make predictions on a cognitive level. The psychometric paradigm focused on the identification of the psychological mechanisms that influence risk perception by highlighting two major factors: dread risk and novelty risk. However, the major level of analysis was on an aggregated level, again neglecting the actual underlying cognitive processes and individual differences. The risk-as-feelings hypothesis, affect heuristic, and availability, in contrast, aim at describing how individuals mentally perceive and judge risks and extends previous models by specifying and testing cognitive process models. Finally, fuzzy-trace theory adapts a dual-process approach to risk perception by distinguishing between verbatim and gist representations. Our understanding of risk perception further requires studying mediating factors such as age, gender, expertise, values, and worldviews.

Despite, or because of, the progress in recent decades, we would like to stress three major approaches for future research on risk perception. First, only limited effort has been spent on integrating different theories and models. Whereas most models have been postulated and tested in isolation, future research may address commonalities and differences and bring together different views to constitute an integrative framework to study risk perception. Thus, the focus should not only be on psychological theories, but it should also apply a multidisciplinary view on risk perception by including concepts from anthropology, sociology, communication research, and technology research. Second, and related, is the fact that most models are perceived as general models that describe and predict risk perception in different domains (i.e., for different risks). However, a more ecological approach might be useful: Just as humans have a wide range of tools in their adaptive toolbox to make decisions and judgments (Gigerenzer, Todd, & the ABC Research Group, 1999; Todd, Gigerenzer, & the ABC Research group, 2012), different tools may exist to assess risks in different situations. Depending on knowledge, time, expertise, and the risk to be judged, different

cognitive strategies may be applied—the key question is when which is used. Third, most research on risk perception has focused on known risks, that is, situations in which the outcome is known and probabilities can be estimated. However, our distinction at the beginning of this chapter highlights that in many situations we do neither know the outcomes nor the probabilities. Up to now, we know only very little how people deal with such truly uncertain situations.

Recommendations for Practice

Based on the knowledge on how the mind perceives risks, we can design environments that facilitate and improve risk perception. For instance, a doctor may overestimate the prevalence of a disease, as she samples patients with the disease disproportionally to the population. After the 9/11 terrorist attacks, many people in the United States avoided flying and switched to their cars instead, resulting in an increase of highway fatalities (Gaissmaier & Gigerenzer, 2012; Gigerenzer, 2006). Understanding the underlying cognitive processes allows improving people's perceptions of risk and design information in such a way to reduce potential flaws in risk judgments.

One illustrative example of how psychological research can help understand and shape debates about public health risk issues was provided by Arkes and Gaissmaier (2012). They investigated the furor that followed when the U.S. Preventive Services Task Force recommended against using the prostate-specific antigen (PSA) test to screen for prostate cancer. Several factors documented by psychological research may have contributed to the public's condemnation of the report, for instance, that an anecdote or two can have a more powerful effect on decision making than a compendium of more reliable statistical data. The information given by the U.S. Preventive Services Task Force that "no trial has shown a decrease in overall mortality with the use of PSA-based screening through 11 years of followup" will not have the same impact as information, say, about the reader's mail carrier's older brother who had a positive PSA test, a biopsy, and a radical prostatectomy, and is now still alive. Psychological research has also developed more effective means to represent statistical information about clinical evidence, including tabular and graphical formats, so that it can be easily understood even by laypeople. Arkes and Gaissmaier suggest that augmenting statistics with these representations might help committees communicate more effectively with the public about health risk issues and with the U.S. Congress and could more generally be used to educate the public and elevate the level of civic discussion. More generally, providing "clean" information would be an important step toward a citizenship that deals with risks in an informed way (Gigerenzer & Gray, 2011).

The other important building block for helping the public understand risk is to teach the psychology and mathematics of risk. It is well documented that, for instance, low statistical numeracy in health distorts perceptions of risks, impedes access to treatments, and is associated with worse health outcomes (Reyna et al., 2009). As Meder and Gigerenzer (2014) put it, "Teaching statistical thinking should be an integral part of comprehensive education, to provide children and adults with the risk literacy needed to make better decisions in a changing and uncertain world" (p. 127). A curriculum that aims at improving people's risk literacy should ideally already start early and target children when they develop their skills and habits (Gigerenzer, 2014). An educated citizen knows which questions to ask and where to get good information and is more strongly protected against undue hopes and anxieties, including distorted perceptions of risk (Gigerenzer, Gaissmaier, Kurz-Milcke, Schwartz, & Woloshin, 2007).

Conclusions

In this chapter, we provided an overview of the psychological theories and models in risk perception research. Risk and risk perception are highly interdisciplinary constructs as they have different connotations in different domains. We reviewed major findings and challenged the individual theories and methods to illustrate their advantages and limitations. The following chapters illustrate the complexity and diversity of risk perception and highlight theoretical approaches to understand the interplay of the mind and the environment and its implications for risk communication.

Suggested Additional Reading

Fischhoff, B. (1995). Risk perception and communication unplugged: Twenty years of process. *Risk Analysis, 15,* 137–145.

Gigerenzer, G. (2002). *Calculated risks: How to know when numbers deceive you.* New York, NY: Simon & Schuster.

Roeser, S., Hillerbrand, R., Sandin, P., & Peterson, M. (2012). *Handbook of risk theory.* London, England: Springer.

References

Alhakami, A. S., & Slovic, P. (1994). A psychological study of the inverse relationship between perceived risk and perceived benefit. *Risk Analysis, 14,* 1085–1096.

Arkes, H. R., & Gaissmaier, W. (2012). Psychological research and the prostate-cancer screening controversy. *Psychological Science, 23,* 547–553.

Bodemer, N., Müller, S. M., Okan, Y., Garcia-Retamero, R., & Neumeyer-Gromen, A. (2012). Do the media provide transparent health information? A cross-cultural comparison of public information about the HPV vaccine. *Vaccine, 30,* 3747–3756.

Bodemer, N., Ruggeri, A., & Galesic, M. (2013). When dread risks are more dreadful than continuous risks: Comparing cumulative population losses over time. *PLoS ONE, 8*(6), e66544. doi:10.1371/journal.pone.0066544

Boholm, A. (1998). Comparative studies of risk perception: A review of twenty years of research. *Journal of Risk Research, 1,* 135–163.

Chambers, J. R., & Windschitl, P. D. (2004). Biases in social comparative judgments: The role of nonmotivated factors in above-average and comparative-optimism effects. *Psychological Bulletin, 130,* 813–838.

Combs, B., & Slovic, P. (1979). Newspaper coverage of causes of death. *Journalism & Mass Communication Quarterly, 56,* 837–849.

Covello, V., von Winterfeldt, D., & Slovic, P. (1987). Communicating risk information to the public. In J. C. Davies, V. Covello, & F. Allen (Eds.), *Risk communication* (pp. 109–134). Washington, DC: Conservation Foundation.

Dillard, A. J., McCaul, K. D., Kelso, P. D., & Klein, W. M. P. (2006). Resisting good news: Reactions to breast cancer risk communication. *Health Communication, 19,* 115–123.

Douglas, M., & Wildavsky, A. B. (1983). *Risk and culture: An essay on the selection of technical and environmental dangers.* Berkeley: University of California Press.

Finucane, M. L., Alhakami, A., Slovic, P., & Johnson, S. M. (2000). The affect heuristic in judgments of risks and benefits. *Journal of Behavioral Decision Making, 13,* 1–17.

Finucane, M. L., Slovic, P., Mertz, C. K., Flynn, J., & Satterfield, T. A. (2000). Gender, race, and perceived risk: The "white male" effect. *Health, Risk & Society, 2*(2), 159–172. doi:10.1080/713670162

Fischhoff, B. (2009). Risk perception and communication. In R. Detels, R. Beaglehole, M. A. Lansang, & M. Gulliford (Eds.), *Oxford textbook of public health* (5th ed., pp. 940–952). Oxford, England: Oxford University Press.

Fischhoff, B., Bruine de Bruin, W., Parker, A. M., Millstein, S. G., & Halpern-Felsher, B. L. (2010). Adolescents' perceived risk of dying. *Journal of Adolescent Health: Official Publication of the Society for Adolescent Medicine, 46,* 265–269.

Fischhoff, B., Slovic, P., Lichtenstein, S., Read, S., & Combs, B. (1978). How safe is safe enough? A psychometric study of attitudes towards technological risks and benefits. *Policy Sciences, 9,* 127–152.

Flynn, J., Slovic, P., & Mertz, C. K. (1994). Gender, race, and perception of environmental health risks. *Risk Analysis, 14*(6), 1101–1108. doi:10.1111/j.1539-6924.1994.tb00082.x

Freudenburg, W. R., Coleman, C.-L., Gonzales, J., & Helgeland, C. (1996). Media coverage of hazard events: Analyzing the assumptions. *Risk Analysis, 16,* 31–42.

Gaissmaier, W., & Gigerenzer, G. (2012). 9/11, Act II: A fine-grained analysis of regional variations in traffic fatalities in the aftermath of the terrorist attacks. *Psychological Science, 23,* 1449–1454.

Galesic, M., & Garcia-Retamero, R. (2012). The risks we dread: A social circle account. *PLoS ONE, 7*(4), e32837.

Galesic, M., Garcia-Retamero, R., & Gigerenzer, G. (2009). Using icon arrays to communicate medical risks: Overcoming low numeracy. *Health Psychology, 28,* 210–216.

Garcia-Retamero, R., & Galesic, M. (2010). How to reduce the effect of framing on messages about health. *Journal of General Internal Medicine, 25,* 1323–1329.

Gardner, G. T., & Gould, L. C. (1989). Public perceptions of the risks and benefits of technology 1. *Risk Analysis, 9,* 225–242.

Gigerenzer, G. (2004). Dread risk, September 11, and fatal traffic accidents. *Psychological Science, 15,* 286–287.

Gigerenzer, G. (2006). Out of the frying pan into the fire: Behavioral reactions to terrorist attacks. *Risk Analysis, 26,* 347–351.

Gigerenzer, G. (2014). *Risk savvy: How to make good decisions.* New York, NY: Penguin Books.

Gigerenzer, G., Fiedler, K., & Olsson, H. (2012). Rethinking cognitive biases as environmental consequences. In P. M. Todd, G. Gigerenzer, & the ABC Research Group (Eds.), *Ecological rationality: Intelligence in the world* (pp. 80–110). New York, NY: Oxford University Press.

Gigerenzer, G., Gaissmaier, W., Kurz-Milcke, E., Schwartz, L. M., & Woloshin, S. (2007). Helping doctors and patients make sense of health statistics. *Psychological Science in the Public Interest, 8,* 53–96.

Gigerenzer, G., & Gray, M. (2011). *Better doctors, better patients, better decisions: Envisioning health care 2020.* Cambridge: MIT Press.

Gigerenzer, G., Mata, J., & Frank, R. (2009). Public knowledge of benefits of breast and prostate cancer screening in Europe. *JNCI Journal of the National Cancer Institute, 101,* 1216–1220.

Gigerenzer, G., Todd, P. M., & the ABC Research Group. (1999). *Simple heuristics that make us smart.* New York, NY: Oxford University Press.

Gøtzsche, P. C., & Nielsen, M. (2011). Screening for breast cancer with mammography. *Cochrane Database of Systematic Reviews,* (1), CD001877.

Hermand, D., Mullet, E., & Rompteaux, L. (1999). Societal risk perception among children, adolescents, adults, and elderly people. *Journal of Adult Development, 6,* 137–143.

Hertwig, R., Pachur, T., & Kurzenhäuser, S. (2005). Judgments of risk frequencies: Tests of possible cognitive mechanisms. *Journal of Experimental Psychology: Learning, Memory, and Cognition, 31,* 621–642.

Hohenemser, C., R., Kates, W., & Slovic, P. (1985). A casual taxonomy. In R. W. Kates, C. Hohenemser, & J. X. Kasperson (Eds.), *Perilous progress: Managing the hazards of technology* (pp. 67–89). Boulder, CO: Westview Press.

Johansson, G., & Rumar, K. (1968). Visible distance s and safe approach speeds for night driving. *Ergonomics, 11,* 275–282.

Kahan, D. M., Braman, D., Gastil, J., Slovic, P., & Mertz, C. K. (2007). Culture and identity-protective cognition: Explaining the white male effect in risk perception. *Journal of Empirical Legal Studies, 4,* 465–505.

Kahan, D. M., Braman, D., Slovic, P., Gastil, J., & Cohen, G. (2009). Cultural cognition of the risks and benefits of nanotechnology. *Nature Nanotechnology, 4,* 87–90.

Kasperson, J. X., Kasperson, R. E., Pidgeon, N., & Slovic, P. (2003). The social amplification of risk: Assessing fifteen years of research and theory. In N. Pidgeon, R. E. Kasperson, & P. Slovic (Eds.), *The social amplification of risk* (pp. 13–46). Cambridge, England: Cambridge University Press.

Knight, F. H. (1921). *Risk, uncertainty, and profit.* Boston, MA: Houghton Mifflin.

Lichtenstein, S., Slovic, P., Fischhoff, B., Layman, M., & Combs, B. (1978). Judged frequency of lethal events. *Journal of Experimental Psychology: Human Learning and Memory, 4,* 551–578.

Loewenstein, G. F., Weber, E. U., Hsee, C. K., & Welch, N. (2001). Risk as feelings. *Psychological Bulletin, 127,* 267–286.

Meder, B., & Gigerenzer, G. (2014). Statistical thinking: No one left behind. In E. J. Chernoff & B. Sriraman (Eds.), *Probabilistic thinking: Presenting plural perspectives* (pp. 127–148). Dordrecht, Netherlands: Springer.

Meder, B., Le Lec, F., & Osman, M. (2013). Decision making in uncertain times: what can cognitive and decision sciences say about or learn from economic crises? *Trends in Cognitive Sciences, 17,* 257–260.

Millstein, S. G., & Halpern-Felsher, B. L. (2002). Judgments about risk and perceived invulnerability in adolescents and young adults. *Journal of Research on Adolescence, 12,* 399–422.

Neumeyer-Gromen, A., Bodemer, N., Müller, S. M., & Gigerenzer, G. (2011). Ermöglichen Medienberichte und Broschüren informierte Entscheidungen zur Gebärmutterhalskrebsprävention? [Do media reports and public brochures facilitate informed decision making about cervical cancer prevention?]. *Bundesgesundheitsblatt—Gesundheitsforschung—Gesundheitsschutz, 54,* 1197–1210.

Pachur, T., Hertwig, R., & Steinmann, F. (2012). How do people judge risks: Availability heuristic, affect heuristic, or both? *Journal of Experimental Psychology: Applied, 18,* 314–330.

Peters, E. (2006). The functions of affect in the construction of preferences. In S. Lichtenstein & P. Slovic (Eds.), *The construction of preference* (pp 454–463). New York, NY: Cambridge University Press.

Peters, E., Vastfjall, D., Slovic, P., Mertz, C. K., Mazzocco, K., & Dickert, S. (2006). Numeracy and decision making. *Psychological Science, 17,* 407–413.

Pidgeon, N. F., Hood, C., Jones, D., Turner, B., & Gibson, R. (1992). Risk perception. In *Risk analysis, perception and management: Report of a Royal Society study group* (pp. 89–134). London, England: Royal Society.

Politi, M. C., Han, P. K. J., & Col, N. F. (2007). Communicating the uncertainty of harms and benefits of medical interventions. *Medical Decision Making, 27*(5), 681–695. doi:10.1177/0272989X07307270

Quadrel, M. J., Fischhoff, B., & Davis, W. (1993). Adolescent (in)vulnerability. *American Psychologist, 48,* 102–116.

Reyna, V. F. (2008). A theory of medical decision making and health: Fuzzy trace theory. *Medical Decision Making, 28,* 850–865.

Reyna, V. F., & Brainerd, C. J. (1995). Fuzzy-trace theory: An interim synthesis. *Learning and Individual Differences, 7,* 1–75.

Reyna, V. F., & Brainerd, C. J. (2011). Dual processes in decision making and developmental neuroscience: A fuzzy-trace model. *Developmental Review, 31,* 180–206.

Reyna, V. F., Estrada, S. M., DeMarinis, J. A., Myers, R. M., Stanisz, J. M., & Mills, B. A. (2011). Neurobiological and memory models of risky decision making in adolescents versus young adults. *Journal of Experimental Psychology: Learning, Memory, and Cognition, 37*(5), 1125–1142. doi:10.1037/a0023943

Reyna, V. F., & Farley, F. (2006). Risk and rationality in adolescent decision making: Implications for theory, practice, and public policy. *Psychological Science in the Public Interest, 7,* 1–44.

Reyna, V. F., Nelson, W. L., Han, P. K., & Dieckmann, N. F. (2009). How numeracy influences risk comprehension and medical decision making. *Psychological Bulletin, 135,* 943–973.

Schwartz, L. M., Woloshin, S., Black, W. C., & Welch, H. G. (1997). The role of numeracy in understanding the benefit of screening mammography. *Annals of Internal Medicine, 127,* 966–972.

Shepperd, J. A., Carroll, P., Grace, J., & Terry, M. (2002). Exploring the causes of comparative optimism. *Psychologica Belgica, 42,* 65–98.

Sjöberg, L. (1996). A discussion of the limitations of the psychometric and cultural theory approaches to risk perception. *Radiation Protection Dosimetry, 68,* 219.

Sjöberg, L. (1998). Risk perception: Experts and the public. *European Psychologist, 3,* 1–12.

Sjöberg, L. (2002a). The allegedly simple structure of experts' risk perception: An urban legend in risk research. *Science, Technology & Human Values, 27,* 443–459.

Sjöberg, L. (2002b). Are received risk perception models alive and well? *Risk Analysis, 22,* 665–669.

Sjöberg, L. (2003). Risk perception is not what it seems: The psychometric paradigm revisited. In K. Andersson (Ed.), VALDOR Conference 2003 (pp. 14–29). Stockholm, Sweden: VALDOR.

Sjöberg, L., Jansson, B., Brenot, J., Frewer, L., Prades, A., & Tönnesen, A. (2000). *Radiation risk perception in commemoration of Chernobyl: A cross-national study in three waves* (Rhizikon: Risk Research Report 33). Stockholm, Sweden: Center for Risk Research.

Sjöberg, L., Moen, B.-E., & Rundmo, T. (2004). *Explaining risk perception: An evaluation of the psychometric paradigm in risk perception research.* Trondheim, Norway: Rotunde.

Slovic, P. (1987). Perception of risk. *Science, 236,* 280–285.

Slovic, P. (1999). Trust, emotion, sex, politics, and science: Surveying the risk-assessment battlefield. *Risk Analysis, 19,* 689–701.

Slovic, P. (2000). *The perception of risk.* London, England: Earthscan.

Slovic, P., Finucane, M., Peters, E., & MacGregor, D. G. (2002). The affect heuristic. In T. Gilovich, D. Griffin, & D. Kahneman (Eds.), *Heuristics and biases: The psychology of intuitive judgment* (pp. 397–420). New York, NY: Cambridge University Press.

Slovic, P., Fischhoff, B., & Lichtenstein, S. (1979). Weighing the risks. *Environment, 21*(5), 17–20, 32–38. (Reprinted in P. Slovic (Ed.). *The perception of risk.* London, England: Earthscan)

Svenson, O. (1981). Are we all less risky and more skillful than our fellow drivers? *Acta Psychologica, 47,* 143–148.

Todd, P. M., & Gigerenzer, G., & the ABC Research Group. (Eds.). (2012). *Ecological rationality: Intelligence in the world.* New York, NY: Oxford University Press.

Tversky, A., & Kahneman, D. (1974). Judgment under uncertainty: Heuristics and biases. *Science, 185,* 1124–1131.

Wahlberg, A. A. F., & Sjöberg, L. (2000). Risk perception and the media. *Journal of Risk Research, 3,* 31–50.

Weinstein, N. D. (1987). Unrealistic optimism about susceptibility to health problems: Conclusions from a community-wide sample. *Journal of Behavioral Medicine, 10,* 481–500.

CHAPTER 2

The Challenge of the Description–Experience Gap to the Communication of Risks

Ralph Hertwig and Renato Frey

Introduction

Experts and the lay public are often at odds with each other when assessing risks. A common explanation for these disagreements in expert and lay opinions is that experts tend to operate on the basis of a technical ("objective") definition of risk. This definition is generally based on a risk's detrimental consequences (e.g., fatalities, injuries, disabilities), weighted by the probabilities of those consequences. Laypeople's assessments of risk—and specifically their perceptions of risk—do not simply follow this metric. Instead, they include other qualitative characteristics of the hazards, such as whether exposure to the risk is voluntary, how controllable the risk is, its catastrophic potential, or its threat to future generations (Slovic, 1987). While acknowledging the importance of this insight that the concept of "risk" means different things to different people, we propose another key factor that may underlie

disagreements between risk experts and the general public. Specifically, information about risks can be acquired via explicit, convenient descriptions of outcomes and their probabilities (e.g., probabilistic weather forecasts, actuarial tables, and mutual fund brochures) or through the sequential experience of the occurrence or nonoccurrence of risky events. Before we explain this distinction (Hertwig, Barron, Weber, & Erev, 2004) in detail, let us describe three instances of expert/lay disagreements. As we will then go on to show, the description–experience distinction offers a key to understanding these disagreements.

Vaccination

Not infrequently, doctors and parents disagree on the benefits and dangers of vaccination. Consider, for example, the decision whether or

Authors' Note: Parts of this text are based on articles by Hertwig and Erev (2009) and Hertwig (2012). We thank Susannah Goss for editing the manuscript and Elsevier and Springer for granting permission rights, and the Swiss National Science Foundation for a grant to the first author (100014–126558).

not to vaccinate a child against diphtheria, tetanus, and pertussis (DTaP). As Hertwig et al. (2004) have described,

> Parents who research the side effects of the DTaP vaccine on the National Immunization Program Web site will find that up to 1 child out of 1,000 will develop high fever and about 1 child out of 14,000 will experience seizures as a result of immunization. (p. 534)

Increasing numbers of parents, after reading such information, decide not to immunize their child. In those U.S. states that permit personal belief exemptions to school and day care immunization requirements, the mean exemption rate increased, on average, by 6% per year, from 0.99% in 1991 to 2.54% in 2004 (Omer et al., 2006). Although doctors have the same statistics at their disposal, they also draw on information not easily available to parents—namely, their personal experience, gathered across many patients, that vaccination rarely results in side effects. Indeed, few doctors have encountered one of the rare cases (1 child in 14,000) of seizures following a vaccination. And even if they have, this experience will be dwarfed by the memory of countless immunizations without side effects. Parents, in contrast, cannot draw on this large stock of personal memories of trouble-free vaccinations.

Terrorism

In the recent past, terrorists have repeatedly targeted tourist centers. In 1997, for instance, terrorists killed 62 people outside the Temple of Queen Hatshepsut at Luxor in Egypt, all but four of them foreigners ("Bloodbath at Luxor," 1997). In 2008, terrorist attacks struck the heart of Mumbai, India's commercial capital, with 166 locals and foreigners being killed in machine-gun and grenade assaults ("Once more to the gallows," 2012). Beyond the lives lost, terrorist attacks exact economic costs—through slumps in the local tourism industry, for example. Yechiam, Barron, and

Erev (2005) analyzed the economic costs of the Al-Aqsa Intifada (uprising), a wave of terrorist attacks in Israel that were "targeted towards specific civilian targets, including hotels, restaurants, cafes, and clubhouses" (p. 432). The costs were operationalized in terms of the number of overnight stays in Israeli hotels before and after the outbreak of the Intifada, separately for domestic and foreign tourists. Domestic tourists might—to use an admittedly rather loose definition—be regarded as "experts on the ground" and foreign tourists as "laypeople." The difference between these two groups was striking: In October 2001, about a year after the onset of the Intifada, the overnight stays of foreign tourists showed an 80% decrease relative to October 2000, as compared with a 20% *increase* for domestic tourists.

Why did "experts" and "laypeople" respond so differently to the threat of terrorist attacks? Acknowledging other contributing factors, Yechiam et al. (2005) proposed that local residents behaved differently because they continued to attend public places such as cafés and markets—where their most common experience was that nothing happened. Terrorist attacks were, fortunately, rare events. Foreign tourists, in contrast, lacked the experience of countless enjoyable or at least uneventful visits to public places. Like parents whose knowledge of vaccination was gleaned from the National Immunization Program website, their primary source of information came via descriptions, here the international media coverage of the most recent terrorist attacks; they did not share the everyday experiences of Israel's residents.

Natural Hazards

Although the most notorious eruption of Mount Vesuvius occurred in 79 CE, destroying Pompeii, the luxurious resort of wealthy Romans, it was not the largest in scope. A Bronze Age eruption around 3780 BCE buried land and villages as far as 25 km (about 16 miles) away, causing the abandonment of the entire area for centuries

(Mastrolorenzo, Petrone, Pappalardo, & Sheridan, 2006). At present, at least 3 million people live within the area that was destroyed by this Bronze Age eruption, and the periphery of Mount Vesuvius includes a significant chunk of the Naples metropolitan area (Bruni, 2003). According to the volcanologists Mastrolorenzo et al. (2006), an eruption comparable in magnitude to the Bronze Age eruption would cause total devastation and mortality within a radius of at least 12 km (about 8 miles). Moreover, volcanologists have argued that it has been roughly 2,000 years since Pompeii, and "with each year, the statistical probability increases that there will be another violent eruption" (Wilford, 2006).

In light of these dire forecasts, one might expect that local residents would be keen to move away from the danger zone. On the contrary, relocating residents has proven extremely difficult, and "in the shadow of Vesuvius, those residents have cultivated a remarkable optimism, a transcendent fatalism and a form of denial as deep as the earth's molten core" (Bruni, 2003). Why the disparity between expert and lay opinions? As we have argued, personal experience or lack thereof may be the key to understanding this and other puzzling disagreements between experts and the lay public. Their personal experience tells residents living in the vicinity of Mount Vesuvius that violent eruptions are extremely rare; in fact, in most people's lifetime, they just do not happen (the last major eruption of the Vesuvius was in 1944; for a similar phenomenon, see the residents of L'Aquila, the Italian town that "had become complacent about the seismic danger" of living near a particular type of fault; Silver, 2012, p. 144). Volcanologists have only numbers (probabilities) and descriptions of possible outcomes to counter the allure of people's personal experience.

The common thread that connects the three introductory examples is that experts and laypeople disagree in their evaluations of the respective risks and that this disagreement may originate in part from the degree to which they rely on description-based versus experienced-based information about risks. Sometimes the

world affords people convenient synopsis descriptions of risky prospects—for example, the side effects detailed in drug package inserts or the risks of adverse weather events (e.g., a hurricane making landfall at a specific location) reported in the media (Gigerenzer, Hertwig, Van Den Broek, Fasolo, & Katsikopoulos, 2005). Equipped with such explicit and quantitative risk information, people can make *decisions from description* (Hertwig et al., 2004). The luxury of such quantified and stated risk information is restricted to just a few domains. In general, we humans have to navigate the perils and opportunities of our environment without tabulated risks. We have to make many consequential decisions, such as whether to marry and have children, as well as countless everyday decisions, such as whether to jaywalk, to back up our computer, or to wear a helmet when cycling, without full knowledge of the whole range of outcomes and their probabilities. To the extent that people's past or present experiences inform their current decisions, people make *decisions from experience* (Hertwig et al., 2004).

Relying on personal experience when assessing risks has interesting implications. Often, but not always, people's samples of personal experience are limited. An individual's experience cannot, generally speaking, approach the scope of the collective, aggregated experience that is encapsulated in tabulated risks. Limited samples, in turn, tend to underrepresent rare (but possibly impactful) events. Therefore, when people draw on their experience, sampled across time, to make decisions involving risks, the chances are that rare events—for example, the eruption of a volcano, the burst of a housing bubble, a vaccination-induced seizure, an accident due to jaywalking, or the loss of vast amounts of data in a computer crash—have *less* impact on people's decisions than they deserve according to their objective probability (see Hertwig & Erev, 2009). But even when a person's immediate experience is sizable (e.g., as in the case of doctors administering hundreds of vaccinations), it may still confer less impact to rare events than explicit descriptions of rare events do (e.g., brochures that inform about the risks of vaccination). Indeed, when people operate on the basis of symbolically described versions of risky events (e.g., distributions of possible outcomes and associated likelihoods), they appear to give rare events *more* weight than they deserve according to their objective probability. This tendency of overweighting of rare events in decisions from description is one of prospect theory's postulates (see Tversky & Kahneman, 1992), the most influential descriptive theory of risky choice; we return to one of the possible explanations of this phenomenon below.

These opposite tendencies regarding the psychological impact of rare events result in a *description–experience gap* (Hertwig et al., 2004): a robust and systematic discrepancy between experience- and description-based choices that has been observed in numerous studies, most (but not all) of them involving monetary gambles (for a review, see Hertwig & Erev, 2009). Before we review the psychology underlying the description–experience gap, let us briefly return to our introductory examples of disagreements between experts and the general public. In many cases, expert and lay decision makers can be distinguished by the degree to which they rely on either experience-based or description-based information, or on both. This difference can go in either direction. As the vaccination example illustrates, expert medical decision makers (i.e., doctors) have access to both statistics on the side effects of vaccination and their personal experience of having administered a vaccine many times. Parents, in contrast, can draw only on the statistics (and possibly the anecdotal experience of other parents, which probably represents a selective sample of experiences of rare adverse side effects; see also Berger, 2007). Similarly, local residents of Israel could draw on their "expert" personal experience as well as on statistics and media reports to gauge the risk of frequenting public places during the Intifada. Foreign tourists, in contrast, only had access to descriptions of events (e.g., newspaper reports). In the case of the Vesuvius, in contrast, it is the local residents and not expert volcanologists who can draw on personal experience of having lived

in the vicinity of the volcano—as well as on experts' "statistical" warnings that the volcano will erupt again.

The relative indifference with which citizens and politicians sometimes consider rare but highly consequential events, such as bursting levees, floods, and eruptions of volcanoes, may be owed to the experience of their rarity. Just as people living in the shadow of Mount Vesuvius have turned down attempts to relocate them, people living in flood plains tend to turn down offers even of federally subsidized flood insurance (Kunreuther, 1984). People who lack pertinent experience have to rely, if available, on descriptions of the possible consequences of risky events and their probabilities (e.g., vaccines and their side effects). In these situations, people appear to overweight the impact of rare events and may then overreact to risks such as side effects of vaccination or the risk of contracting swine flu (H1N1). To understand how people respond to rare but high-consequence events, and to the communication of the respective risks, researchers need to take into account the psychology of people's decisions from experience and from description (Hertwig et al., 2004).

In what follows, we explain the description–experience gap and how it has typically been studied in more detail.

The Description–Experience Gap

Just as biologists use the *Drosophila* as a model organism, behavioral decision researchers have used choice between monetary gambles as a model for risky choice, assuming that many real-world options have the same properties, namely, *n* outcomes and associated probabilities (Lopes, 1983). From this perspective, parents deciding whether not to have their child vaccinated choose between two risky "gambles." The first is to choose vaccination and face two possible outcomes, namely, adverse side effects with a probability p_{SE}, and otherwise a healthy child. The second is to forgo vaccination and face two possible outcomes, namely, the child contracting diphtheria, tetanus, or pertussis with a probability p_{DTaP}, and otherwise a healthy child.

Behavioral decision researchers investigating choice between monetary gambles as a model for risky choice have grown accustomed to presenting

their respondents with one particular genus of the fruit fly: gambles in which all outcomes and their probabilities are stated, and respondents make a single choice, as illustrated in the upper panel of Figure 2.1. And, indeed, parents who

Figure 2.1 A Description-Based Paradigm and Three Experiential Paradigms for Studying Choice

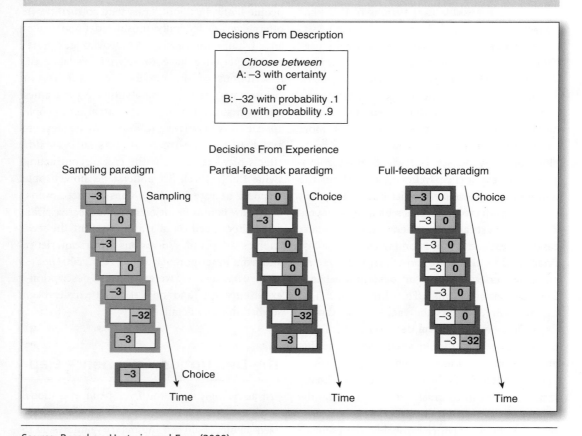

Source: Based on Hertwig and Erev (2009).

Note: How to study decisions from descriptions and experience? The choice task in decisions from description (*upper panel*) typically consists of two monetary gambles with explicitly stated outcomes and their probabilities. In research on decisions from experience (*lower panel*), three paradigms have been employed: The *sampling paradigm* consists of an initial sampling stage (here represented by seven fictitious draws) in which the participant explores two payoff distributions (that offer various monetary outcomes, each one associated with a certain probability) at no cost by clicking on one of two buttons on a computer screen (shown here outlined in light gray). The buttons chosen by the participant are shaded. After terminating sampling, the participant sees a choice screen (here shown outlined in dark gray) and is asked to draw once for real. The *partial-feedback paradigm* collapses sampling and choice; thus, each draw represents an act of both exploration and exploitation. The participant receives feedback on the obtained payoff after each draw (shaded box). The *full-feedback paradigm* is identical to the partial-feedback paradigm, except that it also provides feedback on the forgone payoff (i.e., the payoff that the participant would have received, had he or she chosen the other option; white box).

choose for or against vaccination enjoy the convenience of explicitly described probabilities and outcomes. This is a rare exception, however. In everyday life, people rarely have access to such descriptions of probability distributions. When people decide whether to take out a mortgage or contemplate the success of a first date, there are no tabulated risks to consult. Instead, they need to rely on their previous experience—if existent—of these options. Decisions from experience and decisions from description can be understood as located at opposite ends of a continuum of uncertainty.

In the first years of the new millennium, the observation of systematic and robust differences between decisions based on experience and decisions based on description has drawn decision scientists' interest back to decisions from experience. Before we turn to their findings, let us briefly explain how researchers investigate decisions from experience. In general, they employ a simple experimental tool, a "computerized money machine." Respondents see two buttons on a computer screen, each one representing an initially *unknown* payoff distribution. Clicking a button results in a random draw from the specified distribution. Three variations of this experimental tool have been employed (lower panel of Figure 2.1). In the *sampling paradigm*, participants first sample as many outcomes as they wish and only then decide from which distribution to make a single draw for real (Hertwig et al., 2004; Weber, Shafir, & Blais, 2004). In the *full-feedback paradigm*, each draw contributes to participants' earnings, and they receive draw-by-draw feedback on the obtained and forgone payoffs (i.e., the payoff they would have received had they selected the other option; Yechiam & Busemeyer, 2006). The *partial-feedback paradigm* is identical to the full-feedback paradigm, except that participants are only informed about the obtained payoffs (Barron & Erev, 2003; Erev & Barron, 2005). In contrast to the sampling and full-feedback paradigms, respondents face an exploitation–exploration trade-off partial-feedback paradigm as they negotiate between the two goals associated with every choice: to obtain a desired outcome (exploitation)

or to gather new information about other, perhaps better, actions (exploration; Cohen, McClure, & Yu, 2007).

Across all three experiential paradigms, a robust and systematic *description–experience gap* has emerged in numerous studies. Figure 2.2 illustrates this gap in six decision problems (Erev et al., 2010), each of which offers a choice between a risky option with two outcomes and a safe option. In the risky options, either the desirable outcome or the less desirable outcome occurs with low probability (probability of .1 or less). In all three experiential paradigms, respondents tend to select the risky option when the desirable outcome occurs with high probability but tend to select the safe option when the desirable outcome occurs with low probability. This tendency is reversed in decisions from description. The general pattern can be summarized as follows: In decisions from experience, people behave as if rare events have less impact than they deserve according to their objective probabilities, whereas in decisions from description, people behave as if rare events have more impact than they deserve. By way of illustration, let us consider Problem 1, in which the risky option offers a relatively large gain of 16.5 with a small probability of 1% (and 6.9 otherwise). If the psychological weight of this rare outcome amounts to less than its objective probability, then the overall value of the risky option will become less attractive than the safe bet of 7. Consequently, people will be more likely to choose the safe than the risky option in decisions from experience, and they indeed do (Figure 2.2). If, however, the rare outcome's psychological weight exceeds its objective probability, then the overall value of the risky option will become more attractive, relative to the safe bet of 7. Consequently, people will be more likely to choose the risky than the safe option in decisions from description. The same logic applies to rare events that involve negative consequences (losses), except that people will now be drawn to the safe option in decisions from description and to the risky option in decisions from experience. Figure 2.2 demonstrates this reversal of preferences.

Figure 2.2   The Description–Experience Gap: Proportion of Choices of the Risky Option as a Function of Paradigm (Description vs. Experience) and as a Function of Decision Problems in Which the Rare Event Is Desirable (Maximum) or Undesirable (Minimum)

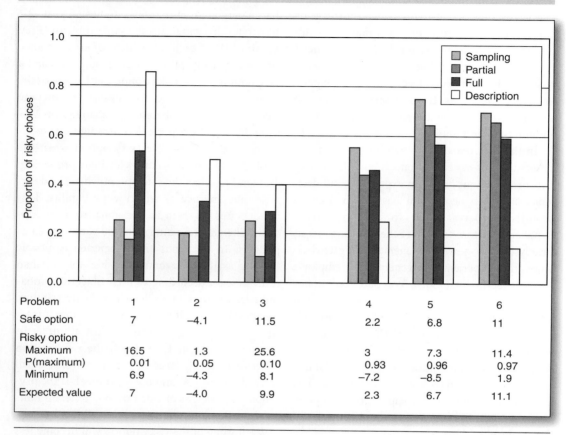

Problem	1	2	3	4	5	6
Safe option	7	−4.1	11.5	2.2	6.8	11
Risky option						
Maximum	16.5	1.3	25.6	3	7.3	11.4
P(maximum)	0.01	0.05	0.10	0.93	0.96	0.97
Minimum	6.9	−4.3	8.1	−7.2	−8.5	1.9
Expected value	7	−4.0	9.9	2.3	6.7	11.1

Source: Based on Hertwig and Erev (2009).

Note: Each decision problem presents a choice between a risky option and a safe option. The decision problems and the expected values of the risky options are displayed below. Each problem was studied using the four paradigms shown in Figure 2.1. Participants (20 per paradigm) were paid (in shekels) the value of one of their choices (which was randomly selected). The partial- and full-feedback paradigms involved 100 choices per problem, and the reported proportions are the means over these choices and participants.

Before we turn to the causes of this reversal, let us briefly review what behavior emerges when respondents receive description *and* experience at the same time. Jessup, Bishara, and Busemeyer (2008) explored how feedback influences repeated decisions from description in a monetary binary choice task. Respondents made 120 repeated choices in response to descriptive information. One group received feedback (indicating their winnings on the previous trial); another group received no feedback. Based on the observed trajectory of choices, the authors concluded, "Apparently, feedback overwhelms descriptive information" (p. 1019), and "individuals who received feedback underweighted small probabilities relative to their no-feedback counterparts" (p. 1019), with the former moving toward linear objective weighting of probabilities.

Similarly, Yechiam et al. (2005) observed that experience limits the effect of description. Using a similar experimental setup as Jessup et al. (2008), Lejarraga and Gonzalez (2011) reached at an even stronger conclusion about the relative impact of description and experience: "Our results suggest that decision makers . . . overlook the descriptive information in an attempt to simplify the cognitive decision process" (p. 289). Whatever the reasons for the observed dominance of experience relative to description, it has potential implications for risk communication; we return to these later.

Reflections for Theory and Research

In this section, we review several factors that have been suggested as contributing to the description–experience gap.

Small Samples

Reliance on small samples has been proposed as one factor that contributes to the attenuated impact of rare events (Hertwig et al., 2004). Across numerous studies employing the sampling paradigm, respondents have typically proved restrained in their information search, with the median number of samples per choice problem typically ranging between 11 and 19 (reviewed in Hau et al., 2010). The chances are that a respondent drawing such small samples will not experience rare events. Even if they do so, the rare event will be encountered less frequently than expected (given its objective probability). This is because the binomial distribution for the number of times a particular outcome will be observed in n independent trials is markedly skewed when p is small (i.e., the event is rare) and n is small (i.e., few outcomes are sampled). For example, let us assume that each of 1,000 players draws 20 times from a distribution in which an attractive outcome occurs with a small probability of .1. Of the

1,000 players, 285 will encounter the event 2 times and could thus estimate its probability accurately. Another 323 will experience the event 3, 4, 5, . . . , or 20 times and would thus most likely overestimate its probability. But 392 players—almost two fifths of the total—will not encounter the event at all, or will encounter it only once, and would thus most likely underestimate its probability.

Interestingly, reliance on small samples has also been discussed as a potential explanation for bumblebees' underweighting of rare events: Having studied the foraging decisions of bees in a spatial arrangement of flowers that promised different amounts of nectar with varying probabilities, Real (1991) concluded that "bumblebees underperceive rare events and overperceive common events" (p. 985). Real (1992) explained this distortion in bees' probability perception as a consequence of their sampling behavior—"bees frame their decisions on the basis of only a few visits" (p. 133)—and suggested that such reliance on small samples can be adaptive:

> Short-term optimization may be adaptive when there is a high degree of spatial autocorrelation in the distribution of floral rewards. In most field situations, there is intense local competition among pollinators for floral resources. When "hot" and "cold" spots in fields of flowers are created through pollinator activity, then such activity will generate a high degree of spatial autocorrelation in nectar rewards. If information about individual flowers is pooled, then the spatial structure of reward distributions will be lost, and foraging over the entire field will be less efficient. In spatially autocorrelated environments ("rugged landscapes"), averaging obscures the true nature of the environment. (p. 135)

In other words, Real (1992) suggested that in environments in which a set of features is clustered together in space, reliance on a small sample is adaptive. Could there be any advantage to frugal sampling in humans' decisions from experience? Hertwig and Pleskac (2008, 2010) proposed one possible advantage that is rooted in the notion of amplification. Unlike Real, however, they argued that amplification offers a cognitive rather than an evolutionary benefit. Through mathematical analysis and computer simulation, Hertwig and Pleskac (2010) showed that small samples amplify the difference between the options' average rewards. That is, drawing small samples from payoff distributions results in experienced differences of sample means that are larger than the objective difference. Such amplified absolute differences make the choice between gambles simpler, thus explaining the frugal sampling behavior observed in investigations of decisions from experience.

This explanation of the description–experience gap in terms of small samples has been the subject of critical debate (Fox & Hadar, 2006). One question is whether the gap observed in the sampling paradigm can in fact be fully attributed to sampling error. Indeed, small samples on average cause the probability of rare events to be underestimated (as illustrated by the above example of 1,000 people and their estimates) and, on average, the smaller the sample, the larger the error. If sampling error were the sole culprit, however, reducing the error by increasing the sample size would attenuate and eventually eliminate the gap. Yet increasing sample sizes substantially (up to 50 and 100 draws per choice problem) reduced, but did not eliminate, the gap (Hau et al., 2010; Hau, Pleskac, Kiefer, & Hertwig, 2008). Were sampling error the sole cause of the gap, moreover, removing the error by aligning the experienced probabilities with the objective probabilities should eliminate it. Yet empirical findings have shown that this is not the case (Ungemach, Chater, & Stewart, 2009). Furthermore, if sampling error were solely to blame, then presenting respondents in the description condition with exactly the same information that others experienced ("yoking") should eliminate the gap. In one study, it did (Rakow, Demes, & Newell, 2008); in another, it did for small but not for large samples

(Hau et al., 2010; see these authors' discussion of "trivial choices" as one possible explanation for the mixed results obtained). Finally, the gap persisted even when people were presented with both descriptions and experience, rather than just descriptions (Jessup et al., 2008).

At this point in the research process, the reality of the description–experience gap across the three experiential paradigms is unchallenged—its cause, however, is debated. Some researchers have argued that the gap in the sampling paradigm is statistical in nature (Fox & Hadar, 2006; Hadar & Fox, 2009; Rakow et al., 2008); others have proposed that the sampling error is not the sole cause (Hau et al., 2008; Hau et al., 2010; Hertwig et al., 2004; Ungemach et al., 2009). Regardless of how this debate advances, it is informative to go beyond the sampling paradigm. Reliance on small samples cannot be the reason behind the description–experience gap in the full-feedback paradigm (see Figure 2.1), for example, in which the impact of rare events is attenuated even after hundreds of trials with perfect feedback. Beyond sampling error, what psychological factors might come into play?

Recency

A psychological factor proposed to contribute to the description–experience gap is *recency* (Hertwig et al., 2004). Ubiquitously observed in memory, belief updating, and judgments (Hogarth & Einhorn, 1992), the recency effect describes the phenomenon that observations made late in a sequence receive more weight than they deserve (i.e., more than $1/n$). Recency is closely related to reliance on small samples: the small sample of recent events can reintroduce the aforementioned skew into large samples of experience. Although the original finding was that people give more weight to outcomes that occurred recently in the flow of their experience than to previous outcomes (Hertwig et al., 2004), later studies showed no or little impact of recency (Hau et al., 2010; Rakow et al., 2008; Ungemach et al., 2009).

Estimation Error

In theory, the description–experience gap could also be the consequence of people systematically *underestimating* the frequency of the rare event that they experienced in the sample (Fox & Hadar, 2006). However, a large stock of studies of frequency and probability assessments report the opposite tendency, namely, overestimation of rare events when people are asked to estimate, for instance, the frequency of lethal events (Hertwig, Pachur, & Kurzenhäuser, 2005; Lichtenstein, Slovic, Fischhoff, Layman, & Combs, 1978). Moreover, studies recording people's estimates of rare events in the sampling paradigm found them to be well calibrated or a little too high relative to the experienced frequency (Hau et al., 2008; Ungemach et al., 2009). That is, people do not systematically estimate rare things to be even rarer.

Reliance on Selective Past Experience

Another factor potentially underlying the description–experience gap, especially in the feedback paradigm, is that people recruit recent and past experiences in similar situations when making decisions (for related notions, see Gilboa & Schmeidler, 1995; Gonzalez & Dutt, 2011). This tendency is likely to be ubiquitous in the wild (Klein, 1999). For example, when firefighters need to predict the behavior of a fire, they appear to retrieve from memory similar instances from the past. Recruiting similar past experiences implies recency and reliance on small sampling to the extent that similarity decreases with time. Furthermore, in dynamic environments (e.g., restless bandit problem; Whittle, 1988), reliance on similar experiences is an efficient heuristic (Biele, Erev, & Ert, 2009). Below, we consider how the process of contingent sampling can be modeled.

Spatial Search Policies

Like any organism, humans can sample information from payoff distributions (e.g., flowers, ponds, other people, gambles) in at least two very different ways. Figure 2.3 depicts two paradigmatic sequential-sampling strategies from two options. In *piecewise* sampling, the searcher oscillates between options, each time drawing (in the most extreme case) the smallest possible sample. In *comprehensive* sampling, in contrast, the searcher samples extensively from one option and only then turns to the other.

Taking these two sampling strategies as a starting point, Hills and Hertwig (2010) suggested that the (spatial) method of sampling foreshadows how people make their final decision. Specifically, they predicted that someone who samples piecewise will make decisions like a judge scoring each round of a boxing match: He or she will determine which option yields the better reward in each round of sampling and will ultimately pick the one that wins the most rounds. In contrast, someone using a comprehensive sampling strategy will gauge the average reward for each option and then choose the one promising the larger harvest. Piecewise and comprehensive sampling strategies thus foster comparisons across different scales of information: rounds versus summaries, respectively. Determining which option is ahead in most rounds versus which yields the largest expected reward can lead to different choices, even when both decision makers experience the exact same information. This is because the piecewise strategy weights each round equally, ignores the magnitude of wins and losses, and thus underweights rare but consequential outcomes. Indeed, Hills and Hertwig (2010) found that individuals who frequently oscillated between options, relative to those who rarely switched, were more likely to choose the roundwise winning options and were also more likely to make choices as if they underweighted rare events.

The Mere-Presentation Effect: Analogical Versus Propositional Representations

All potential causes of the description–experience gap listed so far concern decisions

Figure 2.3 Two Paradigmatic Search Policies in Decisions From Experience

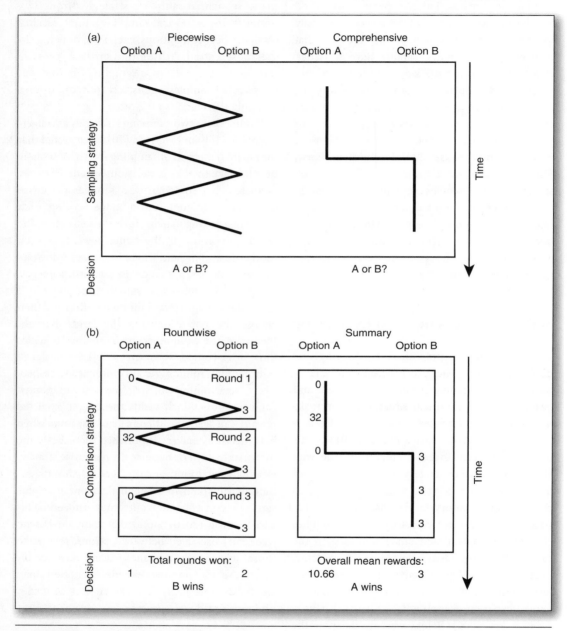

Source: Based on Hills and Hertwig (2010).

Note: (a) Representations of the sampling patterns associated with piecewise and comprehensive sampling strategies. Piecewise strategies repeatedly alternate back and forth between options. Comprehensive sampling strategies take one larger sample from each option. Following the sampling phase, the participants make a decision about which option they prefer. (b) Representations of the comparison strategies associated with roundwise and summary strategies for a set of hypothetical outcomes. Roundwise strategies compare outcomes over repeated rounds and choose options that win the most rounds. Summary strategies compare final values (here, the overall expected value) and choose options with the better final value.

from experience; none deal with the tendency to overweight rare events in decisions from description. But why does this overweighting of rare events occur? The phenomenon has been postulated within prospect theory, the most influential *descriptive* account of how people choose between risky options. Prospect theory deals with empirical violations of the most important *normative* theory of risky choice, namely, expected utility. According to expected utility theory, people making choices behave as if they were multiplying some function of the outcomes' subjective value (utility) with the outcomes' probabilities and value and then maximizing (i.e., choosing the option that promises the highest expected utility). Prospect theory was proposed in response to experimental evidence showing that people systematically violate expected utility theory in their choices. It proposed several modifications of expected utility theory to address these empirical violations. One relates to how people respond to stated probabilities in general and to extreme probabilities in particular. The originators of prospect theory, Kahneman and Tversky (1979) asserted, "Because people are limited in their ability to comprehend and evaluate extreme probabilities, highly unlikely events are either neglected or overweighted, and the difference between high probability and certainty is either neglected or exaggerated" (p. 283). In more formal terms, Kahneman and Tversky argued that people do not take stated probabilities at face value when choosing but that these probabilities enter choices via decision weight. These weights are obtained from the objective probabilities by a nonlinear, inverse S-shaped weighting function that overweights small probabilities and underweights moderate and large ones (resulting in an inverse S shape).

But why should rare events be overweighted when explicitly stated? Hertwig, Barron, Weber, and Erev (2006) and Erev, Glozmann, and Hertwig (2008) suggested that a mere mention of those events lends them weight—a phenomenon they referred to as the *mere-presentation effect*. The *propositional* (symbolic) representations of options in decisions from description—for instance, "32

with probability .1; 0 otherwise"—may put more equal emphasis on the possible outcomes than the actual probabilities of occurrence warrants. If attention translates into decision weight, as some research suggests (Weber & Kirsner, 1996), then, other things being equal, the weights of rare and common events will draw closer together than they should. Decisions from experience, in contrast, rest on an *analogical* representation. For instance, 10 draws from the option "32 with probability .1; 0 otherwise" can be experienced as 0, 0, 0, 0, 0, 32, 0, 0, 0, 0. Information regarding the relative frequency of the option's outcomes can thus be read off directly. Moreover, to the extent that more attention is automatically allocated to the processing of the event that occurs more frequently (i.e., 0) than the rare event (i.e., 32), the resulting weights may more accurately reflect the sample probabilities (and, by extension, the objective probabilities).

In sum, having previously focused on people's responses to descriptions of events, behavioral decision research has more recently turned to decisions from experience, using three experiential paradigms to study how experience affects risky choice. A consistent picture has emerged: Description- and experience-based decisions can drastically diverge, especially when rare events are involved (for the demonstration of the gap with common events, see Ludvig & Spetch, 2011). Several factors have been proposed (e.g., sampling error, recency, reliance on selective past experience, propositional representation) as causing people to give rare events less impact than they deserve (according to their objective probabilities) in decisions from experience but more impact than they deserve in decisions from description. We now discuss the implications of the description–experience gap when extrapolated to the domain of risk communication.

Recommendations for Practice

The psychologist Paul Slovic (2000) described the following experience as the starting point of his influential research program on risk perception:

In 1970, I was introduced to Gilbert White, who asked if the studies on decision making under risk that Lichtenstein and I had been doing could provide insight into some of the puzzling behaviors he had observed in the domain of human response to natural hazards. Much to our embarrassment, we realized that our laboratory studies had been too narrowly focused on choices among simple gambles to tell us much about risk-taking behavior in the flood plain or on the earthquake fault. (p. xxxi)

We are sympathetic to Slovic's sober assessment of the limited value that studying choices among simple gambles has for understanding people's behavior under risk. However, we believe that the discovery of the description–experience gap has led to interesting insights that, if they generalize beyond simple monetary gambles, may immensely benefit our understanding of potential obstacles to successful risk communication. So what are the potential implications of the description–experience gap? Our starting premise is that risk communication typically involves *descriptive* information.

The domains portrayed in our introductory examples differ in the extent to which receivers of risk communication have had the opportunity to personally experience the occurrence and nonoccurrence of the risk in question. In the domain of vaccination, parents—or, more generally, people considering vaccination—typically have no direct experience of the side effects of vaccination. They are thus blank slates, and communication about side effects and the associated probabilities will not compete with direct personal experience. In contrast, most residents of Naples have lifelong experience of living safe and sound in the shadow of the Vesuvius. They will evaluate warnings about the impending danger of a violent eruption against the backdrop of this experience. To predict the impact of a risk warning, communicators therefore need to take into account the receiver's degree of experience and the extent to which the warning may be at odds with this experience.

The issue is not just whether or not people have personal experience of a risk, however, but the rarity of that risk and, relatedly, the scope of personal experience. If the risk in question is a "black swan" (Taleb, 2007), a highly improbable event that occurs on average once in, say, 50 years, then a person may not know of its existence or may consider it to be less likely than it is. If, in contrast, a person has had opportunity to experience a very rare event—or, equally importantly, its nonoccurrence—through, for instance, administering thousands of vaccinations, his or her experienced sampled frequencies ("natural frequencies"; Gigerenzer & Hoffrage, 1995) may reflect the risks' objective frequencies quite accurately. But even considerable experience may result in underrepresentation of the rare risk due to recency (as mentioned above). Because improbable events are less likely to have occurred recently as compared with anytime during one's whole life, recency lessens the event's impact on people's choices. But the opposite also holds. Once a rare, high-impact event has recently occurred, recency is likely to give it a larger impact on behavior than its probability warrants. For instance, after four planes crashed in the terrorist attacks of September 11, 2001, many people stopped flying, at least temporarily, and instead drove some of the miles not flown. According to Gigerenzer's (2004) analysis (see also Gaissmaier & Gigerenzer, 2012), this response caused more people to lose their lives on the road by avoiding the risk of flying than were killed in the four fatal flights on 9/11.

Risk warnings do not operate in a vacuum. Sometimes people have experienced many safe encounters prior to receiving a warning (e.g., the repeated experience of unprotected sex without contracting a sexually transmitted disease); sometimes they receive the warning right after disaster has struck for the first time; sometimes they are blank slates with no experience at all. In all likelihood, how risk communication affects behavior depends on people's past experience. The few available studies that have investigated (focusing on monetary gambles) the relative impact of description and experience when they co-occur suggest that experience tends to overpower description (Jessup et al., 2008; Lejarraga & Gonazlez, 2011). Without understanding the interplay of description and experience, scientists and policymakers will continue to be surprised by how ineffectual risk communication can be (see Barron, Leider, & Stack, 2008).

To date, we know of only one systematic investigation of this interplay that explicitly addressed the context of risk warnings and communication (Barron et al., 2008). The authors concluded that, even after being adequately warned, some people may continue to take risks simply because they have experienced good outcomes after making the same choice in the past (consistent with Jessup et al., 2008; Lejarraga & Gonazlez, 2011). One of their illustrations of the allure of positive experiences is the case of Vioxx, a nonsteroidal, anti-inflammatory drug developed by Merck & Co. When the drug was found to increase the risk of heart attack, an alert was first added to the package insert, and the drug was ultimately taken off the global market. Yet more than 2 million people continued to take the drug until their prescription ran out; presumably because they had taken it for quite some time without adverse consequences. Clearly, behavioral decision research has only just begun to appreciate that in many situations people can recruit descriptive or experienced-based information. What is now needed is a better understanding of the conditions under which these information sources are contradictory and of which source then gets the upper hand.

Let us briefly sketch one important line of future scientific inquiry. Personal experience is a powerful consultant (Weinstein, 1989). But some evolving 21st-century risks, such as the risks brought about by climate change, are "virtually impossible to detect from personal experience, amid the noise of random fluctuation around the central trend" (Weber & Stern, 2011, p. 318). Under such circumstances, personal experience offers the wrong advice and is possibly one key

driver behind the public (e.g., in the United States) lacking the willingness to take action against climate change. One key task for future research is therefore to find out whether and to what extent it may be possible to retrain the powerful consultant of personal experience through experience garnered in virtual realities (Weber & Stern, 2011). These learning environments offer the opportunity to experience various possible future climates—including catastrophic events that, although unlikely, deserve being taken into account: Today's black swans may turn lighter in the future.

Conclusions

Really good things and really bad things happen infrequently. Most of us experience only one true love. Few of us get to graduate from Stanford or Oxford and become rocket scientists, brain surgeons, or CEOs; even fewer make it as movie stars. By the same token, few of us lose our life's savings in a stock market crash, are rendered quadriplegic in an accident, or have a debilitating birth defect. The events of our brightest dreams and darkest nightmares tend to happen rarely. We can learn about such rare opportunities and dangers in at least two ways: (1) through symbolic representations or (2) through personal experience. Research on how people make risky choices has recently arrived at an important insight: These two types of information, description and experience, can prompt qualitatively different choices. Although the original findings pertained to choices among simple gambles, the description–experience gap also applies to the world outside decision scientists' laboratories. We suggest that the description–experience gap is one key to a better understanding of why experts and the general public are often at odds with each other when reckoning with risks. It also explains why risk communications and expert warnings clothed in numbers (probabilities) and descriptions of possible outcomes lack persuasive power.

Suggested Additional Readings

Hertwig, R. (in press). Decisions from experience. In G. Keren & G. Wu (Eds.), *Blackwell handbook of decision making*. Oxford, England: Blackwell.

Weber, E. U. (2013). Doing the right thing willingly: Behavioral decision theory and environmental policy. In E. Shafir (Ed.), *The behavioral foundations of public policy* (pp. 380–397). Princeton, NJ: Princeton University Press.

References

Barron, G., & Erev, I. (2003). Small feedback-based decisions and their limited correspondence to description-based decisions. *Journal of Behavioral Decision Making, 16*, 215–233. doi:10.1002/bdm.443

Barron, G., Leider, S., & Stack, J. (2008). The effect of safe experience on a warning's impact: Sex, drugs, and rock-n-roll. *Organizational Behavior and Human Decision Processes, 106*(2), 125–142. doi:10.1016/j.obhdp.2007.11.002

Berger, C. R. (2007). A tale of two communication modes: When rational and experiential processing systems encounter statistical and anecdotal depictions of threat. *Journal of Language and Social Psychology, 26*, 215–333. doi:10.1177/0261927X06303453

Biele, G., Erev, I., & Ert, E. (2009). Learning, risk attitude and hot stoves in restless bandit problems. *Journal of Mathematical Psychology, 53*, 155–167. doi:10.1016/j.jmp.2008.05.006

Bloodbath at Luxor. (1997, November 20). *The Economist*. Retrieved from http://www.economist.com/node/106278

Bruni, F. (2003, August 26). San Giuseppe Vesuviano journal; Who's afraid of Vesuvius? (Pompeii is history). *The New York Times*. Retrieved from http://www.nytimes.com/2003/08/26/world/san-giuseppe-vesuviano-journal-who-s-afraid-of-vesuvius-pompeii-is-history.html

Cohen, J. D., McClure, S. M., & Yu, A. J. (2007). Should I stay or should I go? How the human brain manages the trade-off between exploitation and exploration. *Philosophical Transactions of the Royal Society B: Biological Sciences, 362*, 933–942. doi:10.1098/rstb.2007.2098

Erev, I., & Barron, G. (2005). On adaptation, maximization, and reinforcement learning among cognitive strategies. *Psychological Review, 112*, 912–931. doi:10.1037/0033–295X.112.4.912

Erev, I., Ert, E., Roth, A. E., Haruvy, E., Herzog, S. M., Hau, R., . . . Lebiere, C. (2010). A choice prediction competition: Choices from experience and from description. *Journal of Behavioral Decision Making, 23*, 15–47. doi:10.1002/bdm.683

Erev, I., Glozmann, I., & Hertwig, R. (2008). What impacts the impact of rare events. *Journal of Risk and Uncertainty, 36*, 153–177. doi:10.1007/s11166–008–9035-z

Fox, C. R., & Hadar, L. (2006). "Decisions from experience" = sampling error + prospect theory: Reconsidering Hertwig, Barron, Weber & Erev (2004). *Judgment and Decision Making, 1*, 159–161.

Gaissmaier, W., & Gigerenzer, G. (2012). 9/11, Act II: A fine-grained analysis of regional variations in traffic fatalities in the aftermath of the terrorist attacks. *Psychological Science, 23*(12), 1449–1454. doi:10.1177/0956797612447804

Gigerenzer, G. (2004). Dread risk, September 11, and fatal traffic accidents. *Psychological Science, 15*(4), 286–287. doi:10.1111/j.0956–7976.2004.00668.x

Gigerenzer, G., Hertwig, R., Van Den Broek, E., Fasolo, B., & Katsikopoulos, K. V. (2005). "A 30% chance of rain tomorrow": How does the public understand probabilistic weather forecasts? *Risk Analysis, 25*, 623–629.

Gigerenzer, G., & Hoffrage, U. (1995). How to improve Bayesian reasoning without instruction: Frequency formats. *Psychological Review, 102*, 684–704. doi:10.1037/0033–295X.102.4.684

Gilboa, I., & Schmeidler, D. (1995). Case-based decision-theory. *Quarterly Journal of Economics, 110*, 605–639. doi:10.2307/2946694

Gonzalez, C., & Dutt, V. (2011). Instance-based learning: Integrating sampling and repeated decisions from experience. *Psychological Review, 118*, 523–551. doi:10.1037/a0024558

Hadar, L., & Fox, C. R. (2009). Information asymmetry in decision from description versus decision from experience. *Judgment and Decision Making, 4*, 317–325.

Hau, R., Pleskac, T. J., & Hertwig, R. (2010). Decisions from experience and statistical probabilities: Why they trigger different choices than a priori probabilities. *Journal of Behavioral Decision Making, 23*, 48–68. doi:10.1002/bdm.665

Hau, R., Pleskac, T. J., Kiefer, J., & Hertwig, R. (2008). The description–experience gap in risky choice: The role of sample size and experienced probabilities. *Journal of Behavioral Decision Making, 21,* 493–518. doi:10.1002/bdm.598

Hertwig, R. (2012). The psychology and rationality of decisions from experience. *Synthese, 187,* 269–292.

Hertwig, R., Barron, G., Weber, E. U., & Erev, I. (2004). Decisions from experience and the effect of rare events in risky choice. *Psychological Science, 15,* 534–539. doi:10.1111/j.0956-7976.2004.00715.x

Hertwig, R., Barron, G., Weber, E. U., & Erev, I. (2006). Decisions from experience: Sampling and updating of information. In K. Fiedler & P. Juslin (Eds.), *Information sampling and adaptive cognition.* New York, NY: Cambridge University Press.

Hertwig, R., & Erev, I. (2009). The description–experience gap in risky choice. *Trends in Cognitive Sciences, 13,* 517–523. doi:10.1016/j.tics.2009.09.004

Hertwig, R., Pachur, T., & Kurzenhäuser, S. (2005). Judgments of risk frequencies: Tests of possible cognitive mechanisms. *Journal of Experimental Psychology: Learning Memory and Cognition, 35,* 621–642. doi:10.1037/0278-7393.31.4.621

Hertwig, R., & Pleskac, T. J. (2008). The game of life: How small samples render choice simpler. In N. Chater & M. Oaksford (Eds.), *The probabilistic mind: Prospects for Bayesian cognitive science* (pp. 209–235). Oxford, England: Oxford University Press.

Hertwig, R., & Pleskac, T. J. (2010). Decisions from experience: Why small samples? *Cognition, 115,* 225–237. doi:10.1016/j.cognition.2009.12.009

Hills, T. T., & Hertwig, R. (2010). Information search in decisions from experience: Do our patterns of sampling foreshadow our decisions? *Psychological Science, 12,* 1787–1792. doi:10.1177/0956797610387443

Hogarth, R. M., & Einhorn, H. J. (1992). Order effects in belief updating: The belief-adjustment model. *Cognitive Psychology, 24,* 1–55. doi:10.1016/0010-0285(92)90002-J

Jessup, R. K., Bishara, A. J., & Busemeyer, J. R. (2008). Feedback produces divergence from prospect theory in descriptive choice. *Psychological Science, 19,* 1015–1022. doi:10.1111/j.1467-9280.2008.02193.x

Kahneman, D., & Tversky, A. (1979). Prospect theory: Analysis of decision under risk. *Econometrica, 47*(2), 263–291. doi:10.2307/1914185

Klein, G. A. (1999). *Sources of power: How people make decisions.* Cambridge: MIT Press.

Lejarraga, T., & Gonzalez, C. (2011). Effects of feedback and complexity on repeated decisions from description. *Organizational Behavior and Human Decision Processes, 116*(2), 286–295.

Lichtenstein, S., Slovic, P., Fischhoff, B., Layman, M., & Combs, B. (1978). Judged frequency of lethal events. *Journal of Experimental Psychology: Human Learning and Memory, 4,* 551–578. doi:10.1037/0278-7393.4.6.551

Lopes, L. L. (1983). Some thoughts on the psychological concept of risk. *Journal of Experimental Psychology: Human Perception and Performance, 8,* 137–144. doi:10.1037/0096-1523.9.1.137

Ludvig E. A., & Spetch M. L. (2011). Of black swans and tossed coins: Is the description–experience gap in risky choice limited to rare events? *PLoS ONE, 6*(6), e20262. doi:10.1371/journal.pone.0020262

Mastrolorenzo, G., Petrone, P., Pappalardo, L., & Sheridan, M. F. (2006). The Avellino 3780-yr-B.P. catastrophe as a worst-case scenario for a future eruption at Vesuvius. *Proceedings of the National Academy of Sciences of the United States of America, 103,* 4366–4370. doi:10.1073/pnas.0508697103

Omer, S. B., Pan, W. K., Halsey, N. A., Stokley, S., Moulton, L. H., Navar, A. M., . . . Salmon, D. A. (2006). Nonmedical exemptions to school immunization requirements. *JAMA, 296*(14), 1757–1763. doi:10.1001/jama.296.14.1757

Once more to the gallows. (2012, November 24). *The Economist.* Retrieved from http://www.economist.com/news/asia/21567104-renewed-unwelcome-enthusiasm-execution-once-more-gallows

Rakow, T., Demes, K. A., & Newell, B. R. (2008). Biased samples not mode of presentation: Re-examining the apparent underweighting of rare events in experience-based choice. *Organizational Behavior and Human Decision Processes, 106,* 168–179. doi:10.1016/j.obhdp.2008.02.001

Real, L. A. (1991). Animal choice behavior and the evolution of cognitive architecture. *Science, 253,* 980–986. doi:10.1126/science.1887231

Real, L. A. (1992). Information processing and the evolutionary ecology of cognitive architecture. *American Naturalist, 140,* 108–145. doi:10.1086/285399

Silver, N. (2012). *The signal and the noise: Why so many predictions fail—but some don't.* New York, NY: Penguin Books.

Slovic, P. (1987). Risk perception. *Science, 236*(4799), 280–285. doi:10.1126/science.3563507

Slovic, P. (2000). *The perception of risk.* London, England: Earthscan.

Taleb, N. N. (2007). *The black swan: The impact of the highly improbable.* New York, NY: Random House.

Tversky, A., & Kahneman, D. (1992). Advances in prospect theory: Cumulative representation of uncertainty. *Journal of Risk and Uncertainty, 5*(4), 297–323. doi:10.1007/BF00122574

Ungemach, C., Chater, N., & Stewart, N. (2009). Are probabilities overweighted or underweighted when rare outcomes are experienced (rarely)? *Psychological Science, 20,* 473–479. doi:10.1111/j.1467-9280.2009.02319.x

Weber, E. U., & Kirsner, B. (1996). Reasons for rank-dependent utility evaluation. *Journal of Risk and Uncertainty, 14,* 41–61. doi:10.1023/A:1007769703493

Weber, E. U., Shafir, S., & Blais, A.-R. (2004). Predicting risk-sensitivity in humans and lower animals: Risk as variance or coefficient of variation. *Psychological Review, 111,* 430–445. doi:10.1037/0033-295X.111.2.430

Weber, E. U., & Stern, P. C. (2011). Public understanding of climate change in the United States. *American Psychologist, 66*(4), 315–328. doi:10.1037/a0023253

Weinstein, N. D. (1989). Effects of personal experience on self-protective behavior. *Psychological Bulletin, 105*(1), 31–50. doi:10.1037/0033-2909.105.1.31

Whittle, P. (1988). Restless bandits: Activity allocation in a changing world. *Journal of Applied Probability, 25A,* 287–298. doi:10.2307/3214163

Wilford, J. N. (2006, March 7). Long before burying Pompeii, Vesuvius vented its wrath. *The New York Times.* Retrieved from http://www.nytimes.com/2006/03/07/science/07volc.html

Yechiam, E., Barron, G., & Erev, I. (2005). The role of personal experience in contributing to different patterns of response to rare terrorist attacks. *Journal of Conflict Resolution, 49,* 430–439. doi:10.1177/0022002704270847

Yechiam, E., & Busemeyer, J. R. (2006). The effect of foregone payoffs on underweighting small probability events. *Journal of Behavioral Decision Making, 19,* 1–16. doi:10.1002/bdm.509

CHAPTER 3

The Feeling of Risk

Implications for Risk Perception and Communication

Stephan Dickert, Daniel Västfjäll, Robert Mauro, and Paul Slovic

Introduction

Being confronted with risks often elicits affective reactions and emotions with varying degrees of strength and valence. Indeed, the link between risk perceptions and emotions is a natural one for the simple fact that emotions serve as beacons for what is dangerous in our surroundings. Affective information is evolutionary; important neural pathways have been prewired in the brain to ensure fast processing of emotionally meaningful information (LeDoux, 1996; Vuilleumier, 2005). However, besides emotions, we also have other, more deliberative means at our disposal to process information related to risk. Contrary to the viewpoint that affective reactions serve only as biases that muddy the water for risk assessors, both affective reactions and deliberative analyses can contribute to rational risk assessments (Slovic, Finucane, Peters, & MacGregor, 2004). One of the challenges for modern theories of risk perception and communication is to identify when and why information about risks sparks affective reactions and when it fails to do so.

The emerging psychological literature on risk perception highlights two fundamentally different ways in which people react to risks: One is characterized by intuitive and instinctual reactions, whereas the other is based on logic, deliberation, and scientific reasoning (Slovic et al., 2004; Slovic & Peters, 2006). The latter is known as *risk-as-analysis*, while the former is strongly related to our experiences and is labeled *risk-as-feelings* (Loewenstein, Weber, Hsee, & Welch, 2001; Slovic et al., 2004; Slovic, Finucane, Peters, & MacGregor, 2002). This distinction is in line with a large body of literature on dual-information processing, postulating that information can be processed and experienced in terms of feelings as well as cognitive faculties (e.g., Epstein, 1994; Evans, 2008; Kahneman, 2003). In what Kahneman

Authors' Note: This research was supported by Grant 1227729 from the U.S. National Science Foundation and by the Swedish Research Council (VR).

(2011) labels the *fast thinking* process, information is quickly and associatively linked to experiences and feelings related to objects. Conversely, a more controlled *slow thinking* process enables careful deliberative analyses as well as judgments and decisions based on reasoning.

Several ways in which affect and emotions may influence information processing have been proposed to indicate why the *feeling of risk* often follows different rules and can produce different risk perceptions than a more analytical approach to risk (Slovic, 2010a). A closer look at the functions of affect and emotions in bringing meaning to reality and in interpreting our surroundings highlights the importance of understanding the role of affect in information processing (e.g., Peters, 2006; Peters, Västfjäll, Gärling, & Slovic, 2006; see also Pfister & Böhm, 2008). Of specific interest for the study of risk perceptions is the notion that affect and emotions can serve as information, as a spotlight for directing our attention, as common currency in the trade-off between different decision alternatives, and as motivation for actions. For example, people can rely on their feelings toward technologies, activities, and objects to make judgments about risk. Likewise, the affect associated with specific outcomes can serve as a spotlight by drawing attention to certain decision attributes at the expense of others. Moreover, when different and mutually exclusive options are present, the associated affect can help decide between different courses of actions (Cabanac, 2002). The notion of affect as a common currency is also supported by neurophysiological approaches to the study of valuations (Montague & Berns, 2002). Last, affect and emotions are fundamental for motivating actions (Damasio, 1994; Zeelenberg, Nelissen, Breugelmans, & Pieters, 2008). These different functions of affect and emotions can explain why risk perceptions that are based on feelings can deviate from more deliberative, analytical judgments. We next introduce the concepts of

feelings in more detail and then explain the role of *risk-as-feeling* in facilitating risk communication.

Affect and Emotion: Definitions and Classifications

In the following section, we focus on the differences between affect and emotion, integral versus incidental affect, and anticipatory versus anticipated affect. Given the widespread disagreement within the field of emotion research on the definition of affective experiences (e.g., Fehr & Russell, 1984), these distinctions are not always clear-cut but rather a guideline of how to conceptualize the different constructs and their relation to risk perception, information processing, and decision making under risk.[1]

The terms *affect* and *emotion* often refer to identical constructs. The conceptual distinctions between affect and emotion are arguably less important than their functions in the perception of risk. Both can serve as powerful and compelling sources of information about risks. Nonetheless, some important differences exist (Dickert, 2010; Västfjäll & Slovic, 2013). As different conceptions of the terminology (especially for the term *affect*) are present in the literature, we will briefly outline the definition used in this chapter. We refer to affect as a relatively brief, conscious or subconscious experience that varies along a positive–negative continuum. Usually, no extensive cognitive work is needed to generate affective responses, as these are often based on automatically activated associations. Note your automatic affective reaction to the words *nemesis* or *vacation*. However, affective reactions might also spring from deliberation (e.g., comparisons between risky options). Affect can dissipate relatively quickly, and it is primarily one-dimensional along a positive–negative valence continuum that signals the goodness or badness of something. The primary distinction between affect and mood states is that affect is often integral to a decision (i.e., the affective reaction springs from the choice options or decision attributes, see below for details). Mood states are longer lasting and often incidental to the decision.

Whereas affect can refer to the first, often automatic appraisal and concomitant response, specific emotions require additional cognitive appraisals and produce increasingly differentiated responses. Emotions are usually conscious, object-related, and specific in their valence, arousal, and cognitive underpinnings. They are conceptualized either as distinct with cognitive and motivational properties (e.g., Frijda, 1986; Lerner & Keltner, 2000, 2001; Zeelenberg et al., 2008) or as a construct based on two dimensions (valence and arousal; Russell, 2003; Russell & Feldman Barrett, 1999), three dimensions (valence, arousal, and locus of control; Osgood, Suci, & Tannenbaum, 1957; Russell & Mehrabian, 1977), or, in complex situations, n-dimensions. For instance, fear can be characterized as a negatively valenced, high-arousal state where an approach/ avoidance motivation is activated, and personal control and certainty are high (Lerner & Keltner, 2001). Unlike affect, the object specificity and conscious experience of emotions tightly connects them to more elaborate cognitive appraisals. Most important among the differences, however, is that emotions are usually more intense experiences than affect. In fact, Slovic and colleagues (2004) called affect a "faint whisper of emotion" (p. 2), which is the underpinning for much of the *risk-as-feeling* approach to risk perception.

Integral Versus Incidental Affect and Emotions

Integral and incidental affective experiences distinguish affect and emotions according to their source. Integral affect and emotions are feelings related to real or imagined stimuli or decision situations. They are object-specific in that the quality of the object, decision attribute, or potential consequence gives rise to affect or distinct emotions. These feelings inform people about specific properties of the stimuli and/or the decision environment. Integral affect is used as information about

risks, especially under time pressure and complex decision environments (Finucane, Alhakami, Slovic, & Johnson, 2000; see also Klein, Orasanu, Calderwood, & Zsambook, 1993), and is essential to rational decision making under risk (Damasio, 1994; Slovic et al., 2004).

Incidental affect and emotions, in contrast, are feelings unrelated to specific stimuli or decision situations and often surface as mood states without a clear source. These mood states can be informative for decision making and risk perception, although they are often not directly relevant for the decision. Typically, they cause risk perceptions and decisions to deviate from more objective considerations. For example, incidental emotions have been shown to bias economic evaluations (Lerner, Small, & Loewenstein, 2004). In risk perception, they can be a source of information, motivation, and direct attention to highlight mood congruent information (Bower & Forgas, 2000; Isen, 2001; Nabi, 2003). Importantly, incidental affect can also have opposite effects on risk perception. A mood congruent probability judgment emerges if people in a positive mood judge risks to be lower than they actually are, and if they exhibit holistic and flexible thinking in positive moods and analytic and detailed thinking in negative moods (Andrade, 2005). However, the reverse pattern may also occur, such that mood has an incongruent effect on probability judgment. Specifically, positive mood can lead to an overestimation of the probability of risk and to risk-averse behavior (i.e., to avert negative consequences and stay in a positive mood). Additionally, negative mood can also lead to risk-seeking behavior (Isen, 2001). Understanding the conditions in which affect-congruent and -incongruent behaviors occur is an important task for future research.

Anticipatory Versus Anticipated Affect and Emotions

Risk perception and decisions under risk are influenced by both anticipatory and anticipated affect and emotions. Affective experiences are often connected to future decision outcomes that represent risky consequences. For example, deciding whether to get vaccinated against a rare but deadly disease and risking serious side effects due to the vaccination is linked to an affective representation of the possible decision outcomes. These representations can be anticipated in future states of well-being as well as anticipatory in the way they influence information processing of decision attributes (Loewenstein et al., 2001; Loewenstein & Lerner, 2003; Västfjäll & Gärling, 2002).

The main difference between anticipated and anticipatory affective experiences is that anticipated affect and emotions are cognitive representations of how one expects to feel in the future, while anticipatory affect and emotions are actually experienced in the moment when decisions are made. Thus, deciding on whether to get vaccinated can depend on one's forecast of an anticipated affective state (e.g., feeling safer due to the vaccination). These cognitive representations constitute part of a decision's outcome utility that can be integrated into the other characteristics of decision outcomes. According to this approach, the decision to buy a lottery ticket depends not only on the price of the lottery ticket, the winning chances, and the price fund but also on how the decision maker anticipates *feeling* if he or she wins or loses. However, these affective predictions are often off the mark because the decision maker is unable to take other characteristics into account that might change the person's well-being (Gilbert, Pinel, Wilson, Blumberg, & Wheatley, 1998; Schkade & Kahneman, 1998; Wilson & Gilbert, 2003).

Conversely, anticipatory affect and emotions are actually experienced in the moment of the decision and directly influence the decision process and cognitive evaluations of the risky consequences (Loewenstein et al., 2001). Anticipatory affect and emotions depend on the vividness of possible decision outcomes (i.e., the quality of mental images), the availability of similar instances stored in memory, and personal experience with the involved risks. Perceptions of risks that are vividly imagined tend to involve anticipatory affect to a higher extent than risks

that are difficult to imagine. Additionally, vividly imagined risks are more prone to be biased.

The Importance of Affect and Emotions in Risk Perception and Communication

The Affect Heuristic and Risk-as-Feeling Hypothesis

People not only engage in analytical evaluations but also consult their feelings about decision consequences when attempting to estimate the severity of risks (Slovic, 2010a). Both the probability component as well as the severity of an outcome can be subject to analytical as well as feeling-based risk perception. These feelings depend on a combination of individual dispositions (e.g., the characteristics of the risk perceiver; Peters & Slovic, 2000), the risk object, and the risk environment (e.g., how information about the risk is presented; Slovic et al., 2002). The affective salience of risks is often used to judge their severity (Slovic, 1987). This mechanism of risk perception was first postulated in the affect heuristic, which states that people refer to their feelings in judgments and decisions (Slovic et al., 2002). It is also possible that the affective quality of risk perception leads to a neglect of probability, such that risks are only judged by their severity and not by their likelihood of occurring (Sunstein, 2003). For example, while the probability of a terrorist attack might be relatively low, the feelings evoked by the images of such an event can lead to an overweighting of the small probability or, in extreme cases, to the complete disregard of the probability dimension (Dieckmann, Slovic, & Peters, 2009). Consequently, catastrophic events might seem more likely than they actually are (in the case of overweighting of small probabilities) or can lead to behavior that assumes they will happen with certainty (in the case of probability neglect).

One aspect of the affect heuristic that has particularly strong relevance to the perception and communication of risks is the relationship between risk and benefit judgments. While in the real world risks and benefits tend to be associated positively, in people's perception they are often negatively related (Fischhoff, Slovic, Lichtenstein, Read, & Combs, 1978). Moreover, this negative relationship is correlated with people's affective evaluation of the risk (Alhakami & Slovic, 1994). The stronger the positive affective association with an activity is, the higher its benefit and the lower its risk are judged. Likewise, negative affective associations lead to lower benefit and higher risk judgments. This has important implications for judgments of risk. Laypeople often do not know the exact risk or benefits from specific activities or policies. If asked whether to support

nuclear power, most people probably do not have enough knowledge about alternatives nor do they know much about the actual relationship between risks and benefits of nuclear power. If the risk is communicated as low (i.e., by presenting information about the relatively low risk of environmental pollution), they might infer that the benefit is high and support nuclear power. Similarly, if presented with information about the potentially high risk of dreaded side effects such as radiation poisoning, they might infer that the benefit of nuclear power is low and decide against it (see Figure 3.1; Finucane et al., 2000).

Figure 3.1   The Affect Heuristic

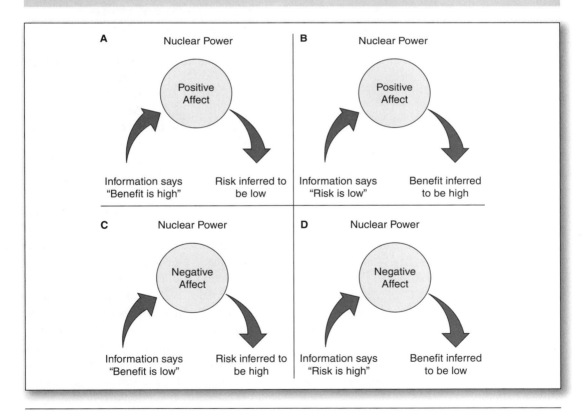

Source: Adapted from Slovic et al. (2002).

Note: A model, based on the affect heuristic, showing how information about benefit (A) and risk (B) could increase the positive affective evaluation of nuclear power and lead to inferences about risk and benefit affectively congruent with the information given. Similarly, information could make the overall affective evaluation of nuclear power more negative (as in C and D), resulting in inferences about risk and benefit that are consistent with this negative feeling.

It is possible that the affect heuristic functions as a sort of "master" heuristic in risk perception and supersedes other strategies to judge risks (for a similar argument about moral reasoning, see Sinnott-Armstrong, Young, & Cushman, 2010). For example, when given several objective criteria for judging the risk–benefit relationship of nuclear power (e.g., the base rate of accidents, radiation pollution, cost-effectiveness, and power output), people could focus only on the most important of these criteria to reduce cognitive complexity (Payne, Bettman, & Johnson, 1988). However, the selection of which of these criteria is most relevant could very well be influenced by the affective meaning of them. Quite plausibly, this could be the amount of dread felt toward nuclear power accidents (Fischhoff et al., 1978). Finally, each criterion can be translated into an affective representation before being integrated into one final judgment (Peters, 2006).

Two additional examples of the affect heuristic as a potential master heuristic in risk perception are its relation to prospect theory (Kahneman & Tversky, 1979; Tversky & Kahneman, 1992) and the appraisal tendency framework (e.g., Lerner & Keltner, 2000, 2001). According to prospect theory, probabilities and outcomes of risky decisions are not objectively represented by people. In fact, both the subjective weighting of the objective probabilities and the subjective evaluation of the potential outcomes are congruent with an affective account of risk perception. In particular, the overweighting of small probabilities of dreaded outcomes is in line with an affect-based explanation of risk perception. Similarly, the subjective valuation of outcomes (as represented by the value function in prospect theory) depends on the affective content of the outcome (Dickert, Västfjäll, Kleber, & Slovic, 2012; Hsee & Rottenstreich, 2004; Slovic, 2007; Slovic & Västfjäll, 2010).

According to the appraisal tendency framework, distinct emotions are connected to a specific cognitive architecture (i.e., appraisals). Closer inspection of the empirical support delineating the specific emotions (i.e., fear, anger, sadness, and disgust) related to risk perception shows that these are ordered among two dimensions postulated by work underlying the affect heuristic (approach–avoidance and unknown risks). Importantly, unknown risks are related to fear, whereas known risks are related to anger. For example, the unknown risks of potential terrorist attacks lead people to be afraid (e.g., it is not clear whether a new terrorist attack will take place, where it might strike, what motivates it, and what the consequences might be). Conversely, if risks are well-known but still condoned by public policymakers (e.g., the identified negative side effects of a vaccine or exposure to second-hand tobacco smoke), people tend to react with anger more than with fear.

Risk Communication: Effects of Presentation Format and Evaluability

Although the notion of risk is present in every decision situation with uncertain outcomes, particular risk domains have attracted specific focus. These include health (e.g., medical and consumer risks), safety (e.g., terrorism, transportation, and recreational risks), environment (e.g., pollution, climate change, natural disasters, and destruction of animal habitats), financial (e.g., stock market and gambling risks), moral (e.g., cheating), and social risks (e.g., jeopardizing social ties, using social network media). These can be further categorized into risk domains that concern physical well-being (e.g., health, safety, and environment), financial well-being, and social well-being (moral and social).

What complicates efficient communication in these domains is often not only the incomplete knowledge of risks on the side of the risk communicators but also the fact that risk perceivers vary in their background knowledge, ability to comprehend the risks, and subjective evaluation thereof. Additionally, the channels and methods of risk communication also vary substantially. Whereas medical risks are often communicated to patients by doctors and through directions for use of medication, safety risks are communicated through agencies (e.g., the Office of Homeland Security, or the Department of Transportation), financial risks are provided by stock brokers and newspapers, and moral risks are often based on personal experience and are just as difficult to quantify as social risks.

When risk can be quantified, the specific consequences and their chances of occurring are usually communicated with statistical information. They can be communicated in different formats, including numbers, images, and text. The specific presentation format is likely to elicit different mental images and affective representations of risk. Research has demonstrated that using frequency formats gives rise to different mental representations than probability formats. For example, psychologists and psychiatrists were less likely to discharge a hospitalized mental patient with some chance of committing an act of violence after discharge if this information was presented with frequencies instead of probabilities (Slovic, Monahan, & MacGregor, 2000). Apparently, a frequency format ("out of 100 mental patients like Mr. Jones, 10 will commit an act of violence") caused participants to have a vivid image of a person committing an act of violence, whereas a probabilistic format ("out of 100 mental patients like Mr. Jones, 10% will commit an act of violence") did not. Similarly, statistical information about causes of death in the United States is likely to remain abstract if presented as a probability. For example, 5.3% of the 2,437,163 deaths in the United States in 2009 were caused by cerebrovascular diseases (e.g., cerebral thrombosis, embolism, and hemorrhage; Kochanek, Xu, Murphy, Minino, & Kung, 2011). Describing this information as a frequency (i.e., 1 in 19 deaths is caused by cerebrovascular diseases) is likely to engage more affective information processing, stronger mental imagery, and affective reactions than the equivalent probability format (5.3%).[2] Another example comes from airline safety. In 2008, 11 airline crashes worldwide cost a total of 439 passengers their lives, equating to a death rate of 0.01 deaths per 100 million passenger-kilometers (U.S. Census Bureau, 2012). Based on these numbers, if one were to fly from New York to Los Angeles, the expected chance of dying in a plane crash would be 1 out of 2,523,977 flights (equating to a chance of .0000004%). When presented with these statistics, people will be more likely to mentally imagine a real plane crash in the frequency format, react affectively (e.g., with fear), and judge its risk to be higher.

The quality of mental representations also depends on other situational factors besides the use of frequency versus probability formats. Numerical information about risks can also be conveyed with graphical images or with text (Dieckmann et al., 2009; Galesic, Garcia-Retamero, & Gigerenzer, 2009). However, what makes this information meaningful is the fact that it can be evaluated. An abstract representation of risk can remain elusive to the perceiver if it is not communicated in a way that carries affective meaning (i.e., if it does not evoke an affective reaction).

Research on the different ways risks can be communicated suggests that the evaluability of information depends on whether alternative outcomes are also presented. For example, Slovic et al. (2002) report an experiment in which participants either rated a gamble with 7/36 chances of winning $9 and 29/36 chances of losing 5¢ or the same gamble without losses (i.e., 7/36 chances of winning $9 and a 29/36 chance to lose nothing). When evaluating these gambles separately, participants rated the gamble with a 5¢ loss as more attractive. Apparently, the addition of a 5¢ loss made the potential gain of $9 affectively more meaningful and evaluable.[3] Similar research also demonstrated that preferences for food quantities (i.e., ice cream) and consumer goods (i.e., dictionaries) depend on the evaluability of the decision outcomes (Hsee, 1996; Hsee & Zhang, 2010). Presenting alternative options jointly (vs. separately) provides information that is useful for comparison purposes and can make risks more evaluable.

Another aspect related to the evaluability of risks is the notion that subjective representations tend to deviate from objective representations when these risks are portrayed in an affect-rich way (e.g., with affect-evoking pictures and visualizations). This seems to be the case for both representations of probability (Rottenstreich & Hsee, 2001) and representations of magnitude[4] (Hsee & Rottenstreich, 2004). These authors demonstrated that participants were less sensitive to changes in probability of an affect-rich versus affect-poor outcome and that magnitudes in outcomes (i.e., whether to save one or four pandas) were less important in participants' responses when these outcomes were presented in an affect-rich manner (i.e., by showing pictures of the pandas) (Figures 3.2 and 3.3). A recent example of how affective salience influences risk perception and risk management policies on a global level is the U.S. government's response to the risk of terrorist attacks. The images of the September 11, 2001, attacks were highly vivid and affect-rich, causing a wave of fear to spread through all levels of risk management. The affect-laden mental representation of terrorism communicated by the government and media has led to concerns that fail to take probability into account.

Similarly, risks that are affect-rich also likely degrade people's sensitivity to the scope of the consequences.

This insensitivity presents a particular set of challenges for risk communicators. The emotional insensitivity to changes in magnitude (i.e., scope or quantity of a stimulus) is clearly visible in situations where large amounts of people (or animals, their natural habitat, or the environment in general) are at risk. The large-scale consequences of genocide and other catastrophes are difficult to mentally represent in a way that evokes affective responses necessary to respond (Slovic, 2007). When presented with statistics of how many people have died in armed conflicts in the past decade or how many victims were homeless after the natural disasters such as the earthquake in Haiti in 2010 or the tsunami disasters in the Indian Ocean (2004) or Japan (2011), these numbers often do not evoke strong affective responses (Slovic, 2010b).

Figure 3.2   Subjective Decision Weighting Functions

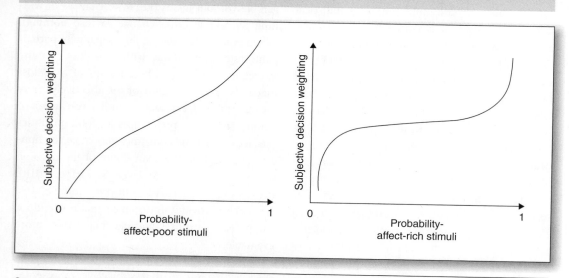

Source: Adapted from Rottenstreich and Hsee (2001) and Peters et al. (2007).

Note: Probability functions for affect-poor and affect-rich decision options. Decision weights are the weight that people put to the probability component in their judgments. Affect-rich decision options lead to insensitivity to changes in probability (*the flat part in the right panel*).

Figure 3.3   Value Functions

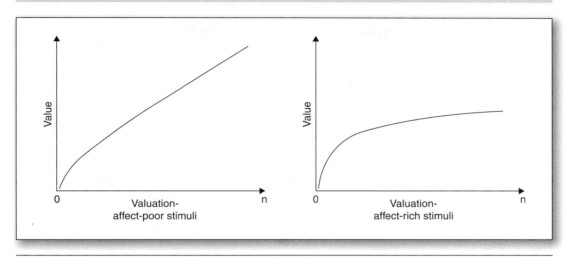

Source: Adapted from Hsee and Rottenstreich (2004) and Peters et al. (2007).

Note: Value functions for affect-poor and affect-rich decision options. *Y*-axis denotes subjective value, *X*-axis denotes quantity of stimulus. Affect-rich decision options lead to insensitivity to changes in magnitude (*the flat part in the right panel*).

In fact, it is likely that abstract statistical representations of victims (i.e., numbers) fail to arouse an emotional response that a single identified victim would (Kogut & Ritov, 2005a, 2005b; Schelling, 1968). Both the effects of singularity and identifiability (i.e., single and identified victims receive more help than statistical victims) can be explained by the affective mechanisms of information processing and mental imagery in particular (Dickert & Slovic, 2011; Slovic & Västfjäll, 2010). Whereas single identified victims elicit vivid mental images and capture attention vital to the generation of emotions (Dickert & Slovic, 2009), groups of victims can remain vague and fail to arouse affective processes that influence the willingness to engage in risk-reducing measures (e.g., donating money).

When risks are presented in ways that do not arouse affective processes, the insensitivity to changes in magnitudes shows in responses that do not differentiate between quantitative changes. For example, Desvouges et al. (2010)

report that people were remarkably insensitive to variations in the number of migratory birds at risk of drowning in oil-contaminated water, and Frederick and Fischhoff (1998) demonstrated the same phenomenon with habitats for wild wolfs in Maine and Wisconsin. In Desvouges et al. (2010), participants were willing to pay virtually the same amount to save 2,000, 20,000, and 200,000 birds ($80, $78, and $88, respectively).

One possible explanation for this insensitivity to changes in quantitative information is the use of a prototype heuristic (Kahneman & Frederick, 2005). According to this explanation, people substitute extensional information (e.g., the amount of lives at risk) with nonextensional information (i.e., a prototype mental image). In the case of endangered birds, people thus may think of one oil-covered bird, which happens to be a rather affect-rich mental image. Showing a singular bird in an oil pond might be at least as effective in communicating environmental risk as showing the relatively affect-poor number of birds at risk.

Interestingly, combining affect-rich images with numerical information has the effect of decreasing emotional engagement of the risk perceiver (Small, Loewenstein, & Slovic, 2007). It appears as though numerical information promotes deliberative information processing and hinders affective processes. As a result, fewer and less intense emotions are generated by the otherwise affect-rich information, and people's motivation to engage in risk-reducing measures declines. This shows that there is no simple way of communicating risks in an affect-rich manner while simultaneously informing about the scope of the problem.

Reflections for Theory and Research

The case of magnitude insensitivity showcases a general phenomenon about boundaries of human perception that has implications for risk perception. Whereas we are generally quite able to distinguish numbers and quantities cognitively (e.g., a 25% chance is greater than a 24% chance), emotionally these differences might be indistinguishable. Moreover, it is quite possible that emotional reactions to risk are bounded in the sense that we are not able to go above and beyond a certain specific emotional reaction. Indeed, it seems as though emotions serve a role in motivating action (vs. inaction) more than in reacting to incremental changes on a particular dimension. A change from *no risk* to *some risk* represents a change in risk category and is therefore perceived quite strongly on an emotional level. This is not the case when the change is incremental and represents a change from *some risk* to *some greater risk* (see also Reyna & Casillas, 2009). Theorizing about the boundaries of human perceptions and emotional reactions is similar to the reasoning behind the value function of prospect theory (Kahneman & Tversky, 1979), but it takes into account the possibility that at a certain level of risk, emotional reactions might cease altogether if the mental images underlying risk perception become too abstract. Of course, individuals differ in their propensity to engage in mental imagery (e.g., Dickert, Kleber, Peters, & Slovic, 2011), which further compounds the problem of effective risk communication.

One important individual difference in risk perception has been linked to people's ability to mentally represent and comprehend numbers (i.e., numeracy; Peters, Västfjäll, Slovic et al., 2006). As most quantitative information about risks is communicated with numbers, the impact of differences in numerical comprehension on risk perception can be substantial. For example, people with low numerical abilities are likely influenced more by incidental affect (e.g., mood states), whereas people with high numerical abilities are more influenced by integral affect (e.g., the comparisons of different risks; Peters et al., 2009). Moreover, for those with low numerical skill, it is even possible that they dislike numbers to such an extent that they experience negative affect simply due to the risk communication format. Instead, they prefer other forms of risk presentations like graphics or text and seem to be better at risk perception when nonnumeric presentation formats are used (e.g., Galesic et al., 2009).

Another individual difference that weighs prominently in risk perception is people's propensity to engage in emotion regulation. When presented with particularly dreadful risks, perceivers are sometimes motivated to reduce their emotional evaluation of these risks. One effective way of doing this is to downplay the severity of catastrophic outcomes or the chances of them occurring. This is habitually done by smokers who are cognitively informed about the risks of smoking yet are unable to quit and rate the risks of contracting lung cancer as low (Slovic, 2001).

Recommendations for Practice

The multidimensionality of risk perception and the underlying psychological processes make it difficult to give specific advice for practice.

However, it is clear that effective risk communication needs to take the role of emotions into account, including the different ways in which emotions are elicited. For example, presenting risks as frequencies (vs. probabilities) can facilitate vivid mental imagery and emotional responses. Moreover, framing risks in an affect-rich way is likely to lead to an underweighting (or neglect) of the associated probability and puts emphasis on the negative consequences. Affect-rich descriptions of risk are also likely to result in a relative insensitivity to incremental changes of risk. However, it should be noted that people are generally less sensitive to incremental changes when numbers are large, regardless of the description of risks. Thus, communicating incremental risks that affect many people can present a great challenge for risk management.

Risk communication that focuses on the *risk-as-feeling* approach reviewed in this chapter highlights how quantitative risk analysis is different from more emotionally driven risk assessments. Risk communication that arouses affective responses is likely to motivate action, but if unguided, this does not guarantee effective risk management or proper risk-reducing measures. Conversely, communicating risks in a way that does not arouse affective responses may not lead to effective risk management, as emotions are important in understanding the meaning of risks.

Conclusions

The research reviewed in this chapter has described how emotions influence risk perception. Whether risks are specific or relatively diffuse, they are naturally intertwined with emotional reactions. To develop effective communication strategies and good risk management, risk communicators must take into account the important ways in which feelings emanating from the presented information determine the meaning of that information.

As the affective side of risk perception can easily be coaxed into supporting even questionable risk management policies, it is vital that individuals and agencies at both sides of the risk communication spectrum (i.e., those who communicate and those who perceive) are aware of the factors that flow into the *feeling of risk*.

Notes

1. By "decision making under risk" we here refer to decisions that have potentially negative consequences (Slovic, 1999). This is not to be confused with another conceptualization of risk, which refers to decision making with known probabilities (vs. decisions under uncertainty).

2. The prevalence of frequency formats to elicit more vivid mental imagery and stronger emotions than probability formats should hold regardless of the actual numbers used. However, evidence exists that mental images and emotions are more vivid with lower numbers, and the effect is strongest when using frequencies in the form of "1 out of x."

3. The notion of evaluability rests on the assumption that individual outcomes are sometimes difficult to evaluate if presented without contextual cues or alternative outcomes. The goodness or badness of a specific outcome of a gamble, if evaluated in isolation, is often more difficult to judge than when other outcomes are also presented. Winning $9 is slightly good for most people; but in the context of not losing 5¢, it becomes really good (Slovic et al., 2002).

4. Magnitude refers to the quantity or scope of a particular outcome. For example, if an earthquake is estimated to affect 300,000 people, then this quantity is referred to as the magnitude or scope.

Suggested Additional Readings

Burns, W. J., Peters, E., & Slovic, P. (2012). Risk perception and the economic crisis: A longitudinal study of the trajectory of perceived risk. *Risk Analysis, 32*(4), 659–677.

Kleber, J., Dickert, S., Peters, E., & Florack, A. (2013). Same numbers, different meanings: How numeracy influences the importance of numerical cues in donations. *Journal of Experimental Social Psychology, 49,* 699–705.

Markowitz, E. M., Slovic, P., Västfjäll, D., & Hodges, S. D. (2013). Compassion fade and the challenge of environmental conservation. *Judgment and Decision Making, 8,* 397–406.

References

Alhakami, A. S., & Slovic, P. (1994). A psychological study of the inverse relationship between perceived risk and perceived benefit. *Risk Analysis, 14,* 1085–1096.

Andrade, E. B. (2005). Behavioral consequences of affect: Combining evaluative and regulatory properties. *Journal of Consumer Research, 32,* 355–362.

Bower, G. H., & Forgas, J. P. (2000). Affect, memory, and social cognition. In E. Eich, J. F. Kihlstrom, G. H. Bower, J. P. Forgas, & P. M. Niedenthal (Eds.), *Cognition and emotion.* Oxford, England: Oxford University Press.

Cabanac, M. (2002). What is emotion? *Behavioural Processes, 60,* 69–83.

Damasio, A. R. (1994). *Descartes' error: Emotion, reason, and the human brain.* New York, NY: Avon.

Desvouges, W. H., Johnson, F., Dunford, R., Hudson, S., Wilson, K., & Boyle, K. (2010). *Measuring nonuse damages using contingent valuation: An experimental evaluation of accuracy* (2nd ed.). Durham, NC: RTI Press.

Dickert, S. (2010). Measuring affect and emotions in decision making: The affective side of intuitive information processing. In A. Glöckner & C. L. Witteman (Eds.), *Tracing intuition: Recent methods in measuring intuitive and deliberative processes in decision making* (pp. 179–198). London, England: Psychology Press.

Dickert, S., Kleber, J., Peters, E., & Slovic, P. (2011). Numeric ability as a precursor to pro-social behavior: The impact of numeracy and presentation format on the cognitive mechanisms underlying donations. *Judgment and Decision Making, 6,* 638–650.

Dickert, S., & Slovic, P. (2009). Attentional mechanisms in the generation of sympathy. *Judgment and Decision Making, 4,* 297–306.

Dickert, S., & Slovic, P. (2011). Unstable values in lifesaving decisions. *Frontiers of Psychology, 2,* 294.

Dickert, S., Västfjäll, D., Kleber, J., & Slovic, P. (2012). Valuations of human lives: Normative expectations and psychological mechanisms of (ir)rationality. *Synthese, 189,* 95–105.

Dieckmann, N. F., Slovic, P., & Peters, E. M. (2009). The use of narrative evidence and explicit likelihood by decision makers varying in numeracy. *Risk Analysis, 29,* 1473–1488.

Epstein, S. (1994). Integration of the cognitive and the psychodynamic unconscious. *American Psychologist, 49,* 709–724.

Evans, J. St. B. T. (2008). Dual-processing accounts of reasoning, judgment, and social cognition. *Annual Review of Psychology, 59,* 255–278.

Fehr, B., & Russell, J. (1984). Concept of emotion viewed from a prototype perspective. *Journal of Experimental Psychology: General, 113,* 464–486.

Finucane, M. L., Alhakami, A., Slovic, P., & Johnson, S. M. (2000). The affect heuristic in judgments of risks and benefits. *Journal of Behavioral Decision Making, 13,* 1–17.

Fischhoff, B., Slovic, P., Lichtenstein, S., Read, S., & Combs, B. (1978). How safe is safe enough? A psychometric study of attitudes toward technological risks and benefits. *Policy Sciences, 9,* 127–152.

Frederick, S. W., & Fischhoff, B. (1998). Scope (in)sensitivity in elicited valuations. *Risk, Decisions, and Policy, 3,* 109–123.

Frijda, N. H. (1986). *The emotions.* Cambridge, England: Cambridge University Press.

Galesic, M., Garcia-Retamero, R., & Gigerenzer, G. (2009). Using icon arrays to communicate medical risks: Overcoming low numeracy. *Health Psychology, 28,* 210–216.

Gilbert, D. T., Pinel, E. C., Wilson, T. D., Blumberg, S. J., & Wheatley, T. P. (1998). Immune neglect: A source of durability bias in affective forecasting. *Journal of Personality and Social Psychology, 75,* 617–638.

Hsee, C. K. (1996). The evaluability hypothesis: An explanation for preference reversals between joint and separate evaluations of alternatives. *Organizational Behavior and Human Decision Processes, 67,* 242–257.

Hsee, C. K., & Rottenstreich, Y. (2004). Music, pandas, and muggers: On the affective psychology of value. *Journal of Experimental Psychology: General, 133,* 23–30.

Hsee, C. K., & Zhang, J. (2010). General evaluability theory. *Perspectives on Psychological Science, 5,* 343–355.

Isen, A. M. (2001). An influence of positive affect on decision making in complex situations: Theoretical issues with practical implications. *Journal of Consumer Psychology, 11,* 75–85.

Kahneman, D. (2003). A perspective on judgment and choice: Mapping bounded rationality. *American Psychologist, 58,* 697–720. doi:10.1037/0003-066x.58.9.697

Kahneman, D. (2011). *Thinking, fast and slow.* New York, NY: Farrar, Straus, & Giroux.

Kahneman, D., & Frederick, S. (2005). *A model of heuristic judgment.* In K. J. Holyoak & R. G. Morrison (Eds.), *The Cambridge handbook of thinking and reasoning* (pp. 267–293). Cambridge, England: Cambridge University Press.

Kahneman, D., & Tversky, A. (1979). Prospect theory: An analysis of decision under risk. *Econometrica: Journal of the Econometric Society, 47,* 263–291.

Klein, G., Orasanu, J., Calderwood, R., & Zsambok, C. E. (1993). *Decision making in action: Models and methods.* Norwood, NJ: Ablex.

Kochanek, K. D., Xu, J., Murphy, S. L., Minino, A. M., & Kung, H.-C. (2011). Deaths: Final data for 2009. *National Vital Statistics Reports, 60,* 1–116. Retrieved from http://www.cdc.gov/nchs/data/nvsr/nvsr60/nvsr60_03.pdf

Kogut, T., & Ritov, I. (2005a). The "identified victim" effect: An identified group, or just a single individual? *Journal of Behavioral Decision Making, 18,* 157–167.

Kogut, T., & Ritov, I. (2005b). The singularity effect of identified victims in separate and joint evaluations. *Organizational Behavior and Human Decision Processes, 97,* 106–116.

LeDoux, J. E. (1996). *The emotional brain: The mysterious underpinning of emotional life.* New York, NY: Simon & Schuster.

Lerner, J. S., & Keltner, D. (2000). Beyond valence: Toward a model of emotion specific influences on judgment and choice. *Cognition and Emotion, 14,* 473–493.

Lerner, J. S., & Keltner, D. (2001). Fear, anger, and risk. *Journal of Personality and Social Psychology, 81,* 146–159.

Lerner, J. S., Small, D. A., & Loewenstein, G. (2004). Heart strings and purse strings: Carryover effects of emotions on economic decisions. *Psychological Science, 15,* 337–341.

Loewenstein, G. F., & Lerner, J. S. (2003). The role of affect in decision making. In R. J. Davidson, K. R. Scherer, & H. H. Goldsmith (Eds.), *Handbook of affective sciences* (pp. 619–642). Oxford, England: Oxford University Press.

Loewenstein, G. F., Weber, E. U., Hsee, C. K., & Welch, N. (2001). Risk as feelings. *Psychological Bulletin, 127,* 267–286.

Montague, P. R., & Berns, G. S. (2002). Neural economics and the biological substrates of valuation. *Neuron, 36,* 265–284.

Nabi, R. L. (2003). The framing effects of emotion: Can discrete emotions influence information recall and policy preference? *Communication Research, 30,* 224–247.

Osgood, C. E., Suci, G. J., & Tannenbaum, P. H. (1957). *The measurement of meaning.* Oxford, England: University of Illinois Press.

Payne, J. W., Bettman, J. R., & Johnson, E. J. (1988). Adaptive strategy selection in decision making. *Journal of Experimental Psychology: Learning, Memory, and Cognition, 14,* 534–552.

Peters, E. (2006). The functions of affect in the construction of preferences. In S. Lichtenstein & P. Slovic (Eds.), *The construction of preference* (pp. 454–463). New York, NY: Cambridge University Press.

Peters, E., Dieckmann, N. F., Västfjäll, D., Mertz, C. K., Slovic, P., & Hibbard, J. (2009). Bringing meaning to numbers: The impact of evaluative categories on decisions. *Journal of Experimental Psychology: Applied, 15,* 213–227.

Peters, E., Romer, D., Slovic, P., Jamieson, K. H., Wharfield, L., Mertz, C. K., & Carpenter, S. M. (2007). The impact and acceptability of Canadian-style cigarette warning labels among US smokers and nonsmokers. *Nicotine & Tobacco Research, 9,* 473–481.

Peters, E., & Slovic, P. (2000). The springs of action: Affective and analytical information processing in choice. *Personality and Social Psychology Bulletin, 26,* 1465–1475.

Peters, E., Västfjäll, D., Gärling, T., & Slovic, P. (2006). Affect and decision making: A "hot" topic. *Journal of Behavioral Decision Making, 19,* 79–85.

Peters, E., Västfjäll, D., Slovic, P., Mertz, C. K., Mazzocco, K., & Dickert, S. (2006). Numeracy and decision making. *Psychological Science, 17,* 407–413.

Pfister, H., & Böhm, G. (2008). The multiplicity of emotions: A framework of emotional functions in decision making. *Judgment and Decision Making, 3,* 5–17.

Reyna, V. F., & Casillas, W. (2009). Development and dual processes in moral reasoning: A fuzzy-trace theory approach. In B. H. Ross (Series Ed.) & D. M. Bartels,

C.W. Bauman, L. J. Skitka, & D. L. Medin (Vol. Eds.), *Psychology of learning and motivation: Vol. 50. Moral judgment and decision making* (pp. 207–239). San Diego, CA: Elsevier Academic Press.

Rottenstreich, Y., & Hsee, C. K. (2001). Money, kisses, and electric shocks: On the affective psychology of risk. *Psychological Science, 12,* 185–190.

Russell, J. (2003). Core affect and the psychological construction of emotion. *Psychological Review, 110,* 145–172.

Russell, J. A., & Feldman Barrett, L. (1999). Core affect, prototypical emotional episodes, and other things called emotion: Dissecting the Elephant. *Journal of Personality and Social Psychology, 76,* 805–819.

Russell, J. A., & Mehrabian, A. (1977). Evidence for a three-factor theory of emotions. *Journal of Research in Personality, 11,* 273–294.

Schelling, T. C. (1968). The life you save may be your own. In S. B. Chase (Ed.), *Problems in public expenditure analysis* (pp. 127–176). Washington, DC: Brookings Institution Press.

Schkade, D. A., & Kahneman, D. (1998). Does living in California make people happy? A focusing illusion in judgments of life satisfaction. *Psychological Science, 9,* 340–346.

Sinnott-Armstrong, W., Young, L., & Cushman, F. (2010). Moral intuitions. In J. Doris & the Moral Psychology Research Group (Eds.), *The moral psychology handbook* (pp. 246–272). New York, NY: Oxford University Press.

Slovic, P. (1987). Perception of risk. *Science, 236,* 280–285.

Slovic, P. (1999). Trust, emotions, sex, politics, and science: Surveying the risk-assessment battlefield. *Risk Analysis, 19,* 689–701.

Slovic, P. (2001). Cigarette smokers: Rational actors or rational fools? In P. Slovic (Ed.), *Smoking: Risk, perception, and policy* (pp. 97–124). Thousand Oaks, CA: Sage.

Slovic, P. (2007). "If I look at the mass I will never act": Psychic numbing and genocide. *Judgment and Decision Making, 2,* 79–95.

Slovic, P. (2010a). *The feeling of risk.* London, England: Earthscan.

Slovic, P. (2010b). The more who die, the less we care. In E. Michel-Kerjan & P. Slovic (Eds.), *The irrational economist: Making decisions in a dangerous world* (pp. 30–40). New York, NY: Public Affairs.

Slovic, P., Finucane, M., Peters, E., & MacGregor, D. G. (2002). The affect heuristic. In T. Gilovich, D. Griffin, & D. Kahneman (Eds.), *Heuristics and biases: The psychology of intuitive judgment* (pp. 397–420). New York, NY: Cambridge University Press.

Slovic, P., Finucane, M., Peters, E., & MacGregor, D. G. (2004). Risk as analysis and risk as feelings. *Risk analysis, 24,* 1–12.

Slovic, P., Monahan, J., & MacGregor, D. G. (2000). Violence risk assessment and risk communication: The effects of using actual cases, providing instructions, and employing probability vs. frequency formats. *Law and Human Behavior, 24,* 271–296.

Slovic, P., & Peters, E. (2006). Risk perception and affect. *Current Directions in Psychological Science, 15,* 322–325.

Slovic, P., & Västfjäll, D. (2010). Affect, moral intuition, and risk. *Psychological Inquiry, 21,* 387–398.

Small, D. A., Loewenstein, G., & Slovic, P. (2007). Sympathy and callousness: The impact of deliberative thought on donations to identifiable and statistical victims. *Organizational Behavior and Human Decision Processes, 102,* 143–153.

Sunstein, C. R. (2003). Terrorism and probability neglect. *Journal of Risk and Uncertainty, 26,* 121–136.

Tversky, A., & Kahneman, D. (1992). Advances in prospect theory: Cumulative representation of uncertainty. *Journal of Risk and Uncertainty, 5,* 297–323.

U.S. Census Bureau. (2012). *Air transportation fatalities and complaints.* Retrieved from http://www.census.gov/compendia/statab/2012/tables/12s1078.pdf

Västfjäll, D., & Gärling, T. (2002). The dimensionality of anticipated affective reactions to risky and certain decision outcomes. *Experimental Psychology, 49,* 228–238.

Västfjäll, D., & Slovic, P. (2013). Emotion and cognition in judgment and decision making. In M. D. Robinson, E. R. Watkins, & E. Harmon-Jones (Eds.), *Handbook of cognition and emotion* (pp. 252–271). New York, NY: Guilford Press.

Vuilleumier, P. (2005). How brains beware: Neural mechanisms of emotional attention. *Trends in Cognitive Sciences, 9*(12), 586–594.

Wilson, T. D., & Gilbert, D. T. (2003). Affective forecasting. *Advances in Experimental Social Psychology, 35,* 345–411.

Zeelenberg, M., Nelissen, R., Breugelmans, S., & Pieters, R. (2008). On emotion specificity in decision making: Why feeling is for doing. *Judgment and Decision Making, 3,* 18–27.

SECTION 2

Risk as Social Construction

CHAPTER 4

Social Construction of Risk

Adam Burgess

Introduction

This chapter concerns understanding risk as a socially constructed phenomenon, that's to say as something that is "made" through the interaction of different actors, ideas, and forces rather than being a simply given risk or danger, as is so often assumed. Below, we elaborate on this way of understanding risk in a more social than literal fashion, using some contemporary examples. We start by explaining why risk is necessarily constructed as an idea about the future and then indicates the origins of this approach more specifically in the "social problems" approach to understanding social issues, the cultural theory of risk, and, finally, the European sociological work of Beck, Luhmann, and Giddens. It's also indicated why, nonetheless, risk actually remains generally still seen in more objectively given terms, and we conclude by emphasizing how strongly particular actors and aspects of contemporary culture object to the idea.

The notion of ideas and even things in our social world being "constructed" is not confined to the study of risk. In fact, as we shall consider, it is less *explicitly* used as a frame of reference here than in many other fields such as literary studies or sociology. There are no books on the subject with the exception of Johnson and Covello (1987a). While some risk-related studies have used the concept to frame their studies, there are few accounts of the idea directly in its own terms (Nelkin, 1989).

Intellectual "construction" is perhaps the easiest to grasp and the least contentious in a field such as literature where the world is described imaginatively, and we can readily accept that words "construct" images and senses of things, and these representations are distinct. Things are more difficult when it comes to social phenomena that have a reality that is, at least partially, given. Even as we must use ideas to order and organize social reality such as class, race, and gender, we know that they do involve actual people who belong to these categories. And despite the lack of explicit constructionist risk research, this category is, actually, a more separate idea—independent of concrete things—than those such as race and class. Risk and risk communication is very much concerned with the *perception* of risk that is independent of any objective hazard. In some shape or form, this perception is, presumably, constructed in one way or another by processes rather than being merely given.

What's more, as we shall elaborate below, the very notion or risk concerns probability—calculating the chance that something may happen *in the future*. It has not yet happened and is therefore an idea rather than fixed reality, "constructed" in the psychology of individuals and through interaction with social influences. In this sense, a constructionist perspective is arguably more important in the study of risk than in other fields—even though the general field of risk analysis is heavily identified with a very objective, scientific view of the world, concerned with precise quantification and often dismissive of less tangible ideas. In this context, construction has been incorporated into risk analysis in the different, and more restricted, sense of social *amplification*, which emerged as a halfway house between the objectivist/psychological roots of risk research and the manifestly social character of risk perception at its heart.

But let's first consider social construction more generally. According to the *Collins Dictionary of Sociology*, it is "a formulation employed within some areas of sociology to emphasize the way in which social institutions and social life generally is socially produced rather than naturally given or determined" (Jary & Jary, 1995, p. 605). The essence of the social construction perspective is to direct us to understand the particular economic, social, political, and cultural influences and actors that lead to the singling out and elevation of some things over others. "Social" here is meant in the broadest sense that includes economic, political, and cultural influences. This is not to say that the character of the object in question does not itself play a role in shaping how we understand and respond. But we should not assume that this role is a determining one; in the risk field, we recognize that the nature of the particular hazard in question is not what solely determines the response to it. This contests the "objectivist" assumptions of conventional risk analysis that focus on the hazard itself; the social construction of risk is at least partly a critique of the kinds of assumed conceptions found in the pages of journals such as *Risk Analysis*, contesting the ways in which risk knowledge is generated along with its claims to objectivity.

Arnoldi (2009) notes how sociologists don't regard risk as an objective given but are interested in the processes of objectification; how calculations are made in industries such as insurance, for example, and what these calculations suggest about the changing ways in which society values and compensates for risk. "This means that risks are socially constructed," he tells us (p. 6). He further defines a constructionist approach as meaning, first, recognition that understanding of any object is influenced by its surrounding culture and meaning, not only it's given qualities, and second, a "strong focus on power and the discursive processes in which reality is constructed ranging from the idea that the culture and meaning influence the perception of reality to the argument that culture and meaning determine our conception of reality" (p. 16). He refers here to the fundamental question of whether things are more or less constructed; in other words, is construction a process of distortion and exaggeration of a "real" social phenomenon or can it be virtually complete, in the way that people see the media as being able to conjure up risk perception at will? We should likely avoid any notion that it is purely and simply constructed; in reality, individuals are bound up with social processes and constraints and cannot simply construct things as they please.

Social construction challenges the "commonsense" notion that social phenomena are simply given by biology, nature, or, in this case, the character of the hazard itself. It indicates how their very "nature" has developed through interaction with changing social processes and assumptions. At its more ambitious, a constructivist perspective doesn't simply assert that these social influences have been important but breaks them down precisely and indicates their relative importance. It is usefully delineated using a comparative framework that indicates how similar phenomena are understood and responded to in quite different terms at different times and in different places. For example, we can indicate how everyday technologies involving radiation evoke quite different reactions in a way that is even inverse to any demonstrable harm that they might cause (Burgess, 2004). Thus, X-ray machines were enthusiastically adopted in the late 19th century at a time of still naïve, prewar enthusiasm for progress and technology—despite the fact that they are proven to be relatively dangerous. In the late 20th century, however, even devices such as mobile phones, for which there is no known mechanism for causing human harm let alone evidence of such, can evoke widespread fears in an individualized "risk society" heavily influenced by media claims and doubts about social cohesion and the future. And within the same contemporary period, there are widely varying reactions in different societies driven by a range of factors from the extent of a culture of litigation (in the United States) to the economic importance of the potential hazard (e.g., in Finland, home of Nokia). Other case studies show that the dramatically different fears about "mad cow disease" are constructed in different sociocultural settings, such as Japan, the United States, and Europe (Ferrari, 2009). Such examples indicate that reactions are shaped far more by prevailing sociocultural norms than the (potential) hazard itself.

In the account of Hilgartner (1992), it is the process of systematically examining the construction of networks of causal attribution that link risk objects to danger. In this sociological perspective, the role of actors and expert knowledge is particularly emphasized. These can result in risks coming to life that are quite detached from evidence and experience. Consider the social construction of nuclear risk around the Fukushima power plant in Japan in 2011. The plant was badly damaged by the devastating tsunami (though not the preceding earthquake) that killed nearly 20,000 people. While Fukushima led to no direct casualties, it was the nuclear *threat* that animated the international media (Burgess, 2011). Why was this, and how did it happen? The background is the distinctive fear associated with anything nuclear in the postwar world. The more direct cause is the establishment of safety standards by the international radiation regulator that bear little relation to any objective threat but are designed to decrease anxiety and safeguard their institutional position. They are calculated to be around 1,000 times what is necessary (Allison, 2009). On the basis of precautionary safety standards, risk can then be created on a daily basis, as an extremely low radiation threshold is regularly breached by levels that pose little actual risk. Dramatic, scary headlines follow, and they obscure the absence of actual harm.

Constructing Social Problems and Risk

Having described some of its characteristics, we will now develop the analysis further by tracing its general and then more specific origins. There are various strands of "constructionist" approach even with the social sciences. Most well-known is the social problems construction perspective. While distinct from risk research, various studies illustrate the interface between the two, such as on the scientific construction of premenstrual syndrome (Jenness, 2003), pregnancy, and endangerment (Brooks Gardner, 1994) and constructing earthquake threats (Stallings, 1995).

Related to the concerns of the sociology of deviance and labelling theory, the constructionist approach emerged in the 1970s (Blumer, 1971; Spector & Kitsuse, 1987). Unlike other more traditional functional and normative understandings, the new framework was not concerned with how problems were functional or otherwise. Social problems needed to be seen less as a *condition* and more as an *activity* (Spector & Kitsuse, 1987, p. 73). In broad terms, the aim was to "shift the focus of analysis from the causes of objective social conditions to the processes by which members of a society define those conditions as problems" (Spector & Kitsuse, 1987, p. 59). Analysis concerns "claims"—the rhetoric used to define social problems and promote policy solutions for them, the "claims makers" who advance these claims, and the crucial issue of how various institutions and people respond. The latter determines whether a problem defined by a group or individual becomes an issue for society at large. Importantly, it is an approach that understands that perception need not have any direct relationship to the problem that it reflects.

Being centrally concerned with the process of claims-making activities, objective conditions are principally of interest with regard to the assertions made about them rather than their actual validity. It is a radical challenge to the conventional understanding of the process of problem creation. In simple terms, it is not that things get so bad that something finally has to be done, as common sense might suggest. The rise of concern about environmental pollution, for example, could not simply have been a response to deterioration in the quality of air and water for there was no such deterioration (Spector & Kitsuse, 1987, p. 128). There is no mechanical relationship between actors and agency. Indeed the conventional assumption of the process of problem creation as a response to new problems can be stood on its head. The existence of purported "problem solvers" is instrumental to the construction of problems themselves. This does not require an active process of agencies manufacturing discontent from nothing. The general pattern of human problem creation and resolution indicates that a problem only becomes defined as such when the possibility of a solution becomes real. Otherwise, conditions are absorbed in a fatalistic fashion; simply "routinely accommodated" (Spector & Kitsuse, 1987, p. 84).

Social construction is sensitive not only to the constructed character of original claims but also to the transformations undergone in the process of a "preproblem" becoming recognized as of wider concern. Using the example of neighborhood complaint about unpleasant smells, Spector and Kitsuse (1987) note how in the process of finding a responsive agency the grievance might be transformed, for example, in accordance with the remit of the particular agency that pursues the problem. The creation of mental health provision within the community might mean that a

complaint that previously would have been directed toward the police is instead laid at the door of health professionals. In the process, a problem of "order" becomes one of "health." Alongside this, local participants framed the issue in the health terms they began to recognize as likely to gain sympathy (Spector & Kitsuse, 1987, p. 84). This process is comparable with how complaints about cell phone towers that originally were economic, aesthetic, and democratic in nature became focused and articulated through the prism of health, and thereby defined as such (Burgess, 2004).

The original outline of the constructionist approach suggested a four-stage typological model (Spector & Kitsuse, 1987, p. 142). It is useful to delineate these different stages because they emphasize social construction as a process that requires a number of stages before being completed, and these are then fleshed out in relation to example for illustration.

Stage 1: Group attempt to assert the existence of some condition; define it as offensive, harmful, or otherwise undesirable; publicize these assertions; stimulate controversy; and create a public or political issue over the matter.

Stage 2: Recognition of the legitimacy of these groups by some official organization, agency, or institution. This may lead to an official investigation, proposals for reform, and the establishment of an agency to respond to those claims and demands.

Stage 3: Reemergence of these claims by the original groups, or by others, expressing dissatisfaction with the established procedures for dealing with the imputed conditions, the bureaucratic handling of the complaints, the failure to generate a condition of trust and confidence in the procedures, and the lack of sympathy for the complaints.

Stage 4: Rejection by complainant groups of the agency's or institution's response, or lack of response to their claims and demands, and the development of activities to create alternative, parallel, or counterinstitutions as responses to the established procedures.

To flesh this model out in relation to risk, consider the example of health concern about electromagnetic fields (EMF) from nonionizing radiation mentioned above, in relation to cell phones. Nonionizing radiation is, by definition, radiation at the "weak" end of the electromagnetic spectrum that is not powerful enough to affect human tissue. Nonetheless, the idea that, somehow, devices using EMF might do so was put forward—in this case by journalists working in the conspiratorial environment of the Cold War (Burgess, 2004). The journalist Paul Brodeur thus "stimulated controversy" and began to "create a public or political issue" about microwaves. In the second stage of the process, these early concerns began to be institutionalized with further scientific research being initiated to confirm their safety and an emphasis on safe levels of exposure put forward by radiation regulators. In the third stage of risk problem construction, health concerns reemerged in relation to new technologies such as microwave ovens and computers, along with a sense that existing guidelines and understanding was simply inadequate for these new challenges. Other individuals and organizations, beyond a lone journalist, began to insist that their concerns be taken seriously, with more research conducted to assure them of safety. New, more sympathetic responses evolved about this issue from scientific authorities in various countries, but these often tended only to strengthen the conviction that there was indeed a serious problem rather than reassure activists that there was nothing to worry about, and all was being taken care of. In the final stage of the process, individuals and organizations become entrenched in their conviction that microwaves are not only dangerous and the official response inadequate but that there is a collusion of interests that demands a determined organizational response. Encouraged by the possibilities of the Internet, a countercultural world of EMF health concern was created dedicated to raising awareness about the dangers of all forms of radiation. At its most extreme, some networks of individuals convinced that they were being made sick by microwaves set themselves physically apart, as far as possible, from the many sources of radiation central to modern living. At all stages of this process, these actors have been instrumental in constructing a sense of risk in relation to cell phones and other devices, most obviously through news media stories often generated by the campaigning individuals.

Since the original elaboration of the social problem approach, differences have emerged, most significantly around the extent to which perception should be treated as independent of reality. The consequence is the demarcation of a "strict" interpretation of constructionism from a "contextual" one that recognized certain assumptions about objective conditions (Best, 1993; Miller & Holstein, 1993). This same distinction applies to the social construction of risk more directly (Johnson & Covello, 1987a). In general, a contextual approach that suggests some engagement with the objectivity of the social problem in question is most widely endorsed (Best, 1995). Even if the claim might be considered to have been "completely" constructed, it remains useful to understand what makes it possible for such a belief to be widely shared. The most well documented subject matter in this regard is Satanism. This case illustrates well that even if claims are proven to be without basis, they need to be located within a particular context such as the wider anxiety about children and abuse, which began in the 1970s (Best, 2000).

The Cultural Approach of Douglas

But the most direct constructionist influence on risk studies is the provocative analysis outlined by Douglas and Wildavsky in their book *Risk and Culture* (1983). This work was the central influence on the only book directly on the subject,

Johnson and Covello's, *The Social and Cultural Construction of Risk* (1987b, p. viii) and confirmed by the unusual inclusion of "cultural" in their title. They didn't oppose the "reigning psychological approach to risk selection and aversion" but called for the cultural perspective to be recognized as a complement to it; an integrated research program that tested established psychometric variables such as the extent of familiarity, immediacy, and individual framing while also considering wider factors such as organizational affiliations, ideology, and institutional context. This was in a context of increasing recognition that risk was about (social) things other than the hazard; as Nelkin (2003) put it, "Narratives of risk are pervaded by concepts of accountability, liability, and blame . . . in many ways, risk is a surrogate issue, a proxy for many other concerns" (p. viii).

Risk and Culture's starting point was the discrepancy between the increasingly safe and healthy lives enjoyed by Americans and their increased perception of risk in the world around them. They examined why Americans chose some risks for concern while ignoring others, and, especially, why industrial pollution and nuclear power were singled out for particular attention. They challenged the assumption that risk can be explained either by the objective nature of the hazard itself or the psychology of those perceiving it, arguing instead that "the perception of risk is a social process" (Douglas & Wildavsky, 1983, p. 6). An important influence was the earlier anthropological research of Mary Douglas, particularly her *Purity and Danger* (1970). All societies, in their view, single out some risks for attention while ignoring others. Such choices do not reflect the scale of the threat or efficacy of how it might be managed so much as beliefs about values, social institutions, nature, and moral behavior. The way we view particular risks reflects what we feel about the activities and institutions associated with it. They identified the example of the Lele tribe of Zaire who focus on only three of the many hazards they face: being struck by lightning, barrenness, and bronchitis.

When these events do occur, they are usually attributed to moral transgression or breaking of taboo rather than a more causal and empirical understanding.

Douglas and Wildavsky ask what sociocultural function selected risks might play in particular cultures. They note how the Hima tribe of Uganda believe that cattle will die if the animal comes into contact with women or if people eat farm produce while drinking milk. These practices were interpreted in Douglas's work as a reinforcement of the existing sexual division of labor, which was central to their way of life, and as a means of cohering their identity against the encroachments of neighboring tribes. Controversially, they applied a similar logic to thinking about modern American society, even though the rationalization of the hazard was fundamentally different. They focus on the key concerns with cancer risks associated with industrial pollution and nuclear power—complex, uncertain, often unproven hazards that, nonetheless, acquired a sense of certain and imminent danger in 1970s America. This was also despite any systematic basis in direct social experience; there was no sudden, significant increase in the numbers of people acquiring such cancers. So how was it that this concern became so prominent, particularly when—unlike many tribal concerns—it was only so recently discovered? These were risks that made little sense or impact in 1950s America, the decade before.

Their first, simplest, and, as it turned out, most controversial explanation was in the rise of environmental groups. It was certainly the case that their rise to prominence was striking, at a time when they were yet to emerge even in Europe. Douglas and Wildavsky described them in comparable terms to any other caste or sect in developing societies, treating their beliefs with no more sympathy. The new American environmental groups were portrayed as secular sects, which sought to sharply define a purpose and identity through the projection of problems and enemies. Their principal enemy was big business—a cultural risk projection that has arguably become far more familiar and universal in the 21st century, particularly after the experience of the tobacco industry's denial of cancer risk.

Less noticed was the broader observation of the rise of what they termed the cultural "periphery" and the corresponding decline of the "center." The periphery here can be equated with the alternative "counterculture" from the 1960s, and the "center" was the traditional probusiness and proscience American elites and their values. They perceptively noted a fundamental shift in the balance between the two at this time and a growing defensiveness within the "center." New consumer and environmental advocates such as Ralph Nader effectively established the assumption that business might put its profits before public safety, such as in his *Unsafe at Any Speed: The Designed-In Dangers of the American Automobile* (Nader, 1965). Seatbelts in cars were to become standard following Nader's critique, indicating the changed cultural perception of risk and its impact. It was not so much a technical argument that was won about car design as a broader cultural one about values and priorities.

But the cultural theory or risk was also concerned with a finer grained analysis that sought to explain how the structures of social organization of which individuals are a part endow them with perceptions that reinforce those structures in competition against alternative ones. Disputes over risk did not have their origins in individual psychology or the character of the hazards themselves, in this view, but in the contestation between adherents of competing ways of life. Douglas developed a framework called the group–grid scheme, which mapped these differences along axes. On one side were groups with egalitarian, collectivist values that tended toward risk aversion in the context of seeing corporate activity furthering social inequality. Against this, individualistic and worldviews accepting of social hierarchies tended to accept risk more readily as they sought to limit state interference and reduce criticism of "natural" hierarchies. In the context of highly applied American risk analysis, cultural theory was obliged to prove itself as a practical instrument. Beginning with

Dake (1991), a graduate student of Wildavsky, there were attempts to empirically substantiate cultural theory (Langford, Georgiou, Bateman, Day, & Turner, 2000; Peters & Slovic, 1996; Poortinga, Steg, & Vlek, 2002). A more recent development has been attempts to integrate psychometric and cultural theories (Kahan, Slovic, Braman, & Gastil, 2006). In this so-called cultural cognition of risk perspective, the psychometric paradigm is seen as the mechanism through which risk perceptions are shaped by cultural worldviews (Peters & Slovic, 1996).

But research directly shaped by the cultural perspective has not established a dominant influence in risk studies, despite the attractions of integration. The group–grid schema has not been very successfully adopted, and it has been, arguably, unfortunate that *Risk and Culture*'s insightful and interesting account of a critical historical moment became reduced to a rather mechanical framework. In this view, it is the general approach and spirit of the defining social constructionist account that is important rather than the predictive capacity of its tools.

We have focused here on the most direct determinants of the social construction perspective. But there are two other key influences that constitute what is understood as the theoretical basis for contemporary social perspectives on risk. The first is a directly sociological influence that effectively introduced the topic of risk to sociology from the German theorist Ulrich Beck, particularly his famous book the *Risk Society*. This was influenced by the complex work of another German theorist, Nicklas Luhmann (2005), and Beck's work, in turn, inspired the most well-known British sociologist Anthony Giddens (1991) to become engaged in the subject. Beck's approach is an ambiguous, rather confused one. It is possible to argue any number of more realist or more constructivist positions from particular quotes in Beck's famous book. On the one hand, Beck portrays risk as all too real, part of a new stage of modernity defined by new threats like climate change that are beyond our capacity to manage. Beck even became synonymous with a catastrophist view of environmental risk, shaped by the particularly one-sided and dramatic reading of the Chernobyl nuclear accident that was central to the "risk society" (Beck, 1992; Burgess, 2006).

On the other hand, there is a much less realist aspect to Beck's work, particularly his emphasis on the process of individualization and the erosion of the norms and assumptions on which classical modernity was based. He understands that this creates social uncertainty, a retreat into self-protection and negotiation that, in turn, shapes perspectives on what may happen in the future (Beck & Beck-Gernsheim, 2001). More broadly, central to both Beck and Giddens's work is the erosion of trust in "expert systems" and government, and this erosion is directly linked to perceptions of risk. In this view, risk is clearly socially and politically constructed rather than simply given. While the contemporary sociological perspective is inconsistent in its constructionist approach to risk, it has further consolidated a nonrealist view of risk in the social sciences.

The third and final key influence on social theories of risk is the "governmentality" perspective associated with (the legacy of) Foucault (Dean, 2009). Foucault himself did not write directly on risk, but some scholars have drawn on his perspective, focusing on how social control is determined through notions of danger and protection. As an example, we might highlight how the global "war on terror" unleashed by George Bush and Tony Blair is also a means of maintaining global hegemony; a "disciplinary regime" made possible by the elevation of a specific and limited hazard into a general, pervasive threat (Dillon & Neal, 2008). The so-called governmentality research is influential in particular areas, particularly health and also criminological perspectives on risk (O'Malley, 2010). In more general terms, Foucault's work is concerned with how power is exercised indirectly, through ideas that bind modern authority to the governed. These are most effective when the governed become engaged—when they become part of a "mentality" (hence "governmentality"). The idea

of external risk clearly has potential to perform such a role, with the governed willingly drawn into a protective relationship to authority. Although, again, rarely employing the explicit language of "social construction," this other social perspective is primarily concerned with what lies behind, particularly what interests lie behind the presentation of risks. Considering all three different approaches, Lupton (1999) describes Beck's approach as having the "weakest" sense of construction, the cultural approach something in the middle, and governmentality the "strongest" sense of how risk can be constructed without any objective basis.

To an extent, all three of these social perspectives on risk remain separate from mainstream risk analysis; it is rare to see research influenced by these ideas in the pages of the journal *Risk Analysis*. On the other hand, risk analysis has, in its own way, become more constructivist, albeit not explicitly. This has not so much been in the form of Slovic's "cultural cognition of risk" but the more basic, but much more successful, idea of the *social amplification of risk*, which he also pioneered, with others (Pidgeon, Kasperson, & Slovic, 2003). The thesis is that hazards have differing potential for amplification and interact with psychological, social, institutional, and cultural processes in ways that can heighten or attenuate public perceptions of risk. This is developed into a social amplification of risk framework (SARF) on the basis of a "signal–receiver" metaphor, with amplification conceived of as a communication phenomenon. As well as the focus on only communication, cultural critics have questioned the assumption of an "appropriate" level of transmission from which amplification deviates among other limitations (Tansey & Rayner, 2008). SARF tends to assume that objectively given risks tend to get amplified, or not, and in this sense, it is a kind of compromise between a realist and constructionist perspective.

SARF can direct us away from what is most interesting—a transformation in the character, not simply the extent or profile of risk. Research by Broer (2007), for example, explores the social construction of (aircraft) noise, illustrating the limitations of focusing only on amplification. This is a good example of how the very character and even the name we attach to something is socially made; "noise" only exists socially, often as a negative expression that develops in the context of mistrust through a process of contestation. If nobody is bothered, "noise" is simply "sound."

Reflections for Theory and Research

Finally, there also exists a problem with our inability to, sometimes, accept the socially constructed nature of risk. Hazards and uncertainties that Western societies previously rationalized as the transgression of taboos or moral injunctions, we now tend to understand in probabilistic terms. In this context, risks are seen as objectively given by their actual nature rather than as symbolic of metaphysical forces; we understand lightning, for example, as a massive electromagnetic discharge rather than as a form of divine transgression or punishment. This advance in understanding is historically positive and progressive, in general terms. But it can also be problematic, particularly when we demand simple, causal accounts of actually complex risks, with at least partly social characters. As is widely recognized, we find it difficult to accept uncertainty. Particularly in a modern culture where other forms of authority have been compromised, "scientific" risk quite uniquely retains its aura of objectivity. This is partly why even those not otherwise positively inclined toward science insist that the risk is "real" with a quite specific cause—as opposed to a psychological disorder with much wider but less definite causes. Thus, campaigners around issues such as war syndromes or health complaints associated with vaccinations or cell phone masts tend to insist that the risk is very real and definite, which for them is equated with insisting on a single physical *cause*—of the vaccination, cell phone mast, or

chemical agent released during conflict. Those who have questioned such complaints as having social as much as physical origins, such as Showalter (1997) and Wesseley (1990), have been the subject of attack, even threat.

In one sense, the social construction of risk can seem relatively straightforward and uncontroversial. But in another sense—and certainly in relation to particular examples—contemporary culture is powerfully resistant to any idea that risk might be "constructed." The misunderstanding here is to equate a process of—in this case psychosocial—construction with a process of artificial, even bogus invention. Curiously, perhaps, in an otherwise psychologically oriented age, we still find it difficult to accept that complaints such as war trauma might be psychosocial in character but, nonetheless, every bit as dramatic in their physical impact as any other. To suggest they are "constructed" suggests that they are illegitimate, and this can be experienced as threatening in environments where identities become bound up with an insistence on causal relations to particular physical causes. More broadly, the idea that something is the product of social rather than only physical causes can be particularly problematic in the world of risk.

Recommendations for Practice

The "practice" of risk communication invariably concerns engaging with, often reassuring, those concerned by "risk objects"—from cell phone towers to additives in their children's food to how the whole Internet might have been consumed by a "millennium bug" or Y2K (MacGregor, 2003). The latter one we now know, in retrospect, to have been a classically "constructed" problem, made by various interested parties who played on institutional ignorance of information technology. At the very least, understanding risk in a socially constructed fashion means we hold back from, and treat skeptically, the latest new hazard that is said to constitute a serious threat. It suggests that we critically investigate the claims that it is a problem, where they originate and who might have an interest in promoting them. And, thinking socially, we understand that it is not exclusively, or even primarily, the characteristics of the risk object itself that determines our reactions. Rather, it is our social circumstances—particularly the anxieties and uncertainties generated by these—that mold, indeed "construct" our reactions. Hard as it may be to accept, it is more likely that anxieties about the risk posed by cell phone towers or food additives, for example, tell us more about wider concerns related to our children, environment, and the future than they do about the technical qualities of microwaves or additives and their potential for harm. The practice of risk communication will be more effective—and interesting—the less it treats its subject matter mechanically and purely in its own terms, as formal risk analysis tends to do, but as a social product that can, under the right circumstances, acquire a life of its own.

Conclusions

In the most recent and authoritative summary of social conceptions of risk, Arnoldi (2009) notes that social construction is a "much used and abused term" (p. 117). It has come to be so widely applied in numerous academic fields that it has, arguably, tended to lose any precision of meaning, slipping into an assertion that difficult and complex social processes can simply be said to have been "constructed" by means of dominant power relations (Hacking, 2000). It is even a kind of charge—widely made in the social sciences and humanities—suggesting an artificial process imposed from above. Yet in explicit terms, at least, it is not a term that is pervasive in social understandings of risk and related fields of risk perception, communication, management, and governance. Arnoldi (2009) makes scant reference to the "social construction" of risk; only twice in his whole book.

It is curious when we consider that the most fundamental concepts of the field are socially

and historically constructed. Risk is often thought of as a thing, most likely a dangerous thing such as a gun or a slippery floor. But that's what we'd called a *hazard*. The risk is the chance of the hazard causing harm, something we calculate by considering how much exposure we might have to the hazard or how large a quantity is involved; how many times the slippery floor is likely to be walked on, for example. A slippery floor on the moon—were there such a thing—cannot cause any harm, so it presents no risk. A hazard only becomes a risk with a particular level of exposure and/or quantity. Otherwise, it is harmless, even something beneficial. Painkillers like aspirin are deadly in large quantities but valuable at the dosage we have established has positive outcomes. As the old adage from Paracelsus, the father of toxicology, goes, "The dosage makes the poison."

So the risk is the chance of a future outcome, generally understood to be a negative one. But this deceptively simple notion is interesting because it tells us that risk is an idea rather than a thing—specifically an idea about the future. How we think about negative outcomes takes different forms and has a history that we can trace. To think in the specific terms of risk presupposes that we are willing and able to think about the future; a real, human future, that is, rather than the metaphysical afterlife that so preoccupied humanity prior to modernity. There was a time when the idea of a risk did not actually exist and other notions took its place. It wasn't always the case that people were able to conceive of the future, or at least conceive of the future in earthly, human terms. Instead, the uncertainties of life were rationalized in metaphysical rather than human terms; very real possibilities of crop failure or disease, for example, were attributed to having somehow offended the gods. In place of risk, premodern cultures such as medieval Europe made sense of uncertainty and misfortune through ideas of fate, providence, and luck. The universe was not then a random one, as everything had its place and happened "for a reason."

Part of a cosmology in which every event and the fate of every individual was depicted as a symbolic representation of God's will. The doctrine of divine providence stipulated that everything happened for a purpose and so every event, however insignificant, was a predetermined part of a grand design, clues to which were to be found in apparently random or "chance" events. (Reith, 2004, p. 386)

Without a clear sense of a changeable future, there can be no concept of different outcomes and therefore no sense of risk.

Yet risk analysis does not easily embrace social construction as a principle or expression. This is because the modern notion of risk is concerned with the mathematically based calculation of probability in fields such as insurance, engineering, medicine, and environmental hazard management. Unsurprisingly perhaps, in these areas, a narrow, frequentist approach to thinking about probability has predominated that has encouraged faith that the correct application of statistical technique will solve problems, discouraging reflection on the problem's terms of reference. The focus of risk analysis has been on the nature of the "risk object" itself and how it can best be managed. Part of that management process has involved considering the psychological effects triggered (outlined in psychometric research), however, and this is understood as being independent of the object of concern. But recognition of how risk perception can depart from the character of the hazard itself is generally a complement to the standard frame of reference rather than as a point of departure for understanding the more fully constructed nature of risk. Risk analysis tends to be accepted as a scientific, data-derived technique that exists independently of social context or framing. A related factor explaining the relative lack of explicit reference to social construction is that while it is multidisciplinary in character, risk research continues to be dominated by the individual terms of reference of the rational or irrational actor, from

psychology and economics (Taylor-Gooby & Zinn, 2006]). Centered in this way, research is directed away from fully embracing a socially constituted approach.

Recognizing the generally limited and often indirect use of social construction in risk research is not to say that social influences are denied; indeed, they have become increasingly undeniable in making sense of risk perception as the field has developed since the 1960s. But these influences have been incorporated principally through the simple notion of *social amplification*, which we can understand to have taken the place of social construction as an explicit framework. The notion of amplification not only works as a cross-disciplinary concept but also sits comfortably with the starting point of the individual, focusing only on what happens to the risk "signal"; whether it is amplified or not. Both the original risk signal and the individual receiver are relatively fixed, indicating a limited sense of construction. Meanwhile, social studies of risk remain set apart in a disciplinary sense from mainstream risk studies, to an extent confined to European social thinking, while risk analysis remains a professional, American-dominated field.

Suggested Additional Readings

Kahan, D.M., Jenkins-Smith, H., & Braman, D. (2011). Cultural cognition of scientific consensus. *Journal of Risk Research, 14,* 147–174.

Longino, H.E. (1990). *Science as social knowledge: Values and objectivity in scientific inquiry.* Princeton, NJ: Princeton University Press.

References

Allison, W. (2009). *Radiation and reason: The impact of science on a culture of fear.* Oxford, England: Wade Allison.

Arnoldi, J. (2009). *Risk.* Oxford, England: Polity Press.

Beck, U. (1992). *Risk society: Towards a new modernity.* London, England: Sage.

Beck, U., & Beck-Gernsheim, E. (2001). *Individualization: Institutionalized individualism and its social and political consequences.* London, England: Sage.

Best, J. (1993). But seriously folks: The limitations of the strict constructionist interpretation of social problems. In G. Miller & J. Holstein (Eds.), *Constructionist controversies: Issues in social problems theory* (pp. 129–1147). New York, NY: Aldine de Gruyter.

Best, J. (Ed.). (1995). *Images of issues: Typifying contemporary social problems* (2nd ed.). New York, NY: Aldine de Gruyter.

Best, J. (2000). *Introduction to globalising social problems.* New York, NY: Aldine de Gruyter.

Blumer, H. (1971). Social problems as collective behavior. *Social Problems, 18,* 298–306.

Broer, C. (2007). Aircraft noise and risk politics. *Health Risk & Society, 9,* 2.

Brooks Gardner, C. (1994). The social construction of pregnancy and fetal development: Notes on a nineteenth century rhetoric of endangerment. In T. Sarbin & J. Kitsuse (Eds.), *Constructing the social* (pp. 45–64). London, England: Sage.

Burgess, A. (2004). *Cellular phones, public fears and a culture of precaution.* New York, NY: Cambridge University Press.

Burgess, A. (2006). The making of the risk-centred society and the limits of social risk research. *Health, Risk and Society, 8,* 329–342.

Burgess, A. (2011). Fukushima fixation: The media focus on radiation risk in tsunami-stricken Japan. *European Journal of Risk and Regulation, 2,* 209–212.

Dake, K. (1991). Orienting dispositions in the perception of risk: An analysis of contemporary worldviews and cultural biases. *Journal of Cross-Cultural Psychology, 22,* 61.

Dean, M. (2009). *Governmentality: Power and rule in modern society.* London, England: Sage.

Dillon, M., & Neal, A. (2008). *Foucault on politics, security and war.* London, England: Palgrave Macmillan.

Douglas, M. (1970). *Purity and danger: An analysis of the concepts of pollution and taboo.* Harmondsworth, England: Penguin Books.

Douglas, M., & Wildavsky, A. (1983). *Risk and culture: An essay on the selection of technological and environmental dangers.* Berkeley: University of California Press.

Ferrari, M. (2009). *Risk perception, culture, and legal change: A comparative study of food safety in the* wake of the mad cow crisis. Farnham, England: Ashgate.

Giddens, A. (1991). *The consequences of modernity.* Oxford, England: Polity Press.

Hacking, I. (2000). *The social construction of "what"?* Cambridge, MA: Harvard University Press.

Hilgartner, S. (1992). The social construction of risk objects: Or, how to pry open networks of risk. In J. F. Short & L. Clarke (Eds.), *Organizations, uncertainties, and risk* (pp. 34–53). Boulder, CO: Westview Press.

Jary, D., & Jary, J. (1995). *Collins dictionary of sociology.* Glasgow, England: HarperCollins.

Jenness, V. (2003). Science constructs PMS. In D. Loseke & J. Best (Eds.), *Social problems: Constructionist readings* (pp. 127–134). New York, NY: Aldine de Gruyter.

Johnson, B., & Covello, V. (Eds.). (1987a). *The social and cultural construction of risk: Essays on risk selection and perception.* Dordrecht, Netherlands: Reidel.

Johnson, B., & Covello, V. (Eds.). (1987b). The social and cultural construction of risk: Issues, methods, and case studies. In *The social and cultural construction of risk: Essays on risk selection and perception* (pp. vii–xiii) Dordrecht, Netherlands: Reidel.

Kahan, D., Slovic, P., Braman, D., & Gastil, J. (2006). Fear of democracy: A cultural critique of SUNSTEIN on risk. *Harvard Law Review, 119,* 1071–1109.

Langford, I. H., Georgiou, S., Bateman, I. J., Day, R. J., & Turner, R. K. (2000). Public perceptions of health risks from polluted coastal bathing waters: A mixed methodological analysis using cultural theory. *Risk Analysis, 20*(5), 691–704.

Luhmann, N. (2005). *Risk: A sociological theory.* Hawthorne, NY: Aldine de Gruyter.

Lupton, D. (1999). *Risk.* London, England: Routledge.

MacGregor, D. (2003). Public response to Y2K: Social amplification and risk adaptation or, 'how I learned to stop worrying and love Y2K. In N. Pidgeon, R. Kasperson, & P. Slovic (Eds.), *The social amplification of risk* (pp. 243–261). Cambridge, England: Cambridge University Press.

Miller, G., & Holstein, J. A. (Eds.). (1993). *Constructionist controversies: Issues in social problems theory.* New York, NY: Aldine de Gruyter.

Nader, R. (1965). *Unsafe at any speed: The designed-in dangers of the American automobile.* New York, NY: Grossman.

Nelkin, D. (1989). Communicating technological risk: The social construction of risk perception. *Annual Review of Public Health, 10,* 95–113.

Nelkin, D. (2003). The social meanings of risk. In B. Harthorn & L. Oaks (Eds.), *Risk, culture and health inequality* (pp. vii–xiv). Westport, CT: Praeger.

O'Malley, P. (2010). *Crime and risk.* London, England: Sage.

Peters, E., & Slovic, P. (1996). The role of affect and worldviews as orienting dispositions in the perception and acceptance of nuclear power. *Journal of Applied Social Psychology, 26*(16), 1427–1453.

Pidgeon, N., Kasperson, R., & Slovic, P. (Eds.). (2003). *The social amplification of risk.* Cambridge, England: Cambridge University Press.

Poortinga, W., Steg, L., & Vlek, C. (2002). Environmental risk concern and preferences for energy-saving measures. *Environment and Behavior, 34*(4), 455–478.

Reith, G. (2004). Uncertain times: The notion of risk and the development of modernity. *Time & Society, 13*(2–3), 383–402.

Showalter, E. (1997). *Hystories: Hysterical epidemics and modern culture.* London, England: Picador.

Spector, M., & Kitsuse, J. I. (1987). *Constructing social problems.* New York: Aldine de Gruyter. (1st ed., 1977)

Stallings, R. A. (1995). *Promoting risk: Constructing the earthquake threat.* New York, NY: Aldine de Gruyter.

Tansey, J., & Rayner, S. (2008). Cultural theory and risk. In R. Heath & D. O'Hair (Eds.), *The handbook of risk and crisis communication* (pp. 69–81). New York, NY: Routledge.

Taylor-Gooby, P., & Zinn, J. (2006). *Risk in social science.* Oxford, England: Oxford University Press.

Wesseley, S. (1990). Old wine in new bottles: Neurasthenia and "M.E." *Psychological Medicine, 20,* 35–53.

CHAPTER 5

The Role of News Media in the Social Amplification of Risk

Andrew R. Binder, Michael A. Cacciatore, Dietram A. Scheufele, and Dominique Brossard

Introduction

Research related to scientific and technological risks is inherently interdisciplinary. Ideally, it produces outcomes relevant to the formation of public policy, features scholars from wide-ranging fields, and focuses on organizational decision making, effective risk communication, and the analysis of public opinion (Freudenburg, 1988). Many risk researchers are particularly interested in rectifying the gap between how experts versus the lay public understand risk (Slimak & Dietz, 2006). Twenty-five years ago, a framework was proposed as a fledgling attempt to define risk in terms of societal factors rather than technical definitions. The social amplification of risk framework (SARF) provided an explanatory model for both the intensification and attenuation of public risk perceptions (Kasperson et al., 1988).

Communication was a central component of the framework, and there have been a variety of studies using the SARF to examine the dissemination of risk information through mass media. The study of news media proves a particularly fitting context for analyzing risk communication, since past communication research has yielded insights into both the production and consumption of news media. These insights will form the basis for the following theoretical and conceptual overview of the role of news media in the social amplification of risk. The current chapter focuses on the narrow goal of explicating what we do and do not know about the news media and risk amplification. This focus necessarily omits several components of the framework, but it nevertheless provides a needed depth for understanding the SARF and the communication of risks more broadly.

With this goal in mind, the present chapter comprises three components. The first involves a review of the concept of news media as an amplification station and the organization of existing

Authors' Note: This material is based on work supported by a grant from the National Science Foundation (Grant No. SES-0820474). Any opinions, findings, and conclusions or recommendations expressed in this material are those of the author and do not necessarily reflect the views of the National Science Foundation.

studies into a typology of SARF research. This organization of existing research will lead into the second component: linking amplification and attenuation processes to communication theories of production and consumption of news media. Finally, we outline a trajectory for future research based on this theoretical overview. The last section focuses specifically on expected outcomes (and potential limitations) of communication in the amplification and attenuation processes of the SARF.

Theoretical Approaches to News, Communication, and Risk

The Social Amplification of Risk

The authors who originally proposed the social amplification of risk sought to provide an explanatory model for the process underlying two possible public reactions to risk (as identified by risk experts): (1) overreaction toward minimal risk hazards and (2) little to no reaction toward substantial risks. The framework's central focus was to address why and how certain risks capture public attention and become either intensified (through an *amplification* process) or ignored (through an *attenuation* process) (Kasperson et al., 1988). Its authors concentrated on two components of risk research: (1) the difference between technical and social definitions of risk and (2) the social mechanisms underlying the communication and reception of risk messages.

The recognition of a socially constructed definition of risk—as opposed to a technical one—was an important component of the framework. The technical definition of risk depends on both the calculation of the probability of the occurrence of a risk and the measurement of the magnitude of its possible effects (Slovic, 2000). This is the definition most commonly used by risk experts. The lay definition of risk, however, is much different. From the perspective of the mass public, "the experience of risk is . . . not an experience of physical harm, but the result of a

process by which individuals or groups learn to acquire or create interpretations of hazards" (Renn, Burns, Kasperson, Kasperson, & Slovic, 1992, p. 140).

These interpretations largely depend on how information is communicated through various "amplification stations," such as social groups, institutions, media outlets, and, ultimately, the individual (Pidgeon, Kasperson, & Kasperson, 2003). Public reactions are thus the product of four components of the framework related to the information at hand: (1) heuristics and values (which are used by individuals to interpret messages), (2) social group relationships (which introduce risks to the political agenda), (3) signal value (which characterizes the risk event), and (4) stigmatization (resulting from negative imagery) (Kasperson et al., 1988). The important process underlying these interconnected facets of information dissemination is communication; people are exposed to information about risks most commonly through their use of mass media (or through discussions with others—a point we will return to later).

News Media as Amplification Stations

Within the framework, risk information is communicated through "amplification stations," defined as social groups, institutions, media outlets, and individuals (Pidgeon et al., 2003). The original treatment of mass media in the SARF comprised three attributes: (1) its *volume*, (2) its *disputed* or *dramatized* nature, and (3) its inclusion of *symbolic connotations* (Kasperson et al., 1988). To build on this conceptualization of news media as amplification station, two assumptions related to these attributes and the news media require clarification.

First is the objective risk or hazard event, which has a corresponding signal value (Slovic, 1987). By *objective risk or hazard events*, we simply refer to any specific occurrences (e.g., accidents or research results) that may garner news media attention. The signal value of a *risk event* may differ from the signal value of the risk itself.

The event's signal value can be repackaged and retransmitted through the news media, and the resulting amplification or attenuation of the signal is the essential process of the social amplification of risk (Kasperson et al., 1988). The second assumption pertains to the *indirect experience* of risk. Risks communicated through mass media are often those with which people have no direct experience. This indirect relationship—between real-world events (e.g., risks events), the media, and the public—is depicted in Figure 5.1. As the figure shows, in the absence of direct experience, the meanings ascribed to these events in news stories and interpreted by audiences are referred to as "mediated reality." This is the view underlying both the spiral of silence theory (Noelle-Neumann, 1974) and cultivation theory (Gerbner, Gross, Morgan, Signorielli, & Shanahan, 2002).

Given these conceptual clarifications, existing research can be categorized in a typology of treatments of news media as an amplification station. Included in the typology are studies that

both explicitly use the SARF as a conceptual framework and incorporate news media as an explanatory mechanism.[1] Studies that meet this criterion can be categorized along two dimensions: (1) the hypothesized outcome (i.e., amplification or attenuation of risk) and (2) the treatment of news media as independent or dependent variable (see Table 5.1).[2]

News Media as Dependent Variable

Research treating news media as a dependent variable focuses on the construction of "mediated reality." These studies generally compare the objective risk event with the volume and tone of media coverage and evaluate the correspondence between the two. These analyses typically take place at the mesolevel, investigating relationships between social groups (especially government, interest groups, and news media). Poumadère et al. (2005) built on existing sociological research to explore story selection related to the 2003 French heat wave, while Bakir (2005) took a qualitative approach to the framing of risk signals in the media and the process of media agenda building as pursued by both Greenpeace and Shell. Berry et al. (2007), through a quantitative content analysis, explored the disproportionate media coverage of SARS and West Nile virus relative to the actual impact on human lives. They focused on the framing of news content in addition to the volume. More recently, Chung and Yun (2013) conducted a descriptive framing analysis of news coverage in South Korea of influenza (H1N1) and bovine spongiform encephalopathy (BSE), concluding that the first risk was presented in terms of health consequences, whereas the second was presented in a political context. Investigating news media treatments of genetically modified food, McInerney et al. (2004) offered the most comprehensive treatment of news media as a dependent variable. Their contributions include the analysis of risk signals' correspondence to the volume—as well as the tenor and tone—of news coverage. These studies represent the bulk of the literature,

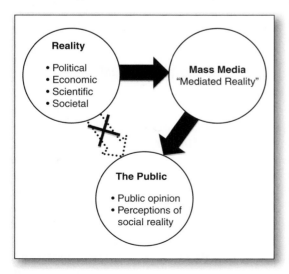

Figure 5.1 Media Constructions of Reality: Links Between Real-World Events, Mass Media, and Public Perceptions

Table 5.1   A Typology of Studies Examining the Social Amplification of Risk and News Media

News Media as	Hypothesized Outcome	
	Risk Amplification	*Risk Attenuation*
Dependent variable	Bakir (2005)	
	Berry, Wharf-Higgins, and Naylor (2007)	
	Chung and Yun (2013)	
	McInerney, Bird, and Nucci (2004)	
	Poumadère, Mays, Le Mer, and Blong (2005)	
Independent variable	Bakir (2006)	
	Barnett and Breakwell (2003)	
	Binder, Scheufele, Brossard, and Gunther (2011)	
	Brenkert-Smith, Dickinson, Champ, and Flores (2013)	
	Busby and Duckett (2012)	
	Busby and Onggo (2013)	
	Chung (2011)	
	Evensen, Decker, and Stedman (2013)	
	Frewer, Miles, and Marsh (2002)	
	Gore, Siemer, Shanahan, Scheufele, and Decker (2005)	
	Gore and Knuth (2009)	
	Hart, Nisbet, and Shanahan (2011)	
	Hooker (2010)	
	Kasperson (2012)	
	Kuhar, Nierenberg, Kirkpatrick, and Tobin (2009)	
	Leiserowitz, Maibach, Roser-Renouf, Smith, and Dawson (2012)	
		Lewis and Tyshenko (2009)
	McComas, Lundell, Trumbo, and Besley (2010)	
	Profeta, Goncharova, Kolyado, Robertus, and McKee (2010)	
		Rickard, McComas, Clarke, Stedman, and Decker (2013)
	Yang and Goddard (2011)	
Both dependent and independent variables	Boyd and Jardine (2011)	
	Burns et al. (1993)	
	Flynn, Peters, Mertz, and Slovic (1998)	
	Kasperson and Kasperson (1996)	
	Trumbo (2012)	

according to our search criteria, looking into how media coverage comes about within the social amplification of risk. While there are some studies looking at how news media acts as an intervening variable (see below), it is evident from our review that there is a lack of research in this particular area.

News Media as Independent Variable

Scholars investigating the effects of media coverage on individual perceptual outcomes treat the news as an independent variable. With few exceptions, these studies often follow an analytic framework similar to agenda-setting studies in political communication, which correlate the volume of coverage with salience among survey respondents. These analyses incorporate a multi-level approach, looking at the relationship between produced news media (mesolevel) and citizens' risk perceptions (microlevel). Bakir (2006) investigates the process of policy agenda setting, especially focusing on impacts of media exposure on public perceptions of risk. Examining the amplification effects caused by a seemingly innocuous letter to doctors about oral contraceptive risks, Barnett and Breakwell (2003) look at both behavioral and affective responses of the public. Gore et al. (2005) investigated potential amplification effects due to a black bear attack in the state of New York but ultimately reported null findings.

In the past 5 years, the biggest increase in studies using SARF have been among those looking at news media as a predictor variable and heightened risk perceptions as an outcome (see Binder et al., 2011; Brenkert-Smith et al., 2013; Busby, Alcock, & MacGillivray, 2009; Busby & Duckett, 2012; Chung, 2011; Gore & Knuth, 2009; Hart et al., 2011; Hooker, 2010; Kuhar et al., 2009; McComas et al., 2010; Profeta et al., 2010). Notably, studies focusing on *attenuated* risk perceptions as a result of news media have also become more common. Lewis and Tyshenko (2009) inquired into Canadian citizens' reactions to the discovery of BSE, concluding that the

population experienced an attenuation of risk associated with eating beef. Rickard et al. (2013) looked at public reactions following the death of a U.S. National Park Service biologist from pneumonic plague. Their in-depth interview data suggested that communication practices led to an attenuated risk perception in the minds of people knowledgeable of the event. Frewer et al. (2002) examined the volume of coverage as it corresponds to risk perceptions of genetically modified food. Theirs is among the few studies to hypothesize and find both amplification and attenuation effects due to news media (operationalized as volume of coverage). A handful of more recent studies took a similar approach and presented evidence for both outcomes as well (Evensen et al., 2013; Kasperson, 2012; Leiserowitz et al., 2012; Yang & Goddard, 2011).

News Media as Intervening Variable

A final category corresponds to studies that take a more global view of the communication process. In these studies, news media are treated as both a dependent and an independent variable. Burns et al. (1993) used a structural equation modeling approach, building news media (operationalized as volume, duration, and half-life) into the model as an intervening variable. Flynn et al. (1998) investigated the stigmatization impacts of an FBI (Federal Bureau of Investigation) raid on a nuclear facility, incorporating a content analysis into their design. Kasperson and Kasperson (1996) looked at both public perceptions of risk and stigmatization related to radioactive contamination of a region of Brazil. They also offer several examples of societal-level attenuation effects (e.g., smoking or handguns). More recently, Trumbo (2012) and Boyd and Jardine (2011) have contributed to this body of research. The former study, through time-series analysis, analyzed rates of influenza infection, news coverage of influenza, and actual doctor visits by patients with symptoms. The data showed that rates of influenza predicted levels of news coverage and that news coverage consequently caused fluctuations in patient visits. The latter study demonstrated how Canadian governmental risk management strategies influenced both media coverage and public perceptions, resulting in neither amplification nor attenuation of risk associated with BSE.

While the social amplification of risk offers a more comprehensive view of the elements of society that give rise to social definitions of risk, it gives short shrift to the complexities of these processes. First, very few empirical studies based on the SARF have examined the risk attenuation (as opposed to amplification) process. Indeed, the typology in Table 5.1 reflects a long-standing criticism of the framework, namely, that it was designed specifically to address the "overblown" reactions of the lay public vis-à-vis minimal risks (Rayner, 1988). Second, the amplification/attenuation dichotomy makes for a useful metaphor, but what added predictive value does it provide? Again, this criticism is hardly new (e.g., Rip, 1988), and it has been dismissed by researchers emphasizing the strengths of a model that incorporates multiple levels of analysis (Renn, 1992). Other questions, however, remain. How theoretically and empirically viable are the relationships that it puts together in a single model? The observation of longitudinal processes (e.g., amplification and attenuation) can be very difficult without a comprehensive methodology that involves data collections at numerous points in time and measuring multiple units of analysis. Moreover, to what degree do we, as researchers, want to prioritize explanatory power over predictive power? If the ultimate goal is to specify a series of conditions both necessary and sufficient for the observation of amplification or attenuation *processes*, then the model in its current formulation lacks the elaboration of such conditions.

One major goal of the present chapter is to explore multiple dimensions of *mass media* as an "amplification station" by incorporating such distinctions as media channels (i.e., newspapers, television, and the Internet), attention and exposure to those channels, and individual reactions based on both. In borrowing these operationalizations of media from theories of mass communication, we explore how they can be useful in understanding the broader communication dynamics of surrounding risk.

Bridging More Recent Communication Theories and the SARF

Communication was given a substantial role in models of the social dynamics of risk such as the SARF, even if the SARF's initial conceptualization was criticized as simplistic and out-of-date (Rip, 1988). Theories of mass communication provide several additional insights into how risk information can be transmitted and transformed through the mass media. This section will focus broadly on two areas of research in mass communication: (1) the production of news in newspapers and television outlets and (2) the consumption of news by mass media audiences.

The Production of News

Scholars have scrutinized the processes underlying news production for several decades (e.g., Fishman, 1980; Tuchman, 1978). Rather than providing an exhaustive review of this literature, we focus specifically on two aspects of news production that have been important features in research on risk communication. Both are located at the mesolevel of analysis, that is, they involve interactions between social groups and societal institutions. The first is the notion of news value, which corresponds somewhat to the signal value of a given risk event. The second is the process of agenda building, which provides a framework for understanding competing social and institutional interests over the news agenda in the wake of a hazard event.

According to media sociologists, reporting on an event as news depends heavily on its news value. The judgment of "what's news" generally corresponds to six broad "yardsticks of newsworthiness": (1) prominence/importance, (2) human interest,

(3) conflict/controversy, (4) the unusual, (5) timeliness, and (6) proximity (Shoemaker & Reese, 1996, p. 111). With some exceptions, the notion of news value, which seems intuitively connected to the signal value of risk and hazard events, has received little attention in risk research. It has been implied to play a role in the social attenuation of risks such as smoking (Kasperson & Kasperson, 1996), which the authors argue have high signal value but low news value. A conceptual distinction should be drawn, however, between the signal value of a *risk* and that of a *risk event*. The latter should be expected to play a large role in determining three common indicators of news coverage used in risk communication studies: (1) the selection of stories, (2) the duration of issue on the news agenda, and (3) the half-life (i.e., the amount of time for the number of stories to decrease by half) (Burns et al., 1993; Freudenburg, Coleman, Gonzales, & Helgeland, 1996). The news value of an event is also exploited by the competing stakeholders through the agenda-building process.

Scholars of media agendas have acknowledged that the agenda is not simply "set" but "built." In other words, rather than suddenly appearing in the news, an agenda "evolves from the interaction of people and organizations in society" (Berkowitz, 1994, p. 84). Various characteristics of the news media constrain the access of news sources, restrict the range of topics available for coverage, make changing these biases difficult, and, in consequence, hide the agenda-building processes from view (Cobb & Elder, 1971). How do competing stakeholders navigate these constraints? Research on interest groups, which often rigorously pursue media coverage, has identified two important factors for success in accessing the media agenda: (1) contacts with the media (an organizational *strategy*) and (2) the establishment of credibility (an organizational *attribute*) (Danielian, 1994). Both factors reflect the research by the routine theorists who observed that journalists defer to official government or industrial sources, who already possess both contacts and credibility (Fishman, 1980; Gans, 1979; Tuchman, 1978).

Of course, the dynamic ebb and flow of issues on the media agenda—as well as the conflict between stakeholders—proves a problem for media researchers. Existing news stories may serve as indicators of who succeeded in reaching the media agenda, but they say little about *why* those groups or individuals succeeded (Nisbet & Lewenstein, 2002). Within the scholarly domain of risk research, apart from initiating risk or hazard event (ranging from accidents to the publication of alarming research), little is known about how risks reach the news agenda or why certain risks endure longer than others. Related research, however, provides some insight.

The concept of the issue–attention cycle, which is related to both news value and the agenda-building process, has received some attention in risk studies. Following an *initiating event*, the cycle consists of various stages of attention that an issue receives over time (Downs, 1972). Applied broadly to science policy issues, the cycle fluctuates between the overtly political policy arena—where public perceptions can play a substantial role—and the administrative policy arena (Nisbet & Huge, 2006). McInerney et al. (2004) use the issue–attention cycle in conjunction with the risk amplification concept to explain the treatment of Bt corn,[3] a genetically modified organism, in the news media; they concluded that "the news media as a whole become a dependent variable subject to the influence by drama and conflict among the various stakeholders" (p. 67). The meaning of a highly publicized story about Bt corn (known as the "Monarch butterfly incident") was driven by narrative because news media were most concerned with telling a good story, and that story involved both news value and conflict between stakeholders.

Why is agenda building important for understanding public reactions to scientific and technological risk? We noted above how the relationship between news value and signal value can shape access to the media agenda, and how the agenda-building perspective adds the elements of *conflict* and *time* to the treatment of news media as a dependent variable. From an agenda-building point of view, risk and hazard events—whether they are fatal accidents or press releases—compete with other events to gain access to the agenda. Once there, however, a risk goes through various phases of packaging and transmission, driven by conflicting interests of stakeholders as much as the need for narrative influences in news media. Thus, a risk event with very low objective signal value, such as crime against the elderly, can have high news value, repackaged to amplify the initially low signal value (Fishman, 1978). At the same time, outcomes related to the volume of coverage are best predicted by objective attributes of the risk (e.g., the number of deaths) than more qualitative or narrative features of stories (Freudenburg et al., 1996). And, as mentioned earlier, risks described with high signal value may receive little to no media coverage.

This review of news production has at least two important implications for the study of news media and the social amplification of risk. First, how do news value and signal value interact to determine the prominence of a risk event on the media agenda? The foregoing overview suggests that the processes that contribute to news production about risk are not only complex but also systematic. Our interest in the complexity of news production is tied to the criticism of reducing communication mechanisms to the rather simplistic dichotomy of amplification or attenuation. It is important, however, to also acknowledge that these processes can be systematically understood through the lens of communication theory. This systematic understanding can be useful for formulating normative recommendations regarding the communication of risk and uncertainty (e.g., Friedman, Dunwoody, & Rogers, 1999). Another facet of its utility, however, is in understanding public reactions to risk information.

The Consumption of News

Scholars of mass communication have looked at the overarching effects of accessibility versus applicability on audiences of news media. These two cognitive constructs underlie three broad research programs in communication research: agenda setting, priming, and framing (Scheufele & Tewksbury, 2007).[4] With the risk amplification concept, accessibility (or salience) of risk issues has been implicitly featured in studies looking at the amplification and attenuation processes. In fact, the authors of the framework suggested accessibility as a necessary condition: "To the extent that risk becomes a central issue in a political campaign or in a conflict among social groups, it will be vigorously *brought to more general public attention* [italics added]" (Kasperson et al., 1988, p. 185). In other words, for a risk to be amplified or attenuated, the public must first be aware of it.

The construct of accessibility is central to agenda-setting effects. The agenda-setting hypothesis proposed that increased news coverage of an issue resulted in increased perceived importance of that issue by the public (McCombs & Shaw, 1972). Initial investigations of agenda setting looked at aggregate trends, that is, the total number of news stories about an issue correlated to the total number of times survey respondents cited that issue as "most important." Risk communication studies have followed suit. The relationship underlies, for example, the quantity of coverage theory: "Increased coverage not only makes the risk salient, but also turns public opinion in a *negative* direction, causing increased opposition to risky technologies and heightened fear of environmental hazards" (Mazur & Lee, 1993, p. 683). As a result, the theory confounds the salience of risks with attitudinal responses to risks.[5]

Elsewhere, the basic components of agenda setting have been called into question, especially regarding the absence of individual-level media use measures and the neglect of individual differences (McLeod, Becker, & Byrnes, 1974; Shaw & Martin, 1992). This is a valuable insight for research on risk communication and the SARF, where the role of the media has most commonly been operationalized as the amount of coverage.

It has, perhaps unsurprisingly, borne out mixed results. In the end, what insight does the agenda-setting function of the media provide to risk communication? The original authors of the SARF, for example, cautioned against conclusions based on the volume of coverage (Kasperson et al., 1988). Such relationships "found little support in the moderate correlations between most risk perception variables and media coverage" (Renn et al., 1992, p. 156). These notions lead to two recommendations for measuring the salience of risks.

First, agenda-setting effects are most commonly found when comparing volume of coverage and issues cited by survey respondents as "most important," but this indicator of salience is rarely used in research on the SARF. It seems plausible, however, that within the context of a risk or hazard event specific to a certain region (as revealed by studies of place; see Lange, Fleming, & Toussaint, 2004; Masuda & Garvin, 2006), media attention to that event could raise it to the status of the most important issue. In addition to this "most important issue" indicator, a second recommendation focuses on linking the salience of risks with attention and exposure to news media. While the volume of coverage may be useful as a unit of analysis, studies of public perceptions of risk should strive to examine both salience and media use through strictly individual-level models.

Of course, salience is only part of the story: "Research must expand beyond calculating the amount of coverage the news media gives selected health topics to an examination of how health messages are constructed" (Berry et al., 2007, p. 36). Thus, the question of *applicability* remains. In other words, how do individuals react to these issues and events as they are presented in mediated reality? To some extent, the answer to this question was suggested in the authors' original conceptualization of the social amplification of risk: "Specific terms or concepts used in risk information may have quite different meanings for varying social and cultural groups. They may also trigger associations independent of those intended" (Kasperson et al., 1988, p. 185). Such

potential reactions to risk messages evoke the theory of media framing effects. Framing has been applied in mass media contexts to both the construction of news discourse and the processing of news content (Pan & Kosicki, 1993; Scheufele, 1999). Frames are used in news stories to define problems, diagnose causes, make moral judgments, and suggest remedies (Entman, 1993). Such effects are summarized in a study looking at the social construction of risks related to nuclear power: "On most policy issues, there are competing packages available in this culture. Indeed, one can view policy issues as, in part, a symbolic contest over which interpretation will prevail" (Gamson & Modigliani, 1989, p. 2). An advantageous aspect of the framing approach is the distinction between *types* of frames.

The distinction between media frames, which are featured in news content, and audience or individual frames, which pertain to how individuals understand such content, has been explored in detail in the communication literature (Druckman, 2001; Scheufele, 1999). Importantly, the frame present in the news story may not always resonate with the frame in the mind of the individual (Price, Tewksbury, & Powers, 1997). This distinction has also been suggested in a risk communication study related to genetically modified foods. News coverage of biotechnology has focused on disagreement between stakeholders, dramatic depictions of risks, and symbolic connotations (Frewer et al., 2002). When the authors investigated the outcomes of these prominent features of news stories about genetically modified food (i.e., the media frames), they concluded that amplified risk perceptions were less likely to occur when people already had established or firmly held views toward the use of biotechnology (i.e., audience frames). Because news stories can bring to mind impressions of past risk events, the frames they highlight may play a substantial role in the amplification of risk process.

The consumption of news, as suggested by agenda-setting and framing effects, can have significant impacts on individuals' risk perceptions with respect to the cognitive mechanisms of accessibility and applicability. This review therefore leads to two specific questions relating to news media use and the communication of risk. First, "What role does the news media play in transmitting the salience of relevant risks to news audiences?" Many existing SARF studies have investigated this question, but concrete results are lacking. Second, "How does the negotiation of meaning (e.g., framing through symbolic connotations) of news content influence audience perceptions of risk?" This question has received less attention in existing research, in spite of the calls from different scholars to begin looking at media use and how it may or may not play a crucial role in predicting risk-related outcomes at the individual level.

Reflections for Theory

As the preceding discussion has highlighted, the SARF has provided a number of advances in our understanding of the role of communication in the risk communication process. There are two we view as the most important to consider. First, the framework provides a useful organizing heuristic for conceptualizing many moving parts in a complex social process. With the many studies published using the SARF as a theoretical framework, its usefulness in helping generate rich hypotheses and research questions is evident. Second, the framework has usefully identified specific potential communication pathways where risk communication messages are transmitted. Especially with regard to risk communication, the framework brings much-needed attention to the inherent communicative aspects of any public debate over risks and hazards.

While these two contributions of SARF have provided demonstrable benefits to our understanding of risk communication processes, they also suggest some theoretical limitations for future research to tackle. Perhaps the most salient limitation concerns the expansive scope of the SARF. In light of its initial introduction as a "fledgling conceptual framework" (Kasperson et al., 1988) over

25 years ago, one might expect that an abundance of research could have caused some fundamental shifts in the framework's structure, for example by eliminating certain factors based on empirical evidence. Our review of the literature suggests that this has not been the case. It is largely for this reason that we have focused our chapter on refining a conceptualization of news media and its role within the framework. Many other communication concepts may benefit from similar theoretical integration into the SARF.

Future research would benefit, for example, from greater attention to interpersonal discussion within the framework of the social amplification of risk. In one of the rare studies looking at how different communication channels influenced awareness of a risk event, 9% of survey respondents indicated that they initially learned of the event through discussions with other people, whereas 53% relied on television and 26% on newspapers (Gore et al., 2005). The differences in magnitude of these outlets' effects on awareness are reflected in communication research; the media make topics salient initially, while interpersonal channels are subsequently used to make informed judgments (Dunwoody & Neuwirth, 1991). Since the SARF is primarily concerned with interpretations of risk events (over and above initial awareness), the role of interpersonal communication in disseminating information and contributing to a socially constructed reaction will likely be substantial. Indeed, Binder and colleagues (2011) investigated the impacts of interpersonal discussion in the context of the SARF. They found that discussion frequency can both amplify and attenuate risk perceptions toward a bio- and agro-defense facility, with such effects contingent on a respondent's initial attitude. Those who were initially opposed to the facility perceived greater risks as their discussion frequency increased, while those who were initially supportive perceived fewer risks the more they discussed the issue. Their findings suggest the promise of exploring risk amplification and attenuation effects based on factors outside of news media, where conceptual overviews such as ours could prove useful in guiding future research in all communicative aspects of the SARF.

Recommendations for Research and Implications for Practice

Our approach to this chapter has revealed two practical organizing principles when it comes to designing, carrying out, or applying new research on news media as an amplification station. First is the treatment of news media as a dependent or independent variable. Second are several relevant concepts from communication theory that can inform future research on the news media and SARF. This section is dedicated to synthesizing these principles into an agenda for future research. The organizational frameworks presented here are certainly not exhaustive but are provided as useful lenses for evaluating past research, guiding future investigation, and aiding practitioners in classifying risk communication phenomena.

Predicting Coverage of Risk in the News Media

The production of news is dependent on news value and agenda building. These notions led to two general research questions regarding news

media as a *dependent variable* in the SARF: (1) "How do news value and signal value interact to determine the prominence of a risk event on the media agenda?" (2) "How does conflict between stakeholders shape the duration and intensity of risk coverage?" News value can be understood as a necessary condition for the increased coverage of risks. Certain risks will gain coverage if journalists and editors see a worthwhile story to tell. But news value is rarely sufficient for predicting coverage. Indeed, the day-to-day competition through agenda building makes it difficult to predict coverage of risks compared with other news stories. Nonetheless, the review of existing literature suggests several outcomes when news media is a dependent variable (see Table 5.2).

The lower left quadrant represents the most commonly investigated outcome: *amplified risk coverage*, which is measured either through the volume or tone of coverage. This outcome is expected especially when the signal value of an event is relatively low but its news value or disputed nature is high. The upper right quadrant depicts the process of *attenuated risk coverage*. Here, high-intensity objective risk signals exhibit relatively little news value or agenda conflict over time, thereby resulting in less news coverage. When an objective risk event has low-intensity signal value and low news value, the result is *suppressed risk coverage*. For risks with

Table 5.2   Predicted Outcomes of the Effects of Objective Risk Signal and News Value/Agenda Conflict on News Media Coverage (Dependent Variable)

News Value or Agenda Conflict	Signal Value of Objective Risk Event	
	Low Intensity	*High Intensity*
Low intensity	Suppressed risk coverage (stasis)	Attenuated risk coverage (change)
High intensity	Amplified risk coverage (change)	Sustained risk coverage (stasis)

Notes: The marginal rows indicate levels of intensity of different attributes of coverage coexistent with objective risk signal. Media coverage outcomes can be observed in many different ways according to the four cells of this table (including analyses of volume, duration, half-life, or framing).

high-intensity signal value and high news value, *sustained risk coverage* is the result.

It is important to emphasize that the first two quadrants depict dynamic changes that occur over time. This aspect contrasts with the expected outcomes in the remaining two quadrants, which remain static. The time factor is crucial and is often overlooked in risk amplification research, although some scholars have demonstrated the amplification of risk coverage through quantitative and qualitative content analyses over time (e.g., Bakir, 2005; McInerney et al., 2004). Evidence for attenuation is more difficult to ascertain. We argue that examples of attenuated risk coverage (e.g., smoking or handguns; see Kasperson & Kasperson, 1996) may be classified more aptly as *suppressed* risk coverage. To be sure, the health risks related to both smoking and handguns may have high signal value in general, but the signal value of a given risk event (e.g., a particular death from smoking or a gun-related fatality) has essentially been reduced through sociocultural processes that leave them with (1) little to no news value, (2) rare agenda conflicts, and, consequently, (3) very little news media coverage. The opposite may be true for an issue like nuclear power, where the intensity of the signal value from one event is reinforced over time, *sustaining* an amplified level of news coverage (e.g., Gamson & Modigliani, 1989). Overall, we present the four-cell matrix in Table 5.2 as a heuristic tool for detecting different outcomes of the SARF by incorporating changes over time and analyses at the mesolevel of analysis.

Predicting Effects of News Media on Individual Perceptions of Risk

The examination of news media influences on individual perceptions focused primarily on accessibility and applicability. These two concepts introduced two broad research questions regarding the SARF and news media as an *independent variable*: (1) "What role does the news media play in transmitting the salience of relevant risks to news audiences?" (2) "How does the framing (e.g., symbolic connotations) of news content influence audience perceptions of risk?" The authors of the SARF suggested accessibility as a necessary condition for the amplification of individual risk perceptions. Awareness of risks may depend on the volume of coverage, its duration, and its half-life, as past studies have suggested (Burns et al., 1993). But does accessibility explain most risk perceptions? The framing literature suggests not, as do SARF studies referring to individual differences (Renn et al., 1992). With these considerations in mind, several outcomes treating news media as an independent variable are expected (see Table 5.3).

Table 5.3   Predicted Outcomes of News Media Coverage (Independent Variable) on Audience Perceptions of Risk

Preexisting Perceptions of Risk	Media Coverage of Objective Risk Event	
	Low Intensity	*High Intensity*
Low intensity	Suppressed risk perception (stasis)	Amplified risk perception (change)
High intensity	Attenuated risk perception (change)	Sustained risk perception (stasis)

Notes: The marginal rows indicate levels of intensity of preexisting audience perceptions of the risk. Perceptual outcomes can be observed in different ways according to the four cells of this table. These may include salience (through agenda setting) or attitudes (through framing).

In this case, the upper right quadrant depicts the commonly expected outcome of *amplified risk perception*. Key factors in this process include high-intensity media coverage (either in volume or tone) and low levels of preexisting individual risk perceptions. The process introduces a relatively new risk to the public and drives perceptual outcomes. The lower left quadrant represents change in the opposite direction. *Attenuated risk perception* should be expected under relatively low-intensity media coverage but heightened preexisting perceptions. Thus, lower levels of media coverage or reassuring media reports are expected to reduce individual risk perceptions. The final two quadrants represent two states of risk perception stasis. *Suppressed risk perception* is the expected outcome of both low-intensity news coverage and low-intensity prior risk perceptions. The opposite result, *sustained risk perception*, is expected to result from high intensity of both predictors.

As with studies emphasizing news media as a dependent variable, an emphasis should be placed on understanding change over time for the two process outcomes. Several studies have demonstrated empirically that individual risk perceptions can be amplified by increased volume of news coverage or attenuated by decreased volume of news coverage (see Table 5.1). But the existing research also demonstrates a bias toward investigating amplification effects of news media. The matrix of expected outcomes presented here, however, suggests that this bias is not necessarily a feature of the SARF itself (as critics have suggested). As with Table 5.2, the matrix in Table 5.3 is illustrative of a variety of expected outcomes of the SARF by incorporating changes over time and analyses at the microlevel of analysis.

Conclusions

The goal of this theoretical and conceptual overview focused on extending our understanding of mass communication—specifically, news media—as a component of the social amplification

of risk. As such, this chapter comprised three components. First, existing SARF research was organized into a typology of (1) treatments of news media as dependent and independent variables and (2) hypothesized amplification or attenuation outcomes. Second, concepts from communication theory were incorporated into the SARF and its treatment of news media as amplification station. Finally, several research questions, as well as expected outcomes, were proposed to guide future research of news media as an amplification station. This overview should be seen as neither a comprehensive treatment of communication within the SARF nor even a definitive conceptual analysis of news media as an amplification station. Rather, our goal was to derive and expand on several organizing principles that have guided research on news media as an amplification station thus far.

The social amplification of risk has received widespread research attention in the 25 years since it was first introduced. Its success should be unsurprising when one considers the depth and breadth of risk issues as they are communicated across all levels of modern society. As this overview has demonstrated, the SARF offers risk communication scholars a useful conceptual tool for examining the social experience of risk, both through "mediated reality" and beyond.

Notes

1. Our primary search criterion was the term *social amplification of risk* in the online database Web of Science, which returned 54 published articles. From these, we identified those that made explicit mention of news media. This second criterion excluded a number of notable articles from the literature (e.g., Flynn, 2003; Lange et al., 2004; Machlis & Rosa, 1990; Masuda & Garvin, 2006; McComas, 2006; McGregor, 2003; Metz, 1996; Raude, Fischler, Lukasiewicz, Setbon, & Flahault, 2004), although insights from these studies will appear in the subsequent discussion where pertinent.

2. The studies listed in Table 5.1 may not represent an exhaustive examination of the literature due to our search criteria and the potential exclusion of

conference papers, books and book chapters, and non–peer-reviewed research articles.

3. This is a type of corn genetically modified to be resistant to pests and herbicides through the insertion of the Bt delta endotoxin, from the bacterium *Bacillus thuringiensis* (Bt), which is toxic to caterpillars. In 1995, Bt corn became the first genetically altered plant to be registered with the Environmental Protection Agency (Bessin, 2004). Controversy has surrounded the product since its introduction, making it particularly useful for studies of risk perception.

4. All of these research programs have insights valuable to the study of risk. Given that priming has focused on the relationship between issue salience and evaluations of officials (rather than perceptions of issues), it is less relevant to this discussion. Of course, priming may play a role in secondary impacts outlined in the amplification process of the SARF and deserves further attention in that context.

5. Although this distinction may not prove to be as important for issues explicitly defined in terms of risk as it is for political issues, it certainly merits testing.

Suggested Additional Readings

Binder, A. R. (2012). Figuring out #Fukushima: An initial look at functions and content of U.S. Twitter commentary about nuclear risk. *Environmental Communication, 6*(2), 268–277. doi:10.1080/175240 32.2012.672442

Nisbet, M. C., Brossard, D., & Kroepsch, A. (2003). Framing science: The stem cell controversy in an age of press/politics. *International Journal of Press/Politics, 8*(2), 36–70. doi:10.1177/1081180X02251047

Runge, K. K., Yeo, S. K., Cacciatore, M. A., Scheufele, D. A., Brossard, D., Xenos, M., . . . Su, L. Y.-F. (2013). Tweeting nano: How public discourses about nanotechnology develop in social media environments. *Journal of Nanoparticle Research, 15*(1), 1–11. doi:10.1007/s11051–012–1381–8

References

Bakir, V. (2005). *Greenpeace v. Shell*: Media exploitation and the social amplification of risk framework (SARF). *Journal of Risk Research, 8*(7–8), 679–691. doi:10.1080/13669870500166898

Bakir, V. (2006). Policy agenda setting and risk communication: Greenpeace, shell, and issues of trust. *International Journal of Press/Politics, 11*(3), 67–88. doi:10.1177/1081180X06289213

Barnett, J., & Breakwell, G. M. (2003). The social amplification of risk and the hazard sequence: The October 1995 oral contraceptive pill scare. *Health Risk & Society, 5*(3), 301–313. doi:10.1080/1369857031000 1606996

Berkowitz, D. (1994). Who sets the media agenda? The ability of policymakers to determine news decisions. In D. J. Kennamer (Ed.), *Public opinion, the press, and public policy* (pp. 81–102). Westport, CT: Praeger.

Berry, T. R., Wharf-Higgins, J., & Naylor, P. J. (2007). SARS wars: An examination of the quantity and construction of health information in the news media. *Health Communication, 21*(1), 35–44. doi:10.1080/10410230701283322

Bessin, R. (2004). *Bt-corn: What it is and how it works.* Retrieved from http://www2.ca.uky.edu/entomology/entfacts/ef130.asp

Binder, A. R., Scheufele, D. A., Brossard, D., & Gunther, A. C. (2011). Interpersonal amplification of risk? Citizen discussions and their impact on perceptions of risks and benefits of a biological research facility. *Risk Analysis, 31*(2), 324–334. doi:10.1111/J.1539–6924.2010 .01516.X

Boyd, A. D., & Jardine, C. G. (2011). Did public risk perspectives of mad cow disease reflect media representations and actual outcomes? *Journal of Risk Research, 14*(5), 615–630. doi:10.1080/13669877.20 10.547258

Brenkert-Smith, H., Dickinson, K. L., Champ, P. A., & Flores, N. (2013). Social amplification of wildfire risk: The role of social interactions and information sources. *Risk Analysis, 33*(5), 800–817. doi:10.1111/j.1539–6924.2012.01917.x

Burns, W. J., Slovic, P., Kasperson, R. E., Kasperson, J. X., Renn, O., & Emani, S. (1993). Incorporating structural models into research on the social amplification of risk: Implications for theory construction and decision-making. *Risk Analysis, 13*(6), 611–623. doi:10.1111/j.1539–6924.1993.tb01323.x

Busby, J., & Duckett, D. (2012). Social risk amplification as an attribution: The case of zoonotic disease outbreaks. *Journal of Risk Research, 15*(9), 1049–1074. doi:10.1080/13669877.2012.670130

Busby, J. S., Alcock, R. E., & MacGillivray, B. H. (2009). Interrupting the social amplification of risk process:

A case study in collective emissions reduction. *Environmental Science & Policy, 12*(3), 297–308. doi:10.1016/j.envsci.2008.12.001

Busby, J. S., & Onggo, S. (2013). Managing the social amplification of risk: A simulation of interacting actors. *Journal of the Operational Research Society, 64*(5), 638–653. doi:10.1057/jors.2012.80

Chung, I. J. (2011). Social amplification of risk in the Internet environment. *Risk Analysis, 31*(12), 1883–1896. doi:10.1111/j.1539–6924.2011.01623.x

Chung, J. B., & Yun, G. W. (2013). Media and social amplification of risk: BSE and H1N1 cases in South Korea. *Disaster Prevention and Management, 22*(2), 148–159. doi:10.1108/09653561311325299

Cobb, R. W., & Elder, C. (1971). The politics of agenda-building: An alternative perspective for modern democratic theory. *Journal of Politics, 33*(4), 892–915. doi:10.2307/2128415

Danielian, L. (1994). Interest groups in the news. In D. J. Kennamer (Ed.), *Public opinion, the press, and public policy* (pp. 63–79). Westport, CT: Praeger.

Downs, A. (1972). Up and down with ecology: The issue–attention cycle. *Public Interest, 28,* 38–50.

Druckman, J. N. (2001). The implications of framing effects for citizen competence. *Political Behavior, 23*(3), 225–256. doi:10.1023/A:1015006907312

Dunwoody, S., & Neuwirth, K. (1991). Coming to terms with the impact of communication on scientific and technological risk judgments. In L. Wilkins & P. Patterson (Eds.), *Risky business: Communicating issues of science, risk, and public policy* (pp. 11–30). Westport, CT: Greenwood Press.

Entman, R. M. (1993). Framing: Toward clarification of a fractured paradigm. *Journal of Communication, 43*(4), 51–58. doi:10.1111/j.1460–2466.1993.tb01304.x

Evensen, D. T., Decker, D. J., & Stedman, R. C. (2013). Shifting reactions to risks: A case study. *Journal of Risk Research, 16*(1), 81–96. doi:10.1080/13669877.2012.726238

Fishman, M. (1978). Crime waves as ideology. *Social Problems, 25*(5), 531–543. doi:10.2307/800102

Fishman, M. (1980). *Manufacturing the news.* Austin: University of Texas Press.

Flynn, J. (2003). Nuclear stigma. In N. F. Pidgeon, R. E. Kasperson, & J. X. Kasperson (Eds.), *The social amplification of risk* (pp. 326–352). New York, NY: Oxford University Press.

Flynn, J., Peters, E., Mertz, C. K., & Slovic, P. (1998). Risk, media, and stigma at Rocky Flats. *Risk Analysis, 18*(6), 715–727. doi:10.1023/B:RIAN.0000005918.67810.6d

Freudenburg, W. R. (1988). Perceived risk, real risk: Social science and the art of probabilistic risk assessment. *Science, 242*(4875), 44–49. doi:10.1126/science.3175635

Freudenburg, W. R., Coleman, C. L., Gonzales, J., & Helgeland, C. (1996). Media coverage of hazard events: Analyzing the assumptions. *Risk Analysis, 16*(1), 31–42. doi:10.1111/j.1539–6924.1996.tb01434.x

Frewer, L. J., Miles, S., & Marsh, R. (2002). The media and genetically modified foods: Evidence in support of social amplification of risk. *Risk Analysis, 22*(4), 701–711. doi:10.1111/0272–4332.00062

Friedman, S. M., Dunwoody, S., & Rogers, C. L. (1999). *Communicating uncertainty: Media coverage of new and controversial science.* Mahwah, NJ: Lawrence Erlbaum.

Gamson, W. A., & Modigliani, A. (1989). Media discourse and public opinion of nuclear power: A constructionist approach. *American Journal of Sociology, 95*(1), 1–37. doi:10.1086/229213

Gans, H. J. (1979). *Deciding what's news: A study of CBS evening news, NBC nightly news, Newsweek, and Time.* New York, NY: Pantheon Books.

Gerbner, G., Gross, L., Morgan, M., Signorielli, N., & Shanahan, J. (2002). Growing up with television: Cultivation processes. In J. Bryant & D. Zillmann (Eds.), *Media effects: Advances in theory and research* (2nd ed.). Mahwah, NJ: Lawrence Erlbaum.

Gore, M. L., & Knuth, B. A. (2009). Mass media effect on the operating environment of a wildlife-related risk-communication campaign. *Journal of Wildlife Management, 73*(8), 1407–1413. doi:10.2193/2008–343

Gore, M. L., Siemer, W. F., Shanahan, J. E., Scheufele, D. A., & Decker, D. J. (2005). Effects on risk perception of media coverage of a black bear-related human fatality. *Wildlife Society Bulletin, 33*(2), 507–516. doi:10.2193/0091–7648(2005)33[507:EORPOM]2.0.CO;2

Hart, P. S., Nisbet, E. C., & Shanahan, J. E. (2011). Environmental values and the social amplification of risk: An examination of how environmental values and media use influence predispositions for public engagement in wildlife management decision making. *Society & Natural Resources, 24*(3), 276–291. doi:10.1080/08941920802676464

Hooker, C. (2010). Health scares: Professional priorities. *Health, 14*(1), 3–21. doi:10.1177/1363459309341875

Kasperson, R. E. (2012). The social amplification of risk and low-level radiation. *Bulletin of the Atomic Scientists, 68*(3), 59–66.

Kasperson, R. E., & Kasperson, J. X. (1996). The social amplification and attenuation of risk. *Annals of the American Academy of Political and Social Science, 545,* 95–105. doi:10.1177/0002716296545001010

Kasperson, R. E., Renn, O., Slovic, P., Brown, H. S., Emel, J., Goble, R., . . . Ratick, S. (1988). The social amplification of risk: A conceptual framework. *Risk Analysis, 8*(2), 177–187. doi:10.1111/j.1539-6924.1988.tb01168.xs

Kuhar, S. E., Nierenberg, K., Kirkpatrick, B., & Tobin, G. A. (2009). Public perceptions of Florida red tide risks. *Risk Analysis, 29*(7), 963–969. doi:10.1111/j.1539-6924.2009.01228.x

Lange, L. J., Fleming, R., & Toussaint, L. L. (2004). Risk perceptions and stress during the threat of explosion from a railroad accident. *Social Behavior and Personality, 32*(2), 117–127. doi:10.2224/sbp.2004.32.2.117

Leiserowitz, A. A., Maibach, E. W., Roser-Renouf, C., Smith, N., & Dawson, E. (2012). Climategate, public opinion, and the loss of trust. *American Behavioral Scientist, 57*(6), 818–837. doi:10.1177/0002764212458272

Lewis, R. E., & Tyshenko, M. G. (2009). The impact of social amplification and attenuation of risk and the public reaction to mad cow disease in Canada. *Risk Analysis, 29*(5), 714–728. doi:10.1111/j.1539-6924.2008.01188.x

Machlis, G. E., & Rosa, E. A. (1990). Desired risk: Broadening the social amplification of risk framework. *Risk Analysis, 10*(1), 161–168. doi:10.1111/j.1539-6924.1990.tb01030.x

Masuda, J. R., & Garvin, T. (2006). Place, culture, and the social amplification of risk. *Risk Analysis, 26*(2), 437–454. doi:10.1111/j.1539-6924.2006.00749.x

Mazur, A., & Lee, J. (1993). Sounding the global alarm: Environmental issues in the United States national news. *Social Studies of Science, 23*(4), 681–720. doi:10.1177/030631293023004003

McComas, K. A. (2006). Defining moments in risk communication research: 1996–2005. *Journal of Health Communication, 11*(1), 75–91. doi:10.1080/10810730500461091

McComas, K. A., Lundell, H. C., Trumbo, C. W., & Besley, J. C. (2010). Public meetings about local cancer clusters: Exploring the relative influence of official versus symbolic risk messages on attendees' post-meeting concern. *Journal of Risk Research, 13*(6), 753–770. doi:10.1080/13669870903551688

McCombs, M. E., & Shaw, D. L. (1972). The agenda-setting function of the mass media. *Public Opinion Quarterly, 36*(2), 176–187. doi:10.1086/267990

McGregor, D. G. (2003). Public response to Y2K: Social amplification of risk adaptation: Or, "how I learned to stop worrying and love Y2K." In N. F. Pidgeon, R. E. Kasperson, & J. X. Kasperson (Eds.), *The social amplification of risk* (pp. 243–261). New York, NY: Oxford University Press.

McInerney, C., Bird, N., & Nucci, M. (2004). The flow of scientific knowledge from lab to the lay public: The case of genetically modified food. *Science Communication, 26*(1), 44–74. doi:10.1177/1075547004267024

McLeod, J. M., Becker, L. B., & Byrnes, J. E. (1974). Another look at the agenda-setting function of the press. *Communication Research, 1*(2), 131–166. doi:10.1177/009365027400100201

Metz, W. C. (1996). Historical application of a social amplification of risk model: Economic impacts of risk events at nuclear weapons facilities. *Risk Analysis, 16*(2), 185–193. doi:10.1111/j.1539-6924.1996.tb01448.x

Nisbet, M. C., & Huge, M. (2006). Attention cycles and frames in the plant biotechnology debate: Managing power and participation through the press/policy connection. *International Journal of Press/Politics, 11*(2), 3–40. doi:10.1177/1081180X06286701

Nisbet, M. C., & Lewenstein, B. V. (2002). Biotechnology and the American media: The policy process and the elite press, 1970 to 1999. *Science Communication, 23*(4), 359–391. doi:10.1177/107554700202300401

Noelle-Neumann, E. (1974). The spiral of silence: A theory of public opinion. *Journal of Communication, 24*(2), 43–51. doi:10.1111/j.1460-2466.1974.tb00367.x

Pan, Z. D., & Kosicki, G. M. (1993). Framing analysis: An approach to news discourse. *Political Communication, 10,* 55–75. doi:10.1080/10584609.1993.9962963

Pidgeon, N. F., Kasperson, R. E., & Kasperson, J. X. (2003). *The social amplification of risk.* New York, NY: Cambridge University Press.

Poumadère, M., Mays, C., Le Mer, S., & Blong, R. (2005). The 2003 heat wave in France: Dangerous climate change here and now. *Risk Analysis, 25*(6), 1483–1494. doi:10.1111/j.1539-6924.2005.00694.x

Price, V., Tewksbury, D., & Powers, E. (1997). Switching trains of thought: The impact of news frames on readers' cognitive responses. *Communication Research, 24*(5), 481–506. doi:10.1177/009365097024005002

Profeta, B., Goncharova, N. P., Kolyado, I. B., Robertus, Y. V., & McKee, M. (2010). Danger from above? A quantitative study of perceptions of hazards from falling rockets in the Altai region of Siberia. *Health Risk & Society, 12*(3), 193–210. doi:10.1080/13698570903329466

Raude, J., Fischler, C., Lukasiewicz, E., Setbon, M., & Flahault, A. (2004). GPs and the social amplification of BSE-related risk: An empirical study. *Health Risk & Society, 6*(2), 173–185. doi:10.1080/1369857042000219760

Rayner, S. (1988). Muddling through metaphors to maturity: A commentary on the social amplification of risk. *Risk Analysis, 8*(2), 201–204. doi:10.1111/j.1539-6924.1988.tb01172.x

Renn, O. (1992). Concepts of risk: A classification. In S. Krimsky & D. Golding (Eds.), *Social theories of risk* (pp. 53–79). Westport, CT: Praeger.

Renn, O., Burns, W. J., Kasperson, J. X., Kasperson, R. E., & Slovic, P. (1992). The social amplification of risk: Theoretical foundations and empirical applications. *Journal of Social Issues, 48*(4), 137–160. doi:10.1111/j.1540-4560.1992.tb01949.x

Rickard, L. N., McComas, K. A., Clarke, C. E., Stedman, R. C., & Decker, D. J. (2013). Exploring risk attenuation and crisis communication after a plague death in Grand Canyon. *Journal of Risk Research, 16*(2), 145–167. doi:10.1080/13669877.2012.725673

Rip, A. (1988). Should social amplification of risk be counteracted. *Risk Analysis, 8*(2), 193–197. doi:10.1111/j.1539-6924.1988.tb01170.x

Scheufele, D. A. (1999). Framing as a theory of media effects. *Journal of Communication, 49*(1), 103–122. doi:10.1111/j.1460-2466.1999.tb02784.x

Scheufele, D. A., & Tewksbury, D. (2007). Framing, agenda setting, and priming: The evolution of three media effects models. *Journal of Communication, 57*(1), 9–20. doi:10.1111/j.1460-2466.2006.00326.x

Shaw, D. L., & Martin, S. E. (1992). The function of mass-media agenda setting. *Journalism Quarterly, 69*(4), 902–920. doi:10.1177/107769909206900410

Shoemaker, P. J., & Reese, S. D. (1996). *Mediating the message: Theories of influences on mass media content* (2nd ed.). White Plains, NY: Longman.

Slimak, M. W., & Dietz, T. (2006). Personal values, beliefs, and ecological risk perception. *Risk Analysis, 26*(6), 1689–1705. doi:10.1111/j.1539-6924.2006.00832.x

Slovic, P. (1987). Perception of risk. *Science, 236*(4799), 280–285. doi:10.1126/science.3563507

Slovic, P. (2000). Perception of risk. In P. Slovic (Ed.), *Perception of risk* (pp. 220–231). Sterling, VA: Earthscan.

Trumbo, C. W. (2012). The effect of newspaper coverage of influenza on the rate of physician visits for influenza 2002–2008. *Mass Communication and Society, 15*(5), 718–738. doi:10.1080/15205436.2011.616277

Tuchman, G. (1978). *Making news: A study in the construction of reality*. New York, NY: Free Press.

Yang, J., & Goddard, E. (2011). The evolution of risk perceptions related to bovine spongiform encephalopathy: Canadian consumer and producer behavior. *Journal of Toxicology and Environmental Health Part A, 74*(2–4), 191–225. doi:10.1080/15287394.2011.529328

CHAPTER 6

Rhetoric of Risk

Robin E. Jensen

Introduction

Rhetoric of risk scholars consider how risks emerge *through* discourse and are therefore discursive. Rather than assuming that risks exist exclusively in the material world, rhetorical explorations of risk are distinguished from other perspectives for their conceptualization of risk as something that comes into being (i.e., is constituted) at the moment of communication. This chapter aims to demonstrate how and to what ends scholarship in this area conceives of risk as a discursive construction. After a brief introduction, I identify the current major lines of research that have emerged from the study of rhetoric and risk—highlighting points of agreement and dissent—and provide an overview of the theoretical deliberations driving this mode of inquiry. Finally, I reflect, briefly, on an important theoretical consideration for future research in this area, and I delineate three promising research directions.

Scholars of rhetoric have long claimed that risk is both a topic and a topoi (i.e., a convention for building arguments) naturally positioned within the purview of their expertise (see, e.g., Danisch, 2011; Gross, 1994; Katz & Miller, 1996). In an overarching sense, rhetorical scholarship tends to focus on exploring what Aristotle described as "the available means of persuasion" in any given situation (Aristotle, trans. 1941, *Rhet.* 1.2, 1355b26f). Rhetorical scholars decipher what symbols might mean to specific audiences in particular contexts and how those symbols develop, circulate, transform, influence, and motivate. No matter the context, the persuasive/motivational process is one that emerges from a sense of uncertainty about past, present, and/or future happenings, as well as from corresponding questions about the most appropriate way to act in response to (or in anticipation of) those happenings. Danisch (2010, 2011) reasoned that the idea of risk—which is only ever probable and always necessarily uncertain—is a constant subject of and source for persuasive endeavors. In this respect, he argued that it makes sense that risk is repeatedly at the center of rhetorical inquiry into discursive interaction.

Indeed, over the past decade, scholars have gone from recognizing that rhetoricians regularly ground their work in topics related to risk framing and perception to delineating a subfield of study specifically dedicated to the rhetoric of risk. Ayotte, Bernard, and O'Hair (2009), for instance, have recently defined the rhetoric of risk as the study of discourses about risk and how they function to shape perceptions of human history. More specifically, they position this area of study as one dedicated to exploring "how particular risks come to be persuasive *as* facts of the world rather than only why a particular rhetorical framing of pregiven facts does or does not move public audiences" (p. 616). Ultimately, this emphasis on understanding *how* risks are constituted via rhetoric over time is one that pervades scholarship in this area. For instance, scholars such as Grabill and Simmons (1998) emphasized the role that context and social factors play in discursive accounts of risk. Similarly, Sauer (2002) published a volume titled *The Rhetoric of Risk* and dedicated it to expanding traditional notions of risk (i.e., the conceptualization of risk as an elite truth delivered in strategic ways to the masses) to account for the role that lay individuals play—via writings, speeches, images, performances, events, and even gestures—in the communication of risk in specific situations and historical moments.

Despite the diversity of their subject matter (e.g., terrorist threats, regulatory communication in the workplace, and educational outcomes), these authors all aim to question the notion of risk as something that can be discovered via mathematical equations or psychometric scales. Risk assessment equations and scales generally attempt to calculate the likelihood of a specific threat or potential hazard in light of the amount of effort or harm that might be incurred by attempts to allay the threat's occurrence. Frequently employed by professionals such as actuaries, governmental committee members, and organizational administrators, these equations are often the factors that decide issues including a person's eligibility for life or health insurance, an airport's security protocol, the grounding of new construction on a known Superfund site, the age at which a woman is encouraged by her doctor to get a mammogram, or the proliferation of a nation's supply of nuclear weapons. The underlying goal in drawing from these equations to make potentially life-altering decisions is on transforming the

unknowable and ephemeral future into something that resembles a predictable fact (see Taylor, 2010). Yet as Schwartzman, Ross, and Berube (2011) have noted, objective risk assessment tools along these lines—as well as the risk assessment plans or "fantasy documents" for which they provide justification (Danisch, 2011; Keränen, 2008, p. 233)—often do not account adequately for human perceptions of and reactions to risk discourse, mostly because, as Grabill and Simmons (1998) have argued, lay perceptions of risk rarely align with risk assessors' perceptions of risk.

Scholarship on the rhetoric of risk, then, is designed to offer a counterpoint to (or at least an opportunity for refining) these more technocratic approaches by accounting for risk as the result of communication—and therefore as symbolic and contextual—rather than as definitive. The major argument uniting rhetoric of risk scholars is that all notions of risk are at least partly discursively constructed and that to communicate about risk is also to create risk. Thus, their work as a whole involves the study of discourse designed to communicate about risk, a task that generally includes close analysis of the symbols employed therein and the implications for framing risk in one way rather than another. Yet, as the following section lays out, there exists within rhetorical scholarship on risk a range of interpretations about the claim that risk is constitutive, as well as a number of different uses to which this claim has been enlisted.

Major Research Areas

Three major areas of research make up the bulk of current scholarship on the rhetoric of risk. These areas emphasize risk as discursively constructed, as the product of deliberation, and as the focus of rhetorical analysis. Although the scholarship within each individual category tends to cluster together under common concerns and assumptions, the categories themselves are not mutually exclusive and so occasionally overlap in terms of findings and points of application.

Risk as Discursively Constructed

While some rhetoric of risk scholars use the constructed nature of risk as a point of departure for analyzing a range of diverse risk-related topics, others have focused more exclusively on theorizing about risk as discursively constructed. The latter tend to begin their theoretical analyses by deconstructing the idea that risk can be empirically identified in the world. In some cases, these authors point to specific analyses of risk communication that they believe are grounded in the idea that risk is primarily a material reality, and they argue why and how this theoretical foundation is faulty. For example, Ayotte et al. (2009) held that Farrell and Goodnight's (1981) research on the 1979 Three Mile Island nuclear plant disaster was grounded in the idea that effective discourse communicates risk as it actually exists in the world. From this perspective, communicative problems are primarily the result of a communicator's inaccurate, unclear, and/or misleading reports. Ayotte et al. (2009) argued that, although such work "can provide useful insights about the ways in which certain rhetorical styles can affect an audience's reception of message," the assumptions on which such work is grounded limit scholars' ability to trace the emergence of social understandings of risk because the possibility that risk is discursively created is negated (p. 615).

At the extreme end of research following in this tradition are scholars who have portrayed themselves as largely reluctant to conceive of risk in a material sense (see, e.g., Danisch, 2010, 2011). These researchers stand in contrast to more moderate risk constructivists who have explicitly recognized a material/physical component of risk. Preda (2005), for example, maintained that risk is real in the sense that some impending, projected dangers do come to pass, the consequences of which are often experienced on a physical, material

level that can be seen, measured, and even predicted to some extent. Yet Preda qualified this claim by noting that risk's "order of reality is not constituted according to a clear-cut distinction between soft and hard worlds that never mingle" (p. 16). Risk, according to Preda, is discursive just as much as it is material, and he held that it is all but impossible to distinguish between the two because they are inherently intertwined. For example, in a discussion about risks associated with HIV/AIDS, Preda posited that the rhetorical nature of risk (e.g., how HIV/AIDS is communicated as threatening) is in constant communication with the material realities of risks realized (e.g., the raw physical pain that can accompany infection). Scientific research findings, mass media portrayals, and the lived experience of danger and crisis come together to constitute risk in the public sphere. In this respect, Preda's work demonstrates that scholars of the rhetoric of risk need not necessarily argue from the position that risk exists *only* because it is discussed. Instead, Preda's conclusions imply that scholars offer increasingly valid and applicable theories of risk when they conceptualize risk as something that is both the product of *and* the catalyst for discourse. In addition, his conceptualization allows for, and perhaps even invites, the development of intra- and interdisciplinary collaboration efforts—efforts that ultimately serve as academic currency for grants, fellowships, publications, and the like.

Current attempts at theorizing risk as a conglomeration of material and discursive conditions seek to explore not only overarching ideas of risk but also the constitution of specific risk categories and groups. The process of forecasting or assessing risk tends to involve the identification of certain behaviors, attributes, or characteristics as particularly perilous. Those who are discursively constructed via risk assessments as members of a high-risk group or as at-risk for experiencing a negative outcome often find themselves simultaneous Other-ed and thereby positioned as abnormal (Douglas, 1992; Lupton, 1999; see also Bell, 2006). Although, as Preda's (2005) work makes clear, there is often an empirical reason that certain individuals are flagged as at-risk for experiencing specific hardships, rhetoric of risk scholars have chronicled the vast discursive repercussions that tend to follow the emergence of such designations. For instance, Treichler (1999) noted that early risk categories for HIV/AIDS not only designated as at-risk those individuals who were not empirically at higher risk for infection than were others (e.g., Haitians) but also failed to include or account for individuals who were empirically at risk for infection (e.g., woman and infants). These discursive choices had costly material implications in terms of unwarranted stigmatization, failed opportunities to encourage preventive behaviors and adherence to treatment, and an escalation in the spread of infection. Fassett and Warren (2005) offered a corresponding example in light of students deemed at-risk for educational failure. They posited that labeling a student at-risk because of variables related to individual demographics or interests was to fail to attend to the context of individuals' opportunities and experiences within the educational system, experiences that may include a lack of educational access or support, a school system driven by student tracking, and/or sociocultural expectations related to variables such as gender, race, religion, and class. Fassett and Warren's analysis of an at-risk student's discussion of her educational experiences and perceived prospects highlights the discursive double bind that the creation of risk categories calls into being. Their conclusion is not that the designation of at-risk groups is entirely negative or somehow avoidable. Instead, they called for scholars and educators to remain ever dedicated to the task of recognizing structural factors that play a role in positioning individuals in this way—factors that often seem to function prophetically when in combination with the discursive creation of risk categories.

Risk as the Product of Deliberation

Several key rhetoric of risk scholars have focused on extending the idea that risk is discursively constructed to encompass the broader value claim that risk is best delineated when it is the product of deliberative (i.e., interactive) decision making. This position is grounded in a critique of risk as defined via unilateral, top-down communication, or what Gross (1994) described as the "deficit model of public understanding" in which experts transfer technical knowledge to passive, uninformed lay publics. More recently, Grabill and Simmons (1998) further categorized top-down risk delineation as either technocratic (e.g., "a one-way flow of technical information from the 'experts' to the public"; p. 421; see also Rowan, 1991) or negotiated (e.g., an interactive collaboration in which anyone who is or might be affected by a risk may participate, regardless of rank, knowledge level, or background). They maintained that even the latter model, which draws theoretically from diverse perspectives via broad participation a la Habermas (1983), offers an essentially top-down explication of risk. Their critique lies in the negotiated model's overarching failure to account for participants' power differences and what Noelle-Neumann (1984) deemed the "spiral of silence" that often results from such differences. Although any individual may participate in deliberations about risk in this framework, many individuals realistically will not participate in light of social pressures to remain silent or to agree with those in power. Such silence, according to Grabill and Simmons, positions those who are neither experts nor leaders within a community without a true say in the process of negotiated knowledge production concerning risk, thereby facilitating the "'oppression' of (typically citizen) audiences" (p. 423).

In response to the failures of technocratic and negotiated risk models, several scholars have offered corrective philosophies of deliberated risk. Grabill and Simmons (1998), for instance, explicated a theory of critical rhetoric for risk communication with the goal of minimizing the widespread acceptance of elitist constructions of risk and maximizing the role that lay publics play in conceptualizing risks both specific and overarching. Their work is based on an ideal of participatory democracy in which risk is contextualized and recognized as something that emerges in the process of deliberation among truly diverse parties. In this conceptualization, lay individuals are not just able or allowed to participate in deliberations, à la the negotiation model, but they are encouraged and even expected to participate because their unique voices and experiences work to legitimize the process and outcome of risk delineation. Although the authors are a bit vague about what this method might look like in practice (as well as what the implications might be of expected participation), their argument that individuals themselves are "the best judge of their own interests" paves the way for continued theorizing about how deliberations concerning risk might be configured to highlight and encourage the discursive contributions of individual stakeholders (p. 429).

Like Grabill and Simmons (1998), Sauer (2002) has also aimed to work from an idea of risk that emerges from the tenets of participatory democracy. In analyzing discourse about mine safety and risk assessment, she echoed Grabill and Simmons's claims about the important role that lay publics (i.e., mine employees) can play in even the very first stages of risk identification and decision making, particularly if risk-related policies are to be created that truly protect and benefit them as stakeholders (see also Simmons, 2007). Yet Sauer resisted attempts to designate an overarching framework for participatory risk delineation for fear that such a model would inadequately accommodate the contextual diversity at play in specific scenarios. Instead, through her own scholarship, she modeled a more flexible understanding of stakeholder contributions and argued that although lay participation in risk deliberations is generally appropriate and necessary, it can, in some cases, be counterproductive. For instance, one might conceive of an unprecedented viral plague spreading rapidly through a community, a plague that can be avoided only via strict adherence to unfamiliar preventative behaviors. Attempts to foster participatory risk identification and assessment in the midst of such a time sensitive, technical scenario would, no doubt, be both unpractical and irresponsible.

Although participatory deliberative practices may be an ideal from which to begin theorizing about risk, scenarios like this one demonstrate that it is not always the best course of action. Ultimately, Sauer concluded that risk specialists (e.g., technical experts such as public health advocates, government officials, and regulatory agency administrators) must decide if a specific situation warrants a top-down delineation of risk in which they, as experts, "represent information that will achieve the desired outcome" (p. 14). In this respect, Sauer's conceptualization of participatory risk delineation accounts for the contingent nature of applied risk communication, while still emphasizing the value in open negotiations about risk. At the same time, however, it could be argued that her approach still positions those with technical (but not necessarily experiential) expertise as solely responsible for the conceptualization and circulation of risk. Despite her emphasis on broad participation and input, Sauer ultimately positioned elites as the ones to determine whether or not lay individuals should be allowed to participate in deliberations about risk delineation in any given case.

In spite of this potential criticism, several scholars have recently echoed and even extended Sauer's (2002) claim, arguing that the ideal of widespread participation in risk communication may sometimes facilitate manipulation or miscommunication on the part of technical experts. For instance, Heiss (2011) demonstrated that, particularly in the realm of marketing and promotion, companies and associations may foster the perception that their ideas about risk are the result of inclusive deliberation, even though the deliberations in question have been strategically orchestrated to communicate a specific risk-oriented outcome. Stratman, Boykin, Holmes, Laufer, and Breen (1995) offered a less egregious example of the potential for miscommunication in participatory deliberation about risk by focusing on the contradictions inherent in attempts to balance organizational expectations with public contributions to and understandings of risk communication. More specifically, they delineated the U.S. Environmental Protection Agency's (EPA) failed attempts to convince Aspen, Colorado, residents of the extreme health risks associated with exposure to local mine waste. In this situation, the EPA's protocol for risk assessment and communication required that regulatory agency employees be the ones to interpret evidence and ultimately lay out steps for risk reduction via public communication efforts. The employees' call to regulate risk and reduce harm for lay citizens was ultimately viewed by many Aspen residents as at-odds with their own contributions to public deliberations about what constituted risk. Although the agency's records encouraged agents to conceive of the public as a partner in the risk-assessment process and to provide opportunities for public participation in risk delineation, the organization's broader goals and standards (which required that EPA employees define and set the terms of a given risk) did not allow for meaningful public input. The authors concluded that the EPA's answer to this impasse "seems to be to let people be heard, but in highly formalized, highly controlled ways that will *not interfere* with either EPA's control of protocol or EPA's ownership of risk determination expertise" (p. 13). Such attempts to create a facade of public participation ultimately do more harm than good, according to Stratman and colleagues, because organizational leaders are not positioned to make use of the information lay publics provide them. Therefore, regulatory agencies often do not understand public perspectives, even though by all accounts they should, and publics continue encountering risk messages that are not informed by their pro-offered perspectives or beliefs. In the end, publics' unique concerns are not addressed and preventative measures are rarely taken.

Stratman and colleagues' (1995) analysis certainly calls into question the practicality of deliberative risk delineation, particularly in the contexts of governmental or regulatory oversight; and other recent scholarship has taken this critique a step further by questioning the overall applicability and generalizability of such a model.

Ding (2009), for instance, complicated basic understandings of risk identification as the product of participatory democracy by considering non-Western contexts and focusing specifically on scenarios in which official discourses of risk are censored and therefore limited or nonexistent. In these situations, the process of fostering public engagement is one that could very well endanger the safety of risk communication advocates themselves, as well as individual members of lay publics who decide to speak up. Ding argued that to participate or invite participation under these conditions "is not a straightforward decision" because information is not widely available, opportunities for participation must be covert to ensure the protection of contributors, and occasions for collaboration are few as governmental and/or regulatory organizations, alternative media outlets, and members of lay publics are generally positioned in adversarial relationships (p. 345). This research highlights not only the current lack of scholarship exploring discourses of risk in international contexts but also the continued need for theorizing about the value (and ethical implications) of public participation when access to official information about potential dangers is unavailable. Ding's work, as well as that of Sauer (2002) and Stratman and colleagues (1995), serves as a reminder that understandings of participatory risk delineation are only ever useful to scholars and practitioners as a context-specific process that resists standardization.

Risk as the Focus of Rhetorical Analysis

Beyond constitutive and participatory conversations about risk, the third major category of ongoing scholarship within the rhetoric of risk subfield involves the identification and delineation of rhetorical strategies for analyzing and managing risk rhetoric. Although some scholars such as Ayotte et al. (2009) have depicted this line of inquiry as limited in terms of what it can offer to broader conceptualizations of symbolic risk construction over time, questions about which rhetorical strategies have been (or might be) used in specific situations and to what end remain relevant to understandings of risk as a discursive creation and persuasive endeavor. On the whole, research in this area generally focuses on rhetorical prescription and application and/or on rhetorical deconstruction, both of which tend to draw heavily from the tomes of classical rhetorical theory.

Hoffman and Ford's (2010) scholarship on organizational rhetoric offers a clear example of prescriptive research in this area as it outlines a number of inductively selected rhetorical strategies that may be used "to manage risk-related situations" (p. 174). Drawing from Bitzer's (1968) foundational work on the "rhetorical situation," Hoffman and Ford conceptualized risks as exigencies (i.e., "imperfection[s] marked by urgency") that rhetors (i.e., communicators) seek to alleviate via symbolic interaction (Bitzer, 1968, pp. 1, 6). Their prescription for diminishing specific risk-oriented exigencies through discourse is grounded heavily in Aristotelian theories of rhetorical invention, style, and delivery. Readers are encouraged, for instance, to attend to the ways that potential risk-oriented messages present their ethos or credibility, as well as the ways in which their messages establish arguments based in appropriate and consistent logos or evidence. Although the authors follow up their suggestions with compelling case studies and specific illustrations, the limitation of prescriptive scholarship along these lines is that inductive advice speaks to so broad an audience and so nebulous a context that direct application of these strategies generally proves to be impractical. To be fair, Hoffman and Ford's work as a whole spans a number of different trajectories, commenting not only on practical application and construction of risk messages but also on the deconstruction of rhetoric about risk and—harkening back to the conceptualization of risk as a product of deliberation—the value in "community participation in controversies over risk" (p. 177). Nevertheless, their conception of risk as a rhetorical exigency is representative of other prescriptive scholarship on rhetoric and risk (see Boyd, 2003; Heath, 2009), scholarship that highlights the need for continued theorizing about risk as an external or constructed exigency and follows existing critiques of the rhetorical situation as a whole (see, e.g., Biesecker, 1989; Edbauer, 2005; Vatz, 1973).

Deconstructive scholarship in this area is essentially the inverse of prescriptive research in that scholars work deductively from risk discourse itself to understand how risk has been constructed and to what symbolic ends. In her scholarship on occupational risk among miners, Sauer (2002) argued that her goal in analyzing risk-oriented documents and the texts of interviews with miners about risk was to "investigate the full range of genres and communication practices that arose in response to particular problems of work, risk, authority, uncertainty, and disaster" (p. 6). She sought to identify and assess the range of rhetorical strategies that mine workers used to negotiate risk in the workplace. Although there are moments in her work when she draws from her findings to justify the prescription of future discourse, her emphasis remains largely on understanding how rhetoric about risk functions and what that means in terms of occupational health and safety.

In his work on the "risky rhetoric" surrounding the surveillance and prevention of HIV/AIDS, Scott (2003) also employed a deconstructive approach to assess the symbolic function of discourse about HIV-testing practices. He focused extensively on exploring how such rhetoric may encourage individuals to identify themselves as at-risk or safe, and what those identifications might mean in terms of discursive and lived health experiences. Like Hoffman and Ford (2010), Scott justified several of his key analytical findings by drawing from Aristotelian constructs, often emphasizing—for example—the role that appeals to kairos (i.e., appropriate timing) play in advertisements and risk-assessment documents (see also Scott, 2006). His conclusions (which highlight how risk rhetoric can encourage those who are not empirically at-risk to spend resources on risk prevention, while correspondingly overlooking those who are most in need of preventative information and services) iterate the value in using rhetorical analytic methods to deconstruct ongoing risk-related discourse.

Reflections for Theory and Research

Ultimately, the most important theoretical task for those studying risk from a rhetorical perspective in the years to come will involve not the creation of a standardized model outlining a single process of risk constitution but, rather, the outlining of multiple ways in which "risk" is, and has been, upheld. Continued and vigilant attention to the criteria used to establish what (and who) is categorized as risky will work to ensure that risk is understood—always—as a product of discursive choices, choices that can and should be changed if they no longer serve the ends to which they were intended.

Related arguments have been made to encourage those studying the so-called rhetorical cannon not only to reassess what sorts of texts and speakers should be included therein but also to reconsider and retheorize the underlying principles or discursive conditions upholding canonical membership in the first place (Biesecker, 1992). To include women's rhetoric, for instance, in a list of canonical texts without considering why women have largely been excluded up until that point does little to ensure that the future of the cannon will be less exclusionary or that the cannon's content will be substantively different. Similarly, adding or subtracting things to the list of recognized risks has few long-term implications if such moves are not preceded by an investigation into both the stated and unstated rules that go into identifying risk. For instance, attempts to adjust the age at which women are encouraged to get a yearly mammogram (and to thereby alter when they are said to be either at a substantial risk for breast cancer and/or at a point at which

mammography offers more benefit than it does risk) likely has more to do with ongoing criteria for establishing medical risk—criteria related to issues such as the cost of false positives—than it has to do with the specific age selected. Scholarly work grounded in an ongoing theoretical dedication to exploring (and constantly reconsidering and readjusting) what factors go into defining risk will uphold a risk-communication process in which little is taken for granted and risk's status is upheld as provisional and oriented, above all else, toward the service of individual and community well-being.

Recommendations for Practice

Although this chapter has already been peppered with several suggestions about the need for specific types of research on the rhetoric of risk, I nevertheless dedicate this section to outlining three broader trajectories that offer compelling opportunities for future scholarly and practical inquiry. These trajectories concentrate on the study of risk and metaphorical communication, the role of the body in the construction of risk, and the conceptualization of risk through the lens of argument sphere theory.

Risk and Metaphorical Communication

The study of metaphorical discourse has a long history in the rhetorical tradition, offering definitions both extended (see, e.g., Rorty, 1989) and succinct (e.g., "giving the thing a name that belongs to something else"; Aristotle, trans. 1941), as well as treatises on usage, function, and pervasiveness (Booth, 1978; Ivie, 1987; Osborn & Ehninger, 1962; Richards, 1936). Despite this extensive body of work, recent scholarship has discussed the continued need for identification of different types of metaphors and their symbolic functions (Jensen, Doss, & Ivic, 2011). Correspondingly, the discursive construction of risk—like many other abstract concepts—is often grounded in metaphor. For example, unprecedented risks such as the emergence of HIV/AIDS are often communicated to the public via equation with more familiar topics such as war or plague (Jensen & King, 2012). Because metaphors function as perceptual lenses, shaping what and how individuals know about a topic (Lakoff & Johnson, 1980), the study of specific risks (or risks in general) as they are presented metaphorically will provide valuable theoretical and applied insight into public understanding of risk. Whether risk is often communicated via a specific type or types of metaphor, or whether metaphorical communication is often generated in light of certain categories of risk (e.g., bodily oriented, environmental), much is to be gained by continued attention to the intersections of metaphor, rhetoric, and risk communication.

The Role of the Body in the Construction of Risk

Whether communicated metaphorically or not, the idea of risk often forecasts a bodily experience such as physical pain, separation from loved ones, or vicissitudes in physiology. Yet there are relatively few scholarly considerations or analyses of the way that the body is symbolized by, or used as a symbol for, the communication of risk. Lupton's (1999) consideration of risk as embodiment offers an excellent starting point for such work, as does Douglas's (1992) discussion of the risks of the flesh standing in for the risks of the body politic. Explorations in this vein might incorporate existing considerations of the types of bodies that have been discursively constituted as at-risk, drawing from works such as Shugart's (2011) analysis of obesity narratives as well as Brouwer's (1998) exploration of HIV/AIDS and self-stigmatizing tattoos. These sorts of bodily oriented risk depictions no doubt play a major role in how individuals identify their own bodies and the physicality of communicated risk.

Conceptualizing Risk via Argument Sphere Theory

On the whole, perhaps the central scholarly debate concerning the rhetorical delineation of risk involves questions about its appropriate argumentative home. Stasis points in this debate revolve around who is qualified to construct risk, and what kinds of information one must understand and have access to in order to responsibly communicate about risk. Some have maintained that risk delineation must be grounded in the realm of technical expertise, while others argue that such delineation makes sense only for those who have lived experience within the community or situation in question. Argument sphere theory—which holds that deliberation tends to occur within or among three spheres of justification (technical, public, or personal) (Goodnight, 1982, 1997)—offers a productive lens for considering these questions, especially in light of risk conceptualizations that emphasize the value in deliberation and argumentation. There are several excellent examples of scholarship that deal implicitly with the rhetorical construction of risk by drawing from elements of argument sphere theory (see, e.g., Endres, 2009; Keränen, 2005; Preda, 2005), but more explicit analyses of argumentation about risk—particularly in terms of how risk discourse emerges and circulates in relationship to evidential expectations—have yet to be realized. In this respect, and many others, although the rhetoric of risk is a relatively young subfield of scholarly exploration, it offers undeniably rich, developed opportunities for the continued delineation of risk communication.

Conclusions

This chapter's aim has been to lay out and consider the major assumption underlying scholarship on the rhetoric of risk, the idea that risk is created via its communication. Existing scholarship in this area takes a variety of different positions concerning the *degree* to which communication is responsible for risk creation, as well as to the content of what "appropriate" or "effective" risk communication consists. Indeed, it should be noted that the ends of such scholarship are as diverse as its foci and applications. A rhetorical approach to risk may be employed, for example, to promote *or* decry the idea that victims of a mugging should play a central role in writing a neighborhood safety manual (and thereby constituting risk in that context and historical moment). What this perspective calls into question is not a certain sociocultural ideal or risk-communication agenda but rather the ways in which risk comes into being and what that discursive constitution means for those who live, speak, and experience society within its reigns. The rhetoric of risk as a subfield functions to increase the possibility that a given risk-assessment is revealed as symbolic as much as it is based on the material or that a specific depiction of a disease or health condition is considered in light of colloquialisms as much as empirical data. Ultimately, an examination of risk as something that exists only (or mainly, or partially) when it is spoken into existence provides a unique and underutilized point from which to consider the many risk-communication conundrums faced by scholars, educators, and public advocates.

Suggested Additional Readings

Lynch, J. A. (2011). *What are stem cells? Definitions at the intersection of science and politics*. Tuscaloosa: University of Alabama Press.

Thornton, D. J. (2011). *Brain culture: Neuroscience and popular media*. New Brunswick, NJ: Rutgers University Press.

References

Aristotle. (1941). *The basic works of Aristotle* (R. McKeon, Ed. & Trans.). New York, NY: Random House. (Original work published n.d.)

Ayotte, K. J., Bernard, D. R., & O'Hair, H. D. (2009). Knowing terror: On the epistemology and rhetoric of risk. In R. L. Heath & H. D. O'Hair (Eds.), *Handbook of risk and crisis communication* (pp. 607–628). New York, NY: Routledge.

Bell, C. (2006). Surveillance strategies and populations at risk: Biopolitical governance in Canada's national security policy. *Security Dialogue, 37,* 147–165. doi:10.1177/0967010606066168

Biesecker, B. A. (1989). Rethinking the rhetorical situation from within the thematic of difference. *Philosophy & Rhetoric, 22,* 110–130.

Biesecker, B. A. (1992). Coming to terms with recent attempts to write women into the history of rhetoric. *Philosophy & Rhetoric, 25,* 140–161.

Bitzer, L. (1968). The rhetorical situation. *Philosophy & Rhetoric, 1,* 1–14.

Booth, W. C. (1978). Metaphor as rhetoric: The problem of evaluation. *Critical Inquiry, 5,* 49–72.

Boyd, J. (2003). The rhetorical construction of trust online. *Communication Theory, 13,* 392–410. doi:10.1111/j.1468–2885.2003.tb00298.x

Brouwer, D. (1998). The precarious visibility politics of self-stigmatization: The case of HIV/AIDS tattoos. *Text and Performance Quarterly, 18,* 114–136. doi:10.1080/10462939809366216

Danisch, R. (2010). Political rhetoric in a world risk society. *Rhetoric Society Quarterly, 40,* 172–192. doi:10.1080/02773941003614456

Danisch, R. (2011). Risk assessment as rhetorical practice: The ironic mathematics behind terrorism, banking, and public policy. *Public Understanding of Science, 21,* 1–16. doi:10.1177/0963662511403039

Ding, H. (2009). Rhetorics of alternative media in an emerging epidemic: SARS, censorship, and extra-institutional risk communication. *Technical Communication Quarterly, 18,* 327–350. doi:10.1080/10572250903149548

Douglas, M. (1992). *Risk and blame: Essays in cultural theory*. London, England: Routledge.

Edbauer, J. (2005). Unframing models of public distribution: From rhetorical situation to rhetorical ecologies. *Rhetoric Society Quarterly, 35,* 5–24. doi:10.1080/02773940509391320

Endres, D. (2009). Science and public participation: An analysis of public scientific argument in the Yucca Mountain controversy. *Environmental Communication, 3*(1), 49–75.

Farrell, T. B., & Goodnight, G. T. (1981). Accidental rhetoric: The root metaphors of Three Mile Island. *Communication Monographs, 48,* 271–300. doi:10.1080/03637758109376063

Fassett, D. L., & Warren, J. T. (2005). The strategic rhetoric of an "at-risk" educational identity:

Interviewing Jane. *Communication and Critical/ Cultural Studies, 2,* 238–256.

Goodnight, G. T. (1982). The personal, technical, and public spheres of argument: A speculative inquiry into the art of public deliberation. *Journal of the American Forensic Association, 18,* 214–227.

Goodnight, G. T. (1997). Opening up the spaces of public dissension. *Communication Monographs, 64,* 270–276.

Grabill, J. T., & Simmons, W. M. (1998). Toward a critical rhetoric of risk communication: Producing citizens and the role of technical communicators. *Technical Communication Quarterly, 7,* 415–441. doi:10.1080/14791420500198597

Gross, A. G. (1994). The roles of rhetoric in the public understanding of science. *Public Understanding of Science, 3,* 3–23. doi:10.1088/0963–6625/3/1/001

Habermas, J. (1983). *Moral consciousness and communicative action* (C. Lenhardt & S. W. Nicholsen, Trans.). Cambridge: MIT Press.

Heath, R. L. (2009). The rhetorical tradition: Wrangle in the marketplace. In R. L. Heath, E. L. Toth, & D. Waymer (Eds.), *Rhetorical and critical approaches to public relations II* (pp. 17–47). New York, NY: Routledge.

Heiss, S. N. (2011). "Healthy" discussions about risk: The Corn Refiners Association's strategic negotiation of authority in the debate over high fructose corn syrup. *Public Understanding of Science, 22,* 219–235. doi:10.1177/0963662511402281

Hoffman, M. F., & Ford, D. J. (2010). *Organizational rhetoric: Situations and strategies.* Thousand Oaks, CA: Sage.

Ivie, R. L. (1987). Metaphor and the rhetorical invention of cold war "idealists". *Communications Monographs, 54*(2), 165–182.

Jensen, R. E., Doss, E. F., & Ivic, R. (2011). Metaphorical invention in early photojournalism: New York Times coverage of the 1876 Brooklyn Theater Fire and the 1911 Shirtwaist Factory Fire. *Critical Studies in Media Communication, 28,* 334–352. doi:10.1080/15295036.2010.515233

Jensen, R. E., & King, A. S. (2012). The authoritative metaphor and social change: Surgeon General C. Everett Koop's direct mailer, "Understanding AIDS." *Health Communication, 28*(6), 592–602. doi:10.1080/10410236.2012.704545

Katz, S., & Miller, C. (1996). The low-level radioactive waste siting controversy in North Carolina: Toward a rhetorical model of risk communication.

In C. Herndl & S. Brown (Eds.), *Green culture: Environmental rhetoric in contemporary America* (pp. 111–140). Madison: University of Wisconsin Press.

Keränen, L. (2005). Mapping misconduct: Demarcating legitimate science from "fraud" in the B-06 lumpectomy controversy. *Argumentation and Advocacy, 42,* 94–113.

Keränen, L. (2008). Bio(in)security: Rhetoric, science, and citizens in the age of bioterrorism—the case of TOPOFF 3. In D. Zarefsky & E. Benacka (Eds.), *Sizing up rhetoric* (pp. 227–249). Long Grove, IL: Waveland Press.

Lakoff, G., & Johnson, M. (1980). *Metaphors we live by.* Chicago, IL: University of Chicago Press.

Lupton, D. (1999). *Risk.* New York, NY: Routledge.

Noelle-Neumann, E. (1984). *The spiral of silence: Public opinion—our social skin.* Chicago, IL: University of Chicago Press.

Osborn, M. M., & Ehninger, D. (1962). The metaphor in public address. *Communication Monographs, 29,* 223–234. doi:10.1080/03637756209375346

Preda, A. (2005). *AIDS, rhetoric, and medical knowledge.* New York, NY: Cambridge University Press.

Richards, I. A. (1936). *The philosophy of rhetoric* (Vol. 3). New York, NY: Oxford University Press.

Rorty, R. (1989). *Contingency, irony, and solidarity.* New York, NY: Cambridge University Press.

Rowan, K. (1991). Goals, obstacles, and strategies in risk communication: A problem-solving approach to improving communication about risks. *Journal of Applied Communication Research, 19,* 300–329. doi:10.1080/00909889109365311

Sauer, B. A. (2002). *The rhetoric of risk: Technical documentation in hazardous environments.* New York, NY: Routledge.

Schwartzman, R., Ross, D. G., & Berube, D. M. (2011). Rhetoric and risk. *Poroi, 7,* 1–7.

Scott, J. B. (2003). *Risky rhetoric: AIDS and the cultural practices of HIV testing.* Carbondale: Southern Illinois University Press.

Scott, J. B. (2006). Kairos as indeterminate risk management: The pharmaceutical industry's response to bioterrorism. *Quarterly Journal of Speech, 92,* 115–143. doi:10.1080/00335630600816938

Shugart, H. A. (2011). Shifting the balance: The contemporary narrative of obesity. *Health Communication, 26,* 37–47. doi:10.1080/1041023 6.2011.527620

Simmons, M. (2007). *Participation and power: Civic discourse in environmental policy decisions.* Albany: State University of New York Press.

Stratman, J. E., Boykin, C., Holmes, M. C., Laufer, M. J., & Breen, M. (1995). Risk communication, meta-communication, and rhetorical stases in the Aspen-EPA superfund controversy. *Journal of Business and Technical Communication, 9,* 5–41. doi:10.1177/1050651995009001002

Taylor, B. C. (2010). "A hedge against the future": The Post-Cold War rhetoric of nuclear weapons modernization. *Quarterly Journal of Speech, 96,* 1–24. doi:10.1080/00335630903512721

Treichler, P. A. (1999). *How to have theory in an epidemic: Cultural chronicles of AIDS.* Durham, NC: Duke University Press.

Vatz, R. E. (1973). The myth of the rhetorical situation. *Philosophy & Rhetoric, 6,* 154–161.

PART II

COMPONENTS OF RISK COMMUNICATION

SECTION 3

Models of Risk Communication

CHAPTER 7

Risk Information Seeking and Processing Model

Sharon Dunwoody and Robert J. Griffin

Introduction

You could be forgiven if a 2006 study published in *Science* about decision making led you to conclude that thoughtful, effortful information seeking and processing were irrelevant to risk judgments. In that study, Dijksterhuis, Bos, Nordgren, and van Baaren (2006) found that simple choices (e.g., choosing among soap brands) were indeed improved if made immediately after conscious thought; complex decisions were not. In their experiment, individuals made better choices of cars (the complex condition) *not* when asked to select a car to buy immediately after considering several models across a dozen attributes but after a distraction took their minds off cars altogether for a period of time.

Put another way, the researchers argued that decisions about complicated things improve if an individual "sleeps on it" and then makes a quick decision, without engaging in conscious pondering. They call this process the "deliberation-without-attention" effect.

That seemingly volitional behaviors can be catalyzed by processes about which actors are unaware is a fascinating idea that may become fertile ground for the next generation of risk communication scholars. But while important decisions may indeed stem from unconscious processing, our brains can pull this off only if they actually have *something* to process; and that something is information. Thus, we argue in this chapter that information seeking and processing are critical components of risk decision making. Individuals vary greatly in the energy expended on these processes, and that variance may spell the difference between the formation of volatile versus stable attitudes about a risk, as well as the difference between acting or not acting in response to a risk.

Below, we examine the concepts of information seeking and processing, with a particular focus on their employment in risk decision making. We then focus on the risk information seeking and processing (RISP) model, devised to explore predictors of these information behaviors within a risk context. In the third part of the chapter, we present some original data analysis in service to testing the consistency of the RISP model across different types of risks and over time. Finally, we return to the "deliberation-without-consciousness" effect to offer a few last words regarding unobtrusive motivators of these information behaviors.

Information Seeking and Processing

Of the two concepts, information processing has received far more attention in the social sciences, in part because it has been a focus of a number of popular psychological theories about social cognition. However, as new information channels make user control increasingly (and, often, disconcertingly) common, the process of information seeking is becoming more salient as a research focus. We take a look at information seeking first and then move on to information processing.

Information Seeking

The concept of "information seeking" can be described as a volitional process of selecting information channels to reach desired informational goals, as well as one of making choices to attend to messages embedded in any particular channel. Although scholars have always assumed that information seeking would be the inevitable outcome of a perceived gap in one's knowledge, studies in information science, in communication, and, most recently, in the subfields of health and risk communication have made it clear that seeking behaviors are complex and contingently driven (Robson & Robinson, 2013). While most individuals, when faced with information gaps, express a desire for additional information, circumstances typically limit the number who progress to actual information seeking behaviors.

Information seeking models describe a number of factors that affect that progress to behavior, such as perceptions of an issue, including judgments of the issue's seriousness; enabling factors that reflect a person's perceived ability to search for information, including an individual's beliefs about the efficacy of available channels; and reinforcing factors such as the perceived utility of the seeking behaviors themselves (see, e.g., Green & Kreuter, 2005; Robson & Robinson, 2013). Many of these models were constructed to serve scholars

in fields such as library sciences and information studies. Within communication, several models have been utilized over the years.

For example, Chaffee (1986) posited two information seeking factors that share much with those articulated above. He argued that, in a search for information, individuals will be guided by two elements: (1) the cost of accessing any particular information channel and (2) the likelihood that a channel will contain information relevant to the need. Here, the term *channel* is not an omnibus term but, rather, is intended to distinguish "channel" from "source." Channels gather, package, and then convey information acquired from sources. While much research has examined source credibility, we argue that audience tendencies to take cognitive shortcuts mean that they may rely on the credibility of channels more than on the credibility of sources. (For an extended discussion of the channel concept, see Dunwoody & Griffin, 2014.)

"Cost," in Chaffee's calculus, means much more than dollars and cents. Searching for a channel can also be costly in terms of time or in terms of the stress induced when folks find themselves searching in ambiguous circumstances. (Key word searches of the electronic universe offer a good example of the latter.) Chaffee's two dimensions handily explain individuals' preference for physicians as channels for health information (high relevance but high cost) and their overwhelming use, instead, of mediated channels, including the Internet (potentially low relevance but low cost) (Hesse et al., 2005).

Another popular framework for information seeking scholarship, the "uses and gratifications" perspective, emphasizes the goodness of fit between an individual's specific information goals and the type of content provided by a channel. It assumes that individuals' channel choices are "goal-directed, purposive and motivated" (Rubin, 2009, p. 167) and that information seekers base future channel choices on an assessment of the ability of any one channel to meet their information needs. A uses-and-gratifications framework, thus, may predict to the employment of different channels for different risk communication goals. A chemical spill may lead a person to emphasize "surveillance" initially and to keep the television tuned to a credible news channel; later, that individual may opt into interpersonal channels for explanatory help and advice about personal protection strategies.

Another "seeking" alternative, of course, is to choose to avoid information about a risk (Case, Andrews, Johnson, & Allard, 2005; Howell & Shepperd, 2013; Sweeny, Melnyk, Miller, & Shepperd, 2010). Although rarely acknowledged in the general information seeking literature, avoidance has become increasingly salient in communication studies of risky situations. Witte's (1992) extended parallel process model offers one rationale for its selection: When highly fearful risks are coupled with few or no means of reducing one's exposure to those risks, individuals may opt to "manage" their fear by avoiding risk information altogether.

Information Processing

The scientific study of the ways people process information began decades ago (see, e.g., Norman, 1976). We find one of the most useful model "types" for communication to be the dual-processing models in psychology. These theories have in common a differentiation between cognitive processes that are fast and automatic versus those that are purposive and effortful. The former are labeled *heuristic*, *reflexive*, and *intuitive*, while the latter are often termed *analytic*, *high effort*, and *rational* (Evans, 2008, p. 257). The duality seems to have evolved, in part, to account for the apparent contradiction between people's capacity to invest time and effort in making meaning and their tendency to, instead, "satisfy their goal-related needs in the most efficient ways possible" (Eagly & Chaiken, 1993, p. 330).

One of the more successful dual-process theories is Shelly Chaiken's heuristic–systematic model (HSM). Chen and Chaiken (1999) differentiate between the two basic modes as follows:

Systematic processing entails a relatively analytic and comprehensive treatment of judgment-relevant information. Judgments formed on the basis of systematic processing are thus responsive to the actual content of this information. Given its nature, systematic processing requires both cognitive ability and capacity. . . . The other basic mode, *heuristic processing*, entails the activation and application of judgmental rules or "heuristics" that, like other knowledge structures, are presumed to be learned and stored in memory. . . . Relative to systematic processing, heuristic processing makes minimal demands on the perceiver. (p. 74)

Most of the dual-processing models (for a comprehensive list and discussion, see Evans, 2008) assume that people can engage in systematic and heuristic processing simultaneously, but the theories typically describe systematic processing as more desirable than its heuristic counterpart. Heuristic processing is seen as a "cognitive shortcut" that may lead to flawed decisions. Wimmer and Shohamy (2012) offer physiological evidence of the role of the brain in facilitating such shortcuts by, for example, increasing the likelihood that past experience will "bias" decisions made in novel situations.

Indeed, although some scholars promote the pragmatic benefits of heuristic decision making (see, e.g., Gigerenzer, 2007; Gigerenzer & Selten, 2002), numerous studies have suggested that systematic processing is more likely to lead to stable attitudes and behaviors (Chaiken, Liberman, & Eagly, 1989; Natter & Berry, 2005), attributes presumably of value in risky situations. The HSM assumes, in fact, that a person's recognition that she has too little information to make a confident judgment about a risk is enough to send her into systematic processing mode; the perception of insufficient information, in other words, will motivate her to devote time and energy to deliberative work (Trumbo, McComas, & Besley, 2008).

In the RISP model described in the next section, we adopt the position that effortful information gathering and processing are not only important precursors to making good risk judgments, but they are also important behaviors *in and of themselves*.

The RISP Model

RISP evolved from a perceived need to make the seeking and processing of risk information central foci of study. Although numerous studies have utilized one or the other of these concepts (see, e.g., Cline & Haynes, 2001; Czaja, Manfredi, & Price, 2003; Kreuter et al., 2007; Matthews, Sellergren, Manfredi, & Williams, 2002), few risk scholars have sought to explore factors that would predict differential use of these two processing strategies. Thus, the model employs risk information seeking and processing as dependent—not independent—variables to better understand the factors that might prompt

individuals to engage in more or less effortful, analytical work when faced with a risk.

An early goal of the model was to avoid reinventing the wheel, so we focused on adapting concepts that existing scholarship had shown to be important to information seeking and processing behaviors. We culled those concepts from several well-known approaches; among them were Slovic's "psychometric paradigm" (Slovic, 1987), the HSM discussed above, and Ajzen's theory of planned behavior (Ajzen, 1988). We now turn to a discussion of the primary components of the model and the theories from which they were gleaned.

Figure 7.1 provides a visual representation of the model. While the original model moved beyond information seeking and processing—with Ajzen's theory of planned behavior as foundational—to predict risk-related coping behaviors (Griffin, Dunwoody, & Neuwirth, 1999), it is the first part of the model, represented in the figure, that has been most rigorously tested and given the RISP label.

Figure 7.1   Risk Information Seeking and Processing Model

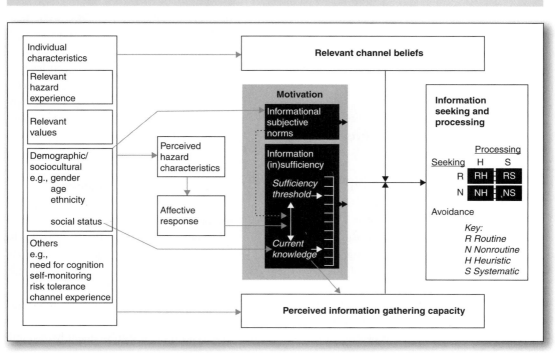

RISP posits that risk information seeking and processing will be driven primarily by a person's subjective assessment of the gap between what he knows about a risk and what he feels he needs to know in order to respond to that risk adequately. That information gap judgment, in turn, will stem from an array of factors, including characteristics of the individual such as socioeconomic status and ideological predisposition, perceptions of the hazards posed by the risk, level of worry about the risk, and perceived social normative pressures to learn about the risk. Finally, the model predicts that beliefs about the available information channels and perceptions of one's ability to gather information effectively will moderate the link between the perceived information gap and a person's information seeking and processing intentions. Although the model takes affect into account, RISP is essentially cognitive in nature.

To make this chapter manageable, we will briefly explain a subset of the model's variables: the information seeking and processing dependent variables; two important motivators, the perceived information gap, labeled "information (in)sufficiency," and informational subjective norms; and two mediating concepts, relevant channel beliefs and perceived information gathering capacity. We direct the reader to other discussions of the model for a fuller explanation of these and additional components (Griffin, Dunwoody, & Yang, 2013; Griffin et al., 1999).

Information Seeking and Processing

Just as information *processing* can have both heuristic and systematic dimensions, so might information *seeking* reflect more or less effortful work. One novel aspect of RISP is its effort to design heuristic and systematic measures of seeking and then to allow those aspects to interact with heuristic and systematic aspects of processing. Thus, someone could seek information heuristically, which the model labels "routine," by encountering information about a risk through her normal surveillance habits, for example, by watching a risk story on a morning TV news program. In contrast, she could engage in more systematic seeking, labeled "nonroutine," by purposely searching for information in channels that she would not normally monitor, for example, by looking for a specific study of the risk in the peer-reviewed literature or contacting someone at a state health agency. Regardless of seeking mode, she can devote varying amounts of time and energy to understanding (via processing) the message.

She can also decide to avoid information about the risk, perhaps because the risk makes her too fearful or because she regards the risk as trivial or unlikely.

Information (In)Sufficiency

Systematic seeking and processing are challenging tasks, so individuals presumably engage in such behaviors only when sufficiently motivated. Although the HSM advances multiple motives for processing, the one most relevant to RISP is the "accuracy motivation," which asserts that a greater or lesser need for accurate attitudes and beliefs catalyzes information processing choices (Chen & Chaiken, 1999). Chaiken et al. (1989) argue that individuals will invest the time and energy needed to achieve their desired degree of judgmental confidence regarding a decision; that chosen level is called the "sufficiency threshold." A low threshold may induce heuristic processing, while a high threshold may catalyze more intensive information gathering and analysis.

Informational Subjective Norms

An important component of Ajzen's theory of planned behavior adapted for the RISP model is subjective norms, a concept that stems from much earlier analyses of social norms in psychology (see, e.g., Asch, 1956; Sherif, 1935). The idea that groups of individuals develop common rules or expectations and that the perception of such social expectations can influence subsequent behavioral choices of individuals remains a compelling focus of research. Many scholars employ norms that reflect the risk behaviors they seek to modify, whether recycling or avoiding texting while driving (Lapinski & Rimal, 2005; Rimal & Real, 2005). Since we are interested in information seeking and processing behaviors, we explore respondent perceptions of whether or not other individuals expect him or her to learn about the risk. We employ the label "informational subjective norms."

Relevant Channel Beliefs

Individuals clearly do not regard all channels as created equal. We develop beliefs about information channels over the course of our lives that can influence our information seeking and processing decisions. Kosicki and McLeod (1990) argued that our judgment of the "quality" of a channel matters, as do beliefs about whether a channel is possibly biased or beholden to special interests. As noted earlier, beliefs about the cost of using a channel may literally drive us into the arms of a more accessible one despite concerns about the relevance of the information available there (Chaffee, 1986; Hesse et al., 2005).

Additionally, we may perceive the utility of channels to vary depending on our specific information needs. While we may not trust government channels to provide "objective" risk information, we may feel comfortable relying on those channels for information about laws and policies relevant to a risk. While we may readily interpret risk stories in mediated channels as informing us generally about a risk, we may nevertheless deem such channels to be less useful for information about our personal risk challenges (Dunwoody & Griffin, 2014).

Perceived Information Gathering Capacity

Of course, another potential roadblock to seeking and processing behaviors is our perception of

our ability to cull the information needed from information channels regardless of their assumed quality. Searches for information about health risks, for example, sometimes take individuals into highly technical prose filled with mathematical representations of disease probability (see Chapter 11, this volume). Perceptions of low self-efficacy in such situations may doom the search to failure, perhaps before it even starts. The concept of "capacity" used here, thus, is driven largely by efficacy.

Self-efficacy has a long history as an important mediator of behavior change (Ajzen, 1988; Bandura, 1982). But while most studies explore individuals' perceptions of their ability to engage in behaviors to, say, reduce smoking or avoid binge drinking, we focus here on information seeking and processing *as behaviors* themselves. Hence, we have adopted the term *perceived information gathering capacity*, thus applying the concept of *capacity* from the HSM (Eagly & Chaiken, 1993) and extending it to both risk information seeking and processing.

A Test of the Model Across Risks and Over Time

Comparatively few survey data sets in the social sciences allow researchers to examine the replication of results over time. Fortunately, two archived studies allow us to do just that with the RISP model. In particular, we will examine the relationships that risk information seeking and processing have with their proximate predictors, as illustrated in Figure 7.1: the motivational variables (information insufficiency and informational subjective norms), relevant channel beliefs, and perceived information gathering capacity. Although some analyses have been published from these data sets, none have compared results across studies and across time in this manner.

One data set, the "Great Lakes" study, employed the RISP model as a framework to investigate the use of risk information concerning health and environmental risks related to the Great Lakes. A professional research organization conducted an annual, three-wave telephone sample survey of a panel of adult residents from two metropolitan areas bordering the Great Lakes (Milwaukee, Wisconsin, and Cleveland, Ohio) from 1996–1997 through 1998–1999. The study was funded by a grant from the federal Agency for Toxic Substances and Disease Registry. The other data set, also employing the RISP model, is from the "Watershed" study. For this project, a professional research organization conducted an annual, two-wave telephone sample survey of a panel of adult residents of two urban river watersheds in the Milwaukee area in the winter of 1999–2000 and again a year later. Questions tapped the respondents' use of information about flooding and environmental risks related to the local rivers and their environs. The study was supported by a STAR (Science to Achieve Results) grant from the U.S. Environmental Protection Agency, the U.S. Department of Agriculture, and the National Science Foundation.

It is important to note that, within each study, respondents were divided into separate "paths" of questions, each path asking about a different risk. In the Great Lakes study, individuals for whom eating Great Lakes fish was a relevant matter were asked about potential health risks to themselves from consuming fish that may contain polychlorinated biphenyls—a family of toxic chemicals that were banned in the United States in the 1970s but that persist nonetheless in the Great Lakes ecosystem. Other respondents, on a random basis, were asked about personal health risks from consuming tap water drawn from the Great Lakes or about ecological risks to the Great Lakes ecosystem itself, an impersonal risk in the sense that the respondent himself or herself was not threatened. In the third wave of this study, interviews were done only with respondents in the fish-related path of questioning. In the Watershed study, individuals in one watershed were randomly assigned to one of two paths of questions: ecological risks to the local river or risks to homes and properties from flooding. In the other

watershed, respondents were asked only about ecological risks to the local river.

Despite these differences in risk topics, the questionnaire items that operationalized variables from the RISP model were otherwise identical or, in the case of one variable, at least comparable. This approach allows us to merge responses across paths for each year of each study to reveal the overarching patterns of relationships between seeking and processing variables and their proximate predictors. Details on the general measurement and analysis strategies used for these data sets, as well as results based on specific risks, can be found elsewhere (e.g., Griffin et al., 2008; Griffin et al., 2013; Griffin, Neuwirth, Dunwoody, & Giese, 2004; Griffin, Neuwirth, Giese, & Dunwoody, 2002; Griffin, Powell, et al., 2004; Kahlor, Dunwoody, Griffin, & Neuwirth, 2006; Kahlor, Dunwoody, Griffin, Neuwirth, & Giese, 2003). On a study-by-study basis, some of those results may vary a bit from the umbrella analyses to be presented in this chapter because of the characteristics of the specific risks examined in those studies and some differences in analysis strategies (e.g., addition or exclusion of some variables). Further information on self-report measures of heuristic and systematic processing of risk information can be found in Smerecnik, Mesters, Candel, De Vries, and De Vries (2011); see also Johnson (2005).

Table 7.1 illustrates a series of analyses that regress information seeking, avoidance, systematic processing, and heuristic processing on the various proximate predictor variables (see Figure 7.1) for each wave of both studies. Except for the operationalization of perceived information gathering capacity, which was changed from the Great Lakes study to the later Watershed study, the same measures are used across all of these analyses. Of particular note is the way that information insufficiency is measured and represented in the analysis. Respondents had been asked to indicate on a 0 to 100 scale how much they currently know about the given risk (current knowledge). Then they were asked, using the same scale, to estimate the total amount of knowledge that they would need in order to achieve an understanding of the

Table 7.1 Performance of Predictors of Risk Information Seeking and Processing Across Two MultiWave Surveys

	Multiple Regression Analyses (betas)									
Dependent Variable	Information Seeking					Information Avoidance				
Study	Great Lakes			Watershed		Great Lakes			Watershed	
Year (Wave)	G1	G2	G3	W1	W2	G1	G2	G3	W1	W2
Information (in)sufficiency										
Current knowledge	.09***	.14***	.11*	.20***	.22***	−.08**	−.09**	−.09	−.15***	−.12**
Information sufficiency threshold	.20***	.21***	.16***	.24***	.24***	−.22***	−.23***	−.15**	−.26***	−.24***
Informational subjective norms	.36***	.32***	.40***	.16***	.20***	−.20***	−.15***	−.22***	−.05	−.13***
Channel beliefs										
Media distort	−.05	−.03	−.08*	−.03	−.04	.12***	.13***	.12**	.06	.12***
Media have processing cues	.00	.01	−.04	.05	−.01	−.10***	−.06	−.05	−.10**	−.04
Perceived information gathering capacity	−.10***	−.15***	−.15***	.16***	.11**	.11***	.09**	.11*	−.15***	−.11**
Adjusted R^2	.26***	.27***	.29***	.25***	.25***	.18***	.15***	.14***	.20***	.18***
N	1,116	878	457	759	717	1,116	878	457	759	717

(Continued)

Table 7.1 (Continued)

Dependent Variable	Systematic Processing					Heuristic Processing				
Year (Wave)	G1	G2	G3	W1	W2	G1	G2	G3	W1	W2
Information (in)sufficiency										
Current knowledge	.08**	.04	.02	.13***	.13***	-.09**	-.09**	-.07	-.18***	-.17***
Information sufficiency threshold	.19***	.21***	.22***	.30***	.29***	-.23***	-.26***	-.25***	-.29***	-.27***
Informational subjective norms	.31***	.27***	.24***	.13***	.22**	-.21***	-.13***	-.25***	-.09**	-.20***
Channel beliefs										
Media distort	-.05	-.04	-.06	-.07*	-.07	.14***	.08**	.08	.06	.11***
Media have processing cues	.16***	.15***	.06	.17***	.11***	.05	.06	.05	-.06	.02
Perceived information gathering capacity	-.07**	-.06	-.06	.15***	.09**	.10***	.16***	.17***	-.13***	-.11***
Adjusted R^2	.24***	.19***	.16***	.27***	26***	.18***	.17***	.23***	.24***	.26***
N	1,116	877	457	759	717	1,116	877	457	759	717

*p = .05; **p = .01; ***p = .001.

risk good enough for their purposes (information sufficiency threshold). With current knowledge controlled in the multiple regressions, the threshold variable represents the relationship of information insufficiency (the information gap) to the dependent variable.

Although the RISP model suggests that motivation (information insufficiency and informational subjective norms), channel beliefs, and capacity might interact to affect risk information seeking and processing, the multiple regressions in Table 7.1 do not examine interactions. Instead, only the direct relationships between the independent and dependent variables are analyzed, with each independent variable controlled by the others in each regression. Since each analysis is based only on cross-sectional data, the results do not reveal patterns of causal direction or influence.

Results in Table 7.1 indicate that the motivation variables have, in general, the strongest and most consistent patterns of relationships with risk information seeking, avoidance, and processing across time and across both studies. Congruent with expectations from the RISP model, the greater the information insufficiency gap (as represented by the threshold variable), the more likely that individuals will seek additional information about the risk, the less likely they will avoid it, the more likely they will process the information systematically, and the less likely they will process it heuristically. The same patterns of relationships with seeking, avoidance, and processing also hold for informational subjective norms, with only one exception—a nonsignificant relationship with avoidance in the first Watershed wave.

The RISP model treats as exploratory the direct and indirect relationships that individuals' channel beliefs might have with seeking, avoiding, and processing risk information. As illustrated in Table 7.1, channel beliefs show somewhat consistent patterns of relationships with three dependent variables. Beliefs that information channels provide cues about the trustworthiness of the information they contain are related positively to systematic processing of

risk information in four of the six comparisons. Similarly, individuals' beliefs that information channels are biased and distort reality tend to be associated with avoiding such channels for risk information (four of six comparisons) and with processing the risk information superficially (three of six comparisons). Although consistent with the model, these relationships are weak, perhaps a function of operationalizing channel beliefs to reflect respondents' general views of mass media content. Indeed, Griffin et al. (2013) have called for a reconceptualization of the channel beliefs components of the RISP model to reflect individuals' expectations about the specific outcomes for themselves from using a wide variety of channels for gathering risk information and how they value those outcomes. Such an approach might adapt Palmgreen and Rayburn's (1982) expectancy value model, which shares its roots with the theory of planned behavior (Ajzen, 1988).

Table 7.1 also illustrates the effects of changing the measures of perceived information gathering capacity between the Great Lakes study and the later Watershed study. For the Watershed study, respondents answered six Likert-scaled items that reflected their self-reported capacity to seek risk information from media, government agencies, and other sources (e.g., knowledge of where to go for the information, having the time to do so), and their capacity to process it (e.g., possessing the abilities to understand the information and to separate fact from fiction). This summated measure of capacity correlates positively with seeking risk information and processing it systematically and negatively with avoiding the information and processing it heuristically, across both waves of the Watershed study. Even though the results are relatively weak, they are consistent with the model. In contrast, the capacity measure used in the Great Lakes study tends to have had the opposite relationships with risk information seeking, avoiding, and processing (especially heuristic). This set of two Likert-scaled measures asked respondents, much more broadly, to indicate how easy or difficult it would be for them to get useful information about the risk from mass media and other sources and to acquire any information they need from those channels if they wanted to. These items emphasize risk information seeking but not necessarily processing.

It is unclear why these two versions of capacity work in contrary ways, albeit weakly, in these analyses. It certainly may be the case that our construction of one or both of these operationalizations is unreliable. Another explanation, however, might be the different loci of control emphasized in the measures: The Watershed capacity scale tends to focus more on internal locus of control and perceived self-efficacy (e.g., Bandura, 1977, 1995), whereas the Great Lakes capacity scale has stronger overtones of external locus of control, that is, the individual being subject to the availability of risk information in media and other sources. A related possibility is that, with the Great Lakes capacity measure, those who perceive greater ease of access to the risk information may not feel the need to expend much effort to get it. Regardless, the Watershed capacity measure (Griffin et al., 2008) seems to be a better fit conceptually for the RISP model, since it details several relevant components of self-efficacy within the individual and includes processing as well as seeking measures. It warrants further exploration and development.

Neither channel beliefs nor perceived information gathering capacity had strong direct relationships with risk information seeking, avoidance, or processing in this analysis. Of course, much of the impact that channel beliefs and capacity might have on these dependent variables could be contained in the proposed interactions these factors may have with the motivational variables (information insufficiency and informational subjective norms). It would also be worth exploring the relationships between capacity and channel beliefs, especially as the latter would become redefined in expectancy value terms. It is possible that an individual's beliefs about the personal outcomes of using various channels for risk information

(e.g., online channels, professional channels, and mass media) could be affected by his or her self-efficacy in getting and processing the information from those channels, or vice versa. For example, as mentioned earlier, individuals typically identify physicians as their preferred channel for health information, yet they are more likely to access health information via mediated channels such as the mainstream media and the Internet (Hesse et al., 2005). The reason—at least in the American culture—is that people do not feel that they can easily access a physician and, thus, are reacting to lower levels of self-efficacy (Hesse et al., 2005). (For a discussion of the relationships between self-efficacy and outcome beliefs, see Williams, 2010.)

Reflections for Theory and Research

Tests of the RISP model over time and across risks indicate that individuals will indeed engage in more effortful information seeking and processing of risk information when they feel social pressures to know about the risk or sense that they have insufficient information for decision making. This is good news for policymakers and for communication professionals who emphasize the importance of providing information as an important catalyst to learning and possible behavior change. Further research might explore other motivations for seeking and processing that might be applicable to risk information, including the defense and impression motivations that complement the HSM accuracy motivation (e.g., Chen, Duckworth, & Chaiken, 1999) and a variety of drivers that stem from the media uses and gratifications models (e.g., McGuire, 1974; Rubin, 2009).

We suspect that many factors influence the relationship between motivations and the seeking and processing of risk information; among them are a person's perception of his ability to find information successfully and beliefs about the nature and quality of available information channels. RISP studies to date support these speculations at only a modest level; additional work is needed to explore the potency of such moderators, especially as they might interact with individuals' motivations to seek and process risk information.

Affect likely also plays a role in people's decisions about information. The RISP model as explored to date is heavily cognitive, since the proximate predictors of seeking and processing, including informational subjective norms, are based essentially on beliefs. RISP has yet to examine affective dimensions to any great extent, although Griffin et al. (2013) have called for such exploration. Mood states, for example, can influence how people seek and process the information they need for making a judgment (e.g., Clore et al., 2001; De Vries, Holland, & Witteman, 2008; Schwarz, 1990). Risk perception researchers have embraced "the affect heuristic" in recent years (see, e.g., Slovic, 2010; see Chapter 3, this volume). Thus, scholars need to find a way to incorporate both cognitive and affective factors in their efforts to understand predictors and outcomes of seeking and processing risk information.

Recommendations for Practice

Studies of information seeking and processing suggest that practitioners who seek to use information to inform or motivate need to be sensitive to such "drivers" as perceived need for information and individuals' senses of efficacy when it comes to finding and using novel information. These factors will come as no surprise to experienced risk communication strategists. But the all-too-common focus in many campaigns on ensuring the credibility of sources may lead practitioners to neglect the critical importance of channel credibility. If, as we suspect, many individuals make decisions based on the credibility of the channel—not the source—then the potency of messages situated in the wrong channel will be greatly reduced.

After decades of research and practical experience, the experienced risk communicator knows a great deal about how to motivate individuals to seek and process information about personal risks. But what courses of action can be effective when the risks of interest are "impersonal," that is, not obviously relevant to the individual? Many practitioners work within this impersonal domain, trying to motivate behavior change in the face of climate change or to confront major public health issues that affect "others." The RISP model offers one clue. Individuals facing, say, an issue affecting the environment may feel no personal involvement in the topic but may ramp up their information seeking and processing behaviors when they believe that others feel they should do so. Informational subjective norms—the perception that others believe one should learn about such a risk—are among the strongest predictors of seeking and processing in these impersonal situations. This suggests that practitioners should seek every opportunity to make audiences aware of their social environment when that environment has declared a particular risk to be important.

Conclusions

As a result of our decades of research on information seeking and processing, we have become intrigued by the potential of informational subjective norms. In our studies, if an individual felt that others expected her to learn about the risk, she was more likely to engage in effortful seeking and processing of information. This suggests that individuals are sensitive to the information management behaviors of others and may take behavioral cues from others even when they, themselves, do not regard a risk as sufficiently salient to require an expenditure of energy.

Also notable is that norms are often unobtrusive. That is, they often operate outside the awareness of the individual. When people are asked to identify factors that influenced their decision to modify their behaviors, they rarely mention their awareness of the behaviors of others (descriptive norms) or a perception that others think they should behave in certain ways (injunctive norms). Yet studies show that these norms are, in fact, among the most powerful predictors (see, e.g., Nolan, Schultz, Cialdini, Goldstein, & Griskevicius, 2008).

This brings us back full circle, to the "deliberation-without-attention" effect (Dijksterhuis et al., 2006) mentioned at the beginning of this chapter, which posits that good decisions about complex problems can happen in the absence of purposive attention and effort. Scholarly interest in unobtrusive motivators of decision making is on the rise, thanks in part to scientists' increased access to brain activity, and there may well be powerful, unobtrusive motivators—in addition to norms—that drive information seeking and processing. We await a new generation of communication researchers-turned-neuroscientists to open those doors.

Suggested Additional Readings

Braun, J., & Niederdeppe, J. (2012). Disruption and identity maintenance in risk information seeking and processing. *Communication Theory, 22,* 138–162.

Chaiken, S., & Trope, Y. (Eds.). (1999). *Dual-process theories in social psychology.* New York, NY: Guilford Press.

Schank, R. C., & Abelson, R. P. (1995). Knowledge and memory: The real story. In R. S. Wyer (Ed.), *Knowledge and memory: The real story: Vol. 8. Advances in social cognition* (pp. 1–85). Hillsdale, NJ: Lawrence Erlbaum.

References

Ajzen, I. (1988). *Attitudes, personality, and behavior.* Milton Keynes, England: Open University Press.

Asch, S. E. (1956). Studies of independence and conformity: I. A minority of one against a unanimous majority. *Psychological Monographs, 70*(9), 1–70. (Whole No. 416)

Bandura, A. (1977). Self-efficacy: Toward a unifying theory of behavioral change. *Psychological Review, 84,* 191–215.

Bandura, A. (1982). Self-efficacy mechanism in human agency. *American Psychologist, 37,* 122–147.

Bandura, A. (1995). Perceived self-efficacy. In A. S. R. Manstead & M. Hewstone (Eds.), *Blackwell encyclopedia of social psychology* (pp. 434–436). Oxford, England: Blackwell.

Case, D. O., Andrews, J. E., Johnson, J. D., & Allard, S. L. (2005). Avoiding versus seeking: The relationship of information seeking to avoidance, blunting, coping, dissonance, and related concepts. *Journal of the Medical Library Association, 93,* 353–362.

Chaffee, S. H. (1986). Mass media and interpersonal channels: Competitive convergent or complementary? In G. Gumpert & R. Cathcart (Eds.), *Intermedia* (3rd ed., pp. 62–80). New York, NY: Oxford University Press.

Chaiken, S., Liberman, A., & Eagly, A. (1989). Heuristic and systematic processing within and beyond the persuasion context. In J. S. Uleman & J. A. Bargh (Eds.), *Unintended thought* (pp. 212–252). New York, NY: Guilford Press.

Chen, S., & Chaiken, S. (1999). The heuristic-systematic model in its broader context. In S. Chaiken & Y. Trope (Eds.), *Dual process theories in social psychology* (pp. 73–96). New York, NY: Guilford Press.

Chen, S., Duckworth, K., & Chaiken, S. (1999). Motivated heuristic and systematic processing. *Psychological Inquiry, 10,* 44–49.

Cline, R. J. W., & Haynes, K. M. (2001). Consumer health information seeking on the Internet: The state of the art. *Health Education Research, 16,* 671–692.

Clore, G. L., Wyer, R. S., Dienes, B., Gasper, K., Gohm, C., & Isbell, L. (2001). Affective feelings as feedback: Some cognitive consequences. In L. L. Martin & G. L. Glore (Eds.), *Theories of mood and cognition: A user's guide* (pp. 27–62). Mahwah, NJ: Lawrence Erlbaum.

Czaja, R., Manfredi, C., & Price, J. (2003). The determinants and consequences of information seeking among cancer patients. *Journal of Health Communication, 8,* 529–562.

De Vries, M., Holland, R. W., & Witteman, C. L. (2008). Fitting decisions: Mood and intuitive versus deliberative decision strategies. *Cognition and Emotion, 22,* 931–943.

Dijksterhuis, A., Bos, M. W., Nordgren, L. F., & van Baaren, R. B. (2006). On making the right choice: The deliberation-without-attention effect. *Science, 311,* 1005–1007.

Dunwoody, S., & Griffin, R. J. (2014). The role of channel beliefs in risk information seeking. In J. Arvai & L. Rivers (Eds.), *Effective risk communication* (pp. 220–233). Abingdon, England: Routledge-Earthscan.

Eagly, A. H., & Chaiken, S. (1993). *The psychology of attitudes.* Fort Worth, TX: Harcourt Brace Jovanovich.

Evans, J. S. B. T. (2008). Dual-processing accounts of reasoning, judgment, and social cognition. *Annual Review of Psychology, 59,* 255–278.

Gigerenzer, G. (2007). *Gut feelings.* New York, NY: Penguin Books.

Gigerenzer, G., & Selten, R. (Eds.). (2002). *Bounded rationality: The adaptive toolbox.* Cambridge: MIT Press.

Green, L. W., & Kreuter, M. W. (2005). *Health program planning: An educational and ecological approach* (4th ed.). Boston, MA: McGraw-Hill.

Griffin, R. J., Dunwoody, S., & Neuwirth, K. (1999). Proposed model of the relationship of risk information seeking and processing to the development of preventive behaviors. *Environmental Research, 80,* S230–S245.

Griffin, R. J., Dunwoody, S., & Yang, Z. J. (2013). Linking risk messages to information seeking and processing. In C. T. Salmon (Ed.), *Communication yearbook 36* (pp. 323–362). New York, NY: Routledge Taylor & Francis.

Griffin, R. J., Neuwirth, K., Dunwoody, S., & Giese, J. (2004). Information sufficiency and risk communication. *Media Psychology, 6,* 23–61.

Griffin, R. J., Neuwirth, K., Giese, J., & Dunwoody, S. (2002). Linking the heuristic-systematic model and depth of processing. *Communication Research, 29,* 705–732.

Griffin, R. J., Powell, M., Dunwoody, S., Neuwirth, K., Clark, D., & Novotny, V. (2004, August). *Testing the robustness of a risk information processing model.* Paper presented at the Communication Theory and Methodology Division, Association for Education in Journalism and Mass Communication annual convention, Toronto, Ontario, Canada.

Griffin, R. J., Yang, Z., ter Huurne, E., Boerner, F., Ortiz, S., & Dunwoody, S. (2008). After the flood: Anger, attribution, and the seeking of information. *Science Communication, 29,* 285–315.

Hesse, B. F., Nelson, D. E., Kreps, G. L., Croyle, R. T., Arora, N. K., Rimer, B. K., & Viswanath, K. (2005). Trust and sources of health information: The impact of the Internet and its implications for health care providers: Findings from the first Health Information National Trends Survey. *Archives of Internal Medicine, 165,* 2618–2624.

Howell, J. L., & Shepperd, J. A. (2013). Behavioral obligation and information avoidance. *Annals of Behavioral Medicine, 45,* 258–263.

Johnson, B. (2005). Testing and expanding a model of cognitive processing of risk information. *Risk Analysis, 25,* 631–650.

Kahlor, L. A., Dunwoody, S., Griffin, R. J., & Neuwirth, K. (2006). Seeking and processing information about impersonal risk. *Science Communication, 28,* 163–194.

Kahlor, L. A., Dunwoody, S., Griffin, R. J., Neuwirth, K., & Giese, J. (2003). Studying heuristic-systematic processing of risk communication. *Risk Analysis, 23,* 355–368.

Kosicki, G. M., & McLeod, J. M. (1990). Learning from political news: Effects of media images and information-processing strategies. In S. Kraus (Ed.), *Mass communication and political information processing* (pp. 69–83). Hillsdale, NJ: Lawrence Erlbaum.

Kreuter, M. W., Green, M. C. Cappella, J. N., Slater, M. D., Wise, M. E., Storey, D., . . . Woolley, S. (2007). Narrative communication in cancer prevention and control: A framework to guide research and application. *Annals of Behavior Medicine, 33,* 221–235.

Lapinski, M. K., & Rimal, R. N. (2005). An explication of social norms. *Communication Theory, 15,* 127–147.

Matthews, A. K., Sellergren, S. A., Manfredi, C., & Williams, M. (2002). Factors influencing medical information seeking among African American cancer patients. *Journal of Health Communication, 7,* 205–219.

McGuire, W. (1974). Psychological motives and communication gratifications. In J. G. Blumler & E. Katz (Eds.), *The uses of mass communication: Current perspectives on gratifications research* (pp. 167–196). Beverly Hills, CA: Sage.

Natter, H. M., & Berry, D. C. (2005). Effects of active information processing on the understanding of risk information. *Applied Cognitive Psychology, 19,* 123–135.

Nolan, J. M., Schultz, P. W., Cialdini, R. B., Goldstein, N. J., & Griskevicius, V. (2008). Normative social influence is underdetected. *Personality and Social Psychology Bulletin, 34,* 913–923.

Norman, D. A. (1976). *Memory and attention: An introduction to human information processing* (2nd ed.). New York, NY: Wiley.

Palmgreen, P., & Rayburn, J. D., II. (1982). Gratifications sought and media exposure: An expectancy value model. *Communication Research, 9,* 561–580.

Rimal, R. N., & Real, K. (2005). How behaviors are influenced by perceived norms: A test of the theory of normative social behavior. *Communication Research, 32,* 389–414.

Robson, A., & Robinson, L. (2013). Building on models of information behavior: Linking information seeking and communication. *Journal of Documentation, 69,* 169–193.

Rubin, A. M. (2009). Uses-and-gratifications perspective of media effects. In J. Bryant & M. B. Oliver (Eds.), *Media effects: Advances in theory and research* (3rd ed., pp. 165–184). New York, NY: Routledge Taylor & Francis.

Schwarz, N. (1990). Feelings as information: Informational and motivational functions of affective states. In E. T. Higgins & R. Sorrentino (Eds.), *Handbook of motivation and cognition: Foundations of social behavior* (Vol. 2, pp. 527–561). New York, NY: Guilford Press.

Sherif, M. (1935). A study of some social factors in perception. *Archives of Psychology, 27,* 1–60.

Slovic, P. (1987). Perception of risk. *Science, 236,* 280–285.

Slovic, P. (2010). *The feeling of risk.* London, England: Earthscan.

Smerecnik, C. M. R., Mesters, I., Candel, M. J. J. M., De Vries, H., & De Vries, N. K. (2011). Risk perception and information processing: The development and validation of a questionnaire to assess self-reported information processing. *Risk Analysis, 32,* 54–66.

Sweeny, K., Melnyk, D., Miller, W., & Shepperd, J. A. (2010). Information avoidance: Who, what, when, and why. *Review of General Psychology, 14*(4), 340–353.

Trumbo, C. W., McComas, K. A., & Besley, J. C. (2008). Individual-and community-level effects on risk perception in cancer cluster investigations. *Risk Analysis, 28,* 161–178.

Williams, D. M. (2010). Outcome expectancy and self-efficacy: Theoretical implications of an unresolved contradiction. *Personality and Social Psychology Review, 14,* 417–425.

Wimmer, G. E., & Shohamy, D. (2012). Preference by association: How memory mechanisms in the hippocampus bias decisions. *Science, 338,* 270–273.

Witte, K. (1992). Putting the fear back into fear appeals: The extended parallel process model. *Communication Monographs, 59,* 329–349.

CHAPTER 8

The Societal Risk Reduction Motivation Model

Hyunyi Cho and Kai Kuang

Introduction

Preventing and controlling risk frequently requires changes in not only individual behaviors but also societal conditions. Extant risk communication theory and research, however, have focused on motivations for individual behavior change; substantially less risk communication theory and research have paid attention to motivations for changing the societal, political, and economic conditions and the contexts and circumstances of risk.

While a main predictor of individual behavior change is personal risk perception, the judgment that one is facing a threat (e.g., Rimal & Real, 2003; Rogers, 1975; Witte, 1992), a main predictor of societal condition change may be societal risk perception, the judgment that society at large is facing a danger. While it has been documented that the media are a primary source of societal risk perception, little theory and research have investigated how the media-influenced societal risk perception can be channeled for changes in the societal conditions and contexts of risk. Risk perception and risk reduction action at the societal level may comprise another route to risk

prevention and control, complementing the path from personal risk perception to personal risk reduction action that has frequently been studied in the extant literature.

Thus, the goal of this chapter is to introduce an initial, rudimentary version of the societal risk reduction motivation model (SRRM) that describes the pathways from societal risk perception to societal risk reduction actions (see Figure 8.1). Building on the theory and research on media effects, social processes, and collective behavior, the SRRM posits the mediators and moderators of the path from societal risk perception to societal risk reduction action.

This chapter begins by distinguishing societal risk perception from personal risk perception and by delineating the role of the media in influencing these perceptions. Next, the parameters and functions of societal risk perception and societal risk reduction action are discussed. On this foundation, the relationships between variables of the model are explained. This chapter concludes by summarizing key contribution of the model, suggesting areas of application of the model, and outlining directions for further model development.

Figure 8.1 The Societal Risk Reduction Motivation Model

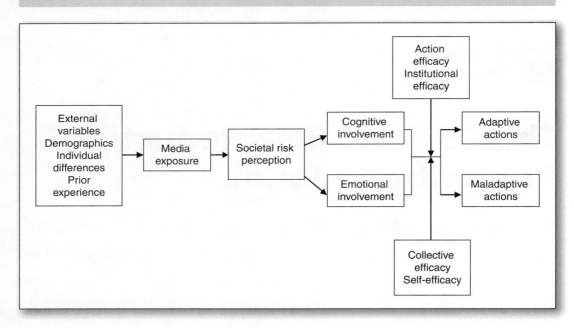

Media and Risk Perceptions at Societal and Personal Levels

The sociality of risk perception has been recognized by various intellectual traditions in social sciences. From the symbolic interaction perspective, Blumer (1971) characterized social problems as collective definitions, not as objective social existences. The social representation theory (Moscovici, 1984) posits a similar perspective in which reality is constructed through communication, interaction, and shared memory. The social amplification of risk framework (Kasperson et al., 1988) proposes that risk perception may rise or fall through psychological, social, organizational, and cultural processes.

A key conduit of the social processes postulated in these perspectives may be mass media. Among different modalities of communication, the media are distinguished for their capacity to create a broad reach and pervasive exposure (Gunther, 1998). Consequently, the media may be able to shape shared and collective perceptions about risk, about what is risky, and about how risky it is, in society.

That media shape judgments about the social world is postulated in the media effects theories of cultivation theory, agenda-setting theory, and the impersonal impact hypothesis. Importantly, a commonality among these models is that they posit the main outcome of media effects as societal-level judgments rather than as personal-level judgments.

Cultivation theory (Gerbner & Gross, 1976) predicts that repeated exposure to the media generates beliefs about society consistent with the media content. Gerbner and Gross (1976), for example, found that repeated exposure to violence on television induced the belief that violence is frequent in society, which is a societal-level risk perception. On the other hand, research did not find a significant direct association between exposure to media violence and fear of becoming a victim of crime, which is a personal-level risk judgment; instead, cultivation effect was found only among survey respondents who resided in high-crime areas or have personally experienced a crime before (Doob & McDonald, 1979; Shrum & Bischak, 2001).

Other studies on cultivation theory illustrate the distinctiveness of societal risk perception and personal risk perception and their sources. For example, on one hand, news exposure predicted societal importance of the issue of crime but not personal fear of becoming a victim of crime; on the other hand, while personal experience of crime predicted fear, it did not predict perceived societal importance of crime (Gross & Aday, 2003). Television viewing predicted fear of crime in distant urban settings but not in one's own neighborhood (Heath & Petraitis, 1987).

Similar to cultivation theory, agenda-setting theory predicts media effects on societal-level judgments. According to agenda-setting theory (McCombs & Shaw, 1972), people learn about important social issues through mass media. Specifically, it is through the media that people learn what issues are important in society and how important they are. For example, after exposure to news media focusing on pollution, national defense, and fiscal inflation, people assigned a greater importance to these social issues than other issues that were not focused on in the news (Iyengar & Kinder, 1987).

Impersonal Impact Hypothesis

The impersonal impact hypothesis (Tyler & Cook, 1984) extends these media effects theories by distinguishing media effects on societal and personal levels of judgments and by positing media effects on risk judgments specifically.[1] The hypothesis predicts that societal and personal risk perceptions are distinct and that the media influence societal risk perception but not personal risk perception. Societal risk perception refers to the beliefs about the importance of a risk issue to the society at large; personal risk perception refers to the beliefs about an individual's likelihood of experiencing harm (Tyler & Cook, 1984). The postulation of differential effects of

the media on personal and societal levels is consistent with evidence observed for the agenda-setting and cultivation effects of the media on societal-level perception (e.g., issue importance in society, event frequency in society) but not on personal-level perception (e.g., fear of becoming a victim of crime).

Support for the impersonal impact hypothesis has been obtained. For example, Coleman (1993) found that among New York state residents, exposure to the media, including newspapers and magazines, predicted the belief that issues such as HIV/AIDS, heart disease, water contamination, and radon would be a serious problem of the country. The same exposure, however, did not predict the residents' beliefs about personally being affected by these problems. Similarly, Morton and Duck (2001) found that among Australian college students, media exposure was associated primarily with the judgments about other Australians' risk of skin cancer but not with personal worry about and vulnerability to skin cancer.

While research has found that the effects of mass media on personal risk perception are limited, theories of behavior change predict that personal risk perception determines individuals' motivations to perform behavior to reduce the risk (e.g., Rogers, 1975; Rosenstock, 1974; Witte, 1992). Consequently, investigations have focused on identifying the conditions under which the media can influence personal risk perception. Generally, this stream of research has identified the kind of content and channels of the media and their interactions with the audience that influence personal risk perception.

For example, Brown and Basil (1995) found that identification with a media celebrity can overcome the impersonal nature of media effects on risk perception. Specifically, after hearing about the basketball player Magic Johnson's HIV infection, college males who identified with Johnson increased their perceived personal vulnerability to HIV. Snyder and Rouse (1995) found that when mass media were differentiated to informational and entertainment media, exposure to entertainment media predicted personal risk perception about HIV. A study extending Snyder and Rouse (1995) found that genre-specific exposure to the media differentially predicted South Korean college students' smoking-related risk perceptions at the personal and societal levels (So, Cho, & Lee, 2011). Together, these studies inform how the media can be utilized to influence personal risk perception. Meta-analyses have reported that personal risk perception influences individuals' attitudes and actions to reduce personal risk (e.g., Floyd, Prentice-Dunn, & Rogers, 2000; Witte & Allen, 2000).

Beyond Personal: Two Routes to Risk Reduction

In contrast to the wealth of research accumulated for personal risk perception, there is a paucity of research that has investigated societal risk perception and its effects. In preventing and controlling risk, changing societal conditions is important in addition to changing individual behaviors because risk may be caused by societal conditions as well as individual behaviors (see Cohen et al., 2000; Sampson, Raudenbush, & Earls, 1997). Furthermore, individual behavior change can be contingent on societal conditions that facilitate or hinder it (e.g., Fishbein & Yzer, 2003).

Distinct judgments of personal risk and societal risk may predict distinct yet complementary routes to risk reduction, comprising personal risk reduction and societal risk reduction action routes. While personal risk perception motivates individual behavior change, societal risk may stimulate societal processes and practices that can generate changes in political, economic, and social conditions surrounding risk. Changes in societal conditions triggered by societal risk perception may facilitate changes in individual behavior as well.

In the existing risk communication literature, however, societal risk perception has been viewed as an end outcome of media exposure and of limited utility in motivating personal risk reduction behavior. Since Tyler and Cook (1984), sparse theory and research have been advanced for the construct of societal risk perception and its role in risk prevention and control. The SRRM attempts to address this void in the current literature by describing the pathways from societal risk perception to societal risk reduction action. This effort first requires laying the conceptual grounds of societal risk perception and societal risk reduction action, the two essential building blocks of the model.

Societal Risk Perception and Societal Risk Reduction Action

Societal Risk Perception

At the societal level, the etiology of risk and approaches to addressing the risk are likely to be outside the control of any one individual. Instead, societal risks are likely to be a product of the conflicts, negotiations, decisions, and actions of individuals, groups, and institutions and interactions between and among them. The causes and control of pollution and contamination of the environment, for example, may involve individuals, groups, and institutions of society operating in multiple sectors. Concurrently, there may be shared consequences of not addressing the risk, as well as shared benefits of addressing the risk, at the societal level.

More than 40 years ago, Hardin (1968) predicted the "tragedy of the commons" in which all shared resources, such as air, water, soil, and climate, are exploited and degraded. These resources comprise public goods, which are properties in the commons, and the outcomes of using them are shared (Marwell & Oliver, 1993; Olson, 1965). Reducing risk in public goods, such as the environment, requires society's collective action (Marwell & Oliver, 1993; Olson, 1965), and a motivator of societal actions may be societal risk perception.

Drawing on Tyler and Cook (1984), societal-level risk perception is defined as judgments about the larger society or collective and about the condition of its members. As an outcome of media exposure, societal risk perception may represent a subtle yet powerful effect of the media (see Katz, 1983, for discussion on this nature of media effects). This effect may stem from the nature of media content and messages, prominent among which are the situations of larger collectives (Mutz, 1998). By presenting phenomena in the larger society, the media influence perceptions about collective conditions, which in turn influence political attitudes (Mutz, 1998).

The effect of societal risk perception may be subtle because it may not have an immediate or direct effect on personal risk reduction behavior; yet it may be powerful because it may influence motivations to change the political, economic, and sociocultural conditions surrounding risk. For example, societal risk perception about the possible or actual "tragedy of the commons" (Hardin, 1968) may spur social processes leading to the establishment of rules and regulations, codification of acceptable conduct, construction of norms, and willingness to comply to the rules, codes, and norms against degradation of the commons or public goods (see Feeny, Berkes, McCay, & Acheson, 1990).

Of note, the distinction between societal and personal risk may not parallel the commonly made differentiation between environmental risk (societal) and health risk (personal) and their respective treatments. Reducing risk in individuals' health, such as heart disease, requires not only personal behavior changes, such as diet, physical activity, and smoking cessation, but also societal actions to change the conditions surrounding the risk, such as labeling of cholesterol content in food packages, providing easy access to physical activity facilities, indoor smoking bans, and so on, which require policy changes. As such, addressing individual health risk can be facilitated by societal-level actions. Consider also the case of HIV. Although condom use is the direct and immediate action that individuals can take to prevent HIV risk, individuals' and society's risk of HIV may be more efficiently reduced through societal actions rather than individual actions alone. Condom use is advocated because of the unavailability of an HIV vaccine; and research, development, and dissemination of an HIV vaccine require a policy commitment that is predicated on support by public opinion, which, in turn, is likely to correlate with societal risk perception about HIV.

Societal Risk Reduction Action

Societal risk reduction action concerns the conditions and contexts surrounding risk. Attitudes and actions to reduce societal risk include willingness to support changes in policies regarding risk, to sign a petition, to join and engage in interest groups, to voice opposition or support for social changes over various avenues, and to vote. SRRM may also activate willingness to donate time, money, and other resources that can be utilized in efforts to facilitate changes and to lower barriers to changes in social, political, and economic environments. Overall, these attitudes and actions seek to directly address the societal contexts of risk rather than to directly address the individual behaviors associated with risk.

Of note, societal risk reduction action is dissimilar to collective action in that the former may subsume the latter. Collective action is frequently defined on the basis of in- and out-group distinctions. For example, collective action "involves behaviors on behalf of the *ingroup* that are directed at improving the conditions of the entire group" (Becker & Wright, 2011, p. 63; see also Wright, Taylor, & Moghaddam, 1990). The goal of collective action is to benefit an in-group that is typically disadvantaged relative to out-groups (Gamson, 1992; Wright et al., 1990). A theoretical foundation of this line of research is intergroup relationships (Gamson, 1992; Tajfel & Turner, 1979).

In comparison, the theoretical foundation of societal risk perception is mass media effects. A unique capacity of the media is their diffusive effects over a wide spectrum of society (Gunther, 1998; Lazarsfeld & Merton, 1949; Mutz, 1998). In contrast, intergroup relationships utilize interpersonal and group communication, which are relatively narrower in scope. Overall, societal actions may subsume collective actions that are based on group distinctions in that groups are important units of the larger society and may have upstream influences on society.

Furthermore, societal risk reduction actions may include those that do not directly benefit the actor. Societal risk reduction actions can include out-group's actions to benefit members of in-groups and other groups. For example, those who participate in actions to remove discrimination against minority groups may not be only the members of the groups that are discriminated; rather, they will include those who value social justice, fairness, and equality and those who expect shared benefit of ensuring these values in society. Connecting people of in- and out-groups through sympathy, empathy, and higher level identities, values, and goals, societal risk reduction actions may hover over the boundaries of in- and out-groups and unite disparate groups.

From Societal Risk Perception to Societal Risk Reduction Action

In previous research, societal risk perception showed sparse effects on individual behaviors that directly reduce risk. For example, a survey of residents of Alberta, Canada, found only a very small correlation between concern for the environment and recycling behavior (Derksen & Gartrell, 1993). This may be because the primary locus in which the effects of societal risk perception occur is societal rather than personal. May the concern better predict support for the increase and wider availability of structured recycling programs, which in turn predict

recycling behavior? In a survey of Connecticut residents, perceived societal significance of the issue of AIDS was not associated with intentions to use condoms to prevent personal AIDS risk (Snyder & Rouse, 1995). May the perceived societal risk of AIDS, however, predict willingness to take societal risk reduction actions, such as donating money and time for AIDS prevention, and to support governmental policies for AIDS research? These questions are based on the postulation that the principal domain of societal risk perception's impact is societal, including societal risk reduction actions that seek to alter the contexts of risk occurrence or risk behavior.

Research on civic and political participation provides evidence supportive of these postulations. For example, those who were more concerned about the federal budget deficit issue in 1988 were more likely to engage in various actions to influence the approaches to addressing the issue, including attendance to public meetings, signing petitions, writing letters, and intentions to vote in the upcoming presidential election (Weaver, 1991). Those who were more concerned about the issues of the state, including crime, drugs, and environment, were more likely to have voted in the 1990 gubernatorial election in Texas (Roberts, 1992). Concern about U.S. involvement in Iraq influenced youth's first voting behavior in the 2004 presidential election (Kiousis & McDevitt, 2008). Across these studies, the actions taken by individuals may not directly address the concern. Rather, these actions may indirectly address the concern by directly influencing the decisions relevant to the concern and the makers of the decisions.

Furthermore, motivations to act on societal risk may be mediated and moderated. The path between societal risk perception and societal risk reduction action may be mediated by cognitive involvement and emotional involvement. Societal risk perception may prime cognitions and emotions that emanate from the societal issue's relevance to self, which then activate willingness to engage in action to reduce the societal risk. The path from cognitive and emotional involvement to societal risk reduction actions may be moderated by efficacy beliefs, which include action efficacy, institutional efficacy, collective efficacy, and self-efficacy. While cognitive and emotional involvement motivates action consistent with the cognition and/or emotion primed, the kind of action to be actualized may be determined by efficacy beliefs. High involvement and high efficacy beliefs may result in the intended actions; high involvement accompanied by low efficacy beliefs actualization may result in inaction or maladaptive reactions, such as fatalistic attitudes or nonnormative actions. Figure 8.1 depicts these posited relationships.

Mediators

Cognitive Involvement

Broadly, cognitive involvement refers to the issue's perceived personal relevance. It is "a motivational state induced by an association between an activated attitude and the self-concept" (Johnson & Eagly, 1989, p. 290). Because society comprises individuals who share the common and public goods, societal risk may have ramifications for individuals. For example, societal risk perception about gun violence may motivate individuals to think about the societal risk issue's implications for their personal lives.

Because cognitive involvement elevates the perceived personal relevance of a societal risk issue, increased cognitive involvement may in turn create a greater motivation to engage in actions to reduce the societal risk. For example, in a French study, people with high cognitive involvement in earthquakes were more likely to exhibit a thought structure for earthquakes that was more practical and more action oriented than people with low cognitive involvement in earthquakes (Gruev-Vintila & Rouquette, 2007).

Cognitive involvement in a societal risk issue may stem from its relevance to a person's value, outcome, or impression. Research found that

cognitive involvement activated by these different kinds of relevance are distinct and are differentially associated with attitudes and actions (Cho & Boster, 2005; Johnson & Eagly, 1989). Values are "mode of conduct and end-state of existence" (Rokeach, 1968, p. 160), while outcomes have consequences for goals and gains. Impression is important to managing one's social life. Thus, depending on the kind of societal risk issue and its personal relevance, different kinds and magnitudes of cognitive involvement may be activated. For example, whereas the more other-focused issues such as organ and tissue donation were associated with value-relevant involvement, the more self-focused issues such as sunscreen use and nutrition were more strongly associated with outcome-relevant involvement (Marshall, Reinhart, Feeley, Tutzauer, & Anker, 2008). People with high other-directedness were more concerned about issues' implications for their social life management (Cho & Boster, 2005).

The kinds and magnitudes of cognitive involvement primed may also influence the direction and strength of attitudes and actions. Research, for example, found that centrality of the issue to one's values predicted extreme attitudes, while the centrality of the issue to one's outcomes predicted greater willingness to seek information (e.g., Cho & Boster, 2005). In a study about Belgian public's opinions about biofuels, the segment of the public with high outcome-relevant involvement with the issue was more likely to express that greater information about biofuels should be available as compared with the segments with high value-relevant involvement or high impression-relevant involvement (Van de Velde, Vandermeulen, Huylenbroeck, & Verbeke, 2011).

Emotional Involvement

In addition to the cognitive involvement in the issue primed through value, outcome, and impression relevance, emotional involvement may also mediate the relationship between societal risk perception and societal risk reduction action. Emotional involvement may come in the form of sympathy or empathy for social groups directly affected by the risk issue, as well as specific discrete emotions evoked for the risk issue itself.

Societal risk perception induced by media exposure may elicit sympathy or empathy for those who are immediately affected. Sympathy and empathy refer to emotional responses arising from the understanding of the emotional states of others. As such, both are other-focused emotional conditions. There are also differences between the two. While sympathy comprises emotional responses that may not be identical with those that others experience, empathy comprises those that others feel; consequently, while sympathy may frequently take the form of concern or sorrows, empathy may take a wider range of emotions (Wispe, 1986). Sympathy and empathy for others who are affected by a risk issue may bolster the willingness to address the risk issue. Eisenberg and Miller (1987), for example, found that empathy promotes prosocial and socially cooperative behavior.

Generally, current research suggests that negative rather than positive emotions may be a stronger mediator of the path from societal risk perception to societal risk reduction action. Negative emotions have been found to increase action tendencies to address risk, as detailed below. In contrast, positive emotions were found to decrease action tendencies. For example, exposure to hostile sexism provoked negative emotions, which increased intentions to distribute flyers and to sign petitions for gender equality, but exposure to benevolent sexism evoked positive emotions, which decreased intentions to perform the same behaviors (Becker & Wright, 2011). While the experience of participation in societal risk reduction actions elicited positive emotions about self, this self-directed positive emotion was a weaker predictor of intentions to participate in future actions than other-directed negative emotions such as anger or fear (Becker, Tausch, & Wagner, 2011).

Although earlier research relied on the dual-emotion perspective of distinguishing positive and negative emotions, more recent research utilizes the discrete emotions perspective (Frijda, 1986; Lazarus, 1991; for reviews, see also Chapter 3, this volume). Briefly, the discrete emotions perspective posits that emotions vary in dimensions, including certainty, attention, effort, and responsibility (for a review, see Lerner & Keltner, 2000).

Depending on the specific negative emotions that it evokes, societal risk perception may indirectly activate differential attitudes and course of actions to reduce societal risk. While fear caused by societal risk perception may motivate actions to avoid the cause of the emotion, anger caused by societal risk perception may motivate actions to approach it (Lerner & Keltner, 2000). After 9/11, Americans who had stronger feelings of anger rather than fear were more likely to endorse punitive policy measures, whereas those who had stronger feelings of fear rather than anger were more likely to support conciliatory policy measures to reduce future terrorism against America (Lerner, Gonzalez, Small, & Fischhoff, 2003).

Guilt and shame may be elicited when societal risk perception produces negative evaluation of self. Guilt is the recognition that one has breached an accepted personal or social principle, while shame concerns failing to meet implicit, as well as explicit, social expectations (Goffman, 1956). Conceptually closer to the public domain of life than guilt, shame promotes social cohesion and consensus, while it can also serve as a means to social control (Cho, 2000).

The experience of guilt and shame may generate motivations to avoid these aversive feelings in future situations (Tangney, Miller, Flicker, & Barlow, 1996). Consequently, the direction of future actions to avoid guilt and shame is likely to be in alignment with perceived norms and expectations in society. For example, guilt has been found to be an important mediator of the association between concern over the environment and intentions to recycle (e.g., Furguson &

Branscombe, 2010; Kaiser, Schultz, Berenguer, Corral-Verdugo, & Tankha, 2008).

Moderators

Efficacy Beliefs

The influence of cognitive and affective involvement on societal risk reduction action may be amplified or attenuated by the levels of efficacy beliefs. Overall, four types of efficacy beliefs may be relevant to societal risk reduction actions: action efficacy, institutional efficacy, collective efficacy, and self-efficacy.

Action efficacy refers to the belief in the action's effectiveness and efficiency in reducing the societal risk under consideration (e.g., "How much will my recycling behavior help in preventing climate change?"). Action efficacy, as a societal-level concept, may differ from response efficacy (Rogers, 1975), which is a personal-level concept. Whereas the appraisal of response efficacy concerns the outcome of adopting a personal risk-reducing action, the appraisal of action efficacy concerns the outcome of adopting a societal risk-reducing action. Compared with the former, the latter may require one to consider a larger set of contingency factors. For example, some societal actions may influence third parties' reactions, while others may not; some may galvanize alliances, while others may prompt opposition movements (Hornsey et al., 2006). In comparison, the outcomes of personal risk-reducing actions (e.g., physical activity and healthy diet) may be less influenced by others' reactions and actions.

Institutional efficacy refers to the citizenry's belief that large societal institutions are fair, just, uncorrupt, trustworthy, and predictable (Rothstein, 2003). Direct and immediate actions to reduce societal risk are frequently not accessible to individual citizens. Rather, individuals engage in actions to influence the institutional decisions and decision makers. Consequently, trust in institutions and institutional decision

makers who will act on the public's expressed attitudes may be a key contingent variable in the public's willingness to voice their attitudes. A survey of citizens of 22 different countries found that perceived institutional quality was a significant predictor of the participation in actions for reducing environmental risk (Duit, 2010). An important predictor of environmental activism was the belief in the competence of national and international agencies, which was operationalized as their openness and responsiveness to citizen voices and capabilities (Lubell, 2002; Lubell, Zahran, & Vedlitz, 2007). This concept of institutional efficacy may be related to social trust (Siegrist, Cvetkovich, & Roth, 2000), which is predicted by perceived similarity between the values held by a member of the public and those held by the institution under consideration.

Collective efficacy refers to individuals' belief that the larger group, organization, or community that they belong to is capable of carrying out a chosen course of action (Bandura, 1986). Societal risk is rarely under one citizens' control, and reducing societal risk frequently requires concerted efforts of citizens. Consequently, collective efficacy can moderate the effect of perceived societal risk on willingness to engage in actions to reduce the societal risk. Indirect evidence of the importance of collective efficacy for societal risk control actions has been obtained as variables akin to collective efficacy have been found to predict actions pertinent to reducing societal risk. For example, the density of social ties tends to predict willingness to engage in collective actions (Marwell, Oliver, & Prahl, 1988). Expected reciprocity, that is, the belief that other members of the collective will return one's own efforts, was a significant predictor of willingness to engage in recycling behavior to reduce the risk of global warming and climate change (Lubell et al., 2007).

Self-efficacy refers to individuals' belief that they themselves are capable of carrying out a chosen course of action (Bandura, 1986). Actions to reduce societal risk frequently require participation by a large number of individuals, and such aggregated individual actions can then influence institutions and policymakers. While individuals may first consider action efficacy and institutional efficacy to choose a particular course of action and then consider self-efficacy, self-efficacy may be a more direct and immediate determinant of whether individuals will actually engage in the chosen course of action or not. That is, the appraisal of action and institutional efficacy may initially determine the decision whether to vote or not for a policy measure. The actual occurrence of voting may then be determined by self-efficacy in voting behavior (e.g., ability to take time out of work to vote, ability to stand in line). Belief in one's own ability, thus, may be one of the elements influencing the occurrence of societal risk reduction action, along with action, institutional, and collective efficacy beliefs.

The relative contribution of these efficacy beliefs toward societal risk control action may be contingent on the kind of risk reduction action under consideration. For example, certain kinds of societal risk reduction may require more collaboration with others (collective efficacy), while others may require more effort of self (self-efficacy). Yet other kinds of societal risk reduction actions are contingent on societal institutions' openness to responding to expressed public opinion (institutional efficacy).

Together, efficacy beliefs may amplify or attenuate the influence of involvement on willingness to engage in action. High efficacy coupled with high involvement may produce actions consistent with the cognition/emotion activated. Low efficacy beliefs coupled with high societal risk may result in inaction or maladaptive reactions to societal risk such as fatalistic attitudes or nonnormative actions. For example, Martin, Brickman, and Murray (1984) found that availability of mobilization resource is an important determinant of collective action against social injustice. Deficiency in efficacy beliefs may engender a range of maladaptive actions. These reactions may range from fatalistic attitudes and inaction (Cho & Salmon, 2006; Rippetoe & Rogers, 1987) to nonnormatively prescribed actions such as violence (Tausch et al., 2011).

Propositions

The discussion above leads to the following propositions:

Proposition 1: Media exposure predicts societal risk perception.

Proposition 2: Societal risk perception predicts willingness to engage in societal risk reduction action.

Proposition 3: The path between societal risk perception and societal risk reduction action is mediated by cognitive involvement and emotional involvement.

Proposition 4: The path between cognitive and affective involvement and societal risk reduction action is moderated by efficacy beliefs.

Proposition 5: High involvement and high efficacy beliefs predict adaptive actions; high involvement and low efficacy beliefs predict maladaptive actions (e.g., fatalism, inaction, and violence).

Proposition 6: Societal risk reduction actions influence political, economic, and sociocultural contexts of risk.

Proposition 7: Changes in political, economic, and sociocultural contexts of risk influence changes in individual behaviors.

Reflections for Theory and Research

The SRRM builds on the unique capacity of the media, which is their influence on societal-level judgments. The SRRM, however, differs from existing theory and research in the following primary ways. Whereas in existing research, societal risk perception has been the end point of the effect of media exposure, the SRRM contends that societal risk perception is the beginning point of the causal process influencing societal risk reduction action (see Figure 8.1). Next, drawing from literatures on social processes and collective behavior, the SRRM proposes the mediating and moderating mechanisms underlying the path between societal risk perception and societal risk control action. Conceptualized this way, societal risk perception is not an example of the limited effect of the media any more. Instead, the SRRM conceives societal risk perception as an indicator of what Katz (1983) termed as *subtle yet powerful* effect of the media. The effects of the media may be subtle in that they often do not directly or immediately affect personal-level motivation. The primary outcome of the media, according to the SRRM, may be societal-level motivation, rather than personal-level motivation. This postulation draws from Mutz (1998): With their coverage of circumstances of larger collectives, the media may shape perceptions about society and its conditions, which in turn influence motivations to address the social conditions.

First, the SRRM has implications on theory and research of new media and social media. On the one hand, the Internet, an increasingly influential source of information, has the potential to influence societal risk perception and personal risk perception in ways distinctive from the television or the print media. Specifically, new media and social media have their unique characteristics, such as interactivity, user-generated content, and easy accessibility. Research should examine the effects of these features on risk perceptions at the personal and societal levels. Might such characteristics exert differential influence on societal risk perception and personal risk perception? Theory and research that address such questions can expand understanding about the utility of new media and social media on risk communication that targets risk perceptions at differential levels.

Second, the SRRM provides opportunities for theory and research at the intersection of risk communication literature and social network literature. Organizational and community social network studies have examined the relational aspects of individuals and network structures in organizational settings. Recently, social network

approach has been applied to risk communication efforts (e.g., the social network contagion theory of risk perception, Scherer & Cho, 2003), yet it has not been widely researched. The SRRM approach may be adopted in conjunction with social network approach to examine the relationship among social network, risk perception, and risk reduction action at the community and societal levels, thus filling this void in the literature. For example, how does social network structure influence and/or potentially moderate media's effect on one's societal risk perceptions? Would network characteristics mediate or moderate societal risk perception's impact on societal risk reduction actions? Future studies that examine such research questions may help explain how and why risk perceptions and actions may vary in different networks.

Third, delineating the mechanisms underlying the path between societal risk perception and societal risk reduction action, the SRRM encourages holistic and systematic examinations of the personal and societal routes to risk reduction. Risk prevention and reduction may require both individual behavior change and societal condition change. Therefore, it is necessary to distinguish the societal and the personal routes, to identify the mechanisms underlying them, and to understand how the two routes could complement each other. Therefore, the relationship between the two routes requires further explication. Substantial individual behavior change may lead to motivations for societal risk reduction action, while societal conditions may facilitate or hinder individual behavior change. Future research that explores the potential interactions between the two pathways may offer more comprehensive understandings on risk prevention and reduction.

Furthermore, the propositions of the SRRM may apply to various cultural settings, since the SRRM encompasses constructs that address potential variability across cultures. For example, cultural attributes such as norms and values about collective group and society may be relevant to individuals' cognitive involvement (e.g., value involvement and impression involvement), which mediates societal risk perception's effect on societal risk reduction action. Additionally, perceived collective efficacy and institutional efficacy in different cultures may vary depending on the cultural and political contexts of risk. Future research can test the SRRM cross-culturally and identify the contextual factors that may influence the propositions of the model.

Recommendations for Practice

That media shape societal risk perceptions, rather than personal-level judgments, has practical implications for risk prevention and control. Risk messages and campaigns that aim at influencing societal risk perceptions should take advantage of mass media's unique capacity. For example, increased media exposure, including both quantity and quality, may contribute to stronger societal risk perceptions.

Another implication for those who communicate risk is that increased societal risk perceptions may or may not necessarily lead to societal risk reduction actions, as the effects are moderated and mediated by cognitive and emotional involvement as well as various efficacy beliefs. Risk messages may need to cognitively and emotionally engage recipients and address various efficacy beliefs in order to motivate actions. Risk communicators need to address these moderating and mediating constructs so that societal risk perceptions can motivate actions.

Viewing the societal route to be distinct from and complementary to the personal route, the SRRM considers societal, political, and economic conditions to be important for risk prevention and control. The SRRM calls for concerted risk communication efforts at both the personal and societal levels. Finally, it should be noted that societal risk reduction action is an outcome of social processes at a certain time and a location, just as societal risk perception is an outcome of social construction. Consequently, the objective validity of societal risk action may

remain elusive, just as societal risk perception may be independent of objective conditions of society.

Conclusions

Preventing and controlling risk requires actions not only at the individual level but also at the societal level. In contrast to the wealth of theory and research on the mechanisms for motivating actions to reduce personal risk, little theory and research have explicated a framework describing the motivational mechanisms for societal risk reduction actions. The SRRM presented in this chapter is an attempt to address this void in the existing literature. SRRM provides a framework for understanding the motivational mechanisms for societal risk reduction actions. Proposing the social and psychological mechanisms through which media influence risk perception and risk reduction action at the societal level, the SRRM provides an innovative approach to addressing the limitations of current theory and research and provides guidance for harnessing the power of the media for addressing collective risk through collective action. Future research can refine the proposed model and empirically test it in cross-cultural contexts; examine the effects of message content, channel, and their interaction on societal risk perceptions; apply the model to risk communication via new media and social media platforms; and explore social network's impact on societal risk perception and actions.

Note

1. The indicators of societal risk perception that Tyler and Cook (1984) used were the perceived importance of societal issues and the importance of governmental actions to address the issues. Notice that the first item in this index is akin to the measure of agenda setting (McCombs & Shaw, 1972), and this measure has been used in subsequent studies of impersonal impact hypothesis (e.g., Coleman, 1993; Park, Scherer, & Glynn, 2001; So et al., 2011).

Suggested Additional Readings

Cho, H., So, J., & Lee, J. (2009). Personal, social, and cultural correlates of self-efficacy beliefs among South Korean college smokers. *Health Communication, 24,* 337–345.

Choi, J., Park, H. S., & Chang, J. (2011). Hostile media perception, involvement types, and advocacy behaviors. *Journalism and Mass Communication Quarterly, 88,* 23–39.

McLeod, J., & Reeves, B. (1980). On the nature of mass media effects. B. Whithey & R. Abeles (Eds.), *Television and social behavior: Beyond violence and children.* Hillsdale, NJ: Lawrence Erlbaum.

References

Bandura, A. (1986). *Social foundations of thought and action: A social cognitive theory.* Englewood Cliffs, NJ: Prentice Hall.

Becker, J. C., Tausch, N., & Wagner, U. (2011). Emotional consequences of collective action participation: Differentiating self-directed and out-group-directed emotions. *Personality and Social Psychology Bulletin, 37,* 1587–1598.

Becker, J. C., & Wright, S. C. (2011). Yet another dark side of chivalry: Benevolent sexism undermines and hostile sexism motivates collective action for social change. *Journal of Personality and Social Psychology, 101,* 62–77.

Blumer, H. (1971). Social problems as collective behavior. *Social Problems, 18,* 298–306.

Brown, W. J., & Basil, M. D. (1995). Media celebrities and public health: Responses to "Magic" Johnson's HIV disclosure and its impact on AIDS risk and high risk behaviors. *Health Communication, 7,* 345–370.

Cho, H. (2000). Public opinion as personal cultivation: A normative notion and source of social control in traditional China. *International Journal of Public Opinion Research, 12,* 299–323.

Cho, H., & Boster, F. J. (2005). Development and validation of value-, outcome-, and impression-relevant involvement scales. *Communication Research, 35,* 235–264.

Cho, H., & Salmon, C. T. (2006). Fear appeals for individuals in different stages of change: Intended and unintended effects and implications on public health campaigns. *Health Communication, 20,* 91–99.

Cohen, D., Spear, S., Scribner, R., Kissinger, P., Mason, K., & Wildgen, J. (2000). "Broken windows" and the risk of gonorrhea. *American Journal of Public Health, 90,* 230–236.

Coleman, C. (1993). The influence of mass media and interpersonal communication on societal and personal judgments. *Communication Research, 20,* 611–628.

Derksen, L., & Gartrell, J. (1993). The social context of recycling. *American Sociological Review, 58,* 434–452.

Doob, A. N., & MacDonald, G. E. (1979). Television viewing and fear of victimization: Is the relationship causal? *Journal of Personality and Social Psychology, 37,* 170–179.

Duit, A. (2010). Patterns of environmental collective action: Some cross-national findings. *Political Studies, 59,* 900–920.

Eisenberg, N., & Miller, P. A. (1987). The relation of empathy to prosocial and related behaviors. *Journal of Personality and Social Psychology, 101,* 91–119.

Feeny, D., Berkes, F., McCay, B. J., & Acheson, J. M. (1990). The tragedy of the commons: Twenty two years later. *Human Ecology, 18,* 1–19.

Fishbein, M., & Yzer, M. C. (2003). Using theory to design effective health behavior interventions. *Communication Theory, 13,* 164–183.

Floyd, D. L., Prentice-Dunn, S., & Rogers, R. W. (2000). A meta-analysis of research on protection motivation theory. *Journal of Applied Social Psychology, 30,* 407–429.

Frijda, N. H. (1986). *The emotions.* New York, NY: Cambridge University Press.

Furguson, M. A., & Branscombe, N. R. (2010). Collective guilt mediates the effect of beliefs about global warming on willingness to engage in mitigation behavior. *Journal of Environmental Psychology, 30,* 135–142.

Gamson, W. A. (1992). The social psychology of collective action. In A. D. Morris & C. M. Muller (Eds.), *Frontiers in social movement theory* (pp. 53–76). New Haven, CT: Yale University Press.

Gerbner, G., & Gross, M. (1976). Living with television: The violence profile. *Journal of Communication, 26,* 172–194.

Goffman, E. (1956). Embarrassment and social organization. *American Journal of Sociology, 62,* 264–271.

Gross, K., & Aday, S. (2003). The scary world in your living room and neighborhood: Using local broadcast news, neighborhood crime rates, and personal experience to test agenda setting and cultivation. *Journal of Communication, 53,* 411–426.

Gruev-Vintila, A., & Rouquette, M. (2007). Social thinking about collective risk: How do risk-related practice and personal involvement impact its social representations? *Journal of Risk Research, 10,* 555–581.

Gunther, A. (1998). The persuasive press inference: Effects of mass media on perceived public opinion. *Communication Research, 25,* 486–504.

Hardin, G. (1968). The tragedy of the commons. *Science, 162,* 1243–1248.

Heath, L., & Petraitis, J. (1987). Television viewing and fear of crime: Where is the mean world? *Basic and Applied Social Psychology, 8,* 97–123.

Hornsey, M. J., Blackwood, L., Louis, W., Fielding, K., Mavor, K., Morton, T., . . . White, K. M. (2006). Why do people engage in collective action? Revisiting the role of perceived effectiveness. *Journal of Applied Social Psychology, 36,* 1701–1722.

Iyengar, S., & Kinder, D. (1987). *News that matters.* Chicago, IL: University of Chicago Press.

Johnson, B. T., & Eagly, A. H. (1989). Effects of involvement on persuasion: A meta-analysis. *Psychological Bulletin, 106,* 290–314.

Kaiser, F. G., Schultz, P. W., Berenguer, J., Corral-Verdugo, V., & Tankha, G. (2008). Extending planning environmentalism: Anticipated guilt and embarrassment across cultures. *European Psychologist, 13,* 288–297.

Kasperson, R. E., Renn, O., Slovic, P., Brown, H. S., Emel, J., Goble, R., . . . Ratick, S. (1988). The social amplification of risk: A conceptual framework. *Risk Analysis, 8,* 177–187.

Katz, E. (1983). Publicity and pluralistic ignorance: Notes on "The Spiral of Silence." In E. Wartella, D. C. Whitney, & S. Windahl (Eds.), *Mass communication review yearbook 4* (pp. 89–100). Beverly Hills, CA: Sage.

Kiousis, S., & McDevitt, M. (2008). Agenda setting in civic development: Effects of curricula and issue importance on youth voter turnout. *Communication Research, 35,* 481–502.

Lazarsfeld, P. F., & Merton, R. K. (1949). Mass communication, popular taste and organized social action. In W. Schramm (Ed.), *Mass communications* (pp. 459–480). Urbana: University of Illinois Press.

Lazarus, R. S. (1991). *Emotion and adaptation.* New York, NY: Oxford University Press.

Lerner, J. S., Gonzalez, R. M., Small, D. A., & Fischhoff, B. (2003). Effects of fear and anger on perceived risks of terrorism: A national field experiment. *Psychological Science, 14,* 144–150.

Lerner, J. S., & Keltner, D. (2000). Beyond valence: Toward a model of emotion-specific influences on judgment and choice. *Cognition & Emotion, 14,* 473–493.

Lubell, M. (2002). Environmental activism as collective action. *Environment and Behavior, 34,* 431–454.

Lubell, M., Zahran, S., & Vedlitz, A. (2007). Collective action and citizen responses to global warming. *Political Behavior, 29,* 391–413.

Marshall, H. M., Reinhart, A. M., Feeley, T., Tutzauer, F., & Anker, A. (2008). Comparing college students' value, outcome, and impression-relevant involvement in health-related issues. *Health Communication, 23,* 171–183.

Martin, J., Brickman, P., & Murray, A. (1984). Moral outrage and pragmatism: Explanations for collective action. *Journal of Experimental Social Psychology, 20,* 484–496.

Marwell, G., & Oliver, P. E. (1993). *The critical mass in collective action: A micro-social theory.* New York, NY: Cambridge University Press.

Marwell, G., Oliver, P. E., & Prahl, R. (1988). Social networks and collective action: A theory of the critical mass. *American Journal of Sociology, 94,* 502–534.

McCombs, M. E., & Shaw, D. L. (1972). The agenda-setting function of mass media. *Public Opinion Quarterly, 36,* 176–187.

Morton, T. A., & Duck, J. M. (2001). Communication and health beliefs: Mass and interpersonal influences on perceptions of risk to self and others. *Communication Research, 28,* 602–626.

Moscovici, S. (1984). The phenomenon of social representations. In R. M. Farr & S. Moscovici (Eds.), *Social representations* (pp. 3–69). Cambridge, England: Cambridge University Press.

Mutz, D. (1998). *Impersonal influence.* New York, NY: Cambridge University Press.

Olson, M. (1965). *The logic of collective action: Public goods and the theory of groups.* Cambridge, MA: Harvard University Press.

Park, E., Scherer, C. W., & Glynn, C. J. (2001). Community involvement and risk perception at personal and societal levels. *Health, Risk & Society, 3,* 281–292.

Rimal, R. N., & Real, K. (2003). Perceived risk and efficacy beliefs as motivators of change. *Human Communication Research, 29,* 370–399.

Rippetoe, P. A., & Rogers, R. W. (1987). Effects of components of protection-motivation theory on adaptive and maladaptive coping with a health threat. *Journal of Personality and Social Psychology, 52,* 596–604.

Roberts, M. S. (1992). Predicting voting behavior via the agenda-setting tradition. *Journalism Quarterly, 69,* 878–892.

Rogers, R. W. (1975). A protection motivation theory of fear appeals and attitude change. *Journal of Psychology, 91,* 93–114.

Rokeach, M. (1968). *Beliefs, attitudes, and values: A theory of organization and change.* San Francisco, CA: Jossey-Bass.

Rosenstock, I. M. (1974). The health belief model: Origins and correlates. *Health Education Monographs, 2,* 336–353.

Rothstein, B. (2003). Social capital, economic growth and quality of government: The causal mechanism. *New Political Economy, 8,* 49–71.

Sampson, R. J., Raudenbush, S. W., & Earls, F. (1997). Neighborhoods and violent crime: A multilevel study of collective efficacy. *Science, 277,* 918–924.

Scherer, C. W., & Cho, H. (2003). A social network contagion theory of risk perception. *Risk Analysis, 23,* 261–267.

Shrum, L. J., & Bischak, V. D. (2001). Mainstreaming, resonance, and impersonal impact: Testing moderators of the cultivation effect for estimates of crime risk. *Human Communication Research, 27,* 187–215.

Siegrist, M., Cvetkovich, G., & Roth, C. (2000). Salient value similarity, social trust, and risk/benefit perception. *Risk Analysis, 20,* 353–362.

Snyder, L. B., & Rouse, R. A. (1995). The media can have more than an impersonal impact: The case of AIDS risk perceptions and behavior. *Health Communication, 7,* 125–145.

So, J., Cho, H., & Lee, J. (2011). Examining contributions of genre-specific media toward perceptions of personal and social risk of smoking among South Korean college students. *Journal of Health Communication, 16,* 533–549.

Tajfel, H., & Turner, J. C. (1979). An integrated theory of intergroup conflict. In W. G. Austin & S. Worchel (Eds.), *The social psychology of intergroup relations* (2nd ed., pp. 33–47). Monterey, CA: Brooks/Cole.

Tangney, J. P., Miller, R. S., Flicker, L., & Barlow, D. H. (1996). Are shame, guilt, embarrassment distinct emotions? *Journal of Personality and Social Psychology, 70,* 1256–1269.

Tausch, N., Becker, J. C., Spears, R., Christ, O., Saab, R., Singh, P., & Siddiqui, R. N. (2011). Explaining radical group behavior: Developing emotion and efficacy routes to normative and nonnormative collective action. *Journal of Personality and Social Psychology, 101,* 129–148.

Tyler, T. R., & Cook, F. L. (1984). The mass media and judgments of risk: Distinguishing impact on personal and societal level judgments. *Journal of Personality and Social Psychology, 47,* 691–708.

Van de Velde, L., Vandermeulen, V., Van Huylenbroeck, G., & Verbeke, W. (2011). Consumer information (in)sufficiency in relation to biofuels: Determinants and impact. *Biofuels, Bioproducts, & Biorefining, 5,* 125–131.

Weaver, D. (1991). Issue salience and public opinion: Are there consequences of agenda-setting? *International Journal of Public Opinion Research, 3,* 53–68.

Wispe, L. (1986). The distinction between sympathy and empathy: To call forth a concept, a word is needed. *Journal of Personality and Social Psychology, 50,* 314–321.

Witte, K. (1992). Putting the fear back into fear appeals: The extended parallel process model. *Communication Monographs, 59,* 330–349.

Witte, K., & Allen, M. (2000). A meta-analysis of fear appeals: Implications for effective public health campaigns. *Health Education & Behavior, 27,* 591–615.

Wright, S. C., Taylor, D. M., & Moghaddam, F. M. (1990). Responding to membership in a disadvantaged group: From acceptance to collective protest. *Journal of Personality and Social Psychology, 58,* 994–1003.

SECTION 4

Audiences of Risk Communication

CHAPTER 9

The Role of Numeracy in Risk Communication

Priscila G. Brust-Renck, Valerie F. Reyna, Jonathan C. Corbin, Caisa E. Royer, and Rebecca B. Weldon

Introduction

Increasing amounts of information are available to the public, and researchers and practitioners alike are concerned about how this information can be used to help improve patient understanding of health risks (Betsch et al., 2012). The complexity of numerical information about risk places demands on people that they are not prepared to meet. Much information about health risks is communicated numerically, such as the effectiveness of treatments, the benefits of lifestyle, and the chances of side effects from medication. A review of the literature, however, has shown that a relatively small number of people have the basic quantitative skills to understand numerical risk (Reyna, Nelson, Han, & Dieckmann, 2009). For example, only 23% of parents can correctly interpret height/weight growth charts, despite the fact that most parents believe growth charts are important when communicating with their physician about their child's physical development (Ben-Joseph, Dowshen, & Izenberg, 2009).

To better communicate numerical risk, it is necessary to be able to identify whether an individual will be able to grasp the meaning behind the number. Measuring differences in the ability to understand and use numbers, or numeracy, provides a metric with which to guide one's approach when communicating risk (Reyna et al., 2009). Communication of complex numerical information confuses low-numerate people, and research suggests that this lack of understanding leads to poor health outcomes (although more work on outcomes is needed; Fischhoff, 2009; Joram et al., 2012; Reyna, 2012b). Therefore, it is important to know which individuals may be more likely to lack essential numerical skills.

Research has uncovered demographic and educational differences with respect to numeracy. For example, older subjects and females are less

Authors' Note: Preparation of this manuscript was supported in part by the National Cancer Institute of the National Institutes of Health under Award Number R21CA149796 to the second author.

accurate when computing risk than younger subjects and males (Keller, Siegrist, & Visschers, 2009; Lipkus, Peters, Kimmick, Liotcheva, & Marcom, 2010; Waters, Weinstein, Colditz, & Emmons, 2006). Furthermore, numeracy differs across countries and cultural groups (Galesic & Garcia-Retamero, 2011; Garcia-Retamero & Galesic, 2010; Garcia-Retamero, Galesic, & Gigerenzer, 2011). Less educated subjects are also more likely to have difficulty interpreting numerical information (Keller et al., 2009; Lipkus et al., 2010; Waters et al., 2006). However, these superficial characteristics can be misleading, and many of these group distributions overlap appreciably. For example, male participants with lower education levels are not more numerate than female participants with higher education, and differences in numeracy across countries are not necessarily cultural, as they could be educational (Reyna & Brainerd, 2007).

The goal of this chapter is to provide a critical review of current theory and evidence regarding how people understand numerical risks. Initially, we present the major theoretical approaches relevant to numeracy in the context of risk communication and discuss a new approach to numeracy based on fuzzy-trace theory (Reyna et al., 2009). We outline these approaches along with their definitions and review how risk comprehension is affected by variations in numerical ability. Finally, we present recommendations for future research and for improving risk communication by enhancing individuals' ability to understand the meaning behind numeric information.

Theoretical Frameworks of Numeracy

To understand the effect of numeracy on risk communication, it is necessary to have a theoretical framework. In this section, we present relevant theories that account for individual differences in understanding numerical information (i.e., numeracy) in the context of risk communication (for a more detailed review, see

Reyna et al., 2009). In particular, we discuss the assumptions of the traditional dual-process approach, which identify high numeracy with analytical processes and low numeracy with intuitive processes (e.g., Peters et al., 2006; Weller et al., 2013). In addition, we discuss a new conception of numeracy based on fuzzy-trace theory—also a dual-process approach, but with the important difference that advanced cognition is intuitive. According to fuzzy-trace theory, understanding numerical risk is a result of extracting the bottom-line meaning (gist) of numbers in addition to the rote (verbatim) computation. This approach to numeracy resolves some important paradoxes, such as the preference of higher numerate individuals for options with worse numerical outcomes (Reyna et al., 2009). We cannot review these theories in exhaustive detail, given the scope of the current chapter. However, we present their theoretical foundations in relation to numeracy and review their implications for risk communication.

Traditional Dual-Process Theories

Traditional dual-process approaches distinguish between intuition and analysis (e.g., Epstein, 1994; Kahneman, 2003, 2011; Sloman, 1996; Stanovich, West, & Toplak, 2011). The distinction between two kinds of reasoning has been made by many authors to account for cognitive processing (for a summary, see Kahneman, 2003, figure 1; Evans & Stanovich, 2013, table 1). According to a broad view of the theories, intuition (or System 1) is impulsive, evolutionarily primitive, and fast, with this system relying on emotion or "gut feelings," which are informed by experience. The analytical component of reasoning (or System 2) is the advanced, slow process that is involved in deliberative thinking and exact computation that can often override intuition (Kahneman, 2003, 2011).

This approach has been extended beyond decision making to numeracy (e.g., Lipkus & Peters, 2009; Peters, Slovic, Västfjäll, & Mertz,

2008). In this view, low numeracy is a result of intuitive processing (System 1) because of its impulsive and emotional way of thinking, whereas high numeracy is a result of analytical thought (System 2) because it involves computational abilities. Although both processes can produce good and bad performance, intuition has traditionally been assumed to be the main source of biases and fallacies. In other words, the more numerate a person is, the more likely she is to inhibit intuitive biases and to compute the correct answer to a numerical problem (Lipkus & Peters, 2009).

Consistent with the dual-process approach, Peters et al. (2006) showed that people with high numeracy were less subject to intuitive biases than those with low numeracy. This effect has been demonstrated in the traditional ratio bias task, whereby participants with high numeracy are less biased when asked to select a "winning" colored jellybean from an objectively inferior selection (9 colored and 91 white beans; i.e., 9% chance) than from a bowl with an objectively higher chance to win (1 colored and 9 white beans; i.e., 10% chance). (Ratio bias is also called numerosity bias in the probability judgment literature.) This empirical effect of ratio bias is a result of individuals neglecting the denominator (i.e., the total number of possible occurrences) and focusing on the numerator (i.e., the number of times an event has occurred; for reviews, see Reyna & Brainerd, 1994, 2008). According to the traditional dual-process approach, low numerate people focus on concrete numbers (e.g., numerators) to make decisions because they seem more real and affectively tempting than abstract large numbers (e.g., denominators; Epstein, 1994; Peters et al., 2006). This effect has implications for judgment of health risks, such as selecting cancer treatment based on different survival rates expressed as ratios (e.g., Bonner & Newell, 2008). The dual-process theories' prediction is that low-numerate people will better understand risk when it is communicated in a way that minimizes biases, for example, using a percentage format when

denominators are different (e.g., choices between 9% and 10% make the risk differences explicit).

However, in a series of other studies, results were not supportive of dual-process predictions that reliance on mathematical or analytical processes results in higher numeracy and reliance on intuitive processes results in biases. For example, Peters et al. (2006) found that participants with higher numeracy rated a loss bet (in which there was a 7/36 probability of winning $9 and 29/36 probability of losing ¢5) as more attractive than a no-loss bet (in which there was a 7/36 probability of winning $9 and 29/36 probability of winning nothing). In this and other examples, participants higher in numeracy actually selected the numerically inferior option, which suggests that differences in traditional dual processes do not fully explain effects of numeracy (see also Cuite, Weinstein, Emmons, & Colditz, 2008; Hess, Visschers, & Siegrist, 2011; Peters et al., 2008; Schapira, Davids, McAuliffe, & Nattinger, 2004; Shiloh, Salton, & Sharabi, 2002).

In sum, although many studies support the dual-process approach prediction that people with high numeracy are less subject to biases because they are more likely to rely on analytical processing, this is not always a consistent finding (see also Cokely & Kelley, 2009; Reyna & Brainerd, 2008). The traditional dual-process approach also does not account for the seeming contradiction between reliance on intuitive processing and better performance on decision problems. The consistent exceptions to the generalization that people higher in numeracy would be better at understanding numerical risk generate crucial concerns for risk communication.

Fuzzy-Trace Theory

Fuzzy-trace theory is a dual-process approach to judgment and decision making that builds on the previous research, including the traditional dual-process theories we have discussed thus far (Reyna, 2012a). This theory distinguishes between two processes: gist and verbatim (Reyna & Brainerd, 1995, 2011). Gist is intuitive and operates on meaningful representations of information. It is also imprecise (i.e., fuzzy) and incorporates factors that affect the meaning of information, such as culture, education, emotion, and experience (e.g., Reyna, 2012a; Reyna & Adam, 2003). However, in contrast to traditional dual-process theories, gist (or intuitive) processing is not considered primitive, but rather, it results from an insightful, advanced means of extracting the essence of information. This process also benefits from background knowledge of the topic and from life experience (e.g., Reyna & Adam, 2003; Reyna & Farley, 2006). Verbatim is analytical and precise, but also rote, in that it does not consist of meaningful interpretation or inference.

According to this theory, people typically encode both verbatim (e.g., 2% chance of side effects) and gist (e.g., small risk of side effects) representations in parallel (Reyna, 2008, 2012a; Reyna & Brainerd, 2011). However, most people prefer to make decisions based on gist—they have a *fuzzy processing preference* (Reyna, 2008; Reyna & Brainerd, 1995). For example, Fraenkel et al. (2012) tested three different methods of communicating the risks and benefits of rheumatoid arthritis treatments based on the predictions of fuzzy-trace theory. Each piece of numerical (or graphical) information used to communicate the benefits from different medications or risks of side effects was accompanied by its essential gist (meaning of the number), as identified by experts and patients. In this study, "2% will experience adverse effects" was accompanied by "a small chance." According to fuzzy-trace theory, people who understand the meaning (gist) of numerical information (e.g., the risk is small) will make more informed decisions than people who rely on rote (verbatim) numbers (e.g., there is a 2% chance of side effects). Results showed that providing the gist increased patient knowledge, willingness to escalate care, and likelihood of making an informed choice in a pre- and posttest comparison (from 35% at pretest to 64% at posttest). Therefore, these results demonstrate that

risk communication based on providing the gist of the message improved understanding, allowing people to make more informed decisions (Reyna, 2008; Reyna & Hamilton, 2001).

In a similar example, Brewer, Richman, DeFrank, Reyna, and Carey (2012) tested several formats of communicating information about the risk of breast cancer recurrence in 10 years. The formats ranged from the commercial test result format, which presented only numerical (verbatim) risk, to a more elaborate report, which included a meaningful (gist) explanation and a simple graph. Results showed that participants were more likely to estimate the correct risk (i.e., low, medium, or high) when presented with the meaningful (gist) form (see also Reyna, 2008; Reyna & Brainerd, 1990). Most people have a fuzzy processing preference—the tendency to rely on the simplest meaningful distinction possible (e.g., some risk vs. no risk, less risk vs. more risk)—that generally facilitates judgments and decisions (Reyna & Ellis, 1994; Reyna et al., 2011; Reyna & Farley, 2006, table 3; Wilhelms & Reyna, 2013).

A new conception of numeracy based on fuzzy-trace theory was proposed by Reyna and Brainerd (2008; see also Reyna et al., 2009). According to this theory, individual differences in numerical understanding are a result of gist and verbatim processing. In this view, higher numeracy is reflected in gist processing (or gist numeracy), because the latter requires understanding the bottom-line (qualitative) meaning of numbers. Lower numeracy can reflect verbatim processing that involves mindless (quantitative) calculation (e.g., Liberali, Reyna, Furlan, Stein, & Pardo, 2011; Reyna, 2008; Reyna & Brainerd, 1995, 2011). (Mindful computation is sometimes required, and naturally, this, too, can be a feature of higher numeracy.) Gist numeracy is about being able to connect the dots within and between quantitative dimensions (e.g., those involving probabilities and ratios) and boiling information down to its essence rather than relying on its rote, verbatim form; people who score high in numeracy who often also have a more precise representation of numbers have been shown to make systematic errors because they do not understand the numbers they are processing (Reyna et al., 2009).

Gist numeracy is not just a matter of using words to represent numbers (e.g., Hawley et al., 2008; Tait, Zikmund-Fisher, Fagerlin, & Voepel-Lewis, 2010), but it is also a matter of choosing the words that accurately reflect the intended meaning of a given number. Many decision makers cannot extract the meaning from precise (verbatim) numerical information on their own because they lack specific knowledge. To determine the right gist, expert physicians and experienced patients in Fraenkel et al.'s (2012) rheumatoid arthritis study used their expertise to evaluate expressions of benefits and risks from treatments and validated the gist generated by the experimenters (which was then used to help another group of patients make decisions). According to fuzzy-trace theory, an informed decision maker should be able to identify whether an option is safe or risky (or low risk or high risk); the gist is the basis of an informed decision about treatment (Reyna & Hamilton, 2001). The gist of the risk depends on the nature of the risk (e.g., the implications of that outcome), not just the objective number.

Regarding the interpretation of risk, after encoding both verbatim numbers and gist, fuzzy-trace theory predicts that people will start their decision process with the simplest distinction between options, identifying the basic categories of risk, such as "some" versus "none" or "will happen" versus "will not happen" (Kühberger & Tanner, 2010; Reyna, 2012a; Reyna & Brainerd, 1991). This simple *categorical* gist (e.g., "even low risk happens to someone") is captured in recently developed scales, which predict healthier outcomes (Mills, Reyna, & Estrada, 2008; Reyna et al., 2011). Studies using the categorical gist scales show that people who engage in predominantly gist thinking are more likely to avoid risk, while people who engage in predominantly verbatim thinking are more likely to take risks. When the options cannot be distinguished categorically (the simplest gist; Reyna et al., 2011), people use an *ordinal* level of discrimination (e.g., "small risk"). One example of this is Fraenkel et al.'s (2012) rheumatoid arthritis study, in which all of the options (treatment vs. no treatment) represented "some" risk. Zikmund-Fisher (2013) presents a series of recommendations about how to communicate risk with different levels of precision based on the kinds of gist we have described, consistent with predictions of fuzzy-trace theory (see also Reyna, 2008; Rivers, Reyna, & Mills, 2008).

Fuzzy-trace theory also acknowledges the impact of affect and basic emotions on numerical processing, in particular by contributing to the gist interpretation of information (Reyna & Rivers, 2008; Rivers et al., 2008). For example, even though the chance of being infected with HIV/AIDS is objectively "small," the gist interpretation of the risk can be "high" because the overall meaning is influenced by emotion—HIV/AIDS is an incurable, deadly disease (Mills et al., 2008; Reyna et al., 2011; see also Wood & Bechara, 2014). However, although emotion augments and amplifies gist, emotion is not essential to explain categorical gist. This categorical distinction is reflected in agreement with the phrase "it only takes once" to get HIV/AIDS (Rivers et al., 2008). Similarly, a diagnosis of Stage III of breast cancer with 60% chance of survival can be interpreted as "survive" because the categorical possibility of life is above chance—50%. Although this interpretation as survival may be augmented by emotion, survival is more likely than mortality. Note that fuzzy-trace theory does not assume that the exact probability (e.g., of 60%) is ignored; it exists in parallel with the categorical perception of survival.

Fuzzy-trace theory also encompasses effects of overlapping classes, such as ratio bias (Reyna & Brainerd, 1994, 2008). According to the theory, ratio bias is a result of the class-inclusion confusion, in which overlapping classes generate confusion about which class constitutes the denominators (e.g., the class of people with a positive test result or the class of people with a disease). In other words, individuals lose track of classes when they exist in relation to one another, and they focus on target classes in numerators (thereby, neglecting the denominator). Consider the ratio bias example presented previously. According to fuzzy-trace theory, the confusion is exacerbated because people focus on the target classes in the numerators (e.g., 9 colored jelly beans in Bowl A and 1 in Bowl B) and neglect the classes in the denominator (e.g., 100 total jelly beans in Bowl A and 10 in Bowl B; Reyna & Brainerd, 1994, 2008). According to fuzzy-trace theory, people who favor the numerically inferior Bowl A are making comparisons of relative magnitude of numerators—wrong comparisons, however, because they neglect the denominators (Reyna & Brainerd, 1990, 1995). Reducing confusion about overlapping classes—by describing classes using labels that are nonoverlapping—has been shown to increase semantic coherence and reduce reasoning fallacies (Reyna & Lloyd, 2006; Wolfe, Fisher, & Reyna, 2013; Wolfe & Reyna, 2010). The fuzzy-trace theory recommendations to tailor risk communication in order to avoid class inclusion errors are described to a greater extent in the Recommendations for Practice section.

In sum, fuzzy-trace theory's predictions of numeracy have been supported by data showing that gist numeracy results in better understanding of the meaning of numerical information rather than relying solely on verbatim calculation, which is associated with those individuals with a more precise representation of numbers. Consistent with the idea of a fuzzy processing preference, most people tend to rely on gist to make decisions, which reduces errors. Because gist processing is based on qualitative distinctions, risk communication should convey absolute (categorical) or relative (ordinal) comparisons rather than only exact, detailed information (see Recommendations for Practice section for more information). Fuzzy-trace theory does not discard the role of calculation, which is sometimes a necessary step (e.g., medication dosage). However, this theory underlines the centrality of

communicating the bottom-line meaning—gist—of risk. Finally, not just any message conveys the gist that leads to informed decision making; the message should express accurate meaning based on expert validation.

Reflections for Theory and Research

An understanding of the risks associated with particular choice options is important for informed decision making, and differences in numerical understanding can influence whether people take or avoid risk (Reyna & Hamilton, 2001). This conclusion is not limited to preference-sensitive decisions (i.e., those involving uncertainty about risks and benefits), as many have claimed. Instead, understanding is a prerequisite to making informed decisions, such as those involving diabetes, in which many patients do not adhere to what are clear recommendations regardless of preferences (Joram et al., 2012). Several information processing models have been developed to account for how individuals process and understand numerical risks that lead to unhealthy decisions (e.g., nonadherence). Research has shown that some people are systematically more susceptible to biases and illusions than others. Some researchers have argued that people do not have stable preferences or judgments (based on the malleability of their decisions; Peters et al., 2006; Peters et al., 2008). However, fuzzy-trace theory predicts and demonstrates that biases are not a result of the absence of preferences, but, rather, that gist representations of risk are combined with gist representations of general values or principles (Reyna & Brainerd, 2007, 2008).

Additional research should be conducted to test fuzzy-trace theory's predictions about the role of numeracy in real-world contexts of risk communication. Applied research should examine how numeracy relates to differences in mental (gist and verbatim) representations, retrieval of gist principles, class inclusion processing, and behavioral inhibition, which have been shown to operate in the laboratory. For example, one question that remains is whether communication methods used in arthritis and heart disease can be exported to diabetes, breast cancer, and orthopedic surgery as well as other nonhealth domains. In addition, more research is needed regarding how to decide the categorical and ordinal gist meaning of risks: Is a 12% chance of breast cancer high or low, and what amount of risk can be considered acceptable? This interpretive endeavor should be distinguished from identifying arbitrary decision thresholds (Reyna & Lloyd, 2006). Meaningfully communicating risk should ultimately promote better life outcomes. However more research on outcomes in health, financial, environmental, technological, and security risks is sorely needed. Moreover, future research should address factors other than demographic descriptors (e.g., age, gender, education, and culture) to assess the underlying causal factors that shape numeracy to provide more individualized assessments of numeracy.

Recommendations for Practice

Fuzzy-trace theory suggests that the gist be presented along with the verbatim information, contrary to some other theories that recommend presenting only numerical information and leaving the decision maker (often with no background knowledge) to interpret its meaning (Reyna & Hamilton, 2001). People often want to extract their own gist. However, providing both numerical information and its meaning increases the likelihood that the risk will be understood regardless of one's numeracy.

As outlined above, numeracy is essential as a means of achieving informed decisions. Therefore, practitioners should be aware that different approaches, beyond gross demographic categories, might be necessary for different individuals in communicating risk. Potential difficulties in decision making that may arise from deficits in numeracy can be resolved through meaningful communication of risk (Cokely, Galesic, Schulz,

Ghazal, & Garcia-Retamero, 2012; Garcia-Retamero & Galesic, 2010; Reyna, 2008; Stone et al., 2003). Problems in risk perception can be remedied by how information is communicated rather than depending only on whether people are numerate or innumerate. According to fuzzy-trace theory, creating narratives that emphasize the bottom-line gist of risk, emphasizing relations among magnitudes, and using methods that convey the meaning behind numeric presentation (e.g., use of appropriate arrays to address specific biases identified in research), should improve understanding and outcomes for both numerate and innumerate individuals.

One way to present information that can improve risk understanding in low- and high-numerate people is to use meaningful narratives that accurately represent risk. Dieckmann, Slovic, and Peters (2009) examined the use of narrative evidence to support risk likelihood estimation about a possible terrorist attack. When narrative evidence was given, both high- and low-numerate participants were better able to understand likelihood ratings. In addition, participants who were less numerate reported that they focused more on the narrative evidence when making decisions about the likelihood of the risk, whereas high-numerate participants focused more on the percentages given. This suggests that the use of meaningful messages (e.g., narratives that reflect the gist of the risk probability) can help both high- and low-numerate individuals make better decisions, which is consistent with fuzzy-trace theory. Naturally, simply including just any narrative information will not necessarily improve the understanding of risk (Dickert, Kleber, Peters, & Slovic, 2011; Scherer et al., 2013).

As predicted by fuzzy-trace theory, studies have shown that representations of risk that clearly distinguish relative risks (i.e., which option has lower risks) help low-numerate patients grasp important information (e.g., Brewer et al., 2012; Fraenkel et al., 2012). Reyna (2008) summarizes research that shows that effective communication formats encourage decision makers to extract specific gist representations: simple bar graphs convey relative magnitude, whereas line graphs convey trends over time (for a review, see Brust-Renck, Royer, & Reyna, 2013). For example, use of simple bar graphs to present information about relative magnitude of risk from different types of surgery allows side-by-side comparison of their differences and increases gist comprehension of options (Brown et al., 2011). Therefore, the use of visual displays such as simple bar graphs emphasizes relationships among magnitudes and aids in making informed decisions.

To aid the comprehension of risk from more complex reasoning problems, fuzzy-trace theory recommends the use of specific tools such as an icon array to represent conditional probabilities (Brust-Renck et al., 2013). Icon arrays disentangle overlapping classes by providing a visual representation of each class separately. However, the icon array per se is not what is effective, but rather, how the array conveys the relations among classes. Icon arrays have been used to disentangle numerators in comparison to their denominators in probability estimates (e.g., number of people with vs. without disease in a population; Lloyd & Reyna, 2001; Reyna & Brainerd, 1994, 2008). The icon arrays can be "tagged" to indicate which classes or sets they belong to, for example, indicating which of the people with a disease would receive a positive diagnostic test result and which would receive a negative result. The confusion of classes accounts for such effects as ratio bias, and these effects should be distinguished from effects of failing to grasp the right gist. Fuzzy-trace theory predicts that simple interventions that separate classes (so that denominators and numerators can be processed discretely) reduce judgment and decision-making errors, which has been confirmed using many different types of displays for information presented as probabilities as well as frequencies (e.g., Reyna & Mills, 2007; Wolfe & Reyna, 2010).

In sum, even though understanding numerical information depends on individual differences in numeracy, the way in which numerical information is communicated (e.g., using the bottom-line gist vs. verbatim, rote representation) can improve risk comprehension. According to fuzzy-trace theory, the key is to convey essential information—the gist—needed to make informed judgments and decisions. The effective communication of the gist of risk depends on presentation format, including the use of meaningful messages and visual displays representing specific gist, which are effective with a wide range of audiences, and, in particular, with the low numerate.

Conclusions

From two theoretical perspectives that are relevant to risk communication and individual differences in numeracy, we examined evidence regarding how effective communication depends on proper understanding. Traditional dual-process approaches predict that people with high numeracy should be less subject to biases because they are more likely to rely on analysis as opposed to relying on intuition (Epstein, 1994; Peters et al., 2006). However, these approaches do not account for the contradictory evidence of reliance on analysis and worse performance on some decision problems (Reyna et al., 2009; Shiloh et al., 2002). The hypothesis that higher numeracy relies on higher analytical processing has not always been supported (e.g., Peters et al., 2006; Peters et al., 2008). Consequently, consistent exceptions to the generalization that people higher in numeracy should be better at understanding numerical risk generate some concerns for risk communication.

Nevertheless, fuzzy-trace theory accounts for standard and paradoxical effects of numeracy on risk communication by explaining that rote computation can lead to a correct risk estimate but cannot help determine what those estimates mean or which kinds of computation to rely on (e.g., Reyna & Brainerd, 2008). According to this theory, most advanced decisions are intuitive in the sense that they are based on bottom-line gist—on simple processing, not simple-minded processing (Reyna, 2008, 2012a). In this view, the ability to extract gist is the key to how well people use and understand risk information conveyed by numbers. It has been repeatedly demonstrated that people have a fuzzy-processing preference; they prefer to reason with the simplest gist that can be used to accomplish a task, given response constraints (Reyna & Brainerd, 2007, 2008). Therefore, it is crucial that we are aware of differences in individuals' ability to grasp the underlying meaning behind numerical information, and when this information is not understood, to know how to present information in such a way that engenders understanding. As we have shown, research on numeracy has begun to pave the way toward this goal, and future work will allow for an even clearer understanding of how to better aid those who have difficulty understanding numbers.

Suggested Additional Readings

Fischhoff, B., Brewer, N. T., & Downs, J. S. (Eds.). (2011). *Communicating risks and benefits: An evidence-based user's guide* (pp. 111–119). Washington, DC: U.S. Department of Health and Human Services, Food and Drug Administration. Retrieved from www.fda.gov/ScienceResearch/SpecialTopics/RiskCommunication/default.htm

Nelson, W., Reyna, V. F., Fagerlin, A., Lipkus, I., & Peters, E. (2008). Clinical implications of numeracy: Theory and practice. *Annals of Behavioral Medicine, 35*, 261–274. doi:10.1007/s12160-008-9037-8

Reyna, V. F. (2004). How people make decisions that involve risk: A dual process approach. *Current Directions in Psychological Science, 13*, 60–66. doi:10.1111/j.0963-7214.2004.00275.x

References

Ben-Joseph, E. P., Dowshen, S. A., & Izenberg, N. (2009). Do parents understand growth charts? A national, Internet-based survey. *Pediatrics, 124*(4), 1100–1109. doi:10.1542/peds.2008-0797

Betsch, C., Brewer, N. T., Brocard, P., Davies, P., Gaissmaier, W., Haase, N., . . . Stryk, M. (2012). Opportunities and challenges of web 2.0 for vaccination decisions. *Vaccine, 30*(25), 372–3733. doi:10.1016/j.vaccine.2012.02.025

Bonner, C., & Newell, B. R. (2008). How to make a risk seem riskier: The ratio bias versus construal level theory. *Judgment and Decision Making, 3*(5), 411–416. Retrieved from journal.sjdm.org/8210/jdm8210.html

Brewer, N. T., Richman, A. R., DeFrank, J. T., Reyna, V. F., & Carey, L. A. (2012). Improving communication of breast cancer recurrence risk. *Breast Cancer Research and Treatment, 133*(2), 553–561. doi:10.1007/s10549-011-1791-9

Brown, S. M., Culver, J. O., Osann, K. E., MacDonald, D. J., Sand, S., Thornton, A. A., . . . Weitzel, J. N. (2011). Health literacy, numeracy, and interpretation of graphical breast cancer risk estimates. *Patient Education and Counseling, 83*(1), 92–98. doi:10.1016/j.pec.2010.04.027

Brust-Renck, P. G., Royer, C. E., & Reyna, V. F. (2013). Communicating numerical risk: Human factors that aid understanding in health care. *Review of Human Factors and Ergonomics, 8*(1), 235–276. doi:10.1177/1557234X13492980.

Cokely, E. T., Galesic, M., Schulz, E., Ghazal, S., & Garcia-Retamero, R. (2012). Measuring risk literacy: The Berlin Numeracy Test. *Judgment and Decision Making, 7*, 25–47. Retrieved from http://journal.sjdm.org/11/11808/jdm11808.html

Cokely, E. T., & Kelley, C. M. (2009). Cognitive abilities and superior decision making under risk: A protocol analysis and process model evaluation. *Judgment and Decision Making, 4*, 20–33. Retrieved from http://journal.sjdm.org/81125/jdm81125.html

Cuite, C. L., Weinstein, N. D., Emmons, K., & Colditz, G. (2008). A test of numeric formats for communicating risk probabilities. *Medical Decision Making, 28*, 377–384. doi:10.1177/0272989X08315246

Dickert, S., Kleber, J., Peters, E., & Slovic, P. (2011). Numeracy as a precursor to pro-social behavior: The impact of numeracy and presentation format on the cognitive mechanisms underlying donation decisions. *Judgment and Decision Making, 6*(7), 638–650. Retrieved from journal.sjdm.org/11/11421a/jdm11421a.html

Dieckmann, N. F., Slovic, P., & Peters, E. M. (2009). The use of narrative evidence and explicit likelihood by decision makers varying in numeracy. *Risk Analysis, 29*(10), 1473–1488. doi:10.1111/j.1539-6924.2009.01279.x

Epstein, S. (1994). Integration of the cognitive and the psychodynamic unconscious. *American Psychologist, 49*, 709–724. doi:10.1037/0003-066X.49.8.709

Evans, J. St. B. T., & Stanovich, K. E. (2013). Dual-process theories of higher cognition: Advancing the debate. *Perspectives in Psychological Science, 8*(3), 223–242. doi:10.1177/1745691612460685

Fischhoff, B. (2009). Risk perception and communication. In R. Detels, R. Beaglehole, M. A. Lansang, & M. Guilliford (Eds.), *Oxford textbook of public health* (5th ed., pp. 940–952). Oxford, England: Oxford University Press.

Fraenkel, L., Peters, E., Charpentier, P., Olsen, B., Errante, L., Schoen, R. T., & Reyna, V. (2012). A decision tool to improve the quality of care in rheumatoid arthritis. *Arthritis Care & Research, 64*(7), 977–985. doi:10.1002/acr.21657

Galesic, M., & Garcia-Retamero, R. (2011). Do low-numeracy people avoid shard decision making? *Health Psychology, 30*(3), 336–341. doi:10.1037/a0022723

Garcia-Retamero, R., & Galesic, M. (2010). Who profits from visual aids: Overcoming challenges in people's understanding of risks. *Social Science & Medicine, 70*(7), 1019–1025. doi:10.1016/j.socscimed.2009.11.031

Garcia-Retamero, R., Galesic, M., & Gigerenzer, G. (2011). Enhancing understanding and recall of quantitative information about medical risks: A cross-cultural comparison between Germany and Spain. *Spanish Journal of Psychology, 14*(1), 218–226. doi:10.5209/rev_SJOP.2011.v14.n1.19

Hawley, S. T., Zikmund-Fisher, B., Ubel, P., Jancovic, A., Lucas, T., & Fagerlin, A. (2008). The impact of the format of graphical presentation on health-related knowledge and treatment choices. *Patient Education and Counseling, 73*(3), 448–455. doi:10.1016/j.pec.2008.07.023

Hess, R., Visschers, V. H. M., & Siegrist, M. (2011). Risk communication with pictographs: The role of numeracy and graph processing. *Judgment and Decision Making, 6*(3), 263–274. Retrieved from journal.sjdm.org/11/10630/jdm10630.html

Joram, E., Roberts-Dobie, S., Mattison, S. J., Devlin, M., Herbrandson, K., Hansen, K., & Eslinger, D. (2012). The numeracy demands of health education information: An examination of numerical concepts in written diabetes materials. *Health Communication, 27*(4), 344–355. doi:10.1080/10410236.2011.586987

Kahneman, D. (2003). A perspective on judgment and choice: Mapping bounded rationality. *American Psychologist, 58*(9), 697–720. doi:10.1037/0003-066X.58.9.697

Kahneman, D. (2011). *Thinking fast and slow.* New York, NY: Farrar, Strauss, & Giroux.

Keller, C., Siegrist, M., & Visschers, V. (2009). Effect of risk ladder format on risk perception in high- and low-numerate individuals. *Risk analysis, 29*(9), 1255–1264. doi:10.1111/j.1539-6924.2009.01261.x

Kühberger, A., & Tanner, C. (2010). Risky choice framing: Task versions and a comparison of prospect theory and fuzzy-trace theory. *Journal of Behavioral Decision Making, 23*(3), 314–329. doi:10.1002/bdm.656

Liberali, J. M., Reyna, V. F., Furlan, S., Stein, L. M., & Pardo, S. T. (2011). Individual differences in numeracy and implications for biases and fallacies in probability judgment. *Journal of Behavioral Decision Making, 2*, 361–381. doi:10.1002/bdm.752

Lipkus, I. M., & Peters, E. (2009). Understanding the role of numeracy in health: Proposed theoretical framework and practical insights. *Health Education and Behavior, 36*, 1065–1081. doi:10.1177/1090198109341533

Lipkus, I. M., Peters, E., Kimmick, G., Liotcheva, V., & Marcom, P. (2010). Breast cancer patients' treatment expectations after exposure to the decision aid program Adjuvant Online: The influence of numeracy. *Medical Decision Making, 30*(4), 464–473. doi:10.1177/0272989X09360371

Lloyd, F. J., & Reyna, V. F. (2001). A web exercise in evidence-based medicine using cognitive theory. *Journal of General Internal Medicine, 16*(2), 94–99. doi:10.1111/j.1525-1497.2001.00214.x

Mills, B., Reyna, V. F., & Estrada, S (2008). Explaining contradictory relations between risk perception and risk taking. *Psychological Science, 19*, 429–433. doi:10.1111/j.1467-9280.2008.02104.x

Peters, E., Slovic, P., Västfjäll, D., & Mertz, C. (2008). Intuitive numbers guide decisions. *Judgment and Decision-making, 3*, 619–635. Retrieved from http://journal.sjdm.org/8827/jdm8827.html

Peters, E., Västfjäll, V., Slovic, P., Mertz, C. K., Mazzocco, K., & Dickert, S. (2006). Numeracy and decision making. *Psychological Science, 17*, 407–413. doi:10.1111/j.1467-9280.2006.01720.x

Reyna, V. F. (2008). A theory of medical decision making and health: Fuzzy trace theory. *Medical Decision Making, 28*(6), 850–865. doi:10.1177/0272989X08327066

Reyna, V. F. (2012a). A new intuitionism: Meaning, memory, and development in fuzzy-trace theory. *Judgment and Decision Making, 7*(3), 332–359.

Retrieved from journal.sjdm.org/11/111031/jdm111031.html

Reyna, V. F. (2012b). Risk perception and communication in vaccination decisions: A fuzzy-trace theory approach. *Vaccine, 30*(25), 3790–3797. doi:10.1016/j.vaccine.2011.11.070

Reyna, V. F., & Adam, M. B. (2003). Fuzzy-trace theory, risk communication, and product labeling in sexually transmitted diseases. *Risk Analysis, 23,* 325–342. doi:10.1111/1539-6924.00332

Reyna, V. F., & Brainerd, C. J. (1990). Fuzzy processing in transitivity development. *Annals of Operations Research, 23*(1), 37–63. doi:10.1007/BF02204838

Reyna, V. F., & Brainerd, C. J. (1991). Fuzzy-trace theory and framing effects in choice: Gist extraction, truncation, and conversion. *Journal of Behavioral Decision Making, 4,* 249–262. doi:10.1002/bdm.3960040403

Reyna, V. F., & Brainerd, C. J. (1994). The origins of probability judgment: A review of data and theories. In G. Wright & P. Ayton (Eds.), *Subjective probability* (pp. 239–272). New York, NY: Wiley.

Reyna, V. F., & Brainerd, C. J. (1995). Fuzzy-trace theory: An interim synthesis. *Learning and Individual Differences, 7,* 1–75. doi:10.1016/1041-6080(95)90031-4

Reyna, V. F., & Brainerd, C. J. (2007). The importance of mathematics in health and human judgment: Numeracy, risk communication, and medical decision making. *Learning and Individual Differences, 17*(2), 147–159. doi:10.1016/j.lindif.2007.03.010

Reyna, V. F., & Brainerd, C. J. (2008). Numeracy, ratio bias, and denominator neglect in judgments of risk and probability. *Learning and Individual Differences, 18*(1), 89–107. doi:10.1016/j.lindif.2007.03.011

Reyna, V. F., & Brainerd, C. J. (2011). Dual processes in decision making and developmental neuroscience: A fuzzy-trace model. *Developmental Review, 31,* 180–206. doi:10.1016/j.dr.2011.07.004

Reyna, V. F., & Ellis, S. C. (1994). Fuzzy-trace theory and framing effects in children's risky decision making. *Psychological Science, 5,* 275–279. doi:10.1111/j.1467-9280.1994.tb00625.x

Reyna, V. F., Estrada, S. M., DeMarinis, J. A., Myers, R. M., Stanisz, J. M., & Mills, B. A. (2011). Neurobiological and memory models of risky decision making in adolescents versus young adults. *Journal of Experimental Psychology: Learning, Memory, and Cognition, 37*(5), 1125–1142. doi:10.1037/a0023943

Reyna, V. F., & Farley, F. (2006). Risk and rationality in adolescent decision-making: Implications for theory, practice, and public policy. *Psychological Science in the Public Interest, 7*(1), 1–44. doi:10.111/j.1529-1006.2006.00026.x

Reyna, V. F., & Hamilton, A. J. (2001). The importance of memory in informed consent for surgical risk. *Medical Decision Making, 21,* 152–155. doi:10.1177/0272989X0102100209

Reyna, V. F., & Lloyd, F. J. (2006). Physician decision making and cardiac risk: Effects of knowledge, risk perception, risk tolerance, and fuzzy processing. *Journal of Experimental Psychology, 12*(3), 179–195. doi:10.1037/1076-898X.12.3.179

Reyna, V. F., & Mills, B. A. (2007). Converging evidence supports fuzzy-trace theory's nested sets hypothesis (but not the frequency hypothesis). *Behavioral and Brain Sciences, 30*(3), 278–280. doi:10.1017/S0140525X07001872

Reyna, V. F., Nelson, W., Han, P., & Dieckmann, N. F. (2009). How numeracy influences risk comprehension and medical decision making. *Psychological Bulletin, 135,* 943–973. doi:10.1037/a0017327

Reyna, V. F., & Rivers, S. E. (2008). Current theories of risk and rational decision making. *Developmental Review, 28*(1), 1–11. doi:10.1016/j.dr.2008.01.002

Rivers, S. E., Reyna, V. F., & Mills, B. A. (2008). Risk taking under the influence: A fuzzy-trace theory of emotion in adolescence. *Developmental Review, 28,* 107–144. doi:10.1016/j.dr.2007.11.002

Schapira, M. M., Davids, S. L., McAuliffe, T. L., & Nattinger, A. B. (2004). Agreement between scales in the measurement of breast cancer risk perceptions. *Risk Analysis, 24*(3), 665–673. doi:10.1111/j.0272-4332.2004.00466.x

Scherer, L. D., Ubel, P. A., McClure, J., Greene, S. M., Alford, S. H., Holtzman, L., . . . Fagerlin, A. (2013). Belief in numbers: When and why women disbelieve tailored breast cancer risk statistics. *Patient Education and Counseling, 92,* 253–259. doi:/10.1016/j.pec.2013.03.016

Shiloh, S., Salton, E., & Sharabi, D. (2002). Individual differences in rational and intuitive thinking styles as predictors of heuristic responses and framing effects. *Personality and Individual*

Differences, 32(3), 415–429. doi:10.1016/S0191-8869(01)00034-4

Sloman, S. A. (1996). The empirical case for two systems of reasoning. *Psychological Bulletin, 119,* 3–22. doi:10.1.1.130.7987

Stanovich, K. E., West, R. F., & Toplak, M. E. (2011). The complexity of developmental predictions from dual process models. *Developmental Review, 31,* 103–118. doi:10.1016/j.dr.2011.07.003

Stone, E. R., Sieck, W. R., Bull, B. E., Yates, J. F., Parks, S. C., & Rush, C. J. (2003). Foreground-background salience: Explaining the effects of graphical displays on risk avoidance. *Organizational Behavior and Human Decision Processes, 90,* 19–36. doi:10.1016/S0749-5978(03)00003-7

Tait, A. R., Zikmund-Fisher, B. J., Fagerlin, A., & Voepel-Lewis, T. (2010). The effect of different risk/benefit trade-offs on parents' understanding of a pediatric research study. *Pediatrics, 125*(6), e1475-e1482. doi:10.1542/peds.2009-1796

Waters, E. A., Weinstein, N. D., Colditz, G. A., & Emmons, K. (2006). Formats for improving risk communication in medical tradeoff decisions. *Journal of health communication, 11*(2), 167–182. doi:10.1080/10810730500526695

Weller, J. A., Dieckmann, N. F., Tusler, M., Mertz, C. K., Burns, W. J., & Peters, E. (2013). Development and testing of an abbreviated numeracy scale: A Rasch analysis approach. *Journal of Behavioral Decision Making, 26,* 198–212. doi:10.1002/bdm.1751

Wilhelms, E. A., & Reyna, V. F. (2013). Fuzzy trace theory and medical decisions by minors: Differences in reasoning between adolescents and adults. *Journal of Medicine and Philosophy, 38*(3), 268–282. doi:10.1093/jmp/jht018

Wolfe, C. R., Fisher, C. R., & Reyna, V. R. (2013). Semantic coherence and inconsistency in estimating conditional probabilities. *Journal of Behavioral Decision Making, 26*(3), 237–246. doi:10.1002/bdm.1756

Wolfe, C. R., & Reyna, V. F. (2010). Semantic coherence and fallacies in estimating joint probabilities. *Journal of Behavioral Decision Making, 23*(2), 203–223. doi:10.1002/bdm.650

Wood, S. M. W., & Bechara, A. (2014). The neuroscience of dual (and triple) systems in decision making. In V. Reyna & V. Zayas (Eds.), *The neuroscience of risky decision making* (pp. 177–202). Washington, DC: American Psychological Association.

Zikmund-Fisher, B. J. (2013). The right tool is what they need, not what we have: A taxonomy of appropriate levels of precision in patient risk communication. *Medical Care Research and Review, 70*(1 Suppl.), 37S–49S. doi:10.1177/1077558712458541

CHAPTER 10

Edgework and Risk Communication

Stephen Lyng, Thomas Workman, and G. H. Morris

Introduction

If there is anything resembling conventional wisdom in the field of risk communication, it would be the idea that the most effective way to reduce the harmful effects of risk-taking behavior is to increase individuals' awareness of the harmful consequences of their risky behavior. It is assumed that participants in most forms of risk taking are not fully aware of the potential outcomes of behavior that can be a danger to themselves or others. This recognition has inspired a large number of efforts to improve the dissemination of knowledge about the dangers of certain life choices, ranging from decisions about the consumption of food and drugs to seat belt use and sexual practices. However, a significant challenge to this conventional wisdom can be found in certain risk-taking activities undertaken by individuals who possess full knowledge of the potentially dangerous consequences of their risk-taking ventures and yet continue to pursue these activities. This occurs not *in spite* of the participant's knowledge, but *because* of it, since an enhanced understanding of the real dangers of the endeavor only serves to heighten its allure.

This chapter will explore the paradoxes that this type of risk taking poses for risk communication research.

In response to the familiar injunction that risk communication should be tailored for specific audiences, we will focus attention on individuals who engage in a type of risk taking that constitutes a unique challenge to agents seeking to reduce harm through effective risk communication. The risks assumed by these individuals derive from their participation in voluntarily chosen pursuits that offer a significant probability of death, serious injury, or other highly consequential outcomes. This form of voluntary risk taking, conceptualized as "edgework" (Lyng, 1990, 2005a, 2005b), has become increasingly prevalent in the postwar era, primarily through the development and expansion of a wide variety of high-risk sports (the so-called "extreme sports") and other leisure activities. As increasing numbers of people are endangered in various ways by freely chosen participation in these high-risk endeavors, we need to better understand the impact of risk communication on individuals involved in such activities.

To address this concern, we will first provide an overview of research on high-risk behaviors classified as edgework by discussing the edgework concept and the broader theoretical perspective on voluntary risk taking spawned by this idea. As we will show, edgework refers to a specific subset of risk-taking behaviors belonging to the far end of the risk continuum in their potential for catastrophic individual outcomes, such as loss of life, serious injury, or other forms of significant impairment. Paradoxically, these activities are, to use Erving Goffman's (1967) phrase, "undertaken for their own sake" without any clear external payoff for the risks incurred. Explaining this apparent paradox has been the specific goal of theoretical investigations of the edgework phenomenon initiated in the past two decades (Lyng, 1990, 2005a). In the section that follows, we turn to the tasks of describing the nature of edgework, the theoretical underpinnings of the concept, and a related interpretive account of the motivations for participating in this form of risk-taking behavior.

What Is Edgework?

As noted above, action that can be classified as edgework is a subset of the more general category of volitional risk-taking behavior, a classification that subsumes a broad range of activities that involve some element of risk. If volitional risk taking possesses any real meaning as a social scientific concept, we must be able to make a distinction between voluntary and involuntary forms of risk-taking behavior. While this distinction may be problematic at an abstract level (it could be asserted that all human behavior, with the exclusion of the basic reflexes, is voluntaristic in nature),[1] we hold that it captures a practically meaningful difference in the everyday experience of social actors. Individuals are often compelled to take risks when important material interests are at stake, as in situations of imminent threat to one's life from a predator or enemy, potential starvation, dangerous exposure to the elements, and

similar situations. It is theoretically possible for individuals in these situations to voluntarily choose *not* to act (and they sometimes make this choice), but people are more likely to act to ensure their survival, even when they must take certain risks to achieve this end. Thus, it could be argued that the deeper one's involvement in risk taking to satisfy one's material needs, the closer one is to the domain of involuntary risk taking.

This suggests the utility of referencing the broad distinction between work and leisure as a way to practically distinguish between involuntary and voluntary risk taking. While risk taking in pursuit of one's livelihood may be compelled by the anticipation of greater resources for satisfying one's material needs, risk–reward calculations are much less relevant to decisions about leisure activities, since leisure involves an escape from the instrumental demands of work. Of course, an examination of the social inequities of occupational choice force us to make a further refinement, if we acknowledge that the degree of choice one has in selecting an occupation depends a great deal on one's location in the social order. Individuals possessing significant amounts of social and cultural capital may have the option to choose careers offering risk-taking experiences that they value, while still remaining financially secure (i.e., a doctor who practices emergency medicine). This kind of workplace risk taking could be considered as voluntary. In contrast, individuals whose life circumstances leave them with minimal social and cultural capital confront significant limitations on occupational choice, which means that they are often forced to engage in the most dangerous forms of paid labor in order to earn a living wage (i.e., commercial fishing). Workplace risk taking of this sort is largely involuntary.

Remaining mindful of these conceptual nuances, we proceed from the assumption that the purest expression of voluntary risk-taking behavior is found in those freely chosen opportunities for chance taking that individuals pursue in their leisure time. Although decisions about the use of one's leisure time are not entirely unconstrained (e.g., in consumer society, the purchase of certain highly valued leisure experiences is usually constrained by one's financial resources), most people have a range of options for amusing themselves in their time away from instrumental demands, and the choices they make often involve some degree of risk taking. Thus, the risk of physical injury is present in sports activities that attract the young and the able-bodied; the risk of financial loss resides in gambling activities enjoyed by young and old alike; and an element of chance can be found in the interpersonal transactions that occur in public places like bars, restaurants, shopping malls, sports arenas, and the like (environments for chance taking that Goffman, 1967, referred to as "fancy milling" [p. 197]). Within this broad class of voluntary risk-taking pursuits, it is possible to identify a more specific form of leisure risk taking that is distinguished by the extreme nature of the dangers that participants confront. This is the domain of edgework.

Development of the Edgework Concept

The concept of edgework refers to a wide range of activities in which individuals voluntarily assume risks that could result in death, serious injury, or major incapacitation. The term *edgework*, which first appeared in Hunter S. Thompson's (1966) journalistic accounts of recreational drug use and related high-risk behaviors among American youth during the late 1960s and the early 1970s, was initially used for social scientific purposes by Stephen Lyng (1990) in a sociological study of high-risk leisure sports, such as skydiving, hang gliding, mountain climbing, motor vehicle racing, and other types of extreme sports and high-risk recreational activities. The edgework perspective arises out of a phenomenologically based theoretical approach that links the experiential "foreground" of risk-taking activities to the historically specific "background" conditions

of these practices (see Katz, 1988, pp. 3–4). In this sense, the edgework approach is best viewed as a micro–macro theory of voluntary risk taking.

Since its introduction into the social scientific literature, the edgework perspective has been applied more broadly to risk-taking activities outside of the leisure domain (see Lyng, 2005b), including dangerous occupations (firefighting, police work, rescue squads, etc.), high-stakes financial transactions (stock and bond trading, high-risk investment schemes, gambling, etc.), intellectual and artistic endeavors (innovative scholarship, avant-garde art, etc.), and certain kinds of criminal enterprises (street crime, gang banging, serial murder, etc.).[2] The expanding use of the edgework concept has been fueled by distinctive social changes in recent decades, including the rapid growth of new forms of voluntary risk-taking behavior, increasing rates of participation in these activities, and the extensive attention of the commercial media to high-risk sports, occupations, and interpersonal relationships.[3]

Edgework can be defined as action focused on negotiating critical boundary lines or "edges" that are highly consequential for human well-being. At the most abstract level, the "edge" is best understood as the boundary between order and disorder, form and formlessness (Lyng, 1990, p. 858), involving more concretely the lines separating life and death, full functionality and permanent disability, consciousness and unconsciousness, or sanity and insanity. Crossing any of these lines clearly represents an "observable threat to one's physical or mental well-being or one's sense of an ordered existence" (Lyng, 1990, p. 857).

Edgework Versus Sensation Seeking: Skills, Boundaries, and Transcendence

With its focus on the experiential dimensions of risk-taking behavior, the edgework approach would appear to share certain similarities with

Marvin Zuckerman's (1994) model of the "sensation-seeking" personality type. While we lack the space for a comprehensive comparison of the sensation-seeking and edgework programs of study, we will briefly describe some of the key differences between these two approaches, with a special focus on the kinds of experiential factors emphasized by each model. At the most basic level, the sensation-seeking and edgework perspectives are distinguished by their different explanatory goals. While Zuckerman does incorporate risk taking into his conceptualization of sensation seeking and posits that the sensation-seeking "drive" is a motivation for certain kinds of risk-taking behavior, his basic theoretical goal is to identify and explain a behavioral preference that he regards as a core dimension of personality. This goal is reflected in Zuckerman's (1994) definition of sensation seeking as "a *trait* [italics added] defined by the seeking of varied, novel, complex, and intense sensations and experiences, and the willingness to take physical, social, legal, and financial risks for the sake of such experience" (p. 27). Noting that risk taking is "a correlate of sensation seeking but not an essential part of the definition" (p. 27), Zuckerman points out that "risk taking is sometimes necessary in order to enjoy some types of sensations and experiences but it is not the essential goal of sensation seeking" (p. 153). In contrast, the theory of edgework was specifically developed as an explanation of voluntary risk-taking behavior. And while not entirely ruling out personality predispositions for risk taking, Lyng (1990) shifts the focus in edgework theory to general social psychological factors as the primary motive forces involved in edgework.

This difference in the theoretical significance of risk taking in each model, that is, Zuckerman's secondary interest in risk taking as just one way to satisfy the desire for intense sensations versus Lyng's direct focus on volitional risk taking as the phenomenon to be explained, is related to an important methodological distinction as well. Much of Zuckerman's conceptual work on sensation seeking was inspired by the earlier

development of his Sensation Seeking Scale (SSS), a factor analytic construct that has gone through several iterations in the past four decades. The different versions of the SSS, which include various combinations of four subscales (Thrill and Adventure Seeking, Experience Seeking, Disinhibition, and Boredom Susceptibility), have demonstrated strong factor reliability and therefore have been regarded as effective tools for assessing sensation seeking in research subjects from a variety of populations. Use of the SSS has yielded an extensive body of empirical research, consisting primarily of correlational studies that relate sensation seeking to a wide range of dependent variables, including sports participation, sexual behavior, criminal activity, health risk behavior, and the form of behavior that seems to underlie all of these activities—volitional risk taking (see Zuckerman, 1994). The endurance of the sensation-seeking concept in recent decades can be attributed in part to the strength of the correlations generated by this body of research.

While empirical and theoretical work on sensation seeking has been dominated by the multivariate, deductive model, the edgework research program has relied primarily on in-depth qualitative studies of risk-taking groups and an inductive approach to theory development. Thus, Zuckerman's (1994) theoretical/methodological strategy is to posit the existence of a "drive with genetical–biological bases" that can be operationalized with a scale consisting primarily of intentional response categories (e.g., "I would like to go scuba diving"), which is then correlated with "various learned . . . expression[s]" of this trait (p. 387). In contrast, the strategy employed by edgework researchers has been to conduct ethnographic and participant observational research on subjects actually involved in voluntary risk taking in order to allow the *subjects* to identify theoretically relevant categories for understanding their participation in risk-taking activities. These two strategies have produced very different results. The sensations and experiences that satisfy Zuckerman's theorized drive—through participation in activities that may involve an element of risk (sex, crime, sports, drug use, etc.)—can be described only in terms of the general qualities of variation, novelty, complexity, and intensity (p. 373). Conversely, ethnographic research on edgeworkers engaged in a wide range of high-risk endeavors has yielded a detailed description of characteristics and sensations that are uniquely associated with the extreme forms of risk taking classified as edgework.

Thus, the empirical research on edgework reveals experiential patterns that are certainly novel and complex but are distinguished by more specific qualities that justifies their classification as "edgework sensations" (Lyng, 1990; see also Lyng, 2005b, for specific empirical studies). As indicated in the ethnographic research, participants often describe sensations that support their sense of edgework as an "other-world" experience that transcends the mundane reality of everyday life. These other-world features include time and space implosions, in which time passes either much faster or slower than normal, and spatial boundaries collapse as the edge is approached. For example, combat soldiers engaged in pitched battles lasting many hours often describe the experience as seeming to last only a few minutes, while skydivers experience 60 seconds of freefall as lasting an eternity. Edgeworkers who employ various forms of technology (racing cars or motorcycles, high-performance airplanes, surgical tools, etc.) describe the blurring of boundaries between themselves and these technologies, leading to a sense of mental control over the machines or tools they use.

Other strong feelings and emotions contribute to the seductive appeal of negotiating the edge. Time and space implosions give a "hyperreal" quality to edgework activities, which are experienced as more "authentic" than everyday reality. The feelings of authenticity are accompanied by a sense that the experience is ineffable—words cannot adequately describe one's experience at the edge. Participants must also manage intense emotions such as fear. The challenge in doing edgework is to cultivate a mind-set that allows

participants to act skillfully and competently by combining intense bodily arousal with focused attention and creative responses to the immediate demands of the moment. Such powerful and unusual sensations acquire a special allure for edgeworkers, and they often claim that being on the edge is when they feel most alive.

Successfully managing fear when negotiating the edge typically produces a sense of omnipotence and control, which leads many edgeworkers to see themselves as members of an elite group. Edgeworkers believe that the power to control seemingly uncontrollable circumstances is innately determined and transferable from one form of edgework to another (Lyng, 1990). Their capacities for control are sometimes attributed a basic "survival skill" that they believe distinguishes true edgeworkers from those who are attracted to risk taking but lack the "right stuff" (Wolfe, 1979) to conduct it successfully.

This last set of edgework sensations brings us to the feature that most clearly distinguishes the sensation-seeking and edgework approaches. As indicated by the previous discussion, individuals who do edgework are most certainly involved in a form of sensation seeking—it is highly unlikely that someone who scores as a "low sensation seeker" on the SSS would be attracted to edgework activities. However, we have seen that the edgework experience is defined by a unique set of sensations, which we can now connect to the core feature of all edgework endeavors—the use of highly developed *skills*, including activity-specific skills (flying one's body in free fall, free-climbing a 1,000-ft. cliff, etc.) and the generic skill of "controlling the seemingly uncontrollable" (the survival skill). At a basic level, edgework practices have evolved as special opportunities for the development and use of complex skills, and this is what edgeworkers value the most. In contrast, developing and using skills is not a defining dimension of sensation seeking, although some forms of sensation seeking do require the use of skills. While one can adopt a passive stance in many kinds of sensation seeking (e.g., ingesting psychotropic drugs), edgework requires an active and skillful engagement with the challenges at hand.

Thus, the special value that edgeworkers place on skill use in high-risk endeavors can be considered as the defining feature of this practice. Indeed, this orientation reinforces the sense that many edgeworkers have of themselves as members of elite groups within society (an orientation sometimes shared by outsiders as well). Edgeworkers typically possess a deep faith in their own ability to skillfully manage chaotic situations, but they are often suspicious of the risk-taking skills of others, especially individuals outside of recognized edgework circles. Consequently, edgeworkers are rarely attracted to the kind of "thrill-ride" activities (roller coasters, bungee jumping, etc.) that offer the best opportunities for sensation seeking because they are unwilling to entrust their fate to individuals who may lack key risk-taking skills (focused attention, hypervigilance, ad hoc abilities, etc.) to ensure successful outcomes.

In short, edgework involves an unusual mix of elements that provides a dramatic contrast to institutionalized routines of work and leisure in modern society. Experiencing themselves as innately skilled in managing fear and chaotic conditions at the edge, participants are drawn to high-risk activities as ways to achieve a heightened sense of self, which is often described as a sense of self-determination or self-actualization. This represents another dimension of the "authentic" character of edgework experiences: In addition to confronting an exaggerated, transcendent reality (a "hyperreality" as it were), edgeworkers also experience a perception of self they often describe as their authentic or "true" self.

The Social and Cultural Context of Edgework Practices

In shifting the analysis to the macrostructural level, attention is directed to the broad-based structural forces that either push or pull (or both

simultaneously) individuals into the pleasurable pursuit of risk. A number of frameworks have been used to explore this dimension. The initial analysis of key structural factors that shape participants' perceptions of the edgework experience relied on ideas drawn from the theoretical perspectives of Karl Marx and G. H. Mead (see Lyng, 1990). The Marx–Mead synthesis offers a way to conceptualize the varied and mutually reinforcing social forces that inspire the search for edgework opportunities. This approach highlights the separations, contradictions, and conflicts in institutionally based action that result in diminished prospects for spontaneous, creative behavior. In a social environment characterized by alienated labor, class conflict, and oversocialization, people struggle for a greater sense of personal agency in their institutionally determined lives. One of the most alluring destinations for those seeking a sense of self-determination is the hyperreality found at the edge, where one's individual skills, powers of concentration, capacities for control, and survival skills are the most critical determinants of one's continued existence. This encounter stands in direct contrast to a more common social experience shaped by the perfunctory performance of institutional roles and routines that seem impervious to the individual's creative powers.

While Marx and Mead give priority to constraints imposed by modern economic relations and community life, respectively, Max Weber (1958) focuses on a structural imperative that shapes a broader range of people's daily affairs. Weber highlights the "rationalization process," which has relegated people to an "iron cage" of routinized behavior and diminished opportunities for creative action. Moreover, by eroding premodern values and reconfiguring people's connections with nature and the cosmos, rationalization also produces a sense of meaninglessness and existential sterility. The ultimate consequence of the rationalization process is a phenomenon that Weber termed as *disenchantment*.

The Weberian perspective adds another dimension to the sociological interpretation of edgework practices, broadening our understanding of edgework as a transcendent experience that emerges against the background structural conditions of modern society (see Lyng, 2005b). Considering the profound contrast that the edgework sensations offer to the dominant reality of rationalized social institutions, it is not surprising that participants perceive edgework as a transcendent experience and often describe it in otherworldly terms. The time and space implosions found in the immediacy of edgework experience occur in unexpected and uncontrolled ways. As an experience that is deeply embodied, largely ineffable, and resistant to techniques of rational control, edgework is an especially powerful way to "re-enchant" the disenchanted world of modern social actors. Thus, the rationalization trend and its disenchanting effects push people to explore alternative realities where they can connect to a domain of mysterious and vibrant experience.

The various classical theoretical interpretations of edgework focus on the fundamental opposition between the institutional world and the alternative space of edgework practices. In considering the possibilities for experiencing human and spiritual agency, these modernist perspectives emphasize the compensatory character of edgework, seeing it as filling a void created by the deforming influences of alienation, reification, oversocialization, and rationalization.

However, it is also possible to employ a macrolevel perspective that envisions edgework experiences not as a radical *contrast* to everyday life but as a purified expression of the form of consciousness and agency that is ascendant in the emerging late modern social universe. Many efforts have been undertaken in recent decades to describe the structural logics of late modernity, but the approach that has proven most useful for understanding the edgework trend has been the "risk society" perspective of Ulrich Beck (1992) and Anthony Giddens (1991). While we lack the space here for a comprehensive overview of the risk society model (see Lyng, 2008, 2012; Lyng & Matthews, 2007, for more extensive discussions of the model's application to edgework),

it is sufficient to note that risk society theorists view the "second modern" era as dominated by a new form of agency and consciousness.

In the risk society, indeterminacy and uncertainty are the overriding qualities of the dominant social reality, and successfully negotiating the uncertainties of daily life becomes the key challenge for many social actors. This challenge is met through an increasing reliance on a form of risk consciousness that treats unpredictability as "cognizable through probabilistic calculation" (Lash, 1994, p. 140). Observing the shift to risk calculation in everyday decision making, Beck and Giddens assert that we have entered a new social reality, increasingly dominated by the logic of risk. Thus, if edgework is contextualized in terms of the risk society, it makes little sense to view it as a form of "counteragency" focused on transcending the dominant reality, since negotiating the reality of everyday life relies on a set of skills not unlike those employed in negotiating the edge. Rather, the more obvious implication of this analysis is that edgework represents the purest expression of the agentic qualities demanded by the risk society.

The connection between edgework and the broader structure of the risk society is perhaps reflected most clearly in an important normative shift that has accompanied the rise of "extreme" leisure pursuits and the growth of institutional uncertainties in contemporary social life: While in an earlier time, risk taking disassociated from the pursuit of material gain was viewed as a sign of irrationality or impulsivity, there is a growing sense today that risk taking is intrinsically valuable because it can be a vehicle of individual liberation and personal growth. By embracing risks rather than avoiding them, in the pursuit of leisure edgework or in the conduct of one's daily life in various institutional domains, one can potentially transcend the constraints of social position and biography. People increasingly see both promise and peril in the growing insecurity of employment, the instability of family life, and the unpredictability of interpersonal relations in the risk society. As one discovers in edgework endeavors, the active embrace of risky circum-stances can yield either new possibilities for self-determination or personal disaster, depending on the degree of skill one exercises in managing the risks. Thus, the skillful action demanded in the immediacy of the edgework experience is merely a purified expression of the kind of agency that is generally valorized within the risk society.

Edgework Communities

Finally, we direct attention to a dimension of social transactions that mediates between the micro/foreground and macro/background of edgework practices—*meso*level interactions between members of edgework groups. Early research has identified the existence of "edge-work communities" that form and are sustained by the collective appreciation or practice of engaging in activity-specific risk behaviors among a group of individuals (Lyng, 1990, 2004, 2005a, 2005b). Perhaps most successful in the edgework research to date has been the docu-mentation of edgework communities that exist across occupational, recreational, and illicit realms. From firefighters to skydivers to motor-cycle gangs to anarchist groups, voluntary risk takers seem to be able to find one another and form a social structure that is centered in the risk-taking activity.

Risk taking within a community of edgework-ers has its own unique benefits in that the indi-vidual risk taker finds acceptance by the group and membership within it through engaging in risky behavior. The risk is collectively celebrated and practiced, increasing the social bond between members. In this way, successful risk taking serves as both a route to personal transformation and to increased social capital among a group of peers who understand and share a particular set of values. Membership in this community may be particularly important to the edgeworker, who may have difficulty accounting for his or her attraction to risk behavior (and may face conster-nation from nonedgeworkers).

Thus, a critical aspect of edgework theory involves understanding the social structures of the edgework community, for it is in this context that risk taking is reified, encouraged, and—most oddly, perhaps—controlled. To make better sense of this, several critical aspects of the inter-actional dimension of edgework must be fully explored.

First, the risk-taking activity in and of itself is less meaningful for the community than the accomplishment of the behavior without the outcome of physical, personal, or legal harm (Lyng, 2005a, 2005b). Thompson's original notion of edgework incorporated his pride in the ability to consume large amounts of alcohol and illicit drugs and drive vehicles at high speeds with little effect (in his mind and the mind of his followers) on his productivity as a journalist and writer; thus, each return from a further edge confirmed a level of skill that became in itself a source of satisfaction, particu-larly as it was celebrated by others in his com-munity. In this way, successful risk activity demonstrates a *skill* that separates members of the community into a hierarchy of accomplish-ment. The more skilled risk taker is better able to defy the odds, overcome the dangers, and successfully cheat the probability of harm through carefully honed abilities. In more for-mal recreational or occupational edgework com-munities, such as test pilots, firefighters, and race car drivers, training and protocol are used to build skill and increase performance, thus lowering the probability of calamity in high-risk behavior (Lyng, 2005a, 2005b). Less formal edgework communities might take a similar informal approach, as more experienced mem-bers mentor the less experienced by sharing their knowledge of risk and skills surrounding harm avoidance (Workman, 2008).

Edgework Practices

Where skill at risk taking increases social capital within an edgework community, unsuccessful risk taking—failure to return from the edge unharmed—destroys that social capital and, in many instances, threatens membership within that community. Researchers at the University of Nebraska found that student reaction to a peer death from acute intoxication or a related behavior was often viewed as the actions of a "stupid drinker" rather than a testament to the level of risk involved in the consumption. An individual who faced significant consequence for his or her risk activity was often shunned by the group and was viewed as a liability rather than as a hero (Workman, 2005a, 2005b). Likewise, research in edgework surrounding illicit drugs found that addiction to the substances also indicated failure, as dependency removed voluntary risk taking from the equation (Reith, 2005).

This presents a unique additional paradox for the edgework community. While the community itself is centered in voluntary risk taking and finds value in an ever-extended edge, those who are unable to defy risk successfully are themselves no longer worthy to be a member of the community. This paradox suggests that edgework communities must not be viewed as collectives where uncalculated risk is celebrated. For the activity to be meaningful, the risk must be managed successfully.

Of particular concern for these communities is risk behavior that threatens the community as a whole. The young and foolish firefighter who runs into the burning building ignoring protocol poses a risk not just to himself but to the entire squad, which now may have to rescue him or her. Similarly, the anarchist who is more enthusiastic than skilled is likely to call attention from the police to the entire group. College fraternities or athletic teams known for their high-risk alcohol consumption and other high-risk exploits learned quickly that the new member with the least experience in drinking, fighting, or sexual conquest was the most likely to be the cause of a sanction against the entire chapter or team, or to the entire fraternal organization or athletic program (Cho et al., 2010). Many fraternal corporations and universities have been litigants in civil lawsuits

for wrongful deaths of students due to drinking activity within a specific group of students (Workman, 2001a, 2005a).

Individual edgeworkers who display high levels of skill by regularly returning from a risky experience unscathed add to their social capital within the community and are likely to build a reputation for the community as a collective able to defy the odds. New members must prove their proficiency by taking a visible risk in front of other members and avoiding harm to gain membership; existing members must maintain or expand their level of risk (and overcome such odds) to gain or maintain prestige and social positioning.

As revealed in the preceding overview of the experiential, interactional, and structural dimensions of edgework practices, individuals involved in risk-taking activities of this type may represent a special challenge for public health officials and risk communication practitioners seeking to develop effective harm reduction strategies. While risk taking of any sort can be experienced as pleasurable by some people, research on edgework has disclosed the highly seductive and, in some cases, addictive nature of this form of extreme risk taking. Recognizing special difficulties presented by this phenomenon, we now turn to a discussion of potential risk communication interventions for addressing edgework practices.

Reflections for Theory and Research

Recognizing the importance of interaction between more experienced and successful edgeworkers and the less skilled, we urge researchers and practitioners to concentrate future research on the nature of this interaction. Qualitative research is warranted to discover how mentors in edgework engage successfully in risk communicative interaction with novices. Such research could reveal how mentors use modeling to demonstrate what skillful performance looks like; how novices engage in questioning of mentors about how to achieve greater control; how mentors provide advice, suggestions, and warnings; and how mentors confront the lesser experienced members who do not take advantage of their advice. These inquiries are just the barest beginnings for how better to understand the nature of interaction in this domain. Armed with such knowledge, risk communication professionals would be better equipped to advise and instruct leaders of edgework communities in how to minimize harms to individuals and communities of voluntary risk taking by living up to their own roles and responsibilities as risk communicators.

The fleshing out of empirical research on edgework communities will be important for refining the harm reduction strategy described in this chapter, but we must also take account of aspects of edgework theory and research that raise questions about the viability of this approach. Although our empirical illustrations have been focused almost exclusively on leisure forms of edgework (relying primarily on illustrative material dealing with high-risk alcohol use among college fraternity and sorority organizations), our review of the edgework literature has shown that the concept has been applied to a wide range of social practices and domains. While extreme sports and other forms of leisure edgework activities are typically dominated by individuals with discretionary time and income, individuals deprived of these resources find other ways to define and negotiate consequential edges. The documented variations in edgework practices relating to gender, class, race, and other social group affiliations and the impact of unique social contextual factors on these practices have important implications for our analysis.

Consider, for example, the various patterns of criminal edgework studied by researchers in recent years (Lyng, 1993, 2004; Miller, 2005; Milovanovic, 2005). On the one hand, it is difficult to conceive of a harm reduction approach to managing criminal risk taking that would be socially and politically viable today, even though the type of novice–mentor relationships and skill transfers we have described are well documented in the

research on criminal edgeworkers. It is not likely that a majority of U.S. citizens would be willing to accept some level of illegal activity by members of criminal subcultures at the cost of making sure that serious crime is better controlled. On the other hand, there could be significant value in encouraging potential novice–mentor relationships among older ex-offenders and young first offenders as a means of transmitting skills for managing life risks in ways that reduce harm to themselves and others. As we become more sensitive to the significant long-term harm often caused by more traditional punitive approaches to less serious crime—as, for example, when individuals incarcerated for minor drug offenses leave prison as hardened criminals—we may find criminal justice authorities and the public more willing to embrace such approaches as alternatives to incarceration.

Finally, as empirical research on edgework activities and practical applications of edgework theory continue to expand, it will be important for scholars to remain cognizant of difficult political–ethical issues posed by the continuing growth of edgework leisure pursuits. One such ethical problem is reflected in the ongoing debate over the appropriate level of regulation that should be imposed on edgework participants and groups. It should come as no surprise that members of edgework communities generally believe that their risk-taking activities should be entirely unregulated, reflecting in part their interest in doing edgework as a way to *escape* life circumstances that they see as overly constrained by social forces. However, this stance is easily criticized by those who point to the externalities generated by the increased participation in high-risk leisure activities. As we have noted in this chapter, highly developed risk-taking skills are a form of social capital in edgework communities, and informal structures for transmitting these skills to novices typically exist within most edgework groups. But this does not ensure that bad outcomes are always prevented. Since the ultimate goal of edgework is to move as close to the edge as possible without actually crossing it, even the most seasoned edgeworkers can miscalculate in negotiating the edge and suffer the serious consequences of their errors in judgment. If they are fortunate enough to survive the experience, their rescue most often requires the heroic efforts of first responders and the extensive resources of the agencies that employ them, all paid for by the nation's taxpayers. Thus, when an edgework endeavor turns out badly, it is not just the participants who suffer the consequences but a larger population of other individuals—family members, first responders, taxpayers—who had no part in deciding whether the risk was worth taking.

In addition to the ethical dilemma linked to the issue of "who pays" for edgework failures, a closely related ethical problem is best understood in terms of the economic concept of "moral hazard." Simply put, moral hazard arises when risk takers' willingness to take chances is influenced by the knowledge that they will be "bailed out" by others if a negative outcome ensues. In the case of edgeworkers, the expectation that they will be rescued by highly trained personnel if they fail in their quest may serve as an incentive for taking risks that they would otherwise not consider—for example, mountain climbers who decide to go for the summit in marginal weather conditions because they know a rescue helicopter will pluck them from the mountain top if necessary. The combination of ethical concerns associated with collectivizing the costs of risk taking and the moral hazard that results from this arrangement provides a strong justification for greater regulation of edgework enterprises of all sorts. It will be important for risk communication researchers and practitioners to remain sensitive to these difficult political–ethical issues as they engage more extensively with edgework communities and further explore the policy implications of edgework research.

Recommendations for Practice

Several aspects of edgework as it appears to operate within a community offer a number of implications for risk communication and harm reduction. There are opportunities to reduce significant harms that can be and have been explored.

First, the social structure of edgework suggests that risk awareness among members of an edgework community is relatively high. Successful edgework requires accurate calculation of risk to whatever degree possible, and an acute awareness of potential disaster always informs the experience. This suggests that more successful edgework communities have found reliable ways in which risk can be calculated, and skills can be developed to lower the probability of harm. One challenge for risk communication professionals, then, is finding ways of feeding risk information to such communities to assist them in this process.

Interestingly, the social structure that promotes risk taking for members of these groups also serves to control the level of risk and increase the chances of survival among those engaging in risk behavior. Although some initial level of skill must be demonstrated to gain entrance into and acceptance of an edgework community, there is evidence that the community provides both knowledge and mentoring across members to increase their success and minimize risk to the community as a whole. This may range from less experienced members observing and imitating the practices of their more skilled peers to direct interaction and instruction by leaders in the community. Often, the instruction comes in the form of drinking stories that are shared at the beginning of a drinking event. The stories highlight "acceptable" forms of intoxication and communicate warnings to new members about the consequences of crossing established boundaries. Likewise, these groups may have an "edge" or level of risky behavior that all members respect and avoid, and this boundary is formally and informally passed along to new members. A classic example of this was a new member of a sorority who was ostracized from the group after "pregaming" (consuming large amounts of alcohol prior to a social event) and vomiting on a transport bus headed to an expensive and carefully planned social event. New fraternity members quickly learn the boundary of approaching another fraternity brother's girlfriend, regardless of the state of intoxication.

This provides a critical opportunity for prevention specialists who are able to supply risk information and harm reduction strategies to the community via established group leadership. Professional training is commonplace for formal occupational or recreational edgework communities, such as pilots, cliff divers, and firefighters; training in risk identification and avoidance is both appreciated and adopted, particularly if the information is valued by leaders in the community. It is equally evident that illicit edgework communities have a heightened understanding of the risks associated with their activities and have members who have discovered successful strategies for negotiating these risks. A classic example in college communities can be found in underage consumption practices. While procurement of alcohol for minors is commonplace, older peers will often modify the amount or type of alcohol provided (and may even refuse to provide alcohol) to minors who appear to lack skill in achieving intoxication without problems. Documenting the strategies employed by these communities may be critical for understanding risk behavior as a whole and the strategies that can reduce the probability of harm.

Unfortunately, this is not the standard approach of most public health efforts to address risk behavior, particularly those behaviors identified as deviant (Workman, 2000) or illicit. Illicit risk behavior is most often studied from an "assumption of malevolence" (Gusfield, 1996) that limits appreciation of the perceived benefits of risk taking and assumes that any probability of harm is problematic (Hanson, 2005). This approach may be particularly ineffective for edgeworkers who find both identity and social capital in the risk activity.

Thus, it is important to note that any communication of risk or risk reduction must not be viewed as antithetical to the edgework community itself. Public health professionals who traditionally view all voluntary risk taking as problematic are quickly rejected by the community. We would argue that, from the edgework perspective, a key aspect of successfully communicating risk to an edgework community is to ensure that the information is seen as enhancing the risk management skills of community members rather than curbing their risk taking, allowing them to maintain their identity as risk takers. In approaching the fraternities and sororities of the University of Nebraska, for example, the team quickly learned that addressing excessive consumption of alcohol was only salient to the members when it could be tied to other outcomes, such as ignoring house maintenance duties, the inability to pay dues, or conflict among a new member class.

Second, the failure of those unable to successfully negotiate risk (which often leads to exclusion from the community) offers a variety of opportunities to interact with both the individual risk taker as well as the community as a whole. Brief motivational interviewing (BMI), which has shown significant efficacy to reduce excessive drinking among college drinkers (Martens, Smith, & Murphy, 2013), may be perfectly suited to address failed edgeworkers. Many colleges and universities routinely conduct BMI on students identified by citation or medical report. Identifying an individual as part of a larger edgework community can add additional material for the interview. Failure that does not lead to death provides a key opportunity for intervention in a variety of forms. Through a failure experience, the edgeworker may discover that they are not quite ready for membership and participation in the edgework community. The individual may also walk away from the failure with a clearer understanding of the risks involved or the gaps in skill that led to the failure, making them better equipped for success in future endeavors.

One challenge to public health and risk reduction efforts is their lack of understanding of the operational definition of failure for many of these communities, which often allows some degree of harm as acceptable rather than problematic. For example, many young adult communities engaging in risky alcohol and other drug behavior do not consider hangovers, vomiting, unconsciousness, or even blackouts as indications of failure, but they do see hospitalization, addiction, significant injury, or death as unacceptable outcomes (Workman, 2001b). The attraction of enforcement personnel or arrest may also not be failure as much as legal conviction and imprisonment. Risk reduction efforts for edgework communities may need to concentrate on harms that have significant salience for skilled risk takers. In the case of reducing the harms of alcohol consumption, public health efforts may be more successful focusing on the more significant physical, legal, and personal harms of acute intoxication, such as car crashes, alcohol poisoning, or unwanted pregnancy or sexual disease. This, too, indicates the need to assist edgework communities in skill development, building into the group structure the ability to assess individual member readiness, setting controls for less skilled members, and inculcating the value of learning from small failures so that future catastrophe is avoided. Research suggests that such values already exist in many edgework communities (Laurendeau, 2006; Milovanovic, 2005; Rajah, 2007), but additional study is needed to determine best approaches available to risk communication professionals for influencing the process.

It is also important to note that edgework communities represent a small minority of their reference populations. Social norms statistics collected at colleges and universities across the nation have found that on average, high-risk alcohol consumption is adopted as a regular practice by a relatively small percentage of students (Perkins, 2003). This, however, indicates the impact of edgework communities on the general culture. From the popularity of extreme sports to the positive depiction of alcohol and other drug use in popular media, edgework communities are often valorized by the broader general population who rarely engage in the risk themselves and see these groups as somehow different from themselves in successfully managing risk (Workman, 2001b, 2005b). Of greatest concern, perhaps, is the attraction of these communities to individuals who are less skilled or less able to calculate risk but who engage in similar behavior to gain entrance to the community and find identity in the practice. The novice edgeworker who lacks the experience and expertise to navigate risk is most likely to suffer harm.

Finally, an important implication of edgework theory for risk communication and harm reduction relates to the role of public health in addressing edgework communities, particularly those communities engaged in illicit activity. While a tolerance for the pursuit of controlled edgework may be critical (and is largely unavoidable as evidenced by the continued growth of these activities despite efforts to eliminate them), society may also need to identify clear boundaries around the practices of these communities. One common approach to doing so can be found in environmental management strategies that employ policy, education, and enforcement that frame edgework within a broader set of social values (DeJong et al., 1998; Newman, Shell, Major, & Workman, 2006). Policies that establish and codify clear values (which must be disseminated and enforced consistently to edgework and nonedgework members of the broader community) set boundaries for edgework communities by increasing consequences for an edgework community member's flagrant disregard for the edge. This enables edgework communities to better control members in order to sustain the community as a whole. An example of this is provided in the section that follows.

An Application: Edgework Theory and College Alcohol Prevention Programs

We conclude the chapter by describing early work done to apply edgework theory in a set of approaches to reduce harms related to high-risk alcohol consumption among college students. Many of the lessons learned from these efforts have led to the evolution of thinking about edgework and the reduction of population harm related to it.

Cho et al. (2010) considered fraternity members as belonging to such a community and identified controlling alcohol consumption as a locus of attention for the community. These authors sought to discover the communities' perspectives on the problems of excessive drinking and possible solutions. Analyzing data from focus groups with members of fraternities, Cho et al. found that members stressed the importance of maintaining control over alcohol consumption and commonly identified lack of control as a problem. They described how members, as freshmen, were more likely than others to drink excessively in order to impress others and how they eventually learned skills necessary to keep from drinking excessively. Members often construed their own fraternities as capable of managing risky behavior, ascribing problems of excessive drinking to other groups. Fraternity members recognized the prudence of having rules and procedures that enabled them to prepare for events in which excessive drinking might occur and to know how to handle out-of-control members. Regarding perceived solutions to problems of excessive drinking, fraternity members expressed a desire to acquire information and skills necessary to control alcohol consumption. For instance, members sought information about alcohol consumption limits and how to care for intoxicated members. In addition, members acknowledged the role of more experienced members in helping freshmen learn control. Those who are better able to take and succeed at carefully controlled risks operate like a central collective of mavens in risk behavior that enables many to escape harm (Reith, 2005; Shewan, Delgarno, & Reith, 2000).

Work done to reduce high-risk drinking and related harms among fraternities and sororities at the University of Nebraska, Lincoln, found within these groups a highly sophisticated social structure where students who were able to drink large amounts of alcohol or take drugs to a level of acute intoxication without long-term negative impact on their health or their academic success had a special notoriety within the group (Workman, 2001a). Similarly, a large number of elite universities have found a common theme of "work hard, play hard" as driving the high-risk behaviors and the resulting social capital of its students. Student interview data suggests that for many of these students, the maintenance of a high grade point average despite weekend after weekend of acute intoxication is a badge of honor, more celebrated than if a student simply focused on academic success without showing equal devotion to "play."

Edgework theory has led to a productive approach in risk communication and in reducing harm with traditional college student populations who engage in high-risk alcohol and other drug consumption (Workman, 2008). Reith (2005) notes that "although the consumption of (illegal) drugs is still regarded as a deviant or marginal form of behavior, ironically, a contrary trend is appearing, the normalization—if not the legalization—of drug use in everyday life," adding that

> weekend drug-taking is part of the leisure habits of many thousands of young people, who frequently indulge in poly-drug use, "picking and mixing" ecstasy, cannabis, amphetamines, LSD, and any number of substances to get the best high. The creation, maintenance, and control of this high is a striking instance of the most demanding of edgework. (p. 235)

Risky alcohol and other drug consumption remains a significant problem for the majority of American colleges and universities, who struggle to find and utilize evidence-based strategies to reduce the harms related to the practice (McCabe, Teter, Boyd, Knight, & Wechsler, 2005). The National Institute for Alcohol Abuse and Alcoholism estimates that 1,825 college students between the ages of 18 and 24 years die annually from alcohol poisoning or alcohol-related unintentional injuries, 599,000 students between the ages of 18 and 24 years are unintentionally injured under the influence of alcohol, and nearly 696,000 students are assaulted by another student who has been drinking (Hingson, Zha, & Weitzman, 2009). A common assumption is that these harms are experienced by the most ardent of risk takers, although this remains unproven. Anecdotal evidence on individual campuses suggests instead that significant harms are more likely to occur among first- and second-year students who, from the edgework perspective, more likely represent less experienced risk takers unsuccessfully attempting to find membership and social capital through risk taking but who lack skill to avoid harm.

Edgework theory is closely aligned with a number of prevention strategies for this population, including small group social norms challenges (Far & Miller, 2003), BMI (LaBrie, Thompson, Huchting, Lac, & Buckley, 2007; Marlatt et al., 1998), alcohol skills training (Fromme, Marlatt, Baer, & Kivlahan, 1994), and other risk reduction strategies that focus on harm protection rather than the abstinence of risk behavior. Given that alcohol and certain other drugs are legal substances, these approaches may be more appropriate for traditional college populations who straddle "legal" consumption laws.

Many of the students studied in these groups followed a clear and uncompromising commitment to drink only on Thursday, Friday, and Saturday nights and completely abstain from the behavior on Sunday, Monday, Tuesday, and often on Wednesday nights. Many spoke of looking forward to the weekend or a special event (including group-based rituals, e.g., new member activation, a birthday, or a formal) as the appropriate time for engaging in high-risk behavior. Yet researchers also quickly learned that certain loose boundaries existed. Fraternity members, regardless of how intoxicated they became, would never "hit on" another member's girlfriend. The rule was known by all the members and was usually obeyed despite high levels of intoxication. Many sororities would "cut a girl off" or take her

home if she began behaving in a way that was embarrassing to the organization. Many women cited the rule that drunken behavior could never occur while a female was wearing her "letters."

Other public health efforts to address high-risk drinking among fraternities and sororities focused on the elimination or total reformation of these organizations. The University of Nebraska, Lincoln, took the opposite approach and sought grant funds from the U.S. Department of Education to intervene with the fraternities and sororities of the university, who realized their membership, along with their reputations across campus, were declining. Critical to this discovery by group leaders, however, was the application of environmental strategies that heightened awareness and enforcement, resulting in sanctions for fraternities and sororities when boundaries were crossed or edgework was unsuccessful.

The effort focused on individual chapters and created separate plans for each chapter based on the identified needs. An early lesson learned was the need to focus on the overall health of the organization rather than the risk behavior of the group. Initial entry into these chapters was accomplished by identifying issues that threatened the organization's ability to sustain itself, such as unpaid dues, small new member classes, conflict within the chapter, and unsuccessful activation of new members who either flunked out or left school during their pledge semester. While many of these issues were not directly related to the risky substance use within the chapter, they were directly related to individuals who engaged in unsuccessful risk behavior and were seen by leaders as indicators that some aspect of harm reduction skills were not being adequately addressed.

Formal and informal leaders of these groups were identified by self-reported consumption surveys and officer and advisor recommendations. Identified leadership met regularly with prevention specialists throughout the program, which ran over an 8-month period in two waves. Leadership meetings were devoted to discussion of risk factors involved in chapter rituals and practices to help the group explore one or more of three responses: (1) the application of new harm reduction strategies, (2) the improvement of intervention approaches with members who fail at negotiating risk successfully, and/or (3) the restructuring of recruitment or social activities that attracted inexperienced risk takers and increased the likelihood of harm to individuals and the chapter as a whole.

At the University of Nebraska and other colleges and universities, peer leaders would serve a vital role in creating and enforcing a set of boundaries for risk taking among members, particularly those members who displayed limited skills in negotiating higher risk behavior. Peers would communicate these boundaries before key events that include substance use such as parties, formals, or chapter rituals and would intervene when appropriate by "cutting off" or sending home a member coming dangerously close to failure.

Critical to the successful adoption of intervention, however, was a continued pressure by the surrounding environment to increase the likelihood of acknowledgeable failure. This included increased enforcement efforts in the community (labeled as *party patrols* by local police); increased sanctions and adjudication for fraternities and other edgework communities that emphasized emergency calls for service without the threat of university sanction; more severe sanctions for peers who did not seek medical attention for individuals who displayed acute intoxication symptoms; and ongoing discussion of risk and normative behaviors across the campus community to emphasize the distinction between the behaviors of edgework communities and the general population. These discussions took many forms, including student forums, cocurricular activities, social norms advertising campaigns, student newspaper articles, and debates held on campus. The campus adopted a definition of "high-risk drinking" that focused on negative consequences rather than on amount consumed. Acute intoxication was expressed as the problematic behavior (Newman et al., 2006).

These efforts have yielded small but significant changes in binge drinking rates among these groups but have had more profound effects on the practices of these groups and the likelihood of tragic events, although they still occur on occasion. Efforts to work with student group leaders to process these events as lessons in failed edgework and the need for additional controls across the membership are ongoing.

Building trust with these edgework communities remains the most difficult challenge, as traditional public health approaches have led many of these groups to believe that the removal of the group or the elimination of risk-taking activity is the ultimate goal of the initiative. Yet the use of peer leaders has allowed prevention professionals to focus trust building on a smaller target, encouraging these students to adopt prevention practices in order to preserve the community.

Equally successful has been the sanctioned counseling of individual students who "fail" at high-risk substance abuse. Most colleges and universities now encourage collaborations between judicial affairs and alcohol counseling staff who sanction students cited for an alcohol or drug policy violation or students who needed emergency medical assistance to attend sessions where the failure can be discussed in light of the students' overall goals and needs. In such cases, failure can be acknowledged, and the individual can be guided in decisions regarding the appropriateness of edgework community membership, other social group options, and future behavior based on the identified limits of skill and experience. Modification of substance use is then seen as a route toward success, increasing the likelihood of adoption.

Conclusions

We began by observing that the more knowledge edgeworkers acquire about the dangers of an activity, the more alluring it becomes for them. After considering some of the social psychological, historical, and societal conditions that propel individuals toward more intense forms of voluntary risk taking, we stressed the central role of skill development in differentiating edgework from mere sensation seeking. Considering possibilities for effective risk communication targeted toward edgework communities, we proposed working within the structure of edgework communities, placing emphasis on developing edgeworkers' skills as an alternative to risk prevention, and identifying risk amelioration strategies tailored to the developmental needs of novices. Finally, we pointed to the moral hazard posed for edgeworkers by their expectation of rescue by first responders when their skills desert them and disaster strikes.

The likelihood is that this moral hazard will become more and more acute as advances in skills and technology allow edgeworkers to move ever closer to the edge. One way to arrest this would be for risk communication and health promotion advocates to find ways to include social costs in edgeworkers' estimations of risk and danger. The most compelling solution to the paradox with which we began this chapter may be that the most intelligent edgeworkers will move back from repeated exposure at the edge when they determine that their self-actualization is not worth the extreme social costs of unsuccessful edgework.

Notes

1. The classic expression of this view is Talcott Parsons's (1937) "voluntaristic theory of action," first explicated in his monograph *The Structure of Social Action*.

2. A representative sampling of this research includes criminology (Rajah, 2007), religious studies (Bromley, 2007), aesthetics (Courtney, 2005), social movements (Yang, 2000), sports studies (Laurendeau, 2006), economics (Zwick, 2005), gender studies (Batchelor, 2007), leisure studies (Holyfield, 1997), juvenile delinquency and youth studies (Ferrell, 1995), urban studies (Hayward, 2004), the sociology of deviance (Williams, 2004), drug issues (Valdez & Kaplan, 2007), and the sociology of risk (Tulloch & Lupton, 2003).

3. These features distinguish contemporary forms of volitional risk taking in sports, occupations, interpersonal relations, and so on, from earlier incarnations of some of these same activities in earlier historical periods. Certain high-risk sports (e.g., mountain climbing, downhill skiing) and high-risk occupations (e.g., soldiering, police work) have long histories that obviously predate the broader societal changes discussed in this chapter. However, at the time of Erving Goffman's (1967) famous study of voluntary risk taking in the 1950s and the early 1960s, he noted that participation in these high-risk endeavors was limited, and practitioners tended to be marginal to mainstream culture (p. 267). What has changed since Goffman published his essay is that extreme risk taking has shifted away from the margins and toward the center of contemporary social life in terms of its growth and development, participation rates, and cultural significance. These changes helped inspire the edgework research program.

Suggested Additional Readings

Alaszewski, A. (2006). Health and risk. In P. Taylor-Gooby & J. O. Zinn (Eds.), *Risk in social science*. Oxford, England: Oxford University Press.

Lupton, D. (2013). *Risk*. New York, NY: Routledge.

Lyng, S. (2008). Edgework, risk, and uncertainty. In J. O. Zinn (Ed.), *Social theories of risk and uncertainty: An introduction* (pp. 106–137). Malden, MA: Blackwell.

References

Batchelor, S. A. (2007). "Getting mad wi'it": Risk seeking by young women. In K. Hannah-Moffat & P. O'Malley (Eds.), *Gendered risks* (pp. 205–27). New York, NY: Routledge-Cavendish.

Beck, U. (1992). *The risk society*. London, England: Sage.

Bromley, D. G. (2007). On spiritual edgework: The logic of extreme ritual performance. *Journal for the Scientific Study of Religion, 46*(3), 287–303.

Cho, H., Wilkum, K., King, A., Bernat, J. K., Ruvarac, A., & Xu, H. (2010). Fraternity drinking as edgework: An analysis of perspectives on risk and control. *Health Communication, 25,* 212–220.

Courtney, D. (2005). Edgework and the aesthetic paradigm: Resonances and high hopes. In S. Lyng (Ed.), *Edgework: The sociology of risk taking* (pp. 89–115). New York, NY: Routledge.

DeJong, W., Vince-Whitman, C., Colthurst, T., Cretalle, M., Gilbreath, M., Rosati, M., & Zweig, K. (1998). *Environmental management: A comprehensive strategy for reducing alcohol and other drug use on college campuses.* Newton, MA: Higher Education Center for Alcohol and Other Drug Prevention.

Far, J., & Miller, J. (2003). The small group norms challenging model: Social norms interventions with targeted high risk groups. In H. W. Perkins (Ed.), *The social norms approach to preventing school and college age substance abuse: A handbook for educators, counselors, clinicians.* San Francisco, CA: Jossey-Bass.

Ferrell, J. (1995). Urban graffiti: Crime, control, and resistance. *Youth and Society, 27*(1), 73–92.

Fromme, K., Marlatt, G. A., Baer, J. S., & Kivlahan, D. R. (1994). The alcohol skills training program: A group intervention for young adult drinkers. *Journal of Substance Abuse Treatment, 11*(2), 143–154.

Giddens, A. (1991). *Modernity and self-identity: Self and society in the late modern age.* Cambridge, England: Polity Press.

Goffman, E. (1967). Where the action is. In E. Goffman (Ed.), *Interaction ritual: Essays on face-to-face behavior* (pp. 149–270). Garden City, NY: Doubleday.

Gusfield, J. (1996). *Contested meanings: The construction of alcohol problems.* Madison: University of Wisconsin Press.

Hanson, D. J. (2005). *Preventing alcohol abuse: Alcohol, culture, and control.* Westport, CT: Praeger.

Hayward, K. (2004). *City limits: Crime, consumer culture, and the urban experience.* London, England: Glasshouse Press.

Hingson, R. W., Zha, W., & Weitzman, E. R. (2009). Magnitude of and trends in alcohol-related mortality and morbidity among U.S. college students ages 18–24, 1998–2005. *Journal of Studies on Alcohol and Drugs, S16,* 12–20.

Holyfield, L. (1997). Generating excitement: Experienced emotion in commercial leisure. In R. J. Erickson & B. Cuthbertson-Johnson (Eds.), *Social perspectives on emotion* (Vol. 4, pp. 257–282). Greenwich, CT: JAI Press.

Katz, J. (1988). *The seductions of crime: Moral and sensual attractions in doing evil.* New York, NY: Basic Books.

LaBrie, J. W., Thompson, A. D., Huchting, K., Lac, A., & Buckley, K. (2007). A group motivational interviewing intervention reduces drinking and alcohol-related negative consequences in adjudicated college women. *Addictive Behaviors, 32*(7), 2549–2562.

Lash, S. (1994). Reflexivity and its doubles: Structure, aesthetics, community. In U. Beck, A. Giddens, & S. Lash (Eds.), *Reflexive modernization: Politics, tradition, and aesthetics in the modern social order* (pp. 110–173). Stanford, CA: Stanford University Press.

Laurendeau, J. (2006). "He didn't go in doing a skydive": Sustaining the illusion of control in an edgework activity. *Sociological Perspectives, 49*(4), 583–605.

Lyng, S. (1990). Edgework: A social psychological analysis of voluntary risk taking. *American Journal of Sociology, 95,* 851–886.

Lyng, S. (1993). Dysfunctional risk-taking: Criminal behavior as edgework. In N. J. Bell & R. W. Bell (Eds.), *Adolescent risk-taking* (pp. 107–130). London, England: Sage.

Lyng, S. (2004). Crime, edgework, and corporeal transaction. *Theoretical Criminology, 8*(3), 359–375.

Lyng, S. (2005a). Edgework and the risk-taking experience. In S. Lyng (Ed.), *Edgework: The sociology of risk taking* (pp. 3–16). New York, NY: Routledge.

Lyng, S. (2005b). Sociology at the edge: Social theory and voluntary risk taking. In S. Lyng (Ed.), *Edgework: The sociology of risk taking* (pp. 17–49). New York, NY: Routledge.

Lyng, S. (2008). Risk taking in sport: Edgework and reflexive community. In M. Atkinson & K. Young (Eds.), *Tribal play: Subcultural journeys through sport* (pp. 83–109). Bengley, England: Emerald Group.

Lyng, S. (2012). Existential transcendence in late modernity: Edgework and hermeneutic reflexivity. *Human Studies, 35*(3), 401–414.

Lyng, S., & Matthews, R. (2007). Risk, edgework, and masculinities. In K. Hannah-Moffat & P. O'Malley (Eds.), *Gendered risks* (pp. 75–97). London, England: Routledge-Cavendish.

Lyng, S., & Snow, D. A. (1986). Vocabularies of motive and high risk behavior: The case of skydiving. In E. J. Lawler (Ed.), *Advances in group processes* (Vol. 3, pp. 157–179). Greenwich, CT: JAI Press.

Marlatt, G. A., Baer, J. S., Kivlahan, D. R., Dimeff, L. A., Larimer, M. E., Quigley, L. A., . . . Williams, E. (1998). Screening and brief intervention for high-risk college student drinkers: Results from a 2-year follow-up assessment. *Journal of Consulting and Clinical Psychology, 66*, 604–615.

Martens, M. P., Smith, A. E., & Murphy, J. G. (2013). The efficacy of single-component brief motivational interventions among at-risk college drinkers. *Journal of Consulting and Clinical Psychology, 81*(4), 691–701.

McCabe, S. E., Teter, C. J., Boyd, C. J., Knight, J. R., & Wechsler, H. (2005). Nonmedical use of prescription opioids among U.S. college students: Prevalence and correlates from a national survey. *Addictive Behaviors, 30*, 789–805.

Miller, W. J. (2005). Adolescents on the edge: The sensual side of delinquency. In S. Lyng (Ed.), *Edgework: The sociology of risk taking* (pp. 153–171). New York, NY: Routledge.

Milovanovic, D. (2005). Edgework: A subjective and structural model for negotiating boundaries. In S. Lyng (Ed.), *Edgework: The sociology of risk taking* (pp. 51–74). New York, NY: Routledge.

Newman, I. M., Shell, D. F., Major, L. J., & Workman, T. A. (2006). Use of policy, education, and enforcement to reduce binge drinking among university students: The NU directions project. *International Journal of Drug Policy, 17*, 339–349.

Parsons, T. (1937). *The structure of social action*. New York, NY: McGraw-Hill.

Perkins, H. W. (2003). *The social norms approach to preventing school and college age substance abuse: A handbook for educators, counselors, and clinicians*. San Francisco, CA: Jossey-Bass.

Rajah, V. (2007). Resistance as edgework in violent intimate relationships of drug-involved women. *British Journal of Criminology, 47*(2), 196–213.

Reith, G. (2005). On the edge: Drugs and consumption of risk in late modernity. In S. Lyng (Ed.), *Edgework: The sociology of risk taking* (pp. 227–246). New York, NY: Routledge.

Shewan, D., Delgarno, P., & Reith, G. (2000). Perceived risk and risk reduction among ecstacy users: The role of drug, set and setting. *International Journal of Drug Policy, 10*, 431–453.

Thompson, H. S. (1966). *Hell's Angels: A strange and terrible saga*. New York, NY: Ballantine Books.

Tulloch, J., & Lupton, D. (2003). *Risk and everyday life*. London, England: Sage.

Valdez, A., & Kaplan, C. (2007). Conditions that increase drug market involvement: The invitational edge and the case of Mexicans in South Texas. *Journal of Drug Issues, 37*(4), 893–918.

Weber, M. (1958). *The protestant ethic and the spirit of capitalism* (T. Parsons, Trans.). New York, NY: Scribner.

Williams, C. R. (2004). Reclaiming the expressive subject: Deviance and the art of non-normativity. *Deviant Behavior, 25*(3), 233–254.

Wolfe, T. (1979). *The right stuff*. New York, NY: Farrar, Straus, & Giroux.

Workman, T. A. (2000). Pleasure versus public health: Controlling collegiate binge drinking. In A. Thio & T. Calhoun (Eds.), *Readings in deviant behavior* (2nd ed., pp. 137–144). Boston, MA: Allyn & Bacon.

Workman, T. A. (2001a). Finding the meanings of college drinking: An analysis of fraternity drinking stories. *Health Communication, 13*(2), 427–448.

Workman, T. A. (2001b). *An intertextual analysis of the college alcohol culture* (Unpublished dissertation). University of Nebraska, Lincoln.

Workman, T. A. (2005a). Death as representative anecdote in the construction of the collegiate binge drinking problem. In L. M. Harter, P. M. Japp, & C. S. Beck (Eds.), *Constructing our health: The implications of narrative for enacting illness and wellness* (pp. 131–152). Mahwah, NJ: Lawrence Erlbaum.

Workman, T. A. (2005b). Drinking stories as learning tools: Socially situated experiential learning and popular culture. In L. Lederman & L. P. Stewart (Eds.), *Changing the culture of college drinking: A socially situated health communication campaign*. Cresskill, NJ: Hampton Press.

Workman, T. A. (2008). To the edge and back: Edgework and collegiate drug use. In R. Chapman (Ed.), *Collegiate drug use: A new look at an old issue* (pp. 25–48). Glassboro, NJ: Rowan University Center for Addiction Studies.

Yang, G. (2000). Achieving emotions in collective action: Emotional processes and movement mobilization in the 1989 Chinese student movement. *Sociological Quarterly, 41*(4), 593–614.

Zuckerman, M. (1994). *Behavior expressions and biosocial bases of sensation seeking*. Cambridge, England: Cambridge University Press.

Zwick, D. (2005). Where the action is: Internet stock trading as edgework. *Journal of Computer-Mediated Communication, 11*(1), 22–43.

SECTION 5

Risk Communication Messages

CHAPTER 11

Numeric Communication of Risk

Torsten Reimer, Christina Jones, and Christine Skubisz

Millions of dollars have been spent to convince American women to repeatedly undergo breast cancer screenings and American men to participate in prostate cancer screenings. The gains of both screenings have been questioned in recent years, though, and recommendations to participate have been withdrawn or reformulated with much more hesitation and often by including a reference to potential risks. From a risk-communication perspective, it is telling to see that campaigns in favor of those screenings have often been based on statistics and numbers that systematically misrepresented risks and misinformed the public. As a prominent example, the advertising tactics used during Susan G. Komen's annual breast cancer awareness month have been analyzed and found to be misleading. In an August 2012 article published in the *British Medical Journal*, Dr. Lisa Schwartz and Dr. Steven Woloshin, both professors of medicine at the Geisel School of Medicine at Dartmouth College, argued that Komen's campaign is best known for promoting mammography screening despite its unclear benefits. The pink-ribbon campaign inaccurately overstates the benefits of mammograms without mentioning the risks. According to Woloshin and Schwartz (2012), "unfortunately, there is a big mismatch between the strength of evidence in support of screening and the strength of Komen's advocacy for it" (p. 345).

The benefits and harms of mammography are so evenly balanced that a major U.S. network of patient and professional groups, the National Breast Cancer Coalition, concluded that there is insufficient evidence to recommend for or against universal mammography for women of any age-group. Mammography's benefits have become an often-debated topic since 2009, when the group of medical advisers who recommended government screening guidelines, the U.S. Preventive Services Task Force, advised against the scans for low-risk women in their 40s. The group concluded that the benefits of screening women in their 40s did not outweigh the risks from unnecessary treatments (Woloshin & Schwartz, 2012).

Komen's breast cancer awareness advertisements only state the benefits of mammography when telling women to get screened and give women no information about the risks associated with screening. One ad, for example, stated,

"What's the key to surviving breast cancer? You" and went on to say the 5-year survival rate for breast cancer caught early is 98%, compared with only 23% survival when it is not. However, the comparison in survival rates between screened and unscreened women is biased. Overdiagnosing cancers that are too slow growing to ever cause a problem skew survival statistics, because the women would have survived after 5 years, regardless of a mammogram. In terms of actual benefit, mammograms can reduce the chances of a woman in her 50s dying of breast cancer over the next 10 years from 0.53% to 0.46%, a difference of 0.07 percentage points. However, the ad claims a 75 percentage point difference. Woloshin and Schwartz (2012) note, "If there were an Oscar for misleading statistics, using survival statistics to judge the benefit of screening would win a lifetime achievement award hands down" (p. 346).

There are profound doubts regarding the benefits of mammography. Where the risk–benefit ratio of mammography is questionable, the twin test of mammography—prostate cancer screening—has seen even more basic critiques in recent years due to the lower performance of the test. A study published in July 2012 in *Cancer* set forth to determine how many cases of prostate cancer might be missed until they metastasized (spread to another area of the body) if prostate specific antigen (PSA) testing were eliminated. Scosyrev, Wu, Mohile, and Messing (2012) analyzed data from the Surveillance, Epidemiology, and End Results Program to determine the prevalence of men who were diagnosed with metastatic prostate cancer as their initial diagnosis, rather than a less invasive form of cancer. Scosyrev et al. (2012) advocated that PSA screening is based on the faulty assumption that cancer starts small, becomes localized in the prostate, advances to nearby regions of the body, becomes metastatic, and then kills. If this were the case, screening studies should have shown that more lives were saved because of the PSA test. According to the authors, the screening studies suggest that there is no difference in mortality. In addition, the largest difference between expected and observed

metastatic cancer was in older age-groups; however, patients who are over 80 years old often have many other health problems that lead to death before even aggressive prostate cancer. On both sides of the debate, researchers agree that men should be informed of the risks and possible benefits of PSA screening and subsequent treatment before they start the process, a challenge when contradictory reports abound.

Scosyrev et al.'s (2012) finding arrived just months after the U.S. Preventative Service Task Force had issued a recommendation *against* using PSA screening, which afforded PSA screening a grade of "D," meaning it does more harm than good for most men. The Food and Drug Administration approved PSA screening in 1986 as a diagnostic test to detect prostate cancer, but it has been controversial from the beginning. The screening has a high false-positive rate because PSA levels rise from nonmalignant prostate growth. Additionally, many prostate cancers grow so slowly that they will never cause problems, and it is nearly impossible to tell which cancers need to be treated and which can be left alone. Surgery or radiation used in treatment can also produce incontinence or impotence. As with any surgery, there is a small risk of death or serious complications, and the procedure is painful, even under the best of circumstances. The task force analyzed several large studies and determined that the benefits of screening and treatment did not outweigh the risks.

As with numerous campaigns for mammography, for-profit as well as not-for-profit organizations have run many campaigns to sway men into participating in prostate cancer screenings (see, e.g., Welch, 2006, for a critical discussion). In the case of mammography as well as prostate cancer screenings, the success of those campaigns is questionable because the benefits and risks have often been presented in a distorted way.

We want to draw attention to four widespread problems and misrepresentations in the communication of quantitative risks that have a high prevalence, particularly in screening campaigns—(1) the presentation of conditional probabilities, (2) the reference class problem, (3) misunderstandings that result from providing information on relative risk reduction, and (4) the use of survival rather than mortality statistics. In all four problem areas, misrepresentations can greatly alter perceptions of risk. Moreover, different from the widespread view that hurdles in the communication of risk are mainly or even exclusively related to the recipient of risk messages, these problems demonstrate that risk communicators are a "serious risk factor" in the risk communication process. The literature on those hurdles offers a theory-based understanding of the underlying mechanisms. Last but not least, there is an alternative way to present information, which can greatly improve understanding. Thus, we summarize research on four communication tools that can help communicators to achieve the goal of informing their audience about quantitative risks. We illustrate the problem areas by using PSA screenings as an example.

Overview of Probability and Frequency Formats

Although presenting numbers in numerically different ways does not change the underlying mathematical nature of the statistics, presentation formats are not equivalent with regard to how message receivers cognitively process and respond to them (Hoffrage, Lindsey, Hertwig, & Gigerenzer, 2000; Skubisz, 2010; Slovic, Monahan, & MacGregor, 2000; see also Peters et al., 2006; Peters et al., 2009). These formats serve as frames through which risk information is perceived, processed, and used in decision making. The most commonly used representations of statistical risk information are probabilities and frequencies.

A probability is a numerical expression of the likelihood that a particular event or outcome will occur. Probability values range from 0 (an outcome will definitely not occur) to 1 (an outcome will definitely occur). In the statement, "there is a .063 probability that a man has prostate cancer," the risk is presented as a probability. Probabilities

can alternatively be expressed as percentages, such as "6.3% of men have prostate cancer." When explaining the results of a PSA test, the screening test for prostate cancer, a doctor could say,

> 81% of men who have a positive test result do not have prostate cancer and 19% of men who have a positive test result have prostate cancer. Therefore, the chance that you have prostate cancer, if you test positive, is about 19%. (Schröder et al., 2009; see Figure 11.1)

Alternatively, a natural frequency is the number of times an event occurs within a sample. Often called naturally sampled frequencies, these numbers result from counting specific cases (e.g., fatal car accidents or cancer deaths) within a specific reference class (e.g., teen drivers or men over age 50). A frequency is often coupled with restrictions concerning the time interval during which the counting has been done; for example, the number of people who die of a specific cancer in a specific year in the United States. A simple frequency is a natural frequency that has been scaled down to smaller numerical values. This is typically done to facilitate cognitive processing. Going back to the man receiving his PSA test results, his doctor could use frequencies for a sample of, say, 1,000 men to explain what a positive result means. The doctor could say,

> Consider 1,000 men with the same prostate cancer risk factors that you have. Of these 1,000 men, about 63 will have cancer. Out of the 63 with cancer, about 13 will test positive. Out of the 937 men who do not have cancer, about 56 will also test positive. Therefore, the chance that you have prostate cancer, if you test positive, is about 1 in 5 (13 out of 13 + 56; see Panel B in Figure 11.1).

When presented with frequencies, physicians as well as patients are better able to recognize the relative degree of uncertainty regarding the conclusions that can be drawn from test results (Casscells, Schoenberger, & Grayboys, 1978; Eddy, 1982; Gigerenzer, 2002; Gigerenzer,

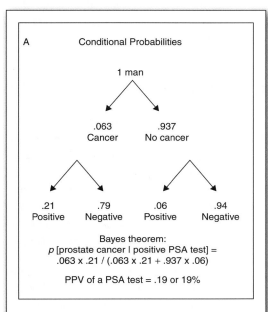

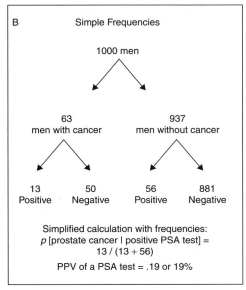

> **Figure 11.1** Representations in the Form of Probabilities and Simple Frequencies

Note: According to Schröder et al. (2009), the base rate for prostate cancer in the general population is 6.3% (see also Arkes & Gaissmaier, 2012).

PSA = prostate specific antigen; PPV = positive predictive value.

Hoffrage, & Ebert, 1998; Skubisz, Reimer, & Hoffrage, 2009). It is important to note that an isolated number (numerator) without a denominator, such as 13 people with cancer who test positive, is not, by itself, a natural frequency. A numerical value becomes a frequency because of its relationship to other numbers that result from counting different cases within the same sample. The denominator must be included when frequencies are presented.

Frequencies Facilitate Statistical Reasoning

There is a growing body of research indicating that patients understand a positive test result (and other conditional probabilities) more easily when the numbers are presented as frequencies such as 50 in 1,000, as opposed to a probability like .05. Brase (2008) proposed a theoretical ordering of numerical formats based on characteristics of the numbers that are used. On one end of the continuum is information that is not encountered in naturalistic environments, is normalized to an artificial reference class (between 0 and 1), is not flexible in its usage, and is not conceptually easy to use. Probabilities and percentages contain all of these disadvantageous characteristics. On the other end of the continuum are formats that are encountered in naturalistic environments, are not normalized, contain information about a reference class, are flexible in usage, and are conceptually easy to use. Naturally sampled frequencies anchor this end of the continuum. Simplified frequencies that have been normalized or scaled down to smaller values, but otherwise include all of the other advantageous features discussed above, also exist on this end of the continuum.

In general, the computations that derive from natural frequencies make it simpler to understand what a positive test result, or other pieces of important numerical information, actually mean. Gigerenzer (1991) argued that people will make rational decisions if the decision is framed in a way that coincides with cognitive mechanisms innately in place in the human mind. Referred to as the *frequency hypothesis* (Gigerenzer & Hoffrage, 1995) or the *evolutionary argument* (Amitani, 2008; Gigerenzer & Hoffrage, 1995), this approach argued that information represented as frequencies was more adaptive over the course of evolutionary history than information represented as percentages. Therefore, humans have built-in mental algorithms to solve frequency problems but do not have these mechanisms for other numerical formats (see also Cosmides & Tooby, 1996; Gigerenzer et al., 1998). This pattern of appreciating frequencies over percentages occurred because frequencies, counts that are not normalized, were more useful to people in their natural environment (Brase, 2002; Gigerenzer & Hoffrage, 1995).

Three main arguments have been provided for why frequency information has been more adaptive than other numerical formats (Brase, 2002). First, people learn from direct experience (Gigerenzer & Hoffrage, 1995; Kleiter, 1994; see Chapter 2, this volume). Consider a physician who observes, case by case, whether or not her patients have a new disease and whether the outcome of a diagnostic test is positive or negative. Frequency information is privileged because this is how people encounter information in the world—people make sense of the world around them by counting events or occurrences (Brase, 2002; Gigerenzer & Hoffrage, 1995; Tooby & Cosmides, 1998). Second, Brase (2002) argued that frequency information is privileged because new frequency information can be easily, immediately, and usefully incorporated with old frequency information. The human mind is a database of information, and it is easier to update this database with frequency information than with percentage information (see Cosmides & Tooby, 1996). Using a method of natural sampling, people count occurrences of events as they encounter them and store the information as natural frequencies for later use (Brase, 2002; see Chapter 2, this volume). Finally, data in a frequency format retain valuable information that is lost in other formats. Specifically, sample sizes are retained with frequency information. For example, a percentage (e.g., 50%) or a likelihood (e.g., .50) could be based on a sample of 1 in 2, 25 in 50, or 500,000 in 1 million. The number that represents the reference class, the category of events to which a probability applies, is preserved with a frequency format.

The Reference Class Problem

With any presentation of risk information, the primary source of confusion for the message receiver surrounds the question of the reference class being discussed (Gigerenzer & Edwards, 2003; Gigerenzer, Hertwig, van den Broek, Fasolo, & Katsikopoulos, 2005). A reference class encompasses the class of events to which a probability applies (von Mises, 1939). Consequently, a reference class must be selected carefully. Each reference class gives the probability of an outcome a different meaning. For example, consider the claim that "smoking accounts for 30% of all cancer deaths." It is possible to interpret this statement in very different ways. Person *A* may understand this message as "of all people who will die of cancer, 30% will die of lung cancer." Person *B* may think that "of all people who will die of cancer, 30% are smokers." Person *C* may interpret it as "of all people who die of cancer, 30% only die because they are smokers." Person *D* may understand the message as "30% of smokers will die of cancer." Finally, Person *E* may think that "30% of all people who have lung cancer will die from it." Persons *A*, *B*, and *C*'s reference classes include all people who die of cancer; Person *D*'s reference class refers to people who smoke, and Person *E* considers only people with lung cancer.

The issue of providing meaning is commonly referred to as the *problem of the reference class* (Reichenbach, 1949) and is one of the primary reasons why statistics can be manipulated with such ease. Statistical inferences depend on how objects, people, or events are categorized. The problem lies in the fact that there is a large number of possible characteristics for which to classify information (Venn, 1876). This is coupled with the fact that no universal, guiding principle exists for valuing particular characteristics (Cheng, 2009). The reference class problem is not restricted to the field of medicine but plagues numerous disciplines and practitioners who depend on numerical information for decision making. Numerical risk information is often central to legal proceedings, for example. The question is which comparison group and, subsequently, which statistic is used in predictions of violence, property valuation, and DNA evidence, among others (Cheng, 2009).

The meaning of a probability hinges on the choice of a reference class. Thus, as a best practice, messages should clearly state which reference class is being described. Information provided as a frequency includes a reference class inherently, by nature of providing the denominator. That being said, care should be taken to ensure that the stated reference class is clearly and precisely described. Simply providing a number does not specify the reference class being discussed or solve the reference class problem. Probability information does not, by the nature of the information, include a reference class. If this format must be presented, a reference class should be explicitly provided alongside the numbers being discussed. In the smoking example above, for instance, one of the specific interpretations (A to E) that provide a reference class should be given rather than the ambiguous statement "smoking accounts for 30% of all cancer deaths."

Conditional Probabilities, Prior Probabilities, Posterior Probabilities, Bayes Theorem

The broad category of probabilities can be divided into prior probabilities and posterior probabilities. A prior probability (the base rate or prevalence) is the probability of an event before any new evidence is obtained. Take the .063 probability that a man will develop prostate cancer (see Figure 11.1). This is a prior probability

for prostate cancer. Conversely, a posterior probability is an updated prior probability—a conditional probability that includes additional evidence or new information. This is sometimes aptly called a *posttest probability*.

In the context of prostate cancer, the additional information or update might be a positive PSA result. A man's prior probability can be updated to a posttest probability by taking the result of a PSA test into account. After a screening test, the primary question of interest is, Given a positive (or a negative) test result, what is the probability of disease? Two values are of particular interest. (1) The positive predictive value (PPV) is the probability of disease (in this case, cancer) among patients with a positive test result. (2) The negative predictive value (NPV) is the probability of no disease (no cancer) among patients with a negative test result.

A man who is given a positive PSA test result has a posttest probability of 19% (p(CANCER | POS) = .19). This is the PPV of the test—the probability that the man actually has prostate cancer given that the test result is positive. The prevalence of prostate cancer in the general population (p(CANCER)) is about .063 (Schröder et al., 2009). Among those who have cancer, the PSA test detects the cancer about 21% of the time, (p(POS | CANCER) = .21). This percentage—the sensitivity of the test—is exceptionally low. Screening tests cannot detect disease with absolute accuracy. Like many screening tests, the PSA test produces false alarms or false positives. If someone does not have cancer, the test yields a positive result in about 6% of such cases (p(POS | NO CANCER) = .06). A doctor could use these numbers to compute the PPV of the test by using the Bayes theorem (Gigerenzer & Hoffrage, 1995; see Panel A in Figure 11.1). However, the information is much easier to process if the numbers are presented in the form of simple frequencies (see Panel B in Figure 11.1). In a sample of 1,000 men, we expect that 69 (13 + 56) test positive. Out of those 69 men, 13 (19%) will have cancer. Most men (56 out of 69; 81%) with a positive test result will not suffer from cancer.

Risk Reduction: Absolute Versus Relative Risks

Information about relative risk describes how two or more risks relate to one another or how a particular risk in one group compares with the same risk in another group (see Gigerenzer, 2002; Sackett, Haynes, Guyatt, & Tugwell, 1991). Risk communicators commonly use this type of information to highlight the risks of certain activities or lifestyles (e.g., Does living next to a nuclear power plant increase the risk of getting leukemia?) or the effectiveness of diagnostic instruments or therapies (e.g., Does breast cancer screening reduce mortality or how useful are oral adjuvant therapies?). In all these cases, researchers compare two or more groups of people with each other with respect to how often a predefined outcome occurs. For example, when seeking information about the benefits of prostate cancer screening, with respect to the risk of dying from prostate cancer, a typical presentation of this information is: An ongoing clinical trial has reported that for men 50 to 74 years old, PSA screening may reduce prostate cancer mortality by 21% (see Schröder et al., 2012). This statement includes information about the relative risk reduction, that undergoing PSA screening may reduce a man's risk of dying from prostate cancer within the next 11 years by 21%. This number, 21%, is derived from a ratio. The proportion of prostate cancer deaths among men who undergo PSA screening (treatment group, T) divided by, or expressed relative to, the proportion of deaths among men who do not receive PSA screening (control group, C).

$$\text{Relative risk reduction} = 1 - \frac{O_T / N_T}{O_C / N_C}.$$

O_T and O_C refer to the number of critical outcomes within a defined time period (participation in screening for 11 years) and a control group (no participation in screening during these same 11 years), respectively. N_T and N_C represent the number of people in the treatment and in the control group, respectively. If the proportion of men dying of prostate cancer in the treatment group is identical to the number of men in the control group who die, then the relative risk reduction of the treatment is zero (or 0% when expressed in percentages). Hence, the two complements, namely the two survival rates, are also identical. Conversely, if the proportion of men dying of prostate cancer in the treatment group is reduced to zero, then the relative risk reduction is 1 (or 100% when expressed in percentages).

Alternatively, the benefits of PSA screening can be framed in terms of *absolute risk reduction*. This is the proportion of men who did not participate in screening and die from prostate cancer minus the proportion of men who die despite being screened:

$$\text{Absolute risk reduction} = \frac{O_C}{N_C} - \frac{O_T}{N_T}.$$

When the benefits of PSA testing are presented in the form of absolute risk reduction, the numbers look quite different. In absolute terms, the risk reduction is 1.07 deaths per 1,000 men at a median follow-up of 11 years. The inverse of the absolute risk reduction is the number needed to treat or number needed to screen in order to save one life within a specified time interval. This means that within an 11-year time frame, 1,055 men must be invited for screening, and 37 cancers need to be detected to prevent 1 death from prostate cancer.

The relative risk reduction (in the present example, 21%) looks more impressive than the absolute risk reduction (.07%). Yet most health expert groups inform patients about the benefits of cancer screening almost exclusively in terms of the relative risk reduction (Kurzenhäuser, 2003; Kurzenhäuser & Lücking, 2004). Perhaps not surprisingly, patients more likely prefer an intervention or treatment if it is advertised in terms of relative risk reduction than in terms of absolute risk reduction (Bucher, Weinbacher, & Gyr, 1994; Ghosh & Ghosh, 2005; Gigerenzer, 2002; Heller, Sandars, Patterson, & McElduff, 2004; Sarfati, Howden-Chapman, Woodward, & Salmond, 1998). Also granting agencies are more likely to fund research on the effectiveness of interventions if the benefits of those interventions have been communicated in terms of relative rather than absolute risk reduction (Fahey, Griffiths, & Peters, 1995). People make more appropriate decisions about whether or not to accept a particular medical treatment when risk reduction is provided in absolute rather than in relative terms (Hembroff, Holmes-Rovner, & Wills, 2004; Sheridan, Pignone, & Lewis, 2003).

Importantly, both absolute and relative representations are mathematically correct. Yet each representation suggests different amounts of benefit or harm, potentially elicits different expectations, and can ultimately lead to different decisions (Hanoch, 2004). Some representations, such as relative risk, typically do not specify the reference class or do not specify any base rate information regarding the reference class. Absolute risk, or both types of information, should be provided whenever possible (Gigerenzer & Edwards, 2003; Paling, 2003).

Survival Rates

In addition to the often misleading presentation of relative risk reduction, screenings are regularly advertised by providing information on survival rates, which are misleading also. To calculate a 5-year survival rate for a specific cancer, the number of patients diagnosed with this cancer still alive after 5 years will be divided by the total number of patients diagnosed with that cancer. For example, the 5-year survival rate for non-Hodgkin's lymphoma is 67%. For every 100 people diagnosed with non-Hodgkin's lymphoma, 67 survived for at least 5 years after diagnosis. Conversely, 33 people died within 5 years of a non-Hodgkin's lymphoma diagnosis. Note that survival rates can be expressed in the form of percentages or frequencies, and, while a 5-year survival rate is the most common survival statistic, there is nothing special about 5 years. The statistic can be calculated for any time frame (Gigerenzer, Gaissmaier, Kurz-Milcke, Schwartz, & Woloshin, 2008). Like with other reference classes, though, the time frame

can greatly influence the numbers and, thus, the comparisons between different classes of people.

Survival rates are often quoted to demonstrate the value of screening. Why are they misleading in the context of screenings? Screening profoundly biases survival in two ways. First, screening affects the timing of diagnosis. Particularly, survival rates can be increased by setting the time of diagnosis *earlier*, even if no life is prolonged or saved (*lead-time bias*). Second, screening affects the nature of diagnosis by including people with nonprogressive cancer (*overdiagnosis bias*).

The lead-time bias can be exemplified with the following example (see Woloshin, Schwartz, & Welch, 2008): Consider a group of individuals with cancer who will all die at age 70; if they receive their first diagnosis at age 67, their 10-year survival rate will be 0%. But if these same individuals had been screened and the cancer was found before they had symptoms, for example, at age 57, then their 10-year survival rate would be 100%, despite the fact that death will still come at 70. Thus, earlier diagnosis always increases survival rates, but it does not necessarily entail that life is prolonged—a common misperception. The lead-time bias may even be exaggerated when more efficacious screening processes are used, for instance, a CT (computerized testing) scan instead of symptom checks. Thus, screening can lead to high survival rates without actually saving lives.

The second phenomenon that leads to spuriously high survival rates is the *overdiagnosis bias*. Overdiagnosis, the detection of pseudodisease, in the context of cancer entails screening-detected abnormalities that meet the pathological definition of cancer but will never progress to cause symptoms in the patient's lifetime. Due to these biases, changes in 5-year survival rates have no reliable relationship to changes in mortality; knowing about changes in survival tells one nothing about changes in mortality (Welch, Schwartz, & Woloshin, 2000). Thus, in the context of screening, survival rates are always a biased metric (Gigerenzer et al., 2008).

Unfortunately, physicians often base their screening recommendations and judgments of a screening's effectiveness on the 5-year survival rate. After presenting physicians with both, survival rates and disease-specific mortality rates, for a screened and an unscreened group of prostate cancer patients, Wegwarth, Gaissmaier, and Gigerenzer (2009) found that across both versions, 66% of the physicians recommended screening when presented with 5-year survival rates, but only 8% of the same physicians made the recommendation when presented with the disease-specific mortality rates. Also, the 5-year survival rates made considerably more physicians (78%) judge the screening to be effective than any other condition and led to the highest overestimations of benefit.

When used for the correct purpose, survival statistics can be helpful (Woloshin et al., 2008). This is true when used to inform a patient regarding his or her individual prognosis and when used as an outcome in a randomized trial. Survival statistics can help a patient evaluate the patient's prognosis and estimate the chance that he or she will survive for a particular amount of time. Statistics are most useful for this purpose when they are based on similar others, particularly in light of the stage of disease development. Survival statistics can also be helpful when interpreting the results of randomized trials comparing a treatment group with a control group. If we assume that randomization has made the two groups similar in every way, then an increased survival rate after a fixed amount of time for those receiving the treatment would indicate it is efficacious over a lessened survival rate for those not using the treatment. However, when used in the context of screenings, mortality rates are more informative (Woloshin et al., 2008).

To see why *mortality rates* are more instructive, imagine a group of patients all diagnosed with cancer on the same day. The proportion of these patients who are still alive 5 years later is the 5-year survival rate. To calculate a mortality rate, imagine another group of people not defined by a cancer diagnosis. The proportion of people in the group who are dead after 1 year (the typical time frame for mortality statistics) is the mortality rate. The key difference to notice between these two kinds of statistics is the word *diagnosed*, which appears in the numerator and denominator of survival statistics but nowhere in the definition of mortality. Ultimately, survival statistics are less informative because they do not tell us whether fewer people are dying from cancer.

As with other problematic numerical presentations, survival rates are often misinterpreted by experts, including physicians. In a study with primary care physicians in the United States, Wegwarth, Schwartz, Woloshin, Gaissmaier, and Gigerenzer (2012) explored to what extent physicians understand cancer screening statistics. The authors report evidence that many primary care physicians are swayed by irrelevant information and base their risk perceptions on survival statistics. Physicians were more enthusiastic about a screening test when they were told that the test increased the 5-year survival rate from 68% to 99% than when they were told that it reduced the cancer mortality from 2 to 1.6 in 1,000 participants. When confronted with survival rates, 69% of physicians recommended the screening compared with 23% when evidence was reported in terms of mortality rates. The vast majority of physicians did not distinguish between irrelevant and relevant screening evidence when asked general knowledge questions. The authors come to the following conclusion: "Most primary care physicians mistakenly interpreted improved survival and increased detection with screening as evidence that screening saves lives. Few correctly recognized that only reduced mortality in a randomized trial constitutes evidence of the benefit of screening" (Wegwarth et al., 2012, p. 341).

Reflections for Theory and Research

Risk information can be presented in many different ways. More research is needed to better understand which format is most effective and appropriate for which audience, situation, and goal. Risk communication can serve several goals including the goals to inform consumers, to persuade, and to build trust (see Weinstein, 1999).

Certain formats may appeal more to specific audiences and may be better suited for certain purposes and goals than others. For example, research indicates that risk communication is more effective when it is tailored to message receivers' numeracy level and cultural background (Lipkus, Samsa, & Rimer, 2001; Peters, 2012; Peters et al., 2006; Reyna, Nelson, Han, & Dieckmann, 2009). More research is needed to improve our understanding of whether effects of frequency formats generalize across different audiences.

Oftentimes, risk communication has not only intended but also unintended effects. Cho and Salmon (2007) offered a typology of unintended effects of health communication campaigns that also applies to risk communication. Unintended effects can include obfuscation, dissonance, boomerang, epidemic of apprehension, desensitization, culpability, opportunity cost, social reproduction, social norming, enabling, and system activation (see Cho & Salmon, 2007). More research is needed to explore the breadth of relevant effects of specific representation formats, in particular because possible unintended effects are often unnoticed. There is some evidence that representation formats can have intended as well as unintended effects. We summarized research in our chapter demonstrating that the presentation of quantitative risk information in a frequency format can greatly increase the accuracy of judgments, in particular when statistics refer to conditional or posterior probabilities (Gigerenzer & Edwards, 2003). At the same time, there is evidence that the use of frequency formats can also have unintended effects—effects that may be difficult to notice. Specifically, Peters, Hart, and Fraenkel (2010) observed that participants low in numeracy perceived a medicine as *more risky* when information about side effects was presented using frequencies rather than percentages. The authors suggest that the frequency format may have elicited greater emotional imagery compared with the more abstract percentage format. The hypothesis that frequency formats elicit more vivid images than probabilities and percentages has been supported by other studies also (Peters, 2012;

see also Chapter 3, this volume). Thus, a specific presentation format may facilitate the accurate perception of quantitative risk information and help a receiver to cognitively understand and interpret quantitative risks. However, the same presentation may also elicit strong feelings (Peters, 2012; see Chapter 3, this volume), which may affect risk perception and decision making. These effects may be moderated by characteristics of the receiver, such as a receiver's numeracy level (see Peters, 2012; Peters et al., 2010).

From a theoretical as well as practical perspective, it is important to further study intended as well as unintended effects of different presentation formats.

Recommendations for Practice

Risk communication can be a risky endeavor. According to Fischhoff (2012), to be considered adequate, risk communication must pass three tests: (1) It must contain the information that users need, (2) it must connect users with that information, and (3) the message has to be understood by users. We focused in our chapter on the last aspect and described a number of hurdles that can prevent receivers of quantitative risk information from understanding and appropriately interpreting risk information. Fortunately, evidence-based tools have been developed that can help overcome the described hurdles. Some of the obstacles that we described in our chapter can be avoided or elevated with proper training about the interpretation and appropriate use of statistical information. Whenever feasible, communicators should translate conditional probabilities into frequencies to make the statistics more understandable. Sedlmeier and Gigerenzer (2001) demonstrated that training people to encode information in terms of natural frequencies can improve the accuracy of their probability judgments.

Moreover, if the goal is to inform an audience, risks should also be communicated in terms of natural frequencies rather than in terms of probabilities to give people a better chance to realistically assess their magnitudes. At a minimum, both types of information should be provided (Edwards, Elwyn, & Gwyn, 1999; Gigerenzer & Edwards, 2003; Paling, 2003; Sackett, 1996).

In addition to proper skills training, risk communicators should adapt their quantitative messages to their audience and monitor if message receivers understand the message. Freimuth, Linnan, and Potter (2000) suggested that effective communication must identify receiver characteristics; deliver accurate, scientifically based messages from credible sources; and reach audiences through familiar channels. If the message arouses fear or other strong emotions (see Chapter 3, this volume), the communicator should provide ways to alleviate the fear.

Fagerlin and Peters (2012) provided a state-of-the art list of recommendations for practitioners that suggests keeping denominators and time frames constant when comparing several risks (see also Gigerenzer & Gray, 2011). It is difficult for receivers to compare risks that use different denominators (e.g., 5 in 100 vs. 70 in 1,000) or fractions and decimals (e.g., .5 in 10,000). Whole numbers are easier to understand (e.g., 5 in 100 or 7 in 1,000). Moreover, the authors stress one aspect that might be easily overlooked by risk communicators: It is critical that providers of risk information think very carefully about which information is central to the argument being made and help receivers focus on that important information.

When information about risk reduction is provided, the following two questions provide excellent guidance for providers as well as receivers. Woloshin and his colleagues (2008) recommended asking the following questions when faced with risk information: (1) *Reduced risk of what?* It is good advice to ask what outcome is being changed and to decide how much one cares about the outcome. (2) *How big is the risk reduction?* A message like "drug X lowers your risk by 42%" is meaningless if no reference class is specified. Moreover, the authors suggested thinking about whether the risk

information applies to a specific audience and whether the benefit of the reduction in risk is worth the downsides that come with the measure or intervention to reduce the risk.

Conclusions

We described four common problems in the communication of quantitative risks. Problems in comprehending conditional probabilities can yield confusion in understanding the benefits and risks of medical tests such as screenings. Conditional probabilities can be much better understood when presented in the form of natural frequencies. Risk communication is often obscured and open to misinterpretation because risks are provided without the specification of a reference class. It should be standard practice to explicitly specify a reference class whenever risks are reported. A related and more specific problem consists in the reporting of relative risk reduction. Relative risk reduction typically comes without the specification of a reference class and produces numbers that are more impressive than reports of absolute risk reduction. At a minimum, the reference class should be specified when a change in risk is reported and risk reduction should not be exclusively reported in relative but also in absolute terms. Last but not least, survival rates should be only reported in situations in which the statistic is relevant and informative. Typically, in the context of screenings and the effectiveness of interventions, mortality rates are more informative than survival rates. The consistent use of these communication tools promises to improve the communication of quantitative risk information.

Suggested Additional Readings

Gaissmaier, W., Anderson, B. L., & Schulkin, J. (2014). How do physicians provide statistical information about antidepressants to hypothetical patients? *Medical Decision Making, 34,* 206–215.

Gigerenzer, G. (2014). *Risk savvy: How to make good decisions.* New York, NY: Penguin Books.

References

Amitani, Y. (2008, November). *The frequency hypothesis and evolutionary arguments.* Paper presented at the Philosophy of Science Association 21st Biennial Meeting, Pittsburgh, PA.

Arkes, H. R., & Gaissmaier, W. (2012). Psychological research and the prostate cancer screening controversy. *Psychological Science, 23,* 547–553.

Brase, G. L. (2002). Which statistical formats facilitate what decisions? The perception and influence of different statistical information formats. *Journal of Behavioral Decision Making, 15,* 381–401.

Brase, G. L. (2008). A field study of how different numerical information formats influence charity support. *Journal of Nonprofit & Public Sector Marketing, 20,* 1–13.

Bucher, H. C., Weinbacher, M., & Gyr, K. (1994). Influence of method of reporting study results on decision of physicians to prescribe drugs to lower cholesterol concentration. *British Medical Journal, 309,* 761–764.

Casscells, W., Schoenberger, A., & Grayboys, T. (1978). Interpretation by physicians of clinical laboratory results. *New England Journal of Medicine, 299,* 999–1001.

Cheng, E. K. (2009). A practical solution to the reference class problem. *Columbia Law Review, 109,* 2081–2103.

Cho, H., & Salmon, C. T. (2007). Unintended effects of health communication campaigns. *Journal of Communication, 57,* 293–317.

Cosmides, L., & Tooby, J. (1996). Are humans good intuitive statisticians after all? Rethinking some conclusions of the literature on judgment under uncertainty. *Cognition, 77,* 197–213.

Eddy, D. M. (1982). Probabilistic reasoning in clinical medicine: Problems and opportunities. In D. Kahneman, P. Slovic, & A. Tversky (Eds.), *Judgment under uncertainty: Heuristics and biases* (pp. 249–267). Cambridge, England: Cambridge University Press.

Edwards, A., Elwyn, G., & Gwyn, R. (1999). General practice registrar responses to the use of different risk communication tools in simulated consultations: A focus group study. *British Medical Journal, 319,* 749–752.

Fagerlin, A., & Peters, E. (2012). Quantitative information. In B. Fischhoff, N. T. Brewer, & J. S. Downs (Eds.), *Communicating risks and benefits: An evidence-based user's guide* (pp. 53–64). Silver Spring, MD: U.S. Department of Health and Human Services, Food and Drug Administration.

Fahey, T., Griffiths, S., & Peters, T. J. (1995). Evidence based purchasing: Understanding results of clinical trials and systematic reviews. *British Medical Journal, 311,* 1056–1059.

Fischhoff, B. (2012). Duty to inform. In B. Fischhoff, N. T. Brewer, & J. S. Downs (Eds.), *Communicating risks and benefits: An evidence-based user's guide* (pp. 19–29). Silver Spring, MD: U.S. Department of Health and Human Services, Food and Drug Administration.

Freimuth, V. S., Linnan, H. W., & Potter, P. (2000). Communicating the threat of emerging infections to the public. *Journal of Emerging Infectious Diseases, 6,* 337–347.

Ghosh, A. K., & Ghosh, K. (2005). Translating evidence-based information into effective risk communication: Current challenges and opportunities. *Journal of Laboratory and Clinical Medicine, 145,* 171–180.

Gigerenzer, G. (1991). How to make cognitive illusions disappear: Beyond "heuristics and biases." *European Review of Social Psychology, 2,* 83–115.

Gigerenzer, G. (2002). *Calculated risks: How to know when numbers deceive you.* New York, NY: Simon & Schuster.

Gigerenzer, G., & Edwards, A. (2003). Simple tools for understanding risk: From innumeracy to insight. *British Medical Journal, 327,* 741–744.

Gigerenzer, G., Gaissmaier, W., Kurz-Milcke, E., Schwartz, L. M., & Woloshin, S. (2008). Helping doctors and patients make sense of health statistics. *Psychological Science in the Public Interest, 8*(2), 53–96.

Gigerenzer, G., & Gray, J. A. M. (2011). Launching the century of the patient. In G. Gigerenzer & J. A. M. Gray (Eds.), *Better doctors, better patients, better decisions: Envisioning health care 2020* (pp. 3–28). Cambridge: MIT Press.

Gigerenzer, G., Hertwig, R., van den Broek, E., Fasolo, B., & Katsikopoulos, K. V. (2005). "A 30% chance of rain tomorrow": How does the public understand probabilistic weather forecasts? *Risk Analysis, 25,* 623–629.

Gigerenzer, G., & Hoffrage, U. (1995). How to improve Bayesian reasoning without instruction: Frequency formats. *Psychological Review, 102,* 684–704.

Gigerenzer, G., Hoffrage, U., & Ebert, A. (1998). AIDS counseling for low-risk clients. *AIDS Care, 10*(2), 197–211.

Hanoch, Y. (2004). Improving doctor–patient understanding of probability in communicating cancer-screening test findings. *Journal of Health Communication, 9,* 327–335.

Heller, R. F., Sandars, J. E., Patterson, L., & McElduff, P. (2004). GP's and physicians' interpretation of risks, benefits, and diagnostic test results. *Family Practice, 21,* 155–159.

Hembroff, L. A., Holmes-Rovner, M., & Wills, C. E. (2004). Treatment decision-making and the form of risk communication: Results from a factorial survey. *BMC Medical Informatics and Decision Making, 4,* 20. doi:10.1186/1472-6947-4-20

Hoffrage, U., Lindsey, S., Hertwig, R., & Gigerenzer, G. (2000). Communicating statistical information. *Science, 22,* 2261–2262.

Kleiter, G. (1994). Natural sampling: Rationality without base rates. In G. H. Fischer & D. Laming (Eds.), *Contributions to mathematical psychology, psychometrics, and methodology* (pp. 375–388). New York, NY: Springer-Verlag.

Kurzenhäuser, S. (2003). *Welche Informationen vermitteln deutsche Gesundheitsbroschüren über die screening-mammographie?* [What information is provided in German health information pamphlets on mammography screening?]. *Zeitschrift für ärztliche Fortbildung und Qualitätssicherung, 97,* 53–57.

Kurzenhäuser, S., & Lücking, A. (2004). Statistical formats in Bayesian inference. In R. Pohl (Ed.), *Cognitive illusions: A handbook on fallacies and biases in thinking, judgment, and memory* (pp. 61–77). Hove, England: Psychological Press.

Lipkus, I. M., Samsa, G., & Rimer, B. K. (2001). General performance on a numeracy scale among highly educated samples. *Medical Decision Making, 21,* 37–44.

von Mises, R. (1939). *Probability, statistics, and truth* (J. Neyman, D. Scholl, & E. Rabinowitsch, Trans.). New York, NY: Macmillan.

Paling, J. (2003). Strategies to help patients understand risks. *British Medical Journal, 327,* 745–748.

Peters, E. (2012). Beyond comprehension: The role of numeracy in judgments and decisions. *Current Directions in Psychological Science, 21,* 31–35.

Peters, E., Dieckmann, N. F., Västfjäll, D., Mertz, C. K., Slovic, P., & Hibbard, J. (2009). Bringing meaning to numbers: The impact of evaluative categories on decisions. *Journal of Experimental Psychology: Applied, 15,* 213–227.

Peters, E., Hart, P. S., & Fraenkel, L. (2010). Informing patients: The influence of numeracy, framing, and format of side-effect information on risk perceptions. *Medical Decision Making, 31,* 432–436.

Peters, E., Västfjäll, D., Slovic, P., Mertz, C. K., Mazzocco, K., & Dickert, S. (2006). Numeracy and decision making. *Psychological Science, 17,* 407–413.

Reichenbach, H. (1949). *The theory of probability.* Oakland: University of California Press.

Reyna, V. F., Nelson, W. L., Han, P. K., & Dieckmann, N. F. (2009). How numeracy influences risk comprehension and medical decision making. *Psychological Bulletin, 135,* 943–973.

Sackett, D. L. (1996). On some clinically useful measures of the effects of treatment. *Evidence-Based Medicine, 1,* 37–38.

Sackett, D. L., Haynes, R. B., Guyatt, G. H., & Tugwell, P. (1991). *Clinical epidemiology. A basic science for clinical medicine* (2nd ed.). Boston, MA: Little, Brown.

Sarfati, D., Howden-Chapman, P., Woodward, A., & Salmond, C. (1998). Does the frame affect the picture? A study into how attitudes to screening for cancer are affected by the way benefits are expressed. *Journal of Medical Screening, 5,* 137–140.

Schröder, F. H., Hugosson, J., Roobol, M. J., Tammela, T. L. J., Ciatto, S., Nelen, V., . . . ERSPC Investigators. (2009). Screening and prostate cancer mortality in a randomized European study. *New England Journal of Medicine, 360,* 1320–1328.

Schröder, F. H., Hugosson, J., Roobol, M. J., Tammela, T. L. J., Ciatto, S., Nelen, V., . . . ERSPC Investigators. (2012). Prostate-cancer mortality at 11 years of follow-up. *New England Journal of Medicine, 366,* 981–990.

Scosyrev, E., Wu, G., Mohile, S., & Messing, E. M. (2012). Prostate-specific antigen screening for prostate cancer and the risk of overt metastatic disease at presentation: Analysis of trends over time. *Cancer, 118,* 5768–5776.

Sedlmeier, P., & Gigerenzer, G. (2001). Teaching Bayesian reasoning in less than two hours. *Journal of Experimental Psychology: General, 130,* 380–400.

Sheridan, S. L, Pignone, M., & Lewis, C. L. (2003). Communicating treatment benefit information to patients: A randomized comparison of patients' understanding of number needed to treat and other common risk formats. *Journal of General Internal Medicine, 18,* 884–892.

Skubisz, C. (2010). Perceptions of risk evidence: Are all statistics considered equal? In D. S. Gouran (Ed.), *The functions of argument and social context* (pp. 476–484). Washington, DC: National Communication Association.

Skubisz, C., Reimer, T., & Hoffrage, U. (2009). Communicating quantitative risk information. In C. Beck (Ed.), *Communication yearbook 33* (pp. 177–212). Mahwah, NJ: Lawrence Erlbaum.

Slovic, P., Monahan, J., & MacGregor, D. G. (2000). Violence risk assessment and risk communication: The effects of using actual cases, providing instruction, and employing probability versus frequency formats. *Law and Human Behavior, 24,* 271–296.

Tooby, J., & Cosmides, L. (1998). Start with Darwin . . . In M. S. Gazzaniga & J. Altman (Eds.), *Brain and mind: Evolutionary perspectives* (Vol. 5, pp. 10–15). Strasbourg, France: Human Frontier Science Program.

Venn, J. (1876). *The logic of chance* (2nd ed.). London, England: Macmillan. (Reprinted New York, NY: Chelsea, 1962)

Wegwarth, O., Gaissmaier, W., & Gigerenzer, G. (2009). Smart strategies for doctors and doctors-in-training: Heuristics in medicine. *Medical Education, 43*(8), 721–728.

Wegwarth, O., Schwartz, L. M., Woloshin, S., Gaissmaier, W., & Gigerenzer, G. (2012). Do physicians understand cancer screening statistics? A national survey of primary care physicians in the United States. *Annals of Internal Medicine, 156*(5), 340–349.

Weinstein, N. D. (1999). What does it mean to understand a risk? Evaluating risk comprehension. *Journal of the National Cancer Institute Monographs, 25,* 15–20.

Welch, H., Schwartz, L. M., & Woloshin, S. (2000). Are increasing 5-year survival rates evidence of success against cancer? *JAMA, 283,* 2975–2978.

Welch, H. G. (2004). *Should I be tested for cancer? Maybe not and here's why.* Los Angeles: University of California Press.

Woloshin, S., & Schwartz, L. M. (2012). How a charity oversells mammography. *British Medical Journal, 345,* 1–3.

Woloshin, S., Schwartz, L. M., & Welch, H .G. (2008). *Know your chances: Understanding health statistics.* Berkeley, CA: University of California Press.

CHAPTER 12

Narrative Communication of Risk

Toward Balancing Accuracy and Acceptance

Hyunyi Cho and L. Brooke Friley

Introduction

Risk communicators have increasingly been interested in narratives for their potential for informing people about risk, for motivating risk reduction, and for overcoming barriers to these tasks that may not be overcome by efforts using other forms of messages. However, evidence for the advantages of narratives over other forms of messages has not been consistent (Allen & Preiss, 1997). As reviewed below, while some studies found narrative advantages, others found no difference or disadvantages. Simultaneously, concern has been voiced over the possibility that narratives may engender biased judgments (Winterbottom, Bekker, Conner, & Mooney, 2008). Together, the expectations for narrative effects, the inconsistent evidence for effectiveness amassed thus far, and the concern over undesirable effects, point to the need for a close examination of narrative communication as related to risk perceptions and practices.

Thus, the goal of this chapter is to review narrative research in divergent disciplines to identify the capacities of and challenges to narrative communication of risk. Instead of intending to be exhaustive, this chapter focuses on the areas of narrative research that are most relevant to risk communication theory and practice. Overall, this chapter recognizes that narrative effects occur at micro-, meso-, and macrolevels. It then explores the mechanisms underlying these effects, including intrapersonal processes and interpersonal and societal-level interactions. On this basis, the characteristics of narratives that may activate these processes and effects are discussed.

Importantly, this chapter distinguishes narrative communication for facilitating *accuracy* in risk judgments from narrative communication for promoting *acceptance* of risk reduction behavior implicitly or explicitly suggested in the message. The *accuracy* goal concerns informed and correct judgments; the *acceptance* goal concerns motivations to adopt and adhere to risk reduction behavior. On this basis, this chapter posits that narrative messages may be less capable of achieving the *accuracy* goal than the *acceptance* goal.

Suggestions for research and practice center on ways challenges for narrative risk communication may be addressed and how the potentials of narratives can be appropriately utilized for risk communication.

Scope of Narratives

Scholars define narratives as stories that connect actions and events involving characters with thematic and temporal sequences (for a review, see Abbott, 2008). Furthermore, scholars consider narratives a fundamental form of human communication (e.g., Fisher, 1984). Humans are storytellers, and it is through stories humans connect and communicate with each other, creating and sustaining shared beliefs, values, and norms (Fisher, 1984).

Perhaps as a result, narratives are found in a wide array of messages. Although recent research focuses on narratives without overt persuasive intent, narratives, including those about risk, are not always communicated in the absence of observable persuasive intent. In fact, historically, research on the processes and effects of narratives involved diverse forms of narratives such as those in news (e.g., Strange & Leung, 1999), advertisements (e.g., Adaval & Wyer, 1998), and testimonials (e.g., Ubel, Jepson, & Baron, 2001), as well as novels (e.g., Green & Brock, 2000) and dramas (e.g., Slater, Rouner, & Long, 2006). Mirroring the divergence, narratives have been referred to as, and taken the form of, anecdotes (e.g., Slater & Rouner, 1996), case histories (e.g., Rook, 1987), exemplars (e.g., Zillmann & Brosius, 2000), vivid messages (e.g., Rook, 1986), and scenarios (e.g., Mevissen, Meertens, Ruiter, Feenstra, & Schaalma, 2009).[1]

Narratives have also been utilized in strategic approaches to influencing changes in individual behaviors and public policies for risk reduction. Two practical frameworks that make use of narratives for risk reduction are entertainment education and media advocacy. Entertainment education uses dramas, rather than didactics, to

influence individuals' beliefs and behaviors for risk reduction (for a review, see Singhal, Cody, Rogers, & Sabido, 2003). Media advocacy uses news stories to gain mass media attention to risk issues and thereby to influence policymakers to change the larger structural and environmental conditions surrounding risk (Wallack & Dorfman, 1996). Whereas persuasive intent has to be covert with entertainment education and does not have to be with media advocacy, central to both approaches are narratives. While entertainment education aims to influence individual behaviors, media advocacy seeks to influence public policy. Although these are different approaches, the goal of both is risk reduction. In sum, the scope of narratives reviewed above suggests that their effects may be relevant to multiple levels of society.

Effects of Narratives

Understanding the effects of the wide array of forms and strategic uses of narratives reviewed above requires an organizing framework. A review of extant research suggests that narrative effects may occur at micro-, meso-, and macrolevels. Microlevel effects include the assessment of probabilities and attitudes, as well as actions related to risk reduction. Mesolevel effects include those on interpersonal and within-community interactions and communication. Macrolevel effects include media attention to risk issues and accompanying public judgments about the causes of and solutions to risk issues in society.

Furthermore, the effects at each level may be both intended and unintended from the risk communicator's standpoint (see Cho & Salmon, 2007, for a conceptual treatment of unintended effects).

Microlevel Effects

One of the key components of risk perception is personal probability estimation, or individuals' assessment of their own likelihood of experiencing harm (Slovic, 1967). Therefore, personal probability estimation has been a criterion with which the efficacy of narrative risk communication was assessed. On the one hand, there are studies that found narrative advantage. For example, exposure to narrative rather than statistical evidence produced higher personal probability estimation of hepatitis B virus infection among men who have sex with men (De Wit, Das, & Vet, 2008). On the other hand, other studies found that narratives were less effective. When messages featuring narratives and frequency statistics about chlamydia were compared, narratives showed less impact on sexually active adults' personal probability estimation of contracting the disease (Mevissen et al., 2009). Other studies have found little difference between narratives and nonnarratives in affecting personal probability of risk (e.g., Golding, Krimsky, & Plough, 1992; Greene & Brinn, 2003).

While a large number of studies have investigated whether narratives *amplify* personal probability, a limited number of studies examined narrative effects on the *accuracy* of probability estimation. Extant evidence, although from differing domains, is not consistent. Sanfey and Hastie (1998) compared various evidence presentation formats, including numeric tables, bar graphs, brief text, and a biographical story, and found that the more accurate judgment of the future performance of marathon runners was reached with text and story rather than with tables and graphs. On the other hand, Dickson (1982) compared narrative and statistical messages about refrigerator failure rates and found that narrative presentation produced an overestimation of the failure rate, while statistical presentation yielded a more accurate estimation of the rate.

In influencing attitudes toward risk prevention behavior, available evidence suggests that narratives may be more effective than nonnarratives when motivation to process information is low rather than high. For example, a vivid rather than an abstract message about osteoporosis was more persuasive for premenopausal women, while both vivid and abstract messages were persuasive for postmenopausal women (Rook, 1986). Similarly, people who were at high risk but wanted to minimize the risk (i.e., in denial) were more persuaded by a case history than an abstract message (Rook, 1987). Greater message engagement was reported by women who read narrative rather than statistical messages about breast cancer screening (Cox & Cox, 2001).

Narrative effects on risk reduction behavior have been reported. In a study comparing entertainment and informational television programs dealing with safe sex, college students who were exposed to an entertainment program indicated more consistent safe sex behavior as compared to those who were exposed to an informational program at a 2-week follow-up (Moyer-Guse & Nabi, 2010). A safety message using a story about a serious injury caused by a mistake produced greater enactment of precautionary behavior than safety messages using nonnarratives that were either concrete or abstract (Ricketts, Shanteau, McSpadden, & Fernandez-Medina, 2010).

Although explaining the inconsistencies in narrative effects highlighted above may be outside the scope of this review, speculations about reasons for these inconsistencies and suggestions for future research may be offered. First, not all narratives may be equal. Narratives, for example, may vary in their ability to elicit emotional engagement, depending on their characteristics (see Characteristics of Narratives section below). Thus, research is needed to investigate what kinds of narratives are most effective, moving beyond the currently predominant question of whether narratives are more effective. Second, in extant research investigating narrative effects, the comparison points have varied. Whereas the aforementioned De Wit et al. (2008) study compared narratives with prevalence statistics, Mevissen et al. (2009) compared narratives with frequency rate statistics. Thus, a question to ask may be what specific other messages are more, or less, effective than narratives. Finally, the goal of risk communication should be considered. For example, the goal of facilitating accuracy in risk judgment may entail encouraging a message-processing strategy different from the goal of facilitating acceptance of risk reduction behavior (see Intrapersonal Processes section below).

Mesolevel Exchanges

Stimulation of exchanges between individuals and within groups and communities may be one of the unique capacities of narratives. As a basic form of human communication, narratives may be more conducive to spurring interactions than other forms of messages. By being grounded in concrete and specific cases and examples, narratives may be a closer representation of reality than other forms of messages that utilize abstractions, and generalizations therefore are a more distal description of reality. Perhaps as a result, narratives may be easier to absorb for self (Cox & Cox, 2001), to retrieve from memory (Rook, 1987), and to relay to others. Furthermore, these mesolevel exchanges may be in the direction intended or unintended by the risk communicator.

Narratives may foster interpersonal communication and interaction consistent with the risk communicator's intention. In this process, narratives, ways to reduce the risk depicted in narratives, and support for enacting risk prevention behavior demonstrated in the narrative may be shared and discussed (Papa et al., 2000). Evidence that narratives promote interpersonal interactions has been reported by experimental and case analysis studies. In an experimental study, exposure to narratives, as compared with nonnarratives, stimulated Belgian college women's conversations with friends and family about skin cancer as reported at a 2-week follow-up (Lemal & Van den Bulck, 2010). A case analysis of an entertainment education radio soap opera, *Tinka Tinka Sukh*, found that exposure to the program facilitated interaction among the audience in an Indian village (Papa et al., 2000). The authors' examination of letters submitted by the listeners of the program suggested that through the interpersonal exchanges, the members of the community constructed a social environment in which ideas for community change could be debated.

Narratives may not only spur intended exchanges but also stimulate unintended interactions and communication about risk, about approaches to reducing the risk, and about efficacies of the risk reduction approaches. An example of such a role of narratives may be antivaccination movements. While the movements date back to the mid-1800s when vaccination became compulsory in the United Kingdom (Wolfe & Sharp, 2002), nowadays, the Internet provides a worldwide avenue in which antivaccination communication and movements take place. Kata's (2010) and Bean's (2011) content analyses of antivaccination websites have found that some of the frequently employed message strategies include personal testimonies, professional testimonies, and reports of adverse vaccination outcomes. Kata (2010), for example, found that the majority of antivaccination websites featured emotional testimonies from parents who felt that their children have been adversely affected by vaccination.

These mesolevel exchanges of narratives, by constructing realities, may have both downstream and upstream influences. On the one hand, the mesoprocesses may impact microlevel individuals' judgments. Emotional narratives about vaccine side effects may have a greater impact on individuals' judgments and decisions about vaccination than statistical presentation of the side effects (Betsch, Ulshofer, Renkewitz, & Betsch, 2011). On the other hand, the mesoprocesses may unite groups with shared realities and mobilize them toward altering and shaping macrolevel public discourse and policies. Philosophical positions against vaccination bolstered by narratives about side effects have resulted in demonstrations, riots, and organized efforts such as antivaccination leagues in Europe and the United States (Wolfe & Sharp, 2002).

Macrolevel Judgments

Narratives may function as a window to the world. Although narratives are episodic anecdotes about specific situations, research suggests that people may form judgments about society in general on the basis of these particulars (Strange, 2002; Strange & Leung, 1999).

Research further suggests that narratives may impact judgments about causes of social problems and their prevalence and importance. For example, after reading one of two narratives about Michael, who was planning to drop out of high school due either to deficiencies in the environment (e.g., lack of school resources and adequately trained teachers) or to deficiencies in individual dispositions (e.g., emotional or motivational issues during adolescence), those who were engaged in the narrative were more likely to assign the cause of school dropouts to the cause focused in the narrative that they read (Strange & Leung, 1999). Readers who were engrossed in a novel about an innocent girl brutally stabbed to death by a psychiatric patient at the mall (*Murder at the Mall*) indicated a higher estimation of the prevalence of stabbing deaths in society than those who were not (Green & Brock, 2000). Furthermore, Strange and Leung (1999) found that compared with those who did not read, those who read narratives about a school dropout rated school dropouts as a more important societal issue than health care, which indicates an agenda-setting effect of narrative exposure.

In addition to judgments about problems in society, narratives may also influence judgments about solutions and willingness to support policies consistent with the solutions. Among people with a liberal ideology, those who read a narrative message about the environmental causes of obesity indicated a stronger belief that societal actors (e.g., government and corporations) were responsible for addressing obesity than those who read an evidence message or a hybrid of narratives and evidence (Niederdeppe, Shapiro, & Porticella, 2011). Green and Brock (2000) found that participants who were engaged in the aforementioned narrative about the death in the mall

(*Murder at the Mall*) were also more likely to support limiting the freedom of psychiatric patients as compared with those who were not engaged in the narrative.

Narrative effects on policy support have been reported. Slater et al. (2006) found that exposure to television dramas increased support for the death penalty by removing the influence of prior ideology and values on participants' position on the issue. Similarly, Shanahan, McBeth, and Hathaway (2011) found that news narratives on the policy concerning snowmobile access to Yellowstone National Park influenced opinions about the policy by either strengthening support for the policy or modifying prior positions about the policy.

Processes of Narrative Effects

Intrapersonal Processes

A range of intraindividual processes have been identified for narrative effects (for a review, see Bilandzic & Busselle, 2013), but the hallmark of narrative message processing may be transportation, the process in which the audience members are carried away from their actual world to the story world (Green & Brock, 2000). Specifically, transportation is "a convergent process where all mental systems and capacities become focused on events occurring in the narrative" (Green & Brock, 2000, p. 701).

Research found that transportation entails emotional responses. In Green and Brock's (2000) study, for example, rather than evaluating the focal beliefs under consideration, readers of the above-described novel *Murder at the Mall* indicated global emotional reactions (p. 707). Similarly, a comparison of narrative and statistical evidence messages for organ donation found that emotional rather than cognitive reactions were more pronounced during narrative processing (Kopfman, Smith, Yun, & Hodges, 1998). To the extent that emotional responses are predominant during narrative processing, narrative communication may foster risk judgments based on feelings rather than those based on analysis, as distinguished by Slovic, Finucane, Peters, and MacGregor (2004). Whereas risk judgments based on analysis rely on logic, reason, abstractions, and quantifications; risk judgments based on feelings rely on affect, emotions, intuitions, images, and narratives (Slovic et al., 2004).

Slovic et al. (2004) argue that affect-based risk judgments may not necessarily be irrational. Evidence consistent with Slovic et al.'s (2004) position is the aforementioned Sanfey and Hastie's (1998) study, in which exposure to narrative rather than numeric information produced the more accurate assessment. Conversely, Dickson (1982) found that exposure to narrative rather than statistical information produced inaccurate assessment of frequency. Evidently, more research is needed to address these inconsistent findings for narratives' role in assisting accurate judgments (see also the Exemplar section below).

Along with eliciting emotional responses, transportation encourages suspension of disbelief. For example, while reading the above-described novel *Murder at the Mall*, participants were asked to circle "false notes," which were parts of a story that contradicted facts or did not make sense (Green & Brock, 2000). The more transported into the narrative, the fewer false notes that the participants indicated. Thus, transportation was inversely related to doubts or questions about the message and to counterarguments.

This capacity of narratives that suppresses the audience's critical processing of the message is considered to be one of their persuasive advantages. By decreasing counterarguments and by increasing emotional engagement, transportation can promote attitudes and actions consistent with the narrative (Green & Brock, 2000). This may be useful when the audience members are resistant to behavior change to prevent well-established risk that harms their health. Transportation can mitigate reactance (Moyer-Guse & Nabi, 2010).

Communication to promote acceptance of recommended risk prevention behavior, however, may differ from communication to help the audience reach an accurate assessment of risk.

For the former, transportation, emotional reactions, and suspension of disbelief may be useful. For the latter, however, risk communicators may need to enable and encourage critical processing and counterarguments, rather than suppressing them. This may be especially true when the risk and its methods of prevention and control under consideration are associated with uncertainties. Considering the range of risk communication situations involving uncertainties, narrative communication of risk may require differentiating between the goals of accuracy and acceptance.

Of note, some findings suggest that when accuracy is the goal, people may not value narrative information as much as they value other, more representative or comprehensive information. In Dickson's (1982) study, narrative information was evaluated to be less representative and less sufficient than statistical information about refrigerator failure rates. Satterfield, Slovic, and Gregory (2000) found that didactic text was rated to be more helpful than narrative text for people to think through different aspects of the issue at hand—the effect of a hydroelectric power plant on the salmon population in a river. A review of verbal and numeric information effects found that people prefer numeric rather than verbal information in making probability estimations (Visschers, Meertens, Passchier, & de Vries, 2009).

Slovic et al. (2004) suggest that analysis-based and feeling-based risk judgments need not be competitive; rather, they can be used in complementary ways so that each can inform the other. Therefore, research should investigate how narratives can be used in combination or conjunction with other forms of messages to facilitate informed decisions and actions related to risk.

Processes Pertinent to Societal Effects

Although direct investigations of narrative effects on societal processes are rare, available theory and research indirectly suggests that narratives may play an important role in these processes. One of the societal processes that narratives activate may be agenda setting (Strange & Leung, 1999). Agenda setting is a process by which a certain subset of issues from the population is selected and communicated to the public by the media (Dearing & Rogers, 1996).

A major factor facilitating an issue's inclusion on the media agenda is the availability of drama, or emotional and vivid stories that exemplify the issue, according to the public arenas model (Hilgartner & Bosk, 1988). Because public arenas have limited capacities (e.g., media space and time, the public's attention and sympathy), the issues with drama are more likely to enter and survive in public arenas (Hilgartner & Bosk, 1988). Dearing and Rogers (1992) argue that the stories about the death of movie actor Rock Hudson and about the discrimination against a Kokomo, Indiana boy, Ryan White, propelled HIV/AIDS to the front line of the national issue agenda. Prior to the stories about Hudson and White, AIDS was not an issue of common concern and relevance to the general public (Dearing & Rogers, 1992, p. 182). Similarly, Nisbet and Huge (2006) argue that the issue of plant biotechnology has retained a low salience status on the national issue agenda because it did not fit the typical political narrative format featuring conflict, drama, climax, and resolutions that are necessary to gain media attention.

It is these capacities of narratives that the practical framework of media advocacy seeks to utilize. Specifically, media advocacy utilizes narratives to gain issue attention from the media and then from policymakers to change the conditions and contexts surrounding the risk and health of individuals (Wallack & Dorfman, 1996). Proponents of media advocacy have recommended a balance between two primary narratives to advance policy change. One is personal narratives of risk experience to gain media attention initially; the other is narratives about the root of the personal risk experience, which are located at societal and structural levels (Wallack, Woodruff, Dorfman, & Diaz, 1999). In sum, narratives may produce macrolevel effects by facilitating an issue's inclusion on the media agenda

and thereby influencing public agenda. Furthermore, being on the public agenda is relevant to an issue's likelihood of becoming policy agenda (Dearing & Rogers, 1996).

Characteristics of Narratives

Understanding the effects and processes of narratives alone may not be sufficient to inform narrative communication of risk. Understanding the characteristics of narratives that activate the micro-, meso-, and macrolevel effects and processes may be necessary. When the characteristics of the message that activate the multilevel processes and effects are identified, theory and research on narrative will advance. Three primary characteristics of narratives may be vividness, realism, and inclusion of an exemplar.

Vividness

Vividness is one of the most frequently used descriptors of narratives. Nisbett and Ross (1980) posit that vivid messages may be more impactful than "pallid and abstract propositions of substantially greater probative and evidentiary value" (p. 44). Vivid messages may be more impactful because they are "(a) emotionally interesting, (b) concrete and imagery-provoking, and (c) proximate in a sensory, temporal, or spatial way" (p. 45).

Vividness has been operationalized in various ways; case histories or narratives are one of the operationalizations of vividness (Taylor & Thompson, 1982). Because narrative messages use concrete language, exciting imagery, and are emotionally engaging, they have been posited to be more effective than abstract messages using facts or statistics. Taylor and Thompson (1982) reviewed seven studies comparing messages with narratives and statistics and found that six reported narrative advantage, but they did not attribute the narrative advantage to vividness because of the lack of evidence for the role of the three variables (e.g., imagery, emotional engagement, and concreteness).

Recent research has investigated imagery and emotional engagement. Imagery did not emerge as a separate facet of narrative processing (Green & Brock, 2000; Strange & Leung, 1999). Evidence of narrative effects on emotional reactions has been obtained (e.g., Green & Brock, 2000). Concreteness of narratives may facilitate message processing when the audience members lack resources to process abstract messages.

Taylor and Thompson (1982) suggested that the effect of vividness may depend on its ability to attract attention. Although earlier research did not find support for this postulation (Frey & Eagly, 1993), recent research found that the effects of vividness on memory and persuasion may be contingent upon the degree to which the vivid elements of a message are consistent with the message content or are central to the main thesis of the message (Guadagno, Rhoads, & Sagarin, 2011; Smith & Shaffer, 2000).

In extant research, vividness has been defined in terms of both message features (e.g., concreteness) and the reactions that the message evokes (e.g., emotional engagement). Future research using vividness as an explanation for narrative effects may need to be specific about what is operationalized as vividness of a given narrative communication. In addition, although previous research frequently treated narratives as vivid and nonnarratives as pallid, all narratives may not be equally vivid.

Realism

Perceived realism refers to the judgment about the degree to which narratives reflect the real world. Earlier research considered realism to be the property of the message and expected that factual narratives would be more realistic and more effective than fictional narratives (Feshbach, 1976). Recent research, however, has found that narratives presented as a fact or a fiction did not have differential effects (Green & Brock, 2000;

Strange & Leung, 1999). Moreover, Pouliot and Cowen (2007) found that fictional rather than nonfiction narratives produced greater recall and emotional arousal.

In addition to the fact versus fiction distinction, narratives may vary on other realism dimensions in meaningful ways. Scholars have argued that the realism of narratives is likely to be multidimensional (e.g., Hall, 2003), and recent research empirically demonstrated that realism comprises the dimensions of plausibility, typicality, factuality, narrative consistency, and perceptual quality, and that these subdimensions differentially predict the processes and outcomes of narratives relevant to risk assessment and prevention (Cho, Shen, & Wilson, 2012, 2013).

Of realism dimensions, typicality is the more stringent criterion as it concerns the representativeness of the narrative event to the population of real-world events; plausibility, on the other hand, is threshold-level realism as it addresses the question whether the event in the narrative could possibly happen in reality (Hall, 2003). Research found that plausibility and typicality predicted differential routes to risk assessment and risk prevention. For risk assessment, typicality was the most important predictor (Cho et al., 2013). Typicality was more strongly associated with personal probability estimation than any other dimensions. Plausibility indirectly contributed to personal probability estimation only by directly decreasing message discounting (e.g., "this story is exaggerated").

While typicality was the strongest predictor of personal probability estimation (Cho et al., 2013), other realism dimensions may also be relevant to narrative effects in other areas related to risk. For example, plausibility as well as typicality contributed toward risk prevention attitudes, although through different paths (Cho et al., 2012). Typicality predicted attitudes via identification but not via emotional engagement; plausibility predicted attitudes via emotional engagement but not via identification. Put differently, typicality primed perceived personal relatedness with the character and situation in the narrative but had little emotional impact; plausibility affected emotions without eliciting relevance to personal realities. However, attitudes toward risk prevention were predicted by both of these paths.

Strange and Leung (1999) did not find that typicality was necessary for societal-level inferences. Specifically, despite the fact that the narrative about a school dropout was not evaluated to be typical, it still influenced the judgment about the locus of responsibility of the dropout. Strange and Leung (1999) attributed this effect of narratives on societal-level inference to the narratives' reminding of the audience's direct or indirect past experience, which is likely to be more similar to plausibility rather than typicality. Research is needed to investigate how differential dimensions of realism may be differentially relevant to narrative effects (e.g., personal vs. societal-level judgments, probability estimation vs. attitudes toward behavior).

Exemplars

Exemplars refer to the persons, characters, or personalities portrayed in a narrative (Zillmann & Brosius, 2000). As narratives frequently describe human experiences, exemplars may be an essential component of any narrative. A growing body of research has investigated the effects of exemplars, and findings suggest that exemplars tend to increase risk estimation and to increase risk prevention intentions. Notably, exemplar research also suggests that exemplars may reduce accuracy in risk assessment.

Research has found that exemplars increase risk estimation. For example, news narratives containing emotionally charged interviews with grieving family members of food poisoning and handgun violence victims led to increased risk perceptions compared to news narratives with nonemotional interviews or no interviews; the risk perceptions included the estimation of the national importance of the issues and personal probability of becoming a victim of the same

risks (Aust & Zillmann, 1996). Readers of a news report with an extreme exemplar of carjacking incidence in which the victim was killed indicated a significantly higher estimation of carjacking as a serious national problem and higher estimation of the rate of fatalities in carjacking incidences than readers of a news report with exemplars who suffered minimal to substantial consequences (Gibson & Zillmann, 1994). These effects of exemplars are facilitated by emotional reactions, and the negative emotions (e.g., fear) elicited through exemplification motivate behavior change (Zillmann, 2006; Zillmann & Brosius, 2000).

Research suggests that for risk prevention purposes, positive exemplars' modeling of prevention behavior can improve narrative effectiveness. For example, news stories with an exemplar who successfully quit smoking were more effective in persuading smokers to form intentions to quit smoking than news stories without such an exemplar (Kim, Bigman, Leader, Lerman, & Cappella, 2012). Furthermore, narratives with an exemplar who succeeded in preventing a risk were more effective than narratives with an exemplar who failed to prevent the risk (Hoeken & Geurts, 2005).

While these studies suggest the significant effects of exemplars, cautions have been issued by researchers about the undesirable effects of exemplars. The cautions are based on the fact that exemplars do not provide a representative or valid summary of risk information and that they may be an unrepresentative or unreliable depiction of reality. Thus, although exemplars may endow suasory power to risk communication through emotional processes, the power may come at the expense of accuracy. Notably, Gibson, Callison, and Zillmann (2011) investigated the effects of exemplars on the accuracy of the estimation of the frequency of negative events. Different probability ratios for illnesses were developed from a newsmagazine story about American volunteers contracting tropical diseases while on a mission trip in Nicaragua. Those who read exemplar-only messages indicated less accurate estimations of the ratio of diarrhea victims and parasite infection victims as compared to those who read baseline-only or both baseline and exemplar messages.

Risk communication research should identify ways to prevent biased judgments arising from unrepresentative exemplars. Evidence gathered by some studies suggests that typicality may be an antidote to unsafe effects of exemplars. For example, Bodenhausen, Schwarz, Bless, and Wanke (1995) found that the thoughts about typicality may mitigate the effects of exemplars. Specifically, they found that exemplar effects vanished when individuals were given the opportunity to think about the atypicality of the exemplars. Furthermore, the judgment about the typicality of the exemplar moderated the accessibility of stereotypical knowledge about the social group and the use of the knowledge to assess a new target person who belongs to the social group (Macrae, Bodenhausen, Milne, & Castelli, 1999). The inclusion of base rate information, on the other hand, did little to mitigate exemplar effects on frequency or prevalence estimation (Brosius & Bathelt, 1994; Zillmann, 2006; Zillmann & Brosius, 2000).

Reflections for Theory and Research

Extant research has frequently focused on determining the relative effectiveness of narratives and nonnarratives. The next step in this research may be to move from the question of *whether* narratives are more effective to *when* narratives are more effective and *what kinds* of narratives are more effective. This stream of investigation may entail the consideration of the following factors: the goal of risk communication (e.g., accuracy vs. acceptance), the kinds of nonnarratives to which narratives are compared with (e.g., prevalence vs. frequency statistics), and the characteristics of narratives (e.g., realism and exemplars). Addressing this question may help identify the characteristics of narratives that activate

intended and unintended processes and effects related to risk communication. These findings can guide risk communicators in determining the situations in which the use of narratives is appropriate and when narratives should be usefully integrated with and used in combination with other forms of messages to promote acceptance based on accuracy.

Recommendations for Practice

Although narratives are increasingly adopted for various communication goals and purposes, the postulations advanced in this chapter suggest that communicators should consider the goal of communication and evaluate whether narratives are the most appropriate message format for a given communication goal. When acceptance is the goal, narratives may be appropriate and efficacious. When accuracy is the goal, however, narratives may not be the most appropriate, as the postulations advanced and evidence reviewed in this chapter suggest that narratives have the possibility of engendering inaccurate risk judgments. Evaluation of risk communication should be mindful of this possibility and should assess a range of outcomes of risk communication rather than just intended goals, such as acceptance. This way, knowledge gained from practice can inform future planning of risk communication.

Conclusions

Risk communication engages multiple goals. Promoting acceptance of risk reduction behavior is one of the goals, but it is not the only goal. Another important goal of risk communication is facilitating accurate judgment of risk. In using narratives for risk communication, these goals should be discerned and distinguished.

Stories may not be told to provide a representative or reliable summary of reality. Rather, stories frequently focus on illustrating details of particular cases. When one is emotionally engaged in stories, disbeliefs are suspended and critical processing and counterarguments are suppressed. This nature and processing of narratives may support the acceptance goal of risk communication, but may encumber the accuracy goal of risk communication. Acceptance should not be encouraged at the expense of accuracy.

Note

1. While it may be possible that these varying forms, lengths, and platforms of narratives produce differential effects, research has yet to investigate this possibility.

Suggested Additional Readings

Chen, S., Duckworth, K., & Chaiken, S. (1999). Motivated heuristic and systematic processing. *Psychological Inquiry, 10,* 44–49.

Larkey, L. K., & Hill, A. (2011). Using narratives to promote health. In H. Cho (Ed.), *Health communication message design: Theory and practice* (pp. 95–112). Thousand Oaks, CA: Sage.

Weinstein, N. D., & Sandman, P. M. (1993). Some criteria for evaluating risk messages. *Risk Analysis, 13,* 103–114.

References

Abbott, H. P. (2008). *The Cambridge introduction to narrative.* Cambridge, England: Cambridge University Press.

Adaval, R., & Wyer, R. S. (1998). The role of narrative in consumer information processing. *Journal of Consumer Psychology, 7,* 207–245.

Allen, M., & Preiss, R. W. (1997). Comparing the persuasiveness of narrative and statistical evidence using meta-analysis. *Communication Research Reports, 14,* 125–131.

Aust, C. F., & Zillmann, D. (1996). Effects of victim exemplification in television news on viewer perception of social issues. *Journalism & Mass Communication Quarterly, 73,* 787–803.

Bean, S. J. (2011). Emerging and continuing trends in vaccine opposition website content. *Vaccine, 29,* 1874–1880.

Betsch, C., Ulshofer, C., Renkewitz, F., & Betsch, T. (2011). The influence of narrative v. statistical information on perceiving vaccination risks. *Medical Decision Making, 31,* 742–753.

Bilandzic, H., & Busselle, R. (2013). Narrative persuasion. In J. P. Dillard & L. Shen (Eds.), *The SAGE handbook of persuasion: Developments in theory and practice* (pp. 200–219). Thousand Oaks, CA: Sage.

Bodenhausen, G. V., Schwarz, N., Bless, H., & Wanke, M. (1995). Effects of atypical exemplars on racial beliefs: Enlightened racism or generalized appraisals? *Journal of Experimental Social Psychology, 31,* 48–63.

Brosius, H.-B., & Bathelt, A. (1994). The utility of exemplars in persuasive communications. *Communication Research, 21,* 48–78.

Cho, H., & Salmon, C. T. (2007). Unintended effects of health communication campaigns. *Journal of Communication, 57,* 293–317.

Cho, H., Shen, L., & Wilson, K. M. (2012). Perceived realism: Dimensions and roles in narrative persuasion. *Communication Research.* Advance online publication. doi:10.1177/0093650212450585

Cho, H., Shen, L., & Wilson, K. M. (2013). What makes a message real? The effects of perceived realism of alcohol and drug related messages on personal probability estimation. *Substance Use & Misuse, 48,* 323–331.

Cox, D., & Cox, A. D. (2001). Communicating the consequences of early detection: The role of evidence and framing. *Journal of Marketing, 65,* 91–103.

De Wit, J. B. F., Das, E., & Vet, R. (2008). What works best: Objective statistics or a personal testimonial? An assessment of the persuasive effects of different types of message evidence on risk perception. *Health Psychology, 27,* 110–115.

Dearing, J. W., & Rogers, E. M. (1992). AIDS and the media agenda. In T. Edgar, M. A. Fitzpatrick, & V. S. Freimuth (Eds.), *AIDS: A communication perspective* (pp. 173–194). Hillsdale, NJ: Lawrence Erlbaum.

Dearing, J. W., & Rogers, E. M. (1996). *Agenda-setting.* Thousand Oaks, CA: Sage.

Dickson, P. R. (1982). The impact of enriching case and statistical information on consumer judgments. *Journal of Consumer Research, 10,* 398–406.

Feshbach, S. (1976). The role of phantasy in response to television. *Journal of Social Issues, 32,* 71–85.

Fisher, W. R. (1984). Narration as a human communication paradigm: The case of public moral argument. *Communication Monographs, 51,* 1–22.

Frey, K. P., & Eagly, A. H. (1993). Vividness can undermine the persuasiveness of messages. *Journal of Personality and Social Psychology, 65,* 32–44.

Gibson, R., Callison, C., & Zillmann, D. (2011). Quantitative literacy and affective reactivity in processing statistical information and case histories in the news. *Media Psychology, 14,* 96–120.

Gibson, R., & Zillmann, D. (1994). Exaggerated versus representative exemplification in news reports: Perception of issues and personal consequences. *Communication Research, 21,* 603–624.

Golding, D., Krimsky, S., & Plough, A. (1992). Evaluating risk communication: Narrative vs. technical presentation of information about radon. *Risk Analysis, 12,* 27–35.

Green, M. C., & Brock, T. C. (2000). The role of transportation in the persuasiveness of public narratives. *Journal of Personality and Social Psychology, 79,* 701–721.

Greene, K., & Brinn, L. S. (2003). Messages influencing college women's tanning bed use: Statistical versus narrative evidence format and a self-assessment to increase perceived susceptibility. *Journal of Health Communication, 8,* 443–461.

Guadagno, R. E., Rhoads, K. V., & Sagarin, B. J. (2011). Figural vividness and persuasion: Capturing the "elusive" vividness effect. *Personality and Social Psychology Bulletin, 37,* 626–638.

Hall, A. (2003). Reading realism: Audiences' evaluations of the reality of media texts. *Journal of Communication, 53,* 624–641.

Hilgartner, S., & Bosk, C. L. (1988). The rise and fall of social problems: A public arena model. *American Journal of Sociology, 94,* 53–78.

Hoeken, H., & Geurts, D. (2005). The influence of exemplars in fear appeals on the perception of self-efficacy and message acceptance. *Information Design Journal, 13,* 238–248.

Kata, A. (2010). A postmodern Pandora's box: Antivaccination misinformation on the Internet. *Vaccine, 28,* 1709–1716.

Kim, H. S., Bigman, C. A., Leaders, A. E., Lerman, C., & Cappella, J. N. (2012). Narrative health communication and behavior change: The influence of exemplars in the news on intention to quit smoking. *Journal of Communication, 62,* 473–492.

Kopfman, J. E., Smith, S. W., Ah Yun, J. K., & Hodges, A. (1998). Affective and cognitive reactions to narrative versus statistical evidence organ donation messages. *Journal of Applied Communication Research, 26,* 279–300.

Lemal, M., & Van den Bulck, J. (2010). Testing the effectiveness of a skin cancer narrative in promoting positive health behavior: A pilot study. *Preventive Medicine, 51,* 178–181.

Macrae, C. N., Bodenhausen, G. V., Milne, A. B., & Castelli, L. (1999). On disregarding deviants: Exemplar typicality and person perception. *Current Psychology, 18*(1), 47–70.

Mevissen, F. E. F., Meertens, R. M., Ruiter, R. A. C., Feenstra, H., & Schaalma, H. P. (2009). HIV/STI risk communication: The effects of scenario-based risk information and frequency-based risk Information on perceived susceptibility to chlamydia and HIV. *Journal of Health Psychology, 14,* 78–87.

Moyer-Guse, E., & Nabi, R. (2010). Explaining the effects of narrative in an entertainment television program: Overcoming resistance to persuasion. *Human Communication Research, 36,* 26–52.

Niederdeppe, J., Shapiro, M. A., & Porticella, N. (2011). Attributions of responsibility for obesity: Narrative communication reduces reactive counterarguing among liberals. *Human Communication Research, 37,* 295–323.

Nisbet, M. C., & Huge, M. (2006). Attention cycles and frames in the plant biotechnology debate: Managing power and participation through the press/policy connection. *Press/Politics, 11,* 3–40.

Nisbett, R. E., & Ross, L. (1980). *Human inference: Strategies and shortcomings of social judgment.* Englewood Cliffs, NJ: Prentice Hall.

Papa, M., Singhal, A., Law, S., Pant, S., Sood, S., Rogeres, E. M., & Shefner-Rogers, C. (2000). Entertainment-education and social change: An analysis of parasocial interaction, social learning, and paradoxical communication. *Journal of Communication, 50,* 31–55.

Pouliot, L., & Cowen, P. S. (2007). Does perceived realism really matter in media effects? *Media Psychology, 9,* 241–259.

Ricketts, M., Shanteau, J., McSpadden, B., & Fernandez-Medina, K. M. (2010). Using stories to battle unintentional injuries: Narratives in safety and health communication. *Social Science & Medicine, 70,* 1441–1449.

Rook, K. S. (1986). Encouraging preventative behavior for distant and proximal health threats: Effects of vivid versus abstract information. *Journal of Gerontology, 41,* 526–534.

Rook, K. S. (1987). Effects of case history versus abstract information on health attitudes and behaviors. *Journal of Applied Social Psychology, 17,* 533–553.

Sanfey, A., & Hastie, R. (1998). Does evidence presentation format affect judgment? An experimental evaluation of displays of data for judgment. *Psychological Science, 9,* 99–103.

Satterfield, T., Slovic, P., & Gregory, R. (2000). Narrative valuation in a policy judgment context. *Ecological Economics, 34,* 315–331.

Shanahan, E. A., McBeth, M. K., & Hathaway, P. L. (2011). Narrative policy framework: The influence of media policy narratives on public opinion. *Politics & Policy, 39,* 373–400.

Singhal, A., Cody, M., Rogers, E. M., & Sabido, M. (Eds.). (2003). *Entertainment education and social change: History, research, and practice.* Mahwah, NJ: Lawrence Erlbaum.

Slater, M. D., & Rouner, D. (1996). Value-affirmative and value-protective processing of alcohol education messages that include statistical evidence or anecdotes. *Communication Research, 23,* 210–235.

Slater, M. D., Rouner, D., & Long, M. A. (2006). Television dramas and support for controversial public policies: Effects and mechanisms. *Journal of Communication, 56,* 235–252.

Slovic, P. (1967). The relative influence of probabilities and payoffs upon the perceived risk of a gamble. *Psychonomic Science, 9,* 223–224.

Slovic, P., Finucane, M. L., Peters, E., & MacGregor, D. G. (2004). Risk as analysis and risk as feelings: Some thoughts about affect, reason, risk, and rationality. *Risk Analysis, 24,* 311–322.

Smith, S. M., & Shaffer, D. R. (2000). Vividness can undermine or enhance message processing: The moderating role of vividness congruency. *Personality and Social Psychology Bulletin, 26,* 769–779.

Strange, J. J. (2002). How fictional tales wag real world beliefs: Models and mechanisms of narrative influence. In M. C. Green, J. J. Strange, & T. C. Brock (Eds.), *Narrative impact: Social and cognitive foundations* (pp. 263–286). Mahwah, NJ: Lawrence Erlbaum.

Strange, J. J., & Leung, C. C. (1999). How anecdotal accounts in news and in fiction can influence judgments of a social problem's urgency, causes, and cures. *Personality and Social Psychology Bulletin, 25,* 436–449.

Taylor, S. E., & Thompson, S. C. (1982). Stalking the elusive "vividness" effect. *Psychological Review, 89,* 155–181.

Ubel, P. A., Jepson, C., & Baron, J. (2001). The inclusion of patient testimonials in decision aids: Effects on treatment choices. *Medical Decision Making, 21,* 60–68.

Visschers, V. H. M., Meertens, R. M., Passchier, W. W. F., & de Vries, N. N. K. (2009). Probability information in risk communication: A review of the research literature. *Risk Analysis, 29,* 267–287.

Wallack, L., & Dorfman, L. (1996). Media advocacy: A strategy for advancing policy and promoting health. *Health Education Quarterly, 23,* 293–317.

Wallack, L., Woodruff, K., Dorfman, L., & Diaz, I. (1999). *News for a change: an advocate's guide to working with the media.* Thousand Oaks, CA: Sage.

Winterbottom, A., Bekker, H. L., Conner, M., & Mooney, A. (2008). Does narrative information bias individual's decision making? A systematic review. *Social Science & Medicine, 67,* 2079–2088.

Wolfe, R. M., & Sharp, L. K. (2002). Anti-vaccinationists past and present. *British Medical Journal, 325,* 430–432.

Zillmann, D. (2006). Exemplification effects in the promotion of safety and health. *Journal of Communication, 56,* s221–s237.

Zillmann, D., & Brosius, H. (2000). *Exemplification in communication: The influence of case reports on the perception of issues.* Mahwah, NJ: Lawrence Erlbaum.

CHAPTER 13

Visual Messaging and Risk Communication

Andy J. King

Introduction

Social critics and researchers suggest that visuals are omnipresent in everyday life (Lester, 2014; Meyer, Höllerer, Jancsary, & van Leeuwen, 2013). For decades, risk communication researchers and practitioners have considered the complexities, drawbacks, and benefits of visually communicating risk information. Much of this research examines the use of graphs, charts, and other visual displays of quantitative information that summarize complex and risk-related statistics and probabilities (see reviews by Ancker, Senathirajah, Kukafka, & Starren, 2006; Lipkus & Hollands, 1999). Other research examines the use of images and illustrations of potential risks or threats, such as atypical moles on one's body (King, 2012), or visual instructions about handling pesticides safely (Grieshop & Winter, 1988). Unlike some other aspects of risk communication, research on the visual presentation of risk is often atheoretical (Ancker et al., 2006; Lipkus, 2007) and, perhaps as a consequence, is still perceived as understudied in a systematic manner.

Given the intensifying visually oriented information environment facing many communicators and assessors of risk, there is a need to push forward research on visual messaging and risk communication by focusing on more theoretically oriented work. Stronger theoretical focus in visual messaging work will improve research and practice. Without improvements in these areas, investigations of visual messaging will likely stall and stagnate, curbing potential innovations and applications in visual messaging research within risk communication contexts. Various fields and disciplines provide a strong knowledge foundation on which to build this systematic pursuit, and communication theory offers a set of theoretical lenses to develop and refine known visual messaging effects and dynamics. This chapter reviews, critiques, and makes suggestions about increasing the theoretical foundations of research on visual messaging and risk communication. The chapter moves through four sections to that end: (1) Previous Research on Visual Messaging and Risk Communication, (2) Relevant Theoretical Frameworks, (3) Reflections for Theory and Research, and (4) Recommendations for Practice.

Previous Research on Visual Messaging and Risk Communication

To distinguish between different types of visuals, reviewed research is organized into two categories: (1) graphical and (2) illustrative displays of risk information. An exhaustive review of either is beyond the scope of this chapter, and readers are encouraged to seek out existing reviews for further information about the topics discussed in this section (see Ancker et al., 2006; Gibson, 2003; Houts, Doak, Doak, & Loscalzo, 2006; Lipkus, 2007; Lipkus & Hollands, 1999). Graphical displays of risk information are data-driven representations of risk information, such as risk ratios, hazard ratios, and other probabilities; frequency comparisons; and multivariate projections of mortality and morbidity. Illustrative displays of risk information include pictures of people to convey information about risk susceptibility, grotesque images that convey risk severity, sequential images that provide instructions about how someone might reduce his or her risk by taking safety precautions (e.g., airplane safety guides), and other visual representations of risk that are nonnumeric and have indexical qualities. See Figure 13.1 for examples of the graphical versus illustrative distinction.

Graphical Displays of Risk Information

Reviewing research on graphical displays of risk information is challenging due to inconsistent theoretical progression (Lipkus & Hollands, 1999) and variability in outcome measures (Ancker et al., 2006). Outcomes of studies examining graphical displays include message perceptions (e.g., Parrott, Silk, Dorgan, Condit, & Harris, 2005), comprehension (e.g., Smerecnik et al., 2010), and behavior change (e.g., Stone, Sieck, Bull, Yates, Parks, & Rush, 2003). Studies often include multiple outcomes. To influence these outcomes, graphical displays of risk information are presented in a variety of formats like bar graphs, line graphs, risk ladders, icon arrays, pie charts, and pictographs (for further discussion of graphical display types, see Kosslyn, 1994, 2006; Lipkus & Hollands, 1999), as well as design features of graphs and charts (Ancker et al., 2006). Many studies engage in comparative testing of graphical presentation formats to determine which is most appropriate for some given context (e.g., low probability events in Dolan & Iadarola, 2008). Given the variety of research done in this area, this section organizes and summarizes findings based on main outcome categories considered: message reception, comprehension, behaviors, and decisions.[1]

Message Reception

Studies interested in people's response to graphical displays of risk information have looked at a variety of message preferences and perceptions.[2] Research found that people preferred certain types of graphical displays over others, although those findings are often specific to the type of information conveyed (e.g., low probability risk events) or the topic of the risk information (e.g., breast cancer). Some research found that people preferred bar graphs over other traditional presentations such as line graphs and survival curves (Fortin, Hirota, Bond, O'Connor, & Col, 2001). Other researchers identified people's preference for bar graphs that were augmented to include some other type of display feature (e.g., flow diagrams in Dolan & Iadarola, 2008), while still others found that icon arrays were preferred over bar graphs (Schapira, Nattinger, & McAuliffe, 2006).

Beyond preferences, research has also examined differing message perceptions depending on graph type. For example, perceived evidence quality and perceived persuasiveness were found to be lower for visual presentations of risk (a bar graph) compared with verbal presentations (Parrott et al., 2005). Focus group studies found that some participants were more likely to perceive higher risk magnitudes when human-shaped figures were used in icon arrays compared with other formats such as bar graphs (Schapira,

Figure 13.1 Examples of Graphical Versus Illustrative Displays of Risk Information

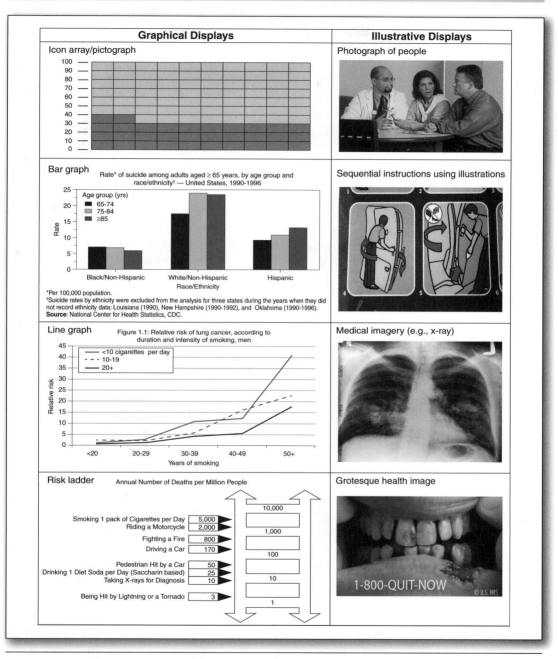

Sources: Photo of people: National Cancer Institute, by Rhoda Baer; bar graph: Centers for Disease Control and Prevention, Dr. Demetri Vacalis; sequential instructions using illustrations: © Scope/Alamy; line graph: Rylander, R., Axelsson, G., Andersson, L., et al. (1996). Lung cancer, smoking and diet among Swedish men. *Lung Cancer, 14* (Suppl. 1), S75–83; medical imagery: National Cancer Institute; risk ladder: adapted from Schultz, W., McClelland, G., Hurd, B., & Smith, J. (1986). *Improving accuracy and reducing costs of environmental benefits assessment*, Vol. 4. Boulder: University of Colorado, Center for Economic Analysis.

Nattinger, & McHorney, 2001). Follow-up research supported that conclusion and extended the work by determining that magnitude of risk was lower if highlighted icons were scattered among an array rather than appearing consecutively (Schapira et al., 2006). Overall, visual influence on message reception of graphical displays of risk information is varied and has yet to yield a consistent pattern of findings.

Comprehension

Comprehension outcomes include assessments of numerical risk estimation accuracy and ability to report correct answers about aspects of information in visual displays. The general conclusion of research reviews in this area is that the inclusion of graphical displays of risk often improves comprehension of information when compared with study conditions excluding visual information. One explanation for graphical displays of risk improving comprehension is that these displays attract and hold attention for longer periods of time, and reduce cognitive load, compared with written risk information (Smerecnik et al., 2010).

Research consistently supports the use of icon arrays—also called pictographs—to communicate risk information. Icon arrays increase comprehension of information about specific, discrete units of statistical information (Fagerlin, Zikmund-Fisher, & Ubel, 2011; Zikmund-Fisher, Ubel, et al., 2008). Additionally, icon arrays improved knowledge of prostate cancer screening compared with a nonvisual comparison message—although the use of icon arrays did not seem to influence screening behavior (Schapira & VanRuiswyk, 2000). Research comparing table, text, and icon arrays supported the superiority of pictographs for improving parent's specific and general understanding of risk information about pediatric postoperative pain control (Tait, Voepel-Lewis, Zikmund-Fisher, & Fagerlin, 2010). Another study suggested that pictographs were most accurately interpreted by men viewing graphical displays in the context of a videotape decision aid

(Pylar et al., 2007). People more accurately estimated risk information when icon arrays or bar graphs were shown as opposed to not being shown and further benefitted from the presented information including the entire population at risk (Garcia-Retamero & Galesic, 2010).

Research has produced conflicting results about the influence of bar graphs on comprehension. Parrott and colleagues (2005) found that the inclusion of a bar graph with text, compared with a text-only condition, resulted in lower comprehension levels of risk information. The opposite has been found in several studies. For example, Sprague, Russo, LaVallie, and Buchwald (2012) found that participants viewing bar graphs along with text were twice as likely to correctly interpret risk compared with a text-only condition. But, again, extant research has not yielded consistent patterns of findings across graph types.

Behaviors and Decisions

Fewer studies have examined the influence of graphical displays of risk information on changing behaviors and future decisions. In this category, in addition to behaviorally oriented outcomes such as intentions and actions, outcomes such as response times and visual attention are included. One study examined visual behavior via eye-tracking technology to determine people fixated more frequently on graphical information than written or other types of presentations (Smerecnik et al., 2010). Stone, Yates, and Parker (1997) found that people were more likely to engage in risk-avoidant behaviors when graphical displays of risk featured stick figures as opposed to numbers. Later work by the same group found that message consumers were more likely to have risk avoidant intentions if graphical displays focused on the number of people harmed and avoided discussion of the complete population at risk (Stone et al., 2003; see also Garcia-Retamero & Galesic, 2010). Carling and colleagues (2009) tested differences between icon arrays and three iterations of bar graphs, finding that bar graphs featuring symptom duration resulted in people making decisions more consistent with their previously expressed values (Carling et al., 2009). In other work, icon arrays presenting risk information incrementally—as opposed to presenting total risk—lowered worry among participants, which likely has positive implications for decision making (Zikmund-Fisher, Fagerlin, Roberts, Derry, & Ubel, 2008).

Illustrative Displays of Risk Information

Research on illustrative displays of risk information has increased significantly in recent years. There are some reviews on illustrative displays in nonrisk contexts, such as pictures and health communication (Houts et al., 2006), photographs and issue perceptions (Gibson, 2003), and intersections of imagery and the design of health communications (Cameron & Chan, 2008). Additionally, there are few studies that classify use of illustrative displays of risk information as relevant to the visual communication of risk. As such, this review features three major illustrative display categories: emotionally evocative, informative, and aesthetics/style.

Emotionally Evocative

Illustrative displays of risk have the potential to influence both the cognitive and emotional components of risk experience (Williams & Cameron, 2009). This claim is supported by a tradition of research in psychology that examines people's varied reactions to pictures (see, e.g., Lang, Greenwald, Bradley, & Hamm, 1993). Fewer studies examine the influence of illustrative displays specifically in risk communication contexts.

Photographs serving as visual exemplars, such as showing people addicted to drugs (Banerjee, Green, & Yanovitzky, 2011), have been found to elicit surprise responses from individuals. Evoking a surprise response is important, as such

a response can lead to someone engaging in preventive behaviors (see Zillmann, 2006). A review and meta-analysis of fear appeals research suggested that the use of grotesque images contributed to increased success of appeals and appraisals of risk severity (Witte & Allen, 2000), although not all studies support the persuasive benefit of illustrative fear appeals (Stephenson & Witte, 1998).

Informative

Illustrative displays of risk information also serve to communicate specific knowledge to various populations. One study examined the use of geographic information system mapping to help communities identify high-risk areas by plotting certain health surveillance data (Parrott et al., 2010). Comprehension of information about cigar-smoking risk was improved by showing comparative information about other smoking options (Strasser et al., 2011). Illustrated instructions improved comprehension and use of unfamiliar medical devices for asthma (Kools, van de Wiel, Ruiter, & Kok, 2006).

Perhaps the most researched aspect about informative illustrative displays is pharmaceuticals and medication instructions. Most of the pictorial aids used in this context are intended to reduce risks connected to the improper use of medication. Pictorial aids are generally believed to enhance comprehension of medication instructions, especially when these pictures are used alongside written or verbal information (Katz, Kripalani, & Weiss, 2006), although some rigorous trials found no benefit to pictorial presentations (e.g., Thompson, Goldszmidt, Schwartz, & Bashook, 2010).

Aesthetics/Style

Of images found in risk and health information pamphlets about cancer, a content analysis indicated that the majority of space is taken up by photographs of people (King, 2012). One explanation for the prominence of these photographs is that it offers some type of aesthetic appeal with the goal of increasing some concept like perceived relevance of health or risk information. Other research suggests that certain visual message features that might seem aesthetically oriented—stylistic properties—actually influence perceptions of textual information relevance (see, e.g., Wang & Peracchio, 2008). For example, interviews with African American women revealed the importance of culturally relevant colors for improving reception of health and risk information (Springston & Champion, 2004).

Relevant Theoretical Frameworks

The focus of the following discussion is on some of the prominent and relevant theories that should be considered in this line of inquiry.

Exemplification Theory

Exemplification theory explains how people use singular event occurrences, experienced personally or vicariously, to form and modify beliefs about various event phenomena (Zillmann, 2006). Research on exemplification theory covers a broad range of nonvisual and visual exemplars (e.g., Parrott et al., 2009; for a thorough overview, see Zillmann & Brosius, 2000), but considerable attention has been paid explicitly to how visual exemplars influence audience reception and perception of news coverage and social issues, such as assessments related to risk and health. For example, one study manipulated the type of visual exemplars displayed during a television news story, where participants were shown either threatening exemplars or "sanitized" exemplars of skin cancer cases (Zillmann & Gan, 1996). Participants did not demonstrate much difference in their risk assessments immediately following exposure, but 2 weeks postexposure, people in the "sanitized" image condition had a significantly lower risk assessment than those

exposed to grotesque exemplars; people who viewed the threatening exemplars maintained their initial risk assessment or increased it slightly.

Other work on exemplification theory has examined the role of victimization in visual exemplars. Zillmann and Gibson, as well as years of research on exemplification theory, suggest that images often convey additional information and have independent effects on people's perceptions of messages (see Gibson, 2003; Gibson & Zillmann, 2000). Exemplification theory also posits explicit relationships between visual exemplars, affective responses, risk assessment, and preventive behaviors. This particular aspect of exemplification theory is yet to be empirically supported for emotional response in general, there is preliminary support that at least one discrete emotion—surprise—seems to mediate the relationship between exemplification exposure and message effectiveness (Banerjee et al., 2011).

Theories of Fear Appeals

Fear appeals research is the most theoretically developed literature in terms of considering visual elements of messages presenting risks and hazards. Going back 60 years to early work on fear-arousing communications, studies used images of poor dental hygiene in message conditions presenting a strong fear appeal (Janis & Feshbach, 1953). Since then, some public health campaign efforts to improve people's understanding of risk information have used scary images with questionable success (see Ruiter, Abraham, & Kok, 2001). Within communication research, a popular theoretical lens with which to study fear appeals has been the extended parallel process model (EPPM). The EPPM predicts the success of fear appeals based on presentation of threat and efficacy message components (see Witte, 1992). Message recipients process threat-related information (e.g., susceptibility and severity of some risk) and efficacy-related information (e.g., beliefs about one's ability to manage a risk and the utility of a suggested risk management strategy). There has been a wealth of research on fear appeals using an EPPM approach and other relevant theories (see Maloney, Lapinski, & Witte, 2011; Witte & Allen, 2000), but most studies focus on verbal and written messages that include images as part of a manipulation rather than a theoretical consideration. Indeed, EPPM theorists suggest that manipulations of the threat component of the model, specifically risk severity, improved over time due to "vivid and often gruesome pictures accompanying fear appeals (as part of the manipulation). These gruesome pictures are likely to be novel and attended to more carefully than other less striking features of the message" (Witte & Allen, 2000, pp. 602–603). Thus far in research on the EPPM and visual messages, this appears to be the most common use of visual presentations of risk: to communicate threat, not efficacy.

Numerous studies suggest the efficiency of presenting risks illustratively through vivid and grotesque pictorials. Recently, researchers found that the grotesque pictorial warnings on cigarette packages, presented alongside a phone number for a quit line service, resulted in an enhanced intervention effect (see, e.g., Miller, Hill, Quester, & Hiller, 2009). Here, the threat component was visually communicated, while the efficacy component was verbally communicated. Acknowledging the potential to communicate efficacy messages visually is important since research suggests that only a marginal threat is needed to increase recipients' risk-protective behaviors (Gore & Bracken, 2005). Previous research supports the possibility that visual information about threats can result in participants feeling manipulated and no more likely to take risk-protective actions (Stephenson & Witte, 1998). A recent study, though, found that high threat messages, with the addition of a medical image of a person's predicted internal body fat, resulted in higher intentions to increase physical activity to recommended levels (Hollands & Marteau, 2013).

Visual Persuasion Framework

A theoretical perspective that continues to gain traction with communication science researchers is Messaris's (1997) theory of visual persuasion.[3] The framework offers a set of propositions and identifies potential causal mechanisms that explain why visual messages influence individuals. Messaris divides consideration of visual influence into two focal points based on semiological theorizing: the semantic and the syntactic properties of visual messages. Semantic properties of images include indexicality and iconicity. Indexical images represent reality in some way: that is, images with indexical properties typically offer proof that what is seen in a picture—whether a person, thing, place, or event—can exist (e.g., a photograph of environmental hazards like contaminated water supplies). Iconic images often have a meaning that is shared by those who see the image (e.g., some corporate logos), or they may be abstractly representative (e.g., male/female stick figures on public bathroom entryways). These semantic image properties have received relatively little attention in communication research. This is disappointing as Messaris (1997) points out that images "possess [indexicality and iconicity] while other modes of communication do not" (p. xvii).

Messaris's theorizing regarding the syntactical features of images—specifically syntactic indeterminacy—has received some attention from communication scholars in health message processing (e.g., Niederdeppe, 2005). Syntactic indeterminacy refers to the lack of explicit, pre-existing rules to process and "read" images (Messaris, 1997). Messaris's (1997) typology of four nonmutually exclusive propositions related to syntactic indeterminacy identified how visual messages can result in people cognitively constructing: (1) causal connections, (2) contrasts, (3) analogies, and (4) generalizations. Niederdeppe (2005) found that message features such as intense imagery and unrelated cuts, which are relevant to syntactic indeterminacy, increased message processing in the context of antitobacco advertisements. Overall, though, there are still few studies that examine Messaris's propositions explicitly or empirically. The framework of visual persuasion offers an avenue for researchers to conduct theoretically grounded work, focusing on juxtapositions, visual tropes, metaphors, and other outlets of innovative visual messaging potentially useful to risk communicators.

Reflections for Theory and Research

There are numerous challenges in studying visual messaging and risk communication for communication science researchers. These challenges include the cost and effort in procuring and producing quality visual stimuli, the ability to include visual displays in research monographs because of journal or creative material copyright issues, the ability to replicate or extend certain findings without having access to original visual stimuli, and a disjointed lexicon of research terms.

The procurement and production of quality visual stimuli can be affected by limited funding for research products, unfamiliarity with information material design software, or lack of understanding of general graphic design principles.[4] One way to overcome this obstacle is to seek grant funding for projects, obviously, but there are other cost-effective ways to manage the inclusion of visual content into messaging stimuli. There are some online databases, such as the National Cancer Institute's (2012) "NCI Visuals Online" site that contains images researchers could use in risk communication contexts. Another source is the Public Health Image Library offered by the Centers for Disease Control and Prevention (2012). Both sites offer images that can be used in message stimuli with minimal (if any) steps required to receive permission for use in publications. Other online tools, like the University of Michigan's "Icon

Array" site, offer the ability to create custom icon arrays (University of Michigan, 2012).

Interdisciplinary collaborations might also address another limitation of current research: diversity in how visual displays are referenced in the literature. For example, some studies use *illustrated pamphlets*, a term that can refer to pictographs and icon arrays with human figures rather than dots (see, e.g., Schapira & VanRuiswyk, 2000) or to (cartoon) illustrations (see, e.g., Delp & Jones, 1996). Neither phrasing is wrong, but it creates confusion in chapters such as this that categorize pictographs as graphical displays and cartoon illustrations as illustrative displays. Similarly, some research refers to graphics in the context of charts and graphs (e.g., Schapira et al., 2006), whereas other research refers to grotesque images as graphic (e.g., Hammond, Fong, McDonald, Brown, & Cameron, 2003).[5] There are no easy solutions to this terminological complexity, but researchers can help clarify these problems by including visual stimuli in research reports or by providing supplementary material through Internet sites.

Theoretically, the next step for visual messaging and risk communication is the more consistent use of existing frameworks to build on the strong empirical foundation of studies concerned with visual displays and risk, as discussed in this chapter and elsewhere in the volume. The goal should be to create predictive models and explicit recommendations to generate future work. Building from message-oriented frameworks like exemplification theory will help researchers identify visual message features, intervening message perceptions and individual differences, and modal explanations for more efficient ways to communicate the complexities and uncertainties of risk information. The strength of a features-based approach to studying visual messages, in line with O'Keefe's (2003) recommendations about message research and theorizing—generally—is that it allows researchers to explore more nuanced shifts, characteristics, and associations in visual messages and visual–verbal interactions. Previous visual message features research in risk contexts and beyond include colors (e.g., Gerend & Sias, 2009), complexity (e.g., Pieters, Wedel, & Batra, 2010), shapes (see Messaris, 1997), perspective (e.g., Schuldt, Konrath, & Schwarz, 2012), and congruency of visual–verbal information (King, Jensen, Davis, & Carcioppolo, in press).

Additionally, there needs to be considerations about advancements in the field of data visualization—and the ability for these visualizations to be interactive. The use of data visualization as a statistical tool for exploring large data sets is popular in disciplines like computer science and statistics, but the potential use of these visualization tools to communicate complex information—like risk information—to the general public are largely unexplored. As these data visualization tools become more widespread, risk communicators need to consider how the public may benefit from layered visual presentations of relevant risk information.

Recommendations for Practice

The disparate, but rich, corpus of past research on visual messaging and risk communication yields few consistent findings. Reviewing research on visual, verbal, and numeric formats of communicating health risk information, Lipkus (2007) presented some general recommendations for best practices based on empirical research: (1) some graphical displays are better at specific tasks, (2) graphical displays should be proportionally display quantities displayed to avoid biased processing by message receivers, (3) icon arrays assist in improving the accuracy of people's numeric estimates, and (4) icon arrays provide clear explanations of graphical display components (e.g., axes, data points). While these recommendations are necessarily broad, they are the product of inconsistent and often atheoretical research findings. Concrete, actionable recommendations are difficult when there are few consistent patterns of findings.

Additionally, the recommendations do not address illustrative displays of risk information (as defined and discussed in this chapter). The upcoming years of research should address this deficiency and focus on systematic, theoretically oriented work that affords more predictive potential and eases the possibility that specific recommendations can be made for risk communicators.

Conclusions

Many reviews on visual communication and visual messaging elements, in a variety of scholarly contexts, end by suggesting that this area of study is in its infancy. While this is somewhat true theoretically, the conclusion is generally inaccurate. This period of infancy is no more, and the perpetuation of the claim that there is not a strong, diverse empirical foundation for future inquiry should end. The foundational—and continuing—work completed in the past five to six decades across disciplines like psychology, engineering, computer science, public health, communication, sociology, medicine, anthropology, nursing, and the decision sciences provides ample entry points to begin systematic research on graphical and illustrative displays of visual risk information, especially from a communication perspective. Research will continue to evolve into visual representations of risk in developing technologies like virtual reality (e.g., Kaphingst et al., 2009) and complex topical areas of study such as ways to convey uncertainty visually (e.g., Deitrick & Edsall, 2008; Spiegelhalter, Pearson, & Short, 2011). Intensifying interest across these domains of inquiry may quickly advance empirical and theoretical understanding of how people process, respond, and act on visual media messages and visualizations about risk, health, science, and complex information in general. This is an encouraging development, as without an understanding of the visual components, there would continue to be an incomplete understanding of the influence and importance of risk communication messages.

Notes

1. On occasion, researchers examine all of the categories identified. For example, Price, Cameron, and Butow (2007) examined preferences for format, comprehension, and response time differences.

2. This section does not talk in detail about individual differences important to the reception and processing of graphical displays of risk information, such as numeracy (see Chapter 9, this volume) and graphicacy (see Aldrich & Sheppard, 2000). Interested readers are directed toward a multidisciplinary review of numeracy (Ancker & Kaufman, 2007) as well as an empirical exploration of graphicacy in health contexts (Brown et al., 2011) as starting points.

3. One concern that warrants mention is the recommendation here to use persuasion strategies and theories in risk communication situations. Readers are encouraged to read further on the role of persuading and informing in the context of risk communication more broadly (see, e.g., Johnson, 1999). Ethical use of visual presentations of risk are paramount, but what is or is not considered ethical may differ based on the hazard or risk being communicated. As such, while there are likely information seeking contexts where persuasion approaches are suboptimal, there may be high risk or crisis situations where such approaches are preferred.

4. Although, it should be noted that most graphic design principles are principles of practice and not theory, there are few studies, if any, that attempt to test graphic design suggestions that might be considered "tried and true" outside of academic settings (e.g., in advertising or marketing).

5. The studies cited to exemplify the occasionally confusing use of similar terms—Delp and Jones (1996), Hammond et al. (2003), Schapira et al. (2006), Schapira and VanRuiswyk (2000)—are used as such because of the high quality of the research presented in those articles. Indeed, given the complexities of talking about visual representations of information, the approaches used by those authors serve as examples of clarity in practice.

Suggested Additional Readings

Bissett, S., Wood, S., Cox, R., Scott, D., & Cassell, J. (2013). Calculating alcohol risk in a visualization tool for promoting healthy behavior. *Patient Education & Counseling, 92,* 167–173.

Garcia-Retamero, R., & Hoffrage, U. (2013). Visual representation of statistical information improves diagnostic inferences in doctors and their patients. *Social Science & Medicine, 83,* 27–33.

Hegarty, M. (2011). The cognitive science of visual-spatial displays: Implications for design. *Topics in Cognitive Science, 3,* 446–474.

Lee, T. J., Cameron, L. D., Wünsche, B., & Stevens, C. (2011). A randomized trial of computer-based communications using imagery and text information to alter representations of heart disease risk and motivate protective behavior. *British Journal of Health Psychology, 16,* 72–91.

References

Aldrich, F., & Sheppard, L. (2000). "Graphicacy": The fourth "r"? *Primary Science Review, 64,* 8–11.

Ancker, J. S., & Kaufman, D. (2007). Rethinking health numeracy: A multidisciplinary literature review. *Journal of the American Medical Informatics Association, 14,* 713–721.

Ancker, J. S., Senathirajah, Y., Kukafka, R., & Starren, J. B. (2006). Design features of graphs in health risk communication: A systematic review. *Journal of the American Medical Informatics Association, 13,* 608–618.

Banerjee, S. C., Greene, K., & Yanovitzky, I. (2011). Sensation seeking and dosage effect: An exploration of the role of surprise in anti-cocaine messages. *Journal of Substance Use, 16,* 1–13.

Brown, S. M., Culver, J. O., Osann, K. E., MacDonald, D. J., Sand, S., Thornton, A. A., . . . Weitzel, J. N. (2011). Health literacy, numeracy, and interpretation of graphical breast cancer risk estimates. *Patient Education & Counseling, 83,* 92–98.

Cameron, L. D., & Chan, C. K. Y. (2008). Designing health communications: Harnessing the power of affect, imagery, and self-regulation. *Social and Personality Psychology Compass, 2,* 262–282.

Carling, C. L. L., Kristofferson, D. T., Flottorp, S., Fretheim, A., Oxman, A. D., Schünemann, H. J., . . .

Montori, V. M. (2009). The effect of alternative graphical displays used to present the benefits of antibiotics for sore throat on decisions about whether to seek treatment: A randomized trial. *PLoS Medicine, 6,* e1000140.

Centers for Disease Control and Prevention. (2012). *Public Health Image Library (PHIL).* Retrieved from http://phil.cdc.gov/

Deitrick, S., & Edsall, R. (2008). Making uncertainty usable: Approaches for visualizing uncertain information. In M. Dodge, M. McDerby, & M. Turner (Eds.), *Geographic visualization: Concepts, tools, and applications* (pp. 277–291). Hoboken, NJ: Wiley.

Delp, C., & Jones, J. (1996). Communicating information to patients: The use of cartoon illustrations to improve comprehension of instructions. *Academic Emergency Medicine, 3,* 264–270.

Dolan, J. G., & Iadarola, S. (2008). Risk communication formats for low probability events: An exploratory study of patient preferences. *BMC Medical Informatics & Decision Making, 8,* 14.

Fagerlin, A., Zikmund-Fisher, B. J., & Ubel, P. A. (2011). Helping patients decide: Ten steps to better risk communication. *Journal of the National Cancer Institute, 103,* 1436–1443.

Fortin, J. M., Hirota, L. K., Bond, B. E., O'Connor, A. M., & Col, N. F. (2001). Identifying patient preferences for communicating risk estimates: A descriptive pilot study. *BMC Medical Informatics & Decision Making, 1,* 2.

Garcia-Retamero, R., & Galesic, M. (2010). Who profits from visual aids: Overcoming challenges in people's understanding of risks. *Social Science & Medicine, 70,* 1019–1025.

Gerend, M. A., & Sias, T. (2009). Message framing and color priming: How subtle threat cues affect persuasion. *Journal of Experimental Social Psychology, 45,* 999–1002.

Gibson, R. (2003). Effects of photograph on issue perception. In J. Bryant, D. R. Roskos-Ewoldsen, & J. Cantor (Eds.), *Communication and emotion: Essays in honor of Dolf Zillmann* (pp. 323–345). Mahwah, NJ: Lawrence Erlbaum.

Gibson, R., & Zillmann, D. (2000). Reading between the photographs: The influence of incidental pictorial information on issue perception. *Journalism & Mass Communication Quarterly, 77,* 355–366.

Gore, T. D., & Bracken, C. C. (2005). Testing the theoretical design of a health risk message: Reexamining the major tenets of the extended parallel process model. *Health Education & Behavior, 32,* 27–41.

Grieshop, J. I., & Winter, D. (1988). Communication for safety's sake: Visual communication materials for pesticide users in Latin America. *Tropical Pest Management, 34,* 249–262.

Hammond, D., Fong, G. T., McDonald, P. W., Brown, S., & Cameron, R. (2004). Graphic Canadian cigarette warning labels and adverse outcomes: Evidence from Canadian smokers. *American Journal of Public Health, 94,* 1442–1445.

Hollands, G. J., & Marteau, T. M. (2013). The impact of using visual images of the body within a personalized health risk assessment: An experimental study. *British Journal of Health Psychology, 18,* 263–278.

Houts, P. S., Doak, C. C., Doak, L. G., & Loscalzo, M. J. (2006). The role of pictures in improving health communication: A review of research on attention, comprehension, recall, and adherence. *Patient Education & Counseling, 61,* 173–190.

Janis, I. L., & Feshbach, S. (1953). Effects of fear-arousing communications. *Journal of Abnormal & Social Psychology, 48,* 78–92.

Johnson, B. B. (1999). Ethical issues in risk communication: Continuing the discussion. *Risk Analysis, 19,* 335–348.

Kaphingst, K. A., Persky, S., McCall, C., Lachance, C., Beall, A. C., & Blascovich, J. (2009). Testing communication strategies to convey genomic concepts using virtual reality technology. *Journal of Health Communication, 14,* 384–399.

Katz, M. G., Kripalani, S., & Weiss, B. D. (2006). Use of pictorial aids in medication instructions: A review of the literature. *American Journal of Health-System Pharmacy, 63,* 2391–2397.

King, A. J. (2012). *Putting the picture together: An investigation of visual persuasion and information in health communication contexts* (Unpublished doctoral dissertation). Purdue University, West Lafayette, IN.

King, A. J., Jensen, J. D., Davis, L. A., & Carcioppolo, N. (in press). Perceived visual informativeness (PVI): Construct and scale development to assess visual health information in printed materials. *Journal of Health Communication.*

Kools, M., van de Wiel, M. W. J., Ruiter, R. A. C., & Kok, G. (2006). Pictures and text in instructions for medical devices: Effects on recall and actual performance. *Patient Education & Counseling, 64,* 104–111.

Kosslyn, S. M. (1994). *Elements of graph design.* New York, NY: W. H. Freeman.

Kosslyn, S. M. (2006). *Graph design for the eye and mind.* New York, NY: Oxford University Press.

Lang, P. J., Greenwald, M. K., Bradley, M. M., & Hamm, A. O. (1993). Looking at pictures: Affective, facial, visceral, and behavioral reactions. *Psychophysiology, 30,* 261–273.

Lester, P. M. (2014). *Visual communication: Images with messages* (6th ed.). Boston, MA: Wadsworth.

Lipkus, I. M. (2007). Numeric, verbal, and visual formats of conveying health risks: Suggested best practices and future recommendations. *Medical Decision Making, 27,* 696–713.

Lipkus, I. M., & Hollands, J. G. (1999). The visual communication of risk. *Journal of the National Cancer Institute Monographs, 25,* 149–163.

Maloney, E. K., Lapinski, M. K., & Witte, K. (2011). Fear appeals and persuasion: A review and update of the extended parallel process model. *Social Psychology & Personality Compass, 5,* 206–219.

Messaris, P. (1997). *Visual persuasion: The role of images in advertising.* Thousand Oaks, CA: Sage.

Meyer, R. E., Höllerer, M. A., Jancsary, D., & van Leeuwen, T. (2013). The visual dimension in organizing, organization, and organization research: Core ideas, current developments, and promising avenues. *Academy of Management Annals, 7,* 489–555.

Miller, C. L., Hill, D. J., Quester, P. G., & Hiller, J. E. (2009). Impact on the Australian Quitline of new graphic cigarette pack warnings including the Quitline number. *Tobacco Control, 18,* 235–237.

National Cancer Institute. (2012). *NCI visuals online.* Retrieved from http://visualsonline.cancer.gov

Niederdeppe, J. D. (2005). Syntactic indeterminacy, perceived message sensation value-enhancing features, and message processing in the context of anti-tobacco advertisements. *Communication Monographs, 72,* 324–344.

O'Keefe, D. J. (2003). Message properties, mediating states, and manipulation checks: Claims, evidence, and data analysis in experimental persuasive message effects research. *Communication Theory, 13,* 251–274.

Parrott, R., Silk, K., Dorgan, K., Condit, C., & Harris, T. (2005). Risk comprehension and judgments of statistical evidentiary appeals: When a picture is not worth a thousand words. *Human Communication Research, 31,* 423–452.

Parrott, R., Volkman, J. E., Hillemeier, M. M., Weisman, C. S., Chase, G. A., & Dyer, A.-M. (2009). Pregnancy intentions and folic acid supplementation exemplars: Findings from the Central Pennsylvania Women's Health Study. *Journal of Health Communication, 14,* 366–383.

Parrott, R., Volkman, J. E., Lengerich, E., Ghetian, C. B., Chadwick, A. E., & Hopfer, S. (2010). Using geographic information systems to promote community involvement in comprehensive cancer control. *Health Communication, 25,* 276–285.

Pieters, R., Wedel, M., & Batra, R. (2010). The stopping power of advertising: Measures and effects of visual complexity. *Journal of Marketing, 74,* 48–60.

Price, M., Cameron, R., & Butow, P. (2007). Communicating risk information: The influence of graphical display format on quantitative information perception—accuracy, comprehension and preferences. *Patient Education & Counseling, 69,* 121–128.

Pylar, J., Wills, C. E., Lillie, J., Rovner, D. R., Kelly-Blake, K., & Holmes-Rovner, M. (2007). Men's interpretations of graphical information in a videotape decision aid. *Health Expectations, 10,* 184–193.

Ruiter, R. A. C., Abraham, C., & Kok, G. (2001). Scary warnings and rational precautions: A review of the psychology of fear appeals. *Psychology & Health, 16,* 613–630.

Schapira, M. M., & VanRuiswyk, J. (2000). The effect of an illustrated pamphlet decision-aid on the use of prostate cancer screening tests. *Journal of Family Practice, 49,* 418–424.

Schapira, M. M., Nattinger, A. B., & McAuliffe, T. L. (2006). The influence of graphic format on breast cancer risk communication. *Journal of Health Communication, 11,* 569–582.

Schapira, M. M., Nattinger, A. B., & McHorney, C. A. (2001). Frequency or probability? A qualitative study of risk communication formats used in health care. *Medical Decision Making, 21,* 459–467.

Schuldt, J. P., Konrath, S. H., & Schwarz, N. (2012). The right angle: Visual portrayal of products affects observers' impressions of owners. *Psychology & Marketing, 29,* 705–711.

Smerecnik, C. M. R., Mesters, I., Kessels, L. T. E., Ruiter, R. A. C., de Vries, N. K., & de Vries, H. (2010). Understanding the positive effects of graphical risk information on comprehension: Measuring attention directed to written, tabular, and graphical risk information. *Risk Analysis, 30,* 1387–1398.

Spiegelhalter, D., Pearson, M., & Short, I. (2011). Visualizing uncertainty about the future. *Science, 333,* 1393–1400.

Sprague, D., Russo, J. E., LaVallie, D. L., & Buchwald, D. S. (2012). Influence of framing and graphic format on comprehension of risk information among American Indian tribal college students. *Journal of Cancer Education, 27*(4), 752–758.

Springston, J. K., & Champion, V. L. (2004). Public relations and cultural aesthetics: Designing health brochures. *Public Relations Review, 30,* 483–491.

Stephenson, M. T., & Witte, K. (1998). Fear, threat, and perceptions of efficacy from frightening skin cancer messages. *Public Health Reviews, 26,* 147–174.

Stone, E. R., Sieck, W. R., Bull, B. E., Yates, J. F., Parks, S. C., & Rush, C. J. (2003). Foreground:background salience: Explaining the effects of graphical displays on risk avoidance. *Organizational Behavior and Human Decision Processes, 90,* 19–36.

Stone, E. R., Yates, J. F., & Parker, A. M. (1997). Effects of numerical and graphical displays on professed risk-taking behavior. *Journal of Experimental Psychology: Applied, 3,* 243–256.

Strasser, A. A., Orom, H., Tang, K. Z., Dumont, R. L., Cappella, J. N., & Kozlowski, L. T. (2011). Graphic-enhanced information improves perceived risks of cigar smoking. *Addictive Behaviors, 36,* 865–869.

Tait, A. R., Voepel-Lewis, T., Zikmund-Fisher, B. J., & Fagerlin, A. (2010). The effect of format on parents' understanding of the risks and benefits of clinical research. *Journal of Health Communication, 15,* 487–501.

Thompson, A. E., Goldszmidt, M. A., Schwartz, A. J., & Bashook, P. G. (2010). A randomized trial of pictorial versus prose-based medication information pamphlets. *Patient Education & Counseling, 78,* 389–393.

University of Michigan. (2012). *Icon array.* Retrieved from http://www.iconarray.com

Wang, K-Y., & Peracchio, L. A. (2008). Reading pictures: Understanding the stylistic properties of advertising images. In E. F. McQuarrie & B. J. Phillips (Eds.), *Go figure! New directions in advertising rhetoric* (pp. 205–226). New York, NY: M. E. Sharpe.

Williams, B., & Cameron, L. (2009). Images in health care: Potential and problems. *Journal of Health Services Research & Policy, 14,* 251–254.

Witte, K. (1992). Putting the fear back into fear appeals: The extended parallel process model. *Communication Monographs, 59,* 329–349.

Witte, K., & Allen, M. (2000). A meta-analysis of fear appeals: Implications for effective public health campaigns. *Health Education & Behavior, 27,* 591–615.

Zikmund-Fisher, B. J., Fagerlin, A., Roberts, T. R., Derry, H. A., & Ubel, P. A. (2008). Alternate methods of framing information about medication side effects: Incremental risk versus total risk of occurrence. *Journal of Health Communication, 13,* 107–124.

Zikmund-Fisher, B. J., Ubel, P. A., Smith, D. M., Derry, H. A., McClure, J. B., Stark, A., . . . Fagerlin, A. (2008). Communicating side effect risks in tamoxifen prophylaxis decision aid: The debiasing influence of pictographs. *Patient Education & Counseling, 73,* 209–214.

Zillmann, D. (2006). Exemplification effects in the promotion of safety and health. *Journal of Communication, 56,* S221–S237.

Zillmann, D., & Brosius, H.-B. (2000). *Exemplification in communication: The influence of case reports on the perception of issues.* Mahwah, NJ: Lawrence Erlbaum.

Zillmann, D., & Gan, S. (1996). Effects of threatening images in news programs on the perception of risk to others and self. *Medienpsychologie: Zeitschrift fur Individual-und Massenkommunkikation, 8,* 288–305.

SECTION 6

Risk Communication and the Media

CHAPTER 14

Media Portrayal of Risk

The Social Production of News

Susanna Priest

Introduction

The study of media content production is important to the study of risk communication because most audience members get much of their information about risk from media accounts. This chapter is concerned with this question: What forces tend to shape that mediated information to begin with, with respect to risk information? While audiences are certainly made up of individuals (and are very often studied at the individual unit-of-analysis level),[1] the processes through which media coverage is shaped reflect complex organizational, institutional, societal, and professional factors, as well as the nature of the broader culture in which these factors play out. The knowledge, assumptions, and beliefs that are widely shared within that culture clearly come into play. Also in play are political and economic constraints that cannot easily be reduced to individual-level decisions. Rather, these are all group or societal processes rather than reflecting primarily the independent influences of individual journalistic actors on individual audience members.

This chapter looks primarily at media coverage of risks associated with emerging technologies, including technology-related problems such as climate change. Studies of media treatments of other types of risks are included only to suggest the many other types of content research that are available and relevant. However, even for emerging technologies risks, this chapter is hardly a complete account. Rather, the intent is to illustrate prominent themes, apparent gaps, and promising areas for future research toward a better theoretical understanding of the social production of risk news in the context of an interest in the social construction of reality more generally.

For purposes of this chapter, framing is less about effects and more about what journalists do to write a story that stresses a particular theme or narrative—a definition not unlike the widely quoted one provided by Entman (1993), which stresses the selection of some "aspects of a perceived reality" in preference to others (p. 52). The present discussion is concerned with understanding the way news is created, in which manipulation of what people think may take place but is generally not strategic in nature.

A Hierarchy of Influences?

Reflecting the proliferation of these and other conceptualizations of media structure and function as influenced by a variety of factors, the "hierarchy of influences" model developed by Shoemaker and Reese (1996) attempted to reestablish academic order by dividing influences on media content into distinct categories arising from various quarters, arranged in a hierarchical order from the most microlevel to the most macrolevel: influences from individual media workers; influences of "media routines," or typical professional practices operating within media organizations; organizational influences, such as the centrality of economic goals to media operations; a broad variety of external influences (sources, interest groups, advertisers, audiences, the government, "the market," and technology); and ideology, referring to the influence of belief systems. This taxonomy is useful in facilitating discussion of studies that concern the micro- to midlevel influences on the general practice of journalism; these influences are the same ones that influence coverage of science and of risk, at least as practiced in developed countries similar to the United States.

However, the lines between levels in the hierarchy are not always firmly drawn. In a well-known analysis, Nelkin (1995) argues that journalists covering science and technology share with the scientific community a conviction that objectivity is both possible and desirable. They also share a belief in the authority and "purity" of science. These are to some extent matters of individual belief but also of shared professional norms and ideals as well as ideology, in Shoemaker and Reese's scheme, in that these beliefs also have political ramifications. In Nelkin's view, these professional beliefs seem to influence science coverage. Rather than inducing disillusionment, Nelkin argues, reports of scientific fraud simply "elicit moral outrage" among journalists in ways that tend to reinforce the image of purity rather than assail it (p. 26), much the same way Gans (1979) argued that coverage of disorder springs from a pervasive concern with order. Yet in showing how journalists' ideological beliefs about scientific objectivity and "purity" influence the

actual practice of their profession, Nelkin is also concerned with everyday work routines influencing the way that stories are selected and developed. Nelkin's focus was on science more generally, but her conclusions also seem relevant to risk.

Singer and Endreny (1993), in their extensive study of journalistic coverage of risk, also emphasize journalistic routines. They discuss the nature of "fact-checking" procedures and conclude that these generally only go so far as to make sure the current account matches prior accounts published elsewhere. (Arguably, such practices are just as pervasive today.) However, they also briefly review the literature on accuracy in scientific reporting from the point of view of scientist sources and conclude that most scientists are more likely to criticize media reports for being incomplete than for being literally factually inaccurate. And in Singer and Endreny's view, "biased" media reporting of risks is more commonly a matter of overemphasizing rare or new risks and underemphasizing common ones rather than getting the essential facts wrong. Consistent with Shoemaker and Reese's "external influences" hypothesis and Gandy's (1982) "information subsidy" hypothesis, both of which paint pictures of media institutions as very strongly influenced by numerous forces external to themselves, the authors of this study found that government officials, followed by industry spokespeople, were the most commonly cited sources in risk stories, with university scientists accounting for just over 7% of sources cited (p. 130).

Is Coverage of Risk and Science Unique?

Dearing (1995) used content analysis and survey research to show how what he terms "maverick" (i.e., fringe minority) scientific views on earthquake prediction, AIDS causation, and "cold fusion" research are lent credibility through media accounts. The same thinking has been applied to coverage of risk, showing how journalists' commitment to "balance" and particular notions of what constitutes a good story have likewise distorted news of climate change (Boykoff & Boykoff, 2007). These are examples of how the professional norms of journalism can distort coverage of science generally and of risk specifically. Balance is often the journalistic operationalization of "objectivity," which itself has roots in political reporting. Arguably, for the purpose of appealing to audiences with a variety of political perspectives, U.S. journalists since the 19th century have moved away from the style of reporting that existed when newspapers had strong political party affiliations, a move often attributed to the desire to attract wider audiences but that has since become canonized as an ethical responsibility.[2]

Within science itself, a different ethic prevails: "Truth" is largely defined by the existence of a scientific consensus, generally (at least in the ideal) following extensive study, discussion, argumentation, review, and replication of results.[3] Individual studies rarely upset the conventional scientific wisdom; once adopted, scientific consensus tends to be robust. Yet journalists may nevertheless feel obligated to seek opposing views to create a "balanced" story, whether before the scientific community has fully engaged in considering a new idea (as in the case of cold fusion) or after a consensus has fully formed (as in the case of climate change). While this chapter has argued till now that news about risk (and science more generally) shares many of its underlying social dynamics with news of other kinds, this issue of the negative power of "balance" appears to be somewhat particular to coverage of science—and of risk.

This dynamic—the desire for balance in the context of information subsidies arising from outside the newsroom—creates opportunities that are regularly exploited by particular interests, whether the case in point is the tobacco industry using news media to put forth a variety of arguments against the further control of smoking, despite the public health data and general medical consensus about its risks (Menashe & Siegel, 1998), or media's coverage of antivaccination groups arguing that an alleged vaccination–autism link has not yet been disproven, again

despite what appears to be a clear scientific consensus on this point, as well as on the risk reduction vaccination offers (Clarke, 2008). Clearly, in some cases, the appearance of contrarian views in news accounts of risk might be counterproductive with respect to reducing the overall societal risk exposure, especially to the extent audiences might not be sophisticated enough to judge available evidence for themselves.

Yet this dynamic also opens the door for public consideration of other contrarian positions that may be entirely correct. One widely publicized case originating in 1989 has involved environmental interests using media publicity to argue that use of the pesticide alar on fresh produce such as apples should be banned because of its carcinogenic potential, particularly with respect to children. However, while the courts have vindicated "60 Minutes" on multiple occasions for running the original story, conventional wisdom often assumes that the story was simply wrong (Nigen, 1996). This is despite the fact that the U.S. Environmental Protection Agency subsequently banned alar based on its carcinogenic potential (U.S. Environmental Protection Agency, 1989). Meanwhile, in as many as 13 U.S. states, and strange as it may sound, disparaging perishable produce has been made illegal, an outcome widely associated with the alar controversy. While journalists need to be responsible about how they present nonmainstream views on scientific controversies, whether from industry, advocacy groups, or other sources, the availability of diverse points of view on risks would appear to be an important societal good in itself. The catch is that public or scientific literacy (see Miller, 1998) may not always suffice to sort out the wisest path forward in all cases.

Risks of Emerging Technologies: A Case in Point

Many risk-related concerns arise in the context of considering emerging technologies. These may appear as part of a formal technology assessment, arise from simple scholarly curiosity, or derive from efforts to envision how future public opinion and policy might develop. Related content studies tend not to be organized around how journalistic accounts of risk are produced (something we need more of and that would help these analyses move beyond description alone) but rather around the life histories of particular technologies. For agricultural biotechnology (genetic engineering of food crops), much controversy has surrounded the reasons why media and public criticism (including concerns over risks) were more prominent in Europe than in the United States. As a result, a large cluster of content studies over the past several decades concerns this technology. Priest (2000) used media content data to examine statements made by the agricultural biotechnology industry early in this history, as reflected in U.S. coverage that was heavily industry dominated. The study concluded that many of these statements tended to attribute criticisms and concerns to public ignorance rather than addressing the criticisms themselves.

Gaskell et al. (2001) speculate that the U.S. press's greater commitment to the notion of "objectivity" (usually defined as two opposing views) meant that the European press was more likely to present a range of views on biotechnology, as on other issues, even at early stages of any controversy. And Priest and Ten Eyck (2004), comparing U.S. and European coverage of both forms of biotechnology, found that coverage of medical biotechnology was generally more positive in both regions and that the differences in general tone of coverage between medical and agricultural biotechnology were of greater magnitude than the differences in coverage between the United States and Europe. Finally, in a recent case study of press coverage in northern Belgium, Maeseele and Schuurman (2012) found challenges to the acceptance of agricultural biotechnology prominent, while a source-driven protechnology bias was more apparent for medical biotechnology.

Objections to biotechnology in both Europe and the United States seem to stem from deeper cultural issues. Food is a sensitive topic, and the idea of altering major components of the food supply in novel ways, especially without broad consultation, is simply troubling to a good share of the population. This issue of "cultural resonance" is largely missing from the hierarchy of influences model, perhaps because it was developed with particular respect to only a single country, the United States. In both regions, however, food biotechnology is seen as problematic, only to varying degrees. One would expect this to be visible in the media coverage of both regions. An open issue is the extent to which U.S. media simply "pasted over" this perception by overreliance on industry sources. Content analysis by itself cannot entirely answer questions like these, although it can provide some insights.

Today, arguably one of the most studied emerging technologies for content researchers is nanotechnology, where significant government investment in both the United States and Europe has gone to research on public reception. However, somewhat ironically, so far nanotechnology seems not to have awakened much concern about risks among the public in either Europe or the United States, a phenomenon that could be attributed to limited coverage of those risks; indeed, experts seem more concerned than lay people. Wilkinson, Allan, Anderson, and Petersen (2007) analyzed British newspaper coverage of nanotechnology from 2003 to 2006; they also asked both scientists and journalists about their views of this coverage. Scientists were concerned about the safety of nanoparticles, but this aspect received little coverage in the press. Media coverage in European countries ranging from Germany (Donk, Metag, Kohring, & Marcinkowski, 2011) to Slovenia (Groboljsek & Mali, 2012) seems similarly positive.

Weaver, Lively, and Bimber (2009), analyzing nanotechnology-related content for the United States, report that at the end of their study period (2008), the most common frame seen was a "generic risk" frame (p. 161). However, Friedman and Egolf (2012), in U.S. data extending through

2011, observe that coverage of nanotechnology-related risk peaked in 2006 but then dropped off steadily. (These authors also provide comparison data for the United Kingdom, but the pattern is more erratic.) Such a pattern suggests that nanotechnology is close to the end point of the "issue–attention cycle," and it may take new developments to put it back into play in the media. Generally, these two groups of studies underscore the possibility that biotechnology had unique cultural characteristics that resonated with at least some segments of the population, keeping it under public scrutiny (and the subject of both media and research attention) longer, whereas nanotechnology appears not to have the same trajectory, at least not as reflected in media representations to date. Furthermore, Europe and the United States do not appear strikingly different in their relative degree of positive versus negative coverage. Once again, this is only a small selection of the studies available, however.

One example of climate change content analysis has already been mentioned above (Boykoff & Boykoff, 2007); there are, of course, many others. In an unusual recent study that helps illustrate the range of content research that can be done looked at reader comments disputing climate change in the United Kingdom's *Daily Mail* (Jaspal, Nerlich, & Koteyko, 2013) rather than at journalist-written content. Dragojlovic and Einsiedel (2013) took a different tack and used experimental methods to study reactions to hypothetical news content about synthetic biology, another alternative approach to studying the importance of risk in the media. The subjects of other recent content studies involving risk range from existing technologies such as nuclear power to a host of more recently emerging technological developments. Further research in this area is needed, however.

Reflections for Theory and Research

These studies illustrate the proliferation of approaches to the study of media production and content, as well as illustrating the range of risk topics that have been considered, particularly those involving technology. However, this essay has not dealt with any of the following: the media component of the vast literature on health and disease risks in much depth; the literature on food risks outside of agricultural biotechnology; the environmental risks not directly associated with emerging technologies; the economic, war, or terrorism risks; and the extensive literature on risks of natural disaster. If Beck (1992) is correct that we have become a "risk society," perhaps the proliferation of risk topics in the news (and in research about the news) shouldn't be all that surprising.

What we can learn from these media and content studies taken together, even this circumscribed set of them, is limited by several factors in addition to the incompleteness of this partial compilation. Content researchers tend to employ different theories and methodologies, creating results that are not directly comparable. Yet every technology, every disease, every natural threat, and every other risk-associated development does have unique characteristics as well as some similarities with previous developments, such that the deployment of a "cookie cutter" set of content categories may or may not be useful; similarly, every nation and culture is a different context. And good content analysis studies (like all good research studies) begin with a theoretical question that is relevant to the context of study and then chooses methods and techniques best suited to that question. Good studies will therefore continue to use alternative methodological approaches and theories, including many not covered in this brief review.

This is not the place to examine contemporary issues in media or content research, but these examples may serve to illustrate that what we know about the dynamics behind media representations of risk is perhaps more and yet less than one might expect, despite the expenditure of a good deal of effort. (For an attempt at meta-analysis studies of media coverage of science in general, however, and its apparent biases, see Schaefer, 2012.) Still, some elements are clear, including the likely resonance between *media* frames and *cultural* perspectives. These are not the same thing and one is not a measure of the other; they appear, however, to be mutually influential.

This discussion used Shoemaker and Reese's hierarchy of influences model to introduce the ways in which the production of news of risk and science are subject to the same institutional and social dynamics as news generally. However, largely missing from the hierarchy of influence analysis—despite the inclusion of "ideology" at the top of the pyramid—is an analysis of cultural influences and a clearly articulated theory of social structure, both of which have proven essential to understanding contemporary societal responses to risk in broad-brush theoretical terms (for key theoretical statements in this regard, see Douglas & Wildavsky, 1983). While ideology, which is usually understood to mean belief systems relative to political and economic systems, is indeed a part of this mix, it is not the entire story. Cultural (shared) beliefs more generally deserve more attention and clearly influence audience reactions to risk; yet most studies of media processes are done within individual nations and cultures not because this is not recognized but because cross-cultural studies have huge logistical, resource, and validation challenges.

Clearly, the field could use more studies of news production as applied to news about risks, more studies of new media (even of relatively old new media, e.g., television), and more systematic comparative studies of media content. We also need more careful consideration of how culture fits into this mix. However, this brief treatment has sought to illustrate that media coverage of risk (as of science generally) is both the same as other types of news coverage and yet different. Many of the institutional and organizational dynamics are similar and are well described by theories of influence developed with respect to news more generally. Yet science has unique features, and the sociology of science is sometimes incomplete without the sociology of news production.

Recommendations for Practice

The proliferation of risks (and concerns about risk) in developed societies, as well as the somewhat different set of risks and concerns characterizing the less developed world, also underscore the need for a critical literacy of risk and science (Priest, 2013). If risks are overreported, underreported, and misreported on a regular basis, then individual consumers and citizens can be disempowered in ways that matter. This suggests that a new emphasis on the ethics of risk communication is in order, as well as a new mode of presentation that goes beyond the "old wine in new bottles" use of new media. What that style should be and what new ethical considerations will arise in developing it are questions for the future.

Conclusions

Despite the limited scope of this chapter, we can suggest several tentative conclusions. The coverage of risk in the news media is generally subject to the same dynamics as the coverage of other types of news. Because the principles of objectivity and balance continue to be important to the practice of journalism, organized interests (from corporations to citizens' advocacy groups) have the opportunity to be heard. New media, which tends to operate by different rules, will continue to change this picture, however, giving groups and individuals the opportunity to do their own newsmaking but complicating audience interpretations and privileging those with the resources to manage websites and other new media in ways that attract those audiences.

At the same time, the coverage of risk is different from other forms of news in that the material is more technical. The scientific community operates on the basis of consensus rather than balance (thus "balanced" news can be seriously distorted, from the point of view of science), and different actors have different access to "news making" resources. This closes down some opportunities but opens up others: In the 21st century, journalists, editors, public relations practitioners, and public information specialists who understand risk issues, as well as the nature of new media, will be in increasing demand. And a new style of reporting may be in order.

Notes

1. This is the case, for example, in almost all, if not all, experimental work on cognition and attitude formation. Even where such studies claim to be concerned with "cultural" factors, individual-level measurements are the norm. Public opinion studies likewise most commonly treat public opinion as the aggregate of individual opinions, as assessed by opinion surveys conducted through one-on-one data gathering, although spiral-of-silence studies and other studies of the opinion "climate" are more sophisticated, as are multilevel studies of media or campaign effects. The concept of "interpretive community" (usually attributed to the work of Stanley Fish on reader-response theory) is a very rich one that is useful in moving our thinking about media audiences from the individual level to the level of the group (see Radway, 1984, for an early example from communication studies, albeit one concerned with romance novels rather than risks).

2. This style has also since spread to Europe and elsewhere. For a brief review of this and other ideas about the origins of "objectivity," including a critique of economic explanations, see Schudson (2001).

3. Complicating this picture further is another dimension of the sociology and philosophy of science: All scientific "truth" is in principle subject to reconsideration and, at least in principal, rejection in favor of a "revised" truth, as famously explored by Kuhn (1962). There is no certain recipe in science—let alone among observers of science, such as journalists—for determining whether today's truth will become tomorrow's error.

Suggested Additional Readings

Dudo, A. D., Dahlstrom, M. F., & Brossard, D. (2007). Reporting a potential pandemic: A risk-related assessment of avian influenza coverage in U.S. newspapers. *Science Communication, 28*(4), 429–454.

Friedman, S. M., Dunwoody, S., & Rogers, C. L. (1999). *Communicating uncertainty: Media coverage of new and controversial science.* Mahwah, NJ: Lawrence Erlbaum.
Krippendorff, K. (2004). *Content analysis: An introduction to its methodology.* Thousand Oaks, CA: Sage.

References

Beck, U. (1992). *Risk society: Towards a new modernity* (Vol. 17). Newbury Park, CA: Sage.
Boykoff, M. T., & Boykoff, J. M. (2007). Climate change and journalistic norms: A case-study of US mass-media coverage. *Geoforum, 38*(6), 1190–1204.
Clarke, C. E. (2008). A question of balance: The Autism-Vaccine Controversy in the British and American elite press. *Science Communication, 30,* 77–107.
Dearing, J. W. (1995). Newspaper coverage of maverick science: Creating controversy through balancing. *Public Understanding of Science, 4,* 4341–4361.
Donk, A., Metag, J., Kohring, M., & Marcinkowski, F. (2011). Framing emerging technologies: Risk perceptions of nanotechnology in the German press. *Science Communication, 34*(1), 5–29.
Douglas, M., & Wildavsky, A. (1983). *Risk and culture: An essay on the selection of technological and environmental dangers.* Berkeley: University of California Press.
Dragojlovic, N., & Einsiedel, E. (2013). Framing synthetic biology: Evolutionary distance, conceptions of nature, and the unnaturalness objection. *Science Communication, 35*(5), 547–571.
Entman, R. M. (1993). Framing: Toward clarification of a fractured paradigm. *Journal of Communication, 43*(4), 51–58.
Friedman, S. M., & Egolf, B. P. (2012, December). *Tracking media and internet coverage of nanotechnology's risks over the years.* Paper presented at the annual meeting of the Society for Risk Analysis, San Francisco, CA.
Gandy, O. H. (1982). *Beyond agenda setting: Information subsidies and public policy.* Norwood, NJ: Ablex.
Gans, H. J. (1979). *Deciding what's news: A study of CBS evening news, NBC nightly news, Newsweek, and Time.* Evanston, IL: Northwestern University Press.

Gaskell, G., Einsiedel, E., Priest, S., Ten Eyck, T., Allum, N., & Torgersen, H. (2001). Troubled waters: The Atlantic divide on biotechnology policy. In G. Gaskell & M. W. Bauer (Eds.), *Biotechnology 1996–2000: The years of Controversy* (pp. 96–115). London, England: Science Museum.

Groboljsek, B., & Mali, F. (2012). Daily newspapers' views on nanotechnology in Slovenia. *Science Communication, 34*(1), 30–56.

Jaspal, R., Nerlich, B., & Koteyko, N. (2013). Contesting science by appealing to its norms: Readers discuss climate science in the *Daily Mail. Science Communication, 35*(3), 383–410.

Kuhn, T. (1962). *The structure of scientific revolutions.* Chicago, IL: University of Chicago Press.

Maeseele, P. A., & Schuurman, D. (2012). Biotechnology and the popular press in Northern Belgium: A case study of hegemonic media discourses and the interpretive struggle. *Science Communication, 29*(4), 435–471.

Menashe, C. L., & Siegel, M. (1998). The power of a frame: An analysis of newspaper coverage of tobacco issues—United States, 1985–1996. *Journal of Health Communication, 3,* 307–325.

Miller, J. D. (1998). The measurement of civic scientific literacy. *Public Understanding of Science, 7,* 3203–3223.

Nelkin, D. (1995). *Selling science: How the press covers science and* technology (2nd ed.). New York, NY: W. H. Freeman.

Nigen, E. (1996). The Alar "Scare" was for real; and so is that "Veggie-Hate-Crime" Movement. *Columbia Journalism Review.* Retrieved from http://www.pbs.org/tradesecrets/docs/alarscarenegin.html

Priest, S. (2013). Can strategic and democratic goals coexist in communicating science? Nanotechnology as a case study in the ethics of science communication and the need for "critical" science literacy. In J. Goodwin, M. F. Dahlstrom, & S. Priest (Eds.), *Ethical issues in science communication: A theory-based approach* (pp. 229–244). Seattle, WA: CreateSpace.

Priest, S. H. (2000). *A grain of truth: The media, the public, and biotechnology.* Lanham, MD: Rowman & Littlefield.

Priest, S. H., & Ten Eyck, T. (2004). Peril or promise: News media framing of the biotechnology debate in Europe and the United States. In N. Stehr (Ed.), *Biotechnology: Between commerce and civil society* (pp. 175–188). New Brunswick, NJ: Transaction Books.

Radway, J. (1984). Interpretive communities and variable literacies: The functions of romance reading. *Daedalus, 113*(3), 49–73.

Schäfer, M. S. (2012). Taking stock: A meta-analysis of studies on the media's coverage of science. *Public Understanding of Science, 21*(6), 650-663.

Schudson, M. (2001). The objectivity norm in American journalism. *Journalism, 2,* 149–170.

Shoemaker, P. J., & Reese, S. D. (1996). *Mediating the message: Theories of influences on mass media content* (2nd ed.). New York, NY: Longman.

Singer, E., & Endreny, P. M. (1993). *Reporting on risk: How the mass media portray accidents, diseases, disasters, and other hazards.* New York, NY: Russell Sage Foundation.

U.S. Environmental Protection Agency. (1989). *Daminozide (Alar) pesticide canceled for food uses.* Retrieved from http://www2.epa.gov/aboutepa/daminozide-alar-pesticide-canceled-food-uses

Weaver, D. A., Lively, E., & Bimber, B. (2009). Searching for a frame: News media tell the story of technological progress, risk, and regulation. *Science Communication, 31*(2), 139–166.

Wilkinson, C., Allan, S., Anderson, A., & Petersen, A. (2007). From uncertainty to risk? Scientific and news media portrayals of nanoparticle safety. *Health, Risk & Society, 9*(2), 145–157.

CHAPTER 15

Framing, the Media, and Risk Communication in Policy Debates

Matthew C. Nisbet

Introduction

Framing—as an area of research and risk communication strategy—spans several scholarly disciplines and professional fields. Frames as they appear in media coverage and policy debates can be thought of as interpretive story lines that set a specific train of thought in motion, communicating why an issue might be a problem or pose a threat, who or what might be responsible for it, and what should be done about it. For many experts and professionals, framing is an unavoidable reality of the communication process, especially for those working in public affairs or on complex policy problems (Nisbet & Scheufele, 2009).

There is no such thing as unframed information, and most successful risk communicators are adept at framing, whether using frames intentionally or intuitively. Lay publics rely on frames to make sense of and discuss an issue; journalists use frames to craft interesting and appealing news reports; policymakers apply frames to define policy options and reach decisions; and experts employ frames to simplify technical details and make them persuasive (Nisbet, 2009a; Scheufele, 1999).

Framing, it should be noted, is not synonymous with placing a false spin on an issue, although some experts, advocates, journalists, and policymakers certainly spin evidence and facts. Rather, in an attempt to remain true to what is conventionally known about a complex topic, as a communication necessity, framing can be used to pare down information, giving greater weight to certain considerations and elements over others (Nisbet, 2009b).

If individuals are given a potentially risky policy dilemma to consider, the different ways in which a message is presented or framed—apart from the content itself—can result in very different responses, depending on the terminology used to describe the problem or the visual context provided in the message. Over the past two decades, research in political communication, science communication, and sociology has added to early work on the psychology of framing effects. The research explains how media portrayals in interaction with cultural forces shape the views of experts, journalists, policymakers, and various segments of the public (Nisbet & Scheufele, 2009).

In many risk-related policy debates, such as those over climate change or food biotechnology, framing plays a central role. In these debates, uncertainty and complexity are high, decisions are often perceived as urgent, and reaching agreement among a plurality of stakeholders is contingent on managing competing interests and values. As a result, public debate features many different competing claims to scientific authority, yet these claims often only obscure underlying political disagreements and values-based differences (Nisbet, 2014).

For risk communication scholars and professionals, navigating the terrain of these complex risk-related policy debates requires a careful understanding of framing as both a cognitive and social process involving the news media and a variety of other related communication processes. Successful efforts at public engagement will depend on being able to manage media and public attention to an issue while also simultaneously framing the issue in advantageous or normatively desirable ways.

With these considerations in mind, I begin by describing media agenda setting and priming as a closely related but unique process from media framing effects. I then describe research focusing on media framing effects as a cognitive and social process, emphasizing the need to carefully consider the relationship between frames as mental models and media packages that might apply to a specific issue and generalizable schema that shape our more global understanding of how society should work. In each case, I use examples from the debates over climate change and food biotechnology to illustrate core concepts and strategies relevant to risk communication professionals working to address complex policy problems.

Establishing the Criteria for Public Evaluations

Among the most relevant findings to risk communication is the ability of the news media to direct the focus of the public to certain issues over others. The news media "may not be successful most of the time in telling people what to think" famously observed Bernard Cohen in 1963 "but it is stunningly successful in telling its readers what to think about" (p. 13). Subsequent research on the "agenda-setting" effect of the media has provided repeated evidence that the issues portrayed in the media shape the issue priorities of the public. By giving attention to some issues over others, the media influences what the public perceives as most pressing and most important (Iyengar & Kinder, 1987; McCombs & Reynolds, 2009; McCombs & Shaw, 1972).

Relative to risk perceptions, a leading example of the agenda-setting influence of the news media is the relationship to public perceptions of crime. In the United States during the 1990s, although statistics tracking real-world incidents of violent crime showed a national decline across the decade, polling showed that the proportion of Americans citing crime as a national problem actually increased from less than 5% in 1990 to 30% in 2000. This increase in public concern corresponded to a rise in coverage of crime at local television and cable news. In sum, public perceptions of crime over the decade followed television trends rather than real-world trends (Iyengar & McGrady, 2007).

Judgments Based on Salience and Accessibility

Journalists will often argue that they do not set the public's agenda but rather follow audience demand for coverage of certain issues over others. Yet multiple lines of research cut against this view. For the past 30 years, studies tracking news attention and public perceptions typically find that a rise in overall news attention to an issue precedes a rise in public concern (McCombs & Reynolds, 2009; Rogers, Dearing, & Bregman, 1993). In addition, laboratory experiments, which are able to demonstrate direct causality, indicate that when subjects are repeatedly shown newscasts over a week, the top issues featured in the newscasts emerge as among the subjects' top national concerns (for discussion, see Iyengar & McGrady, 2007).

Researchers explain the agenda-setting influence of the media by way of a memory-based model of opinion formation, which assumes that (1) some issues or pieces of information are more accessible in a person's mind than others, (2) opinion is to a large degree a function of how readily accessible these certain considerations are, and (3) accessibility is mostly a function of "how much" or "how recently" a person has been exposed to these considerations (Kim, Scheufele, & Shanahan, 2005; Scheufele, 1999).

When individuals are asked to describe the issues of most concern to them, they are most likely to draw on those issues that are most readily accessible in their short-term memory and therefore easily recalled. Research shows that accessibility is typically a direct function of news exposure. Moreover, when the media focuses on issues that are also closely connected to personal experience such as food safety or a volatility in energy prices, accessibility and therefore media agenda setting is magnified (Nisbet & Feldman, 2011).

Media agenda-setting effects matter to public judgments because they "prime" public evaluations. The issues or events that receive the heaviest coverage in the news—because of their greater accessibility in short-term memory—often serve as the criteria by which the public evaluate the performance and credibility of a political leader, government agency, scientific organization, or corporation (Iyengar & Kinder, 1987; Nisbet & Feldman, 2011).

Recognizing and anticipating the priming effects of news attention, when an issue or event rises on the overall news agenda, to protect their public image, political leaders and organizations are likely to take some form of action on the issue, even if only symbolically. For example, in the wake of Hurricane Katrina and the success of Al Gore's *An Inconvenient Truth*, for the first time, major environmental funders and leaders collectively agreed to make climate change their top policy priority, coordinating their lobbying efforts with Congress and the White House, and their investments in programs and initiatives. In this case, apart from their own individual judgments relative to climate change, among environmental leaders there was a recognition that their organization's members would expect more coordinated action (Nisbet, 2011; Nisbet & Feldman, 2011).

Media priming also helps explain why major corporations have invested so heavily in promoting and protecting their social responsibility image. Over the past decade, in correlation to a rise in news attention to issues like sustainable agriculture, fair trade, renewable energy, and climate change, corporations recognize that consumers are more likely to give greater weight to their perceived social responsibility on these issues. As a result, companies have combined real changes in corporate practice with advertising, media, and branding campaigns to promote their environmental records (Nisbet, 2011; Nisbet & Feldman, 2011).

Setting the Context for Perceptions: The Case of Climate Change

Though sometimes confused with agenda setting and priming, media framing effects are a distinct cognitive and social process shaping individual judgments and decisions. With limited time, resources, and ability to process complex information, as we move through our daily lives trying to make sense of an almost constant torrent of ambiguous signals, situations and choices, we are heavily dependent on shifting cues that set the context for our perceptions. When we "frame" a complex science, health, or environment-related issue, we differentially emphasize specific cues relative to that complex subject, endowing certain dimensions with greater apparent relevance than they would have under an alternative frame (Nisbet, 2009a; Scheufele, 1999; Scheufele & Scheufele, 2010).

For example, is climate change a grave environmental risk to animal species and ecosystems that requires regulation of industry to solve or is it a public health threat to children and the elderly that requires government investment in clean energy technology? In the first context or "frame" set for perception, the emphasis is on the *risks to the environment*, protecting *nature* from harm and the need to *limit industry*. In the second frame, the emphasis is on the *risks to humans*, protecting *vulnerable people* from harm and the need to *aid industry* through government support of technological innovation.

The frame-setting process—establishing one context for perception versus another—is fundamentally different from media agenda-setting and priming effects, which via *repetition* make some issues or attributes more *accessible* and *available* in short-term memory. In contrast, a frame, by making some considerations or attributions more *applicable* or *relevant* to an issue, need only be evoked *a few times* to be persuasive (Nisbet & Feldman, 2011).

Frames exist as mental models that organize and interpret information about specific risk-related issues and as discursive, textual, and/or visual packages that structure conversations, news reports, and other media portrayals about an issue. Understanding the relationship between mental models and the interpretative packages available in broader public discourse is fundamental to understanding framing as a process of media effects and the impact on risk perceptions.

As mental models and organizing devices for communication, frames set the context for perception and discussion by selectively activating different cognitive and affective schema. If frames are the software by which we navigate

the complexity of risks posed by a problem like climate change, then schema provide a deeper cognitive architecture, defining for us core concepts, such as the relationship between science and society or the government and the economy. Once activated, schema provide short cuts for reaching an opinion about a complex topic, serving as a basis for inference, and operating as a mechanism for storing and retrieving information from memory. Schema can also be value constructs and moral intuitions that guide evaluations of personal behavior and societal choices (Price, 1992; Price & Tewksbury, 1997; Scheufele & Scheufele, 2010).

In sum then, media and other discursive frames influence our judgments of complex policy debates when they are relevant—or "applicable"—to an individual's specific existing interpretive schema. Framing effects will vary in strength as a partial function of the fit between the schemas a frame suggests should be applied to an issue and the presence of those schemas within a particular audience (Price & Tewksbury, 1997; Scheufele & Tewksbury, 2007).

Media frames, therefore, influence risk perceptions by connecting the mental dots for the public. They suggest a connection between two concepts, issues, or things, such that after exposure to the framed message, audiences accept or are at least aware of the connection. Alternatively, if a frame draws connections that are not relevant to something a segment of the public already values or understands, then the message is likely to be ignored or to lack personal significance (Nisbet, 2009a, 2009c).

For example, environmental organizations working with religious leaders are attempting to generate news stories and media portrayals that emphasize the relationship between the risks posed by climate change and the teachings of specific religious traditions. As an increasing number of news stories, books, and TV accounts emphasizing the connection between the risks posed by climate change and the religious duty to protect the vulnerable or to "care for creation" appear, we would expect that religious Americans would grow more concerned by and accepting of climate change–related risks (Nisbet, 2009a, 2009c).

Communicating About Climate Change as a Public Health Problem

Consider an example where strategic framing is being used to communicate about the risks of climate change in a manner that resonates with issues of already strong concern to the broader public. In a series of studies conducted with George Mason University's Edward Maibach and several colleagues, we investigated how a diversity of Americans understand the health and security risks of climate change and how they react to information about climate change when it is framed in terms of these alternative dimensions. In this research funded by the Robert Wood Johnson Foundation, our goal was to inform the work of public health professionals, municipal managers and planners, and other trusted civic leaders as they seek to engage broader publics on the health and security risks posed by climate change (for overviews, see Nisbet, 2014; Weathers, Maibach, & Nisbet, 2013).

Framing climate change in terms of public health stresses climate change's potential to increase the incidence of infectious diseases, asthma, allergies, heat stroke, and other salient health problems, especially among the most vulnerable populations: the elderly and children. In the process, the public health frame makes climate change personally relevant to new audiences by connecting the issue to health problems that are already familiar and perceived as important. The frame also shifts the geographic location of impacts, replacing visuals of remote Arctic regions, animals, and peoples with more socially proximate neighbors and places across local communities and cities. Coverage at local television news outlets and specialized urban media is also generated (Nisbet, 2009a; Weathers, Maibach, & Nisbet, 2013).

Efforts to protect and defend people and communities are also easily localized. State and municipal governments have greater control, responsibility, and authority over climate change adaptation-related policy actions. In addition, recruiting Americans to protect their neighbors and defend their communities against climate impacts naturally lends itself to forms of civic participation and community volunteering. In these cases, because of the localization of the issue and the nonpolitical nature of participation, barriers related to polarization may be more easily overcome and a diversity of organizations can work on the issue without being labeled as "advocates," "activists," or "environmentalists." Moreover, once community members from differing political backgrounds join together to achieve a broadly inspiring goal like protecting people and a local way of life, then the networks of trust and collaboration formed can be used to move this diverse segment toward cooperation in pursuit of national policy goals (Nisbet, Markowitz, & Kotcher, 2012; Weathers, Maibach, & Nisbet, 2013).

To test these assumptions, in an initial study, we conducted in-depth interviews with 70 respondents from 29 states, recruiting subjects from 6 previously defined audience segments. These segments ranged in a continuum from those individuals deeply alarmed by climate change to those who were deeply dismissive of the problem. Across all 6 audience segments, individuals said that information about the health implications of climate change was both useful and compelling, particularly when locally focused mitigation and adaptation-related actions were paired with specific benefits to public health (Maibach, Nisbet, Baldwin, Akerlof, & Diao, 2010).

In a follow-up study, we conducted a nationally representative web survey in which respondents from each of the six audience segments were randomly assigned to three different experimental conditions allowing us to evaluate their emotional reactions to strategically framed messages about climate change. Though people in the various audience segments reacted differently to some of the messages, in general, framing climate change in terms of public health generated more hope and less anger than framed messages that defined climate change in terms of either national security or environmental threats. Somewhat surprisingly, our findings also indicated that the national security frame could "boomerang" among audience segments already doubtful or dismissive of the issue, eliciting unintended feelings of anger (Myers, Nisbet, Maibach, & Leiserowitz, 2012).

In a third study, we examined how Americans perceived the risks posed by a major spike in fossil fuel energy prices. According to our analysis of national survey data, approximately half of American adults believe that their health is at risk from major shifts in fossil fuel prices and availability. Moreover, this belief was widely shared among people of different political ideologies and was strongly held even among individuals otherwise dismissive of climate change. Our findings suggest that many Americans would find relevant and useful communication efforts that emphasized energy resilience strategies that reduce demand for fossil fuels, thereby limiting greenhouse emissions and preparing communities for fuel shortages or price spikes. Examples include improving home heating and automobile fuel efficiency, increasing the availability and affordability of public transportation, and investing in government-sponsored research on cleaner, more efficient energy technologies (Nisbet, Maibach, & Leiserowitz, 2011).

Framing Strategy in Policy Debates: The Case of Food Biotechnology

In a complementary line of research to the cognitive focus on framing effects just reviewed, scholars following the lead of the sociologist William Gamson have adopted a "social constructivist" approach to media framing and its relationship to risk perceptions. According to this line of research, to make sense of political issues, citizens use as resources the frames available in media coverage but integrate these packages with the mental frames forged by way of personal experience or conversations with others. Media

frames might help set the terms of the debate among citizens, but rarely, if ever, do they exclusively determine public opinion. Instead, as part of a "frame contest," one interpretative package might gain influence because it resonates with popular culture or a series of events, fits with media routines or practices, and/or is heavily sponsored by powerful political actors (Gamson, 1992; Gamson & Modigliani, 1989; Nisbet, 2009c; Price, Nir, & Capella, 2005).

Controlling News Attention and Shaping Perceptions

The strategic framing of social problems and policy debates also influences public attention to risk-related issues while managing the "scope of participation" in a political debate (defined as the types and numbers of groups who are involved in policy making). In fact, across the history of many policy debates, power has turned on the ability to not only control attention to an issue within policy contexts or in the media but also to simultaneously frame the nature of the problem and what should be done (Nisbet, Brossard, & Kroepsch, 2003).

If a coalition relative to a complex problem is favored by the status quo in policy making, it is in their best interest to frame issues in highly technical, scientific, or legalistic ways and to downplay possible risks, since these interpretations tend to deflect wider news attention and attract only narrow constituencies. Under these conditions, journalists lack the dramatic grist to set the storytelling mill in motion, meaning that overall news attention will remain low and sporadic, with coverage originating from the science and business beats or appearing in specialized advocacy media, rather than gaining the attention of political journalists and commentators at the major news outlets (Nisbet & Huge, 2006, 2007).

But, on the other hand, if an interest group is disadvantaged by the status quo in policy making, it is usually in their best interest to reframe the issue in terms of dramatic risks/costs and in moral ways since these interpretations are more likely to shift decision from regulatory arenas to overtly political contexts like Congress or the White House, where arguments emphasizing dramatic risks and morality have more sway. Under these conditions, it becomes potentially easier to mobilize a broader coalition of groups to challenge the status quo and to generate widespread coverage from political journalists and commentators at major media outlets, thereby increasing the status of the issue on the overall news media agenda and shaping the risk perceptions of the wider public (Nisbet & Huge, 2006, 2007).

Consider the example of food biotechnology. Previous research has attempted to understand why the issue has experienced relatively limited political conflict in the United States, especially in comparison with that in the United Kingdom and several European countries. A major reason is that the biotech industry and scientists have been successful at limiting the scope of participation, as early policy decisions framed the issue around the technical aspects of scientific review and patenting rules. This ability to frame the terms of the debate and to limit the scope of attention and participation helped establish a virtual "policy monopoly" within regulatory policy arenas such as the Food and Drug Administration and the Environmental Protection Agency with very little attention from Congress or the White House or beyond the science and business beats at newspapers or small audience advocacy-oriented media outlets (Nisbet & Huge, 2006, 2007).

Though increased media attention to plant biotechnology and more dramatic definitions of the issue have surfaced in recent years, challenging the status quo in U.S. regulation, the ability of the biotech industry and allies in early policy decisions to frame the debate around short-term environmental and health risks have led to lasting and powerful feedback effects (Sheingate, 2006). The early success of biotech proponents in defining the terms of the debate is attributable in part to minimal media coverage, which made

precedent setting 1990s market approvals of genetically modified crops essentially "nondecisions" for the wider public (Nisbet & Huge, 2006, 2007). This is in contrast to the United Kingdom and Europe where, from the beginning, Jasanoff (2005) and others have noted that there was a much wider scope of participation in policy decisions. The early inclusion of environmental, consumer, and labor groups, and the comparatively stronger framing of the issue in terms of transparency and public accountability, led to a very different European regulatory regime that took into account social and economic factors as well as the possibility of unknown future technical risks (Nisbet & Huge, 2006, 2007).

Yet in the United States, there are signs that the scope of participation and framing of the issue may be shifting. Critics have helped expand and intensify the issue of public opposed to food biotechnology even as overall news attention has remained low by framing the issue in the context of parallel food system debates, by taking advantage of niche media, and by shifting the regulatory battle to states. The best-selling authors Michael Pollan, Mark Bittman, and Jane Goodall along with specialized consumer magazines and popular documentaries like *Food Inc.*, all link food biotechnology to ongoing debates over childhood obesity, the survival of traditional farmers, food safety, organics, and animal welfare. Opponents of food biotechnology have also shifted focus to states such as California, Maine, and Washington, where they have mobilized supportive issue publics to lobby on behalf of bills requiring mandatory labeling and/or have sponsored state ballot measures.

A Typology of Cultural Schema and Frames

Identifying the relevant frames in a policy debate as it takes place across various media and political arenas, and the cultural schema that different publics might draw on to make sense of and employ those frames on behalf of their political goals, can be approached both deductively and inductively. Drawing on previous work, studies usually work from a set of cultural schema that appear to reoccur across policy debates and that organize our thinking and conversations about the social implications of science and technology (Nisbet, 2009a, 2009c).

These past studies have referred to these schema as frames. Yet by serving as the deeper cultural architecture and meaning generators by which we sort through the complex relationship between science, technology, and societal risks, they are more accurately characterized as schema.

Originally identified by Gamson and Modigliani (1989) in a study of nuclear energy, the typology of cultural schema was further adapted in studies of food and medical biotechnology in Europe and the United States and in analysis of the debate over climate change (Dahniden, 2002; Durant, Bauer, & Gaskell, 1998; Nisbet, 2009a; Nisbet & Lewenstein, 2002). These cultural schema include the following:

- *Social progress:* Improving quality of life, or finding solutions to problems. Alternative interpretation as harmony with nature instead of mastery, "sustainability."
- *Economic development/competitiveness:* Economic investment, market benefits or risks; local, national, or global competitiveness.
- *Morality/ethics:* Right or wrong; respecting or crossing limits, thresholds, or boundaries.
- *Scientific/technical uncertainty:* A matter of expert understanding; what is known versus unknown; either invokes or undermines expert consensus, calls on the authority of "sound science," falsifiability, or peer review.
- *Pandora's box/Frankenstein's monster/runaway science:* Call for precaution in face of possible impacts or catastrophe. Out of control, a Frankenstein's monster, or as fatalism, that is, action is futile, path is chosen, and no turning back.

- *Public accountability/governance:* Research in the public interest or serving private interests; a matter of ownership, control, and/or patenting of research, or responsible use or abuse of science in decision making, "politicization."
- *Middle way/alternative path:* Finding a possible compromise position, or a third way between conflicting/polarized views or options.
- *Conflict/strategy:* A game among elites, who's ahead or behind in winning debate, battle of personalities, or groups (usually journalist-driven interpretation).

A few key details about this typology are worth noting. First, these cultural schemas are general organizing devices for public debate and should not be confused with specific policy positions. In other words, each schema can relate to pro-, anti-, and neutral arguments, though one set of advocates might more commonly activate one cultural schema over others. This distinction between schema and the valence of arguments becomes clearer after considering a few examples (Nisbet, 2009c).

Specific to food biotechnology, opponents have framed the issue via media reports and specialized niche media in terms of an idealized, pastoral vision of small-scale farms and the "natural," while also emphasizing fears of environmental contamination. These frames of reference activate cultural schema related to *social progress*, in this case specific to living in harmony with nature rather than controlling it and relative to precaution in the face of *scientific uncertainty*. Activists have also focused on the perceived inadequacy of regulation to ensure choice for farmers and consumers and to be responsive to citizens, emphasizing fairness, transparency, and equity. This framing strategy activates cultural schema related to *public accountability*, particularly science serving the public interest rather than private interests (Nisbet, 2011).

Industry and other proponents have countered by emphasizing via media reports and advertising the value of food biotechnology to meet world food demand in an era of climate change and growing population. This frame of reference activates the cultural schema of *social progress* but emphasizes science and technology as a tool for mastering nature's adverse risks and as solving problems. Proponents have also strongly criticized antibiotech activists for destroying crops and research installations, for promoting misinformation, and for generating unfounded public fears. This frame of reference activates cultural schema related to *public accountability*, emphasizing the pollution of science by ideology. In each of the above examples, specific frames are also often efficiently translated and conveyed by way of "frame devices." These triggers of various schema include catch phrases (i.e., "Frankenfood"), metaphors (i.e., comparing food biotech to "playing God in the Garden"), and visuals (i.e., an African farmer standing in an abundant field of crops as an image of social progress) (Nisbet, 2009a; Scheufele, 1999).

Reflections for Theory and Research

As reviewed in this chapter, to fully understand the relevance of media framing to risk communication in policy debates requires scholars and professionals to look across multiple disciplinary approaches to research ranging from the cognitive to the sociological. In this sense, as Stephen Reese (2007) suggests, the study of risk communication and framing effects in policy debates is best addressed through the application of a "bridging model" approach that integrates qualitative, quantitative, and interpretative methods; and psychological, sociological, and critical traditions; while actively drawing connections to professional practice (see also Nisbet, 2009c).

Adopting such a bridging model approach suggests several related areas in need of further investigation by scholars and consideration by

professionals. First, the methods we deployed in our research on reframing climate change as a public health problem as well as the typology first introduced by Gamson are not only useful resources for better understanding public opinion and media coverage, but for scholars, the methods and principles described are also generalizable models for conducting various modes of framing effects of research across risk-related debates. For example, our research on climate change and public health offers a useful methodological model for pairing audience segmentation strategies with the qualitative and experimental testing of different framed messages. Moreover, for many policy debates, Gamson's typology can inform the selection and design of messages tested in experiments, hypotheses generated about media effects evaluated in survey studies, and the identification and coding of open-ended responses generated in qualitative interviews of subjects or in the coding of patterns in news coverage.

Risk communication scholars are also still struggling to catch up with the rapid changes in our media system and what they might mean for understanding framing effects. For example, in complex policy debates such as those over climate change and food biotechnology, the editorial and business decisions at prestige news outlets have likely indirectly amplified differential risk perceptions across segments of the news audience. The *New York Times* and *Washington Post*, most notably, have cut back on news coverage of climate change and other science issues, letting go of many of their most experienced reporters, allowing advocacy-oriented media outlets and commentators to fill the information gap. As a consequence, careful reporting at outlets such as the *New York Times* on the technical details of science and policy have been replaced by morally framed interpretations from bloggers and advocacy journalists at other outlets that often dramatize and distort the risks related to these issues. Online news and commentary are also highly socially contextualized, passed along and preselected by people who are likely to share worldviews and political preferences. If an individual incidentally "bumps" into news about climate change or food biotechnology by way of Twitter, Facebook, or Google+, the news item is likely to be the subject of metacommentary that frames the political and moral relevance of the information (Scheufele & Nisbet, 2012).

Taking advantage of these self-reinforcing spirals, advocacy groups devote considerable resources to flooding social media with politically favorable comments and purposively selected stories, anticipating that many news consumers may incidentally "bump" into these comments and stories by way of their social media networks. This trends, therefore, suggests that in today's social and participatory news system, many news consumers are potentially exposed to multiple frames of reference when engaging with a single news item. Even before engaging with the framing featured in a news story, today's news consumer is potentially exposed to the frame emphasized in the blog post, Tweet, or Facebook feed that called their attention to the new story. If after reading the news story, the individual decides to read the comment section, additional framing effects may occur (Brossard, 2013; Scheufele & Nisbet, 2012).

Even when individuals, prompted by a focusing event like extreme weather or news of a major scientific report do seek out more information about climate change or food biotechnology via Google and other search engines, further selectivity is likely to occur. In this case, for example, liberals might choose to search for information on "climate change" or "frankenfoods" and encounter one set of differentially framed search results; whereas a conservative searching for information on "global warming" or "genetically modified food" encounters an entirely different set of search results. Not only does word choice shape the information returned through Google but so does the past browsing and search history of the individual, adding an additional layer of selectivity and bias to the information encountered (Brossard, 2013).

Recommendations for Practice

For professionals, Gamson's generalizable framing typology and the insights from new research on social media discourse can also serve as valuable and low-cost diagnostic tools. In strategy sessions with colleagues, Gamson's typology, for example, can be used to identify and categorize the types of frames as they are being deployed by multiple parties and groups in a policy debate, to track how these frames appear differentially across different news outlets and websites, and to link these frames back to the deeper cultural meanings that they might trigger. Professionals can do this informally by gathering examples of news coverage and commentary from both the mainstream and advocacy press; by analyzing text, video, and images from websites and advertisements; by gathering a range of polling results and noting differences in responses by question wording; and by observing and analyzing discussion by way of informal focus groups of friends and colleagues.

Conclusions

Looking to the future, risk communication scholars and professionals can learn from each other as they experiment with "big data" analysis tools that can sample, capture, and code social media discussion of risk-related policy debates. A relevant next step in line with the research reviewed in this chapter is to analyze various social media statements and forms of expression by way of carefully developed and generalizable typologies of schema and frames. In this way, patterns of selectively framed discourse about a subject like climate change or food biotechnology can be tracked in real time, by geographic location, and in relation to focusing events across online networks of groups and audience segments. As the 2012 presidential campaign of Barack Obama showed (Carey, 2012), behavioral scientists can work effectively in tandem with practitioners to design and run controlled experiments to test the effects of exposure to differentially framed social media conversations as they might be encountered online. This type of collaboration will likely benefit our overall understanding of the role of media framing in complex policy debates while also fine-tuning the communication strategies of practitioners and leading to methodological innovation.

Suggested Additional Readings

Nisbet, M. C., & Markowitz, E. (2014). Understanding public opinion in debates over biomedical research: Looking beyond partisanship to focus on beliefs about science and society. *PLoS ONE, 9*(2), e88473.

Scheufele, D. A. (2013). Communicating science in social settings. *Proceedings of the National Academy of Sciences, 110,* 14040–14047.

References

Brossard, D. (2013). New media landscapes and the science information consumer. *Proceedings of the National Academy of Sciences, 110*(Suppl. 3), 14096–14101.

Carey, B. (2012, November 12). Academic "dream team" helped Obama's effort. *The New York Times,* p. D1. Retrieved from http://www.nytimes.com/2012/11/13/health/dream-team-of-behavioral-scientists-advised-obama-campaign.html?pagewanted=all

Cohen, B. C. (1963). *The press and foreign policy.* Princeton, NJ: Princeton University Press.

Dahinden, U. (2002). Biotechnology in Switzerland: Frames in a heated debate. *Science Communication, 24,* 184–197.

Durant, J., Bauer, M. W., & Gaskell, G. (1998). *Biotechnology in the public sphere: A European sourcebook.* Lansing: Michigan State University Press.

Gamson, W. A. (1992). *Talking politics.* New York, NY: Cambridge University Press.

Gamson, W. A., & Modigliani, A. (1989). Media discourse and public opinion on nuclear power: A constructionist approach. *American Journal of Sociology, 95,* 1–37.

Iyengar, S., & Kinder, D. (1987). *News that matters.* Chicago, IL: University of Chicago Press.

Iyengar, S., & McGrady, J. (2007). *Media & politics: A citizen's guide.* New York, NY: Norton.

Jasanoff, S. (2005). *Designs on nature: Science and democracy in Europe and the United States.* Princeton, NJ: Princeton University Press.

Kim, S. H., Scheufele, D. A., & Shanahan, J. (2005). Who cares about the issues? Issue voting and the role of news media during the 2000 U.S. presidential election. *Journal of Communication, 55,* 103–121.

Maibach, E., Nisbet, M. C., Baldwin, P., Akerlof, K., & Diao, G. (2010). Reframing climate change as a public health issue: An exploratory study of public reactions. *BMC Public Health, 10,* 299.

McCombs, M., & Reynolds, A. (2009). How the news shapes our civic agenda. In J. Bryant & M. B. Oliver (Eds.), *Media effects: Advances in theory and research* (3rd ed., pp. 1–16). New York, NY: Routledge.

McCombs, M. E., & Shaw, D. L. (1972). The agenda-setting function of mass media. *Public Opinion Quarterly, 36*(2), 176–187.

Myers, T., Nisbet, M. C., Maibach, E. W., & Leiserowitz, A. (2012). A public health frame arouses hopeful emotions about climate change. *Climatic Change Research Letters,* 1105–1121.

Nisbet, M. C. (2009a). Communicating climate change: Why frames matter to public engagement. *Environment, 51*(2), 514–518.

Nisbet, M. C. (2009b). The ethics of framing science. In B. Nerlich, B. Larson, & R. Elliott (Eds.), *Communicating biological sciences: Ethical and metaphorical dimensions* (pp. 51–74). London, England: Ashgate.

Nisbet, M. C. (2009c). Knowledge into action: Framing the debates over climate change and poverty. In P. D'Angelo & J. Kuypers (Eds.), *Doing news framing analysis: Empirical, theoretical, and normative perspectives* (pp. 43–83). New York, NY: Routledge.

Nisbet, M. C. (2011). Public opinion and political participation. In D. Schlosberg, J. Dryzek, & R. Norgaard (Eds.), *Oxford handbook of climate change and society.* London, England: Oxford University Press.

Nisbet, M. C. (2014). Engaging in science policy controversies: Insights for the U.S. debate over climate change. In M. Bucchi & B. Trench (Eds.),

The Routledge handbook of public communication of science and technology (2nd ed.). London, England: Routledge.

Nisbet, M. C., Brossard, D., & Kroepsch, A. (2003). Framing science: The stem cell controversy in an age of press/politics. *Harvard International Journal of Press/Politics, 8*(2), 36–70.

Nisbet, M. C., & Feldman, L. (2011). The social psychology of political communication. In D. Hook, B. Franks, & M. Bauer (Eds.), *Communication, culture and social change: The social psychological perspective* (pp. 284–299). London, England: Palgrave Macmillan.

Nisbet, M. C., & Huge, M. (2006). Attention cycles and frames in the plant biotechnology debate: Managing power and participation through the press/policy connection. *Harvard International Journal of Press/Politics, 11*(2), 3–40.

Nisbet, M. C., & Huge, M. (2007). Where do science policy debates come from? In D. Brossard, J. Shanahan, & C. Nesbitt (Eds.), *The public, the media, and agricultural biotechnology* (pp. 193–230). New York, NY: CABI/Oxford University Press.

Nisbet, M. C., & Lewenstein, B. V. (2002). Biotechnology and the American media the policy process and the Elite Press, 1970 to 1999. *Science Communication, 23*(4), 359–391.

Nisbet, M. C., Maibach, E., & Leiserowitz, A. (2011). Framing peak petroleum as a public health problem: Audience research and participatory engagement in the United States. *American Journal of Public Health, 101*(9), 1620–1626.

Nisbet, M. C., Markowitz, E. M., & Kotcher, J. (2012). Winning the conversation: framing and moral messaging in environmental campaigns. In L. Ahern & D. Bortree (Eds.), *Talking green: Exploring current issues in environmental communication* (pp. 9–36). New York, NY: Peter Lang.

Nisbet, M. C., & Scheufele, D. A. (2009). What's next for science communication? Promising directions and lingering distractions. *American Journal of Botany, 96*(10), 1767–1778.

Price, V. (1992). *Public opinion*. Newbury Park, CA: Sage.

Price, V., Nir, L., & Capella, J. N. (2005). Framing public discussion of gay civil unions. *Public Opinion Quarterly, 69,* 179–212.

Price, V., & Tewksbury, D. (1997). News values and public opinion: A theoretical account of media priming and framing. In G. A. Barnett & F. J. Boster (Eds.), *Progress in communication sciences* (Vol. 13, pp. 173–212). New York, NY: Ablex.

Reese, S. D. (2007). The framing project: A bridging model for media research revisited. *Journal of Communication, 57,* 148–154.

Rogers, E. M., Dearing, J. W., & Bregman, D. (1993). The anatomy of agenda-setting research. *Journal of Communication, 43*(2), 68–84.

Scheufele, B. T., & Scheufele, D. A. (2010). Of spreading activation, applicability, and schemas: Conceptual distinctions and their operational implications for measuring frames and framing effects. In P. D'Angelo & J. A. Kuypers (Eds.), *Doing news framing analysis: Empirical and theoretical perspectives* (pp. 110–134). New York, NY: Routledge.

Scheufele, D. A. (1999). Framing as a theory of media effects. *Journal of Communication, 49*(1), 103–122.

Scheufele, D. A., & Nisbet, M. C. (2012). Online news and the demise of political disagreement. In C. Salmon (Ed.), *Communication yearbook 36* (pp. 45–54). New York, NY: Routledge.

Scheufele, D. A., & Tewksbury, D. (2007). Framing, agenda setting, and priming: The evolution of three media effects models. *Journal of Communication, 57*(1), 9–20.

Sheingate, A. D. (2006). Promotion versus precaution: The evolution of biotechnology policy in the United States. *British Journal of Political Science, 36*(2), 243.

Weathers, M., Maibach, E. W., & Nisbet, M. C. (2013). Conveying the human implications of climate change: Using audience research to inform the work of public health professionals. In D. Y. Kim, G. Kreps, & A. Singhal (Eds.), *Health communication: Strategies for developing global health programs*. New York, NY: Peter Lang.

CHAPTER 16

Social Media and Risk Communication

Stephen A. Rains, Steven R. Brunner, and Kyle Oman

Introduction

The past decade has been marked by the widespread diffusion of a plethora of new channels for risk communication. New communication technologies such as blogs, social network websites, photo- and video-sharing websites, and microblogs are a few of the technologies that have created opportunities for governments, organizations, and individual citizens to communicate about risk. Moreover, there is evidence to suggest that these technologies are playing a significant role in risk communication. Blogs, for example, were a noteworthy resource for communicating about a pet food recall (Stephens & Malone, 2009), and microblogs proved important during the Red River Valley flood (Starbird, Palen, Hughes, & Vieweg, 2010). Social network websites were widely used by the Centers for Disease Control and Prevention (CDC) in their efforts to communicate information about the H1N1 virus (Ding & Zhang, 2010) and by campus community members in the wake of the mass shootings at Virginia Tech University (Palen, Vieweg, Liu, & Hughes, 2009). Online discussion groups dedicated to neighborhood communities were a valuable resource among individuals affected by Hurricane Katrina (Procopio & Procopio, 2007). As these examples suggest, new communication technologies have potentially important consequences for communicating about risk.

This chapter examines contemporary research on the implications of communication technologies—and, in particular, social media—for risk communication. The primary objective of this chapter is to review the existing body of research on this topic with the aim of fostering efforts to develop theory designed to explain and predict the uses and effects of social media for risk communication. Social media is conceptualized broadly in this project as communication technologies that foster the creation and exchange of user-generated content (Kaplan & Haenlein, 2010). Table 16.1 provides an overview of some common forms of social media. Risk communication is defined as the "iterative exchange of information among individuals, groups, and institutions related to the assessment, characterization, and management of risk" (McComas, 2006, p. 76). Although we recognize that there are important differences between risk and crisis

Table 16.1 Forms of Social Media Relevant to Risk Communication

Social Media Type	Function Relevant to Risk Communication	Contemporary Brands
Social network website	System of personal webpages that articulate members' connections and can be viewed and contributed to by members of the system	Facebook, Google+, Orkut
Blog	Dedicated space for a single individual or organization to share information and experiences—contributions are not limited	Blogger, Wordpress, Typepad
Microblog	Dedicated space for a single individual or organization to share information and experiences—contributions are limited to 140 characters	Twitter, Tumblr
Discussion forum or group	Online group dedicated to contributing, viewing, and/or responding to questions, comments, and/or information about a specific topic	Groups.Google, Groups.Yahoo, i-neighbors
Video-sharing website	Website dedicated to viewing, sharing, and/or commenting on videos uploaded by users	YouTube, Google video
Photo-sharing website	Website dedicated to viewing, sharing, and/or commenting on photos uploaded by users	Flickr, Picasa, Photobucket

communication, we review research examining the use of social media for both types of communication. Our decision to do so is driven by the relative paucity of research focused specifically on risk communication and the fact that the two concepts share key similarities (Reynolds & Seeger, 2005). We begin our review by first considering the role of theory and theory development in research on social media and risk communication.

Theoretical Bases

As a relatively recent addition to the broader media landscape, it is perhaps not surprising that few theories have been developed thus far that are dedicated to explaining and predicting the uses and effects of social media for risk communication. One noteworthy exception is the social-mediated crisis communication model (Jin, Liu, & Austin, 2014), which has largely been applied to blogs (Jin & Liu, 2010; Liu, Jin, Briones, & Kuch, 2012). This model outlines the interrelationships between influential social media users, social media followers, traditional news media outlets, and the organization experiencing a crisis. The social-mediated crisis communication model explains why influential social media users (e.g., bloggers) become active in a crisis, how they influence other social media users with whom they are interconnected as well as the news media, and what organizations should do to more effectively manage the presence of these individuals (Jin & Liu, 2010). Although this model represents one useful theoretical framework, developing a complete understanding of the uses and effects of social media for risk communication requires additional theory-building efforts.

A primary goal of this chapter is to review existing research in an effort to identify some potential building blocks that might then be

Table 16.2   Themes in Research on the Uses and Effects of Social Media for Risk Communication

Theme	Dimension(s)
Among governments and organizations	
Dissemination efficacy	• Potential to communicate rapidly with a broad audience • Opportunity to share multiple forms of content (e.g., text, video)
Interactivity	• Opportunity for internal and external shareholders to communicate directly with one another
Credibility/ information accuracy	• Potential for concerns with information accuracy and source quality to become salient
Among individual citizens	
Information sharing	• Ability to reproduce and distribute information from the news media or governmental agencies • Potential to translate technical information for a lay audience • Opportunity to share citizen-generated information
Information acquisition	• Potential to circumvent formal media outlets or information sources (e.g., governmental agencies) • Opportunity to obtain information about individual citizens and their concerns (e.g., missing persons inquiry)
Exchanging social support	• Ability to give and receive emotional support, advice, and/or physical assistance

used for theory construction. To this end, we consider six themes that transcend the body of research examining social media and risk communication. These themes represent trends in the uses and effects of social media in the context of risk communication. Although we do highlight research on specific forms of social media like blogs and social network websites, our objective is to focus on themes that transcend the various types of social media in an effort to better understand this class of communication technologies (Chaffee, 1986). Our review proceeds by focusing on three themes in each of two distinct contexts in which the uses and effects of social media for risk communication have been examined: government and organizational uses of social media and

the use of social media by individual citizens. A summary of the six themes is presented in Table 16.2.

Government and Organizational Uses of Social Media for Risk Communication

A survey of the risk communication literature suggests growing interest in the ways in which governments and organizations are and should be using social media for risk communication. Much of this work focuses on social media use to communicate with external stakeholders (e.g., González-Herrero & Smith, 2008; Roundtree, Dorsten, & Reif, 2011; Strecher,

Greenwood, Wang, & Dumont, 1999; Taylor & Perry, 2005). As opposed to relying on the news media as an intermediary, organizations and governments can deliver official messages directly to citizens through social media such as social network sites and video-sharing sites as well as blogs and microblogs. Throughout this body of scholarship, several themes have emerged. Three related themes we consider in the following paragraphs include (1) the ability to effectively disseminate risk information using social media, (2) potential for audience interactivity, (3) and concerns with credibility and information accuracy.

Dissemination Efficacy

The potential to effectively disseminate risk information has been highlighted as a key benefit of social media for governments and organizations. Social media has been argued to make it possible to communicate information rapidly to a relatively broad audience (Roundtree et al., 2011; Schultz, Utz, & Göritz, 2011). Ding and Zhang (2010), for example, explain that the "timeliness and open accessibility of the social media enable the real-time dissemination of [the] latest updates about risk situations" (p. 84). Timeliness is particularly critical because organizations facing crises need to be able to share information with the public quickly (Taylor & Perry, 2005). Yet timeliness can also be a limitation. Some scholars contend that, in making it easy to disseminate information rapidly and without formal gatekeepers, social media may exacerbate unfounded fears or concerns about risk (González-Herrero & Smith, 2008).

The ability to disseminate information in a timely fashion is likely one reason that social media played an important role in various organizations' efforts to communicate information about the H1N1 outbreak in the United States during 2009. Liu and Kim (2011) examined the use of social media (i.e., Facebook and Twitter) and traditional media (e.g., press releases, fact

sheets, and media advisories) by 13 governmental or corporate organizations. They reported that, of the approximately 750 crisis responses they examined, almost three quarters were communicated using social media. Ding and Zhang (2010) focused specifically on the CDC's efforts and found that the social network website Facebook and the microblogging service Twitter were used to communicate over half of the CDC's message related to H1N1.

In addition to timeliness, the potential to share multiple and various forms of content is a secondary dimension of social media that is pertinent to information dissemination. In their campaign about the H1N1 virus, for example, the CDC used seven different types of social media to share a total of 214 risk communication messages consisting of videos, pictures, audio clips, and/or text documents (Ding & Zhang, 2010). Sugerman et al. (2012) contend that using multiple message formats is important to foster audience compliance with risk messages. Stephens, Barrett, and Mahometa (2013) pursued this idea in their research examining the effects of emergency messages conveyed using different combinations of communication technologies. In the days following a shooting on their campus, Stephens and colleagues surveyed a random sample of students, faculty, and staff. They found a three-way interaction between the source of the notification about the shooting, nature of the medium used to communicate the notification, and notification frequency for respondents' perceptions of urgency regarding the shooting. Respondents who received their first and second notification from an asynchronous official channel (e.g., university e-mail) perceived the crisis to be least urgent. At the third notification, however, the sense of urgency reported by members who received an asynchronous official message was similar to the amount of urgency felt by most other groups. Stephens et al.'s (2013) findings underscore the utility of synchronous technologies and potential limitations of asynchronous technologies to communicate crisis information.

Interactivity

A second theme in the literature examining governmental and organizational uses of social media involves the interactive nature of social media. Several scholars have argued that social media provides opportunities for risk communication because it can be interactive (Ding & Zhang, 2010; González-Herrero & Smith, 2008; Roundtree et al., 2011; Schultz et al., 2011; Strecher et al., 1999; Taylor & Perry, 2005; Waters, Burnett, Lamm, & Lucas, 2009). Interactivity is generally conceptualized in terms of the potential of an organization or government and their external stakeholders to exchange information and concerns about a risk-related event. Traditional risk communication activities by organizations and governments typically have been limited to one-way messages sent from the organization or government to their external stakeholders. The audience is mostly considered to be passive receivers with little opportunity to participate directly (González-Herrero & Smith, 2008). Social media, in contrast, has been argued to "help to break down the linear one-way risk communication and make it multichannel and thus more participatory" (Ding & Zhang, 2010, p. 80). The interactivity of social media provides external stakeholders an opportunity to contribute to the discussion and understanding of the risk-related event. External stakeholders can post messages and reply to information presented by an organization (Roundtree et al., 2011) and participate in chats or view real-time videos (González-Herrero & Smith, 2008). The participation between an organization or government and its external stakeholders has also been argued to foster more democratic decision making regarding risk-related events (Ding & Zhang, 2010).

Relatively few empirical studies have been conducted to explore the implications of interactivity for government and organizations' risk communication efforts. Taylor and Perry (2005) examined the use of the Internet among 50 organizations facing crises between 1998 and 2003.

Almost half of these organizations incorporated some form of two-way communication between the organization and external stakeholders. Other research has found evidence to suggest that social media is particularly critical for directly engaging opinion leaders such as bloggers (Liu et al., 2012) and building relationships with volunteers and local community members (Briones, Kuch, Liu, & Jin, 2011). A number of the 40 Red Cross employees interviewed mentioned responding to posts from influential bloggers during a crisis (Liu et al., 2012). Additionally, Red Cross employees indicated that they used blogs and microblogs as a means to better understand the public's perceptions of the organization and to engage volunteers (Briones et al., 2011). Interactivity has also been examined as an outcome of social media use. Schultz et al. (2011) conducted an experiment in which they manipulated the communication medium and communication strategy used in response to a hypothetical scenario involving car accidents resulting from a faulty part. They found a main effect for communication medium in which information communicated via microblog and blog was less likely to be shared by external stakeholders than when the information was communicated in an online newspaper.

Credibility and Information Accuracy

Credibility and information accuracy is a final theme that has been addressed in scholarship examining government and organizational uses of social media for risk communication. Accurate information and a reliable source are vital to effective risk communication efforts (González-Herrero & Smith, 2008; Williams & Olaniran, 1998). Yet the participatory nature of social media has created challenges for establishing the accuracy of information and credibility of sources (Larson, Cooper, Eskola, Katz, & Ratzan, 2011). In creating opportunities for virtually anyone to participate in the discourse surrounding a crisis or risk event, social media have made it possible to spread information that is inaccurate or, worse, intentionally misleading. Moreover, inaccurate information is easily reproduced via social media such as microblogs and social network websites. As such, Krimsky (2007) claimed that social media are a breeding ground for public skepticism.

Relatively little research has been conducted to empirically examine the implications of social media for source credibility and information quality specifically in the context of risk communication. Sweetser and Metzgar (2007) conducted an experiment focusing on the use of blogs to communicate about organizational crises. They found that participants who were exposed to a blog identified as being written by an individual citizen perceived the crisis to be more significant than when the blog was designated as the official blog for the organization dealing with the crisis. However, readers of the official blog rated the organization more positively. Schultz et al. (2011) conducted an experiment about the use of various types and combinations of social media for organizational crisis communication. They found that participants rated the reputation of organizations who responded to a crisis using a microblog and blog post or online newspaper more positively than when only a microblog or blog was used for the response. Additionally, participants reported being less likely to engage in a secondary reaction to the crisis such as a boycott when a microblog plus a blog or microblog only was used to communicate the message than when the message was shared in a blog or online newspaper.

Social Media Use by Individual Citizens for Risk Communication

In addition to considering organizational and governmental uses of social media for risk communication, researchers have examined the use of communication technologies by individual citizens to communicate about risk-related events (e.g., Procopio & Procopio, 2007; Shklovski, Palen, & Sutton, 2008; Starbird et al., 2010). Blogs, microblogs, social network websites, and other technologies offer individual citizens a means to acquire and share information and, more broadly, participate in the social construction of risk-related events. Three key themes emerged in this literature focusing on the use of social media for: (1) acquiring risk-related information, (2) sharing risk information, and (3) exchanging social support in response to risk. We review research addressing each of these three themes in the following paragraphs.

Acquiring Risk-Related Information

The first theme in research examining use of social media by individual citizens for risk communication focuses on information acquisition. Social media are a means for individual citizens to acquire risk information. Social media may be used to circumvent traditional media outlets or when information from traditional media is perceived to be insufficient (Shklovski et al., 2008; Sutton et al., 2008). Information acquired through social media can be especially critical to help manage citizens' uncertainty (Procopio & Procopio, 2007). Social media may also be used as a means to locate missing persons or check on the well-being of specific individuals (Palen et al., 2009).

Procopio and Procopio (2007) surveyed more than 1,000 individuals who lived in the greater New Orleans area prior to Hurricane Katrina and reported that online discussion forums dedicated to specific neighborhoods were a key resource for information seeking. Respondents reported using the forums to acquire information about damage in their local area, aerial footage, pictures, and accounts from neighbors who stayed during the storm among other types of information. In the case of the mass shootings at Virginia Tech, online forums were used to acquire information about the safety of the campus community (Palen et al., 2009). In the southern California wildfires, the perceived insufficiency of information from traditional news media was one reason social media was used as an information seeking resource (Sutton et al., 2008). Although the news media were an important information source, social media were used by citizens to acquire information about the fires relevant to their specific locale (Shklovski et al., 2008).

Sharing Risk Information

Social media has been identified as a mechanism for individual citizens to share risk information. Social network websites, microblogs, and blogs offer diverse opportunities for information sharing. Facts and data from traditional news media may be reproduced intact or synthesized to produce new insights (Starbird et al., 2010). Information may also be translated from technical language to a form that is more easily understandable by a lay audience (Stephens & Malone, 2009). Additionally, social media may be used to share novel, citizen-generated information with other members of the community (Shklovski et al., 2008).

Several studies have examined the use of social media for information sharing in the context of crises. Sutton et al. (2008) surveyed almost 300 adults affected by the 2007 wildfires in southern California. More than one third of their respondents reported contributing information about the fires through online discussion boards, blogs, photo-sharing websites, and microblogs. Concerns with a perceived lack of useful information from formal sources such as local and national news media was cited as a factor motivating individuals to share the information they acquired. Interviews with approximately 40 people affected by the fires further revealed that social media was critical for distributing information from citizens to other community members (Shklovski et al., 2008). Social media also appears to be particularly valuable for sharing novel information. Only a few hours after the mass shootings at Virginia Tech during 2007, a student-created group was established on the social network website Facebook specifically

so that students and other members of the campus community could self-report their safety (Palen et al., 2009). These information sharing efforts led to the accurate identification of the shooting victims before their names were officially released by the university.

Several studies have been conducted focusing specifically on the use of blogs and microblogs for information sharing. Starbird et al. (2010) conducted an analysis of posts made to the microblogging service Twitter regarding flooding in the Red River Valley and found that a major function of posts was synthesizing outside knowledge—ranging from other microblog posts to information from official news sources and even historical facts. Macias, Hilyard, and Freimuth (2009) examined a sample of blogs authored by individuals and formal news outlets (e.g., *The Times Picayune* newspaper) affected by Hurricane Katrina. Several functions of the blogs they examined were related to sharing information. Blogs were used to contribute information about missing persons, call for rescue, and document experiences. Other activities related to information sharing included posting official news, giving information about damage, and administering information regarding available services. Yet there is other evidence to suggest that blogs may be less widely used than traditional media for specific forms of information sharing. Stephens and Malone (2009) reported that whereas news articles and official press releases contained more instances of technical translation regarding scientific information about a pet food recall, blogs contained fewer instances of translation than would be expected by chance.

Exchanging Social Support

A final theme in the literature on social media use by individual citizens involves the use of social media to exchange social support in response to crises. Social media are argued to provide an avenue through which individuals can connect to others who can provide emotional, informational, and even tangible forms of support (Procopio & Procopio, 2007; Stephens & Malone, 2009). Moreover, in making it possible to connect with others affected by the risk or crisis, social media allows communities to engage in collective forms of coping (Dabner, 2011; Sutton et al., 2008). Social media can serve as a communal space in which individuals can make sense of and manage the uncertainty about the events affecting their community.

Several studies of social media use in response to crises have demonstrated their utility for exchanging forms of emotional support such as reassurance and encouragement, as well as more generally fostering a sense of community. Dabner (2011) reported that a student-created group on the social network website Facebook was an integral resource for support among members of a university community affected by a large earthquake. Posts were used to express gratitude for the response efforts and to reassure one another that normalcy would return. Discussion forums and blogs were used as a collective space for managing stress (Sutton et al., 2008) and fostering a sense of community (Shklovski et al., 2008) among people affected by wildfires in southern California. Research focusing specifically on blogs has demonstrated that the exchange of support is an important use of this technology. Over a quarter of the blog posts examined by Stephens and Malone (2010) about a pet food recall consisted of requests for emotional support. Additionally, Macias et al. (2009) reported that a major function of blogs used among those affected by Hurricane Katrina was for outreach and assistance purposes.

Reflections for Theory and Research

A noteworthy trend in the research reviewed in this chapter is the relative lack of theory applied or developed to explain the implications of social media for risk communication (for exceptions, see Jin et al., 2014; Procopio & Procopio, 2007; Stephens et al., 2013). Yet six themes, which are summarized in Table 16.2, were identified in this body of research that represent a use and/or effect of social media for risk communication. These themes present a foundation from which to begin building novel theories as well as a potential guide for adapting existing theories and frameworks. In the following two sections, we outline several such possibilities.

Developing Novel Theories and Models

The six themes identified in reviewing the body of research on social media and risk communication offer insights that might facilitate efforts at developing novel theories and models to explain the implications of these communication technologies. Several of the themes might serve as the focal point for a theory or model. That is, a model might be constructed with the objective of explicating how, why, and with what effects the theme operates. For example, credibility and information accuracy was a theme in research examining individual citizens' use of social media for risk communication. Researchers might consider developing a model to explain when and how information quality and source credibility become salient as well as the effects of these constructs on individuals' use of social media for risk communication and the outcomes of social media use. Under what conditions does information quality become important? Why are some forms of social media perceived, in general, to be more or less credible than others? What are the consequences of receiving risk information from social media sources that are perceived to be more or less credible—how does this information influence individuals' attitudes and behaviors related to risk? Any or all of these questions might be pursued in attempting to develop a novel model or theory to explicate the role of information quality and source credibility in social media use for risk communication. Beyond information quality and source credibility, several of the other themes (e.g., information dissemination efficacy, exchanging social support) could also function as the focus for a novel model or theory.

More generally, it seems possible that one or more of the themes might serve as a starting point for a model or theory. For example, the social-mediated crisis communication model (Jin et al., 2014; Jin & Liu, 2010) is rooted in the basic notion that social media make possible interactivity between internal and external organizational stakeholders, and such interactivity has important implications for organizational crises and crisis management. Although the authors do not explicitly present the model as being about interactivity, this theme appears to be central to the model. The model presents a detailed framework to explain how influential social media users influence other external stakeholders (e.g., news media, other social media users) and how organizations might respond to these opinion leaders. Interactivity and the other five themes offer a framework to help focus our attention on those uses and effects of social media that are particularly important and, as such, offer a general guide to begin thinking about theory development.

Applying Existing Theories and Models

Researchers studying social media and risk communication might also use the six themes identified in this chapter as a guide for applying and adapting existing theories and models. Each of the themes highlights an important, specific function of social media that might be explained by adapting existing theory. Information sharing, for example, is a theme that pervades the literature on individual citizens' use of social media for risk communication. Theorizing about electronic word-of-mouth communication (eWOM) might be applied to better understand how social media are used by individual citizens to share information and the effects of such sharing. eWOM is rooted in the idea that sharing information person to person can be influential (Dellarocas, 2003). Although research on word of mouth has traditionally focused on face-to-face communication, eWOM is conceptualized as centering on the written word and, more specifically, written accounts from specific individuals that are published electronically (Sun, Youn, Wu, & Kuntaraporn, 2006). eWOM, which is typically studied in contexts such as online reviews for products and services (Zhang, Craciun, & Shin, 2010) or viral forms of marketing (Golan & Zaidner, 2008), has important potential implications for risk communication and, in particular, information sharing. An eWOM framework might be used to better understand why and how groups of people use social media to share their perceptions and experiences of a risk-related event as well as the consequences of such sharing. Theorizing about eWOM might also help us gain insight into the behavior of opinion leaders and their effects on the diffusion of risk information throughout social media networks.

The social amplification of risk framework (Pidgeon, Kasperson, & Slovic, 2003) is a second existing theory that might be fruitfully applied to examine the outcomes associated with individual citizens' use of social media for acquiring risk information. This framework is rooted in the idea that social, psychological, and cultural processes can amplify or reduce individuals' perceptions of risk and subsequent behaviors. It seems plausible that social media—as a channel for information acquisition—may play a noteworthy role in amplification or attenuation processes. Through making it possible to gain access to the perceptions of others with whom one shares a connection, social media might be an important source of information that serves to attenuate or amplify risk perceptions. Learning, for example, that a "friend" in one's social network was influenced by an event such as a product safety recall might make one feel more susceptible to the risk associated with the recall. Social network websites have the potential to personalize a risk by providing people with access to known individuals in their social network who have been affected by the risk. As this example illustrates, the social amplification of risk framework might be fruitfully applied to help better understand the implications of individual citizens' use of social media to acquire risk information.

Recommendations for Practice

In addition to informing theory development, the research reviewed in this chapter implies some recommendations for practitioners of risk communication. Practitioners would benefit from becoming more aware of and responsive to individual citizens' use of these technologies. Two specific recommendations include using social media as tools for surveillance and engagement.

First, social media offer a potentially valuable resource for practitioners to monitor the attitudes and behavior of individual citizens associated with risk-related events and issues (Briones et al., 2011; Liu et al., 2012). A reasonable amount of evidence exists to suggest that individual citizens are using social media to acquire and share risk information as well as to exchange social support. As such, risk practitioners might use these channels to monitor trends in citizens' perceptions of and responses to the risk event. In the event of a product recall, for example, practitioners would benefit from directing attention to bloggers writing about the recall and groups on popular social network websites dedicated to the recall. Monitoring these two technologies would make it possible to better understand the public's general attitudes toward the recall as well as specific areas of confusion or concern. In effect, social media offer one avenue through which practitioners can gain insight into the general public's understanding of and response to risk-related events.

Social media also make it possible for risk communication practitioners to directly engage individuals and groups of citizens. Interactivity was a theme identified in the body of research examining organizational uses of social media. Social media offer avenues through which risk communication practitioners working in or for an organization can circumvent many of the traditional gatekeepers such as news outlets and communicate directly with concerned citizens. In the instance of new recommendations for medical screenings, for example, a practitioner might use one or more microblogging services as a means to broadcast information directly to groups of citizens. Another possibility is to communicate with influential bloggers writing about the screening recommendations. A public discussion in a place such as a blog might be a valuable means of correcting misinformation and addressing common concerns in-depth. As a tool for engagement, social media make it possible for practitioners to communicate directly with citizens and other external stakeholders.

Conclusions

The research reviewed in this chapter suggests the potential of social media for risk communication and underscores the challenges for researchers attempting to study this phenomenon. Although the body of scholarship on this topic is rapidly growing, much of the work has been descriptive in nature and relatively little has integrated existing theories or attempted to build novel models and theories. A central goal of this chapter has been to help facilitate such efforts. Six themes pervading research on social media use for risk communication were considered, and several examples of potential directions for theory and model building were presented. Through developing and applying theory to explain the implications of social media for risk communication, scholars will be well positioned to understand the potential and pitfalls of existing social media as well as new forms developed in the future.

Suggested Additional Reading

Veil, S. R., Buehner, T., & Palenchar, M. J. (2011). A work in-progress literature review: Incorporating social media in risk and crisis communication. *Journal of Contingencies and Crisis Management, 19*, 110–122.

Wendling, C., Radisch, J., & Jacobzone, S. (2013). *The use of social media in risk and crisis communication.* OECD Working Papers on Public Governance, No. 25, OECD Publishing.

References

Briones, R. L., Kuch, B., Liu, B. F., & Jin, Y. (2011). Keeping up with the digital age: How the American Red Cross uses social media to build relationships. *Public Relations Review, 37,* 37–43.

Chaffee, S. H. (1986). Mass media and interpersonal channels: Competitive, convergent, or complementary? In Gumpert & Cathcart (Eds.), *Intermedia* (pp. 62–80). New York, NY: Oxford University Press.

Dabner, N. (2011). "Breaking ground" in the use of social media: A case study of a university earthquake response to inform educational design with Facebook. *Internet in Higher Education, 15,* 69–78.

Dellarocas, C. (2003). The digitization of word-of-mouth: Promise and challenges of online reputation systems. *Management Science, 49,* 1407–1424.

Ding, H., & Zhang, J. (2010). Social media and participatory risk communication during the H1N1 flu epidemic: A comparative study of the United States and China. *China Media Research, 6,* 80–91.

Golan, G. J., & Zaidner, L. (2008). Creative strategies in viral advertising: An application of Taylor's six-segment message strategy wheel. *Journal of Computer-Mediated Communication, 13,* 959–972.

González-Herrero, A., & Smith, S. (2008). Crisis communications management on the web: How internet-based technologies are changing the way public relations professionals handle business crises. *Journal of Contingencies and Crisis Management, 16,* 143–153.

Jin, Y., & Liu, B. F. (2010). The blog-mediated crisis communication model: Recommendations for responding to influential external blogs. *Journal of Public Relations Research, 22,* 429–455.

Jin, Y., Liu, B. F., & Austin, L. L. (2014). Examining the role of social media in effective crisis management: The effects of crisis origin, information form, and source on publics' crisis responses. *Communication Research, 41,* 74–94.

Kaplan, A. M., & Haenlein, M. (2010). Users of the world, unite! The challenges and opportunities of social media. *Business Horizons, 53,* 59–68.

Krimsky, S. (2007). Risk communication in the Internet age: The rise of disorganized skepticism. *Environmental Hazards, 7,* 157–164.

Larson, H., Cooper, L. Z., Eskola, J., Katz, S. L., & Ratzan, S. (2011). New decade of vaccines 5: Addressing the vaccine confidence gap. *Lancet, 378,* 526–535.

Liu, B. F., Jin, Y., Briones, R., & Kuch, B. (2012). Managing turbulence online: Evaluating the blog-mediated crisis communication model with the American Red Cross. *Journal of Public Relations Research, 24,* 353–370.

Liu, B. F., & Kim, S. (2011). How organizations framed the 2009 H1N1 pandemic via social and traditional media: Implications for U.S. health communicators. *Public Relations Review, 37,* 233–244.

Macias, W., Hilyard, K., & Freimuth, V. (2009). Blog functions as risk and crisis communication during Hurricane Katrina. *Journal of Computer-Mediated Communication, 15,* 1–31.

McComas, K. A. (2006). Defining moments in risk communication research: 1996–2005. *Journal of Health Communication, 11,* 75–91.

Palen, L., Vieweg, S., Liu, S. B., & Hughes, A. L. (2009). Crisis in a networked world: Features of computer-mediate communication in the April 16, 2007, Virginia Tech event. *Social Science Computer Review, 27,* 467–480.

Pidgeon, N. F., Kasperson, R. K., & Slovic, P. (2003). *The social amplification of risk.* Cambridge, England: Cambridge University Press.

Procopio, C., & Procopio, S. (2007). Do you know what it means to miss New Orleans? Internet communication, geographic community, and social capital in crisis. *Journal of Applied Communication Research, 35,* 67–87.

Reynolds, B., & Seeger, M. W. (2005). Crisis and emergency risk communication as an integrative model. *Journal of Health Communication, 10,* 43–55.

Roundtree, A. K., Dorsten, A., & Reif, J. (2011). Improving patient activation in crisis and chronic care through rhetorical approaches to new media technologies. *Poroi, 7,* 1–13.

Schultz, F., Utz, S., & Göritz, A. (2011). Is the medium the message? Perceptions of and reactions to crisis communication via Twitter, blogs and traditional media. *Public Relations Review, 37,* 20–27. doi:10.1016/j.pubrev.2010.12.001

Shklovski, I., Palen, L., & Sutton, J. (2008). Finding community through information and communication technology during disaster events. In

Proceedings of the 2008 Conference on Computer Supported Cooperative Work (pp. 127–136). New York, NY: Associations for Computing Machinery.

Starbird, K., Palen, L., Hughes, A. L., & Vieweg, S. (2010). Chatter on the red: What hazards threat reveals about the social life of microblogged information. In *Proceedings of the 2010 Conference on Computer Supported Cooperative Work* (pp. 241–246). New York, NY: Associations for Computing Machinery.

Stephens, K. K., Barrett, A. K., & Mahometa, M. J. (2013). Organizational communication in emergencies: Using multiple channels and sources to combat noise and escalate a sense of urgency. *Human Communication Research, 39,* 230–251.

Stephens, K. K., & Malone, P. (2009). If the organizations won't give us information . . .: The use of multiple new media for crisis technical translation and dialogue. *Journal of Public Relations Research, 21,* 229–239.

Stephens, K. K., & Malone, P. C. (2010). New media for crisis communication: Opportunities for technical translation, dialogue, and stakeholder responses. In T. C. Coombs & S. J. Holladay (Eds.), *Handbook of crisis communication* (pp. 381–395). Malden, MA: Blackwell.

Strecher, V. J., Greenwood, T., Wang, C., & Dumont, D. (1999). Interactive multimedia and risk communication. *Journal of the National Cancer Institute Monographs, 25,* 134–139.

Sugerman, D. E., Keir, J. M., Dee, D. L., Lipman, H., Waterman, S. H., Ginsberg, M., & Fishbein, D. B. (2012). Emergency health risk communication during the 2007 San Diego wildfires: Comprehension, compliance, and recall. *Journal of Health Communication, 17,* 698–712. doi:10.10 80/10810730.2011.635777

Sun, T., Youn, S., Wu, G., & Kuntaraporn, M. (2006). Online word-of-mouth (or mouse): An exploration of its antecedents and consequences. *Journal of Computer-Mediated Communication, 11*(4), 1104–1127.

Sutton, J., Palen, L., & Shklovski, I. (2008). Backchannels on the front lines: Emergent use of social media in the 2007 southern California fires. In F. Fiedrich & B. Van de Walle (Eds.), *Proceedings of the 5th International Information Systems for Crisis Response and Management Conference* (pp. 624–631). Washington, DC: ISCRAM.

Sweetser, K. D., & Metzgar, E. (2007). Communication during crisis: Use of blogs as a relationship management tool. *Public Relations Review, 33,* 340–342.

Taylor, M., & Perry, D. C. (2005). Diffusion of traditional and new media tactics in crisis communication. *Public Relations Review, 31,* 209–217.

Waters, R. D., Burnett, E., Lamm, A., & Lucas, J. (2009). Engaging stakeholders through social networking: How nonprofit organizations are using Facebook. *Public Relations Review, 35,* 102–106.

Williams, D., & Olaniran, B. A. (1998). Expanding the crisis planning function: Introducing elements of risk communication. *Public Relations Review, 24,* 387–400.

Zhang, J. Q., Craciun, G., & Shin, D. (2010). When does electronic word-of-mouth matter? A study of consumer product reviews. *Journal of Business Research, 63,* 1336–1341.

PART III

CONTEXTS OF RISK COMMUNICATION

SECTION 7

Interpersonal Contexts of Risk Communication

CHAPTER 17

Risk Communication in Provider–Patient Interactions

Carma L. Bylund, Erin Maloney, and Emily B. Peterson

Introduction

Provider–patient communication plays a critical role in the achievement of important patient outcomes, such as informed decision making, satisfaction with care, and adherence. Communication skills are regarded as a core competency by accrediting agencies such as the Accreditation Council for Graduate Medical Education, the Liaison Committee on Medical Education, and the American Board of Internal Medicine.

Communication about risk happens regularly in health care consultations, transcending both discipline and provider type. For the purposes of this chapter, we are conceptualizing *risk* in provider–patient communication as including any topic of provider–patient discussion where the outcome is uncertain. For example, a woman may discuss with her obstetrician (OB) the decision to have an amniocentesis to test for genetic abnormalities in her unborn child. Such a discussion would include the risk of harm to the fetus by administering the test, as well as the risk of the undesirable outcome of finding a genetic abnormality. Alternatively, a prostate cancer patient may discuss with his oncologist the risks of

choosing an active surveillance approach to his low-risk prostate cancer and managing his uncertainty about whether or not his low-risk prostate cancer would spread rather than opting for immediate treatment. Our approach overlaps with much that has been written about uncertainty in health care (Han, Klein, & Arora, 2011).

In this chapter, we first provide two theoretical underpinnings for our focus on provider–patient communication and risk discussions. Here, we use several specific health care contexts in which the discussions of risk are prevalent as case examples. For each, we give a basic introduction to the context, followed by a review of what we know from research about risk discussions in this context and what we do not yet know. We conclude with reflections on how the named theoretical approaches can help us and make recommendations for future work that considers additional theories of interpersonal communication.

Theoretical Underpinnings

First and foremost, provider–patient communication is interpersonal and thus is transactional by nature (Gearing, Townsend, MacKenzie, & Charach, 2011). Transactional communication in a health care context means that when a health care provider and patient communicate, both the provider and the patient are affected by and affect the other simultaneously (e.g., Gordon, Street, Sharf, & Souchek, 2006). As the individuals interact, they each create a context for the other and relate to the other within that context (Galvin, Bylund, & Brommel, 2012). Regardless of how much talking each individual does, the impact is mutual.

As an example of transactional communication, imagine a discussion between an oncology nurse and a patient about a clinical trial the patient is considering. The oncologist briefly explains the trial and then leaves the room after telling the patient that the nurse could answer his questions. The patient asks numerous questions of the nurse, based on the reading he has done on the Internet. As the patient continues to pepper the nurse with questions, the nurse becomes increasingly upset—she is new in her position and can't answer some of the questions the patient is asking. As the nurse becomes upset, the patient becomes more frustrated and assertive—he can't believe the doctor would leave him with someone who can't answer his questions about such an important issue. Transactional communication does not necessarily describe a negative impact. Using the same example, we could imagine a nurse speaking empathically to the patient and answering all of his questions, leading to a patient who was more relaxed and trusting. As the patient becomes more relaxed and trusting, the nurse subsequently does more to help the patient.

A second theoretical perspective comes from uncertainty theories. By definition, communication about risk always includes some discussion of uncertainty (e.g., uncertainty in an outcome, uncertainty in a test result). Uncertainty theories focus on how individuals assess, manage, and cope with such ambiguous and complex situations that are inherent in risk communication. One of the most widely used uncertainty theories in communication research is uncertainty

management theory (UMT; Brashers, 2001). UMT differs from other uncertainty theories in that it posits that uncertainty engenders other emotions besides anxiety and that people may not be motivated to decrease their uncertainty in certain situations. UMT also emphasizes that the amount of uncertainty that people feel is independent of the amount of information they have. Thus, it is possible for a person to have a lot of information on a subject and still feel uncertain or have little information but feel certain (Brashers, 2001).

In a health care setting, UMT posits that patients will either evaluate medical uncertainty as negative (causing anxiety or stress), positive (associated with opportunity, hope, or optimism), or as simply a fact of life ("generally speaking, life is uncertain"). Subsequent actions will reflect this appraisal: When the uncertainty is perceived negatively, the patient will seek information to decrease uncertainty, and when the uncertainty is perceived positively, the patient will avoid information to maintain that uncertainty. When uncertainty is perceived as an ongoing fact of life, patients may seek social support to help manage their informational and emotional needs (Brashers, Hsieh, Neidig, & Reynolds, 2006). Additionally, other factors may also influence patients' likelihood to seek information, such as their propensity to defer to the authority of providers, a perceived lack of ability to understand medical information, or a belief that seeking information will be beneficial in managing their health care plan (Brashers, Haas, & Neidig, 1999).

Another key tenet of UMT is that a patient's evaluation of uncertainty is not stable and is likely to change over time. Thus, information seeking can be a balancing act for patients who have multiple and changing health goals, such as preserving hope, maintaining good health, or learning about treatment options. For example, a patient in genetic counseling who avoids information immediately after learning the results of her breast cancer genetic risk test (BRCA 1/2 test) might later actively seek information about options to reduce risk later in life (e.g., prophylactic surgery).

As we elaborate on below, patient uncertainty is prevalent in many types of clinical interactions involving risk, but it is not always understood or managed properly by providers. These theoretical perspectives provide important insight for examining specific risk discussions in health care settings. Transactional communication and UMT can further our understanding of current interactions and provide guidance for future practice.

Health Care Content Areas

Here, we highlight several content areas in which provider–patient discussions about risk may take place: risky lifestyle behaviors, cancer screening, genetic screening, prenatal testing, surgical procedures, and medical imaging tests. For each area, we present specific lines of research as "cases" to examine what has been studied and what could be studied in the future.

Risky Lifestyle Behaviors

Risky lifestyle behaviors such as alcohol consumption, poor diet, lack of exercise, and smoking play a major role in overall health. Despite this, many physicians often do not discuss prevention counseling in clinical interactions (Denny, Serdula, Holtzman, & Nelson, 2003). This may be due in part to physicians' perceived lack of efficacy in producing real behavioral change with patients, role expectations, and external constraints, such as time and availability (Ampt et al., 2009).

There have been relatively few studies examining the discussion of risky behaviors in clinical encounters, and such research focuses primarily on the frequency of the interaction and perceived relevance, without analyzing the substance of the interaction itself. In a rare study, entering medical students were surveyed about their willingness to discuss the risks of lifestyle behaviors with patients (McCurdy, 2012). Students were given four

hypothetical patient vignettes, each focused on a common lifestyle risk factor (a 45-year-old smoker, a 38-year-old with signs of alcoholism, an overweight and sedentary 23-year-old, and a 16-year-old contemplating being sexually active). For each of the vignettes, the students were asked to indicate how likely they would be to provide information in each of four areas of risk communication: first, providing information about the risk; second, recommending elimination of the risky behavior; third, discussing alternative strategies to risk elimination (harm reduction); and fourth, reassuring patients that care will continue regardless of whether the patient accepts and puts into practice the physician's recommendations for lifestyle changes.

Overall, the students indicated strong willingness to communicate about risky behaviors for relatively noncontroversial issues like smoking cessation (78.5%) and exercise (87.1%). However, only 28% of students indicated that they would recommend sexual abstinence for the 16-year-old patient. One possible explanation for this difference is that guidelines with clear recommendations are available for discussing relatively uncontroversial issues such as smoking cessation, yet such guidelines are sparse for more disputed topics such as teen abstinence. For such issues, patients may not be getting uniform messages about the risk associated with the behavior, as the physician's willingness to engage in such controversial subjects may be affected by their own backgrounds and biases (e.g., values, cultural background). As provider–patient communication is also transactional by nature, the physician's willingness to provide recommendations to patients would likely also be affected by the patient's communicative behaviors or demographics (e.g., perceived maturity, patient reticence, sex, age, etc.).

Cancer Screening

Provider–patient discussions can play an important role in whether or not individuals adhere to regular screening recommendations (e.g., Fox &

Stein, 1991). Factors associated with screening intent or adherence include a physician recommending it (Brenes & Paskett, 2000; Cairns & Viswanath, 2006), the enthusiasm of the physician about the screening test (Fox et al., 2009), and the extent to which the patient feels the doctor communicates in a trusting way (Liang, Kasman, Wang, Yuan, & Madelblatt, 2006).

Many have called for shared decision making as the most ethical and sound approach for interactions with patients (Charles, Gafni, & Whelan, 1997). In the case of cancer screening discussions, if shared decision making is the goal, then provider–patient discussions about cancer screening should ideally also contain discussions about risk. Providers may discuss the risk of cancer and the importance of screening tests to detect cancer early; they may also discuss the risk of the screening test itself. In this section, we will focus on three types of cancer screening tests: mammography (X-ray of the breast to detect breast cancer); prostate-specific antigen (PSA; blood test to detect possible prostate cancer); and colonoscopy (examination of the entire colon to detect precancerous and cancerous growths).

Risk of Cancer

Patients may be at varying risks for cancer depending on many factors, including age, family history, and race. Dube and Fuller (2003) found in a qualitative study of 38 standardized patient interactions that these types of risk were always addressed when discussing male cancer screening. Patients' understandings of risk may be improved through provider–patient discussions. It is thought that the actual discussion of cancer risk may lead to a better understanding of cancer risk and ultimately screening (Politi, Clark, Rogers, McGarry, & Sciamanna, 2008).

Risk of Screening Test

In addition to their benefits, cancer screening tests do have risks. According to the National Cancer Institute (2012a), several risks or potential harms, are present with mammography. One is the risk of overdiagnosis and unnecessary treatment, wherein women whose cancers would not have grown are treated with surgery, chemotherapy, and/or radiation (Woloshin & Schwartz, 2012). A second is the risk of false negatives as mammograms miss about 20% of breast cancer tumors. A third risk is false positives, which can cause anxiety and psychological distress. Between 20% and 50% of women who are screened annually for breast cancer over a decade will experience a false positive (Woloshin & Schwartz, 2012). A fourth risk is exposure to radiation, discussed elsewhere in this chapter (National Cancer Institute, 2012a).

PSA tests are used to screen prostate cancer. However, similar to mammography, there are several risks to using the PSA as a screening test (National Cancer Institute, 2012b). Overdiagnosis and unnecessary treatment of cancers that are not life threatening lead to side effects and complications. False negatives and false positives are also risks. In fact, false positives are quite high—about 75% of men with an elevated PSA level who have a biopsy do not have cancer (National Cancer Institute, 2012b).

Colonoscopy, the most widely used screening test for colorectal cancer, differs significantly from mammography and PSA tests. Colonoscopy allows for any precancerous tumors to be removed; mammography and PSA do not. Consequently, there is not the same risk of overtreatment, false positives, and false negatives with colonoscopy as there is with mammography and PSA. However, colonoscopy does have risks associated with the procedure. Most well-known is the risk of the bowel being perforated during the procedure, although that risk is very low (Gatto et al., 2003).

The extent to which risks of cancer screening such as those described above are discussed in provider–patient consultations is not entirely clear, as there have been very few studies that have examined that question. One study examined audio recordings of doctor–patient discussions about colorectal cancer screening and found that overall only 17% had discussion about "pros and cons"—which would include risks (Ling et al., 2008). With patients who had been screened in the past, only 3% of doctors talked about pros and cons. In one small interview study, it was found that most women would have liked to be given information about the most common type of noninvasive breast cancer, ductal carcinoma in situ, when they were invited for breast screening (Prinjha, Evans, & McPherson, 2006).

Genetic Screening

Both environmental and genetic factors contribute to the development of any disease. With the relatively recent completion of human genome sequencing, the development of genetic tests that identify errors in specific genes that elevate an individual's risk for different medical conditions such as breast and ovarian cancer, Alzheimer's disease, cystic fibrosis, and Huntington's disease have become increasingly available.

Genetic testing for heightened susceptibility to develop medical conditions has raised several moral and ethical concerns among scientists as well as the lay public. A number of these concerns involve interpersonal communication about risk among clinicians, patients, family members, and friends. The following sections will review research that has been conducted on this topic, followed by a discussion of areas that need more research to fully understand best practices for communicating about risk in the context of genetic testing.

Testing for genetic factors that elevate one's risk of developing medical conditions is a unique and challenging issue to discuss. Through a series of focus group discussions with genetic counselors, physicians, and nurses, McCarthy, Bartels, and LeRoy (2001) identified the following ethical and professional challenges that arise when patients have genetic concerns: informed consent, withholding information, facing uncertainty, resource allocation, value conflicts,

directiveness/nondirectiveness (i.e., patients vary in the degree of autonomy they want over their health care decisions, and health care professionals also sometimes have strong opinions about the best course of action for patients), determining the primary patient (i.e., when family members are involved, it is sometimes difficult to identify to whom the health care professional's primary obligation lies), professional identity issues (i.e., health care professionals may sometimes question the nature or extent of their professional role), emotional responses, diversity issues, confidentiality, attaining/maintaining proficiency (i.e., genetic testing is constantly changing and evolving. It is often a challenge for health care professionals to keep up with the most up-to-date genetic knowledge, tests, and resources), professional misconduct, discrimination (i.e., genetic status potentially may become a threat to employment or insurance coverage), colleague error (i.e., at times, patients may be misinformed or misguided by other health care professionals, and it must be cleared up), and documentation (i.e., patients may ask for certain information to be left out of their medical record or to be recorded in a particular way).

In addition to doctor–patient discussions about genetic tests and results of these tests, patients are often encouraged, and sometimes required, to meet with genetic counselors before and after testing. The American Society of Human Genetics (1975) has defined genetic counseling as "a communication process which deals with the human problems associated with the occurrence, or risk of an occurrence, of a genetic disorder in the family" (p. 240). Genetic counselors are trained to work with patients to fully comprehend several issues that pose challenges to patient–provider genetic risk discussions, including diagnosis, probable course of a genetic disorder, and available options for management that are appropriate in their view of their risk, their family goals, and their ethical and religious standards; the contribution of genetics to the disorder and which relatives are most at risk for the disorder; and the best possible adjustment to the disorder in the affected family member and/or risk of recurrence (American Society of Human Genetics, 1975).

Meta-analyses have indicated that genetic counseling helps decrease generalized anxiety and increase accuracy of perceived risks with regard to BRCA 1/2 mutation screening (Di Prospero et al., 2001) and improves knowledge without having an adverse effect on cancer-specific worry, general anxiety, distress, and depression with regard to familial cancers in general (Braithwaite, Emery, Walter, Prevost, & Sutton, 2004). Some drawbacks to genetic counseling have also been noted. Di Prospero and colleagues (2001) found that test results increased worry among patients who underwent testing for BRCA 1/2 mutations. However, study participants also noted that they did not regret their decision to undergo testing, were satisfied with the clinical services they received, and had high confidence in cancer surveillance efficacy. At the conclusion of this study, authors stressed the importance of making adequate resources available to clinical programs that offer BRCA 1/2 mutation screening so that they may offer appropriate pretest counseling, timely availability of results, and organization of support groups for people found to have gene mutations.

Previous examinations have identified that the most common concepts discussed in genetic counseling sessions have been fact based, including general population risk for breast cancer, family members' risk of inheriting a mutation, and the elevated risk for disease associated with an inherited mutation (Lobb et al., 2003). Clinicians generally encourage patients to share risk information with blood relatives (Forrest, Delatycki, Skene, & Aitken, 2007). Studies examining the interpersonal communication of results for strongly predictive genetic tests showed that recipients of genetic tests shared results with their family members (Di Prospero et al., 2001; Hughes et al., 2002) and that talking to family members may help reduce distress (van Oostram et al., 2007).

Sharing genetic risk information with relatives, however, sometimes has been shown to be a source of anxiety for the patient. For example, Maloney and colleagues (2012) noted that mothers consistently report worry and fear about communicating genetic testing for BRCA 1/2 mutation information with their adolescent daughters. A prospective study on the impact of genetic susceptibility testing on family relationships found that although some participants (37%) felt that testing had affected familial relationships in a positive way, such as feeling closer, improved communication and support, greater appreciation for relatives, and relief of getting negative results, other sectors reported negative consequences, such as unwanted changes in relationships (19%), problematic situations (13%), or conflicts (4%) (van Oostram et al., 2007). These adverse consequences on family relationships were associated with a lack of open communication between relatives. Thus, it has been suggested that discussions about how to communicate cancer risk information to blood relatives should be added to clinicians' standard repertoire when meeting with patients (e.g., Maloney et al., 2012).

As genetic testing becomes more expansive and available, researchers need to continue exploring the best ways to communicate genetic risk information about specific diseases. Best practices for communicating this information are likely to vary depending on whether the interaction occurs between clinicians and patients or between patients and various blood relatives. Decision aids, such as handouts and Internet resources can be created to help patients and their family members understand their risk levels and convey this risk information to their family members. From a UMT perspective, clinicians and family members should be trained to recognize that in some cases, people may prefer not to hear information about their genetic risk for developing a disease, but this may change over time. For example, most health professionals recommend that women wait until they are 25 years old before undergoing testing for an increased risk of developing breast cancer because even if they are found to have a mutation that puts them at greater risk, they wouldn't be able to be enrolled in an early screening program until they reached 25. By the same logic, adolescent girls may choose uncertainty and avoiding genetic risk information from their mothers until after they are 25 years old, at which point they may begin to seek information about their genetic risk.

Prenatal Testing Risk Discussions

Prenatal testing for chromosomal and genetic conditions has become a routine component of prenatal care in the United States. Similar to other types of screening discussed previously, there are risks associated with prenatal testing. However, decision making in prenatal testing is an especially complex process as the woman must simultaneously consider different risk figures, including the risk of an affected child, the risk of an abnormal test result, and the risk of miscarriage as a result of the testing process (Gates, 2004). Thus, risk discussion about prenatal testing can quickly become complicated and overwhelming to patients (Caughey, Washington, & Kupperman, 2008).

Additionally, available prenatal tests vary not only in their risks (e.g., potential miscarriage) but also in their diagnostic accuracy. While some diagnostic tests, such as amniocentesis and chorionic villus sampling, are able to provide a "yes" or "no" answer with 99% accuracy, screening methods such as nuchal translucency and maternal serum screening merely provide a general probability figure estimate. As outlined by UMT, the way these tests are perceived will differ depending on how the woman perceives prenatal testing uncertainty. For example, a woman who perceives such uncertainty positively may opt out of tests that are high in diagnostic accuracy in an effort to maintain hope, while a woman who perceives uncertainty negatively would prefer these high-accuracy tests.

Despite the inherent complexity to prenatal screening risk discussion, there has been little research devoted to improving provider–patient communication in this context. One area that has been studied is the format in which risk is presented in prenatal care. While most risk information is given to prenatal care patients in a numerical format, the majority of patients lack the skills necessary to adequately process the information (Edwards & Prior, 1997). Even small changes within a numerical format can alter how patients perceive risk. For example, Chase and colleagues (1986) described risk of a birth defect as either 4 per 100 or 40 per 1,000. Less than 25% of the women who were given the risk as 40 per 1,000 were able to identify it as 4%, while 75% of the women given the risk of 4 per 100 were able to identify it correctly. Additionally, numerical proportions are more likely to be accurately interpreted by prenatal care patients when presented with a numerator of one (e.g., "1/25" as opposed to "4/100"; Grimes & Snively, 1999).

A rare study outside of presentation format focused on the "baseline" perceived risks of carrying a Down syndrome–affected fetus and of a procedure-related miscarriage (Caughey et al., 2008). The authors found several factors not associated with actual risk significantly related to perceived risk in these women in a prenatal genetic counseling session. For example, women with higher incomes reported a lower perceived risk of procedure-related miscarriage, and those with higher education reported a lower perceived risk of a Down syndrome–affected baby. Based on these data, the authors note the importance of prediscussion risk preconceptions and argue for patient education to improve actual risk perception accuracy among pregnant women.

Surgical Risk Discussions

Any surgical procedure carries risk with it, and these risks must be discussed by the surgeon with the patient for informed consent to take place. During consultations, surgeons may discuss with patients risk related to mortality, complications, and side effects. Using visual aids to present risks is often recommended

(Paling, 2003), although the way in which the data are presented to the patient may affect their choice (Timmermans, Molewijk, Stigglebout, & Kievit, 2004).

One retrospective study demonstrated that for patients who had undergone laparoscopic surgery to remove the bladder found that although most patients reported that they had received clear and exhaustive information from their physicians, they interpreted the information differently than doctors perceived they gave it (Tuveri et al., 2009). For example, patients perceived a higher risk than the doctors perceived communicating of the need to convert from a laparoscopic to an open surgery to complete the procedure safely. Similarly, patients perceived a higher likelihood of surgical complications than doctors perceived communicating.

One recommendation from surgical oncologists for discussing potential side effects is to divide them into minor and major categories, with only the most common types of aftereffects being verbally reviewed, though making sure the patient understands that other less common complications may occur. These surgeons also recommend to not minimize the possibility of complications; if unanticipated outcomes occur, patients and families will be more frustrated and anxious if the risk of complications was minimized (Heerdt, Park, & Boland, 2010).

Radiation Risk

Medical imaging tests that use radiation, such as X-rays and computed tomography scans, increase one's risk of developing cancer in the future (National Academies of Science & Council, 2006). Yet these same tests are also necessary and highly beneficial because they reduce unnecessary surgical procedures by allowing doctors to diagnose or rule out illnesses (Frush & Applegate, 2004; Malone, Wolf, Malmed, & Melliere, 1992) and save lives by detecting cancer in its earliest stages and by monitoring response to medical treatments (Pastorino et al., 2003).

Use of computed tomography scans has doubled every year since the 1980s (Prokop, 2005), which has led to a corresponding increased concern within the medical community (e.g., Baerlocher & Detsky, 2010) and in media (Dauer et al., 2011) about the risks posed by the radiation in these tests. Medical professionals have noted recent patient expressions of concern about radiation exposure from tests, and some patients have even refused tests that are recommended by their health care providers out of fear of the consequences from radiation exposure, even when the risks associated with refusing these tests are greater than the risks posed by undergoing these tests (Rosenthal, 2006). Research suggests that patients want their physicians to discuss the risks and benefits of imaging tests before ordering them, yet this topic remains largely unaddressed between doctors and patients (Lee, Halms, Monico, Brink, & Forman, 2004). Therefore, current practices do not appear to match patient needs for discussion about this issue or standards of quality informed decision making.

Results from a survey of 456 physicians and radiologists affiliated with three tertiary hospitals in the United States revealed that most physicians do not know if patients in their institutions are informed about cancer from medical imaging, but they feel that informed consent about the cancer risk associated with these tests should be obtained. Most of these study participants felt that consent should be provided by radiology departments rather than through a discussion with the referring physician. From a practical standpoint, however, it has been noted that physicians who refer patients for radiation tests have the most complete medical information about the patient (Baerlocher & Detsky, 2010), and they are trained to carefully consider the risk-to-benefit ratio before prescribing any tests. Therefore, it has been argued that referring physicians (rather than radiology departments or other sources) are the most appropriate clinicians to engage in these conversations with their patients (Baerlocher & Detsky, 2010).

Currently, informed consent about radiation risks before a patient undergoes a radiation test is not mandatory due to the complexity of determining and explaining these risks (Brink, Goske, & Patti, 2011). Rather than a mandatory consent process, however, it has been suggested that effective communication about risks, benefits, and alternative options "promotes patient autonomy, alleviates unfounded patient apprehension, and mitigates medicolegal liability," factors that are associated with quality patient care (Cardinal, Gunderman, & Tarver, 2011, abstract). Thus, although doctors are not required to discuss the risks and benefits of radiation with patients on prescribing a test, evidence suggests that these discussions are helpful for factors associated with quality patient care, and referring physicians are most equipped to engage in these conversations (Baerlocher & Detsky, 2010).

The recommendation that referring physicians discuss the risks of exposure to radiation from medical imaging with patients comes with some caveats. First, consideration must be given to the knowledge base of the physician. Extensive literature indicates that overall physician knowledge of the risks associated with radiation from medical imaging is low (e.g., Arslanoglu, Bilgin, Kubali, Ceyhan, & Ilhan, 2007; Borgen, Stranden, & Espeland, 2010; Lee et al., 2004). Furthermore, research suggests that greater knowledge alone does not necessarily translate into increased interpersonal communication about these risks with patients (Borgen et al., 2010). Thus, there is a need for an intervention to equip physicians with the knowledge needed to engage in conversations with patients about the risks associated with medical radiation imaging and to motivate them to do so. Second, research is needed to determine the most appropriate method for disclosing knowledge about lifetime cancer risk from medical imaging in a manner that does not cause unnecessary stress to the patient. Generally, the risk associated with radiation exposure from medical tests recommended by health care providers is miniscule in comparison with the risks associated with not having the test, including the

inability to detect or diagnose disease in early stages and an inability to monitor treatment effectiveness. However, in some situations, tests may be ordered as an unnecessary precaution (Miller, Holmes, & Derlet, 1997), or patients may demand medical radiation tests that are not necessary for their health because they do not understand that the risk of radiation exposure is greater than this risk of not having the test (Jain, 2012). Thus, it is important for patients to be informed of the risks and benefits of medical imaging tests before they are scanned. It is well established that patients often have difficulty interpreting quantitative risk information, so a simple presentation of risk statistics associated with having a medical imaging test versus skipping it is not likely to enhance patients' ability to make an informed decision about having a test (see Chapter 18, this volume). Although continued efforts are needed to improve patient interpretation of numerical data about risks and benefits associated with medical testing, an interpersonal communication approach is preferred over providing patients with written materials alone. In their investigation comparing patients' understanding of common risk presentation formats, Sheridan, Pignone, and Lewis (2003) noted that although all patients in the study had difficulty comparing and calculating treatment benefits, those who reported having medical discussions with their doctors interpreted treatment benefits correctly more often than those who did not engage in these interactions.

Although some have called for mandatory informed consent on the issue, a UMT perspective would highlight the importance of recognizing that risks of exposure to radiation from medical testing are different across individuals. For example, although children are at greatest risk for developing secondary cancers as a result of radiation exposure from medical testing, parents of children who are undergoing medical scans to monitor the effectiveness of their treatment for terminal cancer most likely will not want (or need) to hear about the risk of developing secondary cancers 20 years in the future when the child is not expected to live another 20 years.

Reflections for Theory and Research

Returning to the two theoretical assumptions we began the chapter with, UMT and transactional theory, it is easy to see how these help us understand risk discussions. First, these discussions are mutually influenced. A provider's discussion about risk with a patient will depend in some part on the patient's questions, responses, even nonverbal cues while the provider is talking. Imagine, for example, a pregnant woman meeting with her OB to discuss the risks of trying to have a vaginal delivery versus a repeat cesarean section (C-section). If the woman seems very nervous and asks a lot of questions about the risk of uterine rupture during vaginal delivery, the OB may think that repeat C-section is better for this patient and downplay the risks of C-section to help the woman feel calm. Because the OB does not emphasize the risks of C-section, the patient may believe that they are not severe and may not ask about them. Because the patient doesn't ask about the risks, the OB assumes that the patient doesn't want to know.

UMT can give us a lens through which to look at many of the contexts of provider–patient risk discussion described to this point in the chapter. Each of the patient–provider risk discussion contexts described in this chapter includes some discussion of uncertainty (e.g., uncertainty in an outcome, uncertainty in a test result) with no clear answer or solution. Thus, it is easy to see how provider–patient risk discussions may do more to increase than to decrease uncertainty. However, this depends on what the uncertainty is about. If the uncertainty is about the outcome itself, a provider–patient discussion may decrease uncertainty. If the uncertainty is about the outcome, a provider–patient discussion about risk may not change or increase the uncertainty.

In addition, the provider–patient discussion about risk has the potential to increase uncertainty by introducing new risks that the patient may not have previously considered. For example, a woman may initiate discussion with her provider about the risks of a mammography false positive, but through her discussion learn of other risks associated with mammographies, such as false negative or radiation risks.

Furthermore, as UMT points out, uncertainty can be appraised differently. Consider the two contrasting examples in the context of genetic counseling. Tom and John both have a family history of the fatal neurodegenerative condition Huntington disease but have not yet been tested for the disease-causing gene expansion. Tom evaluates the uncertainty of having the condition positively; if he does not know whether he has the mutation, he can continue his hope and optimism that he is not affected by the condition and will continue to lead a healthy life. John, however, views this same uncertainty negatively. He has a low tolerance for ambiguity and feels anxious and stressed about the fact that he doesn't know whether he has the mutation. For John, knowing—even if it is bad news—is better than not knowing. Such differences of uncertainty appraisal in cases like this have direct consequences for discussions about risk with providers. For example, Tom may choose to focus pretesting genetic counseling sessions on promising new research being done to increase uncertainty about the potential prognosis if he has the condition. Health care providers must navigate these individual differences during their communication with their patients about risk.

There is still much work to be done to better understand discussions about risk in provider–patient communication and to establish a better evidence base to guide health care providers on how to best present and discuss risk. This research should continue to be done in a variety of health contexts, as best practices for risk presentation may depend on the health issue being discussed. For instance, a health care provider may present risk about radiation along with a strong recommendation for the patient to have the diagnostic test, whereas the same provider may present risk about surgery in the context of working with the patient to make a shared decision about treatment.

Additionally, practitioners may consider individual differences in what patients may hope to gain from their health care conversations and adjust to these preferences accordingly. One theory that may be helpful in this task is goals–plans–action theory. This theory posits that social interactions, including health care conversations, are goal driven. Primary goals, such as changing the other's stance toward an issue, providing counsel, and obtaining permission are often present in patient–provider discussions about risk. For example, a primary care physician may initiate a discussion with a patient who smokes about the risks of tobacco in an attempt to modify the patient's behavior. However, these primary goals are often influenced by secondary goals that shape or limit the interaction. For example, the physician may be concerned about damaging the relationship with his patient or offending his patient and thus modify how he discusses the risks of smoking. Although this theory has not yet been used to study provider–patient risk discussions, it may be useful in fleshing out some of the difficulties that can be encountered when these conversations arise.

Recommendations for Practice

Our recommendations for health care providers who are discussing uncertain outcomes with their patients draw on the notion of patient-centered communication (Epstein & Street, 2007). A patient-centered communication approach proposes that the provider should seek to understand the patient's understanding of his or her disease and preferences for information. Particularly, understanding how a patient views the uncertainty associated with risk is important in knowing how to best communicate. For example, a patient who wants the uncertainty to remain may

not follow through on an appointment for a diagnostic test. If the provider understands this patient's point of view, she can communicate with the patient about the relative advantages and disadvantages of knowing and not knowing.

The area of genetic risk discussions is particularly fruitful regarding recommendations for practice. Several of the ethical and professional challenges that arise from patients with genetic concerns can be alleviated through simple directed conversations between doctors and patients to identify patients' values, desire for autonomy and information, desire and ability to understand complex genetic information, misconceptions based on previous conversations or research, and any cultural, ethnic, or religious factors that may influence their preferred plan of action. In accordance with the principles of transactional communication, asking patients to discuss these issues may lead patients to feel more comfortable in expressing their concerns and personal preferences with their providers. Because of the time restrictions and the difficulty associated with attaining and maintaining proficiency in the area, it will be important to increase patient access to genetic counseling services and to encourage patients to utilize these services. Clinicians should acknowledge the principles of UMT to recognize that over time, different patients may have multiple or changing health goals, preserving hope, maintaining good health, or learning about treatment options.

In accordance with UMT, patients who evaluate uncertainty about the state of their health negatively may be motivated to pressure their health care provides to order unnecessary medical imaging tests in an effort to reduce this uncertainty. Others may evaluate uncertainty about the state of their health positively because they are afraid of receiving news that their treatment isn't working to combat their disease. It is important for health care professionals to understand and acknowledge these motivations when engaging in conversations about whether or not a medical imaging test is necessary.

Conclusions

Provider–patient communication provides many opportunities for discussions about risks or uncertain outcomes. Providers and patients influence each other substantially during these conversations, as they work to manage the uncertainty inherent in health care. Particularly relevant topic areas of provider–patient communication include risky health behaviors, cancer screening, genetic screening, prenatal screening, surgical risk, and radiation risk. Health care providers should strive for communication about risk that is patient-centered and that recognizes the complications of uncertainty management.

Suggested Additional Readings

Baxter, L. A., & Braithwaite, D. O. (Eds.). (2008). *Engaging theories in interpersonal communication: Multiple perspectives.* Thousand Oaks, CA: Sage.

Bylund, C. L., Peterson, E. B., & Cameron, K. A. (2012). A practitioner's guide to interpersonal communication theory: An overview and exploration of selected theories. *Patient Education and Counseling, 87,* 261–267.

References

American Society of Human Genetics, Ad Hoc Committee on Genetic Counseling. (1975). Genetic counseling. *American Journal of Human Genetics, 27*(2), 240–242.

Ampt, A., Amoroso, C., Harris, M. F., McKenzie, S. H., Rose, V. K., & Taggert, J. R. (2009). Attitudes, norms and controls influencing lifestyle risk factor management in general practice. *BMC Family Practice, 10,* 1–8.

Arslanoglu, A., Bilgin, S., Kubali, Z., Ceyhan, M. N., & Ilhan, I. M. (2007). Doctors' and intern doctors' knowledge about patients' ionizing radiation exposure doses during common radiological examinations. *Diagnostic Interventional Radiology, 13,* 53–55.

Baerlocher, M. O., & Detsky, A. S. (2010). Discussing radiation risks associated with CT scans with patients. *JAMA, 304*(19), 2170–2171.

Borgen, L., Stranden, E., & Espeland, A. (2010). Clinicians' justification of imaging: Do radiation issues play a role? *Insights Imaging, 1,* 193–200.

Braithwaite, D., Emery, J., Walter, F., Prevost, A. J., & Sutton, S. (2004). Psychological impact of genetic counseling for familial cancer: A systematic review and meta-analysis. *Journal of the National Cancer Institute, 96*(2), 122–133.

Brashers, D. E. (2001). Communication and uncertainty management. *Journal of Communication, 51,* 477–497.

Brashers, D. E., Haas, S. M., & Neidig, J. L. (1999). The patient self-advocacy scale: Measuring patient involvement in health care decision-making interactions. *Health Communication, 11,* 97–121.

Brashers, D. E., Hsieh, E., Neidig, J. L., & Reynolds, N. R. (2006). Managing uncertainty about illness: Health care providers as credible authorities. In R. M. Dailey & B. A. Le Poire (Eds.), *Applied interpersonal communication matters: Family, health & community relations* (pp. 219–240). New York, NY: Peter Lang.

Brenes, G. A., & Paskett, E. D. (2000). Predictors of stage of adoption for colorectal cancer screening. *Preventive Medicine, 31*(4), 410–416. doi:10.1006/pmed.2000.0729

Brink, J. A., Goske, M. J., & Patti, J. A. (2011). Informed consent for radiologic procedures. *JAMA, 305,* 888–889.

Cairns, C. P., & Viswanath, K. (2006). Communication and colorectal cancer screening among the uninsured: Data from the Health Information National Trends Survey (United States). *Cancer Causes Control, 17*(9), 1115–1125. doi:10.1007/s10552-006-0046-2

Cardinal, J. S., Gunderman, R. B., & Tarver, R. D. (2011). Informing patients about risks and benefits of radiology examinations: A review article. *Journal of the American College of Radiology, 896,* 402–408.

Caughey, A. B., Washington, A. E., & Kupperman, M. (2008). Perceived risk of prenatal diagnostic procedure-related miscarriage and Down syndrome among pregnant women. *American Journal of Obstetrics and Gynecology, 198,* 333.e331–333.e338.

Charles, C., Gafni, A., & Whelan, T. (1997). Shared decision-making in the medical encounter: What does it mean? (or it takes at least two to tango). *Social Science and Medicine, 44*(5), 681–692.

Chase, G. A., Faden, R. R., Holtzman, N. A., Chwalow, A. J., Leonard, C. O., Lopes, C., & Quaid, K. (1986). Assessment of risk by pregnant women: Implications for genetic counseling and education. *Social Biology, 33,* 57–64.

Dauer, L. T., Thornton, R., Hay, J. L., Baleter, R., Williamson, M. J., & St. Germain, J. (2011). Fears, feelings, and facts: Interactively communicating benefits and risks of medical radiation with patients. *American Journal of Roentgenology, 196,* 756–761.

Denny, C. H., Serdula, M. K., Holtzman, D., & Nelson, D. E. (2003). Physician advice about smoking and drinking: Are U.S. adults being informed? *American Journal of Preventive Medicine, 24,* 71–74.

Di Prospero, L. S., Seminisky, M., Honeyford, J., Doan, B., Franssen, E., Meschino, W., . . . Warner, E. (2001). Psychosocial issues following a positive result of genetic testing for BRCA1 and BRCA2 mutations: Findings from a focus group and a needs assessment survey. *Canadian Medical Association Journal, 164*(7), 1005–1009.

Dube, C., & Fuller, B. K. (2003). A qualitative study of communication skills for male cancer screening discussions. *Journal of Cancer Education, 18*(4), 182–187.

Edwards, A., & Prior, L. (1997). Communication about risk: Dilemmas for general practitioners. The Department of General Practice Working Group, University of Wales College of Medicine. *British Journal of General Practice, 47,* 739–742.

Epstein R. M., Street R. L., Jr. (2007). *Patient-centered communication in cancer care: Promoting healing and reducing suffering* (NIH Publication No. 07–6225). Bethesda, MD: National Cancer Institute.

Forrest, L. E., Delatycki, M. B., Skene, L., & Aitken, M. (2007). Communicating genetic information in families: A review of guidelines and position papers. *European Journal of Human Genetics, 15,* 612–618.

Fox, S. A., Heritage, J., Stockdale, S. E., Asch, S. M., Duan, N., & Reise, S. P. (2009). Cancer screening adherence: Does physician-patient communication matter? *Patient Education and Counseling, 75,* 178–184.

Fox, S. A., & Stein, J. A. (1991). The effect of physician–patient communication on mammography utilization by different ethnic groups. *Medical Care, 29*(11), 1065–1082.

Frush, D. P., & Applegate, K. (2004). Computed tomography and radiation: Understanding the issues. *Journal of the American College of Radiology, 1*(2), 113–119.

Galvin, K. M., Bylund, C. L., & Brommel, B. J. (2012). *Family communication: Cohesion and change.* Boston, MA: Allyn & Bacon.

Gates, E. A. (2004). Communicating risk in prenatal genetic testing. *Journal of Midwifery & Women's Health, 49,* 220–227.

Gatto, N. M., Frucht, H., Sundararajan, V., Jacobson, J. S., Grann, V. R., & Neugut, A. I. (2003). Risk of perforation after colonoscopy and sigmoidoscopy: A population-based study. *Journal of the National Cancer Institute, 95*(3), 230–236.

Gearing, R. E., Townsend, L., MacKenzie, M., & Charach, A. (2011). Reconceptualizing medication adherence: Six phases of dynamic adherence. *Harvard Review of Psychiatry, 19,* 177–189.

Gordon, H. S., Street, R. L., Sharf, B. F., Kelly, P. A., & Souchek, J. (2006). Racial differences in trust and lung cancer patients' perceptions of physician communication. *Journal of Clinical Oncology, 24,* 904–909.

Grimes, D. A., & Snively, G. R. (1999). Patients' understanding of medical risks: Implications for genetic counseling. *Obstetrics & Gynecology, 93,* 910–914.

Han, P. K. J., Klein, W. M. P., & Arora, N. K. (2011). Varieties of uncertainty in health care: A conceptual taxonomy. *Medical Decision Making, 31,* 828–838.

Heerdt, A., Park, B., & Boland, P. (2010). Communication in surgical oncology. In D. W. Kissane, B. D. Bultz, P. N. Butow, & I. G. Finaly (Eds.), *Handbook of communication in oncology and palliative care* (pp. 473–478). New York, NY: Oxford University Press.

Hughes, C., Lerman, C., Schwartz, M., Peshkin, B., Wenzel, L., Narod, S., . . . Main, D. (2002). All in the family: Evaluation of the process and content of sisters' communication about BRCA 1 and BRCA 2 genetic test results. *American Journal of Medical Genetics, 107,* 143–150.

Jain, M. (2012, July 2). When patients demand tests and prescriptions, doctors should think twice. *The Washington Post.* Retrieved from http://www.washingtonpost.com/national/health-science/

when-patients-demand-tests-and-prescriptions-doctors-should-think-twice/2012/07/02/gJQAWnfgIW_print.html

Lee, C. I., Halms, A. H., Monico, E. P., Brink, J. A., & Forman, H. P. (2004). Diagnostic CT scans: Assessment of physician and radiologist awareness of radiation dose and possible risks. *Radiology, 231,* 393–398.

Liang, W., Kasman, D., Wang, J. H., Yuan, E. H., & Madelblatt, J. S. (2006). Communication between older women and physicians: Preliminary implications for satisfaction and intention to have mammography. *Patient Education and Counseling, 64,* 387–392.

Ling, B. S., Trauth, J. M., Fine, M. J., Mor, M. K., Resnick, A., Braddock, C. H., . . . Whittle, J. (2008). Informed decision-making and colorectal cancer screening: Is it occurring in primary care? *Medical Care, 46,* S23–S29.

Lobb, E. A., Butow, P. N., Meiser, B., Barratt, A., Gaff, C., Young, M. A., . . . Tucker, K. (2003). Women's preferences and consultants' communication of risk in consultations about familial breast cancer: Impact on patient outcomes. *Journal of Medical Genetics, 40,* e56.

Malone, A. J., Wolf, C. R., Malmed, A. S., & Melliere, B. F. (1992). Diagnosis of acute appendicitis: Value of unenhanced CT. *American Journal of Roentgenology, 160,* 763–766.

Maloney, E., Edgerson, S., Robson, M., Offit, K., Brown, R. F., Bylund, C., & Kissane, D. (2012). What women with breast cancer discuss with clinicians about risk for their adolescent daughters. *Journal of Psychosocial Oncology, 30*(4), 484–502.

McCarthy, V. P., Bartels, D. M., & LeRoy, B. S. (2001). Ethical and professional challenges posed by patients with genetic concerns: A report of focus group discussions with genetic counselors, physicians, and nurses. *Journal of Genetic Counseling, 10,* 97–119.

McCurdy, S. A. (2012). Willingness to provide behavioral health recommendations: A cross-sectional study of entering medical students. *BMC Medical Education, 12,* 1–7.

Miller, E. C., Holmes, J. F., & Derlet, R. W. (1997). Utilizing clinical favors to reduce head CT scan ordering for minor head trauma patients. *Journal of Emergency Medicine, 15*(4), 453–457.

National Academies of Science, Engineering, and Medicine, & Council, National Research. (2006). *BEIR VII, Phase 2: Health risks from exposure to low levels of ionizing radiation.* Washington, DC: National Academies Press.

National Cancer Institute. (2012a). *Fact sheet: Mammogram.* Retrieved from http://www.cancer.gov/cancertopics/factsheet/detection/mammograms

National Cancer Institute. (2012b). *Fact sheet: Prostate-specific antigen (PSA) test.* Retrieved from http://www.cancer.gov/cancertopics/factsheet/detection/PSA

van Oostram, I., Meijers-Heijboer, H., Duivervoorden, H. J., Brocker-Vriends, A. H. J. T., Van Asperen, C. J., Sijmons, R. H., . . . Tibben, A. (2007). A prospective study of the impact of genetic susceptibility testing for BRCA 1/2 or HNPCC on family relationships. *Psychooncology, 16*(4), 320–328.

Paling, J. (2003). Strategies to help patients understand risks. *British Medical Journal, 327,* 745–748.

Pastorino, U., Bellomi, M., Landoni, C., De Fiori, E., Arnaldi, P., Picchio, M., . . . Fazio, F. (2003). Early lung cancer detection with spiral CT and positron emission tomography in heavy smokers: 2-year results. *Lancet, 362,* 593–597.

Politi, M. C., Clark, M. A., Rogers, M. L., McGarry, K., & Sciamanna, C. N. (2008). Patient-provider communication and cancer screening among unmarried women. *Patient Education and Counseling, 73,* 251–255.

Prinjha, S., Evans, J., & McPherson, A. (2006). Women's information needs about ductal carcinoma in situ before mammographic screening and after diagnosis: A qualitative study. *Journal of Medical Screening, 13,* 110–114.

Prokop, M. (2005). New challenges in MDCT. *European Radiology, 15,* E35–E45.

Rosenthal, M. S. (2006). Patient misconceptions and ethical challenges in radioactive iodine scanning and therapy. *Journal of Nuclear Medicine Technology, 34*(3), 143–150.

Sheridan, S., Pignone, M. P., & Lewis, C. L. (2003). A randomized comparison of patients' understanding of number needed to treat and other common risk reduction formats. *Journal of General Internal Medicine, 18,* 884–892.

Timmermans, D., Molewijk, B., Stigglebout, A., & Kievit, J. (2004). Different formats for communicating surgical risks to patients and the effect on choice of treatment. *Patient Education and Counseling, 54,* 255–263.

Tuveri, M., Caocci, G., Efficace, F., Medas, F., Collins, G. S., & Pisu, S. (2009). Different perception of surgical risks between physicians and patients undergoing laparoscopic cholecystectomy. *Surgical Laparoscopy Endoscopy & Percutaneous Techniques, 22,* 305–311.

Woloshin, S., & Schwartz, L. M. (2012). How a charity oversells mammography. *British Medical Journal, 345,* e5132.

CHAPTER 18

Informed Consent

Z. Janet Yang

Introduction

Informed consent is inherently a risk communication issue because individuals' consent to participate in research should be sought and granted based on effective communication of the potential risks and benefits involved. Across all different disciplines, informed consent should include five elements: (1) competence, (2) disclosure, (3) comprehension, (4) voluntariness, and (5) consent (Beauchamp & Childress, 2009). Risk communication, not surprisingly, is closely related to all these elements. However, as this chapter will illustrate, the communication of risk, as involved in the process of obtaining informed consent, is inadequate at times. This inadequacy presents challenges for the protection of participants involved in medical and social science research, as well as in ethnographic and industrial settings.

Historically, informed consent has received distinct attention from researchers in clinical/medical research and social science research. The concept of informed consent was developed mainly for medical research, whereas in social sciences, it is a learned practice adopted from the consent process in the medical field. Medical research provides a natural setting for informed consent because there is an unquestionable need to ensure that participants understand the risks of potential harm that they may be exposed to as well as the potential benefits they may accrue to themselves, to others, and to medical science. These days, in the medical area, the patient's right to know surpasses the doctor's right not to tell, both in the moral and the legal sense (Fluehr-Lobban, 1994). Ethical principles including respects for human dignity and autonomy are at work when medical regulations require voluntary informed consent.

Social sciences often involve direct and long-term studies of human groups, which pose a lot of difficulties to obtain informed consent adequately and naturally (Du Toit, 1980). Therefore, informed consent was not fully incorporated into the code of ethics for many social science areas until much later. Since the 1960s, however, social scientists have been required to inform the participants how the information they provide will be used in the future and their rights to withhold cooperation. The primary goal of social science research is to generate knowledge. Nevertheless, autonomy, comprehension, and competence are still some of the basic requirements for the informed consent process. As Wilson (2001) suggested, "While at one time seeking the 'informed consent' of the studied was unknown, proceeding without it now is almost unthinkable" (Wilson, 2001, p. 80).

To analyze informed consent as a risk communication issue, this chapter will first introduce the institution of informed consent, including its historical background. Based on a review of literature that examines factors that influence informed consent decisions, communication challenges involved in the informed consent process will be discussed through a case example. Finally, the chapter will conclude by offering reflections for theory and research, as well as recommendations for practice.

History of Informed Consent

Informed consent has been a central issue in clinical research and biomedical ethics since the Nazi war crime trials at Nuremberg in 1947. The Nuremberg Code, published in 1948, makes a subject's voluntary consent a primary consideration in research. Even though the Nuremberg Code was limited in its scope, it served as a model for many professional and governmental codes formulated throughout the 1950s and 1960s. In 1964, the World Medical Association adopted the Declaration of Helsinki, which requires consent for all nontherapeutic medical research but not for therapeutic research. This omission of requirement for therapeutic research was a serious flaw, but the Declaration of Helsinki stimulated other medical associations to reflect on informed consent and research ethics (Faden & Beauchamp, 1986).

In comparison, early descriptions of the American Psychological Association's Ethical Standards did not mention informed consent specifically, rather, they were primarily focused on stress and harm, as well as deception used in psychological research (Faden & Beauchamp, 1986). In the 1960s and 1970s, several controversial cases that violated the research participants' rights or harmed their physical or psychological well-being, such as Milgram's Obedience Research, Humphrey's Tearoom-Trade Research, and the Tuskegee Syphilis Study, rekindled public attention and debate

over informed consent, which led to the appointment of a National Commission by the Congress to examine ethics in both behavioral and biomedical research.

On April 18, 1979, the National Commission for the Protection of Human Subjects of Biomedical and Behavioral Research published its official report—the Belmont Report. In this report, informed consent is defined as respect for persons, which "requires that subjects, to the degree that they are capable, be given the opportunity to choose what shall or shall not happen to them. This opportunity is provided when adequate standards for informed consent are satisfied" (The Belmont Report, 1979). The consent process involves three key features: (1) disclosing to participants information needed to make an informed decision, (2) facilitating the understanding of what has been disclosed, and (3) promoting the voluntariness of the decision about whether or not to participate in the research. The Belmont Report requires that informed consent must be legally effective and prospectively obtained. As such, informed consent finally emerged as a major moral rule for human research in both behavioral and biomedical sciences.

The Belmont Report sets clear boundaries between practice (clinical care) and research. While practice refers to interventions designed solely to enhance the well-being of a patient, research is conducted for the purpose of generating knowledge. For research involving human participants, three basic ethical principles are specified—(1) respect for persons, (2) beneficence, and (3) justice. Respect for persons requires that individuals should be treated as autonomous agents, while persons with diminished autonomy are entitled to protection. Beneficence requires researchers to do no harm and maximize possible benefits and minimize possible harms. Justice requires a fair distribution of the benefits and burdens of research (The Belmont Report, 1979).

In medical settings, informed consent requires a patient to have the capacity to make decisions, understand the information disclosed, and voluntarily authorize or refuse the treatment recommended (Beauchamp & Childress, 2009). The patient should be given adequate time to evaluate information received from the medical researcher and to reflect on his or her personal values and goals. At the same time, the medical researcher needs to disclose all information relevant to the decision-making process, including potential benefits and side effects of the treatment recommended and its alternatives. The medical researcher cannot present information selectively to coerce the patient into a treatment (Beauchamp & Childress, 2009). However, even though the requirement to obtain consent is now taken as a given in modern medical ethics, actual consent is not obtained in all cases. Even when consent is obtained, it may not be "adequately informed" or "autonomous" (Veatch, 1995).

Thus, risk communication seems a central issue in the process of obtaining informed consent. However, communication researchers did not pay much attention to studying informed consent until the late 1990s (Hines, Badzek, & Moss, 1997). Past research, however, has indicated that the communication of risk is not always adequate. Next, communication issues related to the five elements of informed consent—competence, disclosure, comprehension, voluntariness, and consent—will be reviewed.

Communication Issues

Competence

Related to informed consent, competence requires an individual to have the ability to make a decision regarding participation in research, and it is especially relevant to research that involves vulnerable populations, such as children, older adults, and individuals with mental disabilities. Compared with other vulnerable populations, there is less research on the evaluation of competence of older adults with diminished decision-making capacity.

Past research has consistently argued for the importance of assessing competence based on individual experiences and specific interventions, especially when children are involved (Alderson, 2007; Miller, Drotar, & Kodish, 2004; Van Staden & Kruger, 2003). In particular, Alderson (2007) pointed out that children's competence and autonomy develop through direct social personal experience and not through age and physical growth. Thus, some children are capable of giving informed consent. However, split views exist among parents regarding children's ability to decide about participation in research. In one study, almost half of the parents from 4,000 families in a longitudinal prospective screening believed that children did not have the competence to understand the consequences for research (Swartling, Helgesson, Hansson, & Ludvigsson, 2009).

From the researchers' end, another relevant concept is *cultural competence*, which emphasizes the need for researchers to balance universal ethical standards with practical and local standards, especially in impoverished settings where participants are more vulnerable to exploitation. Here, informed consent should be achieved with greater flexibility in communication, in terms of both meeting participants' language need and cooperating with their cultural beliefs and values (Adams et al., 2007). For instance, to establish an ethically responsible and culturally appropriate informed consent process for biomedical research in the Tibet Autonomous Region in China, Adams and her colleagues conducted open-ended qualitative interviews and surveys to collect basic cultural information. The key findings from their study indicate that even when using illustrations and culturally appropriate terms, participants with the least formal education consistently showed lower levels of comprehension. Thus, cultural competence presents a unique challenge to the informed consent process, especially in international research.[1]

Disclosure

Disclosure should generally cover the aims and methods of the research, anticipated benefits and risks, anticipated inconvenience or discomfort, and the participants' right to withdraw from the research (Beauchamp & Childress, 2009). However, in a survey of institutional review boards overseeing research that involves human participants from a probability sample of 16 institutions, procedures of the research were not mentioned in 10% of the consent forms, purpose was not mentioned in 23%, benefits of the research were not mentioned in 45%, and risk was not mentioned in 30% (Gray, Cooke, & Tannenbaum, 1978). In some cases, these topics were mentioned only in statements such as "I certify that I have been informed of the purpose, procedures, and risks and benefits of this study."

From this study, it is clear that consent forms for research involving human participants do not always offer sufficient disclosure. Today, a greater challenge for adequate disclosure lies in clinical care practice that evolves to serve research goals, with opportunities embedded for commercial exploitation. For example, situations involving research on cell or tissue samples present complexities regarding what participants are consenting to—the particular use of his or her tissue samples for research into a disease or the banking of these samples for future research. Since the purpose of future research involving these tissue samples may not be specified, a blanket consent may be obtained, which means that research participants may not be fully informed of the possible commercial benefits resulting from the use of these samples. The case of *John Moore v. the Regents of the University of California* illustrates this scenario well. In 1976, John Moore underwent treatment for hairy cell leukemia at the UCLA Medical Center, under the supervision of Dr. David W. Golde. Dr. Golde later developed Moore's cell line, applied for a patent, and negotiated agreements for its commercial development. In 1990, the California Supreme Court ruled that Moore had no right to any share of the profits realized from the commercialization of anything developed from his discarded body parts. In this case, the boundary between practice and research was blurred, and Moore was unknowingly transformed from a patient to a research participant. Here, communication was inadequate due to the lack of disclosure from the researchers to the patient regarding their research goals, methods and sponsorship, and an explanation for future uses and commercial possibilities.

Comprehension

Comprehension requires participants to understand if they have acquired pertinent information and to know the nature and consequences of their actions (Beauchamp & Childress, 2009). Existing communication research has consistently shown that comprehension presents a major challenge for truly informed consent to be obtained. For instance, from a discursive perspective, past research has found that patients often have a lack of understanding of information presented in the consent form (Olufowote, 2008; Schulz & Rubinelli, 2008). Other studies have applied quantitative method to explore the social cognitive factors that influence the informed consent process. For instance, Curbow, Fogarty, McDonnell, Chill, and Scott (2006) found that women's likelihood of accepting to participate in breast cancer clinical trials was negatively related to their knowledge gain from the informed consent document, which suggests that their decisions to participate were not based on in-depth processing of the information presented (Curbow et al., 2006). This result highlights an important communication issue—the difference between receiving the information and understanding the information. Other researchers have raised similar concerns regarding participants' inadequate comprehension of informed consent document, especially among participants with low literacy skills. For instance, in a study of 37 Spanish-speaking individuals, Cortés, Drainoni, Henault, and Paasche-Orlow (2010) found that even among people who understood most of the consent form, they were confused about the extent to which the consent form provided sufficient protections around the issues of confidentiality, risks, and benefits (Cortés et al., 2010).

Other researchers have argued that more innovative and interactive communication procedures are necessary to improve participants' comprehension of consent information. Donovan-Kicken and colleagues found that individuals with higher health literacy reported higher self-efficacy, which was positively related to their feeling more informed about risks and more prepared to make decisions about the procedure. In addition, they argued for giving patients a greater control over how to receive consent information—through the traditional written format or through new multimedia tool (Donovan-Kicken et al., 2012). This sentiment was echoed by other researchers (Jimison, Sher, Appleyard, & LeVernois, 1998; Wanzer et al., 2010). For instance, Wanzer and her colleagues (2010) found that patients who viewed the multimedia presentation of consent information scored higher on an objective test, which included questions related to the risks and benefits of the procedure, showing a greater increase in comprehension. Physicians who were blind to the study conditions also rated these patients significantly higher in their comprehension of the consent information.

Voluntariness

Voluntariness requires the participant to give consent without being under the researcher's influence (Beauchamp & Childress, 2009). This influence does not have to be exerted through outright coercion, other forms of manipulation and persuasion can compromise voluntariness as well. Here, information processing plays a central role in leading to a truly *informed* consent. There is ample evidence that people have problems processing information about risks and probabilities (Kahneman & Tversky, 1984; Tversky & Kahneman, 1974). For instance, patients' preference between hypothetical therapies for lung cancer varied significantly when their probable outcomes were

described in terms of mortality or survival. When treatment outcomes were described in terms of mortality, the riskier surgery option was chosen less than the less risky radiation therapy option. In contrast, when treatment outcomes were described in terms of survival, more patients chose the surgery option. Kahneman and Tversky (1984) argue that this *formulation* or *framing effects* could be exploited deliberately to manipulate the relative attractiveness of different options, which is especially relevant to the process of obtaining informed consent.

Some researchers argue that *nudging*, which refers to the practice of steering patients' decision making in health-promoting ways, offers an important new paradigm for informed consent that combines the advantages of beneficence and autonomy (Cohen, 2013). The argument here is that the doctor can secure a patient's consent to an important intervention by presenting its success rates as opposed to the complementary failure rates when the patient is "unreasonably stubborn" (Cohen, 2013). The concern, obviously, is the extent to which nudging differs from improper manipulation or exploitation of individuals' cognitive weaknesses related to the framing effects mentioned above. Strictly speaking, nudging compromises the voluntariness of the consent because the decision is not completely autonomous.

Another concern related to the voluntariness of informed consent has to do with the advent of the Internet age. As Ploug and Holm (2013) illustrated, informed consent may lose its function as a protection of personal autonomy if it is routinized, which happens when the provision or refusal of consent happens as an unreflective, habitual act. Internet users often have to implicitly or explicitly offer their consent to use a given site or service, which may make the provision of consent become a habitual act. Furthermore, in exchange of the right to use, personal or private information voluntarily offered by the users is often accessed and utilized beyond the users' control. In a study of users of social networking sites, a majority of the participants failed to read the consent documents prior to offering their consent, citing reasons such as "all are the same," which indicated a degree of routinization (Ploug & Holm, 2013).

Consent

Last, researchers have argued that the informed consent process should be a dynamic and interactive process rather than a static and linear transmission of information from researchers to participants (Hines et al., 1997). From the research participants' perspective, their willingness to engage in conversations with the researchers also contributes to a successful informed consent process. Past research has examined this willingness to talk from a risk communication perspective. In particular, based on a probability sample of 500 U.S. adults, McComas and her colleagues (2010) found that individuals' perception of interactional justice, which emphasizes the degree to which they believe that their doctor would communicate with them in an informative, fair, and respectful manner, was associated with greater willingness to talk about clinical trials. This research suggests that when patients believe that their doctors will treat them with respect, kindness, openness, and concern, as well as tailor information to meet their needs, they are more willing to broach sensitive topics or offer their opinions. This way, positive outcomes can emerge from the informed consent process, which leads to better decision making on both the patient's and the doctor's end (Schachter & Fins, 2008).

In ethnographic settings and anthropological studies, informed consent is sometimes difficult to achieve because of the researcher's goal to observe natural behavior. As Du Toit (1980) pointed out, for this type of research, it is important for the researcher to view host population with respect and dignity and to do everything possible to protect confidentiality and trust. The researcher should explain as clearly and informatively as possible the procedure and

implications of the research to the individuals being studied. When covert observation is necessary, retrospective consent should be obtained from the participants. Furthermore, it is important to note that observing "public behavior" without informed consent can be morally problematic because anonymity may be difficult to ensure when individuals are sufficiently distinctive, which makes them potentially identifiable (Schrag, 2009).

When research is conducted in organizational or workplace settings, gaining access through organizational managers is different from obtaining informed consent from individual participants. Individual participants may assent simply because senior management has approved the study, which means the consent is not truly voluntary (Plankey-Videla, 2012). Therefore, as compared with medical settings, informed consent in ethnographic, industrial, and workplace settings may be more difficult to obtain because the relational concerns in these settings may be more complex. Indeed, there is power differentiation in medical settings, but the power dynamics in organizational settings may have greater impact on participants and are more difficult to negotiate. Also, obtaining informed consent in ethnographic research is often an ongoing process because the relationship between the researcher and the participants could evolve to become more intimate and intertwined (Plankey-Videla, 2012; Schrag, 2009).

Case Example

Next, the communication issues discussed above will be illustrated through a case example—seeking informed consent for cancer clinical trials. Low patient accrual in clinical trials poses a serious concern for the advancement of medical science in the United States (National Cancer Institute, 2002). Past research has shown that the informed consent process plays an important role in influencing individuals' decisions about enrollment (see, e.g., Albrecht et al., 2003).

Two competing ethical frameworks govern how key elements of informed consent are presented to potential participants—the contemporary bioethics model and the informed judgment model. Contemporary bioethicists maintain that informed consent should represent nothing less than an "autonomous authorization" by an individual (Beauchamp & Childress, 2009). In contrast, the informed judgment model requires researchers to transfer the necessary expertise to participants so that they could make the decision together (Charles, Gafni, & Whelan, 1999). Clearly, these two frameworks have different implications for risk communication. In the contemporary bioethics model, the most important elements of informed consent are disclosure and voluntariness, which means that any *nudging* from the medical researcher is inappropriate. In terms of the ethical principles laid out in the Belmont Report, beneficence and justice stand second to respect for person because autonomy is of utmost importance. In contrast, the informed judgment model is perhaps more concerned with comprehension and competence. To ensure the inclusion of participants in shared decision making, some nudging might be appropriate.

Because randomization is an important aspect of clinical trials that could influence potential participants' decisions, some researchers argue that it is debatable whether autonomy should take precedence to beneficence in the informed consent process (Corbett, Oldham, & Lilford, 1996). Traditionally, physicians have been more concerned with beneficence, acting in what they construe to be the patient's best interest even when the patient fails to recognize that interest (Zussman, 1992). In clinical trials, the researcher–participant relationship involves a greater disparity in power and control. Because most people share a generalized trust of physicians and medical institutions and trust plays an important role in their enrollment decision (Gordon & Daugherty, 2001; Grady et al., 2006), it becomes even more important for the informed consent process to strike a balance between autonomy and beneficence. A frank description of what

randomization means could deter a lot of people from enrolling in a trial, but it is important for potential participants to understand the process and not to have inflated hope about getting the new treatment.

Between the two ethical frameworks mentioned above, the informed judgment model makes risk communication more relevant, yet also more challenging, to the conduct of seeking informed consent for cancer clinical trials. In an exploratory study of 22 oncology encounters, Barton and Eggly (2009) found that physicians regularly present the purpose, benefits, and risks of their research with a positive valence. In particular, when presenting risks, physicians often mitigate side effects and negative outcomes by indicating that they would be mild or treatable. Similarly, past research has found that physicians often make implicit statements favoring either the standard treatment or the clinical trial, while a general rationale for randomization is described in less than half of the consultations (Brown, Butow, Ellis, Boyle, & Tattersall, 2004). These practices are problematic because they could skew the patients' information processing and lead them to make risk-approaching decisions that are not warranted.

Past research has suggested that patients often exhibit fear of the information included in consent documents (Olufowote, 2008; Schulz & Rubinelli, 2008). In fact, fear is one of the main reasons that deter people to enroll in clinical trials (National Cancer Institute, 2002). Other emotions such as anxiety, worry, and discomfort related to randomization, placebo, and side effects, as well as hope for therapeutic benefits are also key factors that influence individuals' decision to enroll (Catania et al., 2008; Madsen, Holm, & Riis, 2007). Recent research suggests that both negative and positive emotions could motivate more active information seeking and more systematic processing of information about clinical trial enrollment (Yang et al., 2010). Thus, when the goal of informed consent is not solely to convince individuals to blindly enter a trial but to make informed health decisions, emotions could drive them to learn more about the trial and weigh the risks and benefits more carefully.

Last, even when the information is presented without bias and the individuals are given sufficient time to make decisions, the manner in which medical researchers communicate with the participants and their family members still plays an important role (Agrawal et al., 2006; Catania et al., 2008). In particular, fairness perceptions, particularly informational justice and interpersonal justice, could facilitate individuals' risk and benefit evaluation and influence their decisions to communicate with researchers about clinical trials (McComas et al., 2010). Here, informational justice refers to proper disclosure and explanation of the risks and benefits involved in research, while interpersonal justice refers to interpersonal treatment that is based on respect and dignity.

Reflections for Theory and Research

Rosenthal (2006) proposes that informed consent is a philosophical concept as well as a democratizing concept. In both the clinical realm and social science research, as well as in other settings, informed consent should fully explain the purpose of the research and the procedure involved and discuss any risks facing the research participants or any benefits involved. More important, informed consent should be voluntary and based on participants' comprehension of the consent documents. Informed consent is intended to resist the parentalism of professionals, and its fundamental goal is to promote autonomous decision making. However, the practice of informed consent is often stigmatized as an effort from the researchers to exert control over their research participants or to take away the right from their participants to make a final decision. More research is needed to pinpoint why that is the case.

Based on the issues discussed in this chapter, several theoretical frameworks offer pathways for future research. First, future research should pay more attention to how emotion influences individuals' decision-making process. Participants, especially those with lower education and less experience with research, may easily feel overwhelmed by the amount of information they receive, especially when the researcher has limited time to answer their questions. Consent information that is too technical for the participants may also make them feel stressed out, which could make comprehension and decision making even more difficult. Judgments about risk often arouse negative emotions such as fear, anxiety, and worry (Johnson & Tversky, 1983). When self-efficacy is inadequate to lead people into an effective coping mechanism, emotions might steer them into decisions that are not based on rational judgment (Witte, 1994). Thus, future research should examine how emotion affects participants' reactions toward the consent documents and their subsequent decision making.

Second, even when the researchers heed all five elements of informed consent, relational issues can determine the outcome of the informed consent process. Past research has shown that perceived fairness of authorities' behaviors can influence how individuals respond to their interactions with the authorities (Colquitt, Greenberg, & Zapata-Phelan, 2005; Van den Bos, 2005). In particular, when individuals believe that they have a say or can have their opinions heard, they will feel that they have some control, even if the outcome of the interactions is beyond their control (Thibaut & Walker, 1975). Because informed consent is sought prior to research, there is always high uncertainty in what might come out of the research. Thus, participants' perceptions of whether the consent procedure is conducted in a fair manner become even more important (Van den Bos, 2005). Future research should further explore the applicability of the procedural justice framework in guiding how consent is obtained.

Recommendations for Practice

Research reviewed in this chapter also offers practical implications. First, with regard to the presentation of potential risks, in order to reduce the likelihood of biased processing from the participants, both sets of frames (gain or loss, mortality or survival, and clinical trial or standard treatment) should be introduced. In addition, percentage-based or frequency-based expressions of probabilities could produce different risk perceptions depending on individuals' numeracy skills (Keller & Siegrist, 2009; see also Chapter 11, this volume). Researchers seeking informed consent should present probabilities in both numeric and nonnumeric terms. For instance, in addition to saying that "3% of the participants will develop a mild fever," the risk information could be restated as, "3% of the participants will develop a mild fever, which means that out of every 100 participants who go through the procedure, 3 will develop a mild fever and 97 will not." Last, analogies to more familiar risks and comparison with prior experiences could also help research subjects understand the risk at hand (Bostrom, 2008; Thompson, 2002).

Second, in addition to the one-way transfer of information from the researcher to the participant, some sort of self-assessment might be incorporated as part of the informed consent process (Donovan-Kicken et al., 2012). Self-assessment will provide opportunities for the participants to review consent information, gauge their levels of understanding, and receive feedback on things they do not comprehend well. This way, researchers can evaluate participants' comprehension related to the specific research project, which will help them offer additional explanation if needed. To help research participants better manage their emotional reactions, sufficient time should be given to the participants to make a decision. Alternative options (e.g., presenting standard treatment during the consent process for a clinical trial) should also be laid out clearly to ease the amount of fear, anxiety, and worry participants feel. Given the power differentiation that often exists between the researcher and the participants, the researcher should treat each participant with dignity and respect, be truthful, and listen to the participant's

concerns. This last recommendation is particularly important when vulnerable populations are involved.

Last, Sankar (2004) introduced an alternative perspective on how to improve the informed consent process, which suggests that some of the efforts to improve informed consent such as using easier language might have "misidentified their target." She argues that sometimes researchers are not aware that they are misleading participants because their assumption about communication is based on the transmission model that measures successful communication based on the extent, accuracy, and duration of the information recalled. This model does not incorporate the influence on "social interactions of time, personal relations, purpose, or expectations" (Sankar, 2004). Based on this idea, a different communication approach, such as a dialectical communication strategy, might enhance the informed consent experience for both the researchers and the participants. A dialectical communication process would empower people to appreciate different perspectives, weigh contradictory facts, scrutinize opinions with a view to their resolution, and sharpen the skills necessary to make informed judgment. Past studies have shown that dialectical messages are successful in increasing critical thinking, preparing motivated lay audiences to productively participate in public deliberation, and probing the broader questions related to certain issues to gain a greater understanding of the complexity of the issues (McComas, 2004). Incorporating the idea of dialectical communication into the process of obtaining informed consent might help make informed consent a more meaningful and ethical practice.

Conclusions

In sum, informed consent offers a unique case study for risk communication because of issues such as uncertainty, risk and benefit analysis, emotion, information processing, and procedural fairness. Based on a review of existing communication research and a case example focusing on informed consent for cancer clinical trials, this chapter argues that the communication of risk could be improved when researchers keep the formulation effects of framing at guard, pay attention to participants' emotional responses to the risks, and engage in conversations with potential participants in a fair manner.

Note

1. Some community groups are of interest to the medical research community because they exhibit high rates of a particular disease. They may also be bearers of traditional knowledge, which may be highly valuable to researchers or to commercial companies. The old principle of bioprospecting because plants, animals, and other traditional knowledge were part of the global commons has now been overturned with the United Nations recognizing the importance of prior informed consent obtained from a traditional community for use of their knowledge (see Convention on Biological Diversity Nagoya Protocol, Article 7.).

Suggested Additional Readings

Gray, B. H. (1978). Complexities of informed consent. *Annals of the American Academy of Political and Social Science, 437*, 37–48.

Marshall, P. A. (2008). "Cultural competence" and informed consent in international health research. *Cambridge Quarterly of Healthcare Ethics, 17*(2), 206–215.

Maschke, K. J. (2005). Navigating an ethical patchwork: Human gene banks. *Nature Biotechnology, 23*(5), 539–545.

References

Adams, V., Miller, S., Craig, S., Sonam, Nyima, Droyoung, . . . Varner, M. (2007). Informed consent in cross-cultural perspective: Clinical research in the Tibetan Autonomous Region, PRC. *Culture Medicine and Psychiatry, 31*(4), 445–472. doi:10.1007/s11013-007-9070-2

Agrawal, M., Grady, C., Fairclough, D. L., Meropol, N. J., Maynard, K., & Emanuel, E. J. (2006). Patients' decision-making process regarding participation in phase I oncology research. *Journal of Clinical Oncology, 24*(27), 4479–4484.

Albrecht, T. L., Ruckdeschel, J. C., Riddle, D. L., Blanchard, C. G., Penner, L. A., Coovert, M. D., & Quinn, G. (2003). Communication and consumer decision making about cancer clinical trials. *Patient Education and Counseling, 50*(1), 39–42.

Alderson, P. (2007). Competent children? Minors' consent to health care treatment and research. *Social Science & Medicine, 65*(11), 2272–2283. doi:10.1016/j.socscimed.2007.08.005

Barton, E., & Eggly, S. (2009). Ethical or unethical persuasion? The rhetoric of offers to participate in clinical trials. *Written Communication, 26*(3), 295–319. doi:10.1177/0741088309336936

Beauchamp, T. L., & Childress, J. F. (2009). Respect for autonomy. In T. L. Beauchamp & J. F. Childress (Eds.), *Principles of biomedical ethics* (4th ed., pp. 99–148). New York, NY: Oxford University Press.

The Belmont Report. (1979). *The National Commission for the Protection of Human Subjects of Biomedical and Behavioral Research*. Retrieved from http://www.hhs.gov/ohrp/humansubjects/guidance/belmont.html

Bostrom, A. (2008). Lead is like mercury: Risk comparisons, analogies and mental models. *Journal of Risk Research, 11*(1–2), 99–117. doi:10.1080/13669870701602956

Brown, R. F., Butow, P. N., Ellis, P., Boyle, F., & Tattersall, M. H. N. (2004). Seeking informed consent to cancer clinical trials: Describing current practice. *Social Science & Medicine, 58*(12), 2445–2457.

Catania, C., De Pas, T., Goldhirsch, A., Radice, D., Adamoli, L., Medici, M., . . . Nole, F. (2008). Participation in clinical trials as viewed by the patient: Understanding cultural and emotional aspects which influence choice. *Oncology, 74*(3–4), 177–187.

Charles, C., Gafni, A., & Whelan, T. (1999). Decision-making in the physician–patient encounter: Revisiting the shared treatment decision-making model. *Social Science & Medicine, 49*(5), 651–661.

Cohen, S. (2013). Nudging and informed consent. *American Journal of Bioethics, 13*(6), 3–11. doi:10.1080/15265161.2013.781704

Colquitt, J. A., Greenberg, J., & Zapata-Phelan, C. P. (2005). What is organizational justice? A historical overview. In J. Greenberg & J. A. Colquitt (Eds.), *Handbook of organizational justice* (pp. 3–56). Mahwah, NJ: Lawrence Erlbaum.

Corbett, F., Oldham, J., & Lilford, R. (1996). Offering patients entry in clinical trials: Preliminary study of the views of prospective participants. *Journal of Medical Ethics, 22*(4), 227–231. doi:10.1136/jme.22.4.227

Cortés, D. E., Drainoni M., Henault, L. E., & Paasche-Orlow, M. K. (2010). How to achieve informed consent for research from Spanish-speaking individuals with low literacy: A qualitative report. *Journal of Health Communication, 15*(Suppl. 2), 172–182. doi:10.1080/10810730.2010.499990

Curbow, B., Fogarty, L. A., McDonnell, K. A., Chill, J., & Scott, L. B. (2006). The role of physician characteristics in clinical trial acceptance: Testing pathways of influence. *Journal of Health Communication, 11,* 199–218.

Donovan-Kicken, E., Mackert, M., Guinn, T. D., Tollison, A. C., Breckinridge, B., & Pont, S. J. (2012). Health literacy, self-efficacy, and patients' assessment of medical disclosure and consent documentation. *Health Communication, 27,* 581–590.

Du Toit, B. M. (1980). Ethics, informed consent, and fieldwork. *Journal of Anthropological Research, 36*(3), 274–286.

Faden, R. R., & Beauchamp, T. L. (1986). *A history and theory of informed consent.* New York, NY: Oxford University Press.

Fluehr-Lobban, C. (1994). Informed consent in anthropological research: We are not exempt. *Human Organization, 53*(1), 1–10.

Gordon, E. F., & Daugherty, C. K. (2001). Referral and decision making among advanced cancer patients participating in phase I trials at a single institution. *Journal of Clinical Ethics, 12,* 37–38.

Grady, C., Hampson, L. A., Wallen, G. R., Rivera-Goba, M. V., Carrington, K. L., & Mittleman, B. B. (2006). Exploring the ethics of clinical research in an urban community. *American Journal of Public Health, 96*(11), 1996–2001.

Gray, B. H., Cooke, R. A., & Tannenbaum, S. S. (1978). Research involving human subjects. *Science, 201,* 1094–1101.

Hines, S. C., Badzek, L., & Moss, A. H. (1997). Informed consent among chronically ill elderly: Assessing its (in)adequacy and predictors. *Journal of Applied Communication Research, 25,* 151–169.

Jimison, H. B., Sher, P. P., Appleyard, R., & LeVernois, Y. (1998). The use of multimedia in the informed consent process. *Journal of the American Medical Informatics Association, 5,* 245–256.

Johnson, E. J., & Tversky, A. (1983). Affect, generalization, and the perception of risk. *Journal of Personality and Social Psychology, 45*(1), 20–31.

Kahneman, D., & Tversky, A. (1984). Choice, values, and frames. *American Psychologist, 39,* 341–350.

Keller, C., & Siegrist, M. (2009). Effect of risk communication formats on risk perception depending on numeracy. *Medical Decision Making, 29*(4), 483–490. doi:10.1177/0272989x09333122

Madsen, S. M., Holm, S., & Riis, P. (2007). Attitudes towards clinical research among cancer trial participants and non-participants: An interview study using a grounded theory approach. *Journal of Medical Ethics, 33*(4), 234–240.

McComas, K. A. (2004). When even the "best-laid" plans go wrong. *EMBO reports, 5*(Suppl. 1), S61–S65.

McComas, K. A., Yang, Z. J., Gay, G. K., Leonard, J. P., Dannenberg, A. J., & Dillon, H. (2010). Individuals' willingness to talk to their doctors about clinical trial enrollment. *Journal of Health Communication, 15,* 189–204. doi:10.1080/10810730903528058

Miller, V. A., Drotar, D., & Kodish, E. (2004). Children's competence for assent and consent: A review of empirical findings. *Ethics & Behavior, 14*(3), 255–295. doi:10.1207/s15327019eb1403_3

National Cancer Institute. (2002). *Cancer clinical trials: The in-depth program.* Bethesda, MD. Retrieved from https://accrualnet.cancer.gov/education/cancer_clinical_trials_in_depth_program#.U5YU7i8Wdqt

Olufowote, J. O. (2008). A structurational analysis of informed consent to treatment: Societal evolution, contradiction, and reproductions in medical practice. *Health communication, 23,* 292–303.

Plankey-Videla, N. (2012). Informed consent as process: Problematizing informed consent in organizational ethnographies. *Qualitative Sociology, 35*(1), 1–21. doi:10.1007/s11133-011-9212-2

Ploug, T., & Holm, S. (2013). Informed consent and routinisation. *Journal of Medical Ethics, 39,* 214–218. doi:10.1136/medethics-2012-101056

Rosenthal, J. P. (2006). Politics, culture, and governance in the development of prior informed consent in indigenous communities. *Current Anthropology, 47*(1), 119–142.

Sankar, P. (2004). Communication and miscommunication in informed consent to research. *Medical Anthropology Quarterly, 18*(4), 429–446.

Schachter, M., & Fins, J. J. (2008). Informed consent revisited: A doctrine in the service of cancer care. *The oncologist, 13*(10), 1109–1113. doi:10.1634/theoncologist.2008-0101

Schrag, B. (2009). Piercing the veil: Ethical issues in ethnographic research. *Science and Engineering Ethics, 15*(2), 135–160. doi:10.1007/s11948-008-9105-2

Schulz, P. J., & Rubinelli, S. (2008). Arguing "for" the patient: Informed consent and strategic maneuvering in doctor-patient interaction. *Argumentation, 22,* 423–432.

Swartling, U., Helgesson, G., Hansson, M. G., & Ludvigsson, J. (2009). Split views among parents regarding children's right to decide about participation in research: A questionnaire survey. *Journal of Medical Ethics, 35*(7), 450–455. doi:10.1136/jme.2008.027383

Thibaut, J. W., & Walker, L. (1975). *Procedural justice: A psychological analysis.* Mahwah, NJ: Lawrence Erlbaum.

Thompson, K. M. (2002). Variability and uncertainty meet risk management and risk communication. *Risk Analysis, 22*(3), 647–654. doi:10.1111/0272-4332.00044

Tversky, A., & Kahneman, D. (1974). Judgment under uncertainty: Heuristics and biases. *Science, 185*(4157), 1124–1131. doi:10.1126/science.185.4157.1124

Van den Bos, K. (2005). What is responsible for the fair process effect? In M. Greenberg & J. A. Colquitt (Eds.), *Handbook of organizational justice* (pp. 273–300). Mahwah, NJ: Lawrence Erlbaum.

Van Staden, C. W., & Kruger, C. (2003). Incapacity to give informed consent owing to mental disorder. *Journal of Medical Ethics, 29*(1), 41–43. doi:10.1136/jme.29.1.41

Veatch, R. M. (1995). Abandoning informed consent. *Hastings Center Report, 25*(2), 5–12.

Wanzer, M. B., Wojtaszczyk, A. M., Schimert, J., Missert, L., Baker, S., Baker, R., & Dunkle, B. (2010). Enhancing the "informed" in informed consent: A pilot test of a multimedia presentation. *Health Communication, 25,* 365–374.

Wilson, S. (2001). Informed consent. *Natural History, 110*(2), 90.

Witte, K. (1994). Fear control and danger control: A test of the extended parallel process model (EPPM). *Communication Monographs, 61*(2), 113–134.

Yang, Z. J., McComas, K. A., Gay, G., Leonard, J. P., Dannenberg, A. J., & Dillon, H. (2010). Motivation for health information seeking and processing about clinical trial enrollment. *Health Communication, 25,* 423–436.

Zussman, R. (1992). *Intensive care: Medical ethics and the medical profession.* Chicago, IL: University of Chicago Press.

SECTION 8

Organizational Contexts of Risk Communication

CHAPTER 19

Risk Communication in Groups

Tillman Russell and Torsten Reimer

Introduction

The day is May 10, 1996, the place, Mount Everest. Two climb leaders, Scott Fischer and Rob Hall, direct a team of climbers to the top of the infamous mountain. At approximately midday, both men turn their frigid gaze toward the mountain peak and recall the rule agreed on at the outset: Given the scarcity of sunlight, if the group cannot make it to the top by midday, they will turn back so as to not work their way down the mountain in the dark. Desire, expectation, uncertainty, and arrogance converged, generating intense pressure for the crew to either turn back as originally planned or keep going and break the intended strategy. What should Scott and Rob do in this situation?

Under normal circumstances, they would have probably turned back, but the confidence and self-assurance of both men in their expertise and familiarity with the mountain influenced their perception of risk, driving them to press forward up the mountain. The result of the decision would prove fatal. By continuing to climb against their better judgment, many of the leader's clients had to make their way down the treacherous mountain in the dark in a torrential snowstorm. Scott Fischer, Rob Hall, and three team members were tragically buried in the snow and ice on their way down the mountain.

Just a day before the climb, Scott Fischer had expressed his confidence in his ability to lead the group up the mountain. He wildly exclaimed that the leaders had "the big E completely figured out" and that these "days . . . [they'd] built a yellow brick road to the summit" (Krakauer, 1997, p. 65). Similarly, at a previous dinner engagement, when one of the clients, who was responsible for the Everest venture, expressed doubt about attempting to climb the mountain with "limited high altitude experience" (Krakauer, 1997, p. 66), Fischer confidently proclaimed that "experience is overrated. It's not the altitude that's important; it's your attitude bro. You'll do fine. You've done some pretty sick climbs—stuff that's way harder than Everest" (Krakauer, 1997, p. 66).

The communication of confidence combined with an overall desire and expectation to make it to the top of Everest, contributed to an unwise decision with deadly consequences. As the Everest guide Guy Cotter stated in connection with the tragedy on Everest, "It's very difficult to turn someone around high on the mountain. If a client sees that the summit is close and they're dead set on getting there, they're going to laugh in your face and keep going" (Krakauer, 1997, p. 225). The Everest tragedy points to the importance of understanding the role of risk communication in group decision making. How do group members perceive risks, and how do they influence and negotiate their risk perceptions? How do groups communicate about risks, and how do groups form decisions under risk?

In this chapter, we review relevant literature that speaks to these questions. Specifically, we offer a groups as information processors perspective by adapting a general model of information processing to risk communication and risky decision making in groups. Information processing frameworks have been repeatedly used to conceptualize and categorize research on group communication and decision making (see, e.g., Hinsz, Tindale, & Vollrath, 1997; Larson & Christensen, 1993; Reimer, Park, & Hinsz, 2006; see also Propp, 1999). We use the proposed framework to highlight a number of topics related to risk communication and risky decision making in groups. Our chapter does not have the goal to provide a comprehensive overview. Rather, we try to highlight some relevant research themes and to integrate research findings that help conceptualize what we know and what we do not know about risk communication in groups. To this end, we integrate literature that directly addresses risk communication and risky decision making in groups as well as research on group decision making under uncertainty that does not have an explicit focus on risk but is highly relevant and can be readily applied to group risk taking.

conceptualized as involving, at the least, a choice among potential alternatives, the presence of uncertainty, and the possibility of loss (Davis, Kameda, & Stasson, 1992). Information processing models—as there are many—emphasize human symbol (i.e., information) manipulation, comparison, and integration (Gardner, 1987; Pinker, 1997). From an information processing perspective, individual cognition is a process by which sensory input is compared with and integrated with information already stored in memory (Hastie & Dawes, 2010). The information processing model of mind has made substantial contributions to the scientific understanding of human cognition and decision making, including individual risk perception and decision making under uncertainty (see, e.g., Chapters 1, 2, and 3).

Given that information is the "lifeblood" of group decision making (Forsyth, 2010, p. 318), understanding the ways in which groups assess and communicate risk information and decide on potential courses of action is both theoretically and practically important. Our goal in this chapter is to highlight the role of group communication in risky decision making by interpreting relevant group literature from an information processing perspective.

Information processing can be represented and conceptualized in many different ways. We suggest the risk information processing framework displayed in Figure 19.1. This figure will assist in helping to answer the question which factors influence risky decision making in groups and in organizing pertinent empirical literature. In an effort to establish a basis for discussion, we first outline some key phases of our risk information processing framework.

Risk Information Processing in Groups

As the Everest tragedy illustrates, making decisions involving risk is among the critical activities performed by groups. Risk taking can be

Model Components

Risk information processing in groups involves the occurrence of a set of information processes that take place among group members. Figure 19.1 highlights some central features and

Figure 19.1 The Risk Information Processing Model in Groups

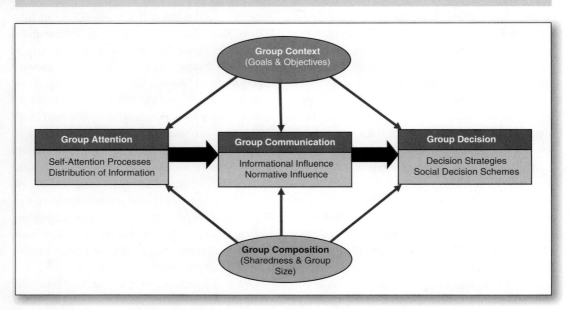

distinguishes among three key phases: (1) group attention, (2) group communication, and (3) group decision making. The *group attention* phase refers to the direction and orientation of individual group member attention. A crucial process, attention opens the door, so to speak, to information processing; without attention to risk-relevant information, processing of risk-relevant information does not occur. During the *group communication* phase, groups gather, exchange, and discuss risk-relevant information. Finally, in the *group decision-making* phase, group members' contributions are combined to form a single group decision on a risky alternative. Decision strategies and schemes are, implicitly or explicitly, employed during this phase for the purpose of arriving at a single group outcome. During all phases, influence processes between members may occur, causing movement toward risky or cautious decision making.

Along with the group attention, group communication, and group decision-making phase, we also include variables that have been shown to affect processes at each phase—we focus here on

characteristics of the *group context* and the *group composition*. The group context (see the top of Figure 19.1), includes group goals and objectives. A group's goals and objectives can affect group attention, risk communication, and group decision making. Similar to individuals, groups process information based on objectives and collective goals (Mackie & Goethals, 1987). Members who have similar objectives and goals, for example, tend to process information in a more similar style than members who pursue different objectives and goals (Hinsz et al., 1997; Levine, Resnick, & Higgins, 1993; Tindale, Sheffey, & Scott, 1993). Group composition (see the bottom of Figure 19.1), includes the concepts of group *sharedness* and *group size*. Extant research has shown that the extent to which group members share the same preferences, gender, race, background, culture, motivation, demographic characteristics, ideas, and cognitive processes can greatly influence group interactions and outcomes (Adamowicz et al., 2005; Hinsz et al., 1997; Janis, 1983; Levine et al., 1993). Along with sharedness, group size has been shown to affect attention, communication, and decision making in groups (Hinsz et al., 1997). Over the next several sections, we describe each phase of the model in detail, highlighting how processes at each phase relate to decision making under risk.

Group Attention

Self-Attention in Groups

The information processing framework applied to group decision making under risk looks at groups as information processing units that choose between risk alternatives. Research indicates that groups attend to threat and opportunity cues relevant for assessing the risk of potential outcomes (Gray, 1987). Many factors can affect a group's orientation to threat and opportunity cues; we focus our discussion on two: (1) *self-attention* and (2) *information distribution* processes. On a very basic level, research suggests that individual group member attention is already influenced by the mere presence of other group members even if members do not interact with each other (Hinsz et al., 1997; Mullen, 1987; Wicklund, 1980). Generally, the mere presence of other group members tends to increase attention to self-presentation (Hinsz et al., 1997). The presence of other group members can be distracting, leading individual members to focus on regulating appearance, rather than solving decision tasks involving risks (Hinsz et al., 1997).

Decision making under risk often involves the consideration of complex information and the assessment of both opportunity and threat. Excessive self-focus can increase individual consideration of stimuli that supports desirable self-presentation while decreasing the consideration of stimuli that threatens desirable self-presentation (Baron, 1986; Hinsz et al., 1997). Group members may feel pressure to conform more closely to a risky group tendency if attention is focused on maintaining identity with the group or increasing the likelihood of cognitive closure

(Kruglanski, Pierro, Mannetti, & De Grada, 2006; Kruglanski, Shah, Pierro, & Mannetti, 2002). Under these circumstances, group member self-attention may be preoccupied with remaining consistent with perceptions of group decision preferences and consequently neglect risk-relevant information.

Scott Fischer and Rob Hall were probably influenced to appear self-assured and confident partially due to the mere presence of their clients, increasing the tendency to focus on reward cues and to ignore potential threat cues. On the other hand, contexts that decrease attention may also increase risk taking (Festinger, Pepitone, & Newcomb, 1952). Processes of *deindividuation*, by decreasing self-awareness and cognizance of social norms, may reduce recognition of threat cues and increase the tendency to form risky decisions (Prentice-Dunn & Rogers, 1989; Zimbardo, 2007). The Everest clients no doubt felt highly connected with the team and to their leaders. Sense of group connection may have decreased the self-awareness of many of the climbers, increasing the likelihood that some of them would make the more risky decision to continue climbing, even in the face of numerous threats. Various leader and client outcomes suggest the key role group composition plays in group risk taking.

Group composition can also affect group risk taking through its impact on attention processes. Typically, groups differ along a number of compositional dimensions, including members' expertise and personalities, basic values and beliefs, cognitive capacity, gender, race, among others (Adamowicz et al., 2005). Compositional differences affect the way attention is oriented and distributed among group members. The more homogeneous a decision-making group, the more likely group members hold similar objectives and, therefore, pay attention to and value similar information (Adamowicz et al., 2005). Along with group composition, group size also affects self-attention processes (Hinsz et al., 1997; Mullen, 1987). As groups get larger, their attention capacity increases. This advantage, however, can be offset by increasing process losses, which include increased distraction and inefficiency (Adamowicz et al., 2005; Hinsz, 1990). A key source of distraction and inefficiency in larger groups results from decreased in-group participation salience. Research suggests that relatively small groups will more likely strengthen individual attention (Hinsz et al., 1997; Mullen, 1991).

Information Distribution

Attention processes in groups are also affected by how information is distributed among group members. Early group risk-taking research suggested that groups took riskier decisions than individuals and that risky decision making in groups was partially the result of the initial distribution of group member preferences (Dahlback, 2003). If the initial distribution of member preferences was inclined in the risk-taking direction, then groups would increase this risk-taking tendency. More recent studies support this line of thinking. Researchers exploring the effects of the information distribution on member attention demonstrated that at least two individual group members need to attend to information for it to be acquired by the group as a whole (Laughlin, 1980; Vollrath, Sheppard, Hinsz, & Davis, 1989).

Crucially for group decision making under risk, research has also shown that groups are more likely to attend to and share information held in common than information held by only one group member, and this effect is enhanced as group size increases (Reimer, Reimer, & Czienskowski, 2010; Stasser, Taylor, & Hanna, 1989). Consequently, groups involved in risky decision making may not attend to threat cues that are only noticed by one group member due to the general tendency for groups to attend to cues shared by several group members. Research suggests that critical but unshared information will be particularly likely to be overlooked in the group deliberation and decision process if it speaks against the decisions and actions that are preferred by most group members. Groups may

not listen to a particularly conservative member who holds relevant information that may decrease the tendency for group risk taking.

Communication

Group decision making involves gathering, sharing, and processing information with the goal of collective response. Compared with individuals, groups provide increased memory capacity (Hollingshead, 2001), augmented information exchange, and enhanced information processing capabilities (Propp, 1999). Consequently, groups are typically viewed as more accurate and efficient decision-making mechanisms than individuals (Kerr, MacCoun, & Kramer, 1996). In the context of group decision making under risk, the gathering of risk-relevant information necessitates group communication, the content of which may refer to the risk situation, requests for clarification, explicit sharing of reasons and arguments, or the mere expression of preferences for one risk alternative (Forsyth, 2010).

Group members who decide on risky alternatives communicate ideas, perspectives, preferences, information, and cognitive processes, which may influence decision making under risk. Two types of social influence processes operating in decision-making contexts identified by group researchers are normative and informational influence (Deutsch & Gerard, 1955; Henningsen & Henningsen, 2003; Kaplan & Miller, 1987). Normative influence appeals to our need to be liked by others and to belong to a group. Informational influence appeals to our need to have accurate views of the world. As both forms of influence function to affect decision making under risk, we will discuss them in detail.

Normative Influence

Normative influence occurs when group members express favored positions with the goal of influencing the group to reach agreement and consensus (Forsyth, 2010). Evidence suggests that a strong initial consensus is associated with normative pressure to maintain group agreement (Henningsen & Henningsen, 2003). Scott Hall and Rob Fischer may have felt normative pressure to keep climbing Everest while ignoring the midday rule established during the planning phase due to their awareness of their client's ardent desire to reach the top of the mountain. Normative pressure may shift a group in the majority direction through the mere disclosure of member supported positions (Henningsen & Henningsen, 2003).

A presupposition of normative influence is the motivation of individuals to have their self, opinion, viewpoint, and perspective perceived as socially acceptable (Isenberg, 1986). Specific contexts increase the likelihood of normative influence (see top of Figure 19.1). For example, research suggests that if a group's processing objective involves the establishment of strong social relations, normative influence will play more of a role in the decision-making process (Kaplan & Miller, 1987; Rugs & Kaplan, 1993). Scott Fischer's prudent client expressed legitimate doubt concerning the feasibility of climbing Everest at the dinner party, yet following Fischer's overly confident response, we can assume that he felt normative pressure to conform to the group norm. Research suggests that position comparison processes among group members can affect the final group decision (Festinger, 1954; Isenberg, 1986). Social comparison leads to the awareness of group *norms* (i.e., standards that indicate appropriate action given a specific context), which can lead members to adapt to perceived norms when positions are made known through communication (Blascovich, Ginsburg, & Howe, 1975; Isenberg, 1986).

If successful, normative influence processes lead individuals to revise their positions to correspond more closely with the position of the majority (Henningsen & Henningsen, 2003). Studies have shown that majority positions favored prior to group discussion will strongly influence group decisions (Gigone & Hastie, 1993; Reimer, Reimer, & Hinsz, 2010). Prediscussion positions can have this influence through mere exposure of the group members to the group average (Isenberg, 1986). Blascovich, Ginsburg, and Howe (1976) found that subjects who bet on Blackjack alone and then in a condition in which member positions were revealed to the group, increased the size of their bets relative to a control condition. In a similar vein, simple communication of group member positions may influence groups to make riskier decisions than individuals (Isenberg, 1986).

Informational Influence

Informational influence is based on a different mechanism than normative influence even though both can work hand in hand and do not exclude each other. Normative influence appeals to our need to belong to a group and to be liked by others. Group members may adhere to the group norm and go with a majority even though they are not convinced that the majority has the best or most accurate position. Informational influence, on the other hand, is based on group members' motivation to have accurate perceptions about the world. Successful informational influence will change a group member's attitude and knowledge about the world. With application to decision making under risk, informational influence can involve the sharing, discussing, and debating of risk-relevant evidence, facts, and arguments with the goal of making the best decision possible (Henningsen & Henningsen, 2003). Operationalized as statements in the process of group discussion that communicate arguments, facts, or evidence (Henningsen & Henningsen, 2003; Kaplan & Miller, 1987; Kelly, Jackson, & Hutson-Comeaux, 1997), informational influence can be based on both shared and unshared information (Stasser & Titus, 1985). Highlighting its crucial role in group risk taking, the distinction between shared and unshared information will be discussed more fully below.

Shared risk information is arguments, facts, or evidence held in common by group members that are potentially relevant to decision making (Henningsen & Henningsen, 2003). Research suggests that shared information will more strongly affect a group's decision than unshared information (Adamowicz et al., 2005; Kerr & Tindale, 2004; Reimer, Reimer, & Czienskowski, 2010). Groups typically are more likely to discuss shared items than unshared items. In addition, items of shared information are often attended to and weighted more heavily in decision making (Henningsen & Henningsen, 2003; Reimer, Reimer, & Hinsz, 2010).

Unshared information refers to arguments, facts, or evidence potentially relevant to decision making that are not held in common by the group but are known to only one group member (Henningsen & Henningsen, 2003). Applied to the risk context, when a group finds information to be risk relevant, it may lead to a revision of initial positions (Henningsen & Henningsen, 2003). Although the consideration of unshared information may assist risk-taking groups to make better risk assessments and decisions, the normative pressure for group validation, unanimity, consensus, and agreement can increase the potential for groups to avoid discussing unshared information. Likewise, conflicting processing objectives and individual group member goals can influence the extent to which groups focus on information that they share in common (Wittenbaum, Hollingshead, & Botero, 2004).

If a member of the group possesses unshared information that may assist in more accurately evaluating the probabilities of various risk alternatives, then a preference for shared information does not bode well for group decision making under risk. Let us suppose that one of Scott Fischer's Everest clients had expertise in meteorology and was the only member of the group who possessed information about weather conditions that would change the group's risk perception. In this case, the tendency for the group to spend more time discussing shared information than unshared information may have worked against an accurate assessment of the risk of potentially fatal outcomes. In a situation like this, it is crucial for the group's welfare that the individual who has the critical piece of information speaks up and shares the critical evidence with the group. Moreover, the group has to consider and integrate that information in their decision making. Research indicates that unshared information is often ignored by a group when it is shared if it does not resonate with the preference that is favored by a majority (see Reimer, Reimer, & Hinsz, 2010). So, even if the meteorologist in our example spoke up, chances are that Fischer and the remaining clients would have downplayed or ignored the warnings.

Group Decision Making

Decision Strategies and Social Decision Schemes

The third phase in the information processing framework refers to decision making (see Figure 19.1). Social decision schemes are ways in which groups act to combine and integrate preferences and choices provided by individual members into a collective group response (Davis, 1973). Groups may rely on delegating decisions, averaging decisions, plurality decisions, unanimous decisions (consensus), or random decisions (Hastie & Kameda, 2005). Delegation of decision refers to a social decision scheme in which an external decision-making unit, whether individual or group, decides who makes the group decision. This can be either an expert or a committee formed for the purpose of deciding for the group (Forsyth, 2010). Under conditions of extensive time pressure, immense compositional diversity, and large group size, group decision making under risk may benefit from the immediate application of expert judgment.

Averaging of decision refers to a scheme in which each member of a group generates a response, and these responses are summed and averaged to produce a group response

(Forsyth, 2010). A key component of social decision schemes including averaging is the fact that discussion among group members is not a necessary component of producing a group decision (Forsyth, 2010). Plurality of decision refers to a scheme in which each member votes, either publically or privately, and the group will decide based on which alternative receives the most votes (Davis, 1973; Kerr, Stasser, & Davis, 1979; Stasser, Kerr, & Davis, 1989). Majority votes can be defined in various ways. For example, some majorities are defined by either a two-thirds or a three-fourths majority rules scheme (Forsyth, 2010). Considered to be one of the most popular decision schemes, research suggests that even if a small group explicitly decides to use a scheme other than the majority rule, the subset of the group with the plurality typically wins out (Kameda, Tindale, & Davis, 2003; Kerr & Tindale, 2004).

Accurate and efficient decision strategies are an important element of adaptive group decision making (Reimer & Hoffrage, 2006, 2012a). As indicated in Figure 19.1, context variables can affect decision-making processes; one way of which is to render a comprehensive consideration of all risk-relevant cues superfluous. In these contexts, the ability for groups to adapt their strategy to fit the environment is paramount (Reimer & Hoffrage, 2006). *Simple group heuristics* are simple group decision strategies that permit groups to be adaptive given contextual constraints. Simple group heuristics are based in the *Fast and Frugal* research program, which seeks to model cognitive processes within the constraints of bounded rationality. Reimer and Hoffrage (2006) found that accuracy of group decision making depended on the distribution of cue validities and the quality of shared information. Moreover, they showed that performance of different decision strategies depended on the ecological fit between the group heuristic selected and the structure of the information environment (Reimer & Hoffrage, 2006).

In the following section, we will provide two research examples that looked directly into group decision making under risk and further illustrate how the risk information processing approach can assist in understanding risk communication in groups. Research on group polarization as well as research on approach and avoidance motivations can be utilized to answer a basic question: Under which conditions are groups taking riskier decisions than individuals?

Risky Shift and Group Polarization

Early group decision-making research assumed that groups would be a more discerning and conservative decision-making mechanism than single individuals (Davis et al., 1992; Stoner, 1961). One fascinating discovery was the tendency for groups to shift toward more risk-inclined behavior subsequent to discussion and deliberation of risk alternatives (Myers & Lamm, 1975; Stoner, 1961). The observation of this *risky shift*—that is, riskier decisions in groups than in individuals—was unexpected and even counterintuitive (Isenberg, 1986; Myers & Lamm, 1975; Stoner, 1961; Sunstein, 1999). Many replications supported the initial findings, and it seemed that groups had a general propensity to make riskier decisions than individuals (Isenberg, 1986). Yet scholars also began to detect shifts not only in the risky direction but also in the cautious direction, if there was a predeliberative tendency to be cautious (Myers & Lamm, 1975).

Risky shifts and cautious shifts were, consequently, reinterpreted as instances of *group polarization* (Forsyth, 2010; Moscovici & Zavalloni, 1969; Myers & Lamm, 1975). Group polarization is the tendency for groups to be more extreme than individuals in the direction of the predeliberative average (Forsyth, 2010; Reimer, Bornstein, & Opwis, 2005). If there is no clear predeliberative tendency for a group to choose particularly risky or cautious alternatives, no polarization is expected. Scholars have developed two primary explanations for group polarization: (1) the social comparison theory (SCT; Baron & Roper, 1976;

Jellison & Arkin, 1977; Sanders & Baron, 1977) and (2) the persuasive arguments theory (PAT; Burnstein & Vinokur, 1977; Isenberg, 1986; Sanders & Baron, 1977).

Social Comparison Theory

SCT suggests that group polarization is the consequence of normative influence in groups. Groups tend to increase risk seeking (if that is the predeliberative direction) compared with individuals due to the motivation to be viewed as socially acceptable. The SCT approach illustrates the way objectives, goals, and motivation (see top of Figure 19.1) direct attention to cues that indicate the positions of other members. As group members' choices are shared in the group, group members adjust their own position so as to be perceived as more socially acceptable (Sunstein, 1999). The information about other member's inclinations triggers a revision of the original position in light of the disclosure. SCT is supported by information processing theory, which suggests that what individuals pay attention to in a group affects outcomes (Hinsz et al., 1997).

Persuasive Arguments Theory

PAT suggests that group polarization is the consequence of informational rather than normative influence in groups. Context variables (see top of Figure 19.1) affect how arguments are assessed. Research suggests that groups exaggerate the tendency of individuals to weight argument quality over quantity on decision items for which individuals are risk inclined (Hinsz & Davis, 1984). Group composition (see bottom of Figure 19.1) also affects informational influence in groups that form decisions under risk. When groups collectively discuss the merits of a particular action, individual group members are exposed to more arguments for specific alternatives than any single individual typically possesses. The influence of the number of persuasive arguments heard by group members shifts the group in a more extreme position relative to the prediscussion average.

Research on the risky shift phenomenon and on group polarization provides key insights into the question of whether and why groups are typically more risky than individuals. Both SCT and PAT seek to offer basic mechanisms through which groups enhance or decrease risk-taking tendencies. More recently, researchers have suggested that activation of distinct motivational systems associated with the perception of reward and threat may provide additional theoretical and empirical comprehension of risky decision making in groups (Park & Hinsz, 2006).

BIS/BAS and Risk Communication in Groups

Well-established and more recent empirical and theoretical investigations of approach and avoidance motivation suggest a common psychological process that connects these motivational systems to affective, cognitive, and behavioral tendencies (Beck, Smits, Claes, Vandereycken, & Bijttebier, 2009; Carver & White, 1994; Park & Hinsz, 2006). The *behavioral approach/activation* system, or BAS, is a motivational system associated with approach tendencies in goal-directed behavior. Increased BAS activation is associated with increases in the perception of individual efficacy and in the perception and attention to cues signaling goal-related opportunities (Derryberry & Reed, 1994; Gray, 1987). The *behavioral avoidance/inhibition* system, or BIS, in contrast, is associated with avoidance tendencies in goal-directed behavior. Increased BIS activation is linked with increases in the perception of danger and a heightened attention to threat cues signaling the presence of peril or the absence of rewards. By increasing the perception of and attention to cues indicating potential negative outcomes, the activation of the BIS system is linked with the inhibition of behaviors that would lead to negative outcomes (Gray, 1987; Park & Hinsz, 2006).

Although the BIS/BAS framework was primarily concerned with individual differences in approach and avoidance motivations, recent group research has suggested that belonging to, and interacting in, a group may be associated with the activation of BAS. Specifically, Park and Hinsz (2006) suggest that BAS activation should theoretically increase in groups, as groups tend to increase perceived access to resources and facilitation of goal attainment (see also Thrash & Elliot, 2004). Individual beliefs concerning the benefits of group collaboration on reward access and goal attainment (e.g., "there is strength and safety in numbers") should lead to differential (or increased) group member communication and an overall increase in approach motivation and behavioral tendencies (Kimbrel, Mitchell, & Nelson-Gray, 2010; Park & Hinsz, 2006). Group communication and interaction does not automatically increase approach motivation; rather it affects approach behavior when groups provide access to rewards and resources, increase the perception of potential goal attainment, and facilitates ease of information processing (Park & Hinsz, 2006; Winkielman & Cacioppo, 2001).

If group communication influences approach and avoidance motivation, then it should also consequently affect the risk perception of group members. Park and Hinsz (2006) suggest that the perception of opportunity affects risk-seeking choices (see also Xie & Wang, 2003); thus the activation of BAS should consequently increase the perception, attention, and elaboration of opportunity cues and increase risky decision making. Conversely, group communication should decrease the awareness and elaboration of threat cues, reducing BIS activation and decreasing risk avoidance. These predictions still have to be tested (see Park & Hinsz, 2006).

Assuming the reciprocal effect of BIS/BAS activation on group interaction and group interaction on BIS/BAS activation, the motivational systems provide a provocative explanation for the occurrence of risky shifts in groups (Park & Hinsz, 2006). In group decision-making contexts, beliefs concerning the inherent rightness of

member consensus offer a sense of strength to individual preferences. When individuals endorse a decision through the communication of preferences, a feeling of unanimity of opinion can occur. This sense of strength may increase the activation of BAS and decrease the activation of BIS; as a consequence, the felt strength increases the likelihood of riskier decisions and preferences overall (Park & Hinsz, 2006). Along these lines, recent research has suggested that social unanimity can be experienced as pleasurable and its lack, as painful. Yanagisawa and colleagues (2011) found that BAS activation is associated with increased pleasure in social inclusion, and BIS activation is associated with increased pain in social exclusion.

Beyond the felt strength, communication among group members can also increase the sense of safety from punishment for negative outcomes. Working and interacting in a group provides a sense of protection from the threat of judgment and evaluation by diffusing individual responsibility for a group product, thereby decreasing avoidance tendencies (Bem, Wallach, & Kogan, 1965; Park & Hinsz, 2006). When individuals believe that they are free to act without full responsibility for their actions, BIS should decrease and risky decision making should increase. Individual group members should feel safer to take risks when not held ultimately accountable for their decisions and preferences. These hypotheses received some indirect support from the literature but still have to be directly tested (see Park & Hinsz, 2006).

Reflections for Theory and Research

Seeking to interpret empirical literature through the lens of our risk information processing framework, we discussed two research examples that directly focused on risk communication in groups. A key question that may guide future investigations is the following: Is there a general propensity for groups to be riskier than individuals? The 1960s and 1970s saw an explosion of interest in the risky shift phenomenon (Lamm & Myers, 1978) and the question of why groups allegedly tend to take greater risks compared with individuals. Several theoretical mechanisms were put forward to explain the shift, including social support (Bem et al., 1965), diffusion of responsibility (Wallach, Kogan, & Bem, 1964), and social comparison processes (Brown, 1965). Researchers also began to consider evidence for shifts in both risky and cautious directions after group discussion, partially giving rise to the conceptualization of a general polarization process.

Recently, group researchers have begun to call into question the comprehensiveness of the polarization explanation of risky shift (Dahlback, 2003; Park & Hinsz, 2006). Some researchers even suggest a general propensity of groups to provide conditions for greater risk taking (Park & Hinsz, 2006). In light of these developments, we pose again the original question: *Does working and interacting in groups generally increase risk-taking preferences? What are the potential boundary conditions for a risky shift? How can differences between groups and individuals in their risk perceptions and risk taking be explained?* Group researchers have suggested looking to the individuals who compose a group for potential explanatory constructs. Park and Hinsz (2006), for example, point toward the activation of individual motivational systems as a potential explanation for the risky shift. These predictions have not received empirical treatment. Research is therefore needed to explore whether groups on average have a greater tendency toward risk taking than individuals and why this occurs.

Recent research exploring adaptive decision making in groups point to the key role *ecological rationality* plays in understanding group dynamics (Reimer & Hoffrage, 2012b; Reimer & Katsikopoulos, 2004). In line with this tradition, we propose empirical investigations of representative samples of individuals and groups to analyze their risk-taking tendencies. As polarization occurs when a prediscussion tendency is intensified in the process of discussion, it is important to sample individuals and groups that represent the population to see whether groups are, in general, more inclined toward risk taking than individuals. Predicting how groups may increase risk taking requires statistical base rate information derived from representative samples. Therefore, more research that explores whether individuals in existing groups are typically risk inclined, and how these groups are composed are important steps in predicting risk taking in groups.

Recommendations for Practice

Groups may cause individuals to focus attention on self-presentation (Mullen, 1987; Wicklund, 1980). Individuals in positions of responsibility may benefit from assigning a member the role of bringing awareness of the group to potential threat cues. Research suggests that experts typically provide this important function to groups (Forsyth, 2010). In addition, as we have seen, compositional diversity and group size can both affect group attention orientation (Adamowicz et al., 2005). Groups may benefit from compositional diversity and smaller group size as it should decrease the likelihood that group members would pay attention only to reward cues and ignore the presence of threat cues.

Groups often pay attention to shared information more than unshared. For groups seeking to increase the likelihood of attention to unshared threat information should take steps to make these information items known to all group members (Forsyth, 2010). As research suggests, at least two group members need to be aware of the information for it to have an impact on the assessment of risk alternatives (Henningsen & Henningsen, 2003). As the discussion of unshared information may drastically shape the risk perception of the group, mechanisms that increase the likelihood that group members would discuss crucial unshared information items can be critical (Reimer, Reimer, & Czienskowski, 2010). Moreover, research suggests that the extent to which group members have formed strong and stable preferences before entering a group discussion can greatly shape how the group deliberates risky choice alternatives (Reimer & Hoffrage, 2012b; Schulz-Hardt, Frey, Lüthgens, & Moscovici, 2000). Groups that are composed of members with strong preferences have a tendency to negotiate and integrate their individual preferences. Conversely, groups that enter discussions without individual preferences, focus more on information received at the meeting (Milch, Weber, Appelt, Handgraaf, & Krantz, 2009; Reimer, Reimer, & Hinsz, 2010). In situations in which it is crucial for a group to consider unshared information in order to be able to form good group decisions, it may be wise to introduce a decision task as new business and to ask group members to deliberate the task without forming individual preferences and opinions. To increase group decision quality, it may be necessary to compose groups based on the extent to which group members do have or do not have strongly formed preferences for a decision alternative prior to discussion.

Conclusions

As the Everest tragedy indicates, decision making under risk is a crucial task that groups perform. In this chapter, we have highlighted the ways in which group objectives, goals, sharedness, and size affect the attention and communication of information leading to collective group response under risk. We have seen that groups may provide conditions for increased likelihood of risky group decision making. While group researchers have tended to categorize this risky shift in group decision making as an instance of group polarization, more recently, scholars have also pointed toward a reconsideration of whether, in general, groups increase risky decision making. Existing empirical research suggests a number of

potential implications for practitioners. Implications including, but not limited to utilizing experts, increasing compositional diversity, making information known to all group members, and forming groups based on a consideration of group preference structure prior to group discussion of decision alternatives.

Suggested Additional Readings

Frey, L. R., Gouran, D. S., & Poole, M. S. (Eds.). (1999). *The handbook of group communication theory and research.* Thousand Oaks, CA: Sage.

Poole, M. S., & Hollingshead, A. B. (Eds.). (2005). *Theories of small groups: Interdisciplinary perspectives.* Thousand Oaks, CA: Sage.

References

Adamowicz, W., Hanemann, M., Swait, J., Johnson, R., Layton, D., Regenwetter, M., . . . & Sorkin, R. (2005). Decision strategy and structure in households: A "groups" perspective. *Marketing Letters, 16*(3–4), 387–399.

Baron, R. S. (1986). Distraction-conflict theory: Progress and problems. *Advances in Experimental Social Psychology, 19,* 1–39.

Baron, R. S., & Roper, G. (1976). Reaffirmation of social comparison views of choice shifts: Averaging and extremity effects in an autokinetic situation. *Journal of Personality and Social Psychology, 33*(5), 521–530.

Beck, I., Smits, D. J., Claes, L., Vandereycken, W., & Bijttebier, P. (2009). Psychometric evaluation of the behavioral inhibition/behavioral activation system scales and the sensitivity to punishment and sensitivity to reward questionnaire in a sample of eating disordered patients. *Personality and Individual Differences, 47*(5), 407–412.

Bem, D. J., Wallach, M. A., & Kogan, N. (1965). Group decision making under risk of aversive consequences. *Journal of Personality and Social Psychology, 1*(5), 453–460.

Blascovich, J., Ginsburg, G. P., & Howe, R. C. (1975). Blackjack and the risky shift, II: Monetary stakes. *Journal of Experimental Social Psychology, 11*(3), 224–232.

Blascovich, J., Ginsburg, G. P., & Howe, R. C. (1976). Blackjack, choice shifts in the field. *Sociometry, 39*(3), 274–276.

Brown, R. (1965). *Social psychology*. New York, NY: Free Press.

Burnstein, E., & Vinokur, A. (1977). Persuasive argumentation and social comparison as determinants of attitude polarization. *Journal of Experimental Social Psychology, 13*(4), 315–332.

Carver, C. S., & White, T. L. (1994). Behavioral inhibition, behavioral activation, and affective responses to impending reward and punishment: The BIS/BAS Scales. *Journal of Personality and Social Psychology, 67*(2), 319–333.

Dahlback, O. (2003). A conflict theory of group risk-taking. *Small Group Research, 34*(3), 251–289.

Davis, J. H. (1973). Group decision and social interaction: A theory of social decision schemes. *Psychological Review, 80*(2), 97–125.

Davis, J. H., Kameda, T., & Stasson, M. F. (1992). Group risk-taking: Selected topics. In J. Yates (Ed.), *Risk-taking behavior* (pp. 164–199). San Francisco, CA: Wiley.

Derryberry, D., & Reed, M. A. (1994). Temperament and attention: Orienting toward and away from positive and negative signals. *Journal of Personality and Social Psychology, 66*(6), 1128–1139.

Deutsch, M., & Gerard, H. B. (1955). A study of normative and informational social influences upon individual judgment. *Journal of Abnormal and Social Psychology, 51*(3), 629–636.

Festinger, L. (1954). A theory of social comparison processes. *Human Relations, 7*(2), 117–140.

Festinger, L., Pepitone, A., & Newcomb, T. (1952). Some consequences of de-individuation in a group. *Journal of Abnormal and Social Psychology, 47*(2), 382–389.

Forsyth, D. R. (2010). *Group dynamics*. Belmont, OH: Wadsworth.

Gardner, H. (1987). *The mind's new science: A history of the cognitive revolution*. New York, NY: Basic books.

Gigone, D., & Hastie, R. (1993). The common knowledge effect: Information sharing and group judgment. *Journal of Personality and Social Psychology, 65*(5), 959–974.

Gray, J. A. (1987). *The psychology of fear and stress* (2nd ed.). New York, NY: Cambridge University Press.

Hastie, R., & Dawes, R. M. (Eds.). (2010). *Rational choice in an uncertain world: The psychology of judgment and decision making*. Thousand Oaks, CA: Sage.

Hastie, R., & Kameda, T. (2005). The robust beauty of majority rules in group decisions. *Psychological Review, 112*(2), 494–508.

Henningsen, D. D., & Henningsen, M. L. M. (2003). Examining social influence in information-sharing contexts. *Small Group Research, 34*(4), 391–412.

Hinsz, V. B. (1990). Cognitive and consensus processes in group recognition memory performance. *Journal of Personality and Social Psychology, 59*(4), 705–718.

Hinsz, V. B., & Davis, J. H. (1984). Persuasive arguments theory, group polarization, and choice shifts. *Personality and Social Psychology Bulletin, 10*(2), 260–268.

Hinsz, V. B., Tindale, D. A., & Vollrath, R. S. (1997). The emerging conceptualization of groups as information processors. *Psychological Bulletin, 121*(1), 43–64.

Hollingshead, A. B. (2001). Cognitive interdependence and convergent expectations in transactive memory. *Journal of Personality and Social Psychology, 81*(6), 1080–1089.

Isenberg, D. J. (1986). Group polarization: A critical review and meta-analysis. *Journal of Personality and Social Psychology, 50*(6), 1141–1151.

Janis, I. L. (1983). *Groupthink*. Boston, MA: Houghton Mifflin.

Jellison, J., & Arkin, R. (1977). Social comparison of abilities: A self-presentation approach to decision making in groups. In J. M. Suls & R. L. Miller (Eds.), *Social comparison processes: Theoretical and empirical perspectives* (pp. 235–257). Oxford, England: Hemisphere.

Kameda, T., Tindale, R. S., & Davis, J. H. (2003). Cognitions, preferences, and social sharedness: Past, present, and future directions in group decision making. In S. L. Schneider & J. Shanteau (Eds.), *Emerging perspectives on judgment and decision research* (pp. 458–486). Cambridge, England: Cambridge University Press.

Kaplan, M. F., & Miller, C. E. (1987). Group decision making and normative versus informational influence: Effects of type of issue and assigned decision rule. *Journal of Personality and Social Psychology, 53*(2), 306–313.

Kelly, J. R., Jackson, J. W., & Hutson-Comeaux, S. L. (1997). The effects of time pressure and task differences on influence modes and accuracy in decision-making groups. *Personality and Social Psychology Bulletin, 23*(1), 10–22.

Kerr, N. L., MacCoun, R. J., & Kramer, G. P. (1996). Bias in judgment: Comparing individuals and groups. *Psychological Review, 103*(4), 687–719.

Kerr, N. L., Stasser, G., & Davis, J. H. (1979). Model testing, model fitting, and social decision schemes. *Organizational Behavior and Human Performance, 23*(3), 399–410.

Kerr, N. L., & Tindale R. S. (2004). Group performance and decision making. *Annual Review of Psychology, 55*, 623–655.

Kimbrel, N. A., Mitchell, J. T., & Nelson-Gray, R. O. (2010). An examination of the relationship between behavioral approach system (BAS) sensitivity and social interaction anxiety. *Journal of Anxiety Disorders, 24*(3), 372–378.

Krakauer, J. (1997). *Into thin air*. New York, NY: Anchor Books.

Kruglanski, A. W., Pierro, A., Mannetti, L., & De Grada, E. (2006). Groups as epistemic providers: Need for closure and the unfolding of group-centrism. *Psychological Review, 113*(1), 84–100.

Kruglanski, A. W., Shah, J. Y., Pierro, A., & Mannetti, L. (2002). When similarity breeds content: Need for closure and the allure of homogeneous and self-resembling groups. *Journal of Personality and Social Psychology, 83*(3), 648–662.

Lamm, H., & Myers, D. G. (1978). Group-induced polarization of attitudes and behavior. *Advances in Experimental Social Psychology, 11*, 145–195.

Larson, J. R., & Christensen, C. (1993). Groups as problem-solving units: Toward a new meaning of social cognition. *British Journal of Social Psychology, 32*(1), 5–30.

Laughlin, P. R. (1980). Social combination processes in cooperative problem-solving groups on verbal intellective tasks. In M. Fishbein (Ed.), *Progress in social psychology* (pp. 127–155). Hillsdale, NJ: Lawrence Erlbaum.

Levine, J. M., Resnick, L. B., & Higgins, E. T. (1993). Social foundations of cognition. *Annual Review of Psychology, 44*(1), 585–612.

Mackie, D. M., & Goethals, G. R. (1987). Individual and group goals. In C. Hendrick (Ed.), *Group processes: Vol. 8. Review of personality and social psychology* (pp. 144–167). Newbury Park, CA: Sage.

Milch, K. F., Weber, E. U., Appelt, K. C., Handgraaf, M. J. J., & Krantz, D. H. (2009). From individual preference construction to group decisions: Framing effects and group processes. *Organizational Behavior and Human Decision Processes, 108*(2), 242–255.

Moscovici, S., & Zavalloni, M. (1969). The group as a polarizer of attitudes. *Journal of Personality and Social Psychology, 12*(2), 125–135.

Mullen, B. (1987). Self-attention theory: The effects of group composition on the individual. In B. Mullen & G. R Goethals (Eds.), *Theories of group behavior* (pp. 125–146), New York, NY: Springer.

Mullen, B. (1991). Group composition, salience, and cognitive representations: The phenomenology of being in a group. *Journal of Experimental Social Psychology, 27*(4), 297–323.

Myers, D. G., & Lamm, H. (1975). The polarizing effect of group discussion: The discovery that discussion tends to enhance the average prediscussion tendency has stimulated new insights about the nature of group influence. *American Scientist, 63*(3), 297–303.

Park, E. S., & Hinsz, V. B. (2006). "Strength and safety in numbers": A theoretical perspective on group influences on approach and avoidance motivation. *Motivation and Emotion, 30*(2), 135–142.

Pinker, S. (1997). *How the mind works*. New York, NY: Norton.

Prentice-Dunn, S., & Rogers, R. W. (1989). Deindividuation and the self-regulation of behavior. In P. B. Paulus (Ed.), *Psychology of group influence* (pp. 87–109). Hillsdale, NJ: Lawrence Erlbaum.

Propp, K. M. (1999). Collective information processing in groups. In L. Frey, D. S. Gouran, & M. S. Poole (Eds.), *The handbook of group communication: Theory and research* (pp. 225–250). Thousand Oaks, CA: Sage.

Reimer, T., Bornstein, A.-L., & Opwis, K. (2005). Positive and negative transfer effects in groups. In T. Betsch & S. Haberstroh (Eds.), *The routine of decision making* (pp. 175–192). Mahwah, NJ: Lawrence Erlbaum.

Reimer, T., & Hoffrage, U. (2006). The ecological rationality of simple group heuristics: Effects of group member strategies on decision accuracy. *Theory and Decision, 60,* 403–438.

Reimer, T., & Hoffrage, U. (2012a). Ecological rationality for teams and committees: Heuristics in group decision making. In P. M. Todd, G. Gigerenzer, & the ABC Research Group (Eds.), *Ecological rationality: Intelligence in the world* (pp. 335–359). New York, NY: Oxford University Press.

Reimer, T., & Hoffrage, U. (2012b). Simple heuristics and information sharing in groups. In R. Hertwig, U. Hoffrage, & the ABC Research Group (Eds.), *Simple heuristics in a social world* (pp. 266–286). New York, NY: Oxford University Press.

Reimer, T., & Katsikopoulos, K. (2004). The use of recognition in group decision-making. *Cognitive Science, 28*(6), 1009–1029.

Reimer, T., Park, E., & Hinsz, V. (2006). Shared and coordinated cognition in competitive and dynamic task environments: An information-processing perspective for team sports. *International Journal of Sport and Exercise Psychology, 4,* 376–400.

Reimer, T., Reimer, A., & Czienskowski, U. (2010). Decision-making groups attenuate the discussion bias in favor of shared information: A meta-analysis. *Communication Monographs, 77,* 121–142.

Reimer, T., Reimer, A., & Hinsz, V. (2010). Naïve groups can solve the hidden-profile problem. *Human Communication Research, 36*(3), 443–467.

Rugs, D., & Kaplan, M. F. (1993). Effectiveness of informational and normative influences in group decision making depends on the group interactive goal. *British Journal of Social Psychology, 32*(2), 147–158.

Sanders, G. S., & Baron, R. S. (1977). Is social comparison irrelevant for producing choice shifts? *Journal of Experimental Social Psychology, 13*(4), 303–314.

Schulz-Hardt, S., Frey, D., Lüthgens, C., & Moscovici, S. (2000). Biased information search in group decision making. *Journal of Personality and Social Psychology, 78*(4), 655–669.

Stasser, G., Kerr, N. L., & Davis, J. H. (1989). Influence processes and consensus models in decision-making groups. In P. B. Paulus (Ed.), *Psychology of group influence* (2nd ed., pp. 279–326). Hillsdale, NJ: Lawrence Erlbaum.

Stasser, G., Taylor, L. A., & Hanna, C. (1989). Information sampling in structured and unstructured discussions of three-and six-person groups. *Journal of Personality and Social Psychology, 57*(1), 67–78.

Stasser, G., & Titus, W. (1985). Pooling of unshared information in group decision making: Biased information sampling during discussion. *Journal of Personality and Social Psychology, 48,* 1467–1478.

Stoner, J. A. (1961). *A comparison of individual and group decision involving risk* (Unpublished master's thesis). Massachusetts Institute of Technology, Cambridge. Retrieved from http://dspace.mit.edu/bitstream/handle/1721.1/11330/33120544.pdf?sequence=1

Sunstein, C. R. (1999). The law of group polarization. *Journal of Political Philosophy, 10*(2), 175–195.

Thrash, T. M., & Elliot, A. J. (2004). Inspiration: Core characteristics, component processes, antecedents, and function. *Journal of Personality and Social Psychology, 87*(6), 957–973.

Tindale, R. S., Sheffey, S., & Scott, L. A. (1993). Framing and group decision-making: Do cognitive changes parallel preference changes? *Organizational Behavior and Human Decision Processes, 55*(3), 470–485.

Vollrath, D. A., Sheppard, B. H., Hinsz, V. B., & Davis, J. H. (1989). Memory performance by decision-making groups and individuals. *Organizational Behavior and Human Decision Processes, 43*(3), 289–300.

Wallach, M. A., Kogan, N., & Bem, D. J. (1964). Diffusion of responsibility and level of risk taking in groups. *Journal of Abnormal and Social Psychology, 68*(3), 263–274.

Wicklund, R. A. (1980). Group contact and self-focused attention. In P. Paulus (Ed.), *Psychology of group influence* (pp. 189–208). Hillsdale, NJ: Lawrence Erlbaum.

Winkielman, P., & Cacioppo, J. T. (2001). Mind at ease puts a smile on the face: Psychophysiological evidence that processing facilitation elicits positive affect. *Journal of Personality and Social Psychology, 81*(6), 989–1000.

Wittenbaum, G. M., Hollingshead, A. B., & Botero, I. C. (2004). From cooperative to motivated information sharing in groups: Moving beyond the hidden profile paradigm. *Communication Monographs, 71*(3), 286–310.

Xie, X. F., & Wang, X. (2003). Risk perception and risky choice: Situational, informational and dispositional effects. *Asian Journal of Social Psychology, 6*(2), 117–132.

Yanagisawa, K., Masui, K., Onoda, K., Furutani, K., Nomura, M., Yoshida, H., & Ura, M. (2011). The effects of the behavioral inhibition and activation systems on social inclusion and exclusion. *Journal of Experimental Social Psychology, 47*(2), 502–505.

Zimbardo, P. G. (2007). *The Lucifer effect: Understanding how good people turn evil.* New York, NY: Random House.

CHAPTER 20

Crisis Communication

Timothy L. Sellnow

Introduction

In essence, crises occur when risk is manifested (Heath & O'Hair, 2009). Unlike other risk contexts that afford an extended decision-making period, crises occur with surprise, pose considerable threat, and limit response time (Hermann, 1963). The shocking and destructive nature of crises compel victims to first seek information on how to protect themselves, followed by victims and observers alike demanding answers to questions such as how or why such events occur and what can be done to better prepare for or avoid similar mayhem in the future. Although crises can decimate entire regions or destroy organizations, in many cases, they serve as "forces for constructive change, growth, and renewal" (Sellnow & Seeger, 2013, p. 1). Risks that were unobserved prior to the crisis are made apparent by creating opportunities for learning and meaningful change.

Much of the research on crisis communication focuses on organizations and government agencies. From this perspective, a crisis is "a specific, unexpected and nonroutine organizationally based event or series of events which creates high levels of uncertainty and threat or perceived threat to an organization's high priority goals" (Seeger, Sellnow, & Ulmer, 1998, p. 233).

The threat induced by a crisis may be life threatening in cases such as natural disasters or recalls of deadly food products. At times, the threat may be restricted to an organization or agency's reputation. For example, improper use of funds, profound failure to meet the mission of an organization, or other actions that fall outside the public's norms of acceptability can cause reputational crises. Regardless of their cause, crises demand a public response from the troubled organization or agency.

This chapter begins by laying the theoretical foundations of crisis communication. Next, this chapter discusses the communication demands, opportunities, and challenges of pre-, during, and postcrisis phases. In doing so, relevant theoretical perspectives for each phase are summarized. The chapter provides suggestions for theory and research and recommendations for the practice of crisis communication, particularly from the perspective of risk management.

The Intersection of Crisis and Risk Communication

Crisis communication theories are generally focused on three areas: (1) reputation, (2) media, and (3) risk management. Theories focusing on reputation emphasize organizational legitimacy and the potential for organizations to lose social legitimacy in the wake of a crisis. Organizations are seen as legitimate when their actions "reflect public values such as telling the truth, not following the flow of capital, and damaging the environment" (Hearit, 2006, p. 13). Organizations experience reputational crises when their "stakeholders perceive an incongruity to exist between a corporation's values, as evidenced in its acts, and those of the social system" (Hearit, 2006, p. 13). Theories of apologia such as Image Repair Theory (Benoit, 1995), or Situational Crisis Communication Theory (Coombs, 2012) identify strategies that enable organizations to repair their images. Strategies such as denial, reducing offensiveness, emphasizing community service, differentiating the accusations from a severe level to a lesser form, and transcending the issue altogether are some of the most common strategies of apologia. A Discourse of Renewal section provides a comprehensive view of how organizations move from apologia to long-term risk management.

The media plays a key role in theorizing about crisis communication. News framing, focusing events, and uses and gratifications are theories frequently applied to understand the role of the media in crisis communication. News framing theory observes how competing interpretations of the crisis are framed or portrayed by the publicity provided by organizations and the media's coverage of the crisis (Hallahan, 2005). Focusing events occur when crises reach a level of public attention and outrage in the media sufficient to inspire lawmakers to reconsider existing policies (Birkland, 1997). Uses and gratification theory is applied during crises to observe how and why individuals seek information through the media during crises (Spence & Lachlan, 2009).

Theories such as organizational learning and sensemaking focus on crisis outcomes. From this perspective, crises are seen as epistemic or as having the capacity to alter the way organizations

or communities see themselves (Sellnow & Seeger, 2013). Sensemaking, from a crisis communication perspective, describes the sudden loss of understanding caused by crises (discussed later in the chapter) and how that meaning is reconstructed. As meaning is reconstructed, Weick (1995) explains that observers subconsciously answer, "How can I know what I think until I see what I say" (p. 18). Organizational learning theory is applied in crises essentially to learn from failure (Sitkin, 1996). As we discuss later in the chapter, this learning process, and the mindfulness it creates, exposes risks that were previously unknown or ignored. Exposing and responding to these risks during and after a crisis is essential to effective risk management.

The strength of existing crisis communication theory rests in the capacity of these theories to explain retrospectively what occurred and why it occurred from a communication perspective. For practitioners engaged in risk as well as crisis communication, however, understanding the function of continuous dialogue and how to rapidly disseminate messages for self-protection are essential (Coombs, 2009; Sellnow & Sellnow, 2010). Issues of crisis communication ethics and inclusivity in both risk and crisis circumstances are also prevalent at the intersection of risk and crisis communication. In the next section, we discuss the alignment of dialogue and instruction in risk and crisis communication.

Precrisis: Risk Communication as Dialogue

An effective crisis response typically unfolds in three stages: precrisis, crisis, and postcrisis (Ulmer, Sellnow, & Seeger, 2011). The precrisis stage involves the identification, management, and reduction of risks facing the organization or community. From a communication perspective, the ultimate objective during precrisis is to enhance "the quality of risk decisions through better communications" (Palenchar & Heath, 2002, p. 129). Because risk decision making involves multiple stakeholders, communication in the precrisis phase is best depicted as a dialogue. Should the organization or agency fail to effectively contend with risk in the precrisis period, a full-blown crisis is likely. During the crisis stage, organizations urgently provide an explanation of how to minimize the danger to stakeholders affected by the crisis. Thus, much of the risk communication in the crisis phase focuses on instructions for self-protection. Such messages of self-protection are intended for those within or near the organization who are in danger as well as any consumer possessing a dangerous product that has been or will be recalled. The postcrisis period is a time of reflection to comprehend how the risks preceding the crisis were overlooked. The postcrisis period focuses on learning from the crisis and apologizing for avoidable failures. As such, this period emphasizes lessons learned and opportunities to fortify resilience as well as expressions of regret and compensation to those who were harmed. As organizations move beyond the postcrisis phase, the process of risk management begins anew with a restructured precrisis period.

Risk communication in the precrisis phase is focused largely on recognizing potential threats and recommending actions for managing or minimizing those threats. Dialogue is at the center of precrisis risk management because crisis planning, resource allocation decisions, and the determination of acceptable thresholds for risk tolerance are based on an extended dialogue among subject matter experts, government officials, and those citizens and consumers who are asked to bear the risk. Such dialogue is possible because a crisis has not yet occurred. Thus, the urgency and short response time indicative of crisis are not constraints in the precrisis phase. When precrisis dialogue functions at its best, "individuals recognize rapidly changing conditions in the environment, follow safe practices, and control and manage hazards" (Sauer, 2003, p. 51). To approach this ideal level, precrisis dialogue must, at minimum, be inclusive, based on quality information, and cognizant of consistent claims.

Inclusivity

For effective dialogue to take place in the precrisis phase, the communication process must account for the capacity of all stakeholders to receive, comprehend, and respond to essential information. From this perspective, anyone whose life could be affected by the risk under discussion is a stakeholder who should be welcome to participate in the precrisis dialogue. Arnett (2012) argues that this inclusive approach to precrisis communication has the potential to overcome what he calls the "tyranny of self-importance" (p. 165). Conversely, a failure to engage and actively consider all points of view in risk decision making can yield "the odd combination of arrogance and ignorance" typically resulting in organizational "hubris" (Arnett, 2012, p. 168). Such hubris diminishes an organization's capacity for managing risk issues effectively and results in severe reputational damage when crises occur (Ulmer et al., 2011).

Inclusivity in precrisis risk dialogue should consider all aspects of the stakeholders, including culture, ethnicity, and race. Liu and Pompper (2012) argue that such sensitivity to diversity "is not solely about mitigating reputational damage, but also about building genuine, long-term relationships with communities and media of various ethnicities and cultures, and others who can enhance communication before, during, and after crises" (Liu & Pompper, 2012, p. 141). To do so, organizations must move "beyond any managerial bias (especially that shaped by a Caucasian/white majority), to develop expanded sensitivities and worldviews beyond their own comfort zone as a normative function" (Liu & Pompper, 2012, p. 143). Liu and Pompper (2012) admonish organizations that, if they are to overcome the "tyranny of self-importance" described by Arnett (2012) above, their dialogue with diverse populations "must be sincere and not simply self-serving" (Liu & Pompper, 2012, p. 143).

Quality of Information Exchanged

Through an inclusive dialogue, organizations and government agencies can ideally serve as "honest broker[s]" of information for stakeholders (Horlick-Jones, Sime, & Pidgeon, 2003, p. 283). Absent of direct coercion, risk communication during the precrisis phase, at its worst, is deceptive, tricking the public into accepting levels of risk that, if understood more fully, would not be tolerated. Such deception is irrefutably unjust. There are, however, other forms of seemingly harmless risk communication that fall far short of the expectations for dialogue described above. Heath (1995) advises organizations and government agencies to shun the temptation to see risk communication as "a linear, hypodermic communication process, whereby technical information can be injected into non-technical audiences" (p. 269). To overcome this organizational bias, organizations must consider the ability of stakeholders to comprehend the evidence presented to them. If organizations fail in this effort, they have not met the standards for dialogue. As Heath, Bradshaw, and Lee (2002) assert, "Without understanding, information is not knowledge" (p. 325).

Nilsen (1974) establishes a set of criteria for exchanging information through dialogue in high-risk situations. He explains that such circumstances require stakeholders to make significant choices about their well-being. Thus, he argues that organizations must meet five ethical standards. Specifically, (1) all information is made available to stakeholders, (2) the speaker's motives are made known, (3) all reasonable alternatives are discussed, (4) both long- and short-term consequences are identified, and (5) stakeholders are free from physical and mental coercion. By emphasizing these ethical standards, Nilsen contends that organizations can avoid providing "misinformation" to stakeholders

(p. 71). Examples of problematic misinformation include incomplete or biased information, statistical units that are incomplete or inadequately defined, vague or ambiguous terminology, implied relationships that are not substantiated, a false sense of urgency, and highly emotionalized language (pp. 71–72). Engaging in any of these strategies for misinformation is incongruent with ethical communication.

Multiple Messages

The nature of risk invites multiple interpretations of the same problem. This variance in points of view emerges because uncertainty is "the central variable" in all risk situations (Palenchar & Heath, 2002, p. 131). If we are certain of an outcome, there is no risk involved. By contrast, risk situations have an unpredictable quality. Thus, communication in risk situations typically involves contrasting points of view resulting in multiple messages. Precrisis communication, then, is characterized by messages to which stakeholders must attend.

Multiple messages focused on risk issues are rarely scrutinized to the level where one viewpoint is unanimously identified as correct. Rather, these messages coexist as interacting arguments presented to stakeholders (Sellnow, Ulmer, Seeger, & Littlefield, 2009). Although some listeners may align with a single point of view, most observers acknowledge that competing sides in an issue share some degree of credibility. In a context where risk messages compete for credibility, the most convincing or persuasive messages are those that converge or are shared by multiple parties (Sellnow et al., 2009). For example, those who experienced Hurricane Katrina found the points of convergence in messages delivered by national agencies and local media most convincing in the early stages of their recovery (Anthony & Sellnow, 2011). In short, the uncertainty of risk fosters multiple points of view. Listeners cope with these competing messages by either adopting one point of view or by seeing points of convergence in multiple points of view.

Crisis: Risk Communication as Instruction

As explained at the outset of this chapter, crises occur when risk is manifested. In other words, our inability or our unwillingness to address risks in the precrisis stage often results in crisis. During the crisis stage, the well-being of an organization's stakeholders is threatened. This threat intensifies without actions to limit harm. From a communication standpoint, instructing those at risk on how to protect themselves reduces threat. Coombs (2009) argues that organizations should prioritize instructional communication during the most acute phase of a crisis. He explains, "Instructing information uses strategies that seek to tell stakeholders what to do to protect themselves from the crisis" (p. 105). For example, urging residents to "evacuate the area or to shelter in-place" are instructional messages (p. 105). From the standpoint of crisis communication, the right instructions, communicated in the right way, at the right time can and does save lives. For instructional communication to function effectively, the organization must move from dialogue to explicit directives, target the message to the most relevant audience when possible, and establish a collaborative relationship with the media.

Shifting From Dialogue to Instruction

Perrow (1999) explains that the interdependency created by our increasingly globalized society makes crises more common, severe, and sudden. He explains that organizations are now tightly coupled with other organizations and the communities they serve. This tight coupling removes buffers that, in the past, may have slowed the spread of a crisis. Crises now explode onto the scene leaving little response time. As Perrow explains, "When systems are tightly coupled failures can cascade faster than any safety device or operator can cope with them" (p. 357). This urgency makes dialogue impractical. Instead, organizations must respond with urgency, sharing whatever information is known, in hopes of avoiding or limiting the harm caused by the crisis (Sellnow & Sellnow, 2010).

The importance of instructional messages during acute phase of the crisis is heightened by the shock and accompanying threat they create. Weick (1993) characterizes these feelings of alarm and distress as cosmology episodes. The reaction to such episodes is, "I've never been here before, I have no idea where I am, and I have no idea who can help me" (Weick, 1993, pp. 634–635). Thus, those experiencing the onset of a crisis are often unable to fully comprehend what is happening because their existing knowledge cannot account for the disarray around them. Instructional messages counter this peculiarity by instructing those who are at risk to take appropriate protective actions (Seeger, 2006).

Comprehending Instructional Messages

For instructional messages to serve their protective purpose, they must meet several criteria. Foremost, those at risk must receive the best information available. Unfortunately, fears of litigation make some organizations reticent to communicate during crises. For example, during a nationwide recall of peanut paste included in more than 100 products, Peanut Corporation of America, the supplier of the tainted product, communicated very little with the public. Government agencies and other members of the industry filled this void. Serving as proxy communicators, government agencies and other members of the peanut industry provided information about what products were contaminated and how to avoid consuming them (Millner, Veil, & Sellnow, 2011). Although, such communication voids can and will be filled by other parties, the organization closest to the crisis typically has the best information and can share it with the least delay.

Once the instructions for self-protection are made available, Mileti and colleagues (Mileti & Fitzpatrick, 1991; Mileti & Sorensen, 1990) explain that the messages must meet several criteria. First, the public must receive the information. Any warning or alert system, for example, must take into account varying levels of media access and language proficiency in the target population. Second, the audience must understand the message. For example, messages should account for limitations in literacy and numeracy (see Chapter 9, this volume).

Developing Targeted Instructional Messages

Recent research suggests that targeting instructional messages during the acute phase of crises enhances comprehension and intention to act (Sellnow, Sellnow, Lane, & Littlefield, 2012). Risk and crisis communication scholars base their work with targeting on the research done in health communication. The primary assumption is that simply presenting the facts to individuals is not necessarily enough to motivate a behavioral response. A considerable body of work indicates that targeting messages to audiences with conditions that increase their level of risk is highly effective (Roberto, Krieger, & Beam, 2009). As we discussed above, the urgency of the crisis makes gathering such data and adapting messages impossible. Still some adaptation or targeting is possible in the crisis phase.

The primary objective in targeting a message during crises is aligning the instructional message with an emphasis on the risks at hand for a particular audience. Sellnow et al. (2012) argue that "in cases where one may suspect that motivation is low, instructive messages should emphasize both self-efficacy and the novel or increased level of risk" (p. 642). For instance, the distinctive danger of a recalled food product, traced to a specific region that is contaminated with a particularly

virulent strain of *Escherichia coli* can and should be emphasized as part of the instructional message. Emphasizing this heightened danger and personalizing the instructional message regionally has been shown to increase the likelihood that individuals will avoid or discard the worrisome product. In addition to emphasizing novel risk associated with the crisis, varying the source of the message can also enhance the response of some segments of the audience. For example, Lachlan and Spence (2011) explain that "underserved communities such as the poor, recent immigrants, and ethnic minorities" are particularly vulnerable to crises (p. 448). They also observe a notable "reliance of these groups on religious organizations in coping with stress" (p. 450). Thus, from a message targeting perspective, they encourage "crisis communication researchers, practitioners, and first responders to investigate the means in which faith-based communities and spirituality can be used to recover from crises" (p. 450). Such strategies as adapting the message to target those at greatest risk and altering the source of the message to enhance credibility can be applied in the acute phase of a crisis.

The shock and threat of crises create an urgent need for instructional messages that give individuals advice for self-protection. Targeting the content and source of the instructional messages to account for audience diversity increases comprehension and the likelihood of an appropriate response. As the acute phase of the crisis dissipates, the communication shifts from instruction to an emphasis on learning.

Postcrisis: Risk Communication as Learning

When the threat and calamity of the crisis stage give way, organizations have the opportunity to identify lessons learned from the crisis and engage in meaningful change. Those organizations that engage in contemplative reflection on how and why the crisis occurred actually have the opportunity to reduce uncertainty. Risks that were underestimated, misunderstood, or missed altogether are revealed. Thus, organizations have the opportunity to emerge from a crisis more resilient than in the past.

The revelation of such knowledge makes crises epistemic or a way of knowing for organizations (Seeger, Sellnow, & Ulmer, 2003). Sauer (2003) explains that, following a crisis, organizations often develop standards based on lessons learned. She explains that the articulation of these lessons for both employees and external stakeholders constitutes a rhetoric of risk that is "both epistemic and inventional" (p. 83). The rhetorical expression of learning in the postcrisis phase is critical because doing so creates a novel understanding of why the crisis occurred. Saur explains, "When individuals represent knowledge in new rhetorical forms, they see the world differently through the lens of new representations; they produce new knowledge and new understanding in the transformation" (p. 83).

In this section, we discuss postcrisis learning from the perspectives of learning, unlearning, and renewal. Learning from failure is a process of adopting new strategies for avoiding similar crises in the future. Unlearning involves reconsidering some foundational assumptions that may have actually hindered rather than helped the organization in risk management. Finally, we offer a discourse of renewal as a systematic means for embracing the opportunities revealed by crises.

Learning From Failure

Sitkin (1996) contends that failure, particularly minor failures, should not be feared or ignored in organizations. Instead, Sitkin insists that failure is necessary for learning. He explains, "Failure is an essential prerequisite for effective organizational learning and adaptation" (p. 541). Sitkin argues further that in fact "the absence of failure experiences can result in decreased organizational resilience" (p. 542). This diminished resilience occurs because risks are often identified through the recognition of

minor failures. If no such failures are detected, organizations may miss out on opportunities for diminishing risk. Learning from failure can occur from both direct and indirect experiences.

In the postcrisis phase, direct learning occurs by reflecting on the failures that lead to crisis. Organizations seek to understand how minor failures that were undetected manifested the crisis. If this process is effective, positive changes occur, making the organization more resilient to similar risks in the future. However, organizations face two potential errors that can limit the learning process. Larsson (2010) characterizes these errors as "underlearning" and "overlearning" (p. 714). Underlearning occurs when organizations fail to comprehend the magnitude of the risks that lead to the crisis. From the perspective of apologia, those organizations that fail to reach the levels of corrective action or mortification are in danger of underlearning. For example, some crises go unnoticed because by chance or good fortune an organization or community experiences a near miss (Dillon & Tinsley, 2008). Dillon and Tinsley (2008) explain that, in many cases, the magnitude of near misses goes unrecognized, resulting in underlearning. The problem is that, when similar circumstances align in the future, good fortune may not be present. The result is a full-blown crisis. For example, Dillon and Tinsley argue that NASA failed to account for earlier near misses that could have prevented the space shuttle Columbia accident. Ironically, overlearning is often manifested by a highly successful crisis response. Larsson (2010) explains that organizations may develop an inflated opinion of their ability to manage crises, thereby abating their sense of exigency for managing risks. In either case, the direct learning experience is misconstrued. For example, the city of Fargo, North Dakota, managed several sizable floods from 1997 to 2007. The successful defense of these floods led city managers to believe that additional flood protection for the city was unnecessary. When, in 2008, a flood of proportions unseen in over a century occurred, the city was ill-prepared and was nearly overwhelmed.

Indirect learning occurs when organizations observe the misfortune of other companies within their industry. Such vicarious learning is accomplished "by watching what happens to individuals when they engage in different behavior patterns, the learner comes to understand that a certain strategy leads to success while another leads to failure, without engaging in either strategy personally" (Weick & Ashford, 2001, p. 712). Seeing a similar organization suffer the consequences of a crisis can and should motivate the leadership of observing organizations to consider their vulnerability to similar crises. In some cases, indirect learning can reach throughout an industry in the form of best practices. For example, many organizations in the food processing industry embrace a set of best practices known as Hazard Analysis & Critical Control Points. This set of carefully crafted best practices is designed to avoid contamination of the food supply at all stages of processing through "the analysis and control of biological, chemical, and physical hazards from raw material production, procurement and handling, to manufacturing, distribution and consumption of the finished product" (U.S. Food and Drug Administration, n.d., para. 1). When an outbreak occurs, the best practices are reviewed, and findings are shared throughout the industry by agencies such as the U.S. Food and Drug Administration. Sharing information through such systems of best practices allows for a sophisticated and well-organized system of vicarious learning.

Unlearning

Although routines are essential to organizational efficiency, they can also cause organizational members to overlook minor failures. Thus, part of organizational learning involves identifying problematic routines and inspiring members of the organization at every level to heighten their sensitivity and to unlearn the habits and routines that contributed to the crisis (Argyris, Putman, & Smith, 1985). Unlearning requires much more effort than eliminating one routine in favor of another. Rather, unlearning requires changing both procedures and attitudes.

Attitudinal change requires organizational members to adopt an attitude of greater mindfulness. By mindfulness, we are not referring to a type of hypervigilance that exhausts resources at all levels. Instead, when we are mindful, "our attention naturally goes to what is different and out of balance" (Langer, 2009, p. 13). For mindful employees, subtle changes or warnings are not masked by a calloused awareness. When mindful employees observe something out of the ordinary, they take note and report the occurrence. By doing so, organizational members display a "high level of sensitivity to errors, unexpected events, and—more generally—to subtle cues suggested by the organization's environment or its own processes" (Levinthal & Rerup, 2006, p. 503). Unlearning is necessary in organizations where routine behaviors have made such levels of observation and reporting unlikely or uncomfortable. Unlearning problematic routines and reporting procedures can be difficult because they are often a part of an organization's culture. Nevertheless, such change is needed for an organization to enhance its resilience against the occurrence of similar crises in the future. The Centers for Disease Control and Prevention (CDC) in the United States underwent an unlearning process in response to the anthrax crisis in 2001. During the anthrax crisis, the CDC was criticized for communicating slowly and for sending inconsistent messages. Members of the CDC tasked with speaking publicly about the crisis felt unprepared. In response to the crisis, the CDC reconsidered its information processing and expanded its focus beyond emerging infectious diseases to include bioterrorism. The leadership of the CDC pledged to update equipment, conduct coordinated communication monitoring, and expedite the vetting process for public messages (Freimuth, 2003).

A Discourse of Renewal

At the most advanced level, learning takes the discursive form of organizational renewal. Organizations engage in a discourse of renewal when they respond to crises by seeking "higher stages progressively and to preclude a decline toward a lower stage" (Lippitt, 1969, p. 28). Crises expedite the renewal process by exposing risks of "exceptional importance" to organizations requiring them to "recognize, confront, and cope with a paramount critical concern" (Lippitt, 1969, p. 28). A discourse of renewal is not akin to recreating the organization. Rather, crises often reveal points where an organization has drifted away from its primary mission or core beliefs. Toelken, Seeger, and Batteau (2005) explain that crises "point out fallacious assumptions or unforeseen vulnerabilities" while reestablishing core values and precipitating "consensus, cooperation, and support" (p. 47). Ultimately, a discourse of renewal "creates an opportunity after a crisis to fundamentally reorder the organization down to its core purpose" (Seeger, Ulmer, Novak, & Sellnow, 2005, p. 92). For a discourse of renewal to take hold and modify an organization's risk management, the organization's leadership must be willing to learn from the crisis, reflect on the organization's ethical responsibility, establish a prospective vision, and represent that vision rhetorically (Ulmer et al., 2011). Each of these components is described in the following paragraphs.

Renewal and Learning. Organizations that engage in a discourse of renewal demonstrate a "desire to change and improve as a result of the crisis" (Ulmer, Sellnow, & Seeger, 2010, p. 692). This improvement begins by making "sense of a crisis through the lessons it can teach" (Veil, Sellnow, & Heald, 2011, p. 170). Without devoting the time to discern these compelling lessons, organizations cannot initiate a discourse of renewal. The lessons become part of an organization's memory. In doing so, they permeate the organization's culture and alter the way

decisions are made. If the memory of lessons learned from a crisis fade over time or if those with a vivid memory of the lessons leave or are replaced, the organization is vulnerable to what Lippitt (1969) described as a "decline toward a lower stage" (p. 28).

Ethical Communication. A discourse of renewal "has a strong value orientation" (Seeger, Sellnow, & Ulmer, 2010, p. 496). Organizations return to their core values in an attempt to better serve their stakeholders. In doing so, they seek to identify any distractions from their value system such as avarice, hubris, or injustice that contributed to the crisis. With these ethical breaches in mind, organizations realign their cultures with positive values as their foundation. Because values are paramount, "organizations that institute strong, positive value positions with key organizational stakeholders, such as openness, honesty, responsibility, accountability, and trustworthiness, before a crisis happens are best able to create renewal following the crisis" (Ulmer et al., 2011, p. 215). In contrast, organizations without a value structure that is stakeholder centered have a much more difficult time establishing a discourse of renewal. For example, British Petroleum was involved in several crises prior to the 2010 gulf disaster. The company was faulted in the previous crises for deemphasizing safety standards. Thus, when the gulf crisis occurred, the company was already weakened from a public relations perspective by the value structure it had displayed in prior crises.

Prospective Vision. The postcrisis phase is often plagued by a retrospective discourse of blame and denial. A prospective vision shifts the focus toward building a more resilient organization or community. The message is one of "hope and optimism to customers, employees, publics, and other stakeholders" (Reierson, Sellnow, & Ulmer, 2009, p. 116). The goal is to become stronger and more resistant to the risks that were manifested in the crisis. In a discourse of renewal, "communication processes are central to framing a prospective vision for how organizations may be reconstituted following a crisis" (Seeger et al., 2010, p. 496). A prospective vision allows organizations to commit their resources to returning to profitability and community service.

Organizational Rhetoric. Strong, visible, and ethical leadership is essential to a discourse of renewal. Through their rhetoric, organizational leaders model the commitment and vision needed to return the organization to prominence (Ulmer, Sellnow, & Seeger, 2009). Essentially, the rhetorical activities of the organization's leaders create "a particular reality for organizational stakeholders and publics," in an attempt to inspire "stakeholders to stay with an organization through a crisis, as well as rebuilding it better than it was before" (Ulmer et al., 2011, p. 219). The rhetoric of renewal embodies all elements of the renewal process. The messages are based on what was learned, the organization's values, and a hope for the future.

Organizational learning is foundational to postcrisis communication. Although organizations may be tempted to defend their reputations through such strategies as denial or shifting the blame, an emphasis on learning and newfound resilience is far more comforting to the public. If organizations are able to reach the level of organizational renewal, the learning they acquire from the crisis can actually make them better organizations than they were before the crisis.

Completing the Cycle: Returning to Precrisis Dialogue

If organizations learn effectively in the postcrisis phase, they experience a "fresh sense of purpose and direction" (Ulmer et al., 2011, p. 213). This fresh sense of purpose allows the organization to return to the precrisis phase. The precrisis phase represents a separation from crisis recovery and a return to risk management. For example, in 2003, the U.S. Department of Agriculture revealed that

a cow with bovine spongiform encephalopathy (mad cow disease) was identified at a U.S. slaughterhouse. Consequently, beef exports from the United States plummeted, creating a financial crisis for the beef industry. The postcrisis phase involved reworking the monitoring process for cattle shipped to U.S. slaughterhouses. Once the changes were in place and confidence was restored, beef exports returned to normal. The new precrisis phase involved the implementation of these improved monitoring techniques. In 2012, another cow infected with bovine spongiform encephalopathy was identified. The U.S. Department of Agriculture announced that the new monitoring techniques kept the cow from ever entering the food supply. As a result, beef exports were not significantly affected by this case. The precrisis phase places more attention to minor failures and the risks they reveal. Moreover, as organizations return to the precrisis phase, they have the capacity to model their renewed resilience for other organizations in their industry.

Most important, a return to the precrisis stage is the opportunity to reengage with stakeholders in a dialogue about risk and risk tolerance. Wheatley (2007) contends that dialogue with stakeholders both inside and outside the organization fosters self-organization. Self-organization occurs when organizations "respond continuously to change" (p. 33). She argues that "a troubled system needs to start talking to itself, especially to those it didn't know were even part of itself" (p. 93). If organizations fail in this information exchange, they are more likely to experience new crises. Thus, a key objective for organizations returning to the precrisis phase is to "increase the number, variety and strength of connections within the system" (p. 93).

Reflections for Theory and Research

The essence of effective risk communication is dialogue. All parties affected by a crisis or potential crisis have a right to be heard. This dialogue, however, functions best during the precrisis and postcrisis periods. As an actual crisis erupts, the most critical information is often shared by emergency responders who offer instructions for self-protection. Once the most dangerous periods of the crisis pass, returning to an inclusive dialogue is warranted. Theories addressing risk communication during the acute phase of crises should account for this brief suspension of dialogue in favor of instructions for self-protection.

The inherent uncertainty in the discussion of risk issues invites multiple, often competing, messages on the same topic. Reconciling these messages can be difficult for audiences. Health, science, and media literacy all vary widely in large audiences. Audience members with lower literacy levels in any or all of these areas are at a disadvantage in comprehending debates over risk issues. In crisis situations, individuals who are confused by multiple messages are placed at higher risk. Theoretical discussion of risk communication in crisis situations must account for variance in an audience's capacity to comprehend and respond to risk messages. Failing to do so results in a lack of inclusivity.

Finally, crises are threatening and disturbing events. They also create opportunities for learning that might otherwise never occur. Theoretical discussion of risk in crisis circumstances should account for these opportunities. Discussion focused solely on a return to normal after a crisis may fail to recognize the fact that returning to the way things were done before the crisis misses an opportunity for renewal that can improve the resilience of a community or organization.

Recommendations for Practice

Risk communication functions best in the form of dialogue where all audiences are included and information is shared openly. Practitioners must, however, recognize that, during crisis situations, the priority must shift to messages of self-protection. Consideration of how these messages might be crafted, targeted, and shared

can and should be a part of risk management and precrisis planning.

Risk communicators have an increasing capacity to target message for those who are most at risk. As such targeted messages are developed, risk communicators can account for variability in the health, science, and media literacy. Attending to other distinct aspects of the targeted audience can also enhance comprehension and compliance with risk messages intended for self-protection.

Risk communicators should remain open to learning. Every crisis creates an opportunity to reconsider the risk management strategies in place before a crisis. Clearly, many crises are unpreventable, but all crises provide the prospect for learning and improvement.

Conclusions

Exploring the life cycle of crises and the risk communication therein reveals that, to some extent, crises are "predictable surprises" (Bazerman & Watkins, 2004, p. 1). Risk is a natural component of the organizing process. When these risks manifest into crises, the capacity of organizations to instruct their stakeholders on how to protect themselves and their willingness to learn from the crises are essential to organizational survival. The precrisis phase gives organizations an opportunity to monitor risks in their environments and to engage stakeholders at all levels in sincere dialogue. This dialogue should also account for underrepresented populations whose access to information and ability to communicate may be complicated by cultural differences (Littlefield, Reierson, Cowden, Stowman, & Long Feather, 2009). Crises are inevitable as are the surprise threat and short response time they create. The harm caused by crises can, however, be diminished by the willingness of organizations to engage in precrisis dialogue, to respond expediently and openly with the information stakeholders need to protect themselves in the event of a crisis, and to dedicate the organization to identifying and implementing the lessons learned from crises. Without these actions, organizations can actually intensify the risks they wish to abate.

Suggested Additional Readings

Anthony, K. E., Sellnow, T. L., & Millner, A. G. (2013). Message convergence as a message-centered approach to analyzing and improving risk communication. *Journal of Applied Communication Research, 41,* 346–364. doi:10.1080/00909882.2013.844346

Venette, S. J. (2008). Risk as an inherent element in the study of crisis communication. *Southern Communication Journal, 73*(3), 197–210. doi:10.1080/10417940802219686

Westerman, D., Spence, P. R., & Van Der Heide, B. (2013). Social media as information source: Recency of updates and credibility of information. *Computer-Mediated Communication, 19*(2), 171–183. doi:10.1111/jcc4.12041

References

Anthony, K. E., & Sellnow, T. L. (2011). Information acquisition, perception, preference, and convergence by Gulf Coast residents in the aftermath of the Hurricane Katrina crisis. *Argumentation and Advocacy, 48,* 81–96.

Argyris, C., Putman, R., & Smith, D. M. (1985). *Action science: Concepts, methods and skills for research and intervention.* San Francisco, CA: Jossey-Bass.

Arnett, R. C. (2012). Communication ethics as Janus at the gates. In S. A. Groom & J. H. Fritz (Eds.), *Communication ethics and crisis* (pp. 161–180). Madison, NJ: Fairleigh Dickinson University Press.

Bazerman, M. H., & Watkins, M. D. (2004). *Predictable surprises: The disasters you should have seen coming and how to prevent them.* Boston, MA: Harvard Business School Press.

Benoit, W. L. (1995). *Accounts, excuses, and apologies: A theory of image restoration strategies.* Albany: State University of New York Press.

Birkland, T. A. (1997). *After disaster: Agenda setting, public policy and focusing events.* Washington, DC: Georgetown University Press.

Coombs, W. T. (2009). Conceptualizing crisis communication. In R. L. Heath & H. D. O'Hair (Eds.), *Handbook of risk and crisis communication* (pp. 99–118). New York, NY: Routledge.

Coombs, W. T. (2012). *Ongoing crisis communication: Planning, managing, and responding.* Thousand Oaks, CA: Sage.

Dillon, R. L., & Tinsley, C. H. (2008). How near-misses influence decision making under risk: A missed opportunity. *Management Science, 54*(8), 1425–1440. doi:10.1287/mnsc.1080.0869

Freimuth, V. (2003). Epilogue to the special issue on anthrax. *Journal of Health Communication, 8,* 148–151. doi:10.1080/10810730390225045

Hallahan, K. (2005). Framing theory. In R. L. Heath (Ed.), *The encyclopedia of public relations* (pp. 340–343). Thousand Oaks, CA: Sage.

Hearit, K. M. (2006). *Crisis management by apology: Corporate response to allegations of wrongdoing.* Mahwah, NJ: Lawrence Erlbaum.

Heath, R. L. (1995). Corporate environmental risk communication: Cases and practices along the Texas Golf Coast. In B. R. Burelson (Ed.), *Communication yearbook 18* (pp. 255–277). Thousand Oaks, CA: Sage.

Heath, R. L., Bradshaw, J., & Lee, J. (2002). Community relationship building: Local leadership in the risk communication infrastructure. *Journal of Public Relations Research, 14,* 317–353.

Heath, R. L., & O'Hair, H. D. (Eds.). (2009). *Handbook of crisis communication.* New York, NY: Routledge.

Hermann, C. F. (1963). Some consequences of crisis which limit the viability of organizations. *Administrative Science Quarterly, 8,* 61–82.

Horlick-Jones, T., Sime, J., & Pidgeon, N. (2003). The social dynamics of environmental risk perception: Implication for risk communication research and practice. In N. Pidgeon, R. E. Kasperson, & P. Slovic (Eds.), *The social amplification of risk* (pp. 262–285). Cambridge, England: Cambridge University Press.

Lachlan, K. A., & Spence, P. R. (2011). Crisis communication and the underserved: The case of partnering with institutions of faith. *Journal of Applied Communication Research, 39,* 448–451.

Langer. E. J. (2009). *Counterclockwise.* New York, NY: Ballantine Books.

Larsson, L. (2010). Crisis learning. In W. T. Coombs & S. J. Holladay (Eds.), *The handbook of crisis communication* (pp. 713–718). Oxford, England: Wiley-Blackwell.

Levinthal, D., & Rerup, C. (2006). Crossing an apparent chasm: Bridging mindful and less-mindful perspectives on organizational learning. *Organization Science, 17*, 502–513.

Lippitt, G. L. (1969). *Organizational renewal: Achieving viability in a changing world.* New York, NY: Appleton-Century-Crofts.

Littlefield, R. S., Reierson, J., Cowden, K., Stowman, S., & Long Feather, C. (2009). A case study of the Red Lake, Minnesota, school shooting: Intercultural learning in the renewal process. *Communication, Culture & Critique, 2,* 361–383.

Liu, B. F., & Pompper, D. (2012). The crisis with no name: Defining the interplay of culture, ethnicity, and race on organizational issues and media outcomes. *Journal of Applied Communication Research, 40,* 127–146.

Mileti, D. S., & Fitzpatrick, C. (1991). Communication of public risk: Its theory and its application. *Sociological Practice Review, 2,* 18–20.

Mileti, D. S., & Sorensen, J. H. (1990). *Communication of emergency public warnings: A social science perspective and state-of-the-art assessment* (ORNL-6609). Oak Ridge, TN: Oak Ridge National Laboratory.

Millner, A. G., Veil, S. R., & Sellnow, T. L. (2011). Proxy communication in crisis response. *Public Relations Review, 37,* 74–76. doi:10.1016/j.pubrev.2010.10.005

Nilsen, T. R. (1974). *Ethics of speech communication* (2nd ed.). Indianapolis, IN: Bobbs-Merrill.

Palenchar, J. J., & Heath, R. L. (2002). Another part of the risk communication model: Analysis of communication processes and message content. *Journal of Public Relations Research, 14*(2), 127–158.

Perrow, C. (1999). *Normal accidents.* Princeton, NJ: Princeton University Press.

Reierson, J. L., Sellnow, T. L., & Ulmer, R. R. (2009). Complexities of crisis renewal over time: Learning from the case of tainted Odwalla apple juice. *Communication Studies, 60,* 114–129.

Roberto, A. J., Krieger, J. L., & Beam, M. A. (2009). Enhancing web-based kidney disease prevention messages for Hispanics using targeting and tailoring. *Journal of Health Communication, 14,* 525–540. doi:10.1080/10810730903089606

Sauer, B. (2003). *The rhetoric of risk: Technical documentation in hazardous environments.* Mahwah, NJ: Lawrence Erlbaum.

Seeger, M. W. (2006). Best practices in crisis and emergency risk communication. *Journal of Applied Communication Research, 34,* 232–244.

Seeger, M. W., Sellnow, T. L., & Ulmer, R. R. (1998). Communication, organization, and crisis. In M. E. Roloff (Ed.), *Communication yearbook 21* (pp. 231–276). Thousand Oaks, CA: Sage.

Seeger, M. W., Sellnow, T. L., & Ulmer, R. R. (2003). *Communication and organizational crisis.* Westport, CT: Praeger.

Seeger, M. W., Sellnow, T. L., & Ulmer, R. R. (2010). Expanding the parameters of crisis communication: From chaos to renewal. In R. L. Heath (Ed.), *Public relations handbook* (2nd ed., pp. 489–500). Thousand Oaks, CA: Sage.

Seeger, M. W., Ulmer, R. R., Novak, J. M., & Sellnow, T. L. (2005). Post-crisis discourse and organizational change, failure and renewal. *Journal of Organizational Change Management, 18*(1), 78–95.

Sellnow, T. L., & Seeger, M. W. (2013). *Theorizing crisis communication.* Malden, MA: Wiley-Blackwell.

Sellnow, T. L., & Sellnow, D. D. (2010). The instructional dynamic of risk and crisis communication: Distinguishing instructional messages from dialogue. *Review of Communication, 10*(2), 111–125.

Sellnow, T. L., Sellnow, D. D., Lane, D. R., & Littlefield, R. S. (2012). The value of instructional communication in crisis situations: Restoring order to chaos. *Risk Analysis, 32*(4), 633–643. doi:10.1111/j.1539-6924.2011.01634.x

Sellnow, T. L., Ulmer, R. R., Seeger, M. W., & Littlefield, R. S. (2009). *Effective risk communication: A message-centered approach.* New York, NY: Springer Science+Business Media.

Sitkin, S. B. (1996). Learning through failure: The strategy of small losses. In M. D. Cohen & L. S. Sproull (Eds.), *Organizational learning* (pp. 541–578). Thousand Oaks, CA: Sage.

Spence, P. R., & Lachlan, K. A. (2009). Presence, sex, and bad news: Exploring the responses of men and women to graphic news stories in varying media. *Journal of Applied Communication Research, 37,* 239–256.

Toelken, K., Seeger, M. W., & Batteau, A. (2005). Learning and renewal following threat and crisis: The experience of a computer services firm in response to Y2K and 9/11. In B. Van de Walle & B. Carle (Eds.), *Proceedings of the 2nd International*

ISCRAM Conference (pp. 43–51). Brussels, Belgium: Information Systems for Crisis Response and Management.

Ulmer, R. R., Sellnow, T. L., & Seeger, M. W. (2009). Post-crisis communication and renewal: Understanding the potential for positive outcomes in crisis communication. In R. L. Heath & D. H. O'Hair (Eds.), *Handbook of risk and crisis communication* (pp. 302–322). New York, NY: Routledge, Taylor & Francis Group.

Ulmer, R. R., Sellnow, T. L., & Seeger, M. W. (2010). Consider the future of crisis communication research: Understanding the opportunities inherent to crisis evens through the discourse of renewal. In W. T. Coombs & S. J. Holladay (Eds.), *Handbook of crisis communication* (pp. 691–697). Malden, MA: Wiley-Blackwell.

Ulmer, R. R., Sellnow, T. L., & Seeger, M. W. (2011). *Effective crisis communication: Moving from crisis to opportunity* (2nd ed.). Thousand Oaks, CA: Sage.

U.S. Food and Drug Administration. (n.d.). *Hazard analysis & critical control points (HACCP)*. Retrieved from http://www.fda.gov/food/guidanceregulation/haccp/default.htm

Veil, S. R., Sellnow, T. L., & Heald, M. (2011). Memorializing crisis: The Oklahoma National Memorial as Renewal Discourse. *Journal of Applied Communication Research, 39,* 164–183.

Weick, K. E. (1993). The collapse of sensemaking in organizations: The Mann Gulch disaster. *Administrative Science Quarterly, 38,* 628–652.

Weick, K. E. (1995). *Sensemaking in organizations.* Thousand Oaks, CA: Sage.

Weick, K. E., & Ashford, S. J. (2001). Learning in organizations. In F. M. Jablin & L. L. Putnam (Eds.), *The new handbook of organizational communication: Advances in theory, research, and methods* (pp. 704–731). Thousand Oaks, CA: Sage.

Wheatley, M. J. (2007). *Leadership for an uncertain time.* San Francisco, CA: Barrett-Koehler.

SECTION 9

Risk Communication in the Public Sphere

CHAPTER 21

Social Movements and Risk Communication

Hilary Schaffer Boudet and Shannon Elizabeth Bell

Introduction

Scholarship on social movements, as it is practiced today, is a relatively young but growing field. Born in the wake of the large-scale rights-based protest movements of the 1960s, social movement scholars departed from the existing characterization of mobilization as chaotic and disorganized riot behavior to an understanding of social protest as a legitimate form of political activism.

How is such scholarship on social movements relevant to risk communication? As Kasperson (1986) notes, in public participation processes about risky endeavors, like siting hazardous waste facilities or investing in research into new technologies, "risk communication often becomes a vehicle of protest by which community groups create resources with which to bargain with government in the risk management process" (p. 276). In addition to becoming fodder for protest, risk communication efforts are often aimed at creating or taking advantage of social mobilization processes to encourage behavior changes—such as dietary restrictions or disaster preparedness—to

mitigate and adapt to risks. Yet at the same time, Kasperson (1986) laments,

> Much more is known about the response to risk by members of the public as individuals than as members of social groups. Improved understanding is needed of the social dynamic of risk consideration in the context of actual controversies and community processes. (p. 280)

Social movement scholarship, which focuses on the underlying structural factors and dynamic processes that drive mobilization, can provide just this sort of information.

In this chapter, we present an overview of social movement theory, with an emphasis on those areas most relevant for risk communication scholars. We then offer two examples of the application of social movement theory to better understand community response to the risky endeavor of energy production. Finally, we provide thoughts about what social movement theory can offer risk communication scholars, as well as what social movement scholars can learn from the risk communication literature.

Defining and Studying Social Movements

As with most sociological terms, definitions of the term *social movement* abound. However, as pointed out by McAdam and Snow (1997),

> Most conceptual efforts [to define social movements] include the following elements: (1) collective or joint action; (2) change-oriented goals; (3) some degree of organization; (4) some degree of temporal continuity; and (5) some extra-institutional collective action, or at least a mixture of extra-institutional (protesting in the streets) and institutional (political lobbying) activity. Blending these elements together, we can define a social movement as a collectivity acting with some degree of organization and continuity outside of institutional channels for the purpose of promoting or resisting change in the group, society, or world order of which it is a part. (p. xviii)

Thus, social movements can simultaneously be studied as agents of change, groups acting outside of institutional channels, and organizations or organized activity. The main question of interest to social movement scholars has been *Under what conditions do movements emerge?* Secondary questions include *Who participates in social movements and why? What tactics do participants use to make claims and why? What ultimate impact do movements have?* We will focus our review of the literature on these questions.

Despite the proliferation of literature on the subject of social movements, the phenomenon itself is actually quite rare (Bell, 2010; McAdam & Boudet, 2012; Sherman, 2011). Protesting requires time, resources, sympathy for and identification with the movement's goals and tactics, and belief in the movement's ability to accomplish them. Participants often have previous experience with this type of political activity and/or strong ties to experienced people or organizations. Participation can have significant repercussions—most recently

exemplified by Tim DeChristopher who spent 2 years in prison for disrupting an oil and gas lease auction—and movements often face powerful competing interests—like the oil and gas industry. Successful collective action requires members with organizational skills and political acumen to frame issues in a manner that is salient to others, recognize potential allies in positions of power, exploit existing political cleavages, and ultimately bring together large numbers of people. In addition, aspects of the political, social, and economic contexts are also important. For example, the success of the Civil Rights Movement was due in part to the Cold War because racism at home had become incompatible with America's interest in spreading democracy abroad (McAdam, 1982/1999). For these reasons, examples of the large-scale social movements—such as the Civil Rights struggle or the French Revolution—that have been the focus of a tremendous volume of scholarship are few and far between.

Nevertheless, the tenets and theories that have been developed by social movement scholars are applicable to a broader category of events, referred to as "episodes of contention." An episode of contention, according to McAdam, Tarrow, and Tilly (2001), is a period of emergent, sustained contentious interaction between at least two collective actors utilizing new and innovative forms of action vis-à-vis one another. *Emergent* refers to the fact that these episodes are understood by the parties involved to represent some qualitative break from whatever relationship, if any, that prevailed in the past. A shared sense of uncertainty about the relationship and the relative power or privileges enjoyed by the conflicting parties is the hallmark of any episode. *New and innovative forms* of action include the wide array of tactics available to challenging groups outside of the institutionalized public participation processes, including demonstrations, protests, civil disobedience, and even violent activity. So while the response of a single community to a proposal for a hazardous facility within its borders may not be considered a social movement, it can fall into this more inclusive category of an episode of contention. In this way, these theories can be applied beyond the rare instances of a social movement to other more common forms of contentious politics.

Competing and Complementary Theories

Overall, three different theories have dominated explanations of how and why social movements emerge: (1) strain or grievance, (2) resource mobilization, and (3) political opportunity. In the early 20th century, when scholars were focused on explaining the rise of movements such as Nazism and fascism, social strain or "breakdown" became a major explanatory factor of movement development (Meyer, 2004; Tarrow, 1998). Scholars in this era argued that when strains or grievances (specifically related to economic depressions) became too much to bear, normal social controls vanished, and crowds, riots, and mobs developed (Buechler, 2007). The idea of a strain or grievance providing the catalyst for a movement is relevant in the context of risk communication. Our society presents many different grievances or "threats" (e.g., to public safety, health, environment, and quality of life) around which people can mobilize. Indeed, local environmental action is often initiated in response to a perceived health risk or threat—as epitomized by the actions of Lois Gibbs and other local citizens in Love Canal (Carmin, 2003; Freudenburg, 1984; Walsh & Warland, 1983; Walsh, Warland, & Smith 1993). Almeida (2003) defines threat as "the probability that existing benefits will be taken away or new harms inflicted if challenging groups fail to act collectively" (p. 347). Defined this way, the idea of threat is very much akin to risk and provides an important starting point for understanding mobilization.

With the emergence of the rights-based movements of the 1960s, social movement scholars began to discredit earlier strain theories. They argued that, because there was a continuous supply of grievances in society at any given time,

public perception of these grievances must be manipulated by motivated individuals or organizations to *provoke* mobilization (McCarthy & Zald, 1977; Meyer, 2004; Turner & Killian, 1972). For example, the senior citizen groups that lobbied for Medicare were initially organized by a branch of the AFL-CIO (American Federation of Labor and Congress of Industrial Organizations) in response to the American Medical Association's claims that seniors were not complaining about existing care (McCarthy & Zald, 1977, p. 1215). Thus, the emergence of this movement was rational and calculated—unlike the irrational "mob behavior" that some earlier scholars argued characterized social movements.

Theorists began to explain the emergence of social movements by focusing on the importance of resources provided by elite actors and organizations (e.g., elected officials, regulators, foundations, etc.) to potential protesters, specifically in terms of organizational infrastructure, funding, information, and experience (Carmin, 2003). Many scholars of this resource mobilization perspective viewed the presence of existing organizations—like the AFL-CIO in the above example, or black churches in the case of Civil Rights (McAdam 1982/1999)—that can be drawn into movement activities, via social appropriation, as particularly important for mobilization (McAdam et al., 2001; Tarrow, 1998; Walsh et al., 1997).

At the same time resource mobilization theory was developing, social movement scholars also began studying how aspects of the broader political context, or "political opportunity structure," influenced movement emergence (Eisinger, 1973; Meyer, 2004). Political opportunity refers to "elements of the political environment that impose constraints or provide opportunities for activism" (Carmin, 2003, p. 47). For example, in the first use of the term, Eisinger (1973) showed that the number of riots in American cities was related to the openness of urban governments to more conventional forms of political participation (e.g., the presence of an elected mayor as opposed to an appointed manager). He showed that governments that invited participation pre-empted protest, while closed governments repressed it. Thus, cities with the highest levels of protest activity were those in the middle, with both open and closed aspects to their governance. The concept of political opportunity structure has since grown to encompass other dimensions, as outlined by McAdam (1996a), including "the stability or instability of that broad set of elite alignments that typically undergird a polity, the presence or absence of elite allies, and the state's capacity and propensity for repression" (p. 27). For example, as discussed above, the desire of U.S. State Department officials to establish America's leadership role on the world stage after World War II and the incompatibility of racism at home with democratic messages abroad during the Cold War created a set of elite allies for the Civil Rights Movement.

McAdam (1982/1999) combined these concepts of threat, resource mobilization, and political opportunity into a single political process model of mobilization. In his studies of the U.S. Civil Rights Movement, he shows how broader social changes (e.g., the collapse of the cotton economy in the South, African American migration to northern cities, and a decline in the number of lynchings) both "lowered the costs and dangers of organizing for African Americans and increased their political value as an electoral constituency" (Meyer, 2004, p. 129). At the same time, elite actions like the Supreme Court decision in *Brown v. Board of Education* legitimized the struggle and provided a sense of hope for progress. Drawing on existing social networks and organizations (e.g., black churches, black colleges, and southern chapters of the National Association for the Advancement of Colored People), organizers brought together large numbers of people for contentious action. According to this model, prerequisites for community mobilization include the following: (a) expanding political opportunities for challenges to the status quo, (b) a perceived threat to the interests of challenging groups and/or previously uninvolved groups, (c) social appropriation

of existing mobilizing structures that include both the informal and formal networks through which people mobilize, and (d) collective interpretive processes that create feelings of both grievance and optimism within the local community about the prospects for collective action (Aminzade & McAdam, 2001; McAdam, 1982/1999).

In practice, despite the inclusion of McAdam's fourth prerequisite, the political process model has largely been applied as a structural theory of mobilization, as scholars have sought to identify objective environmental factors that facilitate mobilization. However, the recent interpretive turn in social science—which has pushed scholars to consider not just the role of structural factors but human agency and subjective interpretation in behavior—has also been mirrored in the study of social movements, resulting in an increased emphasis on an area that should be of interest to risk communicators—framing.

Framing and Frame Alignment

Framing has been defined and studied in various ways in divergent disciplines of social science. As conceptualized by social movement theorists, *framing* is the process whereby social movement actors assign meaning to events and circumstances with the intent of mobilizing possible supporters, acquiring the sympathy of bystanders, and demobilizing opponents (Snow & Benford, 1988). For example, Civil Rights activists framed their confrontations with the racist system in ways that "created powerful and resonant images that triggered critically important reactions" in the media and the American public (McAdam, 1996b, p. 354). By luring southern segregationists to engage in appalling acts of racist violence against a group of nonviolent protestors, they created a dramatic visual "juxtaposition of peaceful black demonstrators and virulent white attackers" (McAdam, 1996b, p. 354). The media flocked to these dramatic confrontations and, in the process, won over the

American public, who, in turn, pressured a reluctant federal government to take action.

Through the process of "frame alignment," social movement organizations attempt to connect the activities, goals, and ideology of the social movement with the values, beliefs, and interests of constituents (Snow, Burke Rochford, Worden, & Benford, 1986).[1] In the case of the Civil Rights Movement, Martin Luther King Jr. worked to construct his message in a way that resonated with a wide variety of publics. By blending a variety of culturally familiar and widely held beliefs—including Christian themes, conventional democratic theory, and the philosophy of nonviolence—King was able to bring "an unusually compelling, yet accessible, frame to the struggle" (McAdam, 1996b, p. 347). This multiplicity of themes accorded both the media and the public a number of different points of potential identification with the movement.

Benford and Snow (2000) elucidate three core framing tasks of social movement organizations and actors. The first is *diagnostic framing*, in which an aspect or condition of social life is diagnosed as being unjust or problematic and in need of change. In the case of the Civil Rights Movement, the unequal and violent treatment of blacks was the social condition to which activists aimed to bring public attention and outrage. The second core framing task is *prognostic framing*, wherein a solution to the diagnosed problem is proposed. Civil Rights organizations offered legislation such as the Civil Rights Act of 1964 and the Voting Rights Act of 1965 as solutions. The final core framing task of social movement organizations is *motivational framing*, which is the "'call to arms' or rationale for engaging in ameliorative collective action" (pp. 615–617). As described above, Civil Rights organizations engaged in this type of framing through exposing the atrocities of white-on-black violence.

Snow and Benford (1988) argue that variation in a social movement's success in mobilizing participants depends on how well these three core framing tasks are performed. The stronger and more thoroughly developed these framing tasks are, the more effective the mobilization effort will be.

Framing Risk

The above examples from the Civil Rights Movement reveal the ways in which social movement organizations framed a particular injustice and the ameliorating solutions to this injustice to mobilize support and action. But how do social movement actors and those they target frame *risk*? To extend the concept of framing to the role it plays in risk communication, we provide two examples from the energy sector. The first, drawn from opposition to liquefied natural gas (LNG) import projects in the United States, shows the dynamic and context-specific nature of the framing process as an opposition group matures and attempts to attract participants. The second, drawn from the coal sector, shows how industry stakeholders counter claims made by movement activists using risk-based arguments—in this case, the risk of *not* developing the resource.

Scaling up the Risk of LNG

With more than 50 proposed for U.S. coastal locations in the early 2000s, LNG importation terminals were touted by industry and government officials as the future of natural gas and a bridge to renewable energy. To produce LNG, natural gas is cooled to cryogenic temperatures for transportation in tankers. Offload terminals receive these tankers and vaporize the LNG for distribution. Many LNG proposals faced fierce resistance.

The risks associated with an LNG offload facility are largely concentrated in the local host community and offer a plethora of options for the diagnostic framing activities of the opposition. Local concerns include safety, terrorism, environmental impacts, and neighborhood quality-of-life issues. A wider environmental concern has to do with continued reliance on fossil fuel energy resources. Some environmentalists view the construction of LNG terminals as taking a step back from renewable sources. So the question remains: Which of these risks did opponents choose? The answer, based on a systematic examination of opposition to projects around the country, is it changes over time and depends on the local and regional context (Boudet, 2011; Boudet & Ortolano, 2010; McAdam & Boudet, 2012).

For example, in a cross-case comparison of two successful opposition efforts to LNG proposals in California—the Mare Island Energy Project in Vallejo and the Cabrillo Port proposal offshore of Malibu and Oxnard, Boudet and Ortolano (2010) show how, despite very different objective risk profiles, the framing of risk changed over time in both locations in the same way—from concern about a high consequence, low probability explosion with mainly local impacts to more chronic, persistent

and broader impacts related to air pollution and neighborhood quality. Figure 21.1, which is based on letters to the editor in local newspapers, shows the similarity in shifts in opponents' framing of threat over time. That opposition groups in both cases settled on air quality impact as the most effective frame for their concerns reflects the high salience of air pollution issues through much of California. It also reflects the powerful role often played by human well-being—and particularly health-related issues—in siting debates. However, perhaps more revealing for risk communicators is that, in both cases, activist framing of the risks posed by the facility transitioned away from low probability, high consequence, localized threats— that seem to motivate a small but vocal minority— to more chronic, persistent, and broader impacts—that seem most likely to sustain and grow mobilization efforts, as well as have a greater impact on decision makers.

Figure 21.1 Comments About *Safety* and *Terrorism* and *Air* and *Neighborhood Quality* Concerns Over Time by Opponents to Two Liquefied Natural Gas Facilities in California

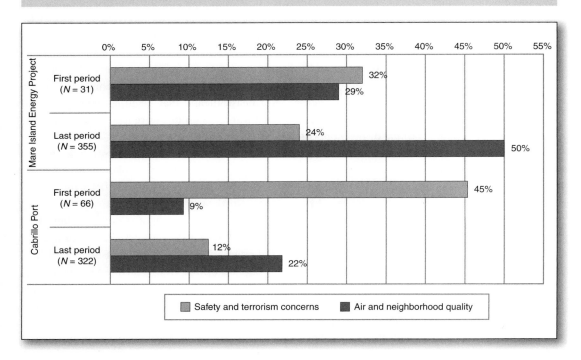

In a subsequent analysis of regional mobilization against LNG, Boudet (2011) underlines the importance of coalition building—a combination of brokerage and frame bridging—in differentiating successful efforts on the West and Gulf Coasts from unsuccessful attempts in the Northeast. *Brokerage* is the building of social connections between previously unconnected persons or sites; *frame bridging* occurs when a collective action frame (the product of framing efforts) is successfully applied to a seemingly separate issue or conflict. In the case of LNG siting, because U.S. energy regulators allowed market demand to determine the number of facilities that would eventually be built, facility proponents raced to obtain permits and begin construction, while affected communities competed to deny and delay the proposals. This competitive aspect of the siting process meant that cooperation between communities to create a larger regional mobilization against LNG more generally was difficult, although not impossible.

In the Gulf Coast, fisheries regulators played a key role in providing a salient bridging frame of potential impact on fisheries and brokering an unlikely alliance between the environmental and fishing communities. For residents throughout the Gulf Coast, the impact on the fisheries was a salient issue; as was the threat to sport fishing. As in the Gulf Coast, West Coast brokers, in the form of an energy regulator and regional environmental activists, helped opponents move beyond localized concerns about safety and land use to fashion a broader framing of LNG opposition that included concerns about need, cost, air pollution, supply chain impacts, greenhouse gas emissions, and LNG's potential impact on efforts to promote renewable energy. One leader of the West Coast opposition effort explained the framing as follows: "The mantra for all campaigns was that we don't need it. It wasn't about one LNG versus another LNG; it was about LNG versus renewable. We framed it that way" (quoted in Boudet, 2011).

This broader oppositional frame, which included diagnostic and prognostic elements, was deployed across multiple cases and had implications beyond the locally affected communities, especially considering Governor Schwarzenegger's efforts to limit greenhouse gas emissions in California.

In contrast, neither of these key mechanisms was evident in the Northeast. No broker successfully connected disparate opposition groups. No consistent framing of the issue emerged across multiple projects. Beyond the absence of these mechanisms, however, two important contextual factors also impeded the development of a coordinated movement within the region. The first is simply the fact that the projects proposed for the region were located in so many different states, each characterized by a different regulatory regime. These varying regimes made lessons learned and tactics employed by opponents in one state much less relevant to potential activists elsewhere. In contrast, on both the West Coast and Gulf Coast, multiple projects were proposed for the same states. Lessons learned and the momentum generated by one project were easily transferred to another because decision-making structures and thus oppositional strategies remained more constant and relevant across multiple sites. The second contextual factor is the Northeast's dependence on coal for electricity generation and oil for residential heating (especially when compared with the West Coast's energy supply mix). The prospect of a cleaner-burning supply of natural gas from LNG in the Northeast meant that regional regulators and environmental groups were loath to disparage all LNG proposals. These groups evaluated each proposal individually, thus preventing them from serving the all-important brokerage role for the development of a regional anti-LNG movement in the Northeast.

This second example of regional mobilization against LNG not only shows the importance of context-specific framing of an issue (e.g., fisheries impacts on the Gulf Coast, renewable energy on the West Coast) but also the critical role played by the frame's messenger. Coalition building cannot be accomplished by any entity but requires the *right* individual or group to be successful, probably an actor less vested in opposition to a specific project and with a geographically broader, and seemingly less partisan, view of the issue at stake. In the two successful examples, this role was filled by a regulator. In the Northeast, unsuccessful attempts at coalition building were undertaken largely by leaders of project-specific opposition efforts in a particular community.

Astroturfing and Friends of Coal

Activists are not alone in engaging in framing work to garner support for their cause. Within the context of energy production, constituents on both sides of the issue devote time, energy, and money to framing the project in differing ways. For instance, industry stakeholders may frame their messaging on the risks of *not* doing the project, focusing on the jobs that will *not* be created or the dangers of *not* meeting the nation's energy needs.

One of the primary weapons used by industries in the framing war against social movement organizations is "astroturfing." An astroturf organization is a false grassroots coalition that is manufactured for the purpose of feigning widespread public support for an issue or industry (Beder, 1998; McNutt & Boland, 2007). In recent decades, it has become standard operating procedure for corporations to spend enormous sums of money to hire public relations firms to manufacture "grassroots" campaigns on their behalf (Beder, 1998; McNutt & Boland, 2007). These astroturf organizations allow corporations to engage in public debates and government hearings under the guise of concerned citizens.

A key purpose of astroturf activities is to defuse the efforts of social movement organizations (Beder, 1998). By hiring "scientific experts" to cast doubt on the hazard claims of activist groups and by enlisting local or national celebrities to speak on their behalf, these astroturf organizations attempt to manipulate the public's trust and gain support for their cause. Enlisting public relations

methodologies, including audience analysis, news media, advertising, and e-marketing, astroturf organizations create the impression of widespread public support for the purpose of influencing public policy in ways that favor corporate interests (Beder, 1998; McNutt & Boland, 2007). Many of these groups work to directly counter the framing activities of social movement organizations that oppose the industries or practices they represent. Astroturf organizations target the diagnostic framing (or problem definition) and prognostic framing (or problem resolution) efforts of social movement organizations, calling into question the truthfulness of their claims against industry and creating counterframes that articulate the importance of the industry. The intended consequence of these efforts is to disrupt the motivational framing (or call to action) efforts of social movement organizations.

The "Friends of Coal" campaign in Central Appalachia is a prime example of an astroturf organization that was created to counter the claims of environmental justice organizations fighting irresponsible mining practices. During the summer of 2002, in response to the impending threat of stricter enforcement of coal truck weight limits, large declines in coal-related employment due to the increased mechanization of mining practices, and the increasing influence of environmental justice groups, the West Virginia Coal Association developed the idea for the "Friends of Coal," an organization that would serve to influence public perceptions about the coal industry's importance to the economy and identity of West Virginia residents (Bell & York, 2010). Now in neighboring Appalachian states, the Friends of Coal has expanded its reach and influence to other constituencies and policymakers.

There are two major ways the Friends of Coal directly counters the claims of environmental justice groups: (1) by hiring scientists to question the validity of studies that have found negative health impacts associated with coal mining and coal processing in order to create doubt and (2) by promulgating arguments about the risks of *not* mining coal. Television commercials created by the

Friends of Coal demonstrate this industry-generated risk communication in action. In one of these commercials, Jeremy Starks, a professional bass fisherman and "conservation team representative" of the Bass Angler Sportsman Society, appears on a stream bank fishing with five children. This image alternates with images of the coal mining process as Starks says,

> Hi. I'm Jeremy Starks—a Friend of Coal and a pro fisherman who's concerned about the environment. . . . This clear stream is proof that sustaining water quality is a big part of the reclamation process. Scientific tests have shown that this water quality is better now than it's ever been. And this is after 22 million tons of coal have been mined in nearby land . . . with responsible practices in place, we can safely mine coal while restoring our land for future generations. (Quoted in Bell & York, 2010, pp. 133)

Through this commercial, a local celebrity and self-proclaimed conservationist dismisses the diagnostic framing claims of environmental groups, assuring the viewer that not only can coal mining and a healthy environment coexist, but the coal industry actually *improves* water quality.

Retired Air Force General "Doc" Foglesong is chosen as the narrator of another Friends of Coal television commercial titled "American Hero." As Foglesong speaks, various images of hard-working male coal miners appear. He states,

> You could say the West Virginia coal miners are modern-day pioneers. Men and women of courage, pride and adventure, who safely go where no one's been before and harvest the coal that powers our nation. . . . In fact, if these miners didn't produce coal, our nation would be in trouble. More than half of the nation's electricity is generated by coal. West Virginia is the national leader in underground coal-mining production, and America needs that energy—today more than ever. (Quoted in Bell & York, 2010, p. 131)

In this commercial, the coal industry is presented as "defending" the United States from the risks associated with *not* having access to this energy source. Furthermore, as Bell and York (2010) assert, choosing a retired military general to be the narrator patently reveals the messages the Friends of Coal seeks to communicate: "The coal industry defends the 'American way of life' just as the military does. Thus, coal is more than an energy source—it is a *patriotic* energy source!" (Bell & York, 2010, p. 132).

This representation of the coal industry as a defender of the American way of life is also apparent in another Friends of Coal television commercial titled "Tracking the Source." The narrator states,

> Without West Virginia coal, our nation's economic status as a leader would be in jeopardy. It may seem like a daunting task to supply the nation with energy. But clean coal technology continues to gain momentum, helping us reduce our dependence on foreign oil and creating jobs for the men and women who proudly call themselves coalminers. (Quoted in Bell & York, 2010, p. 132)

Thus, the Friends of Coal is able to counter the social movement organizations' messages about the risks of coal mining by creating its own diagnostic frame: If we do *not* mine coal, the nation will most certainly face economic disaster and foreign conflict over oil.

As the risk perception literature reveals, a person's propensity to view an industry or practice as harmful is influenced by the degree to which that individual perceives personal or economic benefit from the hazard (Alhakami & Slovic, 1994). Thus, one of the main functions of astroturf organizations is to amplify the perceived benefits of the relevant industry. As described above, a number of factors prevent would-be constituents from engaging in activism. Industry framing efforts, such as those of the Friends of Coal, aim to defuse grievances against polluting companies by convincing the public that they bring more good than harm. For example, the Friends of Coal attempts to give the impression that the coal industry provides more economic contributions and local employment than it actually does by pervading the social landscape with its presence. First, they ensure that the Friends of Coal logo is seen across the region by distributing car decals, hats, clothing, yard signs, and selling Friends of Coal license plates at the Department of Motor Vehicles. Second, they sponsor a wide variety of cultural events, community improvement projects, scholarships, sporting events, and other projects to draw public attention to the organization. And, finally, they enter public school classrooms through the Coal Education Development and Resource Program of Southern West Virginia, which provides public school teachers with grants and the possibility of cash prizes for implementing the curriculum (Bell & York, 2010). By being persistently visible across all facets of life in this region, the Friends of Coal is able to give the impression that there is widespread grassroots support for the coal industry and that the industry provides resources for all people, regardless of whether they or their family members actually work in coal. Through this tactic, the coal industry attempts to persuade the public into believing that the benefits associated with mining outweigh any risks.

Reflections for Theory and Research

Given the mutual interests between the fields of social movements and risk communication regarding what facilitates or impedes collective action, we hope that this brief overview will begin a much longer conversation between these two research communities. Social movement scholars could contribute expertise on *collective* framing processes, as well as an understanding of the structural and contextual factors like political opportunity and resources that are relevant for collective mobilization. Risk communication

scholars could provide critical information about *individual* interpretation and attribution of risk, particularly related to its social amplification (Kasperson et al., 1988; see also Chapter 5, this volume), cultural cognition (Douglas & Wildavsky, 1982; see also Chapter 1, this volume), and the mental models that shape public perceptions of less familiar and higher dread risks (Morgan, Fischhoff, Bostrom, & Atman, 2002), the actualization of which often provides the impetus for mobilization. The rejection of grievance-based explanations of mobilization by resource mobilization and political process theorists described above has left a corresponding gap in the literature in terms of theorizing threat and its attribution (Wright & Boudet, 2012)—a gap that risk communication scholarship could readily fill.

In addition, the divergent methodological choices between the two fields—(1) social movement scholars tend to focus on historical case studies and event history analysis of successful movements and (2) risk communication scholars often utilize surveys and experiments of decontextualized, hypothetical risks—could also inspire fruitful collaborations. For example, combining nationally representative survey data about public perceptions and actions related to hydraulic fracturing with an in-depth analysis of the strategic framing efforts and activities of anti-fracking organizations could provide a much more comprehensive analysis of the drivers of mobilization and its impacts than one or the other alone.

We conclude with one final example to show the synergies that could exist between these two fields. Schutz and Wiedemann's (2008) experiment showed that characterizing businesses involved in nanotechnology endeavors as "small" or "large" affected public risk perceptions. Just imagine how this research could be deepened by incorporating Schurman's (2004) work conceptualizing how industry structures (a form of political opportunity structure) affected the success of the antibiotechnology movement in Western Europe. Schurman argues that, for example, the movement—in addition to targeting the life sciences firms that produce genetically modified organisms—purposefully and successfully focused efforts on consumer-oriented activism to affect the highly competitive food-processing and retail sectors that purchase and sell genetically modified foods. Conversely, Schurman's arguments could also be made stronger by incorporating Schutz and Wiedemann's techniques.

Recommendations for Practice

We offer two recommendations from the literature on social movements for practicing risk communicators. The first is the importance of considering structural factors that facilitate or impede mobilization—such as political opportunities and resources—in designing risk communication programs. For example, Eisinger's (1973) finding of the curvilinear relationship between political openness and protest, which has been replicated in other contexts (Kriesi, 2004), has important implications for participatory designs. Tentative steps toward more open decision-making procedures will likely encourage mobilization. In other words, participation is not something that can be done halfway. Similarly, communities with past experience successfully mobilizing, even in a relatively unrelated area, can transfer these organizational skills and resources to subsequent efforts. Communicators who are new to a community should spend time getting to know it not only in terms of the issue at hand but also in terms of political activity more generally.

A second recommendation relates to framing. Framing is not just about getting the facts right, testing messages, and disseminating them. It is a context-specific, dynamic, and contested process. Risk communicators must continually monitor their own framing efforts, as well as those of others, to ensure that their messages are salient and motivating to those they are trying to reach. One of the key mechanisms of mobilization is a collective interpretation of injustice combined with hope for change—and framing is key to establishing or avoiding such interpretations.

Several ethical implications result from this type of research. In particular, examining factors that impede mobilization can be problematic, depending on who uses such research and how the findings are presented. For instance, a potential unintended consequence could be inadvertently providing information that oil and gas companies could use to limit community action against development proposals. At the same time, however, information about the strategies used by industry proponents may be useful to affected communities. We must carefully consider the groups and people we may hurt or help through our research choices. Another question to consider is, given the importance of the framing process in shaping mobilization, how do we monitor and vet inaccurate or false claims during contentious processes? As Futrell (2003) noted in his study of attempts to site chemical weapons disposal facilities in the United States, the "information haze" of "conflicting, contradictory, multiparty, multidirectional communications that fail to clarify the risks associated with a project" often results in a shift from public requests for additional information to "more contentious, active resistance" (p. 365).

Conclusions

In this chapter, we have provided a brief overview of the theoretical underpinnings of the study of social movements with a focus on framing—an area we felt would be of particular interest to risk communication scholars—and real-world examples from the energy sector. Through these examples, we have shown the context-specific, dynamic, and contested nature of the framing of risk and how these facets relate to the spread of contention. We also provided some ideas about areas of potential collaboration between risk communication and social movement scholars. We concluded with some implications for the practice of risk communication from studies of social movements and contentious politics.

Note

1. Communication scholars will note similarities with Asen's (2000) work on "counterpublics," which emphasizes the important role of discourse in establishing collective identification as opposed to involuntary classification as a subordinated group.

Suggested Additional Readings

Klandermans, B., & Roggeband, C. M. (Eds.). (2007). *The handbook of social movements across disciplines*. New York, NY: Springer.

Snow, D., Soule, S. A., & Kriesi, H. (Eds.). (2004). *The Blackwell companion to social movements*. Malden, MA: Wiley-Blackwell.

References

Alhakami, A. S., & Slovic, P. (1994). A psychological study of the inverse relationship between perceived risk and perceived benefit. *Risk Analysis, 14*, 1085–1096.

Almeida, P. D. (2003). Opportunity organizations and threat-induced contention: Protest waves in authoritarian settings. *American Journal of Sociology, 109*(2), 345–400.

Aminzade, R. R., & McAdam, D. (2001). Emotions and contentious politics. In R. R. Aminzade, J. A. Goldstone, D. McAdam, E. J. Perry, W. H. J. Sewell, S. Tarrow, & C. Tilly (Eds.), *Silence and voice in the study of contentious politics* (pp. 14–50). Cambridge, England: Cambridge University Press.

Asen, R. (2000). Seeking the "counter" in counterpublics. *Communication Theory, 10*(4), 424–446.

Beder, S. (1998). Public relations' role in manufacturing artificial grassroots coalitions. *Public Relations Quarterly, 43*(2), 21–23.

Bell, S. E. (2010). *Fighting king coal: The barriers to grassroots environmental justice movement participation in central Appalachia* (Doctoral dissertation).

University of Oregon, Eugene. Retrieved from http://search.proquest.com/docview/816357349

Bell, S. E., & York, R. (2010). Community economic identity: The coal industry and ideology construction in West Virginia. *Rural Sociology, 75*(1), 111–143.

Benford, R., & Snow, D. (2000). Framing processes and social movements: An overview and assessment. *Annual Review of Sociology, 26*, 611–639.

Boudet, H. S. (2011). From NIMBY to NIABY: Regional mobilization against liquefied natural gas facility siting in the U.S. *Environmental Politics, 20*(6), 786–806.

Boudet, H. S., & Ortolano, L. (2010). A tale of two sitings: Contentious politics in liquefied natural gas facility siting in California. *Journal of Planning Education and Research, 30*, 5–21.

Buechler, S. M. (2007). The strange career of strain and breakdown theories of collective action. In D. A. Snow, S. A. Soule, & H. Kriesi (Eds.), *Blackwell companion to social movements* (pp. 47–66). Oxford, England: Blackwell.

Carmin, J. (2003). Resources, opportunities and local environmental action in the democratic transition and early consolidation periods of the Czech Republic. *Environmental Politics, 12*(3), 42–64.

Douglas, M., & Wildavsky, A. B. (1982). *Risk and culture: An essay on the selection of technical and environmental dangers*. Berkeley: University of California Press.

Eisinger, P. K. (1973). The conditions of protest behavior in American cities. *American Political Science Review, 67*, 11–28.

Freudenburg, N. (1984). Citizen action for environmental health: Report on a survey of community organizations. *American Journal of Public Health, 74*(5), 444–448.

Futrell, R. (2003). Framing processes, cognitive liberation and NIMBY protest in the U.S. chemical-weapons disposal conflict. *Sociological Inquiry, 73*(3), 359–386.

Kasperson, R. E. (1986). Six propositions on public participation and their relevance for risk communication. *Risk Analysis, 6*(3), 275–281.

Kasperson, R. E., Renn, O., Slovic, P., Brown, H. S., Emel, J., Goble, R., . . . Ratick, S. (1988). The social amplification of risk: A conceptual framework. *Risk Analysis, 8*(2), 177–187.

Kriesi, H. (2004). Political context and opportunity. In D. A. Snow, S. A. Soule, & H. Kriesi (Eds.),

The Blackwell companion to social movements (pp. 67–90). Malden, MA: Blackwell.

McAdam, D. (1996a). Conceptual origins, current problems, future directions. In D. McAdam, J. D. McCarthy, & M. N. Zald (Eds.), *Comparative perspectives on social movements: Political opportunities, mobilizing structures, and cultural framings* (pp. 23–40). New York, NY: Cambridge University Press.

McAdam, D. (1996b). The framing function of movement tactics: Dramaturgy in the American Civil Rights Movement. In D. McAdam, J. D. McCarthy, & M. N. Zald (Eds.), *Comparative perspectives on social movements: Political opportunities, mobilizing structures, and cultural framings* (pp. 338–356). New York, NY: Cambridge University Press.

McAdam, D. (1999). *Political process and the development of black insurgency, 1930–1970.* Chicago, IL: University of Chicago Press. (Original work published 1982)

McAdam, D., & Boudet, H. S. (2012). *Putting social movements in their place: Explaining opposition to energy projects in the United States, 2000–2005.* Cambridge, England: Cambridge University Press.

McAdam, D., & Snow, D. A. (1997). *Social movements: Readings on their emergence, mobilization and dynamics.* Los Angeles, CA: Roxbury.

McAdam, D., Tarrow, S., & Tilly, C. (2001). *Dynamics of contention.* New York, NY: Cambridge University Press.

McCarthy, J. D., & Zald, M. N. (1977). Resource mobilization and social movements: A partial theory. *America Journal of Sociology, 82*(6), 1212–1241.

McNutt, J., & Boland, K. (2007). Astroturf, technology and the future of community mobilization: Implications for nonprofit theory. *Journal of Sociology & Social Welfare, 34*(3), 165–179.

Meyer, D. (2004). Protest and political opportunities. *Annual Review of Sociology, 30,* 125–145.

Morgan, G., Fischhoff, B., Bostrom, A., & Atman, C. J. (2002). *Risk communication: A mental models approach.* Cambridge, England: Cambridge University Press.

Schurman, R. (2004). Fighting "Frankenfoods": Industry opportunity structures and the efficacy of the Anti-Biotech Movement in Western Europe. *Social Problems, 51*(2), 243–268.

Schutz, H., & Wiedemann, P. M. (2008). Framing effects on risk perception of nanotechnology. *Public Understanding of Science, 17*(3), 369–379. doi:10.1177/0963662506071282

Sherman, D. J. (2011). *Not here, not there, not anywhere: Politics, Social Movements, and the disposal of low-level radioactive waste.* Washington, DC: RFF Press.

Snow, D. A., & Benford, R. (1988). Ideology, frame resonance, and participant mobilization. *International Social Movement Research, 1,* 197–217.

Snow, D. A., Burke Rochford, E., Jr., Worden, S. K., & Benford, R. D. (1986). Frame alignment processes. *Annual Sociological Review, 51,* 464–481.

Tarrow, S. (1998). *Power in movement: Social movements and contentious politics.* In P. Lange (Ed.), *Cambridge studies in comparative politics.* Cambridge, England: Cambridge University Press.

Turner, R. H., & Killian, L. M. (1972). *Collective behavior* (2nd ed.). East Rutherford, NJ: Prentice Hall.

Walsh, E. J., & Warland, R. H. (1983). Social movement involvement in the wake of a nuclear accident: Activists and free riders in the TMI area. *American Sociological Review, 48,* 764–780.

Walsh, E. J., Warland, R. H., & Smith, D. C. (1997). *Don't burn it here: Grassroots challenges to trash incinerators.* University Park: Penn State University Press.

Wright, R. A., & Boudet, H. S. (2012). To act or not to act: Context, capability, and community response to environmental risk. *American Journal of Sociology, 118*(3), 728–777.

CHAPTER 22

Public Engagement in Risk-Related Decision Making

John C. Besley

Introduction

Both practical and legal concerns make ensuring that citizens have the opportunity to engage with decision makers central to the study of risk communication. Similarly, the challenge of coming to social consensus around health and environmental concerns has meant that those interested in public engagement often focus on issues of risk. In both cases, the expectation is that community dialogue will help decision makers and those affected by decisions take positions that reflect their interests and values. Given this expectation, as well as normative arguments about peoples' right to be involved in decision making related to risks that might affect what they care about, developed countries have developed laws, regulations, and norms that mandate public engagement when citizens may be faced with new perceived risks (Lundgren & McMakin, 2009; Organisation for Economic Cooperation and Development, 2009). Given the importance of public engagement to risk management, the current chapter highlights connections between risk-focused work and discussions within the broader social science literature on public engagement. It argues that risk researchers will benefit from greater attention to this foundational literature.

To this end, this chapter first discusses the challenge of providing a working definition of the term *public engagement* aimed at helping researchers and practitioners identify relevant research and then briefly turns to a history of public engagement practice and research to help explain current interest in the topic within risk research. The chapter then provides an overview of risk communication research on public engagement with a focus on both direct, face-to-face engagement as well as engagement that is mediated by traditional or newer communication technologies. For reasons of space and focus, the current chapter focuses primarily on how social scientists have studied public engagement related to risk, although it is clear that scholars with a focus on topics like critical theory, rhetorical analysis, and history have also addressed issues of engagement in substantive and useful ways (e.g., Hauser & Benoit-Barne, 2002), especially in the realm of environmental communication (e.g., Depoe, Delicath, & Elsenbeer, 2004).

The Current Literature

The fact that public engagement can encompass an enormous range of activities can make it difficult for both scholars and practitioners to distill the available evidence into usable knowledge. The challenge stems from several features of the literature. First, public engagement can be defined to include relatively low-involvement activities such as donating money or signing a petition to high-involvement activities such as attending a series of public meetings or sitting on advisory boards. As part of this, some writers may attempt to differentiate "engagement" from "participation" or some other term, but at this point in the development of the literature, it seems more productive to take a pragmatic, inclusive approach and focus on the underlying ideas rather than the label. Second, scholars from a range of different disciplines study public engagement in both risk and nonrisk contexts with substantial contributions coming from across the social sciences as well as areas such as political theory (e.g., Gutmann & Thompson, 2004; Mutz, 2006) and various disciplines within the humanities (e.g., Schudson, 1998). Finally, while scholars may want to improve the quality of public engagement, most efforts at engaging the public occur in real-world settings where there is little opportunity to systematically test novel approaches against competing approach or to spend limited resources on enhancing theoretical or analytical rigor.

It is noteworthy that both the National Research Council of the National Academy of Sciences (2008) and the Organisation for Economic Cooperation and Development (2009) have produced comprehensive summaries of the public engagement literature with some focus on health and environmental risk in recent years. Also, several teams of researchers have attempted to provide their own frameworks for assessing the impact of engagement efforts (e.g., McComas, Arvai, & Besley, 2009; Rowe & Frewer, 2005). A number of reviews of the literature on "deliberative democracy" are also available to provide insight into the relationship between democratic theory related to engagement and empirical research (e.g., Delli Carpini, Cook, & Jacobs, 2004; Thompson, 2008). The goal here is to avoid repeating the findings of such work while highlighting areas where risk researchers are active and where additional risk-focused work seems needed.

Defining Public Engagement

A simple way to define public engagement is to look at how several prominent reviews have defined public engagement and to consider whether these definitions are too broad or too narrow for the current purposes. The National Research Council of the National Academy of Sciences (2008), in its review of "public participation" in environmental assessment, for example, defines participation to include only an "organized process adopted by elected officials, government agencies, or other public- or private-sector organizations to engage the public in environmental assessment, planning, decision-making, management, monitoring and evaluation" (p. 11). This is similar to the definition provided by Creighton (2005) in a general handbook on public participation that defines the subject as "the process by which public concerns, needs and values are incorporated into governmental and corporate decision making. It is two-way communication and interaction, with the overall goal of better decisions that are supported by the public" (p. 7). These definitions thus clearly highlight both the importance of thinking about public engagement as a process of communication and one that is linked to policy discussions.

Rather than focus on finding a single definition, another way to understand public engagement suggests thinking about the concept along a continuum. A classic article on participation thus differentiates mechanisms by the degree to which they give citizens control over decisions. The lowest level of the "ladder" includes nonparticipative mechanisms that emphasize educating or persuading citizens to go along with what decision makers choose, while higher levels of the ladder include mechanisms where decision makers allow citizens to have a meaningful voice (Arnstein, 1969; Creighton, 2005, p. 9). Rowe and Frewer (2005) similarly distilled three classes of engagement—public communication, public consultation, and public participation—based on the degree to which decision makers aim to truly communicate with the public. McComas and her colleagues (2009) simply proposed a hierarchy based on the degree to which participants are able to meaningfully "deliberate" about the key issues at play with decision makers. Near the low end of this hierarchy are techniques such as decision maker–controlled focus groups that offer little opportunity for participant-controlled dialogue, while formal deliberative procedures such as consensus conferences (Einsiedel & Eastlick, 2000) lie at the other end. The dominant theoretical framework in the field of public relations—including the crisis communication, which is often tied to risk communication—further argues that organizations that get closest to two-way, symmetrical communication are more likely to succeed (Grunig, Grunig, & Dozier, 2006). Finally, the focus on a continuum is consistent with one recent attempt by Delli Carpini and his colleagues (2004) to untangle public engagement and integrate the associated body of literature on "deliberative theory." The Delli Carpini review describes deliberation as an idealized form of "discursive participation" where there is "debate and discussion aimed at producing reasonable, well-informed opinions in which participants are willing to revise preferences in light of discussion, new information, and claims made by fellow participations" (Chambers, 2003, p. 309). Consistent with a continuum idea, this definition emphasizes that "deliberation" is an ideal and that most instances of actual engagement will fall short.

A final way to think about what we mean by public engagement is to look at how major research projects have operationalized the concept. The American National Election Study

(2010) is a primary resource for the study of public participation in the United States (e.g,. Verba, Schlozman, & Brady, 1995). It includes a battery of political participation measures that address whether survey participants had voted, tried to persuade someone else to vote for or against a candidate, displayed campaign buttons, stickers or lawn signs, gone to meetings or rallies, done work for a party or candidate, or given money to some related group (American National Election Study, 2010). Similar questions are asked as part of the European Social Survey (2012).

What gets excluded from such lists, however, are engagement activities where the main purpose is *not* to "improve things . . . or help prevent things from going wrong" (European Social Survey, 2012). Belonging to a fraternal organization or church group and volunteering for a charity may have political dimensions, but these are typically studied as a separate set of behaviors. All of these activities involve the potential for communication between the public and decision makers and thus could be relevant to risk-related decision making. Furthermore, while most of the risk communication literature seems to focus on engagement organized by decision makers in government, the private sector, or nongovernmental organizations, it does not seem reasonable to ignore citizen-directed activities. Unsolicited letter writing, protests, and boycotts seem most likely to occur when citizens feel they do not have an adequate voice through traditional mechanisms of engagement. Such activities deserve attention from engagement scholars because they still involve members of the public attempting to engage with decision makers (see also Bucchi & Neresini, 2008).

Furthermore, any complete list of engagement activities should also include organized efforts to engage the public about risk even if they occur prior to the announcement of formal decision-making processes. These might include efforts by museums, universities, or other science-related organizations to engage with nonscientists on novel issues (Bell, Lewenstein, Shouse, & Feder, 2009) and are similar to "community relations" efforts in the field of public relations where the focus is on building relationships (Heath & Ni, 2009). Another purpose of such "upstream engagement" may be to begin societal dialogue about potential issues before they become the subject of, for example, formal risk assessment or decision-making processes and before they become firmly established in the public mind (Pidgeon & Rogers-Hayden, 2007). Engagement might also occur as part of "citizen science" projects where members of the public interact with scientists to collect real data through activities such as bird counts (Haywood & Besley, 2014; Shirk et al., 2012). In each case, participants may have a desire to influence policy, even if the path to such influence may be several steps removed from the activity itself.

In summary, there are a broad range of potential subjects that could be and are studied by risk communication scholars interested in engagement. What differentiates this area of scholarship from others is that it focuses on procedures through which decision makers and other actors communicate around current or potential policy question.

The History of Public Engagement Research in Risk Communication

One potential criticism of risk communication research is that it often fails to adequately draw on foundational political theory, as well as literature from the broader social sciences, when discussing public engagement (Biegelbauer & Hansen, 2011). Doing so deprives the risk community from being part of a wider academic discussion and may result in a failure to ask how risk-focused engagement might be different from engagement involving other complex issues, or to identify relevant ideas from non–risk-related discussions.

Pateman (1970) highlights the origins of theories of participation in the works of Rousseau and his contemporaries' efforts to understand how individuals can come to take collective action to govern themselves, but she argues that broadening and enhancing participation became a point of discussion in the late 1960s as social and environmental issues took center stage in political debates (see also Schudson, 1998). The "deliberative renaissance" that seems to have occurred in the late 20th century likely had its origins in changes in technologies that made communication more immediate, in a culture that was becoming more complex, and a political system that was grappling with declines in trust (Gastil & Keith, 2005).

In the context of risk communication, an influential 20-year summary of the field suggests that risk managers have gone through related stages of thinking. The initial phases, according to this argument, focused on technical accuracy and clear explanation. Eventually, it became clear that they also needed to treat people nicely, and then they learned that they needed to do all of these things while also bringing the public into the decision-making process (Fischhoff, 1995). A similar overview of 25 years of "public understanding of science" research traces the discussion from a focus on literacy to a broader emphasis on "understanding" and then, finally, to a focus on the role of "science in society." This final phase emphasized using public engagement to both make better decisions and build trust (Bauer, Allum, & Miller, 2007).

Such summaries, however, note that implementing meaningful engagement, even when provided substantial resources, remains fraught with challenges (e.g., Horlick-Jones et al., 2007). Furthermore, while some science and risk communication scholars appear to endorse efforts to enhance the quality and quantity of engagement, not all political theorists believe that we should expect much success from such efforts. One important argument highlights the fact that Western political systems were designed on the idea of representative democracy rather than participatory or deliberative democracy and that it is unrealistic to expect substantial input from citizens (Biegelbauer & Hansen, 2011; Mutz, 2006). Underlying this argument is the evidence that citizens say that they not only want to be better consulted about politics but also want to be left alone (Hibbing & Theiss-Morse, 2002). A primary set of counterarguments to such positions are that (a) citizens increasingly expect to have opportunities to engage and that (b) fostering such engagement is needed to deal with the complex issues faced by society (e.g., Beierle & Cayford, 2002; Gutmann & Thompson, 2004). Another important critique argues that efforts at engagement are likely to re-create inequalities, because it is unlikely that organizers will be able to overcome existing power dynamics (Sanders, 1997) or that they might exacerbate existing disagreements (Mendelberg & Oleske, 2000; Mutz, 2006).

The Impact of Engagement

A dual focus on decision quality and individuals' attitudes and beliefs is at the heart of many of the attempts to summarize the impacts of public engagement. Gutmann and Thompson (2004), in this regard, argue that an ongoing shift toward deliberative democracy represents both an effort to create policies that citizens can accept as legitimate while also helping find solutions that serve their needs. This focus has manifested itself in the risk research in, for example, Beierle and Cayford's (2002) emphasis on outcomes such as the incorporation of values in decisions, improving the substantive quality of decisions (i.e., consistency with available evidence), and resolving conflict between parties from citizen-level outcomes such as building trust in decision-making institutions and learning (see also Rowe & Frewer, 2000). Engagement's impact on decision quality and on the individual are discussed, in turn, below.

The Impact of Public Engagement on Decision Quality

In practice, it is harder to study the effect of engagement on decision quality than engagement's impact on the individual. The types of issues around which decision makers are hoping that political participation can help are "wicked problems" for which no ideal solution exists (Beierle & Cayford, 2002, p. 5). Even the concept of a "better" decision is problematic inasmuch as there are almost always many potential metrics for what would constitute quality (i.e., cost, social impact, environmental impact, etc.).

Attempts to assess decision quality therefore often sidestep the "quality" question and focus on whether public input gained through engagement mechanisms gets incorporated into decisions. For example, one risk study that looked at a group of Canadians brought together to discuss a medical issue (xenotransplantation) found that the process appeared to have resulted in "institutional learning" within the government department that sponsored it and was highlighted on a website and in internal meetings (Einsiedel & Ross, 2002). Similar "technology assessment" work now occurs in many countries (Joss & Belluci, 2002), but many continue to struggle at how to integrate the lessons of such processes into decision making (Mejlgaard & Stares, 2012). Ultimately, including multiple stakeholders takes substantial commitment from decision makers (e.g., Lauber & Knuth, 1999; Murdock, Wiessner, & Sexton, 2005). One important area of research focuses on developing tools (e.g., simple modeling software) that decision makers can use to help members of the public work through complicated issues (McComas et al., 2009).

Participants care about whether their advice gets taken. Several studies about attempts to foster discussion of complex technologies have noted that participants, in particular, often worry about whether their efforts would contribute to policy (e.g., Horlick-Jones et al., 2007; Rowe, Marsh, & Frewer, 2004). Journalists covering public engagement exercises also say that weak links to decision making limit their willingness to cover such events (Besley & Roberts, 2010). Finally, it is clear that different types of decision makers and other stakeholders expect different things out of risk engagement processes (Besley, McComas, & Trumbo, 2012; Tuler & Webler, 1999; Webler & Tuler, 2006).

One perspective is that the process of integrating public views into decision making should be understood as a long-term, largely mediated process through which the decision makers, the public, and other actors develop social consensus (Yankelovich, 1991). This literature is partly built on the idea of "opinion quality" and focuses on assessing the degree to which citizens hold opinions that are grounded in individual and group debate (Delli Carpini & Keeter, 1996). Fishkin (1997), in particular, links the two literatures in his efforts to popularize "Deliberative Polls," in which representative samples of citizens are brought together to learn and discuss issues with a goal of trying to assess where public opinion is likely to move as it becomes more informed (see also Sturgis, Roberts, & Allum, 2005).

Also, while research on the question is limited, considering public input does not, of course, automatically mean "better" decisions. There will be cases where members of the public ultimately call for a plan that experts might not see as optimal. For example, the Brent Spar disposal controversy in the United Kingdom involved substantial public debate, but Shell and Exxon ultimately felt forced by public pressure to choose an option—dismantling the oil platform onshore, rather than sinking it—that risk analysts suggested put people and the environment at more risk than would other available options. In this case, one challenge may have been that key proponents—namely, the government and Shell oil—may not have had enough trust to withstand a media challenge initiated by Greenpeace (Lofstedt & Renn, 1997). More generally, many experts may see technologies such as those associated with nuclear energy or biotechnology as relatively safe compared with alternatives, but the public may still push for alternative paths.

The Impact of Public Engagement on the Individual

The potentially rich nature of public engagement means that it can have many different impacts on participants. Karpowitz and Mendelberg's (2011) review of research found that a range of potential benefits included helping individuals become (a) more tolerant and empathetic, (b) more knowledgeable, (c) better able to connect attitudes and personal objectives, (d) better able to understand opponents' perspectives, (e) more empowered and efficacious in pursuing their objectives, (f) more public spirited, (g) more willing to compromise for the common good, and (h) more willing to participate in the future (Karpowitz & Mendelberg, 2011). Another review suggests a possible set of reciprocal relationships where engagement is both the cause and the consequence of such effects (Burkhalter, Gastil, & Kelshaw, 2002; see also Delli Carpini, 2004). Within the political communication literature, Verba and his colleagues' (1995) "Resource Model" research showed that involvement in civic life fosters the development of resources—attitudes and skills—that increase the likelihood that they will continue to engage in civic life in the future.

Any number of risk studies suggests that participating in engagement has impacts on participants. Much of this work has drawn in a general way on the broad public participation and deliberation literature to suggest potential effects (e.g., Zorn, Roper, Weaver, & Rigby, 2012). Given the range of potential impacts, Besley and his colleagues have, for example, argued that the literature on procedural justice—which distinguishes perceptions of "distributive fairness" from non-distributive forms of fairness such as procedural and interpersonal fairness—provides one body of theory for choosing which variables to use to assess the impact engagement related to risk. Specifically, this work argues that practitioners should focus on ensuring that participants see decision makers as willing to listen and be respectful (Besley, 2010; Besley, Kramer, Yao, & Toumey, 2008), although novel experimental research on risk-related engagement suggests that providing a fair process may not make as much difference as might be hoped (Arvai & Froschauer, 2010). There is also evidence that fairness concerns matter more when respondents may be uncertain about the underlying science (i.e., they do not have strong preexisting attitudes) (Besley, 2012; Doble, 1995).

Also, the types of effects associated with engagement connect the literature on public engagement to research on media effects. This work explores the relationships between various forms of media use, efficacy, and trust in various actors (Cho et al., 2009) and argues that mediated communication behavior appears to enhance some of the same skills and attitudes summarized by those who study the effect of direct engagement (Brossard & Dudo, 2012; Satterfield, Kandlikar, Beaudrie, Conti, & Herr Harthorn, 2009). The literature on the relationships between media use and views about decision makers is also a primary site for the debate about appropriate risk communication goals: How much should direct or mediated engagement focus on imparting raw information (i.e., educating) versus trying to shape how people think about issues (i.e., through careful framing of messages) and decision makers (i.e., through careful portrayals of key actors)? Research clearly shows that knowledge about science and risk are only minor predictors of views about science (Sturgis, Brunton-Smith, & Fife-Schaw, 2010), and we also know that affective reactions to risk topics (Finucane, Alhakami, Slovic, & Johnson, 2000) and factors such as trust (Earle, Siegrist, & Gutscher, 2007) and fairness (Webler, 2013) are more central to how people understand risk. Unfortunately, while risk researchers know that experts see their job as transferring information to rectify deficiencies in the public's knowledge (Besley & Nisbet, 2013), it is not clear that decision makers prioritize using their interactions with others to communicate potential heuristic cues such as trustworthiness or their respect for others.

Predicting Engagement

Individual-level variables are also sometimes used to predict engagement behavior. Many of the variables already discussed—trust in decision makers, a sense of personal efficacy, personal knowledge, and media use—are an important part of this work. In general, the social science literature suggests that the more people trust decision makers, the more they feel like they can make a difference, and the more they know, the more likely they are to engage (Delli Carpini et al., 2004). As Burkhalter et al. (2002) suggest, the evidence is that the effects of engagement are also its predictors. For example, just as trust may be a desired consequence of engagement, those who trust more are more likely to engage. Such research is also that age drives engagement type, with younger generations preferring to try and shape their society through volunteering and community activism, as well as consumer behavior, rather than through traditional political routes (Zukin, Keeter, Andolina, Jenkins, & Delli Carpini, 2006). Recent research in this vein suggests that online mobilization efforts were only effective at fostering online engagement and not offline engagement (Vissers, Hooghe, Stolle, & Mahéo, 2012). Other efforts have explored which factors might lead experts and other decision makers to engage with the public in meaningful ways. At present, the evidence suggests that scientists' internal motivation and sense of efficacy are key drivers of getting involved in engagement efforts (e.g., Besley, Oh, & Nisbet, 2013; Webler, Tuler, Shockey, Stern, & Beattie, 2003).

At the larger level, it is also clear that different cultures have different approaches to engagement that affect both who is likely to participate and how that participation is likely to be structured (Einsiedel & Eastlick, 2000; Hagendijk & Irwin, 2006; Joss & Belluci, 2002).

Online Engagement

Despite early hyperbole, it has become clear that we should not expect online engagement to provide a panacea for challenges associated with getting the public involved in public decision making (Hindman, 2009; Zavestoski, Shulman, & Schlosberg, 2006) and that the online engagement arena remains as fragmented as the offline engagement arena (Susha & Grönlund, 2012). Nevertheless, progress continues to be made.

In the risk context, people are using online tools to discuss health and environmental risks, and decision makers can contribute to these discussions (Runge et al., 2013). Furthermore, it is clear that many opportunities exist to communicate risk by means that will be able to interact with the public in new or improved ways (Neeley, 2014). Indeed, it would be seen as odd if large-scale engagement attempts did not include meaningful online elements (Horlick-Jones et al., 2007), and scholars have attempted to adapt face-to-face engagement models such as consensus conferences to online environments with both limited success and some frustration (Delborne, Anderson, Kleinman, Colin, & Powell, 2011). The types of decision-support tools used to help nonexperts work through risks mentioned above are also being implemented in online environments (e.g., Aguirre & Nyerges, 2011; Brown, Montag, & Lyon, 2012). It also seems clear, however, that the public's ability to get information online may also shape how risk gets discussed, including the information that people bring to the table and the tone of the discussion (Brossard & Scheufele, 2013). One specific concern is that such forms may result in less respectful discussion on some topics (Anderson, Brossard, Scheufele, Xenos, & Ladwig, 2013).

Reflections for Theory and Research

The various attempts to define public engagement described above, as well as the later discussion of engagement effects, emphasize that at the heart successful public engagement is honest, respectful dialogue with the public. Much of the literature thus represents examples of efforts to implement processes where experts and the public were able to meet on relatively equal ground and come to some agreement on a path forward (Morton, Airoldi, & Phillips, 2009) or when problems emerged because of a failure to create a

discursive framework participants saw as reasonable (e.g., Einsiedel & Ross, 2002; Goven, 2003; Horlick-Jones et al., 2007). No single technique or methodology, in this regard, should be seen as inherently superior, but rather, the focus should be on ensuring a procedure that participants see as fair over the long term (McComas et al., 2009).

Moving forward, it should be expected that public engagement will remain an active topic for risk communication research and practice. The risks with which societies are dealing are simply too enmeshed into how we live to expect experts to solve problems on their own. However, the popularity of engagement research—driven by the ubiquity of engagement practice—means that practitioners (and scholars) interested in engagement need to commit themselves to gaining insight from a range of fields.

This interdisciplinary mind-set also needs to accompany a commitment to systematic, empirical testing of ideas (e.g., Arvai & Froschauer, 2010). A productive path forward would be to hone in on specific relationships of interest and study these systematically. In other words, consistent with research in areas such as public health where controlled field trials are common, it would be helpful if risk-focused engagement scholars were to learn to isolate and manipulate just key variables of interest in their work. There have been some attempts to provide comparable case studies (e.g., Biegelbauer & Hansen, 2011; Kurath & Gisler, 2009; Webler & Tuler, 2006) or even experiments in which an engagement technique was systematically manipulated (e.g., Arvai, 2003; Arvai & Froschauer, 2010; French & Bayley, 2011), but more needs to be done. At this point in the study and practice of engagement, it seems likely that risk communication scholars will continue to make only incremental gains unless they begin to pull apart engagement and find ways to test what really works.

Recommendations for Practice

Just as researchers and theorists may need to pay more attention to testing ideas, so too should practitioners develop an empirical mind-set that prioritizes ensuring real impacts over, for example, creativity in designing new mechanisms for engagement. A commitment to impacts also means a commitment to adopting engagement practices that have demonstrated success in the past as well as rigorous assessment. Planning, implementing, and assessing engagement needs to be recognized as a professional activity rather than as an afterthought or something that can be done by anyone. This is similar to the argument that, while many people know how to communicate, this does not mean they know how to communicate effectively or strategically. The risk context may change some aspects of engagement—by increasing its importance in certain stakeholders' minds, for example—but the key goals (e.g., share knowledge, listen to those with concerns and potential insight, build trust, etc.) seem general, and therefore the needed guidance should be sought out in range of places.

Conclusions

The current chapter argued that those interested in risk-related engagement need to pay attention to a broad range of research on public engagement from across the social sciences (as well as various disciplines from the humanities). Doing so can ensure that we take full advantage of insights from relevant work. It may also allow us to maximize the impact of our own work by contributing to the broader dialogue. It was also argued that public engagement itself needs to be understood broadly because doing so may help direct attention to the many ways in which the public may attempt to have a voice in decision-making processes and where risk communicators may wish to engage. Ultimately, while there is substantial opportunity to use engagement practices to provide participants with structured access to high-quality risk information, the literature also highlights the fact that providing high-quality opportunities for engagement is where outcomes such as trust in decision makers and

personal efficacy may be developed. Furthermore, these same outcomes are also believed to contribute to future engagement in what has the potential to be a reinforcing cycle.

Suggested Additional Readings

Gastil, J. (2008). *Political communication and deliberation*. Los Angeles, CA: Sage.

Renn, O., Webler, T., & Wiedemann, P. M. (1995). *Fairness and competence in citizen participation: Evaluating models for environmental discourse*. Boston, MA: Kluwer Academic.

The Royal Society. (1985). *The public understanding of science ("The Bodmer Report")*. London, England: Author.

References

Aguirre, R., & Nyerges, T. (2011). Geovisual evaluation of public participation in decision making: The grapevine. *Journal of Visual Languages and Computing, 22*(4), 305–321. doi:10.1016/j.jvlc.2010.12.004

American National Election Study. (2010). *Time series cumulative data file*. Retrieved from http://www.electionstudies.org/studypages/cdf/cdf.htm

Anderson, A. A., Brossard, D., Scheufele, D. A., Xenos, M. A., & Ladwig, P. (2013). The "nasty effect": Online incivility and risk perceptions of emerging technologies. *Journal of Computer-Mediated Communication*. doi:10.1111/jcc4.12009

Arnstein, S. (1969). A ladder of citizen participation. *Journal of the American Institute of Planners, 35*, 216–224.

Arvai, J. L. (2003). Using risk communication to disclose the outcome of a participatory decision-making process: Effects on the perceived acceptability of risk-policy decision. *Risk Analysis, 23*(2), 281–289.

Arvai, J. L., & Froschauer, A. (2010). Good decisions, bad decisions: The interaction of process and outcome in evaluations of decision quality. *Journal of Risk Research, 13*(7), 845–859. doi:10.1080/13669871003660767

Bauer, M. W., Allum, N., & Miller, S. (2007). What can we learn from 25 years of PUS survey research? Liberating and expanding the agenda. *Public Understanding of Science, 16*(1), 79–95. doi:10.1177/0963662506071287

Beierle, T. C., & Cayford, J. (2002). *Democracy in practice: Public participation in environmental decisions*. Washington, DC: Resources for the Future.

Bell, P., Lewenstein, B. V., Shouse, A. W., & Feder, M. (Eds.). (2009). *Learning science in informal environments*. Washington, DC: National Academies Press.

Besley, J. C. (2010). Public engagement and the impact of fairness perceptions on decision favorability and acceptance. *Science Communication, 32*(2), 256–280. doi:10.1177/1075547009358624

Besley, J. C. (2012). Does fairness matter in the context of anger about nuclear energy decision making? *Risk Analysis, 32*(1), 25–38. doi:10.1111/j.1539-6924.2011.01664.x

Besley, J. C., Kramer, V. L., Yao, Q., & Toumey, C. (2008). Interpersonal discussion following citizen engagement on emerging technology. *Science Communication, 30*(4), 209–235. doi:10.1177/1075547008324670

Besley, J. C., McComas, K. A., & Trumbo, C. W. (2012). Citizen views about public meetings. *Journal of Risk Research, 15*(4), 355–371. doi:10.1080/13669877.2011.634516

Besley, J. C., & Nisbet, M. C. (2013). How scientists view the public, the media and the political process. *Public Understanding of Science, 22*(6), 644–659. doi:10.1177/0963662511418743

Besley, J. C., Oh, S. H., & Nisbet, M. C. (2013). Predicting scientist' participation in public life. *Public Understanding of Science, 22*(8), 971–987. doi:10.1177/0963662512459315

Besley, J. C., & Roberts, M. C. (2010). Qualitative interviews with journalists about deliberative public engagement. *Journalism Practice, 4*(1), 66–81. doi:10.1080/17512780903172031

Biegelbauer, P., & Hansen, J. (2011). Democratic theory and citizen participation: Democracy models in the evaluation of public participation in science and technology. *Science and Public Policy, 38*(8), 589–597. doi:10.3152/030234211x13092649606404

Brossard, D., & Dudo, A. D. (2012). Cultivation of attitudes toward science. In M. Morgan, J. Shanahan, & N. Signorielli (Eds.), *Living with television now: Advances in cultivation theory & research* (pp. 120–146). New York, NY: Peter Lang.

Brossard, D., & Scheufele, D. A. (2013). Science, new media, and the public. *Science, 339*(6115), 40–41. doi:10.1126/science.1232329

Brown, G., Montag, J. M., & Lyon, K. (2012). Public participation GIS: A method for identifying ecosystem services. *Society & Natural Resources, 25*(7), 633–651. doi:10.1080/08941920.2011.621511

Bucchi, M., & Neresini, F. (2008). Science and public participation. In E. J. Hackett (Ed.), *The handbook of science and technology studies* (3rd ed., pp. 449–472). Cambridge: MIT Press. (Published in cooperation with the Society for the Social Studies of Science)

Burkhalter, S., Gastil, J., & Kelshaw, T. (2002). A conceptual definition and theoretical model of public deliberation in small face-to-face groups. *Communication Theory, 12*(4), 398–422.

Chambers, S. (2003). Deliberative democratic theory. *Annual Review of Political Science, 6,* 307–326.

Cho, J., Shah, D. V., McLeod, J. M., Mcleod, D. M., Scholl, R. M., & Gotlieb, M. R. (2009). Campaigns, reflection, and deliberation: Advancing an O-S-R-O-R model of communication effects. *Communication Theory, 19*(1), 66–88. doi:10.1111/j.1468-2885.2008.01333.x

Creighton, J. L. (2005). *The public participation handbook: Making better decisions through citizen involvement* (1st ed.). San Francisco, CA: Jossey-Bass.

Delborne, J. A., Anderson, A. A., Kleinman, D. L., Colin, M., & Powell, M. (2011). Virtual deliberation? Prospects and challenges for integrating the Internet in consensus conferences. *Public Understanding of Science, 20*(3), 367–384. doi:10.1177/0963662509347138

Delli Carpini, M. X. (2004). Mediating democratic engagement: The impact of communications and citizens' involvement in political and civic life. In L. L. Kaid (Ed.), *Handbook of political communication research* (pp. 395–434). Mahwah, NJ: Lawrence Erlbaum.

Delli Carpini, M. X., Cook, F. L., & Jacobs, L. R. (2004). Public deliberation, discursive participation, and citizen engagement: A review of the empirical literature. *Annual Review of Political Science, 7,* 315–344. doi:10.1146/annurev.polisci.7.121003.091630

Delli Carpini, M. X., & Keeter, S. (1996). *What Americans know about politics and why it matters.* New Haven, CT: Yale University Press.

Depoe, S. P., Delicath, J. W., & Elsenbeer, M.-F. A. (2004). *Communication and public participation in environmental decision making*. Albany: State University of New York Press.

Doble, J. (1995). Public opinion about issues characterized by technological complexity and scientific uncertainty. *Public Understanding of Science, 4*, 95–118.

Earle, T. C., Siegrist, M., & Gutscher, H. (2007). Trust, risk perception and the TCC model of cooperation. In M. Siegrist, T. C. Earle, & H. Gutscher (Eds.), *Trust in cooperative risk management: Uncertainty and scepticism in the public mind* (pp. 1–50). London, England: Earthscan.

Einsiedel, E. F., & Eastlick, D. L. (2000). Consensus conferences as deliberative democracy: A communications perspective. *Science Communication, 21*(4), 323–343.

Einsiedel, E. F., & Ross, H. (2002). Animal spare parts? A Canadian public consultation on xenotransplantation. *Science and Engineering Ethics, 8*(4), 579–591.

European Social Survey. (2012). *ESS cumulative data wizard.* London, England: Author. Retrieved from http://ess.nsd.uib.no/downloadwizard/

Finucane, M. L., Alhakami, A., Slovic, P., & Johnson, S. M. (2000). The affect heuristic in judgments of risks and benefits. *Journal of Behavioral Decision Making, 13*(1), 1–17. doi:10.1002/(sici)1099-0771(200001/03)13:1<1::aid-bdm333>3.0.co;2-s

Fischhoff, B. (1995). Risk perception and communication unplugged: Twenty years of process. *Risk Analysis, 2*, 137–144. doi:10.1111/j.1539-6924.1995.tb00308.x

Fishkin, J. S. (1997). *The voice of the people: Public opinion and democracy* (2nd ed.). New Haven, CT: Yale University Press.

French, S., & Bayley, C. (2011). Public participation: Comparing approaches. *Journal of Risk Research, 14*(2), 241–257. doi:10.1080/13669877.2010.515316

Gastil, J., & Keith, W. M. (2005). A nation that (sometimes) likes to talk: A brief history of public deliberation in the United States. In J. Gastil & P. Levine (Eds.), *The deliberative democracy handbook* (pp. 3–19). San Francisco, CA: Jossey-Bass.

Goven, J. (2003). Deploying the consensus conference in New Zealand: Democracy and de-problematization. *Public Understanding of Science, 12*(4), 423–440.

Grunig, J. E., Grunig, L. A., & Dozier, D. M. (2006). The excellence theory. In C. H. Botan & V. Hazleton (Eds.), *Public relations theory II* (pp. 21–62). Mahwah, NJ: Lawrence Erlbaum.

Gutmann, A., & Thompson, D. (2004). *Why deliberative democracy.* Princeton, NJ: Princeton University Press.

Hagendijk, R., & Irwin, A. (2006). Public deliberation and governance: Engaging with science and technology in contemporary Europe. *Minerva, 44*(2), 167–184. doi:10.1007/s11024-006-0012-x

Hauser, G. A., & Benoit-Barne, C. (2002). Reflections on rhetoric, deliberative democracy, civil society, and trust. *Rhetoric and Public Affairs, 5*(2), 261–275.

Haywood, B. K., & Besley, J. C. (2014). Education, outreach, and inclusive engagement: Towards integrated indicators of successful program outcomes in participatory science. *Public Understanding of Science, 23*(1), 92–106. doi:10.1177/0963662513494560

Heath, R. L., & Ni, L. (2009). Community relations and corporate social responsibility. In R. L. Heath & D. H. O'Hair (Eds.), *Handbook of risk and crisis communication* (pp. 557–568). New York, NY: Routledge.

Hibbing, J. R., & Theiss-Morse, E. (2002). *Stealth democracy: Americans' beliefs about how government should work.* New York, NY: Cambridge University Press.

Hindman, M. S. (2009). *The myth of digital democracy.* Princeton, NJ: Princeton University Press.

Horlick-Jones, T., Walls, J., Rowe, G., Pidgeon, N. F., Poortinga, W., Murdock, G., & O'Riordan, T. (Eds.). (2007). *The GM debate: Risk, politics and public engagement.* New York, NY: Routledge.

Joss, S., & Belluci, S. (Eds.). (2002). *Participatory technology assessment: European perspectives.* Gateshead, England: Athenaeum Press/Centre for the Study of Democracy.

Karpowitz, C. F., & Mendelberg, T. (2011). An experimental approach to citizen deliberation. In J. N. Druckman, D. P. Green, J. H. Kuklinski, & A. Lupia (Eds.), *Cambridge handbook of experimental political science* (pp. 258–272). New York, NY: Cambridge University Press.

Kurath, M., & Gisler, P. (2009). Informing, involving or engaging? Science communication, in the ages of atom-, bio- and nanotechnology. *Public Understanding of Science, 18*(5), 559–573. doi:10.1177/0963662509104723

Lauber, T. B., & Knuth, B. A. (1999). Measuring fairness in citizen participation: A case study of moose management. *Society & Natural Resources, 12*(1), 19–37.

Lofstedt, R. E., & Renn, O. (1997). The Brent Spar controversy: An example of risk communication gone wrong. *Risk Analysis, 17*(2), 131–136.

Lundgren, R. E., & McMakin, A. H. (2009). *Risk communication: A handbook for communicating environmental, safety, and health risks* (4th ed.). Columbus, OH: Battelle Press.

McComas, K. A., Arvai, J. L., & Besley, J. C. (2009). Linking public participation and decision making through risk communication. In R. L. Heath & D. H. O'Hair (Eds.), *Handbook of crisis and risk communication* (pp. 364–385). New York, NY: Routledge.

Mejlgaard, N., & Stares, S. (2012). Performed and preferred participation in science and technology across Europe: Exploring an alternative idea of "democratic deficit." *Public Understanding of Science.* doi:10.1177/0963662512446560

Mendelberg, T., & Oleske, J. (2000). Race and public deliberation. *Political Communication, 17*(2), 169–191.

Morton, A., Airoldi, M., & Phillips, L. D. (2009). Nuclear risk management on stage: A decision analysis perspective on the UK's Committee on Radioactive Waste Management. *Risk Analysis, 29*(5), 764–779. doi:10.1111/j.1539-6924.2008.01192.x

Murdock, B. S., Wiessner, C., & Sexton, K. (2005). Stakeholder participation in voluntary environmental agreements: Analysis of 10 Project XL case studies. *Science, Technology & Human Values, 30*(2), 223–250.

Mutz, D. C. (2006). *Hearing the other side: Deliberative versus participatory democracy.* New York, NY: Cambridge University Press.

National Research Council of the National Academy of Sciences. (2008). *Public participation in environmental assessment and decision making.* Washington, DC: National Academy Press.

Neeley, L. (2014). Risk communication and social media. In J. L. Arvai & L. Rivers (Eds.), *Effective risk communication* (pp. 143–164). New York, NY: Earthscan/Routledge.

Organisation for Economic Cooperation and Development. (2009). *Focus on citizens: Public engagement for better policy and services.* Paris, France: Author.

Pateman, C. (1970). *Participation and democratic theory.* Cambridge, England: Cambridge University Press.

Pidgeon, N., & Rogers-Hayden, T. (2007). Opening up nanotechnology dialogue with the publics: Risk communication or 'upstream engagement'? *Health, Risk & Society, 9*(2), 191–210. doi:10.1080/13698570701306906

Rowe, G., & Frewer, L. J. (2000). Public participation methods: A framework for evaluation. *Science, Technology & Human Values, 25*(1), 3–29.

Rowe, G., & Frewer, L. J. (2005). A typology of public engagement mechanisms. *Science, Technology & Human Values, 30*(2), 251–290.

Rowe, G., Marsh, R., & Frewer, L. J. (2004). Evaluation of a deliberative conference. *Science, Technology & Human Values, 29*(1), 88–121.

Runge, K. K., Yeo, S. K., Cacciatore, M. A., Scheufele, D. A., Brossard, D., Xenos, M., . . . Su, L. Y. F. (2013). Tweeting nano: How public discourses about nanotechnology develop in social media environments. *Journal of Nanoparticle Research, 15*(1), 1–11. doi:10.1007/s11051-012-1381-8

Sanders, L. M. (1997). Against deliberation. *Political Theory, 25*(3), 347–376.

Satterfield, T., Kandlikar, M., Beaudrie, C. E., Conti, J., & Herr Harthorn, B. (2009). Anticipating the perceived risk of nanotechnologies. *Nature Nanotechnology, 4*(11), 752–758. doi:10.1038/nnano.2009.265

Schudson, M. (1998). *The good citizen: A history of American civic life.* New York, NY: Free Press.

Shirk, J. L., Ballard, H. L., Wilderman, C. C., Phillips, T., Wiggins, A., Jordan, R., . . . Bonney, R. (2012). Public participation in scientific research: A framework for deliberate design. *Ecology and Society, 17*(2), 29–48. doi:10.5751/es-04705-170229

Sturgis, P., Brunton-Smith, I., & Fife-Schaw, C. (2010). Public attitudes to genomic science: An experiment in information provision. *Public Understanding of Science, 19*(2), 166–180. doi:10.1177/0963662508093371

Sturgis, P., Roberts, C., & Allum, N. (2005). A different take on the deliberative poll: Information, deliberation, and attitude constraint. *Public Opinion Quarterly, 69*(1), 30–65.

Susha, I., & Grönlund, Å. (2012). eParticipation research: Systematizing the field. *Government Information Quarterly, 29*(3), 373–382. doi:10.1016/j.giq.2011.11.005

Thompson, D. F. (2008). Deliberative democratic theory and empirical political science. *Annual Review of Political Science, 11*(1), 497–520. doi:10.1146/annurev.polisci.11.081306.070555

Tuler, S., & Webler, T. (1999). Voices from the forest: What participants expect of a public participation process. *Society & Natural Resources, 12*(5), 437–453.

Verba, S., Schlozman, K. L., & Brady, H. E. (1995). *Voice and equality: Civic voluntarism in American politics.* Cambridge, MA: Harvard University Press.

Vissers, S., Hooghe, M., Stolle, D., & Mahéo, V.-A. (2012). The impact of mobilization media on off-line and online participation: Are mobilization effects medium-specific? *Social Science Computer Review, 30*(2), 152–169. doi:10.1177/0894439310396485

Webler, T. (2013). Why risk communicators should care about the fairness and competence of their public engagement processes. In J. L. Arvai & L. Rivers (Eds.), *Effective risk communication* (pp. 124–141). Oxford, England: Earthscan.

Webler, T., & Tuler, S. (2006). Four perspectives on public participation process in environmental assessment and decision making: Combined results from 10 case studies. *Policy Studies Journal, 34*(4), 699–722.

Webler, T., Tuler, S., Shockey, I., Stern, P., & Beattie, R. (2003). Participation by local governmental officials in watershed management planning. *Society & Natural Resources, 16*(2), 105–121.

Yankelovich, D. (1991). *Coming to public judgment: Making democracy work in a complex world.* Syracuse, NY: Syracuse University Press.

Zavestoski, S., Shulman, S., & Schlosberg, D. (2006). Democracy and the environment on the Internet: Electronic citizen participation in regulatory rulemaking. *Science, Technology & Human Values, 31*(4), 383–408.

Zorn, T. E., Roper, J., Weaver, C. K., & Rigby, C. (2012). Influence in science dialogue: Individual attitude changes as a result of dialogue between laypersons and scientists. *Public Understanding of Science, 21*(7), 848–864. doi:10.1177/0963662510386292

Zukin, C., Keeter, S., Andolina, M., Jenkins, C., & Delli Carpini, M. X. (2006). *A new engagement? Political participation, civic life, and the changing American citizen.* New York, NY: Oxford University Press.

Glossary

Accuracy goal The communication purpose in which the intent of the sender is to convey accurate information for the receiver.

Accuracy motivation A person's drive to learn and process information to gain sufficient confidence that his/her judgments are accurate.

Action efficacy The belief in the effectiveness and efficiency of certain behavior in reducing the risk under consideration.

Adherence goal The communication purpose in which the intent of the sender is to move the receiver's attitudes and actions in the direction desired by the sender.

Collective efficacy Individuals' belief that the larger group, organization, or community that they belong to is capable of carrying out a chosen course of action.

Crisis communication A specific, unexpected, and nonroutine organizationally based event or series of events that create high levels of uncertainty and threat or perceived threat to an organization's high priority goals.

Cultivation theory The theory of cultivation, proposed by George Gerbner, focuses on the role that television plays in shaping viewer's perceptions of social reality. The theory predicts that those who spend more time watching television will be more likely to view reality in terms of the very images that television portrays.

Decision from description Choices between risky options that are based on symbolic and complete descriptions of options and their probabilities (e.g., graphical representations, numerical representations).

Decision from experience Choices between uncertain options that are based on various sources of experience about possible outcomes and their probabilities (e.g., on-line samples from the options, samples of relevant experience from memory, and samples of relevant vicarious experience).

Deliberative democracy A body of political theory that focuses on the role of public dialogue in decision making about public issues and on which risk communication scholars have drawn insight when designing public engagement mechanisms.

Deliberative risk delineation A procedure for identifying and constructing risk that works from the claim that risk is best delineated in any given case when it is the product of participatory democracy and deliberative decision making.

Discourse of renewal A means by which organizations, after experiencing a crisis, recognize fallacious assumptions or unforeseen vulnerabilities while reestablishing core values.

Edgework High-risk activities undertaken voluntarily that involve a clearly observable threat to one's physical or mental well-being or one's sense of an ordered existence.

Edgework communities Networks of risk takers who assist one another in skill development, build group structures for assessing individual member readiness for high-risk behavior, set controls for less skilled members, and inculcate the value of learning from small failures so that future harms are avoided.

Ethics Coming from the Greek word *ethos*, which means character, ethics addresses morality questions such as right and wrong or good and evil. Ethical issues in risk communication often entail fair distribution of risks and benefits, empowerment of recipients of risk communication messages, and adequate disclosure of information that enables informed decision making.

Framing The process whereby social movement actors assign meaning to events and circumstances with the intent of mobilizing possible supporters, acquiring the sympathy of bystanders, and demobilizing opponents.

Fuzzy-trace theory A theory that integrates reasoning and decision making in a new way to explain numeracy by distinguishing between meaning-based gist representations, which support fuzzy (yet advanced) intuition, and superficial verbatim representations of information, which support precise analysis.

Genetic counseling The professional provision of assistance and guidance in resolving human problems associated with a genetic disorder or the heightened risk of a genetic disorder in an individual or family.

Graphical displays of risk information Data-driven visual message elements featuring numerical information, such as risk ratios, hazard ratios, and other probabilities; frequency comparisons; and multivariate projections of mortality and morbidity.

Group polarization The tendency of a group to move toward a more extreme position compared with the average individual group member. The direction of the shift is determined by the majority of the members' predeliberation preferences.

Illustrative displays of risk information Visual messages and visual message features conveying information related to threats, hazards, or risk avoidance that are not numerical in nature, such as pictures of people alongside textual information to influence perceptions of risk susceptibility, grotesque images that convey risk severity, as well as sequential images that provide instructions about how someone might reduce his or her risk by taking safety precautions (e.g., airplane safety guides) and other visual representations of risk that are nonnumeric and have indexical qualities.

Impression involvement The extent to which one is concerned with other people's impression of his or her publicly expressed attitude.

Information dissemination The relative reach, rapidity, and timeliness of information sharing. Social media can provide a means of distributing information about risk to large audiences in a quick and timely manner.

Information processing The mental process of manipulating, storing, and retrieving information. The process may or may not integrate information into existing mental models already maintained by the individual.

Information seeking An effort—usually conscious—to acquire information in response to a need or gap in knowledge.

Information subsidy Information provided to journalists, without any investment of money or effort on the journalists' part, in the hope of influencing what they cover and how they cover it; press releases distributed by public relations staff fall into this category.

Informed decision making Primarily discussed in health care settings, informed decision making aims at increasing individuals' participation in decision making at a level they desire. Supported by adequate information, informed decision making promotes decisions that are consistent with individuals' values and preferences.

Institutional efficacy Belief that large societal institutions are fair, just, and reliable.

Interactivity The degree to which stakeholders in an organization can communicate directly with one another. Interactivity is an affordance of social media that can be used by organizations or governments to communicate with their audience(s) in a two-way fashion that allows for information exchange.

Media framing Involves the process of selectively emphasizing one aspect or dimension of a complex subject over another. Media "frames" set a specific train of thought in motion, communicating why an issue might be a problem or pose a threat, who or what might be responsible, and what should be done.

Media priming The issues or events at any given moment that are receiving the greatest amount of media attention often serve as the criteria by which the public evaluate the performance and credibility of a political leader, government agency, scientific organization, or corporation.

Media routines The set of professional practices typical of day-to-day journalistic work by which journalists and editors choose news topics, create narrative stories framed in particular ways out of "raw" information, and select sources and statements to include in those stories.

Narratives Stories that connect actions and events involving characters with thematic and temporal sequences.

Numeracy The ability to understand and use numbers.

Outcome involvement The extent to which the issue under consideration is important to one's goals.

Personal risk perception Judgments that one is facing a threat.

Probability neglect The idea that probabilities are ignored when judging consequences of decisions. Affect-rich presentations of risk can evoke probability neglect in risk perception.

Public engagement A broad area of study focused on the procedures through which decision makers and other actors communicate around current or potential policy question. Health and environmental risks are common topics for public engagement.

Reference class When determining the probability of a negative event or outcome, as a first step, a risk communicator must begin by choosing a reference class. The reference class determines which numbers will be presented. For example, the frequencies of plane crashes can be computed by month, year, or decade; air company; category of distance traveled; or plane size. All these categories specify different reference classes. Often, misunderstandings about the meaning of a particular risk message can be attributed to confusion about the identity of the reference class.

Rhetoric of risk A subfield of scholarship grounded in the assumption that risk is, to some extent, discursively constructed and dedicated to exploring the symbolic constitution of risk over time and in specific historical moments.

Risk Defined as the probability and the magnitude of harm, where harm refers to threats to humans and things they value. Risks are generally measurable, that is, outcomes and their probabilities are known.

Risk as feeling The hypothesis that risks are experienced affectively. These feelings intuitively influence how dangerous risks are perceived.

Risk perception Refers to the subjective assessment of the probability and the magnitude of harm. Risk perceptions include people's beliefs, attitudes, and judgments regarding risky events. Theories of risk perception acknowledge that the interdependence of the individual with societal and cultural contexts may amplify or attenuate individual perception.

Risky shift phenomenon The tendency of groups to form riskier decisions than their average group member.

Shared and unshared information Shared information refers to information items that are known to several group members prior to group deliberation. Unshared information refers to items that are only known to individual group members.

Societal risk perception Judgments that the society or collective at large is facing a threat.

Societal risk reduction action Behaviors to reduce the threat faced by the larger society by changing the conditions and contexts surrounding the threat, such as willingness to support changes in policies regarding risk; to voice opposition or support for social changes; to donate time, money, and other resources that can be utilized in efforts to facilitate changes; and to lower barriers to changes in social, political, and economic environments.

Spiral of silence The spiral of silence, authored by Elisabeth Noelle-Neumann, is a communication theory describing the process by which a point of view can become dominant in society. The theory posits that the willingness of an individual to express his or her opinion is a function of how he or she perceives the climate of opinion. Out of an innate fear of isolation, people tend to remain silent when they believe that their views are in the minority, but they are more vocal when they believe that their opinions are similar to those of the majority.

Survival rate The proportion of patients who are alive after a fixed period (e.g., 5 or 10 years) after they have been diagnosed with a disease. Survival rates are misleading as a measure of how well screenings work. Survival rates will increase whenever cancers are diagnosed earlier, even if the time of death is not postponed.

Transactional communication In interpersonal communication, each individual simultaneously influences and is influenced by the other. It is within this mutually constructed context that the individuals relate to each other.

Uncertainty In contrast to risk, uncertainty is not measureable as either the probabilities of outcomes and/or the outcomes are unknown. A more relaxed definition allows for a quantification of uncertainty in form of confidence intervals, ranges, or expert confidence ratings.

Uncertainty management theory Uncertainty theories focus on how individuals assess, manage, and cope with ambiguous and complex situations inherent in risk communication. Uncertainty management theory is one of the most widely used uncertainty theories, and it posits that uncertainty engenders other emotions besides anxiety and that people are not always motivated to decrease their uncertainty.

Value involvement The extent to which the issue under consideration is related to one's perspective on how the world should operate.

Author Index

Subject Index

Note: In page references, f indicates figures and t indicates tables.

About the Editors

Hyunyi Cho is a professor of communication at Purdue University. Her program of research focuses on risk communication and health communication. Her current research investigates effects of communication on judgments and actions relevant to environmental risk and health risk and the role of messages and the media in social change and behavior change processes.

Torsten Reimer is an associate professor of communication and psychology at Purdue University. His research focuses on the role of communication in decision making. His research program has the overarching goal to explore how communication principles facilitate decision making by guiding information processing and reducing information overload.

Katherine A. McComas is a professor of communication at Cornell University. Her research program examines how people communicate about health, science, and environmental risks. Her current projects examine ways to develop risk messages about infectious and zoonotic disease that promote awareness of the interconnectedness of public, animal, and environmental health.

About the Contributors

Shannon Elizabeth Bell is an assistant professor of sociology at the University of Kentucky. Her research falls at the intersection of environmental sociology, gender, and social movements, with a particular focus on understanding the ways in which environmentally destructive industries acquire and maintain their power and discovering strategies for increasing the political participation of communities most affected by environmental injustices.

John C. Besley is the Ellis N. Brandt Chair in public relations at Michigan State University. His program of research focuses on how perceptions about decision-making processes shape views about science and risk. His current research explores how scientists' views about the public and public engagement affect willingness to engage.

Andrew R. Binder is an assistant professor in the Department of Communication at North Carolina State University. He conducts research on controversial science topics, including how information about those topics is communicated through various communication channels and what impact that communication has on risk perception and public understanding of science.

Nicolai Bodemer is a visiting researcher at the Harding Center for Risk Literacy at the Max Planck Institute for Human Development. His research focuses on the transparent and intuitive communication of (health) risks and uncertainty.

Hilary Schaffer Boudet is an assistant professor of climate change and energy in the School of Public Policy at Oregon State University. Her research interests include the environmental and social impacts associated with energy development, public participation in environmental and energy decision making, and sustainable behavior change.

Dominique Brossard is a professor and chair in the Department of Life Sciences Communication at the University of Wisconsin, Madison. Her research program concentrates on the intersection between science, media, and policy.

Steven R. Brunner is a doctoral student of communication at the University of Arizona. His research focuses on the implications of new communication technologies on interpersonal relationships.

Priscila G. Brust-Renck is a PhD student in developmental psychology at Cornell University, working in the Laboratory for Rational Decision Making. Her research focuses on judgment and decision making and numerical cognition with implications for health risk communication and development.

Adam Burgess is currently reader in social risk research at the University of Kent, specializing in sociological studies of "risk behaviors" and anxieties, and the role of media and institutions like public inquiries in the making of social risk perceptions and controversies. His main current research project is a historical account of the rise of a more probabilistic way of making sense of uncertainty and misfortune, and the corresponding decline of a moral one.

Carma L. Bylund is associate director, medical education at Hamad Medical Corporation and associate professor of communication studies, Weill Cornell Medical College-Qatar, Doha, Qatar.

Her research focuses on health care communication, with an emphasis on physician and nurse communication skills training.

Michael A. Cacciatore is an assistant professor in the Department of Advertising & Public Relations at the University of Georgia. His research focuses on risk communication with an emphasis on media coverage of risk and opinion formation for risk topics.

Jonathan C. Corbin is a PhD candidate in the Department of Human Development at Cornell University. He currently works in Dr. Valerie Reyna's Laboratory for Rational Decision-Making. His research interests include cognitive development and the relationships between human memory, decision making, and individual differences in cognition.

Stephan Dickert is an assistant professor of marketing at the WU Vienna University of Economics and Business in Austria. He currently also holds a visiting professorship at the Psychology Department at Linköping University, Sweden. His research focuses on affective information processing in judgment and decision making.

Sharon Dunwoody is Evjue-Bascom Professor Emerita of Journalism and Mass Communication at the University of Wisconsin–Madison. She studies both the construction and impacts of mediated science and environmental messages, with particular focus on how individuals use risk information to make judgments and to act.

Renato Frey is a postdoctoral fellow at the Max Planck Institute for Human Development, Berlin. His research focuses on experience-based risky choice and on investigating learning and decision processes using computational models of cognition.

L. Brooke Friley is a PhD candidate in communication at Purdue University. Her research focus is on health communication with areas of interest related to health campaign message design and patient decision making. Current research investigates patient disclosure to providers and factors influencing patients' treatment decision-making processes.

Wolfgang Gaissmaier is a full professor of social psychology and decision sciences at the University

of Konstanz, Germany. His research focuses on how people make decisions under risk and uncertainty and how risks can be communicated more effectively to help people make better decisions, particularly in the domain of health.

Robert J. Griffin is professor of communication at Marquette University in Milwaukee, Wisconsin. His research program focuses on the ways in which individuals seek and process information about risks to health and to the natural environment, as well as the antecedents and outcomes of those activities.

Ralph Hertwig is director at the Max Planck Institute of Human Development, Berlin. He has written widely on the topic of bounded and social rationality, experience-based and description-based decision making under risk and uncertainty and the experimental practices of the social sciences.

Robin E. Jensen is an associate professor of communication at the University of Utah. She studies historical and contemporary discourses concerning health, science, and gender. Her research program investigates how technical, popular, and vernacular arguments interact in the formation of narratives related to sex education policy, HIV/AIDS prevention, and fertility awareness.

Christina Jones is an assistant professor of communication at University of Wisconsin, Whitewater. Her research focuses on health disparities, culture-centered approaches to health communication, and community-based health interventions. Her current studies evaluate health communication campaigns and the effectiveness of behavioral health theories in health promotion.

Andy J. King is an assistant professor of public relations at Texas Tech University. His research examines visual information and messaging in health and risk contexts. Current projects investigate visual information about cancer prevention, public campaign effectiveness in promoting organ donation, and visual framing influence on environmental message processing.

Kai Kuang is a PhD candidate in communication at Purdue University. Her research interest includes risk and health communication and communication campaigns. Her current research focuses on risk amplification and attenuation process and the effects of narrative evidence in health and risk communication.

Stephen Lyng is a professor of sociology at Carthage College. His current research examines the connections between risk and reflexivity in late modernity, especially the influence of voluntary risk-taking practices on self-reflexivity. This line of inquiry is part of an ongoing program to expand the theory of edgework.

Erin Maloney is the research director in the Tobacco Center of Regulatory Science at the University of Pennsylvania. Her program of research focuses on identifying and applying social influence techniques to design effective health and risk communication messages. Her current research examines positive and negative effects of electronic cigarette advertising and use of narrative and testimonial communication styles to combat misinformation about tobacco products.

Robert Mauro is a research scientist at Decision Research and an associate professor of psychology at the University of Oregon. He conducts basic and applied research in decision making, risk perception, and human emotion. He has also worked on the development of risk assessment tools for use in high-risk environments.

G. H. Morris is a professor of communication at California State University, San Marcos. A discourse analyst, his research explores accounts, narratives, and practices of positive organizational communication.

Matthew C. Nisbet is an associate professor of communication studies, public policy, and urban affairs at Northeastern University. His current research focuses on two broad questions: (1) How are urban areas and coastal communities debating actions that would make themselves more resilient, sustainable, and secure places to live? and (2) How do publics living in "innovation" cities understand and make sense of advances in fields like biomedicine, genetics, and information technology?

Kyle Oman is co-owner and operator of Armory Pacific social media consultants.

Emily B. Peterson is a doctoral candidate in communication at George Mason University in Fairfax, VA. Her research focuses on the design of effective messages for public communication campaigns, patient–provider communication, and maternal and child health.

Susanna Priest is presently a visiting scholar at the University of Washington. She has held tenured positions at Texas A&M University, the University of South Carolina, and the University of Nevada. Her research focuses on public responses to emerging technologies and science-related controversies, and she edits the international journal *Science Communication: Linking Theory and Practice*.

Stephen A. Rains is an associate professor of communication at the University of Arizona. His research examines the implications of new communication technologies for health communication.

Valerie F. Reyna, director of the Human Neuroscience Institute and co-director of the Center for Behavioral Economics and Decision Research at Cornell University, is a developer of fuzzy-trace theory, applied in law, medicine, and public health. Her recent work has focused on numeracy, medical decision making, risk communication, risk taking, neurobiological development, and neurocognitive impairment.

Caisa E. Royer is a PhD/JD student in the Department of Human Development at Cornell University. Her research interests focus on the communication of information and how that information influences decisions made in legal contexts, including the influence of suggestive information, false memories, and legal expertise.

Tillman Russell is a doctoral student in the Brian Lamb School of Communication at Purdue University. His research explores the relationship between communication and cognition, specifically the role of semantic networks in persuasion and decision making. His research also examines the connection between group communication, shared mental models, and heuristic information processing.

Dietram A. Scheufele is the John E. Ross Professor in Science Communication at the University of Wisconsin, Madison, and honorary professor at the Technische Universität Dresden, Germany. He is currently also serving as co–principal investigator of the Center for Nanotechnology in Society at Arizona State University. His research deals with the interface of media, policy, and public opinion.

Timothy L. Sellnow is professor of communication and risk science in the College of Communication and Information at the University of Kentucky. His research focuses on bioterrorism, precrisis planning, and communication strategies for risk management and mitigation in organizational and health settings.

Christine Skubisz is an assistant professor of Communication at Emerson College. Her research focuses on message design and effects in health contexts. Her current projects investigate how individuals process and use information to make health-related decisions and how to present health information to facilitate comprehension and use.

Paul Slovic is founder and president of Decision Research. He studies human judgment, decision making, and risk analysis. He and his colleagues worldwide have developed methods to describe risk perceptions and measure their impacts on individuals, industry, and society. He also serves as a consultant to industry and government.

Daniel Västfjäll is a research scientist at Decision Research and professor of cognitive psychology at Linköping University in Sweden. His research focuses on the role of affect, and especially mood, in judgment and decision making, perception, and psychophysics.

Rebecca B. Weldon is a postdoctoral associate at Cornell University, working with Dr. Valerie Reyna in the Human Neuroscience Institute. Her current research investigates risky decision making in brain and behavior. She is interested in the motivational, developmental, and cognitive factors that contribute to decision making.

Thomas Workman is the principal communication researcher in the Health and Human Development Program of the American Institutes for Research. His research and practice focuses on stakeholder-driven health and health care and environmental approaches to behavioral health. He has extensive experience in the area of substance abuse in higher education.

Z. Janet Yang is an assistant professor of communication at University at Buffalo. Her program of research focuses on the communication of risk information in science, environmental, and health contexts. Her current research investigates the impact of climate change communication on public support for environmental adaptation and mitigation.